Postcolonial Literatures of Climate Change

Cross/Cultures

READINGS IN POST/COLONIAL
LITERATURES AND CULTURES IN ENGLISH

Edited by

Bénédicte Ledent and Delphine Munos

Founding Editors

Gordon Collier
Geoffrey Davis†
Hena Maes-Jelinek†

Advisory Board

David Callahan (*University of Aveira*) – Stephen Clingman (*University of Massachusetts*) – Marc Delrez (*Université de Liège*) – Gaurav Desai (*University of Michigan*) – Russell McDougall (*University of New England*) – John McLeod (*University of Leeds*) – Irikidzayi Manase (*University of the Free State*) – Caryl Phillips (*Yale University*) – Diana Brydon (*University of Manitoba*) – Pilar Cuder- Dominguez (*University of Huelva*) – Wendy Knepper (*Brunel University*) – Carine Mardorossian (*University of Buffalo*) – Maria Olaussen (*University of Gothenburg*) – Chris Prentice (*Otago University*) – Cheryl Stobie (*University of KwaZulu-Natal*)

VOLUME 218

The titles published in this series are listed at *brill.com/cc*

Postcolonial Literatures of Climate Change

Edited by

Russell McDougall, John C. Ryan and Pauline Reynolds

BRILL

LEIDEN | BOSTON

Cover illustration: https://pixabay.com/photos/bird-humming-bird-animal-2711789/ (cocoparisienne)

Library of Congress Cataloging-in-Publication Data

Names: McDougall, Russell, editor. | Ryan, John (John Charles) (Poet),
   editor. | Reynolds, Pauline, editor.
Title: Postcolonial literatures of climate change / edited by Russell
   McDougall, John C. Ryan, and Pauline Reynolds.
Description: Leiden ; Boston : Brill, [2022] | Series: Cross/cultures, 0924-1426 ;
   volume 218 | Includes bibliographical references and index.
Identifiers: LCCN 2022018193 (print) | LCCN 2022018194 (ebook) |
   ISBN 9789004514171 (hardback) | ISBN 9789004514164 (ebook)
Subjects: LCSH: Climatic changes in literature. | Ecology in literature. |
   Postcolonialism in literature. | Environmentalism in literature. |
   Environmental literature–History and criticism. | Ecocriticism. |
   LCGFT: Literary criticism.
Classification: LCC PN56.C612 P68 2022 (print) | LCC PN56.C612 (ebook) |
   DDC 809/.9335–dc23/eng/20220605
LC record available at https://lccn.loc.gov/2022018193
LC ebook record available at https://lccn.loc.gov/2022018194

Typeface for the Latin, Greek, and Cyrillic scripts: "Brill". See and download: brill.com/brill-typeface.

ISSN 0924-1426
ISBN 978-90-04-51417-1 (hardback)
ISBN 978-90-04-51416-4 (e-book)

Copyright 2022 by Koninklijke Brill NV, Leiden, The Netherlands.
Koninklijke Brill NV incorporates the imprints Brill, Brill Nijhoff, Brill Hotei, Brill Schöningh, Brill Fink,
Brill mentis, Vandenhoeck & Ruprecht, Böhlau and V&R unipress.
All rights reserved. No part of this publication may be reproduced, translated, stored in a retrieval system,
or transmitted in any form or by any means, electronic, mechanical, photocopying, recording or otherwise,
without prior written permission from the publisher. Requests for re-use and/or translations must be
addressed to Koninklijke Brill NV via brill.com or copyright.com.

This book is printed on acid-free paper and produced in a sustainable manner.

Dedicated to Geoffrey V. Davis (1943–2018)

∴

Contents

Acknowledgements IX
List of Illustrations X
Notes on Contributors and Editors XI
Dear Matafele Peinam XVI
   Kathy Jetñil-Kijiner

1 Introduction
  Postcolonial Literatures of Climate Change 1
    Russell McDougall, John C. Ryan and Pauline Reynolds

2 "The Imagining of Possibilities"
  Writers as Activists 56
    Geoffrey V. Davis

3 River Writing
  Culture, Law and Poetics 93
    Chris Prentice

4 Which Island, What Home?
  Plantation Ecologies and Climate Change in Australia and Nauru 120
    Paul Sharrad

5 Island Life and Wild Time
  Crossing into Country in Tim Winton's Island Home 135
    Stephen Harris

6 Islands Within Islands
  Climate Change and the Deep Time Narratives of the Southern Beech 162
    John C. Ryan

7 Refashioning Futures with Sargassum
  A Caribbean Poetics of Hope 192
    Kasia Mika and Sally Stainier

8 "Kāne and Kanaloa Are Coming"
  Contemporary Hawaiian Poetry and Climate Change 219
    Craig Santos Perez

VIII CONTENTS

9 Monsoonal Memories and "the Reliable Water"
Reading Climate Change in Selected Malaysian Literature 251
   Agnes S. K. Yeow

10 Aswan High Dam and Haggag Oddoul's *Stories from Old Nubia*
*Redefining the Line between Immediate Catastrophe and Slow
Violence* 281
   Amany Dahab

11 Caring for the Future
Climate Change, Kinship and Inuit Knowledge 311
   Renée Hulan

12 Fictional Representations of Antarctic Tourism and Climate Change
To the Ends of the World 334
   Hanne E.F. Nielsen

13 Ice Islands of the Anthropocene
The Cultural Meanings of Antarctic Bergs 361
   Elizabeth Leane

Index 383

Acknowledgements

The editors are grateful to the University of New England, Armidale, NSW, and the Flinders University of South Australia, for their financial support of the South Pacific Association for Commonwealth Literature and Language Studies (SPACLALS) Conference ("The Two Canaries of Climate Change: Island and Polar Places") held at the UNE FutureCampus, Parramatta in February 2018. We would also like to thank Gillian Dooley, for her assistance with the event (which led directly to this book); Julie Love, for her care and attention to the manuscript and her devotion to its cause; and Jess Klaassen-Wright for the index.

Russell McDougall thanks Christa Stevens for her continuing support and enthusiasm; Gareth Griffiths and Helen Tiffin, for their sustaining friendship and intellectual camaraderie; Greta Thunberg, Ursula Rakova and Kathy Jetñil-Kijiner for inspiration.

John C. Ryan acknowledges the School of Arts and Social Sciences at Southern Cross University, Australia, and the Nulungu Research Institute at the University of Notre Dame, Australia, for their support and encouragement. He also thanks SPACLALS, for drawing his attention to scholarship in postcolonial ecocriticism.

Pauline Reynolds thanks Russell McDougall and John C. Ryan for their expertise and guidance. In addition, she is grateful to SPACLALS and its members past, present and future.

Illustrations

7.1   Sainte-Anne, Guadeloupe—2018. © Sally Stainier, 2018   193
7.2   Saint-François, Guadeloupe—2018. © Sally Stainier, 2018   193
12.1 Antarctic tourists in a zodiac craft, Antarctic Peninsula. © Hanne Nielsen, 2016.   339
12.2 The remains of boilers from whaling days, Whaler's Bay, South Shetland Islands, Antarctica. © Hanne Nielsen, 2017.   350

Notes on Contributors and Editors

Amany Dahab

is an architect and PhD candidate in comparative literature at the University of Western Ontario, Canada. Her main research interest is the convergence of literary and architectural spaces. In her early work, she focused on exploring Expressionism as an approach to Contemporary Architecture. Currently, she is working on a project entitled Unfolding Infinity: Expressionism in Sufi Poetics and Islamic Architecture. She is also interested in exploring the impact of built environment on altering ecological topographies and mobilising the change of social and cultural patterns; and the representation of such impact in visual art, cinema and literature.

Geoffrey V. Davis

taught at universities in Austria, France, Germany and Italy and held research fellowships at Cambridge University, Curtin University and the Harry Ransom Center, University of Texas at Austin. He wrote his doctorate in German studies on *Arnold Zweig in der DDR* and his postdoctoral dissertation (Habilitation) on *Voices of Justice and Reason: Apartheid and Beyond in South African Literature.* He was for many years co-editor of the influential Brill/Rodopi book series, "Cross/Cultures: Readings in Post/Colonial Literatures and Cultures in English," and of *MATATU: Journal for African Culture and Society.* He was the Chair of the Association for Commonwealth Literature and Language Studies (ACLALS), 2008–2011; and of its European branch (EACLALS), 2002–2008 and 2011–2014. From 2007 until his death in 2018, he also worked closely with the Bhasha Research Centre in Baroda (India), an NGO involved in education for tribal people (Adivasis). His scholarly interests were vast, producing books on African, Canadian, Australian, New Zealand, South Asian, Indigenous as well as Black and Asian British literatures and cultures. Among his many co-edited books are *Performing Identities: The Celebration of Indigeneity* (2015) and *The Language Loss of the Indigenous* (2016).

Stephen Harris

is an Adjunct Lecturer in the field of literary and cultural studies, with particular interests in American literature and contemporary fiction. He has published books on the work of Gore Vidal and the historical novel in American culture, plus numerous articles and reviews. His recent research focuses on the relationship between literature and the environment, with a focus on ecocritical themes in Australian literature. He is also a member of the interdisciplinary research WRaIN (Water Research and Innovation Network) at the University of New England (UNE), and, as part of that group, has co-edited and contributed to a collection of interdisciplinary essays on the subject of water in *Australia, Water Policy, Imagination and Innovation: Interdisciplinary Approaches* (2017). He is presently collaborating on a book of essays focusing on wilderness.

Renée Hulan

is Professor in the Department of English Language and Literature at Saint Mary's University (Halifax, Canada). She is the author of *Climate Change and Writing the Canadian Arctic* (2018), *Canadian Historical Writing: Reading the Remains* (2014) and *Northern Experience and the Myths of Canadian Culture* (2002). She has also edited *Native North America: Critical and Cultural Perspectives* (1999) and, with Renate Eigenbrod, *Aboriginal Oral Traditions: Theory, Practice, Ethics* (2008).

Kathy Jetñil-Kijiner

is a poet and performance artist of Marshall Islander ancestry whose work focuses on climate change, colonialism and social injustice in the Marshall Islands. She has a Master's degree in Pacific Island Studies from the University of Hawai'i and is a PhD student at the Australia National University. Her first collection of poetry, *Iep Jāltok: Poems from a Marshallese Daughter*, was published in 2017 by the University of Arizona Press. She serves as Climate Envoy for the Marshall Islands Ministry of Environment and is co-founder and Director of *Jo-Jikum*, a non-profit Marshallese youth environmental organisation.

Elizabeth Leane

is Associate Professor of English at the University of Tasmania. She holds an ARC Future Fellowship split between the School of Humanities and the Institute for Marine and Antarctic Studies. She is interested in building bridges between disciplines, and bringing the insights of the humanities to the study of the Antarctic. She is the author of *South Pole: Nature and Culture* (2016), *Antarctica in Fiction* (2012), *Reading Popular Physics* (2007) and co-editor of *Considering Animals* (2011) and *Imagining Antarctica* (2011). She is Arts and Literature editor of the *Polar Journal* and co-chair of the Humanities and Social Science Expert Group of the Scientific Committee on Antarctic Research.

Russell McDougall

is Professor Emeritus in the School of Arts, Humanities and Social Sciences at the University of New England in Australia. He has published widely on African, Australian and Caribbean literatures. His monograph, *Letters from*

Khartoum: D.R. Ewen, Teaching English Literature, Sudan, 1951–1965, was published by Brill in 2020. His most recent edited book (with Sue Thomas and Anne Collett) is *Tracking the Literature of Tropical Weather: Typhoons, Hurricanes and Cyclones* (2017).

Kasia Mika

is a Lecturer in Comparative Literature at Queen Mary University of London (UK). Prior to that, she was a Lecturer in Literary and Cultural Analysis at the University of Amsterdam and a postdoc in Comparative Caribbean Studies at KITLV (The Royal Netherlands Institute of Southeast Asian and Caribbean Studies). Her monograph, *Disasters, Vulnerability and Narratives: Writing Haiti's Futures* (2018) uses narrative responses to the 2010 Haiti earthquake as a starting point for an analysis of notions of disaster, vulnerability, reconstruction and recovery. In her analysis, she turns to concepts of hinged chronologies, slow healing and remnant dwelling, offering a vision of open-ended Caribbean futures, full of resolve. Her articles have appeared in *Area, Journal of Haitian Studies, Moving Worlds* and other journals.

Hanne E.F. Nielsen

specialises in representations of Antarctica in advertising, media and popular culture. She completed her PhD at the University of Tasmania, where she examined representations of Antarctica in advertising, as part of Elizabeth Leane's "Integrating the Humanities into Antarctic Studies" project. Hanne is a member of the Scientific Committee on Antarctic Research (SCAR) Humanities and Social Sciences Expert Group; a 2017 SCAR Fellowship holder; and 2017/18 President of the Association of Polar Early Career Scientists (APECS). She spends her summers in the Antarctic Peninsula, working as a tour guide, and her winters in Hobart.

Craig Santos Perez

is a Professor of English at the University of Hawai'i, Mānoa, where he teaches creative writing, Pacific Islander literature and environmental poetry. He is the author of five books of poetry and the co-editor of five anthologies.

Chris Prentice

researches and teaches postcolonial literatures at the University of Otago, New Zealand. Her research has focused on uses of culture in contemporary Indigenous discourses and politics of decolonisation in settler-invader contexts, and she has published journal articles and book chapters on aspects of this topic. Her recent work has moved into areas of postcolonial disaster studies and cultural memory studies. She coordinates the Postcolonial Studies Research Network at Otago, and was the Chair of ACLALS (2016–2019).

Pauline Reynolds

recently completed her PhD by Creative Practice at the University of New England. She was formerly the Postgraduate Representative for SPACLALS. An historian, textile artist and Churchill Fellow, she is best known for her academic and creative work around Pacific history and barkcloth. Her most recent collaborations with the University of Cambridge and the British Museum allowed her to explore how objects can help reveal the voices of those who have been left out of historical narratives.

John C. Ryan

is Adjunct Associate Professor at Southern Cross University, Australia, and Adjunct Senior Research Fellow at Nulungu Institute, Notre Dame University, Australia. His research focuses on Aboriginal Australian literature, Southeast Asian ecocriticism, environmental humanities, ecopoetics and critical plant studies. His recent book publications include *Introduction to the Environmental Humanities* (2021, co-authored with J. Andrew Hubbell), *The Mind of Plants: Narratives of Vegetal Intelligence* (2021, co-edited with Monica Gagliano and Patrícia Vieira) and *Nationalism in India: Texts and Contexts* (2021, co-edited with Debajyoti Biswas). In 2020, he published the botanical poetry collection *Seeing Trees: A Poetic Arboretum* with Western Australian author Glen Phillips.

Paul Sharrad

is a Senior Fellow in the Faculty of Law, Humanities and the Arts, University of Wollongong where he taught postcolonial literatures for many years. His research centres on India, the Pacific and Australia, and his monographs feature Raja Rao, Albert Wendt and Thomas Keneally. He edited New Literatures Review (1989–2001), was co-editor of Volume 12 of the *Oxford History of the Novel in English: The Novel in Australia, Canada, New Zealand, and the South Pacific Since 1950* (2017), co-editor *Of Indian Origin: Writings from Australia* (2018) and co-editor of *Transnational Spaces of India and Australia* (2022). He is also a regular contributor to the postcolonial section of *The Year's Work in English Studies*.

Sally Stainier

is a PhD candidate in Political Science at Université des Antilles in Guadeloupe (French West Indies). Based on local teachers' social representations of language and formal education, her dissertation examines French and Creole glottopolitics as examples of top-down and bottom-up public policy. Other research interests include collective memory, (re)construction and futures-making explored through notions of disaster, sovereignty and diasporic identity. An all-around language professional and teacher at heart, she is the founder of URURIMI and works as a conference interpreter, translator and writer specialising in the Greater Caribbean.

Agnes S. K. Yeow
is a Senior Lecturer with the English Department, Faculty of Arts and Social Sciences at the University of Malaya in Kuala Lumpur, Malaysia. Her research focuses on Modernist fiction and ecocritical readings of Malaysian literature.

Dear Matafele Peinam

Kathy Jetñil-Kijiner

Dear Matafele Peinam,

You are a seven month old sunrise of gummy smiles
you are bald as an egg and bald as the Buddha
you are thighs that are thunder and shrieks that are lightning
so excited for bananas, hugs and
our morning walks past the lagoon

Dear Matafele Peinam,

I want to tell you about that lagoon

that lucid, sleepy lagoon lounging against the sunrise

Men say that one day
that lagoon will devour you

They say it will gnaw at the shoreline
chew at the roots of your breadfruit trees
gulp down rows of your seawallsand crunch your island's
    shattered bones

They say you, your daughter
and your granddaughter, too
will wander
rootless
with only
a passport
to call home

Dear Matafele Peinam,

Don't cry

Mommy promises you

no one
will come and devour you

no greedy whale of a company sharking through political seas
no backwater bullying of businesses with broken morals
no blindfolded bureaucracies gonna push
this mother ocean over
the edge

no one's drowning, baby

no one's moving
no one's losing
their homeland
no one's gonna become
a climate change refugee

or should I say
no one else

to the Carteret Islanders of Papua New Guinea
and to the Taro Islanders of the Solomon Islands
I take this moment
to apologize to you
we are drawing the line
here

Because baby we are going to fight
your mommy daddy
bubu jimma your country and president too
we will all fight

and even though there are those
hidden behind platinum titles
who like to pretend
that we don't exist
that the Marshall Islands
Tuvalu
Kiribati
Maldives

Typhoon Haiyan in the Philippines
Floods of Pakistan, Algeria, Colombia
and all the hurricanes, earthquakes, and tidalwaves
didn't exist

still
there are those
who see us

hands reaching out
fists raising up
banners unfurling
megaphones booming
and we are
canoes blocking coal ships

the radiance of solar villages

the rich clean soil of the farmer's past
petitions blooming from teenage fingertips
families biking, recycling, reusing,
engineers dreaming, designing, building,
artists painting, dancing, writing
and we are spreading the word

and there are thousands

out on the street
marching with signs
hand in hand
chanting for change NOW

and they're marching for you, baby
they're marching for us

because we deserve

to do more

than just
survive

we deserve
to thrive

Dear Matafele Peinam,

you are eyes heavy
with drowsy weight
so just close those eyes, baby
and sleep in peace

because we won't let you down

you'll see

> Kathy Jetñil-Kijiner, *Poems from a Marshallese Daughter* (Arizona: U of Arizona P (2017): 70–73

CHAPTER 1

Introduction

Postcolonial Literatures of Climate Change

Russell McDougall, John C. Ryan and Pauline Reynolds

A blood-red sky glows above Mallacoota, a small coastal town in the East Gippsland region of Victoria, Australia. On an otherwise empty wharf, a family prepares to flee the highly unpredictable firestorm aboard a small motorboat.[1] On the beach nearby as many as four thousand people huddle together anxiously, trapped by the encroaching flames. These haunting images capture just a single traumatic moment of the broad-scale crisis that befell Australia during the 2019–2020 bushfire season known colloquially as the "Black Summer."[2] From July 2019 to March 2020—winter to autumn in Australia—more than 11,000 conflagrations devastated approximately 18.6 million hectares (46 million acres) of country, including 5.4 million hectares in the state of New South Wales alone. Eighty-one percent of the Blue Mountains World Heritage Area and 54 percent of the remnant Gondwana Rainforests of NSW and Queensland also went up in flames.[3] The total death tally of the inferno was thirty-four human and an estimated one billion non-human animals. The conditions that conspired to cause this tragedy, exacerbated by a prolonged drought, were, according to the Australian Bureau of Meteorology, those associated with anthropogenic (human-induced) climate change.[4] Indeed, the year 2019 was the hottest and driest on record, with precipitation levels registering 40 percent below the national average.[5]

The editors of this volume, all based in northern New South Wales, witnessed this national tragedy unfolding first-hand. But we begin with the Australian example not simply for the reason of local impact but also because

---

1 ABC News, "Families Board Boat in Mallacoota," *ABC News* (December 31, 2020), www.abc.net.au/news/2019-12-31/families-board-boat-in-mallacoota-1/11833952.

2 Lesley Hughes, Annika Dean, Will Steffen, Ella Weisbrot, Martin Rice and Greg Mullins, *Summer of Crisis Report* (Potts Point, NSW: Climate Council of Australia Ltd, 2020).

3 Hughes, et al., *Summer of Crisis Report*, iv.

4 Geert Jan van Oldenborgh, et al., "Attribution of the Australian Bushfire Risk to Anthropogenic Climate Change," *Natural Hazards and Earth System Sciences* 21.3 (2021): 941–960.

5 Hughes, et al., *Summer of Crisis Report*, 3.

© KONINKLIJKE BRILL NV, LEIDEN, 2022 | DOI:10.1163/9789004514164_002

it has global implications. The 2019–2020 Australian bushfire season contributed significantly to the global increase of carbon dioxide (CO_2) in the atmosphere, emitting 250m tonnes of it in fact (almost half of the country's annual emissions), which of course will have a knock-on effect upon global warming.[6] Scientists have observed the same kind of effects in relation to the 2019 fire season in Siberia and Eastern Russia, Alaska and Greenland. Researchers associated with the Copernicus Atmosphere Monitoring Service (CAMS) in Europe advise that, in the first three weeks of June alone, fires within the Arctic Circle released approximately 100 megatons (or 100 million metric tons) of carbon dioxide into the atmosphere.[7]

Globally, the decade 2010–2019 was the warmest on record, eight of the ten hottest known years occurring during this period.[8] According to independent studies conducted by NASA and the National Oceanic and Atmospheric Administration (NOAA), the average surface temperature of the Earth in 2019 ranked second highest since recorded observations began in 1880.[9] More precisely, 2019 measured 0.95 degrees Celsius (1.7 degrees Fahrenheit) above the twentieth-century average.[10] Satellite data reveal that, during the summer of 2019 in the Northern Hemisphere, Greenland lost 600 gigatonnes (600 billion tonnes) of ice, causing a global sea level rise of 2.2 millimetres in just two months.[11] The situation is similar in the Southern Hemisphere. In February 2020, weather stations at the northern tip of the Antarctic Peninsula transmitted a reading of 18.4 degrees Celsius (65.1 degrees Fahrenheit), the highest known temperature for the ice-covered continent that contains 90 percent of the world's fresh water. The Antarctic Peninsula is one of the most rapidly

---

6   Adam Morton, "Australian Bushfires to Contribute to Huge Annual Increase in Global Carbon Dioxide," *Guardian* Australian edition (January 24, 2020), https://www.theguardian.com/australia-news/2020/jan/24/australian-bushfires-to-contribute-to-huge-annual-increase-in-global-carbon-dioxide.

7   Jordan Davidson, "Unprecedented Wildfires in Arctic Have Scientists Concerned," *EcoWatch* (July 25, 2019), https://www.ecowatch.com/arctic-wildfires--2639340124.html?rebelltitem=1#rebelltitem1.

8   Nick Watts, et al., "The 2019 Report of *The Lancet* Countdown on Health and Climate Change: Ensuring That the Health of a Child Born Today Is Not Defined by a Changing Climate," *Lancet* 394 (2019): 1836.

9   NOAA, "Global Climate Report—Annual 2019," *NOAA*, January 2020.

10   NOAA, "Global Climate Report."

11   Isabella Velicogna, et al., "Continuity of Ice Sheet Mass Loss in Greenland and Antarctica from the GRACE and GRACE Follow-On Missions," *Geophysical Research Letters* 47.8 (April 28, 2020): 1–8.

INTRODUCTION

warming places on Earth (see Chapter 12 and 13 of this volume.)[12] From the expanding desertification of Africa to the eroded seashores caused by rising sea levels in Southeast Asia and the island nations of the Pacific and Indian Oceans, from the accelerated melting of Greenland and Antarctica to the increasing frequency and intensity of extreme weather events in many other parts of the world, climate change continues to have an impact on people, plants and animals everywhere.[13] Scientific studies have linked climate change to increased human mortality from heat stress, air pollution and viral transmissions.[14] The World Health Organization, furthermore, has implicated climate change in the spread of infectious diseases—such as the deadly coronavirus that grew to pandemic status in 2020.[15] The increase in global temperatures is linked to an increase in the frequency and intensity of extreme precipitation events (such as hurricanes and floods), which "not only cause direct injuries" but also "spur disease outbreaks and produce lingering mental health problems, as people lose their homes," their livelihoods and their loved ones.[16] As the 2009 report of *The Lancet* and University College London Institute for Global Health Commission stated categorically: "climate change is the biggest global health threat of the 21st century."[17]

The hard data of the scientific consensus on climate change would seem irrefutable. But scientific discourse is perhaps inadequate to communicate the perceptual, emotional, interpersonal and cultural ramifications of climate change. With this in mind, researchers have begun to embrace alternative descriptions such as "climate disruption" to underscore the disturbance of those global processes that make life on Earth possible,[18] and "climate crisis"

---

12   World Meteorological Organization, "New Record For Antarctic Continent Reported," World Meteorological Organization (February 14, 2020), https://public.wmo.int/en/media/news/new-record-antarctic-continent-reported.

13   David Eckstein, Marie-Lena Hutfils and Maik Winges, *Global Climate Risk Index 2019 Briefing Paper* (Bonn, Germany: Germanwatch, 2018).

14   Nick Watts, et al., "The 2019 Report of *The Lancet* Countdown on Health and Climate Change:" 1836–1878.

15   World Health Organization, "Climate Change and Human Health," *World Health Organization*, https://www.who.int/news-room/fact-sheets/detail/climate-change-and-health.

16   Laurie Goering, "Climate Change 'Biggest Global Health Threat' of Century, Doctors Warn," Reuters, (November 29, 2018), https://in.reuters.com/article/global-climatechange-health/climate-change-biggest-global-health-threat-of-century-doctors-warn-idINL8N1Y346F.

17   Anthony Costello et al, "Managing the Health Effects of Climate Change," *The Lancet* 373 (2009): 1693.

18   Alistair Woodward, "Climate Change: Disruption, Risk and Opportunity," *Global Transitions* 1 (2019): 44.

to illuminate the manifold urgencies that the term "change" underplays.[19] U.S. Senator, Al Gore, was promoting the environmental "crisis" discourse long before his ascension to the Vice Presidency in 1993. But policy-makers in the U.S. and Australia, hampered by the denialists in their ranks, have been slow to respond. A report published by the Universal Ecological Fund in November 2019 concluded that 136 of the 184 nations that had pledged climate action to limit global warming in accordance with the 2015 Paris Agreement had failed to develop policy frameworks adequate to the task.[20]

Climate change today is radically fracturing the lives and livelihoods of both human and more-than-human worlds. This volume focuses attention on the contribution that literature offers to the evolving climate debate. In this age of ecological disarticulation that paleobiologists postulate as the Anthropocene epoch,[21] literature has become an enabling instrument for readers attempting to make sense of—and possibly even come to terms with—the immense spatiotemporal reach of the climate catastrophe. Literature, inter alia, functions as a medium to render transparent the imperialist blocked formations of black-and-white thinking on the relationship between Nature and Culture that subtend the crisis; to re-invigorate that relationship as it has been destabilised by the climate crisis; and to voice the concerns of those marginalised societies and cultures that are often the most intensely pressured by the crisis, namely the Indigenous peoples of the Global South—in Africa, large parts of Asia, Central and South America, and much of the Middle East. Literature also has the potential to elicit empathy for non-human protagonists, imperilled by climate change yet often excluded from the discourses surrounding the issue. It serves not only to record but also to mourn the loss of habitat and species, and as a mnemonic device for remembering, thereby possibly even stimulating action to bring about their recovery.[22] In his study of climate narratives, ecocritic Matthew Schneider-Mayerson argues that novels, plays, poetry, short stories and other diverse literary genres inculcate climate consciousness and

---

19 Rabah Arezki, Patrick Bolton, Karim El Aynaoui and Maurice Obstfeld, eds. *Coping With the Climate Crisis: Mitigation Policies and Global Coordination* (New York: Columbia UP, 2018).

20 "The Truth Behind the Climate Pledges", https://feu-us.org/our-work/behind-the-climate -pledges/.

21 Jan Zalasiewicz, "Commentary on the 'Anthropocene in Chile' Manifesto," *Environmental Humanities* 11.2 (2019): 498–500.

22 See, for example, John C. Ryan, " 'The Pained and Silent Song of a Branch': Ecological Precarity in the Poetry of Taufiq Ismail and Khairani Barokka," *Journal of Postcolonial Writing* 56.4 (2020): 488–502.

INTRODUCTION

generate an ecologically sustainable politics and practices.[23] This volume aims precisely to activate that capacity for building a critical climate consciousness.

1 Literary/Critical Activism

In his 1982 essay, "Subversion and Legitimation: The Avant-garde in Postmodern Culture," Charles Russell asserted that "the primary model of post-modern literary and critical activism" was "the semiological analysis of discourse."[24] Barbara Eckstein took him to task, lamenting the absence of any "true activism" in American letters at that time, and expressing alarm that "any apolitical post-structuralism" should be described as "activism."[25] This, in Eckstein's view, was symptomatic of the historical amnesia of humanism in the United States, a forgetting of history and its causes that had led to focusing on decontextualised psychological effects and reducing political conflicts to personal dilemmas. Forgetting the existential reality of historical positioning is a luxury, as Eckstein also observed, clearly impossible in war-torn nations such as Lebanon or El Salvador. But this was also the case in most other postcolonial nations. In the 1980s, in South Africa, Apartheid was still the ruling ideology, which no writer could for a moment forget. In Australia, Aboriginal literature had begun "pulling white Australian history away from its protective ethnocentric moorings,"[26] challenging the national "cult of forgetfulness,"[27] and encouraging Australian writers to remember the nation's troubled history. In the Caribbean, where literature is the product of many nations and consequently much more diverse (racially, linguistically, culturally, geographically), the first scholarly proposals of a unifying thesis for the field also began to appear in the 1980s.[28] More generally, while postcolonial styles of discourse analysis were coming into their own in the 1980s, focusing on the discursive construction of colonialism, these

---

23   Matthew Schneider-Mayerson, "The Influence of Climate Fiction: An Empirical Survey of Readers," *Environmental Humanities* 10.2 (2018).

24   Charles Russell, "Subversion and Legitimation: The Avant-garde in Postmodern Culture," *Chicago Review* 33.2 (1982): 55.

25   Barbara Eckstein, "What Humanists Help America to Forget," *The Literary Review: An International Journal of Contemporary Writing* 28.4 (1985): 591.

26   J.J. Healy, " 'The True Life in Our History': Aboriginal Literature in Australia," *Antipodes* 2.2 (1988): 84.

27   W.H. Stanner, *After the Dreaming* (Sydney: Australian Broadcasting Commission, 1972): 25.

28   See Selwyn R. Cudjoe, *Resistance and Caribbean Literature* (Athens, OH, Chicago and London: Ohio UP, 1981) and O. R. Dathorne, *Dark Ancestor: The Literature of the Black Man in the Caribbean* (Baton Rouge and London: Louisiana State UP, 1981).

"did not seek to replace or exclude other forms" and expressions of colonialism (historical, geographical, economic, military or political).[29] Indeed, as Robert J.C. Young argues, postcolonial discourse analysis has provided "a significant framework" for analysis of these other forms by emphasising that "all perspectives on colonialism share and have to deal with a common discursive medium which was also that of colonialism itself."[30] This is one aspect of postcolonial literary/critical activism. Another, as Young also argues, has been its transformation of "the Eurocentrism and ingrained cultural assumptions of the West" and its advocating of "greater tolerance and understanding of people who displayed ethnic and cultural differences."[31] To progress this political agenda, of course, authors and critics have often worked hand in hand. They have demonstrated a remarkable capacity for operating flexibly across multiple political fronts, attacking all forms of oppression, and making postcolonialism itself "the locus of activism," as well as a transformational politics for addressing diverse colonialist injustices.[32] The targets of intervention are too broad to enumerate, but they include for example: land and water rights, massified tourism impacts on traditional Indigenous lands, reparations for slavery and the slave trade, animal othering and commodification, museum decolonisation and indigenisation, refugee policies and practices, statelessness, sovereignty, violence against women, ecofeminist citizenship, (homo)sexuality, liberation theology, corporate capitalism, globalisation, developmentalism, neoliberal technology, biochemical violence, bio- and geo-piracy, sex trade, food security, and many more issues.

The achievements of literary activism are often difficult to prove. But some texts, for example Harriet Beecher Stowe's novel *Uncle Tom's Cabin* (1852), Simone de Beauvoir's *The Second Sex* (1949) and Rachel Carson's *Silent Spring* (1962), have a demonstrable influence, raising consciousness, either at a governmental or a grass-roots level, or both, and in some cases stimulating action to bring about change. In postcolonial contexts, literary/critical activists who have had an indisputable impact in one political arena or another include: Ngũgĩ wa Thiong'o (Kenya), Dennis Brutus (South Africa), Wole Soyinka (Nigeria),

---

29 Bill Ashcroft, Gareth Griffiths and Helen Tiffin, eds. *Postcolonial Studies. The Key Concepts*, second ed. (London and New York: Routledge, 2007): 109.

30 Robert J.C. Young, *Colonial Desire: Hybridity in Theory, Culture and Race* (London: Routledge, 1995): 163.

31 Young, "Postcolonial Remains," in *Reviewing Imperial Conflicts*, eds. Ana Cristina Mendes, Cristina Baptista (Newcastle upon Tyne: Cambridge Scholars Publishing, 2014): 18.

32 Paul F. Banida, "Afterword. Postcolonialism, Activism, and Translation," in *The Routledge Handbook of Translation and Activism*, eds. Rebecca Ruth Gould, Kayvan Tahmasebian, (London and New York: Routledge, 2020): 518.

INTRODUCTION

Efua Sutherland (Ghana), Oodgeroo Noonuccal (Australia), Walter Rodney (Guyana), Claribel Alegría (Nicaragua/El Salvador), John Trudell (Indigenous America), Paulo Freire (Brazil), and many others. Some were arrested for their efforts, others tortured, killed or exiled.

2 Literary/Critical Responses to Climate Change

Sixteen years ago, nature writer Robert Macfarlane lamented the increasingly visible "deficiency of a creative response to climate change," a deficiency all the more obvious in contrast to "the abundance of literature produced in response to the other great eschatological crisis of the past half-century—the nuclear threat."[33] Over the last decade, the situation has changed dramatically, with the evolution of a whole new species of fiction, climate fiction (cli-fi, for short), a term coined by Dan Bloom in 2008 with reference to Hollywood movies that focus on major environmental change, like *The Day After Tomorrow* (dir. Roland Emmerich, 2004). In 2012, Bloom gave the term a literary twist in his press release for U.S. author, Jim Laughter's climate-themed novel, *Polar City Red*. Climate scientist, Judith Curry (President of Climate Forecast Applications Network), picked up on this, promoting the new "fledgling" genre on her *Climate Etc.* blog. The exemplars she gave at that time were Michael Crichton's *State of Fear* (2004), Rachendra Pachauri's *Return to Almora* (2010), Rex Fleming's *Exposure* (2012), Ian McEwan's *Solar* (2010) and Barbara Kingsolver's *Flight Behaviour* (2012).[34]

In order to reflect the social distortions of climate change, the genre departed the literary mainstream of realism to join science fiction (sci-fi) as a new species of speculative (future-oriented) fiction. In a way, this played into the hands of the denialists' contention that climate change is not real. As Christine Shearer argues, the "discourse of doubt" produced by the fossil fuel industry and its allies employs "certainty" as "the only acceptable standard for acknowledging and thus acting" on the problem, "simultaneously manufacturing uncertainty" to ensure that certainty is never achieved, and that—despite the high level of scientific consensus about global warming—the science

---

33 Robert Macfarlane, "The Burning Question," *Guardian* Australian edition (24 September 2005): para. 5, www.theguardian.com/books/2005/sep/24/featuresreviews.guardianrevie w29#maincontent.

34 Judith Curry, "Cli-Fi," *Climate Etc.* Blog (December 23, 2012), https://judithcurry.com/2012/ 12/23/cli-fi/.

is cast into doubt.[35] In the context of this highly organised manufacture of uncertainty, cli-fi is easily discredited by its association with science fiction, pigeonholed as a species of "popular" fiction (like fantasy) which many readers and critics assume is less "serious" than "literary" fiction. Thus, in 2016, the acclaimed Indian novelist, Amitav Ghosh, lamented the literary exile of the subject, climate change, from "the mansion where serious fiction has long been in residence."[36] In other words, the climate crisis is also a crisis of culture and imagination. Of course, as Ghosh acknowledges, the list of those who *have* sought to communicate a sense of urgency about the issue includes a number of clearly "serious" authors—Margaret Atwood, Doris Lessing, Cormac McCarthy and others. Still, Ghosh insists, the literary mainstream remains as broadly indifferent to the "the crisis on our doorstep as the population at large."[37] Is it possible, then, he wonders, that the arts generally, by "moving forever forward, in irreversible time, by means of innovation and the free pursuit of imagination," are blinded by their own diverse engagements with the future to what *actually* lies ahead?[38]

In the political arena this kind of blindness manifests most obviously in the marginalisation of Indigenous peoples from national and international climate change policy and decision-making, when the key to a sustainable future quite possibly lies with traditional and local knowledge practices. After all, Indigenous people manage over 76 percent of the world's tropical forests, which account for around half of the world's carbon reserves. Before the dispossessions of "colonial capitalism,"[39] Indigenous people's localised understandings of climate impacts, and their "low-carbon" adaptation strategies for managing the environment, had enabled them to live sustainably for thousands of years. Thus, the United Nations body charged with assessing the science related to climate change, the Intergovernmental Panel on Climate Change (IPCC), stated categorically in its Special Report of August 2019 on Climate Change and Land: without secure land rights for Indigenous peoples,

---

35 Christine Shearer, *Kivalina: A Climate Change Story* (Chicago: Haymarket Books, 2011): 16. See also William R. Freudenburg, Robert Gramling and Debra J. Davison, "Scientific Certainty Argumentation Methods (SCAMs): Science and the Politics of Doubt," *Sociological Inquiry* 78.1 (2008): 16ff.

36 Amitav Ghosh, *The Great Derangement: Climate Change and the Unthinkable* (Chicago: Chicago UP, 2016): 24.

37 Ghosh, *The Great Derangement*, 125.

38 Ghosh, *The Great Derangement*, 125.

39 Onur Ulas Ince, *Colonial Capitalism and the Dilemmas of Liberalism* (Oxford: Oxford UP, 2018), provides an insightful analysis of the relations between colonialism and capitalism.

INTRODUCTION

any effort to adapt to climate change and to mitigate its effects globally will be in vain.[40]

Since Ghosh's 2016 lament concerning the dearth of "literary" fiction focusing on climate change, there has been a considerable attempt to redress the situation, by both Indigenous and non-Indigenous writers. Much of this literature takes place in a dystopian future. In Métis writer, Cherie Dimaline's fiction for young adults, *The Marrow Thieves* (2017), for example, global warming has not only ravaged the physical world but has also deprived non-Indigenous people of their capacity for dreaming.[41] To regain that capacity, they begin hunting the Indigenes, whose bone marrow they harvest to make a dream serum. Australian Waany author, Alexis Wright's novel, *The Swan Book* (2013), also takes place in a climatically-disturbed future, where the "living land" has been devastated not only by climate change but also by the invasion of the Australian army into Aboriginal communities.[42] This refers to the controversial Intervention authorised by the 2007 Northern Territory National Emergency Response Act (which, despite the modifications of the "Stronger Futures in the Northern Territory" Act of 2012, remains in essence operational). Initially motivated by a sense of social crisis in Aboriginal communities, the Intervention in fact eroded the land rights of the people it sought to assist by introducing compulsory leasing of community land. In *The Swan Book*, the living land has been violated, like Oblivia, the Aboriginal rape victim who is its protagonist. The climate change that causes its desertification is twinned with military intervention in the lives of its Traditional Owners, as manifestations of the what the Guyanese author Wilson Harris calls "conquistadorial ego."[43] That is to say, they are inseparable, for they are both defining aspects of imperialism.

The "living land" of *The Swan* Book evokes the Aboriginal concept of Country, which embraces a traditional way of being completely different from Western concepts of land, territory and property. As Deborah Bird Rose writes:

> Country in Aboriginal English is not only a common noun but also a proper noun. People talk about country in the same way that they would talk about a person: they speak to country, sing to country, visit country,

---

40   *Special Report on Climate Change and Land from Indigenous Peoples* (August 2019), https://www.ipcc.ch/srccl/.

41   Cherie Dimaline, *The Marrow Thieves* (Toronto, Ont.: Dancing Cat Books, 2017).

42   Alexis Wright, *The Swan Book: A Novel* (New York: Atria Books, 2016): 15.

43   Wilson Harris, *The Womb of Space: The Cross-Cultural Imagination* (Westport, Connecticut: Greenwood Press, 1983): 137.

worry about country, feel sorry for country, and long for country. People say that country knows, hears, smells, takes notice, takes care, is sorry or happy. Country is not a generalised or undifferentiated type of place, such as one might indicate with terms like 'spending a day in the country' or 'going up the country'. Rather, country is a living entity with a yesterday, today and tomorrow, with a consciousness, and a will toward life. Because of this richness, country is home, and peace; nourishment for body, mind, and spirit; heart's ease.[44]

Settler literatures abound with the sense of place. But Country is more than place, and it is more-than-human. As Bird Rose explains: "It consists of people, animals, plants, Dreamings, underground, earth soils, minerals and waters, surface water, and air."[45] Country is relational, like kinship. As Palyku novelist and lawyer, Ambelin Kwaymullina, puts it:

> Country is filled with relations speaking language and following Law, no matter whether the shape of that relation is human, rock, crow, wattle. Country is loved, needed, and cared for, and country loves, needs, and cares for her peoples in turn. Country is family, culture, identity. Country is self.[46]

Caring for Country is caring for self, individually and collectively, all things being related; and healing desecrated Country, violated, for example, by the extractive processes of fossil capitalism that lead to climate change, is self-healing. It means advocating for greater respect for Indigenous land rights, more involvement by Indigenous people in the management of their homelands, greater recognition of Indigenous cultural knowledge (including knowledge of environmental cycles and processes), and the redress of historical injustices, as well as escalations of climate injustice. Country includes climate; and caring for Country means taking care of the climate also. It means insisting on Climate Justice.

In other parts of the world Indigenous peoples have different ideas of "living land," but they all include climate as a key element of their non-binary apprehension of Nature and Culture. Living land is a term used in one form

---

44   Deborah Bird Rose, *Nourishing Terrains: Australian Aboriginal Views of Landscape and Wilderness* (Canberra, Australia: Australian Heritage Commission, 1996): 7.

45   Bird Rose, *Nourishing Terrains*, 7.

46   Ambelin Kwaymullina, "Seeing the Light: Aboriginal Law, Learning and Sustainable Living in Country," *Indigenous Law Bulletin* 6.11 (2005): 12.

INTRODUCTION

or another by the Sami people of Lapland, the Kluane of the Canadian Yukon, the Kichwa of the Ecuadorian Amazon and many other Indigenous peoples around the world. "Dead land," by contrast, to the Kantu of West Borneo, is land that has been given over to rubber plantations.[47] But climate change also is already killing Indigenous land, which accounts for up to 22 percent of the world's land area, and accounts for 80 percent of the world's biodiversity.[48] In Australia, for instance, Indigenous peoples have reported the erosion of beaches by rising seas, "which for turtles that always return to the same beach to breed is potentially disastrous, not just to the species, but to the Indigenous peoples who hunt them for food and cultural purposes."[49] In the Pacific, whole islands have already been lost, as land is washed out to sea. Land drowned by the ocean is dead land. Dead land is land that has been brutalised, whether by colonial plantation practices, neocolonial extraction technologies or anthropocentric climate change. But Indigenous voices are often not heard in climate debates, which makes Indigenous climate change literature like *The Swan Book* all the more important. Oblivia, the violated protagonist, knows intuitively and for a fact that the black swan is a climate refugee, "banished from where it should be singing its stories ... searching for its soul in her."[50]

In the Caribbean/South American context, Wilson Harris's theorisation of "living landscapes" has its roots (as Melanie Otto states) in "an indigenous-inflected episteme."[51] The living land, as Harris understands it, is not passive. It is active. Always moving, never static. But its music—the sound of trees in the wind, of rivers flowing through rocks—is unscalable. Its dance also is often invisible, like the movement of rocks in deep time to make way for rivers. Living landscapes thread through immeasurable space and time. They witness history, but are not contained by it. Their music derives from "an orchestra of species," articulating a parable of being or "a sacrament of subsistence" that Indigenous peoples, who inherited it from their ancestors, know how to cultivate.[52] Their

---

47 See Michael R. Dove, "Living Rubber, Dead Land, and Persisting Systems in Borneo; Indigenous Representations of Sustainability," Bijdragen tot de taal-, land- en volkenkunde, *Journal of the Humanities and Social Sciences of Southeast Asia* 154.1 (1998): 20–54.

48 "Indigenous Peoples: The Unsung Heroes of Conservation," *UN Environment Programme* (January 9, 2017), https://www.unep.org/zh-hans/node/477.

49 Melissa Nursey-Bray, R. Palmer, T. F. Smith and P. Rist, "Old Ways for New Days: Australian Indigenous Peoples and Climate Change," *Local Environment* 24.5 (2019): 473486.

50 Wright, *The Swan Book*, 15.

51 Melanie Otto, "Poet-Shamanic Aesthetics in the Work of Gloria Anzaldúa and Wilson Harris," *The CLR James Journal* 23.1–2 (Fall 2017): 135.

52 Wilson Harris, "The Music of Living Landscapes," in *Selected Essays of Wilson Harris: The Unfinished Genesis of the Imagination*, ed. Andrew Bundy (London: Routledge, 1999): 41.

ear is attuned to it, and so—when "Nature erupts into Nemesis"[53]—they hear it coming. To resist the climate crisis that has been thrust upon us by the imperialist and industrialist forces of the "civilised" world we must repudiate the "dumbness or passivity with which we subconsciously or unconsciously robe the living world."[54] We must challenge "the hubris of one-sided tradition" and re-sensitise our consciousness and our technologies so that they resonate to "the life of the planet."[55]

But "living land" is also a concept that has been appropriated by First World discourses like those of the "Living Land" coalition—founded by BirdLife (Europe and Central Asia), the World Wide Fund for Nature (Europe) and the European Environmental Bureau—with the aim of reforming the European Union's Common Agricultural Policy (CAP). Organisations seek to address climate change by reforming agriculture, yet they pay little if any attention to Indigenous peoples, who are the frontline of resistance to it.

The postcolonial reading practices that evolved in the 1990s in response to the literary outpourings of cultures struggling to shake off the shackles of their colonial past also provided a lens to critique the hidden power relations of European literary tradition. Similarly, from the development of climate consciousness and the evolving genres of climate literature a new reading optic has begun to emerge. As the foremost imprint of the Anthropocene, climate change is a boundary-defying omnipresence with ecological, political, social, cultural and *literary* implications. Positioning climate change in terms of a critical reading practice—rather than simply as a literary topic or style—contributors to this volume articulate the increasingly profound effects of climate-related formations on literary consciousness, production and analysis.

Ecocritics Adeline Johns-Putra,[56] George B. Handley[57] and others have observed already how the unambiguous climate consciousness of various contemporary writers has made their work readily identifiable as climate fiction, climate poetry and so on. Philip Mead, for example, characterises *The Swan Book* as an "Anthropocene novel."[58] Likewise, Kathy Jetñil-Kijiner's *Iep*

---

53 Harris, "The Music of Living Landscapes," 43.

54 Harris, "The Music of Living Landscapes," 44.

55 Harris, "The Music of Living Landscapes," 44.

56 Adeline Johns-Putra, *Climate Change and the Contemporary Novel* (Cambridge, UK: Cambridge UP, 2019).

57 George B. Handley, "Climate Change, Cosmology, and Poetry: The Case of Derek Walcott's *Omeros*," in *Global Ecologies and the Environmental Humanities: Postcolonial Approaches*, ed. Elizabeth DeLoughrey, Jill Didur and Anthony Carrigan (New York: Routledge, 2015).

58 Philip Mead, "Unresolved Sovereignty and the Anthropocene Novel: Alexis Wright's *The Swan Book*," *Journal of Australian Studies* 42.4 (2018).

INTRODUCTION

Jāltok: Poems from a Marshallese Daughter is readily identifiable as climate poetry in its advocation of climate consciousness.[59] The climate crisis has also spawned a new kind of theatre, with locally specific plays responding to the unique climate challenges of the local environments in which they are produced and performed. The Bennde Mutale Theatre Group, for example, which is located in the Kruger National Park, works to bring environmental education to the local community near the Mozambican and Zimbabwean borders of South Africa, particularly concerning global warming and climate change, and their impact on local environmental and health issues. Other new theatre groups are operating transnationally to address climate change, like the Arctic Cycle group (founded by French-Canadian playwright, Chantal Bilodeau), which aims "to foster dialogue about our global climate crisis, create an empowering vision of the future, and inspire people to take action."[60] The Climate Change Theatre Action alliance is another transnational institution, soliciting new plays from all over the world, and organising performances biennially to coincide with the United Nations Conference of the Parties (COP) meetings, wherever they may be held. There has also been a burgeoning of politically engaged plays—most obviously in Britain, Europe and the U.S., but also in many other countries—for example, *Kayak* (Jordan Hall, Canada, 2010); *Between Two Waves* (Ian Meadows, Australia, 2012); *Bare Spaces* (Angella Emurwon, Uganda 2017); *Earth: A Children's Story for Adults* (Kashyap Raja, India, 2020); and *Hibernation* (Finegan Kruckemeyer, 2021). Indigenous writers have been at the forefront of this movement, with plays like *Calling All Polar Bears* (by Iñupiaq playwright, Allison Akootchook Warden, 2011); *The Unplugging* (by Algonquin playwright, Yvette Nolan); and process-driven performance pieces like *Cut the Sky* (by the Australian Indigenous theatre company, Marrugeku, 2015), and *Min Duoddarat III* (by the Sami National Theatre of Norway, Beaivváš Sámi Našunálateáhter, 2011).

For Indigenous theatre aiming to stimulate climate consciousness, multimedia collaborations also are increasingly important. A case in point is *Moana: The Rising of the Sea*, written by Vilsoni Hereniko (former director of the Oceania Centre for Arts, Culture and Pacific Studies at the University of the South Pacific) and choreographed by Peter Rockford Espiritu (Director of the Oceania Dance Theatre, at the same University), which had its world premiere on 6 December 2013 in Suva to coincide with the European Consortium for Pacific Studies (ECOPAS) conference, "Restoring the Human to Climate

---

59   Kathy Jetñil-Kijiner, *Iep Jāltok: Poems from a Marshallese Daughter* (Tucson, AZ: U of Arizona P, 2017).

60   The Arctic Cycle. "Our Mission," https://www.thearcticcycle.org/mission.

Change." The performance began with a direct address to the audience, written by the Marshall Islands poet and climate activist, Kathy Jetñil-Kijiner (who has kindly allowed us to preface this volume with another of her poems):

> *tell them about the water*
> *how we have seen it rising*
> *flooding across our cemeteries*
> *gushing over the sea walls*
> *and crashing against our homes*
> *tell them what it's like*
> *to see the entire ocean level with the land*
> *tell them*
> *we are afraid*[61]

Along with poetry, *Moana: The Rising of the Sea* incorporated video imagery, song and dance styles from the Solomon Islands, Kiribati, Niue, Samoa and Fiji to enact a powerful plea for recognition for a place that has already begun to disappear under the ocean, and for a people facing forced migration, from a place that most outside of the region would not even know how to find on a map.

> *but most importantly tell them*
> *we don't want to leave*
> *we've never wanted to leave*
> *and that we*
> *are nothing without our islands.*[62]

Eco-theatre generally attempts to focus climate and environmental justice issues on the stage in an attempt to re-shape the audience's attitudes toward the environment and stimulate an acceptance of how entangled human lives are with other animal lives in the context of a much larger ecological community. Indigenous eco-drama, however, as Melissa Colleen Campbell rightly points out, is even more ambitious:

---

61   Kathy Jetñil-Kijiner, "Tell Them," *Iep Jāltok: Poems from a Marshallese Daughter* (Tucson, AZ: Arizona University Press, 2017): 66. This is the poem that Jetñil-Kijiner read at the Global Call for Climate Action (GCCA) protest outside the venue of the 2015 United Nations Climate Change Conference (COP 21).

62   Jetñil-Kijiner, "Tell Them," 67.

Indigenous eco-drama recognizes that Indigenous sovereignty and protection of the environment go hand-in-hand. At its core, Indigenous eco-drama connects the colonization and displacement of Indigenous people with the need to redress one of the most pressing contemporary concerns for Indigenous people globally: the ecological crisis.[63]

Needless to say, the climate crisis, which from a scientific perspective might be seen to subsume all other crises, is only one aspect of the ecological affront that Indigenous peoples have to contend with, from logging and mining corporations and a host of other colonialist/capitalist enterprises.

As Barbara Eckstein points out, "Anthropogenic climate change and the study of literary genre occupy, more or less, the same timescale. They are not an odd couple."[64] On the other hand, "if we give all climate change its due in the history of the Earth, temporal reorientation is required to couple it with the study of genre—or any human act of making and framing."[65] Taking a "deep history" perspective, therefore, it is possible to read even the texts and genres that preceded the contemporary climate crisis—in fact all of the cultural productions of the Anthropocene Epoch—through the lens of climate change.

In recent years a number of literary scholars have begun to take up this challenge. Ken Hiltner's work on air pollution in London in the seventeenth-century, for example, has drawn attention to how the pastoral poets of the period shied away from climate crisis, and how the success of this turn gave literary historians a distorting lens through which to view the bigger picture.[66] Hiltner's salvage of non-canonical texts that did *not* turn their backs on the true environmental problem—like Sir John Denham's topographical poem, *Cooper's Hill* (1642)—is important for this reason. A historicised understanding of the Anthropocene reveals signs of emergent climate consciousness in periods previous to our own that might provide valuable insights for the crisis we find ourselves in today. David Higgins's study of the relationship between British Romanticism and climate change connects Byron, Shelley and other

---

63   Melissa Colleen Campbell, "Reclaiming Indigenous Voices and Staging Eco-activism in Northern Indigenous Theatre," *Seismopolite* 8 (December 2014), http://www.seismopolite.com/reclaiming-indigenous-voices-and-staging-eco-activism-in-northern-indigenous-theatre.

64   Barbara Eckstein, "Introduction—Genres of Climate Change," *Philological Quarterly* 93.3 (Summer 2014): 247.

65   Eckstein, "Introduction—Genres of Climate Change," 247.

66   Ken Hiltner, *What Else Is Pastoral?: Renaissance Literature and the Environment* (Ithaca, NY: Cornell UP, 2011).

writers of the period to current debates in the environmental humanities.[67] As well, a number of other scholars have begun to revisit Victorian Literature with climate change in mind.[68] As Handley suggests, "rereading in light of the challenges posed by the Anthropocene ... may be one of the most important tasks for an environmental humanities."[69] In the light of this challenge, we aim in this volume to extend the possibilities of "rereading" by orchestrating a timely convergence of postcolonial analysis with climate consciousness.

3 Postcolonial Literary Studies and Climate Consciousness: A Timely Convergence

Postcolonial literary studies call attention to the functioning of power in narrative, to the investments of ideology in colonialist discourse and to the marginalised agency of colonised subjects. It is a field that adopts a critical stance in relation not only to the experience of imperialism and colonialism in the past but also toward the ongoing aftermaths of that experience. Postcolonial literature, generally speaking, is a literature of resistance, evolving out of the lived experience of colonial subjugation. It enables the voicing of "small" narratives that have been historically marginalised or silenced by the "big" narratives of colonial mastery.[70] The contemporary task of postcolonial literature is to render—in narrative, poetic or dramatic form—the far-reaching reverberations of diverse experiences of colonialism around the world as they remain embedded in economic militarism, neoliberal development, resource commodification and other destructive operations that work within the "dialectic of invisibility and visibility."[71] The work of postcolonial scholarship, therefore,

---

67   David Higgins, *British Romanticism, Climate Change, and the Anthropocene: Writing Tambora* (London: Palgrave Macmillan, 2017).

68   See for example Daniel Williams, "Victorian Ecocriticism for the Anthropocene," *Victorian Literature and Culture* 45.3 (September 2017): 667–684; Heidi C. M. Scott, "Industrial Souls: Climate Change, Immorality, and Victorian Anticipations of the Good Anthropocene," *Victorian Studies* 60.4 (Summer 2018): 588–610; Tina Young Choi and Barbara Leckie, "Slow Causality: The Function of Narrative in an Age of Climate Change," *Victorian Studies* 60.4 (Summer 2018): 565–587; Peter Adkins and Wendy Parkins, "Introduction: Victorian Ecology and the Anthropocene," *Interdisciplinary Studies in the Long Nineteenth Century* 26 (2018): 1–15.

69   Handley, "Climate Change, Cosmology, and Poetry," 342.

70   Ato Quayson, "Introduction: Postcolonial Literature in a Changing Historical Frame," *The Cambridge History of Postcolonial Literature*, ed. Ato Quayson (Cambridge, UK: Cambridge UP, 2012): 6.

71   Robert J.C. Young, "Postcolonial Remains," *New Literary History* 43.1 (2012): 23.

INTRODUCTION

as Robert J.C. Young maintains, is "to reconstruct Western knowledge formations, reorient ethical norms, turn the power structures of the world upside
down, refashion the world from below."[72] Postcolonial critics operate generally
with a view to change things. The ideal of social transformation that drives
postcolonial scholarship intersects comfortably with the political aims of environmentalism and ecocriticism. Indeed, an ecological perspective now seems
critical to understanding the continuing impacts of colonialism, particularly in
terms of the conventional Nature/Culture divide.[73]

The first international conference to focus on "Commonwealth Literature"—
a nomenclatory precursor for Postcolonial Literature—took place in Leeds,
just two years after the publication of Rachel Carson's *Silent Spring* (1962), the
book that inspired the environmental movement.[74] Yet postcolonialism has
been historically reticent to develop explicitly environmentalist positions, and
ecocriticism has been equally cautious in its embrace of postcolonialism. In
2004, in the first book-length treatment of ecocriticism, Greg Garrard identified "the postcolonial politics of resistance to economic globalisation" as
"an avenue as yet inadequately explored in ecocriticism."[75] A year later Rob
Nixon[76] attributed the "mutually constitutive silences" between environmentalism and postcolonialism to four key differences. First, whereas postcolonialism has traditionally emphasised hybridity and cross-culturation, ecocriticism
historically has favoured more purist discourses concerning wilderness preservation. Second, postcolonialism's concern with displacement contrasts sharply
with ecocriticism's privileging of place in literature.[77] Third, postcolonial critics have "tended to favour the cosmopolitan and the transnational," and have
been typically critical of nationalism, whereas "the canons of environmental
literature and criticism developed within a national (and often nationalistic)
American framework."[78] Fourth, whereas postcolonialism has attended to the

---

72   Young, "Postcolonial Remains," 20.

73   Elizabeth DeLoughrey and George B. Handley, "Introduction: Towards an Aesthetics of the
      Earth," in *Postcolonial Ecologies: Literatures of the Environment*, ed. Elizabeth DeLoughrey
      and George B. Handley (New York: Oxford UP, 2011): 3–41.

74   Rachel Carson, *Silent Spring* (Boston: Houghton Mifflin, 1962).

75   Greg Garrard, *Ecocriticism*, 1st ed. (London: Routledge, 2004): 118.

76   Rob Nixon, "Environmentalism and Postcolonialism," in *Postcolonial Studies and Beyond*,
      ed. Ania Loomba, Suvir Kaul, Matti Bunzl, Antoinette Burton and Jed Esty (Durham,
      NC: Duke UP, 2005): 235.

77   Garrard goes so far as to say that the ecocritical preoccupation with a conception of place
      as a localised phenomenon resulted in an impoverished sense of translocal planetary
      place, *Ecocriticism*, 178.

78   Nixon, "Environmentalism and Postcolonialism," 236.

excavation and re-imagining of marginalised pasts ("often along the transnational axes of migrant memory") ecocriticism has mostly preferred to subordinate history to a timelessness of internalised communion with the natural world.[79] "What would it mean to bring environmentalism into dialogue with postcolonialism?" Nixon asks.[80] His answer was to posit a "transnational ethics of place," as a means to reformulate binary oppositions between "bioregionalism and cosmopolitanism, between transcendentalism and transnationalism, between an ethics of place and the experience of displacement."[81]

It might be thought that Nixon and Garrard overstated the mutual disregard of ecocriticism and postcolonialism, by paying insufficient attention to studies focusing on settler and/or Indigenous representations of land and water, and overlooking attempts to learn from Indigenous environmental stewardship. But Indigenous Studies in some countries regards "postcolonial" scholarship with suspicion, if not hostility, primarily for two reasons. First, because many scholars (including some who identify as "postcolonial") habitually over-simplify the meaning of the prefix ("post"), implying that the time of colonialism has passed (which, for many Indigenous peoples, clearly it has not). Needless to say, our own understanding of the postcolonial in this volume acknowledges the continuing operation of neocolonialist forces in the contemporary moment. Second, as Anna Källén writes: "Postcolonial theory, with its complicating anti-essentialist discourse analysis, can ... easily appear confusing or in conflict with the immediate interests of the indigenous movement (simply because they believe in different routes to solve the problem of domination and oppression)."[82] As we have indicated already with regard to Indigenous theatre, Indigenous activists have a broader notion of collective Earth stewardship and responsibility, which they pursue often at a global level, through trans-Indigenous and/or intercultural coalitions. From an Indigenous perspective the dominant discourses on climate change are themselves colonising. In the Pacific, for example, settler environmentalism focusing on the plight of small island nations faced with the invasion of their homelands by rising seas takes little if any account of how the historical legacies of nuclear imperialism and extractive capitalism have multiplied the risks of climate change, and made its impact more immediately and intensely dangerous.[83] The

---

79   Nixon, "Environmentalism and Postcolonialism," 235.
80   Nixon, "Environmentalism and Postcolonialism," 233.
81   Nixon, "Environmentalism and Postcolonialism," 239, 247.
82   Anna Källén, "Postcolonial Theory and Sámi Archaeology—A Commentary," *Arctic Anthropology* 52.2 (2015): 81.
83   See Aimee Bahng, "The Pacific Proving Grounds and the Proliferation of Settler Environmentalism," *Journal of Transnational American Studies* 1.2 (2020): 45–69.

conservation efforts of settler environmentalist organisations often overlook local Indigenous stakeholders, which is why Indigenous spokespeople tend to regard their efforts as expressions of an outdated "Racialised Neocolonial Global Conservation" movement, the success of which is inevitably undermined by its failure to take account of Indigenous understandings of place and place-making.[84] Postcolonial scholarship properly endorses this Indigenous view by providing studies of the institutional apparatus and the public discourse of global environmentalism that, in many parts of the world, reveal not only their colonial origins and underpinnings but also their continuing neocolonial influence "in the context of globalisation and development."[85]

Over the last fifteen years—particularly in response to climate change as the dominant signature of the Anthropocene—the lack of convergence between postcolonialism and environmentalism lamented by Nixon and Garrard has to some extent been rectified by the emergence of postcolonial ecology and postcolonial environmental humanities as transdisciplinary fields. As Garrard himself noted, in his 2014 Introduction to *The Oxford Handbook of Ecocriticism*, postcolonial critics such as Pablo Mukherjee, Elizabeth DeLoughrey, Rob Nixon and Lizabeth Paravisini-Gebert have successfully disrupted "the canonical and theoretical constructs of first-wave ecocriticism," the Anglo-American dominance of which came to be seen as "intellectually limiting and politically problematic."[86]

One of the earliest efforts to expand the boundaries of postcolonial critique to encompass ecological concerns and methodologies was a special issue of *SPAN* devoted to "Gardening in the Colonies."[87] Published in 1998, and edited by Anne Collett, it provided an early illumination of the vital function of ecology and more-than-human ontologies in literary texts by Australian, Pacific Island and Caribbean authors. Ten years later Graham Huggan was

---

84　See Prakash Kashwan, Rosaleen V. Duffy, Francis Massé, Adeniyi P. Asiyanbi, and Esther Marijne, "From Racialized Neocolonial Global Conservation to an Inclusive and Regenerative Conservation," *Environment: Science and Policy for Sustainable Development* 63.4 (2021): 4–19.

85　See, for example, Maija Anneli Hyle, "Conceptual Reflection on Responsive Environmental Governance," *International Journal of Public Administration* 39.8 (2016): 610–619; also, Prakash Kashwan, et al. "From Racialized Neocolonial Global Conservation to an Inclusive and Regenerative Conservation," 4–19.

86　Greg Garrard, "Introduction", in *The Oxford Handbook of Ecocriticism*, ed. Garrard (Oxford: Oxford UP, 2014): 1–26.

87　SPAN was for many years the journal of the South Pacific Association for Commonwealth Literature and Language Studies (SPACLALS). See Anne Collett, ed. "Gardening in the Colonies" *SPAN* 46 (1998).

able to report the "greening" of postcolonial studies.[88] In the meantime, he and Helen Tiffin introduced the term "green postcolonialism."[89] It referred to new "forms of environmentally oriented postcolonial criticism which insist on the factoring of cultural difference into both historical and contemporary ecological and bioethical debates."[90] But the foundational book-length study of the field, *Postcolonial Ecocriticism: Literature, Animals, Environment*, had to wait until 2010, by which time, as Huggan and Tiffin acknowledged in their Introduction, global warming had become an "impending catastrophe."[91] That year too *Postcolonial Green: Environmental Politics and World Narratives* appeared, a collection of essays edited by Bonnie Roos and Alex Hunt that demonstrated the "green" turn of postcolonialism in literary critical practice.[92] The five-year period that followed was the hottest on record. The World Health Organization reported that its "record temperatures were accompanied by rising sea levels and declines in Arctic sea-ice extent, continental glaciers and northern hemisphere snow cover."[93] There was a growing sense of urgency, in the light of which Huggan and Tiffin began to work towards a revised edition of *Postcolonial Ecocriticism*, in which they might devote more space to postcolonial literature's increasingly innovative engagements with climate change. They timed its publication to coincide with the United Nations Framework Convention on Climate Change's (UNFCCC) Conference of Parties (COP21) in Paris in December 2015.

For Huggan and Tiffin, "green postcolonialism" is a term that mediates the friction between politics and aesthetics that had characterised postcolonial and environmental literary studies alike.[94] It delineates conceptual potentialities for a real-world transformation that might realise both social and environmental justice.[95] In this way, it can be seen as a precursor to postcolonial ecocriticism.

---

88   Graham Huggan, "Greening" Postcolonialism: Ecocritical Perspectives," MFS. *Modern Fiction Studies* 50.3 (2004): 701–733.

89   Graham Huggan and Helen Tiffin, "Green Postcolonialism," *Interventions* 9.1 (2007): 1–11.

90   Huggan and Tiffin, "Green Postcolonialism," 9.

91   Graham Huggan and Helen Tiffin, *Postcolonial Ecocriticism: Literature, Animals, Environment*, 1st ed. (London: Routledge, 2010): 191.

92   Bonnie Roos and Alex Hunt, *Postcolonial Green: Environmental Politics and World Narratives*, ed. Roos and Hunt (Charlottesville, VA: U of Virginia P, 2010).

93   "The Global Climate 2011–2015: Heat Records and High Impact Weather," World Health Organization Press Release (November 8, 2016), https://public.wmo.int/en/media/press-release/global-climate-2011-2015-hot-and-wild.

94   Huggan and Tiffin, "Green Postcolonialism," 10.

95   Huggan and Tiffin, "Green Postcolonialism," 10.

INTRODUCTION

In fact the term was coined in the same year that Cara Cilano and Elizabeth DeLoughrey outlined their own ideas for a postcolonial ecocriticism, in their introduction to a special section of *Interdisciplinary Studies in Literature and Environment*.[96] The most advantageous convergence between postcolonial and ecocritical discourses, they argued, is one characterised by dialogue around the production of heterogeneous forms of local and global knowledge, integrating perspectives from both the social and environmental sciences.[97] "Interdisciplinary, transnational and comparative" (as Cilano and DeLoughrey see it), postcolonial ecocriticism "refuses the nostalgia of pure landscape even while it grapples with the best ways of addressing the representation of the nonhuman environment."[98]

In 2011, in their introduction to *Postcolonial Ecologies: Literatures of the Environment*, DeLoughrey and Handley theorised the postcolonial praxis of ecology as one that contextualises the object of study—relations between human and non-human agents and their environment—by its attention to historical processes of ecocultural mobility, translocation and consumption, and by its acknowledgement that spatial imaginings are only "made possible by the experience of place."[99] Postcolonial ecology, as DeLoughrey and Handley conceive of it, aims to recuperate "the alterity of both history *and* nature, without reducing either to the other."[100] The fundamental principle is to re-imagine human experiences of place at the same time as restoring agency to the more-than-human communities *displaced* by colonialism and globalisation.[101]

The postcolonial approach to the environmental humanities (as outlined by DeLoughrey, Jill Didur and Anthony Carrigan in 2015) gives similar prominence to the potential of the irreducible difference of human and more-than-human subjects.[102] While ecocriticism falls within the broad ambit of the environmental humanities, however its evolution has followed a different path. Ecocriticism arose out of literary departments in the U.S. and U.K. during the 1990s and since then has diversified into specialisms including zoocriticism

---

96   Cara Cilano and Elizabeth DeLoughrey, "Against Authenticity: Global Knowledges and Postcolonial Ecocriticism," *ISLE: Interdisciplinary Studies in Literature and Environment* 14.1 (2007): 73–74.

97   Cilano and DeLoughrey, "Against Authenticity," 74.

98   "Against Authenticity," 80, 79.

99   DeLoughrey and Handley, "Introduction: Toward an Aesthetics of the Earth," 4.

100 DeLoughrey and Handley, "Introduction: Toward an Aesthetics of the Earth," 4.

101 DeLoughrey and Handley, "Introduction: Toward an Aesthetics of the Earth," 4–6.

102 DeLoughrey, Didur and Carrigan, "Introduction: A Postcolonial Environmental Humanities," in *Global Ecologies and the Environmental Humanities: Postcolonial Approaches*, ed. Elizabeth DeLoughrey, Jill Didur and Anthony Carrigan (New York: Routledge, 2015): 3.

(studies of animals and literature) and affective ecocriticism (examining the role of affect, embodiment and emotions in literature as related to ecology). Its focus remains resolutely literary, evolving ways of reading from the perspectives of environmental justice, ecological relationality, ecofeminism, and more recently the urgencies of the Anthropocene including climate change. The environmental humanities, on the other hand, encompass ecocinema (studies of environment and film), ecojournalism, environmental communication, environmental history, environmental philosophy, ecotheology, as well as ecocriticism.

The postcolonial humanities, as distinct from postcolonial criticism, is equally multi-disciplinary. It embraces trauma studies, migration studies, religious studies, history, anthropology and many other disciplines.[103] Where the postcolonial and environmental humanities come together, in terms of a postcolonial environmental humanities, is in their seeking to interrogate the emerging historical, social and epistemological uncertainties provoked by the radically divergent—indeed unfamiliar and alienating—temporal scale of climate change.[104] The role of postcolonial ecocriticism here is vital, exposing how climate narratives are entangled with colonial practices, imperialist formations and globalised exchanges.[105]

As DeLoughrey, Didur and Carrigan argue, postcolonial ecocriticism operates on two fronts as one, the social and the environmental. It interrogates the historical underpinnings of anthropocentrism and it contextualises climate debates in deep geological time. It emphasises voices dispossessed by climate injustice, particularly those of Indigenous peoples, and the diasporic communities formed by climate refugees, environmental migrants and other subaltern subjects pushed beyond the periphery of the urban centres of technocratic elitism.[106] Furthermore, postcolonial ecocriticism questions the grounding of the climate change debate in positivist and masculinist paradigms, as with such organisations as the IPCC, which provides "governments at all levels with scientific information that they can use to develop climate policies" as well seeking to influence "international climate change negotiations."[107]

---

103   For survey of specific disciplinary contributions to the field of postcolonial studies, see Huggan, "Introduction" to *The Oxford Handbook of Postcolonial Studies*, ed Huggan (Oxford: Oxford UP, 2013): 1–26.

104   DeLoughrey, Didur and Carrigan, "Introduction: A Postcolonial Environmental Humanities," 12.

105   DeLoughrey, Didur and Carrigan, "Introduction: A Postcolonial Environmental Humanities," 6.

106   "Introduction: A Postcolonial Environmental Humanities," 6.

107   IPCC, "About the IPCC," para 1, https://www.ipcc.ch/about/.

INTRODUCTION   23

Broadly speaking, the aim of the postcolonial environmental humanities—including postcolonial ecocriticism—is to advance our understanding of "the complex intergenerational ethical issues" of that problem.[108] Ethical frameworks call attention to human responsibility (for climate change triggers), obligation (to future generations and other species) and equity (in handling the global burden of adaptation).[109] For philosopher Stephen Gardiner, the ethical formidability of climate change is that it is a transnational problem of inherent interdisciplinarity, challenging science, economics, politics, law and other knowledge domains.[110] Among these, it is important to recognise literary studies, and more particularly postcolonial literary studies, for climate change is not only an interdisciplinary challenge but also a postcolonial concern. As Michael Woolcott has shown, the global capitalist networks underlying climatic transformation are predicated upon the subjugation of people and the commodification of natural systems.[111] In other words, the pernicious processes of colonial oppression have shapeshifted into modern forms of techno-industrial servitude, laying the groundwork for climate malaise and extremism.[112] As Bruno Latour puts it, "the climate question is at the heart of all *geo*political issues and [...] is directly tied to questions of injustice and inequality."[113] The achievement of climate justice and equality, as visualised by the postcolonial environmental humanities, is contingent upon decolonising processes that reject the idea of human exceptionalism and work to undo the Nature/Culture binarism, and which act out of a sense of the urgencies of the present. As Deborah Bird Rose declaims eloquently in *Reports from a Wild Country*, "the ethical challenge of decolonisation illuminates a ground for powerful presence. Against domination it asserts relationality, against control it asserts mutuality, against hyperseparation it asserts connectivity, and against

---

108   Denis Arnold, "Introduction: Climate Change and Ethics," in *The Ethics of Global Climate Change*, ed. Denis G. Arnold (Cambridge, UK: Cambridge UP, 2011): 1.

109   Arnold, "Introduction: Climate Change and Ethics," 10.

110   Stephen Gardiner, Ethics and Global Climate Change," in *Climate Ethics: Essential Readings*, ed. Stephen M. Gardiner, Simon Caney, Dale Jamieson and Henry Shue (Oxford, UK: Oxford UP, 2010): 3.

111   Michael Northcott, *A Moral Climate: The Ethics of Global Warming* (Maryknoll, NY: Orbis Books, 2007).

112   George B. Handley, "Climate Change, Cosmology, and Poetry: The Case of Derek Walcott's *Omeros*," in *Global Ecologies and the Environmental Humanities: Postcolonial Approaches*, eds Elizabeth DeLoughrey, Jill Didur and Anthony Carrigan (New York: Routledge, 2015): 339.

113   Bruno Latour, *Down to Earth: Politics in the New Climate Regime,* trans. by Catherine Porter (Cambridge UK: Polity Press, 2018): 2, 3, italics original.

claims that rely on an imagined future it asserts engaged responsiveness in the present."[114]

Climate change is deeply rooted in colonial violence.[115] Nixon characterises the incremental violence of climate change as a "slow violence," for it "occurs gradually and out of sight, a violence of delayed destruction that is dispersed across time and space, an attritional violence that is typically not viewed as violence at all."[116] It is "neither spectacular nor instantaneous, but rather incremental and accretive, its calamitous repercussions playing out across a range of temporal scales."[117] The slow registering of this violence of anthropogenic climate change offers a particular challenge to the imagination of writers and artists, as well as activists and concerned citizens.[118] As we indicated earlier, the poorer and less-developed nations of the Global South make them particularly vulnerable to climate catastrophe, where extreme weather events can cause the displacement of communities, conflicts over resources, food and water shortages and disease outbreaks with epidemic potential.[119] There has been much debate about the use of this term, the "Global South." A number of critics find it too homogenising, downplaying the many significant differences between the nations that it attempts to incorporate—not least their different experiences of colonialism. As Siba Grovogu argues, however, it is a deliberately "symbolic" designation, mobilised with postcolonial "political intent." The idea of the Global South attempts to capture a cohesion that began to emerge in the mid-twentieth century as formerly colonised nations began to embrace "political projects of decolonization," moving toward the realisation of a new (postcolonial) world order.[120] In other words, the "Global South" is part of a counter-discourse to precisely the kinds of violence of which we are speaking. Climate change has been a colonial project and it continues to be wielded as a political tool causing untold damage to the peoples of the Global

---

114   Deborah Bird Rose, *Reports from a Wild Country: Ethics for Decolonisation* (Sydney: U of New South Wales P, 2004): 213.

115   Handley, "Climate Change, Cosmology, and Poetry," 337.

116   Rob Nixon, *Slow Violence and the Environmentalism of the Poor* (Cambridge, MA: Harvard UP, 2011): 2.

117   Nixon, *Slow Violence and the Environmentalism of the Poor*, 2.

118   Nixon, *Slow Violence and the Environmentalism of the Poor*, 9–10.

119   Shouraseni Sen Roy, *Linking Gender to Climate Change Impacts in the Global South* (Cham, Switzerland: Springer Nature, 2018): 2–3.

120   Siba Grovogu, "A Revolution Nonetheless: The Global South in International Relations," *The Global South* 5 (Spring 2011): 175.

INTRODUCTION   25

South.[121] It is therefore imperative that postcolonial forms of critique respond to and focus upon it.

As the human species shapes the natural world now on a planetary scale, the longstanding humanist demarcation between natural and human history collapses.[122] The sense of global geological precarity has become an aspect of everyday consciousness. It therefore behoves us all as "geological agents," Dipesh Chakrabarty argues, "to scale up" our "imagination of the human."[123] This scale of the problem tests the limits of our ability to even imagine how we might begin to remedy and transform the situation. We now comprehend— if only vaguely or abstractly—that vast, geological scales of millions of years are imbricated with the quotidian choices and actions of individuals, societies and nations.[124] For Chakrabarty, "the current conjuncture of globalization and global warming leaves us with the challenge of having to think of human agency over multiple and incommensurable scales at once."[125] As a consequence, postcolonial studies must urgently confront humankind's "contradictory registers: as a geophysical force and as a political agent, as a bearer of rights and as author of actions."[126]

Echoing Chakrabarty's emphasis on scale, Ghosh contends in *The Great Derangement* that "the climate crisis is also a crisis of culture, and thus of the imagination."[127] As we have observed already, Ghosh calls into question the capacity of fiction to address the environmental collapse brought on by climate change, and whether the narrative imagination is capable even of absorbing the temporal complexities of the Anthropocene. But climate change fiction is, in Chakrabarty's terms, attempting "to scale up our imagination of the human." Indeed, it has emerged prominently as a "mobilizing idiom,"[128] assisting readers to imagine other forms of life, the potential decline of the human species and the perils of anthropocentrism. Adeline Johns-Putra defines cli-fi as "fiction concerned with anthropogenic climate change or global warming as we

---

121 See, for example, Israel's operationalising of climate change to displace Palestinian Bedouins, Eyal Weizman and Fazal Sheikh, *The Conflict Shoreline: Colonialism as Climate Change* (Göttingen: Steidl, 2015).

122 Dipesh Chakrabarty, "The Climate of History: Four Theses," *Critical Inquiry* 35.2 (2009): 201.

123 Dipesh Chakrabarty, "Anthropocene Time," *History and Theory* 57.1 (2018): 206.

124 Chakrabarty, "Postcolonial Studies and the Challenge of Climate Change," 4.

125 Chakrabarty, "Postcolonial Studies and the Challenge of Climate Change," 1.

126 Chakrabarty, "Postcolonial Studies and the Challenge of Climate Change," 14.

127 Amitav Ghosh, *The Great Derangement: Climate Change and the Unthinkable* (Chicago, IL: U of Chicago P, 2016): 9.

128 DeLoughrey, Didur and Carrigan, "Introduction: A Postcolonial Environmental Humanities," 14.

now understand it."[129] It is not so much a literary genre unto itself as a categorisation demonstrating how the subject of climate increasingly figures into other genres (particularly in science fiction, dystopian and post-apocalyptic fiction, fantasy, memoir).[130] Through narratives of social instability, economic uncertainty and technological utopianism, fictions of climate change challenge readers to struggle with ethical, psychological and political dilemmas.[131] For Johns-Putra, the effectiveness of climate change fiction is its decentring of Anthropos and its problematising of human exceptionalism as a destructive metanarrative that subtends the environmental crisis.[132] Intersecting with postcolonial concerns, cli-fi sheds light on how racism and imperialism function towards global ecological degradation.[133] As Ghassan Hage argues, "racial and ecological domination have the same roots. They emanate from what is today the dominant mode of inhabiting the world," which he calls "generalized domestication."[134] Its key features are domination and othering, for the transcendent purpose of making the world yield up value to ourselves. Climate change novels intervene in dominant climate discourses to instil in their readers a sense of obligation to future generations.[135]

Climate change poetry, on the other hand—or cli-po as Craig Santos Perez terms it in Chapter 8 of this volume—has evolved as a discrete branch of ecopoetry. Scott Knickerbocker, in his influential elaboration of ecopoetry, theorises the term "sensuous poiesis" to signify the ways in which poetry enacts "through formal devices such as sound effects the speaker's experience of the complexity, mystery, and beauty of nature."[136] Sensuous poiesis is also a vital dimension of cli-po, in which poems approximate—in their arrangement, lineation and other stylistic features—the complexity, magnitude, disorder and disarray of climate-related catastrophe. Cli-po is marked by the interchange between lyrical descriptions of nature and lament over the destruction caused by human activities.[137] It recognises "the permeability and constitution of the

---

129   Johns-Putra, "Climate Change in Literature and Literary Studies: From Cli-Fi, Climate Change Theatre and Ecopoetry to Ecocriticism and Climate Change Criticism," *WIRES Climate Change* 7 (2016): 267.

130   Johns-Putra, "Climate Change in Literature and Literary Studies," 267.

131   Johns-Putra, "Climate Change in Literature and Literary Studies," 269.

132   Johns-Putra, "The Rest Is Silence: Postmodern and Postcolonial Possibilities in Climate Change Fiction," *Studies in the Novel* 50.1 (2018): 40.

133   Johns-Putra, "The Rest Is Silence," 32.

134   Ghassan Hage, *Is Racism an Environmental Threat?* (Cambridge: Polity Press, 2017): 1.

135   Johns-Putra, *Climate Change and the Contemporary Novel*, 39–40.

136   Scott Knickerbocker, *Ecopoetics: The Language of Nature, the Nature of Language* (Amherst, MA: U of Massachusetts P, 2012): 13.

137   Johns-Putra, "Climate Change in Literature and Literary Studies," 272.

INTRODUCTION

self within systemic exchanges" while—in a postcolonial sense—voicing the experiences of those impacted by climatic disruption and its subjacent imperialisms.[138] Jetñil-Kijiner's collection, *Iep Jāltok,* offers a compelling example of climate change poetry, foregrounding the urgencies of an island nation threatened by rising sea levels. Her poem "Two Degrees," for instance, opens with the image of the speaker's fever-stricken toddler, an affective strategy for narrating the implications of a warming climate on the low-lying topography of the Marshall Islands. The speaker poignantly evokes the importance of poetry and narrative more generally in a world confronted by conflicting messages about climate: "So that people / remember / that beyond / the discussions / numbers / and statistics / there are faces."[139]

Memoir also is an increasingly persuasive form for focussing on climate change, not only alerting readers to the realities but also encouraging them to action. Climate change memoir is an emerging genre—a sub-genre of environmental life writing, as Stephen Siperstein explains, or ecobiography— that explores "what it means, and what it feels like, to be an individual in the Anthropocene, entangled in communities of human and nonhuman beings."[140] The most highly profiled example of the genre perhaps is the Swedish family memoir, *Our House Is on Fire: Scenes of a Family and a Planet in Crisis* (2020) by Malena Ernman, Beata Ernman, Svante Thunberg and Greta Thunberg. But there are others. In Canada, for example: Carrie Saxifrage's *The Big Swim: Coming Ashore in a World Adrift* (2015), Sheila Watt-Cloutier's *The Right to Be Cold: One Woman's Fight to Protect the Arctic and Save the Planet from Climate Change* (2015) and Bren Smith's *Eat Like a Fish: My Adventures as a Fisherman Turned Restorative Ocean Farmer* (2019).

4 Climate Change as Postcolonial Resistance Discourse

Political scientists Heather W. Cann and Leigh Raymond observe that the "denial of climate change science has long been seen as a central impediment to the development of climate-energy policy."[141] By promoting climate change

---

138 Heidi Lynn Staples, "Preface," in *Big Energy Poets: Ecopoetry Thinks Climate Change*, ed. Heidi Lynn Staples and Amy King (Buffalo, NY: Blazevox Books, 2017): 14.

139 Jetñil-Kijiner, *Iep* Jāltok, 78–79.

140 Stephen Siperstein, "Climate Change in Literature and Culture: Conversion, Speculation, Education," Unpublished PhD Dissertation (University of Oregon, 2016): 85.

141 Heather W. Cann and Leigh Raymond, "Does Climate Denialism Still Matter? The Prevalence of Alternative Frames in Opposition to Climate Policy," *Environmental Politics* 27.3 (2018): 433.

scepticism, anti-science movements work to stifle the growth of ecologically-inflected paradigms, policies, practices and possibilities. Cann and Raymond have also observed a rising trend towards personal attacks on the integrity of climate researchers and their supporters.[142] Not limited to Trump-inspired right-wing populism, anti-science climate denialism has permeated Australian politics, especially since Prime Minister Scott Morrison took office in 2018. During the 2019–20 Australian bushfires, the role of climate denialism in perpetuating the catastrophe came into full view, as a consequence of which Australia has been described as a nation "pioneering the denial of climate disaster."[143] The Deputy Prime Minister at the time, Michael McCormack, ridiculed the linking of drought and fire to climate change as the fanaticism of "inner-city raving lunatics."[144]

Research has shown a systematic gender correlation with anthropogenic climate change scepticism: men are much more likely to be in climate change denial than women. Denialists are also likely to be political conservatives, endorsing ideologies that favour maintenance of the status quo. In other words, climate denial is associated with "social dominance orientation and system justification."[145] Typically, system justifications widespread in Western societies involve self-serving beliefs or ideologies (for example: market-driven processes and outcomes are inherently equitable and just; or success is an indicator of individual application and accomplishment rather than of social class, or race, or gender, or ethnicity). These are the kind of ideologies that gravitate against collective action, preserving and legitimating inequality, and generally they are regarded as cross-cultural ideologies. In New Zealand researchers have discovered that there are also some system-justifying ideologies that are specific to postcolonial cultures, such as "historical negation" (the denial of the contemporary relevance of past injustices) and "symbolic exclusion" (the rejection of Indigenous cultures from the nation's identity).[146] But they also undermine action on climate change, not only because they marginalise the

---

142   Cann and Leigh Raymond, "Does Climate Denialism Still Matter?," 449.
143   Ketan Joshi, "Something Else Is Out of Control in Australia: Climate Disaster Denialism," *Guardian* Australia edition (January 8, 2020).
144   Michael McCormack qtd. in David Crowe, "Deputy PM Slams People Raising Climate Change in Relation to NSW Bushfires," *Sydney Morning Herald* (November 11, 2019).
145   Taciano L.Milfont, Wokje Abrahamse and Edith A. MacDonald, "Scepticism of Anthropogenic Climate Change: Additional Evidence for the Role of System-Justifying Ideologies," *Personality and Individual Differences* 168 (2021): 110237.
146   Danny Osborne, Kumar Yogeeswaran and Chris G. Sibley, "Culture-Specific Ideologies Undermine Collective Action Support: Examining the Legitimizing Effects of Postcolonial Belief Systems," *Group Processes & Intergroup Relations* 20.3 (2017): 333–349.

INTRODUCTION

communities most often in closest relationship with their environment and at most immediate risk, but also because, more generally, they are motivated by a desire to maintain the social hierarchies and preserve the social systems that provide their socially dominant adherents with power. Needless to say, it is the most privileged people and nations—the most powerful—that have the most opportunity to mitigate climate change, and to adapt to it.[147]

In this volume we conceive of anthropogenic climate change as a discourse of resistance, an inherently postcolonial discourse. Resistance discourses aim generally to countervail hegemonic imperialisms, while affirming "a general need for a critique of domination."[148] We see particularly significant possibilities for literary activism in postcolonial climate narratives. Denialists remain stubbornly indifferent to scientific consensus.[149] Science on its own has proved insufficient to resist the power of denialism. It needs other voices and discourses to assist; and if, as Tom Cohen proposes, climate change has "something like a literary structure," driving towards the seemingly inevitable closure of ecocide,[150] literary criticism has a key role to play in deconstructing that narrative. In any case, *Postcolonial Literatures of Climate Change* seeks to challenge mainstream denialism and open the climate change narrative to critical scrutiny in the light of the interrelated subjugations of people and land in the Anthropocene context.

A core feature of postcolonial literature is its inscription of the pervasive traces of climate change. Colonialism, neo-imperialism, capitalism and climate change are imbricated in a manner that critics are only now beginning to comprehend. But the reality is, as Australian novelist, Jennifer Mills, argues: "All novels are Anthropocene novels."[151] The prefixed genres of literature discussed above (cli-fi, cli-po, and so on) have in this sense already ceased

---

147 See Kirsti M. Jylhä and Nazar Akrami, "Social Dominance Orientation and Climate Change Denial: The Role of Dominance and System Justification," *Personality and Individual Differences* 86 (2015): 108–111.

148 Andrew Biro, "Introduction: The Paradoxes of Contemporary Environmental Crisis and the Redemption of the Hopes of the Past," in *Critical Ecologies: The Frankfurt School and Contemporary Environmental Crises*, ed. Andrew Biro (Toronto: U of Toronto P, 2011): 4.

149 Greg Garrard, Axel Goodbody, George B. Handley and Stephanie Posthumus, *Climate Change Scepticism: A Transnational Ecocritical Analysis* (London: Bloomsbury, 2019).

150 Tom Cohen, "Trolling "Anthropos"—Or, Requiem for a Failed Prosopopeia," in *Twilight of the Anthropocene Idols*, ed. Tom Cohen, Claire Colebrook and J. Hillis Miller (London: Open Humanities P, 2016): 26.

151 Jennifer Mills, quoted in Broede Carmody, "How Climate Anxiety is Changing the Face of Australian Fiction," *Sydney Morning Herald* (June 20, 2019), https://www.smh.com.au/entertainment/books/how-climate-anxiety-is-changing-the-face-of-australian-fiction-20190619-p51z44.html.

to apply, as it becomes increasingly clear that climate change is a less of a problem than it is a condition of life in the Anthropocene Era. As Australian writer and environmentalist, Jane Rawson, maintains, "All novels written now should be climate change novels ... Realist novels that don't have climate change as part of the contemporary landscape are fantasies, genre novels."[152] There is nothing wrong with genre fiction (cli-fi, sci-fi, fantasy and so on) except that, until recently at least, it has often not been taken seriously as literature. Still, that too is changing, and has been now for some time. The critical reception of texts like Margaret Atwood's MaddAddam Trilogy (2003, 2009, 2013), Cormac McCarthy's novel *The Road* (2006) and Barbara Kingsolver's *Flight Behaviour* (2012) prove this point.

Genre fiction generally reaches a wider audience than literary fiction, which may be one reason so many writers have chosen apocalyptic (and post-apocalyptic) science fiction as a means to address climate change. Or is it, as McKenzie Wark argues, that "climate change exceeds what the form of the bourgeois novel can express?"[153] In *The Great Derangement* Ghosh characterises the birth of the modern novel—that is, the realist novel, which developed to dominance in the nineteenth century—in terms of "the banishment of the improbable and the insertion of the everyday."[154] This means that the true motor of the narrative is concealed by what Franco Moretti calls "fillers," which function to maintain the illusion of life being under control. Moretti understands that all cultural forms "are the abstract of social relationships: so, formal analysis is in its own modest way an analysis of power."[155] With the onset of climate change, the world is demonstrably out of control; and the novel, which has never before had "to confront the centrality of the improbable,"[156] has been struggling to adapt, even with the "cultural turn" of climate studies. In this context, the growing fascination of genre fiction might be seen as a sign of the literary novel's looming obsolescence.

---

152   Jane Rawson, quoted in Ben Brooker, "Climate Change Was So Last Year: Writers' Festivals and the Great Derangement," *Overland* (September 3, 2018), https://overland.org.au/2018/09/climate-change-was-so-last-year-writers-festivals-and-the-great-derangement/.

153   McKenzie Wark, "On the Obsolescence of the Bourgeois Novel in the Anthropocene," *Verso* (August 16, 2017), https://www.versobooks.com/blogs/3356-on-the-obsolescence-of-the-bourgeois-novel-in-the-anthropocene. See also Wark, "The Engine Room of Literature: On Franco Moretti," *Los Angeles Review of Books* (June 5, 2013), https://lareviewofbooks.org/article/the-engine-room-of-literature-on-franco-moretti/.

154   Ghosh, *The Great Derangement*, 17.

155   Franco Moretti, "Conjectures on World Literature," *New Left Review* 1. (January/February 2000): 66.

156   Ghosh, *The Great Derangement*, 23.

INTRODUCTION

In fact, the literary novel, the bourgeois novel, the modern novel—essentially the realist novel—has been out of favour with postcolonial authors and critics for decades. Wilson Harris, for example, regarded the continuing dominance of realism in the modern novel as evidence of a widespread "addiction to imperium."[157] Realism, in his view, is one of the trappings—indeed, "it is the bastion"[158] —of imperialism. It is linked irrevocably to both the ideology of "extreme materialism"[159] and the "linear bias"[160] of progress. It is one of the primary modes of oppression. Realism, as Harris sees it, confines the imagination to "objective" reality, thus disenabling any genuine innovation or vision of social change. In other words, realism prevents genuine action on climate change.

Much work has been done on how postcolonial genres serve as social devices to articulate the kinds of fears and desires that feed into differing nation formations.[161] The renewed focus on genre, in order to understand the effectiveness of different forms of cultural expression in organising the discourses of climate change, is now a matter of urgency.[162] But if we want to know which genres are the most effective at stimulating conversions of belief, transformations of attitudes and real action to mitigate climate change we need something more than genre studies. We need more empirical reception studies, which are localised to particular reading communities. After all, no genre can reach every reader, because every society of readers incorporates a range of different interpretive communities, whose selves are shaped by multiple variables and allegiances, of race, gender, ethnicity, class, age, and so on. Reception studies of climate genres are therefore increasingly important;[163] and a postcolonial perspective will hopefully assist reception studies to avoid the tendency toward globalised and ahistorical findings.

---

157 Harris, "On the Beach," *Landfall* 39.3 (155) (September 1985): 335.
158 Harris, "On the Beach," 335.
159 Harris, "On the Beach," 335.
160 Wilson Harris, "The Fabric of the Imagination," in *The Radical Imagination: Lectures and Talks*, eds. Alan Riach and Mark Williams (Liège, Belgium: L3- Liège Language and Literature, 1992): 72.
161 See for example Sarah Ilott, *New Postcolonial British Genres: Shifting the Boundaries* (London: Palgrave Macmillan, 2015); Saskia Schabio and Walter Goebel, ed., *Locating Postcolonial Narrative Genres* (London: Routledge, 2015).
162 See for example Sune Auken and Christel Sunesen, eds. *Genre in the Climate Debate* (Warsaw, Poland: De Gruyter Open Poland, 2021).
163 See for instance Michael T. Bravo, "Voices from the Sea Ice: The Reception of Climate Impact Narratives," *Journal of Historical Geography* 35.2 (April 2009): 256–278; Matthew Schneider-Mayerson, "The Influence of Climate Fiction: An Empirical Survey of Readers," *Environmental Humanities* 10.2 (November 2018): 473–500.

Postcolonial Literatures of Climate Change conceptualises climate change as a discourse of resistance to social orders that maintain the illusion of everyday gradualism, that foster neo-colonial denialism, that practise climate colonialism, and that maintain their own wealth and stability by neoliberal modes of global governance (or dominance). We see significant possibilities for literary activism in postcolonial climate narratives, which dramatise the "incorporation of subaltern lives into the market logics of transnational capital, albeit shrouded in the narrative of development."[164] Some chapters here focus directly on climate texts, such as Jetñil-Kijiner's poem "Two Degrees" (discussed above). Other chapters provide readings—analyses, re-imaginings—that proceed through the contemporary climate optic. After all, climate change as we now know it is the effect of a fossil fuel economy that took shape in nineteenth-century Britain, "through its coal-powered factories, railways, and steamships, which drove the emergence of modern consumer capitalism."[165] Imaginative literature enables writers and readers to envisage possibilities beyond climate denialist politics. In short, climate change in our view is a site of resistance and transformation, as well as a fountainhead of potentiality and hope.

5   Overview of Chapters

In this vein, Geoffrey V. Davis imagines the possibilities that unfold when writers turn to activism in the Anthropocene era. As editors, we are honoured to feature Davis's chapter, the final academic piece he completed before his death in 2018. Highly personal and reflective at times, the discussion takes to heart Huggan and Tiffin's cue that literature can function as "a catalyst for social action."[166] Davis suggests that the writings of authors such as Ganesh Devy, Arundhati Roy, Ken Saro-Wiwa, Helon Habila and Amitav Ghosh have in common a view of literature and the writing process as a means to raise public awareness of the ecological urgencies disproportionately impacting the Global South. Informing the chapter is Davis's own collaboration with Ganesh Devy, an Indian scholar-activist who in 1996 began working with the Denotified and

---

164   Mohan J Dutta, Jagadish Thaker and Kang Sun, "Neoliberalism, Neocolonialism, and Communication for Social Change: A Culture-Centered Agenda for the Social Sciences," *Global Media Journal* (2014): 1–13.

165   Philip Steer, "Reading Classic Novels in an Era of Climate Change," *The Conversation* (May 23, 2017), https://theconversation.com/reading-classic-novels-in-an-era-of-climate-change-75843.

166   Huggan and Tiffin, *Postcolonial Ecocriticism*, 35.

Nomadic Tribes (DNT) and Adivasis of India. Devy's shift to activism inspired Davis's interest in Indigenous peoples, observing in particular: their social deprivation through lack of access to education and the loss of traditional lands; and the endangerment of their languages through cultural fragmentation. Confronting climate change, environmental pollution and Indigenous agency, the interventions made by these writers, in Davis's view, exemplify the contribution that literature can make—by its insistent reading of materialities—to urgent societal concerns.

Contemporary climate change at the biospheric level is occurring alongside a transformation in the climate of the humanities, both in their institutional downgrading (in education) and in the perception of their contribution to social and cultural debate. The confluence of climate change, literature, activism and Indigenous cultures considered in Davis's chapter similarly forms the basis of Chris Prentice's "River Writing: Culture, Law and Poetics." Prentice brings postcolonial literature and climate change into generative dialogue with legal discourse. Through analysis of New Zealand's Whanganui River Claims Settlement Act of 2017, the chapter articulates a new transdisciplinary mode of re-reading in response to Anthropocene exigencies. The Act enshrines the ancestral status of the Whanganui River for the Whanganui people. Prentice's discussion critically considers the legal document in connection to literary texts that narrativise the agencies of rivers within more-than-human worlds, focusing specifically on poems by the Māori poet Hone Tuwhare, and on the novel *Carpentaria*, by Indigenous Australian (Waanyi) writer, Alexis Wright. Spanning the discursively binarised registers of law and poetics—language in the services, respectively, of settlement and unsettlement—these literary writings attend less to recognisable climate change phenomena than to the enmeshment of historical, cultural and political factors with questions of human "being" among elemental and environmental "beings" and phenomena. Prentice meticulously traces how writers such as Tuwhare and Wright deploy language to evince the relational ontology and temporal dynamism urgently needed as humanity confronts the consequences of climatic disruption.

The implications of climate change for postcolonial analysis in the Pacific Ocean region is the subject of Paul Sharrad's chapter, "Which Island, What Home? Plantation Ecologies and Climate Change in Australia and Nauru." Sharrad develops the idea of "plantation ecologies" to illustrate how writers now grapple with the question of aesthetics while talking back to power differentials in science, technology, environment and material culture. Sharrad, like many of the contributors to this volume, considers how colonialist-imperialist systems fuel the ecocidal acceleration of the present. He reasserts the value of postcolonial literary analysis as a decolonising apparatus through a focus on the literature of Nauru. Sharrad's close reading of literary works from Nauru illuminates the strategies developed by Pacific writers to story the ecological depredations leading to climate catastrophe.

"Islandness" (the characteristics of being an island, like Nauru, as distinct from a continent), postcoloniality and climate change converge uniquely in Stephen Harris's chapter, "Island Life and Wild Time: Crossing into Country in Tim Winton's *Island Home*." Harris emphasises the implicit intertwining of the geographical and the autobiographical in Australian writer-activist Tim Winton's landscape memoir. For Harris, Winton's memoir challenges traditional conceptions of life writing in the climate change era while questioning prevailing assumptions about Nature and Culture. Harris propounds that a conception of more-than-human beings and elements as "family" invites non-Indigenous Australians particularly to learn to "see" Country—that is, to transform their frame of mind, allowing deeper and more nuanced perceptions of place. In Harris's view, the premise of "family" at the heart of Winton's *Island Home* implies ethical obligations, challenging governments and communities to respond to climate disturbance. Incorporating a deep geological temporal perspective into life writing, Harris contends, enables Winton to expand upon the potential of imaginative literature to enhance our understanding of alternative temporalities and ontologies of place (such as "island life" and "wild time"). Indeed, climate extremification—an urgency underlying Winton's memoir—demands that Australians, and all other global citizens, accept their place within the Earth-family.

Extending Harris's attention to the literary mediation of "island life" and "wild time" in a climate-disturbed world, John C. Ryan's chapter, "Islands Within Islands: Climate Change and the Deep Time Narratives of the Southern Beech," develops a "Gondwanan" approach to the postcolonial environmental humanities. Ryan analyses the deep time poetics of the "southern beech tree"—the vernacular name for a genus of trees (*Nothofagus* spp.) that has survived the disintegration of the Gondwanan supercontinent and endured the climatic transformations of innumerable millennia. Deep time narratives are of burgeoning interest to climate change scholars, for they engage the registers of geological time as it manifests in places, things and bodies. Ryan traces the arboreal narratives of poets James K. Baxter and Ruth Dallas (New Zealand), Pablo Neruda and Gabriela Mistral (Chile) and Peter Kama Kerpi and Steven Edmund Winduo (Papua New Guinea). He argues that their poetry constructs deep time not as a temporal abstraction but as a perceivable formation of everyday experience—one that becomes palpable especially through human sensory interactions with ancient trees. Inflected by the urgency of botanical loss in the Anthropocene, Ryan's re-reading of these poets, through a southern

INTRODUCTION

beech tree focus, hinges on a dual sense of vulnerability and vitality. The trees figure simultaneously as resilient witnesses to the climatic disruptions of the past and as potential casualties of the anthropogenic climate change of the nearing future. Notwithstanding the precarious ecological conditions of Gondwanan trees in Chile, New Zealand, Papua New Guinea and elsewhere, poetry, in Ryan's assessment, can empower the public to envisage possibilities for responding to a climate-disturbed future in dialogue with the wisdom of plants.

As Ryan traces the registers of deep time in southern beech tree narratives, so Kasia Mika and Sally Stainier foreground the non-linear temporality of algal narratives, specifically in relation to the seaweed genus *Sargassum*. In "Refashioning Futures with Sargassum: A Caribbean Poetics of Hope," they postulate "coiled temporality" as a temporal mode predicated on interconnected archipelagic time(s). Their formulation extends the revered Martinican poet and novelist Édouard Glissant's theorisation of time, colonialism and imperial resistance in the Caribbean but also takes into account the more-than-human other (sargassum) and its oceanic histories. Crucially, their approach calls attention to the demarcation between "weather" and "climate"—a distinction also explored by Agnes S. K. Yeow in the Malaysian context (see Chapter 9). Seasonal storms might give warning, strike, then subside but climate change never leaves, inexorably shaping visions of (im)possible futures of life on Caribbean islands. Mika and Stainier bring anthropological texts into conversation with Caribbean literary and philosophical works to enunciate a new analytical lexicon for thinking about interwoven human-non-human vulnerabilities in an era of intensive—yet unevenly distributed—climate change impacts. The generative notion of "coiled temporality" resists linear constructions of Caribbean futures, opening upon unexpected moments of time folding in upon itself.

The transformation of "islandness" in response to climatic disturbance is also emphasised in Craig Santos Perez's chapter, " 'Kāne and Kanaloa Are Coming': Contemporary Hawaiian Poetry and Climate Change." Perez emphasises the significance of *ʻike ʻāina* (environmental knowledge), *wahi pana* (place stories), *malama ʻāina* (respect for land) and *aloha ʻāina* (love of land). His discussion brings crucial attention to Hawaiʻi—a place routinely neglected in global media accounts of climate change in the Pacific. Perez begins by examining how the *Hawaiʻi Sea Level Rise Vulnerability and Adaptation Report* of 2017 depicts Kānaka Maoli (Native Hawaiian) culture and *ike ʻāina*. He then turns to the work of Kānaka Maoli writers—Kealiʻi Mackenzie, Joe Balaz and Brandy Nālani McDougall—who articulate a Hawaiian climate change poetics, giving prominence to the interconnections between Hawaiian identity, culture, genealogy and ecology. For Perez, their poetry critiques persistent environmental injustices relating to climate change, including "carbon colonialism"—that is, the insistence on carbon reductions in the Global South to offset the carbon emissions of the Global North.[167] As the *Report* makes clear, the denial of Indigenous Hawaiian self-determination abjures the rights of Hawaiian people to shape the archipelago's future. Hawaiian cli-po articulates a discourse of resistance to recuperate the Indigenous sovereignty necessary to confront climate issues in the Pacific.

Complementing Perez's discussion of climate poetry in Hawai'i, Agnes S. K. Yeow proposes the terms "socio-climatic poetry" and "socio-climatic literature" in her chapter, "Monsoonal Memories and 'the Reliable Water': Reading Climate Change in Selected Malaysian Literature." Within the context of a push in Malaysian politics towards climate sustainability, Yeow considers literary works that narrativise the climate-disturbed ecologies of postcolonial Malaysia. Yeow grounds her analysis in the Malay term for homeland *tanahair*, denoting "landwater" and reflecting the fluid character of the tropical country. Yeow draws attention to how the Malaysian-American writer Shirley Geok-lin Lim's diasporic identity invigorates her memories of Asian monsoons and the coastal ecologies of her childhood. Her experience of the unseasonal warmth of an American city elicits recollections of ancestral *tanahair*, inculcating critical awareness of the global reach of climate disruption. Similarly, Yeow draws attention to poet Muhammad Haji Salleh's interest in the anthropogenic destabilisation of "reliable water," a reference to the ancient hydrological system that, in turn, serves as a metonym for the country as a whole. In Yeow's assessment, the poetry of Muhammad and Lim brings postcolonial environmental justice to bear on the climatic future of Malaysia. Placing critical attention on the many victims of climate trauma, their work represents the possibilities of "socio-climatic" literature.

Amany Dahab's chapter "Aswan High Dam and Haggag Oddoul's *Stories from Old Nubia*: Redefining the Line between Immediate Catastrophe and Slow Violence," traces the slow violence of climate change in the Nile Valley, focusing on the Egyptian writer Haggag Oddoul's *Nights of Musk*. Oddoul's short stories confront the prolonged catastrophic consequences of the Aswan High Dam, often lauded as an icon of resistance to British colonialism. By Dahab's analysis, the catastrophe of the dam is both protracted and attritional, with its contribution to climate change the most pernicious effect. Dahab examines

---

167   See Heidi Bachram, "Climate Fraud and Carbon Colonialism: The New Trade in Greenhouse Gases," *Capitalism Nature Socialism* 15.4 (2004): 5–20.

INTRODUCTION

the attritional catastrophes that have been obscured by temporal, geographical and rhetorical factors—the neocolonial slow violence of the dam affecting subsequent generations. Indeed, as Emad Elba, Brigitte Urban, Bernd Ettmer and Dalia Farghaly point out, "Egypt is likely to become one of the most vulnerable countries in the world in the next several decades. Many climate scenarios predict that climate change will severely affect rainfall in the Nile basin and the flow of the Nile River in general and the High Aswan Dam Reservoir (HADR) in particular."[168] Dahab explicates Oddoul's storying as a means to confront the paradox of the dam's origins in Egyptian nationalism and Anglo-American imperialism while, at the same time, exposing its climatic disruptions. Her historically-nuanced reading of *Nights of Musk* draws attention to the power of the literary imagination not only to presage but also to make present the devastating consequences of climate interference.

From Egypt's Aswan High Dam, *Postcolonial Literatures of Climate Change* turns next to the Canadian Arctic, with Renée Hulan's "Caring for the Future: Climate Change, Kinship and Inuit Knowledge." Hulan begins by acknowledging a tendency within Canadian literature, culture and politics to underplay what John McCannon has termed "Arcticide."[169] Contemporary Canadian literary fiction typically figures climate change as a backdrop to human affairs, rather than focusing on the more-than-human consequences of the continuing degradation of the Arctic environment. Hulan contrasts this denialism with Indigenous Canadian attitudes to Arcticide, foregrounding the climate consciousness of Inuit artists, Tanya Tagaq and Zacharias Kunuk as integral to understanding climate change in the Canadian Arctic. In her analysis of their work, Hulan underscores the dangers of scholarship in the environmental humanities that perpetuates the colonialist attitudes that have caused the ecological disaster in the first place. For Hulan, a lack of engagement with the material and cultural contexts of First Nations climate narratives prompts ethical questions about the role of Indigeneity in theorisations of the Anthropocene. This chapter shows how Indigenous scholars have created frameworks for understanding the narratives of Tagaq and Kunuk as a challenge to denialism, drawing attention to the shared consequences of the climate crisis. For Hulan, Indigenous Canadian narratives illuminate the

---

168   Emad Elba, Brigitte Urban, Bernd Ettmer and Dalia Farghaly, "Mitigating the Impact of Climate Change by Reducing Evaporation Losses: Sediment Removal from the High Aswan Dam Reservoir," *American Journal of Climate Change* 6 (May 2017): 230.

169   John McCannon, *A History of the Arctic: Nature, Exploration and Exploitation* (London: Reaktion, 2013): 280.

potential of creative expression and collaboration to engender an ethics of care for the Arctic in the Anthropocene.

From the Artic, *Postcolonial Literatures of Climate Change* moves to the Antarctic. Hanne E. F. Nielsen's "Fictional Representations of Antarctic Tourism and Climate Change: To the Ends of the World" considers the ways Antarctic tourism has contributed to, and been depicted in, literary fiction. She focuses on the Bulgarian-German writer and translator Ilija Trojanow, who grew up in Kenya. For Nielsen, Trojanow's work re-centres Antarctica, inviting readers to understand the southernmost continent as part of broader global systems of power, labour and climate. Elizabeth Leane's chapter, "Ice Islands of the Anthropocene: The Cultural Meanings of Antarctic Bergs," on the other hand, takes as its point of departure the media frenzy that surrounded the calving of a large iceberg as it broke free of the Larsen B Ice Shelf in 2017. From the disintegration of the ice shelf, this giant iceberg (A68) formed, measuring "more than 2,300 square miles (6,000 square km) in area."[170] A68 was conferred an identity, a cultural value and a narrative agency that its counterparts have generally been refused. Its calving, for Leane, constitutes a "cryo-historical moment" that needs to be understood socioculturally as well as scientifically. A "cryobiographical" appreciation of A68 affirms the extent to which bergs are interconnected with human desires. These concluding chapters, by Leane and Nielsen, reflect a relatively new and unsettling postcolonial engagement with Antarctica,[171] demonstrating how it has been subjected to competing and often overlapping colonising projects and agendas, fueled by desires for territory, knowledge and resources.

6   Coda: Climate in the Time of Covid-19

When we started on this Introduction at the beginning of 2020 it seemed immediately appropriate to open with a brief retrospect on Australia's "Black Summer" of 2019–2020. Since then, the climatic disasters have just kept coming: record-breaking hurricanes, cyclones, floods and fires. The rainforests of Brazil experienced their worst fires in a decade. By October 2020,

---

170   Brandon Specktor, "The World's Largest Iceberg May Have Just Begun Its Death March" *Live Science* (4 April 2020), https://www.livescience.com/worlds-largest-iceberg-dying .html.

171   See Klaus Dodds, "Post-Colonial Antarctica: An Emerging Engagement," *Polar Record* 42 (2006): 59–79; also, Dodds and Christy Collis, "Post-Colonial Antarctica," in K. Dodds, P. Roberts, and A. Hemmings, eds. *Handbook on the Politics of Antarctica.* (London, UK: Edward Elgar Publishing, 2017): 50–68.

INTRODUCTION   39

the Amazon (which crosses the borders of nine countries) had 28,892 active
fires. In November, Cyclone Amphan, which had already caused havoc in the
Philippines and Vietnam, moved across the Bay of Bengal to Bengal to wreak
further devastation in India and Bangladesh. It was the biggest cyclonic storm
over the Bay of Bengal in two decades. That same month, in Central America,
Hurricane Eta smashed its way across Guatemala, Mexico, El Salvador, Panama,
Nicaragua and Costa Rica, leaving destruction its wake. The Atlantic hurricane
season of 2020 turned out to be one of the worst on record. Now as we write,
eighteen months after we began, the climate disasters are again shaping up
to be of unprecedented magnitude. Europe, China, India, the Philippines: all
have been inundated by torrential rains, causing mass evacuations and food
insecurities. Wildfires are raging across the United States. Three million acres
have burned this year, and the fire season is far from over. Forest fires are also
burning out of control in Siberia, which is experiencing the worst fire season
in memory—more than 200,000 fires so far, and that is just within the Russian
Republic of Sakha (Yakutia). Needless to say, these blazes are also emitting
"record amounts of carbon while their smoke transits the North Pole."[172] Mark
Parrington, a senior scientist with the Copernicus Atmosphere Monitoring
Service, which uses satellites to track wildfire emissions, puts the figure at 108
megatons between 1 June and 1 August.[173] Turkey and Greece are in flames.
So is the Amazon—in Brazil, Bolivia, Peru and Colombia. For the first time
ever, the Amazon rainforest is emitting more carbon dioxide than it is able to
absorb.[174]

On 9 August 2021, the IPCC released the first instalment of its Sixth
Assessment Report. It provides the clearest picture yet of past, present and
future climate, serving as an essential map for where we are headed, what can
be done, and how we can prepare.[175] It issues a stark warning: climate change
is already affecting every region on Earth, in multiple ways; and "unless there
are immediate, rapid and large-scale reductions in greenhouse gas emissions,"
it will be impossible to hold the increase in global warming to 1.5°C (or even
2°C). What would that mean? "For 1.5°C of global warming, there will be

---

172   Kasha Patel, "Siberia Endures 'Nasty Burning' Amid Worst Fire Season in Decades,"
      Washington Post (August 10, 2021), https://www.washingtonpost.com/weather/2021/08/
      10/siberia-sakha-fires-record-carbon/.
173   Patel, "Siberia Endures 'Nasty Burning' Amid Worst Fire Season in Decades.".
174   Luciana V. Gatti, et al. "Amazonia as a Carbon Source Linked to Deforestation and Climate
      Change," *Nature* 595 (2021): 388–393.
175   "Climate Change Widespread, Rapid, and Intensifying—IPCC," https://www.ipcc.ch/
      2021/08/09/ar6-wg1-20210809-pr/.

increasing heat waves, longer warm seasons and shorter cold seasons. At 2°C of global warming, heat extremes would more often reach critical tolerance thresholds for agriculture and health."[176] Another scientific study, also released in August 2021, has found that global warming has so weakened the Atlantic Meridional Overturning Circulation (AMOC)—the system of ocean currents that transports warm surface water north from the tropics into the North Atlantic, and which plays a crucial role in regulating climate globally—that it may be approaching a tipping point from which there can be no return.[177] The environmental and socioeconomic impacts of this would be devastating. As Damian Carrington writes: "Such an event would have catastrophic consequences around the world, severely disrupting the rains that billions of people depend on for food in India, South America and West Africa; increasing storms and lowering temperatures in Europe; and pushing up the sea level off eastern North America. It would also further endanger the Amazon rainforest and Antarctic ice sheets."[178]

This book, like many others in recent times, has been produced in difficult circumstances. The first human victims of coronavirus disease were identified in China late in December 2019. A month later the World Health Organization declared a "public health emergency of international concern" and on 11 March it declared a pandemic. By June two of our editorial team were in lockdown in Australia and the third was trapped in Indonesia. With Covid-19 raging out of control there it was the worst place to be in Southeast Asia. A year later he is still there, unable to leave, as Indonesia crumbles under the pressure of the disease, while in Australia, where the disease is surging for the third time, the other editors are again in lockdown. Universities, libraries, archives are closed. But there are other reasons also that this book has been difficult to bring to completion. As will be clear from the previous paragraph, keeping pace with the acceleration of climate change is a major challenge. In June last year, in lockdown, we inserted a brief comment into this Introduction to the effect that climate change had been implicated in the spread of zoonotic diseases (that is, diseases transmitted between species, from animals to humans and from humans to animals). Today the evidence of causal connection between climate change, environmental resilience and public health is completely

---

176   "Climate Change Widespread, Rapid, and Intensifying—IPCC".
177   Niklas Boers, "Observation-Based Early-Warning Signals for a Collapse of the Atlantic Meridional Overturning Circulation," *Nature Climate Change* 11 (2021): 680–688.
178   Damien Carrington, "Climate Crisis: Scientists Spot Warning Signs of Gulf Stream Collapse," *The Guardian* (August 6, 2021), https://www.theguardian.com/environment/2021/aug/05/climate-crisis-scientists-spot-warning-signs-of-gulf-stream-collapse/.

INTRODUCTION

compelling.[179] The root causes of climate change and pandemics are the same: deforestation, habitat loss, large-scale livestock farming, global warming, melting ice, rising seas, all pushing migration (human and nonhuman) and causing novel cross-species encounters that provide multiple opportunities for pathogens, especially those forced by species extinctions to find new hosts.[180] The urgency of the situation had led to a range of new disciplinary interventions. And this is another reason for our difficulty in bringing this project to completion: the pace of new research on climate change, especially in the past year, across so many disciplinary fronts, and at the crossroads of new interdisciplinary formations. Climate and health scientists, for example, are seeking to define "climate and health literacy" for policy makers and activists alike.[181] Economists argue that "countries in which individuals look after each other and the environment, creating sustainable societies, are better able to cope with climate and public health emergencies."[182] Social scientists propose that a "resetting of economic and social structures" and a more thorough "cross-sectoral framing of issues" are called for if the world is to avoid, as Joseph Stiglitz puts it, leaping "from the COVID frying pan into the climate fire."[183] Philosopher Slavoj Zizek cautions against continuing down the path of "barbarian capitalism," with its "zombie investment" in the use of cheap fossil fuels and unsustainable "shovel ready projects" as an accelerant to post-coronavirus growth and a means of putting people back to work.[184] We knew that "the neoliberal market ideologies of the news outlets were at times pitted

---

179   A.L. Ramanathan, S. Chidambaram, M.P. Jonathan, M.V. Prasanna, Pankaj Kumar, S Chidambaram, *Environmental Resilience and Transformation in times of COVID-19. Climate Change Effects on Environmental Functionality* (Amsterdam: Elsevier Science, 2021).

180   "Coronavirus, Climate Change, and the Environment: A Conversation on COVID-19 with Dr. Aaron Bernstein," Harvard T.H. Chan School of Public Health (Harvard Chan C-CHANGE), https://www.hsph.harvard.edu/c-change/subtopics/coronavirus-and-climate-change/.

181   Vijay S. Limaye, Maggie L. Grabow, Valerie J. Stull and Jonathan A. Patz, "Developing A Definition Of Climate And Health Literacy," *Health Affairs* 12 (2020): 2182–2188.

182   Aydin Ozkan, Gulcin Ozkan, Abdullah Yalaman and Yilmaz Yildiz, "Climate Risk, Culture and the Covid-19 Mortality: A Cross-Country Analysis," *World Development*, 141 (May 2021). See also Carl Benedikt Frey, Giorgio Presidente and Chinchih Chen, "Covid-19 and the Future of Democracy," VOX, CEPR Policy Portal (May 20, 2020), https://voxeu.org/article/covid-19-and-future-democracy.

183   David Selby and Fumiyo Kagawa, "Climate Change and Coronavirus: A Confluence of Crises as Learning Moment," in *COVID-19 in the Global South Impacts and Responses,* Pádraig Carmody, Gerard McCann, Clodagh Colleran and Ciara O'Halloran, eds. (Bristol: Bristol University P, 2021): 24.

184   David Selby and Fumiyo Kagawa, "Climate Change and Coronavirus," 23.

against the public health ethic of collectivism and practices of state intervention."[185] Recent media research has confirmed, however, that the news outlets that have been challenging meaningful state intervention to address climate change are the same as those now undermining public health interventions in relation to Covid-19, challenging their legitimacy and blaming governments for the restriction of civil liberties.[186] Psychologists, puzzled by the widespread refusal of science, are now assessing how people process and respond to scientific information, how "doomsday messages" decrease public engagement, and how the loss of stability and of a predictable future causes "climate grief" (or "eco-anxiety," or "eco-guilt.")[187] Anthropologists, reflecting on their discipline's stake in and influence on transitions to a different world in the aftermath of the Covid-19 pandemic, have begun to ask how they might "work with and alongside the climate justice movement" to foment social change and offer political alternatives.[188] For historians, one key question is whether this is only the first zoonotic pandemic driven by climate change—that is, "expressive of biodiversity ecosystems coming under uncontrollable stress."[189] Tom Holland puts it like this: "the question is whether in 100 years, people will look back and see this as being the first of a number of epidemics [caused by] humanity crashing into ecosystems that previously humans were not part of."[190]

As the climate crisis has worsened, and its connection with the spread of disease has been better understood, so too research on the relationship between climate and colonialism has intensified, on the basis that the crisis is itself a result of colonialism. As Keila Mcfarland Dias writes:

---

185 Joseph Thwaites, "Public Interest in the Pandemic: A Comparative Framing Analysis of COVID-19 Public Health Interventions by the Victorian State Government and Australian Digital News Outlets," MSc. (Media and Communication, Lund University, 2021): 60.

186 Thwaites, "Public Interest in the Pandemic," 61.

187 See for example Hannah Comtesse, Verena Ertl, Sophie M.C. Hengst, Rita Rosner and Geert E. Smid, "Ecological Grief as a Response to Environmental Change: A Mental Health Risk or Functional Response?" *International Journal of Environmental Research and Public Health* 18 (2021): 734.

188 Lilian Von Storch, Lukas Ley and Jing Sun, "New Climate Change Activism: Before and After the Covid-19 Pandemic," *Social Anthropology* 29 (2021): 205–209.

189 Esther Addley, "'A Very Dangerous Epoch': Historians Try to Make Sense of Covid," *The Guardian* (February 13, 2021), https://www.theguardian.com/world/2021/feb/13/a-very-dangerous-epoch-historians-try-make-sense-covid. In fact, many diseases previously identified as "endemic" (that is, as restricted to a particular region) have been unofficially upgraded to "epidemic" and even "pandemic" status. See, for example, D.R. Hamilton, "Lyme Disease. The Hidden Pandemic," *Postgraduate Medicine* 85.5 (1989), 303–314; Scott A. Ritchie, "Dengue: Australia's Other Pandemic," *Microbiology Australia* 30, (September 2009): 114–117.

190 Addley, "'A Very Dangerous Epoch'".

INTRODUCTION 43

Climate change is widely perceived as a byproduct of our contemporary socio-economic model, which rotates around the exploitation of nature, unrestrained extractivism, excessive pollution, deforestation, and land degradation. Nevertheless, the environmental crisis is in itself a consequence of colonialism, as imperial expansion heavily relied on the widespread plunder of colonies' natural resources, thus marking the genesis of environmental destruction.[191]

Recognising climate change among the multi-generational legacies of colonialism, environmentalists join with human rights advocates to denounce "colonial conservation" policies and practices that compound the climate injustice of racialised inequalities:

> between the winners of the rapacious global capitalist system and those who are impoverished by it, those who produce the greatest environmental burdens and those who bear its worst consequences; those who make claim to 'global' resources and those whose claims to territory, livelihood and wellbeing are extinguished at the local level; those whose luxury is being protected and those whose survival is being sacrificed.[192]

The Green Deal, for instance, launched in December 2019 with the aim of making the entire European Union "climate neutral" by 2050, has been criticised for its neo-colonial logic, adopting a falsely "apolitical narrative on climate change" that disguises the potential of its policy initiatives to have a detrimental impact on "other parts of the world, where resources for this economic shift will have to be extracted."[193] In other words, according to Myriam Douo, a steering group member of Equinox Initiative For Racial Justice, the Green Deal is premised on continuing "climate colonialism."[194] Using this term (in

---

191 Keila Mcfarland Dias, "Environmentalism And The Legacy Of Colonialism," *Human Rights Pulse* (December 7, 2020), https://www.humanrightspulse.com/mastercontent blog/environmentalism-and-the-legacy-of-colonialism.

192 Adeniyi Asiyanbi, "Decolonising the Environment: Race, Rationalities and Crises," Sheffield Institute for International Development (SIID) Blog (August 7, 2019), http://siid .group.shef.ac.uk/blog/decolonising-the-environment-race-rationalities-and-crises/.

193 Myriam Douo, "Climate Colonialism and the EU's Green Deal," *Aljazeera* (June 23, 2021), https://www.aljazeera.com/opinions/2021/6/23/the-eus-green-deal-could-propagate -climate-colonialism.

194 Christoph Rehmann-Sutter, "*Stoppt den Klima-Kolonialismus!*" ["Stop Climate Colonialsim!"], *Tagesan Zeiger* (24 July 2019), https://www.imgwf.uni-luebeck.de/filead min/oeffentlich/Publikationen/Rehmann-Sutter/CRS_Stoppt_den_Klima-Kolonialismu s__-_Kultur_Diverses_-_tagesanzeiger.ch.pdf.

preference to "climate change") reframes the problem in order to focalise cultures and ideologies that are not only "fatally impacted" by the climate solutions of the developed world but also silenced and marginalised in debates about the problem. It is a change of terminology intended, as Doreen Martinez puts it, to underline the fact that the climate is not simply changing, rather it is being *forced* to change.[195] The problem that now preoccupies climate justice advocates around the world is how to prevent climate solutions (relying on technology or taxes) that would perpetuate colonialism and imperialism and instead to devise alternative solutions (based on genuine social, economic and political change) in order to avoid that trap.

There is a good indication here of one thing that literary studies can offer: discourse analysis, a deconstruction of block formations of thought and language, the revelation of the hidden ideological underpinnings and a narratological modelling of alternatives to the kind of narrative mastery that justifies the development model that drives climate colonialism. David Higgins, Tess Somervell and Nigel Clark provide a timely reminder that "climate and climate change are inevitably mediated and remediated through cultural forms: particular narratives, vocabularies, images, objects, and symbols."[196] Again, the bread and butter of literary studies. "If we do not understand the cultural politics of how climate change is framed, and the role of racialised, colonial, and extractivist ideologies in those framings," say Higgins et al, "then we can hardly expect to move forward."[197] Postcolonial literary theory has been influential in opening our eyes to the cultural politics of framing strategies, focusing particularly on identities of nation, race and gender, but also to the historical and geographical constructions of disease, among other disorders.

In the midst of the Covid-19 pandemic, it is worth remembering what the plague literature of the past tells us. Homer opens the *Iliad* with a plague upon the city of Thebes, sent by Apollo, the Plague God, as a punishment upon the Greek army for Agamemnon's insult of an Apollonian priest. But it is Sophocles, in the tragic drama of *Oedipus Rex*, who provides the real

---

195   Doreen E. Martinez, "The Right to Be Free of Fear: Indigeneity and the United Nations," *Wičazo Ša Review* 29.2 (Fall 2014): 79.

196   David Higgins, Tess Somervell and Nigel Clark, "Introduction: Environmental Humanities Approaches to Climate Change," *Humanities* 9.3, 94 (2020), https://www.mdpi.com/2076 -0787/9/3/94/htm.

197   Higgins, Somervell and Clark, "Introduction: Environmental Humanities Approaches to Climate Change."

INTRODUCTION

reason for plagues, when he has the blind prophet, Teiresias, berate the arrogant King as the cause of his own downfall. Or as Stephen Berkoff has the Sphinx say in *Greek*, recasting the Oedipal tragedy in the 1980s: "you are the plague."[198] It is the same with the banana plague in Gabriel Garcia Marquez's novel, *One Hundred Years of Solitude* (1967), where the downfall of the Colombian town of Macondo is brought about by a foreign banana company, an allegorical representation of capitalist industrialisation and neocolonialism.[199] It is the same again in Albert Camus's novel, *The Plague* (1949), set in French Algeria, where the pestilence is understood allegorically as an expression of Nazism.

Over the past couple of decades postcolonial scholars have realised that the colonial and imperial issues of the past were in fact always environmental issues.[200] More generally, we have known for centuries that dystopias and utopias are deeply related. It is certainly possible for us to reimagine ourselves in a range of different ways—writers do it all the time—and the literature of climate change help us to do that, to choose how we will live in the future. But we need also to know how to read the narratives of our past through the lens of climate change, in order to know how we got to where we are now. If new models of community are needed to address climate change—because after all (as Mike Hulme has shown) climate is as much a social and cultural construction as it is a physical phenomenon[201]—postcolonial literature has already shown itself adept at devising strategies of resistance to entrenched oppressions, challenging perceptions of how we live in the world and imagining alternative identities and realities. We are climate change; we invented it, and we are fighting for control of its narrative as the reality itself affects us. We are the agents of change—its origins, its pace—and ultimately, we hold within our grasp all the possibilities of its denouement.

September 15, 2021

---

198 Stephen Berkoff, *Decadence and Other Plays: East, West, Greek* (London: Faber, 1982): 168.

199 See Dean Irvine, "Fables of the Plague Years: Postcolonialism, Postmodernism, and Magical Realism in *Cien años de soledad*," in *One Hundred Years of Solitude—Gabriel Garcia Marquez*, ed. Harold Bloom (Broomall, PA: Chelsea House, 2009): 140.

200 Upamanyu Pablo Mukherjee makes this point emphatically in *Postcolonial Environments: Nature, Culture and the Contemporary Indian Novel in English* (London: Palgrave Macmillan, 2010): 39; See also Graham Huggan, "Greening" Postcolonialism: Ecocritical Perspectives." *MFS. Modern Fiction Studies* 50.3 (2004): 701–733.

201 See Michael Hulme, *Why We Disagree about Climate Change. Understanding Controversy, Inaction and Opportunity* (Cambridge: Cambridge University Press, 2009).

Works Cited

ABC News. "Families Board Boat in Mallacoota." *ABC News* (December 31, 2020), www.abc.net.au/news/2019-12-31/families-board-boat-in-mallacoota-1/11833952.

Addley, Esther. " 'A Very Dangerous Epoch': Historians Try to Make Sense of Covid." *The Guardian* (February 13, 2021), https://www.theguardian.com/world/2021/feb/13/a-very-dangerous-epoch-historians-try-make-sense-covid.

Adkins, Peter and Wendy Parkins. "Introduction: Victorian Ecology and the Anthropocene," *Interdisciplinary Studies in the Long Nineteenth Century* 26 (2018): 1–15.

Arezki, Rabah, Patrick Bolton, Karim El Aynaoui and Maurice Obstfeld, ed. *Coping With the Climate Crisis: Mitigation Policies and Global Coordination* (New York: Columbia UP, 2018).

Arnold, Denis. "Introduction: Climate Change and Ethics," in *The Ethics of Global Climate Change*, ed. Denis G. Arnold (Cambridge, UK: Cambridge UP, 2011): 1–15.

Ashcroft, Bill, Gareth Griffiths and Helen Tiffin. *Post-Colonial Studies: The Key Concepts*, 2nd ed. (London: Routledge, 2007).

Asiyanbi, Adeniyi. "Decolonising the Environment: Race, Rationalities and Crises." Sheffield Institute for International Development (SIID) Blog (August 7, 2019), http://siid.group.shef.ac.uk/blog/decolonising-the-environment-race-rationalities-and-crises/.

Auken, Sune and Christel Sunesen, eds. *Genre in the Climate Debate*. (Warsaw, Poland: De Gruyter Open Poland, 2021).

Bachram, Heidi. "Climate Fraud and Carbon Colonialism: The New Trade in Greenhouse Gases," *Capitalism Nature Socialism*, 15.4 (2004): 5–20.

Bahng, Aimee. "The Pacific Proving Grounds and the Proliferation of Settler Environmentalism," *Journal of Transnational American Studies* 1.2 (2020): 45–69.

Banida, Paul F. "Afterword. Postcolonialism, Activism, and Translation," in Rebecca Ruth Gould, Kayvan Tahmasebian, eds. *The Routledge Handbook of Translation and Activism*. (London and New York: Routledge, 2020): 515–520.

Berkoff, Stephen. *Decadence and Other Plays: East, West, Greek*. (London: Faber, 1982).

Biro, Andrew. "Introduction: The Paradoxes of Contemporary Environmental Crisis and the Redemption of the Hopes of the Past," in *Critical Ecologies: The Frankfurt School and Contemporary Environmental Crises*, ed. Andrew Biro (Toronto: U of Toronto P, 2011): 3–19.

Boers, Niklas. "Observation-Based Early-Warning Signals for a Collapse of the Atlantic Meridional Overturning Circulation," *Nature Climate Change* 11 (2021): 680–688.

Bravo, Michael T. "Voices from the Sea Ice: The Reception of Climate Impact Narratives," *Journal of Historical Geography* 35.2 (April 2009): 256–278.

Brooker, Ben. "Climate Change Was So Last Year: Writers' Festivals and the Great Derangement," *Overland* (September 3, 2018), https://overland.org.au/2018/09/climate-change-was-so-last-year-writers-festivals-and-the-great-derangement/.

Campbell, Melissa Colleen. "Reclaiming Indigenous Voices and Staging Eco-activism in Northern Indigenous Theatre," *Seismopolite* 8 (December 2014), http://www.seismopolite.com/reclaiming-indigenous-voices-and-staging-eco-activism-in-northern-indigenous-theatre.

Cann, Heather W. and Leigh Raymond. "Does Climate Denialism Still Matter? The Prevalence of Alternative Frames in Opposition to Climate Policy." *Environmental Politics* 27.3 (2018): 433–454.

Carmody, Broede. "How Climate Anxiety is Changing the Face of Australian Fiction." *Sydney Morning Herald* (June 20, 2019), https://www.smh.com.au/entertainment/books/how-climate-anxiety-is-changing-the-face-of-australian-fiction-20190619-p51z44.html.

Carrington, Damien. "Climate Crisis: Scientists Spot Warning Signs of Gulf Stream Collapse." *The Guardian* (August 6, 2021), https://www.theguardian.com/environment/2021/aug/05/climate-crisis-scientists-spot-warning-signs-of-gulf-stream-collapse.

Carson, Rachel. *Silent Spring.* (Boston: Houghton Mifflin, 1962).

Chakrabarty, Dipesh. "The Climate of History: Four Theses." *Critical Inquiry* 35.2 (2009): 197–222.

Chakrabarty, Dipesh. "Postcolonial Studies and the Challenge of Climate Change." *New Literary History* 43 (2012): 1–18.

Chakrabarty, Dipesh. "Anthropocene Time." *History and Theory* 57.1 (2018): 5–32.

Choi, Tina Young and Barbara Leckie. "Slow Causality: The Function of Narrative in an Age of Climate Change," *Victorian Studies* 60.4 (Summer 2018): 565–587.

Cilano, Cara, and Elizabeth DeLoughrey. "Against Authenticity: Global Knowledges and Postcolonial Ecocriticism." *ISLE: Interdisciplinary Studies in Literature and Environment* 14.1 (2007): 71–87.

"Climate Change Widespread, Rapid, and Intensifying—IPCC." *2021 Intergovernmental Panel on Climate Change (IPCC),* https://www.ipcc.ch/2021/08/09/ar6-wg1-20210809-pr/.

Cohen, Tom. "Trolling "Anthropos"—Or, Requiem for a Failed Prosopopeia," in *Twilight of the Anthropocene Idols*, ed. Tom Cohen, Claire Colebrook & J. Hillis Miller (London: Open Humanities Press, 2016).

Collett, Anne, ed. "Gardening in the Colonies." *SPAN* 46 (1998).

Comtesse, Hannah, Verena Ertl, Sophie M.C. Hengst, Rita Rosner and Geert E. Smid. "Ecological Grief as a Response to Environmental Change: A Mental Health Risk or Functional Response?" *International Journal of Environmental Research and Public Health* 18 (2021).

"Coronavirus, Climate Change, and the Environment: A Conversation on COVID-19 with Dr. Aaron Bernstein." Harvard T.H. Chan School of Public Health (Harvard Chan C-CHANGE), https://www.hsph.harvard.edu/c-change/subtopics/coronavirus-and-climate-change/.

Costello, Anthony et al. "Managing the Health Effects of Climate Change." *The Lancet*, 373 (2009): 1693–1733.

Crowe, David. "Deputy PM Slams People Raising Climate Change in Relation to NSW Bushfires," *Sydney Morning Herald* (November 11, 2019), https://www.smh.com.au/politics/federal/raving-inner-city-lunatics-michael-mccormack-dismisses-link-between-climate-change-and-bushfires-20191111-p539ap.html.

Cudjoe, Selwyn R. *Resistance and Caribbean Literature.* (Athens, OH, Chicago and London: Ohio UP, 1980).

Curry, Judith. "Cli-Fi," *Climate Etc.* Blog (December 23, 2012), https://judithcurry.com/2012/12/23/cli-fi/.

Dathorne, O.R. *Dark Ancestor: The Literature of the Black Man in the Caribbean.* (Baton Rouge and London: Louisiana State UP, 1981).

Davidson, Jordan. "Unprecedented Wildfires in Arctic Have Scientists Concerned," *EcoWatch* (July 25, 2019), https://www.ecowatch.com/arctic-wildfires--2639340124.html?rebelltitem=1#rebelltitem1.

DeLoughrey, Elizabeth, Jill Didur and Anthony Carrigan. "Introduction: A Postcolonial Environmental Humanities," in *Global Ecologies and the Environmental Humanities: Postcolonial Approaches*, ed. DeLoughrey, Didur and Carrigan (New York: Routledge, 2015): 1–32.

DeLoughrey, Elizabeth and George B. Handley. "Introduction: Toward an Aesthetics of the Earth," in *Postcolonial Ecologies: Literatures of the Environment*, ed. DeLoughrey and Handley (New York: Oxford UP, 2011): 3–41.

Dias Mcfarland, Keila. "Environmentalism And The Legacy Of Colonialism." *Human Rights Pulse* (December 7, 2020), https://www.humanrightspulse.com/mastercontentblog/environmentalism-and-the-legacy-of-colonialism.

Dimaline, Cherie. *The Marrow Thieves* (Toronto, Ont.: Dancing Cat Books, 2017).

Dodds, Klaus. "Post-Colonial Antarctica: An Emerging Engagement," *Polar Record* 42 (2006): 59–79.

Dodds, Klaus and Christy Collis. "Post-Colonial Antarctica," in *Handbook on the politics of Antarctica,* eds. K. Dodds, P. Roberts and A. Hemmings (London, UK: Edward Elgar Publishing, 2017): 50–68.

Dutta, Mohan J., Jagadish Thaker and Kang Sun. "Neoliberalism, Neocolonialism, and Communication for Social Change: A Culture-Centered Agenda for the Social Sciences." *Global Media Journal* (2014): 1–13.

Douo, Myriam. "Climate Colonialism and the EU's Green Deal." *Aljazeera* (June 23, 2021), https://www.aljazeera.com/opinions/2021/6/23/the-eus-green-deal-could-propagate-climate-colonialism.

Dove, Michael R. "Living Rubber, Dead Land, and Persisting Systems in Borneo; Indigenous Representations of Sustainability," Bijdragen tot de taal-, land- en volkenkunde / *Journal of the Humanities and Social Sciences of Southeast Asia* 154.1 (1998): 20–54.

Eckstein, Barbara. "What Humanists Help America to Forget." *The Literary Review: An International Journal of Contemporary Writing* 28.4 (1985): 591–605.

Eckstein, Barbara. "Introduction—Genres of Climate Change." *Philological Quarterly* 93.3 (Summer 2014): 247–259.

Eckstein, David, Marie-Lena Hutfils and Maik Winges. *Global Climate Risk Index 2019 Briefing Paper* (Bonn, Germany: Germanwatch, 2018).

Elba, Emad, Brigitte Urban, Bernd Ettmer and Dalia Farghaly. "Mitigating the Impact of Climate Change by Reducing Evaporation Losses: Sediment Removal from the High Aswan Dam Reservoir," *American Journal of Climate Change* 6 (May 2017): 230.

Freudenburg, W. R., R. Gramling and D. Davison. "Scientific Certainty Argumentation Methods (SCAMs): Science and the Politics of Doubt," *Sociological Inquiry* 78.1 (2008).

Frey, Carl Benedikt, Giorgio Presidente and Chinchih Chen. "Covid-19 and the Future of Democracy." *VOX, CEPR Policy Portal* (May 20, 2020), https://voxeu.org/article/covid-19-and-future-democracy.

Gardiner, Stephen M. "Ethics and Global Climate Change," in *Climate Ethics: Essential Readings*, eds. Stephen M. Gardiner, Simon Caney, Dale Jamieson and Henry Shue (Oxford, UK: Oxford UP, 2010): 3–35.

Garrard, Greg. *Ecocriticism*, 1st ed. (London: Taylor and Francis, 2004).

Garrard, Greg. "Introduction," in *The Oxford Handbook of Ecocriticism*, ed. Garrard (Oxford: Oxford UP, 2014): 1–26.

Garrard, Greg, Axel Goodbody, George B. Handley and Stephanie Posthumus. *Climate Change Scepticism: A Transnational Ecocritical Analysis.* (London: Bloomsbury, 2019).

Gatti, Luciana V., Luana Basso, John Miller, Manuel Gloor, Lucas Gatti Domingues, Henrique Cassol, et al. "Amazonia as a Carbon Source Linked to Deforestation and Climate Change." *Nature* 595 (2021): 388–393.

Ghosh, Amitav. *The Great Derangement: Climate Change and the Unthinkable* (Chicago, IL: U of Chicago P, 2016).

Goering, Laurie. "Climate Change 'Biggest Global Health Threat' of Century, Doctors Warn," Reuters (November 29, 2018), https://in.reuters.com/article/global-climatechange-health/climate-change-biggest-global-health-threat-of-century-doctors-warn-idINL8N1Y346F.

Grovogu, Siba. "A Revolution Nonetheless: The Global South in International Relations." *The Global South* 5.1 (Spring 2011): 175–190.

Hage, Ghassan. *Is Racism an Environmental Threat? (Debating Race)*. (Cambridge: Polity Press, 2017).

Handley, George B. "Climate Change, Cosmology, and Poetry: The Case of Derek Walcott's *Omeros*," in *Global Ecologies and the Environmental Humanities: Postcolonial Approaches*, ed. Elizabeth DeLoughrey, Jill Didur and Anthony Carrigan (New York: Routledge, 2015): 333–351.

Harris, Wilson. *The Womb of Space: The Cross-Cultural Imagination* (Westport, Connecticut: Greenwood Press, 1983).

Harris, Wilson. "On the Beach." *Landfall* 39.3 (155) (September 1985): 335–341.

Harris, Wilson. "The Fabric of the Imagination," in *The Radical Imagination: Lectures and Talks*, eds. Alan Riach and Mark Williams (Liège, Belgium: L3- Liège Language and Literature, 1992): 69–79.

Harris, Wilson. "The Music of Living Landscapes" in Wilson Harris, *The Unfinished Genesis of the Imagination*, ed. Andrew Bundy (London: Routledge, 1999): 40–46.

Healy, J.J. " 'The True Life in Our History': Aboriginal Literature in Australia," *Antipodes* 2.2 (1988): 19–85.

Higgins, David. *British Romanticism, Climate Change, and the Anthropocene: Writing Tambora* (London: Palgrave Macmillan, 2017).

Higgins, David, Tess Somervell and Nigel Clark. "Introduction: Environmental Humanities Approaches to Climate Change," *Humanities* 9.3.94 (2020), https://www.mdpi.com/2076-0787/9/3/94/htm.

Hiltner, Ken. *What Else Is Pastoral? Renaissance Literature and the Environment* (Ithaca, NY: Cornell UP, 1916).

Huggan, Graham. "Greening Postcolonialism: Ecocritical Perspectives." *MFS. Modern Fiction Studies*, 50 3 (2004): 701–733.

Huggan, Graham. Introduction to *The Oxford Handbook of Postcolonial Studies*, ed. Huggan (Oxford: Oxford UP, 2013): 1–26.

Huggan, Graham and Helen Tiffin. "Green Postcolonialism," *Interventions* 9.1 (2007): 1–11.

Huggan, Graham and Helen Tiffin. *Postcolonial Ecocriticism: Literature, Animals, Environment*, 1st ed. (London: Routledge, 2010).

Huggan, Graham and Helen Tiffin. *Postcolonial Ecocriticism: Literature, Animals, Environment*, 2nd ed. (London: Routledge, 2015).

Hughes, Lesley, Annika Dean, Will Steffen, Ella Weisbrot, Martin Rice and Greg Mullins. *Summer of Crisis Report*. (Potts Point, NSW: Climate Council of Australia Ltd, 2020), https://www.climatecouncil.org.au/wp-content/uploads/2020/03/Crisis-Summer -Report-200311.pdf.

Hulme, Michael. *Why We Disagree about Climate Change. Understanding Controversy, Inaction and Opportunity*. (Cambridge: Cambridge University Press, 2009).

Hyle, Maija Anneli. "Conceptual Reflection on Responsive Environmental Governance." *International Journal of Public Administration* 39.8 (2016): 610–619.

Ilott, Sarah. *New Postcolonial British Genres: Shifting the Boundaries*. (London: Palgrave Macmillan, 2015).

Ince, Onur Ulas. *Colonial Capitalism and the Dilemmas of Liberalism.* (Oxford: Oxford UP, 2018).

"Indigenous Peoples: The Unsung Heroes of Conservation," UN Environment Programme, (January 9, 2017), https://www.unep.org/zh-hans/node/477.

IPCC. 2019. "About the IPCC," https://www.ipcc.ch/about/.

Irvine, Dean. "Fables of the Plague Years: Postcolonialism, Postmodernism, and Magical Realism in *Cien años de soledad*" in *One Hundred Years of Solitude—Gabriel Garcia Marquez*, ed. Harold Bloom (Broomall, PA: Chelsea House, 2009).

Jetñil-Kijiner, Kathy. *Iep Jāltok: Poems from a Marshallese Daughter.* (Tucson, AZ: U of Arizona P, 2017).

Johns-Putra, Adeline. "Climate Change in Literature and Literary Studies: From Cli-Fi, Climate Change Theatre and Ecopoetry to Ecocriticism and Climate Change Criticism." *WIRES Climate Change* 7 (2016): 266–282.

Johns-Putra, Adeline. "The Rest Is Silence: Postmodern and Postcolonial Possibilities in Climate Change Fiction." *Studies in the Novel* 50.1 (2018): 26–42.

Johns-Putra, Adeline. *Climate Change and the Contemporary Novel.* (Cambridge, UK: Cambridge UP, 2019).

Joshi, Ketan. "Something Else Is Out of Control in Australia: Climate Disaster Denialism," *Guardian* Australian edition (January 8, 2020), https://www.theguardian.com/commentisfree/2020/jan/08/australia-climate-disaster-denial-bushfires-online-rightwing-press-politicians.

Jylhä, Kirsti M. and Nazar Akrami. "Social Dominance Orientation and Climate Change Denial: The Role of Dominance and System Justification." *Personality and Individual Differences* 86 (2015): 108–111.

Källén, Anna. "Postcolonial Theory and Sámi Archaeology—A Commentary." *Arctic Anthropology* 52.2 (2015): 81–86.

Kashwan, Prakash, Rosaleen V. Duffy, Francis Massé, Adeniyi P. Asiyanbi, and Esther Marijnen. "Racialized Neocolonial Global Conservation to an Inclusive and Regenerative Conservation." *Environment: Science and Policy for Sustainable Development* 63 (2021): 4–19.

Knickerbocker, Scott. *Ecopoetics: The Language of Nature, the Nature of Language.* (Amherst MA: U of Massachusetts P, 2012).

Kwaymullina, Ambelin. "Seeing the Light: Aboriginal Law, Learning and Sustainable Living in Country." *Indigenous Law Bulletin* 6.11 (2005): 12–15.

Latour, Bruno. *Down to Earth: Politics in the New Climate Regime.* trans. Catherine Porter (Cambridge UK: Polity Press, 2018).

Limaye, Vijay S., Maggie L. Grabow, Valerie J. Stull and Jonathan A. Patz. "Developing A Definition Of Climate And Health Literacy," *Health Affairs* 12 (2020): 2182–2188.

Macfarlane, Robert. "The Burning Question," *Guardian* Australian edition (24 September 2005), www.theguardian.com/books/2005/sep/24/featuresreviews.guardianreview29#maincontent.

Martinez, Doreen E. "The Right to Be Free of Fear: Indigeneity and the United Nations," *Wíčazo Ša Review* 29.2 (Fall 2014): 63–87.

McCannon, John. *A History of the Arctic: Nature, Exploration and Exploitation.* (London: Reaktion, 2013).

McCormack, Michael quoted in David Crowe. "Deputy PM Slams People Raising Climate Change in Relation to NSW Bushfires." *Sydney Morning Herald* (November 11, 2019).

Mead, Philip. "Unresolved Sovereignty and the Anthropocene Novel: Alexis Wright's *The Swan Book,*" *Journal of Australian Studies* 42.4 (2018): 524–538.

Milfont, Taciano L., Wokje Abrahamse and Edith A. MacDonald. "Scepticism of Anthropogenic Climate Change: Additional Evidence for the Role of System-Justifying Ideologies." *Personality and Individual Differences* 168 (2021): 110237.

Moretti, Franco. "Conjectures on World Literature." *New Left Review* 1. (January/February 2000): 54–68.

Morton, Adam. "Australian Bushfires to Contribute to Huge Annual Increase in Global Carbon Dioxide." *Guardian* Australian edition (January 24, 2020), https://www.theg uardian.com/australia-news/2020/jan/24/australian-bushfires-to-contribute-to -huge-annual-increase-in-global-carbon-dioxide.

Mukherjee, Upamanyu Pablo. *Postcolonial Environments: Nature, Culture and the Contemporary Indian Novel in English.* (London: Palgrave Macmillan, 2010).

Nixon, Rob. "Environmentalism and Postcolonialism," in *Postcolonial Studies and Beyond.* eds. Ania Loomba, Suvir Kaul, Matti Bunzl, Antoinette Burton and Jed Esty (Durham, NC: Duke UP, 2005): 233–251.

Nixon, Rob. *Slow Violence and the Environmentalism of the Poor.* (Cambridge, MA: Harvard UP, 2011).

NOAA. "Global Climate Report—Annual 2019." *NOAA* (January 2020), https://www .ncdc.noaa.gov/sotc/global/201913.

Northcott, Michael. *A Moral Climate: The Ethics of Global Warming.* (Maryknoll, NY: Orbis Books, 2007).

Nursey-Bray, Melissa, R. Palmer, T. F. Smith and P. Rist. "Old Ways for New Days: Australian Indigenous Peoples and Climate Change." *Local Environment* 24.5 (2019): 473–486.

Osborne, Danny, Kumar Yogeeswaran and Chris G. Sibley. "Culture-Specific Ideologies Undermine Collective Action Support: Examining the Legitimizing Effects of Postcolonial Belief Systems." *Group Processes & Intergroup Relations* 20.3 (2017): 333–349.

Otto, Melanie. "Poet-Shamanic Aesthetics in the Work of Gloria Anzaldúa and Wilson Harris." *The CLR James Journal* 23 1–2 (Fall 2017): 135–156.

Ozkan, Aydin, Gulcin Ozkan, Abdullah Yalaman and Yilmaz Yildiz. "Climate Risk, Culture and the Covid-19 Mortality: A Cross-Country Analysis." *World Development* 141 (May 2021): 105412.

Patel, Kasha. "Siberia Endures 'Nasty Burning' Amid Worst Fire Season in Decades." *Washington Post* (August 10, 2021), https://www.washingtonpost.com/weather/2021/08/10/siberia-sakha-fires-record-carbon/.

Quayson, Ato. "Introduction: Postcolonial Literature in a Changing Historical Frame," in *The Cambridge History of Postcolonial Literature*, ed. Ato Quayson (Cambridge, UK: Cambridge UP, 2012): 1–29.

Ramanathan, A.L., S. Chidambaram, M.P. Jonathan, M.V. Prasanna, Pankaj Kumar, S Chidambaram. *Environmental Resilience and Transformation in times of COVID-19. Climate Change Effects on Environmental Functionality* (Amsterdam: Elsevier Science, 2021).

Rehmann-Sutter, Christoph. "*Stoppt den Klima-Kolonialismus!*" ["Stop Climate Colonialsim!"], *Tagesan Zeiger.* (July 24, 2019), https://www.imgwf.uni-luebeck.de/fileadmin/oeffentlich/Publikationen/Rehmann-Sutter/CRS_Stoppt_den_Klima.

Roos, Bonnie and Alex Hunt, eds. *Postcolonial Green: Environmental Politics and World Narratives.* (Charlottesville, VA: U of Virginia P, 2010).

Roos, Bonnie and Alex Hunt. "Introduction: Narratives of Survival, Sustainability, and Justice," in *Postcolonial Green: Environmental Politics and World Narratives*, ed. Roos and Hunt (Charlottesville, VA: U of Virgina P, 2010): 1–13.

Rose, Deborah Bird. *Reports from a Wild Country: Ethics for Decolonisation.* (Sydney: U of New South Wales P, 2004).

Rose, Deborah Bird. *Nourishing Terrains: Australian Aboriginal Views of Landscape and Wilderness.* (Canberra, Australia: Australian Heritage Commission, 1996).

Roy, Shouraseni Sen. *Linking Gender to Climate Change Impacts in the Global South.* (Cham, Switzerland: Springer Nature, 2018).

Russell, Charles. "Subversion and Legitimation: The Avant-garde in Postmodern Culture." *Chicago Review* 33.2 (1982): 54–59.

Ryan, John Charles. "'The Pained and Silent Song of a Branch': Ecological Precarity in the Poetry of Taufiq Ismail and Khairani Barokk," *Journal of Postcolonial Writing* 56.4 (2020): 488–502.

Scott, Heidi C. M. "Industrial Souls: Climate Change, Immorality, and Victorian Anticipations of the Good Anthropocene." *Victorian Studies* 60.4 (Summer 2018): 588–610.

Schabio, Saskia and Walter Goebel, eds. *Locating Postcolonial Narrative Genres.* (London: Routledge, 2015).

Schneider-Mayerson, Matthew. "The Influence of Climate Fiction: An Empirical Survey of Readers." *Environmental Humanities* 10.2 (2018): 473–500.

Selby, David and Fumiyo Kagawa, "Climate Change and Coronavirus: A Confluence of Crises as Learning Moment" in *COVID-19 in the Global South Impacts and Responses,* eds. Pádraig Carmody, Gerard McCann, Clodagh Colleran and Ciara O'Halloran (Bristol: Bristol University Press, 2021): 17–28.

Shearer, Christine. *Kivalina: A Climate Change Story.* (Chicago: Haymarket Books, 2011).

Siperstein, Stephen. "Climate Change in Literature and Culture: Conversion, Speculation, Education." PhD thesis (University of Oregon, 2016).

Special Report on Climate Change and Land from Indigenous Peoples. (August 2019), https://www.ipcc.ch/srccl/.

Specktor, Brandon. "The World's Largest Iceberg May Have Just Begun Its Death March." *Live Science* (April 4, 2020), https://www.livescience.com/worlds-largest -iceberg-dying.html.

Stanner, W.H. *After the Dreaming.* (Sydney: Australian Broadcasting Commission, 1972).

Staples, Heidi Lynn. "Preface," in *Big Energy Poets: Ecopoetry Thinks Climate Change*, eds. Heidi Lynn Staples and Amy King (Buffalo, NY: Blazevox Books, 2017): 13–16.

Steer. Philip. "Reading Classic Novels in an Era of Climate Change." *The Conversation* (May 23, 2017), https://theconversation.com/reading-classic-novels-in-an-era-of -climate change-75843.

The Arctic Cycle. "Our Mission." https://www.thearcticcycle.org/mission.

"The Global Climate 2011–2015: Heat Records and High Impact Weather." World Health Organization Press Release (November 8, 2016), https://public.wmo.int/en/media/ press-release/global-climate-2011-2015-hot-and-wild.

Thwaites, Joseph. "Public Interest in the Pandemic: A Comparative Framing Analysis of COVID-19 Public Health Interventions by the Victorian State Government and Australian Digital News Outlets." MSc. (Media and Communication, Lund University, 2021).

van Oldenborgh, Geert Jan, et al. "Attribution of the Australian Bushfire Risk to Anthropogenic Climate Change," *Natural Hazards and Earth System Sciences* 21.3 (2021): 941–960.

Velicogna, Isabella, Yara Mohajerani, A. Geruo, Felix Landerer, Jeremie Mouginot, Brice Noel, Eric Rignot, et al. "Continuity of Ice Sheet Mass Loss in Greenland and Antarctica From the GRACE and GRACE Follow-On Missions." *Geophysical Research Letters* 47.8 (April 28, 2020): 1–8.

Von Storch, Lilian, Lukas Ley and Jing Sun. "New Climate Change Activism: Before and After the Covid-19 Pandemic." *Social Anthropology* 29 (2021): 205–209.

Wark, McKenzie. "On the Obsolescence of the Bourgeois Novel in the Anthropocene," *Verso* (August 16, 2017), https://www.versobooks.com/blogs/3356-on-the-obsolesce nce-of-the-bourgeois-novel-in-the-anthropocene.

Wark, McKenzie. "The Engine Room of Literature: On Franco Moretti," *Los Angeles Review of Books.* (June 5, 2013), https://lareviewofbooks.org/article/the-engine -room-of-literature-on-franco-moretti/.

Watts, Nick, et al. "The 2019 Report of *The Lancet* Countdown on Health and Climate Change: Ensuring That the Health of a Child Born Today Is Not Defined by a Changing Climate." *Lancet* 394 (2019): 1836–1878.

Weizman, Eyal and Fazal Sheikh. *The Conflict Shoreline: Colonialism as Climate Change.* (Göttingen: Steidl, 2015).

Williams, Daniel. "Victorian Ecocriticism for the Anthropocene." *Victorian Literature and Culture* 45.3 (September 2017): 667–684.

Wright, Alexis. *The Swan Book: A Novel* (New York: Atria Books, 2016).

Woodward, Alistair. "Climate Change: Disruption, Risk and Opportunity," *Global Transitions* 1 (2019): 44–49.

World Health Organization. "Climate Change and Human Health," *World Health Organization*, www.who.int/globalchange/summary/en/index5.html.

World Meteorological Organization. "New Record For Antarctic Continent Reported," *World Meteorological Organization* (February 14, 2020), https://public.wmo.int/en/media/news/new-record-antarctic-continent-reported.

Young, Robert J.C. "Postcolonial Remains." *New Literary History* 43.1 (2012): 19–42.

Young, Robert J.C. *Colonial Desire: Hybridity in Theory, Culture and Race.* (London: Routledge, 1995).

Zalasiewicz, Jan. "Commentary on the 'Anthropocene in Chile' Manifesto." *Environmental Humanities* 11.2 (2019): 498–500.

CHAPTER 2

"The Imagining of Possibilities"
Writers as Activists

Geoffrey V. Davis

In Memoriam: Eckhard Breitinger
"A writer is his cause."[1]
"You start to understand the world through stories."[2]
"Once you've seen certain things, you can't un-see them,
and saying nothing is as political an act as speaking out."[3]

∵

In their seminal study *Postcolonial Ecocriticism*, Helen Tiffin and Graham Huggan describe their aim as "to strike a balance between the study of literature, the application of science, and the role of social activism,"[4] and, while demonstrating how ecological issues have become central to the work of an increasing number of scholars in the humanities, they draw attention to some of the numerous postcolonial writers who have made "a valuable contribution to ongoing debates about social and economic development in many regions of the formerly colonized world."[5] Imaginative literature, they argue, can act as "a catalyst for social action."[6] Following their lead, I would like in this chapter to discuss the work of a diverse selection of writers from Africa and India who share that aim and seek to raise awareness of ecological and Indigenous issues. What can be learnt from their commitment?

---

1   Ken Saro-Wiwa, *A Month and a Day: A Detention Diary* (Harmondsworth: Penguin, 1995): 82.
2   Helon Habila speaking at the Library of Congress, May 1, 2012.
3   Arundhati Roy, *The Shape of the Beast: Conversations with Arundhati Roy* (New Delhi: Penguin, 2009): 49.
4   Graham Huggan and Helen Tiffin, *Postcolonial Ecocriticism: Literature, Animals, Environment.* 2nd ed. (Abingdon and New York: Routledge, 2015): vii.
5   Huggan and Tiffin, *Postcolonial Ecocriticism,* 35.
6   Huggan and Tiffin, *Postcolonial Ecocriticism,* 12.

© KONINKLIJKE BRILL NV, LEIDEN, 2022 | DOI:10.1163/9789004514164_003

"THE IMAGINING OF POSSIBILITIES" 57

In view of the publication last year of *Literary Activism: Perspectives*, a collection of essays edited by Amit Chaudhuri,[7] I should first point out that the focus of that volume on the way writers, critics and publishers function as advocates of literature, for instance in Derek Attridge's choosing to write about the work of Zoë Wicomb with the conscious purpose of contributing to a rise in her reputation[8] or Chaudhuri's own campaign to have the Indian poet Mehrotra elected Professor of Poetry at Oxford,[9] is not my concern here. My interest lies rather in the work of writers who, faced with the dire threats to humanity posed by climate change, globalization, the political dispensation in their countries and social injustice especially towards Indigenous people, have chosen to become activists themselves, or have espoused activist positions in their literary work. I mean the kind of writers whose social commentary, to borrow a phrase from Njabulo Ndebele, "prods the reader towards an activist understanding."[10] One should bear in mind too that with their critical interventions they may be running the risk of harassment, imprisonment or even death.

As Mary C. Joyce observes, "Activism is all around us, but its mechanics are little understood and explanations are often idiosyncratic ..."[11] The general concept of activism is rarely articulated. Indeed, the word itself did not appear until the early twentieth century, although obviously people at various times long before that were taking direct action to achieve their social and political goals. As Harry Ritter points out, even the idea of "revolution," in its social meaning, is "a product of the modern era ... [I]ts crystallization was only possible in the context of a specifically modern outlook on the world."[12] Similarly, Joyce notes scholarly research on activism did not begin until the 1960s. Activism, as we understand it today, grew out of the youth movements and protests of that time, emerging with the "new" social movements of the post-industrial age—among them the peace movement, the civil rights movement, the women's liberation movement, the animal rights movement and the environmental movement. But the idea of activism originated, according to Astra Taylor, a century ago, with the German philosopher Rudolf Eucken, "who preferred the

---

7   Amit Chaudhuri, *Literary Activism: Perspectives* (New Delhi: Oxford UP, 2017).

8   Chaudhuri, *Literary Activism: Perspectives*, 45–69.

9   Chaudhuri, *Literary Activism: Perspectives*, 215–246.

10   Njabulo S. Ndebele, "Preface," *Fine Lines from the Box: further thoughts about our country* (Roggebaai: Umuzi, 2007): 11.

11   Mary C. Joyce, "Activism Success: A Concept Explication" MA thesis (University of Washington, 2014): 7.

12   Harry Ritter, *Dictionary of Concepts in History* (New York, Greenwood Press, 1986): 389.

mystical to the material; and that preference lingers on, for many still believe that action, even when disconnected from any coherent strategy, can magically lead to societal awakening."[13] The distinction here is between activism and organising, which has its roots in trade union and labour politics—that is, "between self-expression and movement-building."[14] Activism flourished "as people moved away from what they felt were dated political ideologies,"[15] particularly those of the Left, which had been more concerned with economics and public policy than with cultural and identity issues. In postcolonial cultures, however, activism had roots in earlier anti-colonial resistance rather than in the liberative individualism of the '60s.[16] Resistance in these contexts has historically been an organised and collective struggle against structural oppression (colonialist attitudes, institutions, policies and practices)—which, in many places, is ongoing. Recent research has shown clearly that climate change impacts on islands of the Caribbean and southwestern Indian Ocean "are magnified by historical environmental injustice and colonial legacies, which have heightened the vulnerability of human and other biotic communities."[17] In these cultures, shaped by colonial oppression, climate change activists have also to be decolonial activists to be effective. And if their medium of resistance is literature (or any other of the arts) they need to develop "a decolonial practice," a kind of "aesthetic activism" that works towards uncoupling colonialism from modernity.[18]

Many would argue that the relationship between literature and activism is intrinsic. (That is why despots burn books: to forestall change.) Literary ethicists such as Dorothy Hale argue that reading literary fiction strengthens the capacity for empathy, and that empathy is a "pre-condition for positive social

---

13 Astra Taylor, "Get Out There and Organise," *Le Monde diplomatique*, July 2016, https://mondediplo.com/2016/07/14activism.

14 Astra Taylor, "Get Out There and Organise".

15 Astra Taylor, "Get Out There and Organise".

16 As Timothy Forsyth argues, "academics have often inferred models of social movement evolution based on the so called 'new social movements' of Europe and North America to developing countries without acknowledging the differences between societies"— "Environmental Social Movements in Thailand: How Important is Class?" *Asian Journal of Social Science* 29.1 (2001): 35.

17 Kristina Douglassa and Jago Cooper, "Archaeology, Environmental Justice, and Climate Change on Islands of the Caribbean and Southwestern Indian Ocean," *Proceedings of the National Academy of Sciences of the United States of America* 117.15 (April 14, 2020): 8254.

18 Allyson Green, "Exceeding the Limits of Reconciliation: 'Decolonial Aesthetic Activism' in the Artwork of Canadian Artist Meryl McMaster," *Cultural Studies Review* 25 (July 2019): 5.

"THE IMAGINING OF POSSIBILITIES" 59

change."[19] Of course, not everyone agrees. D.A. Miller, for instance, regards the novel as an instrument of the state's policing power, maintaining normative social relations and ensuring social control.[20] But in postcolonial contexts the novel—and other literary genres: plays and poems and so on—are more usually agents of change. Sociologists are only now beginning to clarify the broad patterns of activism with regard to the achievement of goals and the realisation of benefits.[21] But clearly some actions succeed, while others fail, and the effects are often cumulative, the result of many contributors. Alan Paton's novel, *Cry, the Beloved Country* (1948), did not on its own end Apartheid in South Africa, but it certainly focused international attention on its evils. Chinua Achebe's novel, *Things Fall Apart* (1958), challenged the fake universalism of the value system underpinning the canons of English literature and, as one of the most widely set texts in universities and colleges across the world, helped to bring about an understanding of the injustices of British imperialism from the point of view of those on the receiving end in Nigeria. But it was not the only post-colonial text to bring that kind of refractive index to bear on English literature. Jean Rhys's *Wide Sargasso Sea* (1966) worked to similar effect, rewriting Charlotte Brontë's narrative of the white creole in *Jane Eyre* (1847). Many writers have combined a literary career with activism in other spheres of influence; some have abandoned literature in order to devote more time to their activism; and others have kickstarted a literary career to support their activism.

I have shaped this chapter around a discussion of the work of Indian writers Ganesh Devy, Arundhati Roy and Amitav Ghosh; and African writers Ken Saro-Wiwa and Helon Habila. Although this choice may be thought somewhat eclectic, it has the advantage of displaying a range of approaches by writers to central issues of our time. Their texts, both fictional and non-fictional,[22] illustrate some of the ways writers have chosen to intervene and have confronted

---

19   Dorothy J. Hale, "Fiction as Restriction: Self-Binding in New Ethical Theories of the Novel," *Narrative*, 15.2 (2007): 189.

20   D.A. Miller, *The Novel and the Police* (Berkeley: University of California Press, 1988).

21   Joyce, "Activism Success," 7.

22   I have reluctantly opted to exclude both poetry and drama. However, I would refer to *Sustaining the Earth: An Anthology of Green Poems in English,* edited by Norbert H. Platz, Birgit Fiddelke and Anne Unfried (Kiel: L&F Verlag, 1998), which includes texts from across the English-speaking world, gives a good idea of just how much there is, and also to *Enacting Nature: Ecocritical Perspectives on Indigenous Performance,* edited by Birgit Däwes and Marc Maufort, *Dramaturgies* 33 (Bruxelles: Peter Lang, 2014) which brings together articles on Indigenous plays from North America, Australia, New Zealand and the Pacific but regrettably not from Asia or Africa, has begun to explore "the interconnections between ecocritical methodologies and Indigenous theatre, drama and performance" (13).

such urgent issues as climate change, environmental pollution and Indigenous agency in their literary work. They exemplify the kind of contribution literature can make to such urgent social debates.

Few have embraced social activism as wholeheartedly as the Indian scholar and writer, Ganesh Devy, and the force of his example is powerful. His commitment to the cause of the tribal people of India and the combination of writing and social activism, representing the twin poles of his work which led him to resign his professorship of English at the university in Baroda, is likely to cause one to question the efficacy of one's own activities in one's own country. As the US-based scholar Rajeswari Sunder Rajan has written, "I am constrained [...] by my sense that his renunciation of an academic career in favour of full-time commitment to social work is a reproach to those of us who pursue our careers in greener pastures abroad."[23] Many of those who have encountered Devy will have felt the same. Certainly, I did.

Devy is a man of great intellectual energy, ever given to radical thinking and the initiation of innovative projects. Much inspired by Gandhi, by the Bengali writer and activist Mahasweta Devi and by the anthropologist Verrier Elwin, an anthology of whose works he has edited, his decision to quit his university position seems very much in the mould of Elwin's own earlier forsaking of an academic life. Elwin wrote:

> I knew that India was a poor country and much as I looked forward to a donnish career at Oxford, I had begun to feel that the academic life was not enough. I was filled with a desire to do something to make reparation for what my country and my class had done to India.[24]

For Devy too, it would seem that a "donnish career" was not enough.

Who are the tribal people with whom Devy began to work? Among its vast population India numbers just over one hundred million tribal people who (as of 2011) constituted 8.6 percent of the population.[25] Many of them are traditionally forest dwellers. Known as adivasis, they have, as Vibha Chauhan puts it, "remained on the margins of the social, economic and political march

---

23   "Foreword," *The G.N. Devy Reader* (Hyderabad: Orient BlackSwan, 2009): xiii.

24   Verrier Elwin, "Leaves from the Jungle, Foreword to the Second Edition," *The Oxford India Elwin* (Delhi: Oxford UP, 2009): 1.

25   Statistical Profile of Scheduled Tribes in India 2013 (New Delhi: Ministry of Tribal Affairs Statistics Division, 2013), https://tribal.nic.in/downloads/Statistics/StatisticalProfileof STs2013.pdf.

of independent India";[26] impoverished and alienated, they occupy the lowest rung on the ladder of development; over half of them live below the poverty line; their literacy rate is barely half that of the general population and is particularly poor in the case of women; living in rural areas they are increasingly vulnerable to encroachment by industrial and mining interests on tribal land, including sacred sites. The issues with which they have to contend are thus demonstrably similar to those faced by Indigenous communities across the world.

In outlining the basic problem facing those who, like himself, devote themselves to bettering the lot of tribal people, Devy has commented:

> It is indeed a matter of great concern for every sensitive citizen of India that the social and economic situation of the adivasis should remain plagued with underdevelopment, starvation and lack of opportunities for progress. On the other hand, the general condition of life in the centres of urban concentration has been so dehumanizing that one may easily feel attracted to the grace and simplicity of the adivasi culture. Any policy for welfare and development drafted for the adivasis will be required to reconcile the two positions.[27]

He further argues that the adivasis, who have long been voiceless in Indian society, should be allowed "to speak for themselves," pointing out that "whether or not to continue the traditional way of life, whether or not to modernize and accept the values and life styles of the technology driven industrial society should be a choice that adivasis themselves have to make."[28] Devy believes in Indigenous agency and his own aim has simply been to provide a platform for this to function.

Devi's activism on behalf of the adivasis is deeply related to issues of climate change in India. As in many other parts of the world, where Indigenous peoples are battling to maintain control over their natural resources, the adivasis are struggling to adapt effectively "to erratic rainfall, drought and other projected impacts of global warming" while at the same time contending with

---

26 Vibha Chauhan, "Crystallizing Protest into Movement: Adivasi Community in History, Society and Literature" in *Indigeneity: Culture and Representation*, eds. G.N. Devy, Geoffrey V. Davis and K.K. Chakaravarty (New Delhi: Orient BlackSwan, 2009): 56.

27 "Foreword," *Adivasis. Legal Provisions, Languages, Locations. A Reference Document for the Status of Adivasis and Denotified and Nomadic Jatis in India* (Vadodara: Adivasi Academy and Bhasha Research and Publication Centre, 2004): 3.

28 "Foreword," 3.

"colonial and corporate attempts to nationalize or privatize" their environmental assets.[29] Eco-spiritual beliefs of Indigenous peoples traditionally link to local ecologies and biodiversity. The Kaani people of the Kanyakumari forests of the Great Escarpment (the Western Ghats) of India is one apt example. "They live in consonance with Nature and derive everything from nature for their sustenance and livelihood"[30]—their material and spiritual wellbeing, their stories, their rituals, even their history, as the Indigenous forest people of the mountains. In the first of the five volumes that I coedited with Devy for the Routledge "Key Concepts in Indigenous Studies" series, we focused jointly on the environments and belief systems of Indigenous peoples, factoring in climate change impacts on religion, ritual and cultural practice, art and design as well as natural resources. In his own chapter, titled "Forests Now Speak English,"[31] Devy asks a number of historical questions, directly relating to climate change today, about the deforestation of India by European colonising powers—as part of their effort to tame, "civilise" and possess the territories where the forests grew. But for the answers to these questions—the background to climate change—he tells us, it is pointless to look into the legitimating histories of British colonialism that were spoon-fed to the children of his generation in Indian schools. Rather, one must look to literature—to the novels of the Bengali author and activist, Mahasweta Devi, for example, like *Jungle Ke Davedar* (*The First Claimants of the Forests*) (2008).

An idea of Devy's thinking on adivasis based on his many years of working with them as a teacher and activist in such areas as education, health, artistic expression and microfinance may be gained from the essays in *A Nomad Called Thief* (2006), which he dedicated to his mentor, Mahasweta Devi. Conscious of the fact that the majority of Indians are ignorant of the social structures, knowledge systems and culture of tribal people, Devy believes that "there is much in the adivasi way of life that the country needs to emulate."[32] "Devy's mission," Rajeswari Sunder Rajan has suggested, "is to show [...] the relevance and value of the Adivasi world view in contemporary India."[33] Thus Devy praises the

---

29 Govind Kelkar, *Adivasi Women Engaging with Climate Change* (New Delhi: United Nations Development Fund for Women, 2009): 2.

30 S. Davidson Sargunam and S. Suja, "Eco-spirituality in the Face of Climate Change: Learning from the Kaani Tribe of Kanyakumari District—Tamil Nadu," https://indiantribalheritage.org/?p=18372#gsc.tab=0.

31 G.N. Devy, "Forests Now Speak English: The Indigenous at Odds with the State," *Environment and Belief Systems* (New Delhi: Routledge India, 2020): 76.

32 G.N. Devy, *A Nomad called Thief: Reflections on Adivasi Silence* (Hyderabad: Orient Longman, 2006): 4.

33 "Foreword," *The G.N. Devy Reader*, xv.

adivasis' sense of community welfare, their preservation of Indigenous knowledge and culture, their lack of a caste system, their harmonious relationship with the natural world and their careful husbanding of the environment.

Devy is painfully aware of the deprivation and marginalisation which the adivasis have suffered first under the colonial Criminal Tribes Act and later under the hardly less discriminatory post-Independence Habitual Offenders Act. He points to the environmental dangers posed by the fact that "most deposits of minerals [lie] in Adivasi areas" and the locations of all of the big dams"—like the Narmada—lie "close to their habitations."[34] Coal India is the largest coal producer in the world and although solar prices hit a record low in 2020, so that coal is no longer the cheapest source of energy, it still provides around 70 percent of the country's electricity. As Amnesty International's 2016 report on coal mining in India states:

> About 70 percent of India's coal is located in the central and eastern states of Chhattisgarh, Jharkhand and Odisha, where over 26 million members of Adivasi communities live, nearly a quarter of India's Adivasi population. Adivasi communities, who traditionally have strong links to land and forests, have suffered disproportionately from development-induced displacement and environmental destruction in India.[35]

It is difficult to secure systematic information about the displacement of adivasis by dams and other development projects but certainly India has more large dams than any other nation except China and the US; and the displacement they cause impacts disproportionately upon adivasi communities.

Devy has been vocal in condemning the usurpation of the adivasi's rights over their forest habitats, as well as the lack of recognition of their languages in the Constitution, the absence of any provision for their artistic practices and the contempt with which they have generally been regarded as primitive. He is severely critical of those social and economic forces which compel them to migrate to the cities and consign them to such long-standing practices as bonded labour. And he deplores the fact that they are largely deprived of primary education and primary healthcare.

In an effort to remedy such deprivation, Devy calls for the creation of Adivasi academies and the formation of self-help groups to render the villages

---

34 Devy, *A Nomad Called Thief,* 12.
35 "When Land is Lost, Do We Eat Coal? Coal Mining and Violations of Adivasi Rights in India" (Bangalore: Amnesty International India, 2016): 6.

more viable; it is, he argues, "possible to create a new life in one's own village"[36] through initiating "development from within"[37] rather than swelling the ranks of exploited labourers in Indian cities.

His first major step towards the realisation of this "mission" was the foundation of a Research and Publication Centre at Baroda in 1996. This organisation, which is staffed largely by tribal people, is called Bhasha, a term usually translated as "language", "speech" or "voice". Its establishment, which began in a very modest fashion operating as it still does out of a small suburban house, was to have far-reaching consequences. The organisation's initial objectives were set out in an initial statement as the "documentation of linguistic, literary and artistic heritage of tribal communities in India and publish[ing] documented materials" as well as the establishment of "a campus for creating an institute for the promotion of tribal languages, literature, arts and culture with a view to initiating formal education in the area of conservation of tribal imagination."[38]

Through the inauguration of a publication programme, Bhasha set out to pioneer the dissemination of literary and educational materials in tribal languages such as translations from the oral tradition, the preparation of pictorial glossaries, dictionaries, grammar books, textbooks for primary and secondary education as well as little magazines. This has entailed designing scripts for use in hitherto unscripted languages. To date Bhasha has brought out publications in nineteen non-scheduled languages.[39] Devy has also edited a useful anthology under the title *Painted Words: An Anthology of Tribal Literature*,[40] which brings together translations of oral narratives and writings by adivasis in an effort to showcase the creativity of tribal communities which has remained largely unknown in India. A related project has been the digitalisation of the holdings of the eighteen tribal museums in India, which resulted in the publication of a National Inventory of Tribal Art.[41]

Madhu Ramnath has argued that there is something wrong with the language of climate change: it is "about ensuring, implementing and monitoring commitments—in fact, it is about avoiding them—and pushing the limits

---

36   Devy, *A Nomad Called Thief,* 139.

37   Devy, *A Nomad Called Thief,* 141.

38   "Foreword," *Adivasis. Legal Provisions, Languages, Locations,* 5.

39   These are Rathwi, Garasia, Chaudhari, Dungri Bhili, Panchmahali Bhili, Kukna, Gamit, Wanjhari, Madari, Naiki, Bhantu, Ahirani, Dehwali, Gor Banjara, Pavri, Chattisgarhi, Garhwali, Khasi, Kinnari, Mizo, Saora and Warli.

40   G.N. Devy, *Painted Words: An Anthology of Tribal Literature* (New Delhi: Penguin, 2002).

41   *Tribal Arts in India,* The National Inventory of Tribal Museums project (Baroda: Bhasha Publications, 2012).

of narrow national and political goals."[42] It effectively excludes the rural and Indigenous peoples who are most closely linked to the forests and oceans, who are the most knowledgeable about those environments, and who have so much to lose from their loss, not only their livelihoods but their cultural and spiritual sustenance. As Peter Coveney and Roger Highfield pointed out thirty years ago, the risk involved in this kind of exclusionary discourse is that it will overlook the richness of the real world with the result that the very essence of the subject under scrutiny (in this case, climate change) will be lost.[43] Could this paucity of language be one reason that so many people remain apparently indifferent to what is at stake in (or worse, in denial about) climate change? In Himachal Pradesh, the northernmost Indian state, there are 220 terms for snow. "Who knows how important these diverse terms for snow will be," Devy asks, "to tackle climate change that is impacting glaciers and snowmelt and precipitation?"[44]

In 1999 the government of Gujarat assigned to Bhasha a plot of land at the village of Tejgadh, which lies on the border of the states of Gujarat and Madhya Pradesh some ninety kilometres to the east of Baroda and which with its surrounding area is inhabited largely by tribal people. Working with the help of a well-known Baroda architect, work soon began there on the building of an Adivasi Academy. This was intended to function as a training and research institution, but would also house a museum of adivasi arts, and a library. The Academy would aspire to become a centre of learning in Tribal Studies focusing on "the history, culture, metaphysics, arts, languages, medicine, economy, development and traditions"[45] of the adivasis, and in realising this aim it would seek to evolve new methodologies of learning and research making particular use of oral traditions, performing arts, handicrafts and visual arts. Since its inception, it has added sustainable agriculture and women's development to its curriculum. Crucial to this project was the concern that "study and research undertaken at the Academy [should be translated] into action-oriented interventions for empowerment of marginalised communities,"[46] which in practice meant that most of those educated at the Academy would

---

42   Madhu Ramnath, "Something is Wrong with the Language of Climate Change," *Vikalp Sangam* (October 18, 2020), https://vikalpsangam.org/article/something-is-wrong-with-the-language-of-climate-change/.

43   Peter Coveney and Roger Highfield, *Arrow of Time. A Voyage Through Science to Solve Time's Greatest Mystery* (New York: Fawcett Books, 1991).

44   Devy, quoted by Ashish Kothari, "The Language of Diversity," *India Together* (December 22, 2015), http://www.indiatogether.org/language-of-diversity-op-ed.

45   "Foreword," *Adivasis. Legal Provisions, Languages, Locations*, 6.

46   "Foreword," *Adivasis. Legal Provisions, Languages, Locations*, 6.

return to their villages to apply what they had learnt there. Since its foundation the Academy has expanded rapidly and a clinic manned by volunteer doctors has been set up to deal with health issues such as sickle cell anaemia, which is widespread in the area. Bhasha's work in health, which has involved an effort to relate modern medicine to the tribals' understanding of health, has been extended to numerous surrounding villages and has created much good will.

An Indian writer who has taken up some of the same issues as Devy and who, until 2017 with the publication of her second novel, *The Ministry of Utmost Happiness*, seemed similarly to have abandoned a successful career, at least as a writer of fiction, is Arundhati Roy. Her essays "The Greater Common Good" of 1999 and "The End of Imagination" of 1998 have been described by Huggan and Tiffin as "probably [...] the most eye-catching ecocritical intervention by a recognized postcolonial writer to date."[47] That is an accolade of course which today might equally apply to Ghosh's *The Great Derangement*, a book in which, incidentally, he praises Roy as "one of the finest prose stylists of our time ... passionate and deeply informed about climate change."[48]

Roy is a writer who has addressed social and political concerns in both her fiction and her non-fiction. Climate change is prominent among those. But climate change for Roy is a "civilizational" issue. To counter it, one needs to resist the dominant ideology of progress, which is corporate capitalism. Progress, she says, has become a "kind of church," for the worshippers of capitalism.[49] Its adherents are afflicted by a kind of fundamentalist psychosis that makes them impervious to reason, so that they refuse "to understand that the survival of the species is connected to the survival of the planet."[50] They can only see the bauxite in the mountain; and so it is on that basis alone that they are able to calculate the mountain's value. Whereas the people who live around that mountain, who *know* that mountain, realise that it sustains not only themselves, that it is not only a question of their own displacement. Rather, it is a question of how the mountain—"which stores water and waters the plains all around it, which grows the food"—sustains a whole population.[51] Roy, like Devy, regards the difficulty inherent in the global conversation about climate change in part

---

47   Huggan and Tiffin, *Postcolonial Ecocriticism*, 46.

48   Amitav Ghosh, *The Great Derangement: Climate Change and the Unthinkable* (Gurgaon: Allen Lane, 2016): 11.

49   Arundhati Roy, "Capitalism Is a 'Form of Religion' Stopping Solutions to Climate Change and Inequality," *Democracy Now* (May 13, 2019), https://www.democracynow.org/2019/5/13/arundhati_roy_capitalism_is_a_form.

50   Roy, "Capitalism Is a 'Form of Religion' ".

51   Roy, "Capitalism Is a 'Form of Religion' ".

"THE IMAGINING OF POSSIBILITIES" 67

as a linguistic one, in that the language used is a language of tribal exclusion. "The language around climate change," she writes, "is being militarized."[52] This is because "every conflict, which appears to be a conflict between a tribe and a tribe, or a country and a country," is underpinned increasingly by climate change, with its "shrinking of resources and people collecting together to claim them, and therefore the growth of this kind of nationalistic or identity or tribal politics."[53]

To those who suggest that Roy made a clear transition from the success of her novel *The God of Small Things* to a life of activism,[54] she responds: "I don't see a great difference between *The God of Small Things* and my non-fiction. I try [...] to tell politics like a story";[55] and elsewhere she asserts that *The God of Small Things* is "no less political than any of my essays."[56] And indeed, that novel can be read in microcosm as a quintessentially postcolonial narrative of India's struggle for political identity. In the period between the publication of the two novels (1997–2017), however, Roy became a renowned activist and devoted all her considerable energies to a great variety of causes in India, wrote numerous "political" essays, and appeared on a number of different public platforms. Her eminence as a Booker Prize-winning novelist and her literary skills served her well in her activism. It is probably true to say that in her own country she has almost always been controversial since she chose to engage with issues on which she outspokenly adopted unpopular positions at variance from those of the state and from those of many Indians, so much so that Ramachandra Guha advised her "to stop writing political essays and go back to literature."[57] Whether one agrees with the positions she takes or not, it is impossible to read her work without being impressed by her commitment to social justice and by the courage with which she articulates her ideas. It is hardly surprising that the latest US edition of her work bears endorsements by authors such as Alice Walker, Naomi Klein, Noam Chomsky, Howard Zinn and John Berger.

Roy has had much to say on writing and activism, although she rejects the label "writer-activist,"[58] which she contends diminishes "the scope, the range,

---

52   Roy, "Capitalism Is a 'Form of Religion'".
53   Roy, "Capitalism Is a 'Form of Religion'".
54   The suggestion was made for instance by David Barsamian in "The Colonization of Knowledge"—Roy, *The Shape of the Beast*, 36.
55   Roy, *The Shape of the Beast*, 36.
56   Roy, *The Algebra of Infinite Justice*, rev. and updated edition (New Delhi: Penguin Books India, 2002): 196.
57   Roy, *The Shape of the Beast*, 13.
58   Roy, *The Algebra of Infinite Justice*, 196.

the sweep, of what a writer is and can be."[59] In her view one is involved in "huge political and social upheavals" not because one is a writer or an activist, but because one is a human being. "Writing about it," she asserts, "just happens to be the most effective thing a writer can do."[60] Time and again she returns to the role of the writer in society. The writer, she believes, has the ability to render complex issues comprehensible, to communicate through stories that everyone can understand. She formulates the duty for the writer to speak out and take sides memorably: "Once you've seen certain things, you can't un-see them, and saying nothing is as political an act as speaking out."[61] Writers should therefore "push at the frontiers" and in a felicitous phrase "worry the edges of the human imagination."[62] And they should not be afraid of political engagement even if it involves the kind of risks she has been prepared to take upon herself.

In the essays that make up *The Algebra of Infinite Justice*, Roy stakes out the issues she would consistently engage with. Thus, she contrasts India's mega-projects such as nuclear weapons and dam building with its neglect of more urgent basic problems such as illiteracy and poverty, the provision of sanitation and the lack of drinking water. She involves herself in the campaign against the building of the enormous Sardar Sarovar Dam on the Narmada River and condemns the resulting displacement of vast numbers of people, mainly adivasis, and "the charade of [their] rehabilitation."[63] For her the "fight over the fate of a river valley [...] began to raise doubts about an entire political system,"[64] which caused her to question the development model India had adopted. She opposes the privatisation of the energy sector, criticises the financial participation of US corporations and asks pertinently whether, in a country like India, "corporate globalization [is] going to close the gap between the privileged and underprivileged, between the upper castes and the lower castes, between the educated and the illiterate."[65] She demonstrates how Indigenous and environmental issues are invariably linked with the example of the adivasis, 117,000 of whom were displaced to facilitate the construction of the Sardar Sarovar Dam; their villages were submerged and they ended up living in slums and

---

59   Roy, *The Algebra of Infinite Justice*, 209.
60   Roy, *The Algebra of Infinite Justice*, 210.
61   Roy, *The Shape of the Beast*, 49.
62   Roy, *The Algebra of Infinite Justice*, 191.
63   Roy, *The Shape of the Beast*, 4.
64   Roy, "Lies, Dam Lies and Statistics," *The Guardian* (June 5, 1999), https://www.theguard ian.com/books/1999/jun/05/arundhatiroy.
65   Roy, *The Algebra of Infinite Justice*, 199.

"THE IMAGINING OF POSSIBILITIES" 69

working as wage labour for a pittance, all in the name of the "greater common good." In taking up the cause of the adivasis, Roy denies the charge that she is "romanticizing Adivasi lifestyles"[66] and in a country where "the politics of 'representation' is fraught," she is careful not to cast herself "as a representative of the voiceless,"[67] insisting that she writes in the cause of social justice on her own behalf.

Roy's essay "My Seditious Heart: An Unfinished Diary of Nowadays," published as the introduction to a US compendium of her essays in 2016,[68] provides a useful overview of her thinking on contemporary Indian politics through the time of the Bharatiya Janata Party (BJP) government led by Narendra Modi. In her view, the country is "at the mercy of what looks like a democratically elected government gone rogue,"[69] by which she is referring to the efforts not only of the ruling BJP but also to the Rashtriya Swayamsevak Sangh or National Self-Help Group (RSS), which aids and abets it, and which she regards as "the ideological holding company of Hindu nationalism,"[70] spreading its ideology of Hindutva and thus transforming India into a Hindu rather than a secular state. She compiles an angry chronicle of events since the BJP first came to power: the nuclear tests which "altered the tone of public discourse in India";[71] the assaults on Christians; Modi's election as chief minister of Gujarat; and the attack on parliament in 2001, which was blamed on Pakistan. She graphically describes the horrendous 2002 riots in Gujarat, which involved the killing of thousands of Muslims, and the Mumbai attacks of 2008. And she rightly alleges that Modi's election as prime minister in 2014, which brought the BJP back into power after ten years, has created a political atmosphere in which right-wing organisations feel they can act with impunity. An example of such actions was the assassination of the philosopher M.M. Kalburgi in Dharwad in 2015, after he had received threats from extreme right-wing Hindu organisations. This led directly to what Roy welcomes as "a new kind of resistance,"[72] when numerous writers spontaneously returned their literary awards to the Sahitya Akademi as a sign of protest. As a sign of the times, Ganesh Devy, who was among them, received a visit from the security police after he did so; Roy herself had already refused to accept her award for *The Algebra of Infinite*

---

66 Roy, *The Shape of the Beast,* 16.
67 Roy, *The Shape of the Beast,* 53.
68 Arundhati Roy, *The End of Imagination* (Chicago: Haymarket Books, 2016).
69 Roy, *The End of Imagination,* 2.
70 Roy, *The End of Imagination,* 5.
71 Roy, *The End of Imagination,* 7.
72 Roy, *The End of Imagination,* 16.

Justice. She is particularly incensed at the BJP government's perceived "instinctive hostility towards intellectual activity,"[73] and she cites a series of repressive actions towards several of India's top universities in support of this. She highlights the suicide of a Dalit student, Rohith Vemula, who was expelled from the University of Hyderabad and whose death and particularly his moving suicide note sparked widespread protest. She also exposes the BJP's repeated attempts to discredit student organisations at the Jawaharlal Nehru University which it regards as a bastion of radical left-wing protest against growing Hindu nationalism. And she notes: "It isn't just students. All over the country, lawyers, activists, writers, and filmmakers—anybody who criticizes the government— is being arrested, imprisoned, or entangled in spurious legal cases."[74] As in her previous writings Roy proves to be greatly in sympathy with the plight of adivasis, aligning herself with their ongoing struggle against mining companies and criticising the state for falsely equating them with "Maoist terrorists."[75] The core of Roy's argument, then, is that the BJP is pursuing policies which are legitimating the far right in the name of Hindu nationalism and dividing the nation.

If she sees reason for hope at such a desperate time it lies in "the excitement of witnessing the dawn of a new era of people's resistance,"[76] and she elaborates on this in her essay on Democracy:

> It means giving a forum to the myriad voices from the hundreds of resistance movements across the country who are speaking about *real* things—about bonded labour, marital rape, sexual preferences, women's wages, uranium dumping, unsustainable mining, weavers' woes, farmers' worries. It means fighting displacement and dispossession and the relentless everyday violence of abject poverty.[77]

Many of the issues she addresses in her essays also inform her novel, *The Ministry of Utmost Happiness* (2017). Among these are self-determination for Kashmir, Maoist Naxalite rebellion,[78] corporate globalisation exemplified in her references to the nuclear, mining and dam building industries, the Gujarat

---

73 Roy, *The End of Imagination*, 16.
74 Roy, *The End of Imagination*, 34.
75 Roy, *The End of Imagination*, 30.
76 Roy, *The Shape of the Beast*, vii.
77 Roy, *The Algebra of Infinite Justice*, 287.
78 For Roy on the Naxalites, see her long essay "Walking with the Comrades" in *Outlook* (March 29, 2010).

"THE IMAGINING OF POSSIBILITIES" 71

riots and the exploitation of adivasis in the cities and Hindu nationalism.[79] But she remains active on the issue of climate change also. In 2018, for instance, in the midst of the catastrophic flooding in her home state of Kerala, she was particularly outspoken:

> Unbridled greed, the shocking denuding of forest land for mining and illegal development of resorts and homes for the wealthy, illegal construction that has blocked all natural drainage, the destruction of natural water storage systems, the blatant mismanagement of dams, have all played a huge part in what is happening.[80]

One year after the floods, a year in which, according to Oxfam, billionaire fortunes in India had increased by 35 percent, while the poorest had remained in debt, Roy was asked to comment on the connection between climate change and increasing inequality in the world. "The connection is just capitalism, isn't it?" It was a rhetorical question, which many undoubtedly would have found blasphemous. But then, according to Roy, any talk of equality of justice these days has that effect—because capitalism has become "a form of religion that will brook no questioning."[81]

Huggan and Tiffin have likened Arundhati Roy in India to Ken Saro-Wiwa in Nigeria, not only as "probably the two most visible postcolonial writer-activists in the field,"[82] but also as writers who "show that ecological disruption is co-extensive with damage to the social fabric."[83] Roy has received death threats, been charged with contempt and sedition, and in 2002, as a warning after being found guilty of contempt for India's Supreme Court, she was even jailed for a day after speaking out against the Sardar Sarovar Dam construction. But in Nigeria, Saro-Wiwa paid the ultimate price: he was executed in Port Harcourt on 10 November 1995. In a trial widely condemned as "a travesty of justice"[84] he had been found guilty of murder on trumped-up charges for a crime he did not commit by a government-appointed "special tribunal" which

---

79   See Roy, *The Ministry of Utmost Happiness* (London: Hamish Hamilton, 2017): 44–45, 63, 81, 98, 105, 113, 116, 151, 165, 421.

80   Roy, "The Deadly Flood in Kerala May Be Only A Gentle Warning," *Climate & Capitalism* (August 23, 2018), https://climateandcapitalism.com/2018/08/23/arundhati-roy-the-deadly-flood-in-kerala-may-be-only-a-gentle-warning/.

81   Roy, "The Deadly Flood in Kerala May Be Only A Gentle Warning".

82   Huggan and Tiffin, *Postcolonial Ecocriticism: Literature, Animals, Environment*, 19.

83   Huggan and Tiffin, *Postcolonial Ecocriticism*, 54.

84   See for example *Wole Soyinka, The Open Sore of a Continent: A Personal Narrative of the Nigerian Crisis* (New York: Oxford UP, 1996): 146.

allowed no possibility of appeal. He was, the novelist William Boyd wrote in the *New Yorker* obituary, "an innocent man."[85] He paid with his life for his convictions and his attempts to protect his people. After his death, innumerable tributes were paid to him. Bernth Lindfors captured the spirit of the man:

> In his writing, in his politics, in his impulses Saro-Wiwa was truly a man of the people [...] he was also, first and foremost, a man for the people. He wrote to move people—to make them laugh, think, protest, act. And in his political work he moved to help people, defending them from injustice by pleading their case in the most conspicuous public arenas. In word and deed he excelled as a champion of the little man and as an advocate of human rights for all people.[86]

Kwame Anthony Appiah, drew a lesson from his death:

> we can do him no greater honor than to reflect [...] on what has happened to the people of his native land [...] and to commit ourselves, each in our own way, to the struggle for justice.[87]

Not surprisingly, Saro-Wiwa with his strong sense of justice and his commitment to non-violence has come to be regarded as "a global symbol of the general struggle for human rights and social [and] ecological justice."[88]

Saro-Wiwa's campaign for environmental justice in the Niger Delta and specifically his criticism of multi-national oil companies like Shell which collaborated with military dictators made activists of us all. In Germany, where I live, and where the writer had memorably attended a conference in Bayreuth in 1992, our students took to the streets when he was put on trial and called on our local Members of Parliament to take action. Fortunately, at that time Aachen was represented both in the Federal and in the European Parliaments by members of the Green Party. And they did take action. When one of them wrote an article for *Die Zeit*, a major German weekly, calling for a national boycott of Shell, this elicited an immediate response from the company which

---

85   *The New Yorker* (November 27, 1995); reprinted as the Introduction to Saro-Wiwa, *A Month and a Day*, vii.

86   Bernth Lindfors, "Ken Saro-Wiwa–in Short, A Giant," reprinted in *Ogoni's Agonies: Ken Saro-Wiwa and the Crisis in Nigeria*, ed. Abdul Rasheed Na'Allah (Trenton NJ: Africa World Press, 1998): 197.

87   Kwame Anthony Appiah, "Preface" in *Ogoni's Agonies*, xxi.

88   Huggan and Tiffin, *Postcolonial Ecocriticism*, 37.

"THE IMAGINING OF POSSIBILITIES" 73

promptly dispatched three of its senior managers from Hamburg, the UK and Nigeria to Aachen in a vain attempt to disclaim any responsibility for human rights violations in Ogoniland. Suffice it to say that, faced with extremely well-versed Members of Parliament, they did not get very far. Rereading the great amount of documentation which we acquired through working with MPs for that campaign, which included the report of QC Michael Birnbaum sent by the Law Society of England and Wales to observe the trial,[89] appeals for clemency from the Bundestag, press releases from Shell,[90] and from the Nigerian government, as well as material from Amnesty International, and the Greenpeace publication "Shell-Shocked," not to mention the leaked internal police memos and court documents from the Special Tribunal, brings it all movingly back to me. Needless to say, I still cannot bring myself to patronise Shell.

In spite of the fact that so much has been written about him,[91] no discussion of "writers as activists" can ignore Saro-Wiwa's significance. He was a novelist, playwright, poet, environmentalist and tireless campaigner for human rights. He held firm views on the function of literature and spoke frequently of the relationship between his literary practice and his activism. He believed that his books provided what he called "the philosophical underpinnings [of the protest movement]"[92] and that his literary ability enabled him to "re-establish the identity of the Ogoni in national and international circles,"[93] which he certainly did. In one of his last letters to William Boyd, from prison, he wrote "The most important thing for me is that I've used my talents as a writer to enable the Ogoni people to confront their tormentors. I was not able to do it as a politician or a businessman. My writing did it."[94]

His activism was grounded in the view that in a country like Nigeria literature should not be "divorced from politics."[95] Moreover, in a region where few people knew how to read and write, the writer, he said, "must be l'homme engagé: the intellectual man of action."[96] He must play "an interventionist

---

89   Michael Birnbaum QC, *Nigeria: Fundamental Rights Denied. Report of the Trial of Ken Saro-Wiwa and Others* (London: Article 19, the International Centre against Censorship, June 1995).

90   See also *Shell and the Environment* (London: Shell International Petroleum Company Limited, 1995).

91   Most recently by Rob Nixon in his excellent chapter on Saro-Wiwa in his book *Slow Violence and the Environmentalism of the Poor* (Cambridge MA and London: Harvard UP, 2011): 103–127.

92   Ken Saro-Wiwa, "We will defend our oil with our blood," *Ogoni's Agonies,* 347.

93   Saro-Wiwa, *A Month and a Day,* 111.

94   Saro-Wiwa, *A Month and a Day,* xv.

95   Saro-Wiwa, *A Month and a Day,* 81.

96   Saro-Wiwa, *A Month and a Day,* 81.

role,"[97] and involve himself in mass organisations, which is why Saro-Wiwa founded the Movement for the Survival of the Ogoni People (MOSOP). The theme of the writer as activist was one he frequently visited. In a 1993 interview, for instance, he declared:

> I think writers are led into different things. In my case, it has made me an activist, not every writer needs this kind of activism. You react to your situation [...] if you're a writer, even in that sort of society, like the Ogoni society, then I think you must go into activism, because if you're not into activism, then you're irresponsible.[98]

Saro-Wiwa was aware that in describing the combined actions of the Nigerian government and the oil companies as genocide, as in the title of his book *Genocide in Nigeria: The Ogoni Tragedy* (1992), he would be open to criticism or, at the very least misinterpretation. He was therefore careful to define what he meant by it. In his view—and here he felt he was in line with the UN definition of the term—if, in the case of the Ogoni, "you pollute their air, you pollute their streams, you make it impossible for them to farm or to fish, which is their main source of livelihood, and then what comes out of their soil you take entirely away,"[99] you are driving them towards extinction. Such a link—between "ecocide" and genocide—has been accepted by legal experts. In her book *Environmental Justice and the Rights of Indigenous Peoples*, for instance, Laura Westra accepts that, where environmental degradation threatens the survival of a people, "ecocide" can be regarded as a form of genocide,[100] and she confirms that such conditions do exist in Ogoniland.

Saro-Wiwa's book, *Genocide in Nigeria,* gives a good idea of the nature of his campaign against carbon pollution. It includes a brief geographical and historical description of the Ogoni lands, an indictment of British colonial responsibility, an account of Ogoni suffering in the Nigerian Civil War and a description of the pollution of the Niger Delta region. It also accords some space to Shell's arguments, which are remarkable for their efforts to shift responsibility on to government, for their protestations that their operations cause "minimal disturbance"[101] and their assertion that they provide employment opportunities

---

97   Saro-Wiwa, *A Month and a Day*, 81.
98   Saro-Wiwa, "They Are Killing My People," *Ogoni's Agonies*, 341.
99   Saro-Wiwa, "We Will Defend Our Oil With Our Blood," 351.
100   Laura Westra, *Environmental Justice and the Rights of Indigenous Peoples,* (Abingdon: Earthscan, 2008): 56, 173.
101   Saro-Wiwa, *Genocide in Nigeria: The Ogoni Tragedy* (Port Harcourt: Saros International Publishers, 1992): 51.

"THE IMAGINING OF POSSIBILITIES" 75

for Ogonis.[102] All of which Saro-Wiwa dismisses as "Shellspeak."[103] The final chapter of the book reprints the "Ogoni Bill of Rights," which summarizes the "tribulations" of the Ogoni people and demands that they be granted political autonomy, including "the right to protect the Ogoni environment and ecology from further degradation."[104]

In taking up the Ogoni struggle, Saro-Wiwa had recognised that he would have to fight on two fronts: against "the complete devastation of the environment by the oil companies prospecting for and mining oil in Ogoni, notably Shell and Chevron"; and against "the political marginalization and economic strangulation of the Ogoni, which was the responsibility of succeeding administrations in the country."[105] In his criticism of the Nigerian state, he was scathing, polemically describing the country as a "modern slave-state"[106] that practiced "domestic colonialism."[107] Accordingly, he regarded the incorporation of the Ogoni into the multi-ethnic Rivers State as unworkable. Critics have argued, rightly I think, that it was his decision to take on the Nigerian federal state and demand political autonomy for the Ogoni minority that finally brought him down. Quayson argues that he "triggered processes well beyond his control that in the end came to destroy him,"[108] while Apter concludes that "for Ken Saro-Wiwa the Ogoni struggle would remain that of persecuted minorities against the so-called ethnic majority."[109] In the end, it was "the combination of Shell,[110] the military regime, the three major language groups (Hausa, Igbo and Yoruba) [that] played different roles to frustrate Saro-Wiwa's efforts."[111]

Saro-Wiwa has become a global symbol of environmental activism, including the struggle for climate justice, which his children, inspired by his example, have taken up. His son, Ken Saro-Wiwa Jr. (aka Ken Wiwa), is a writer and journalist. His daughter, Zina Saro-Wiwa, is a video artist and filmmaker. And both are activists for climate justice. Both have struggled with their father's

---

102   Saro-Wiwa, *Genocide in Nigeria,* 55, 57.
103   Saro-Wiwa, *Genocide in Nigeria,* 56.
104   Saro-Wiwa, *Genocide in Nigeria,* 95.
105   Saro-Wiwa, *A Month and a Day,* 80.
106   Saro-Wiwa, *A Month and a Day,* 7.
107   Saro-Wiwa, *A Month and a Day,* 73.
108   Ato Quayson, "For Ken Saro-Wiwa: African Postcolonial Relations Through a Prism of Tragedy" in *Ogoni's Agonies,* 69.
109   Andrew Apter, "Death and the King's Henchmen: Ken Saro-Wiwa and the Political Ecology of citizenship in Nigeria" in *Ogoni's Agonies,* 132.
110   Westra notes that in spite of the international campaign against Shell after the death of Saro-Wiwa "no nation had 'halted purchases of Nigerian oil or sales of drilling equipment as a result of the hangings' " (287).
111   Abdul-Rasheed Na'Allah, "Introduction" to *Ogoni's Agonies,* 15.

legacy. It was clear by the time of his death that greenhouse gas emissions were a major contributor to climate change. What was not clear was the specific effects of climate change at particular locations. Today Saro-Wiwa Snr.'s environmental activism takes on new meaning, for the devastations of the Niger Delta stand revealed in such apocalyptic proportion as to render the prevailing language of climate change—the language of scientific modelling and speculative projection—completely anachronistic. But as Philip Aghoghovwia argues, this "apocalyptic realism" might also be read as "an organizing trope" for apprehending anthropogenic climate change according to a different kind of logic,[112] of "quotidian reality" as opposed to "imminent occurrence."[113] We perhaps should not be surprised to find that Zina Saro-Wiwa's artistic practice responds directly to that logic, conceiving of "new ways of being ... beyond the ken of modernity that the oil ontology inscribes in the Niger Delta."[114] "It is time to decolonize Environmentalism!" she proclaims.[115]

For many Nigerian writers,[116] the "judicial murder" of Ken Saro-Wiwa marked a watershed moment in the political and indeed in the literary history of their country. Certainly, this was true for Helon Habila, whose novel, *Oil on Water* (2010), quite evidently shares Saro-Wiwa's activist concerns about the continuing exploits of multinational oil companies, the ensuing environmental pollution and widespread corruption in the government, the army and the police. Aghoghovwia groups him with Zina Saro-Wiwa, as an apocalyptic realist, envisaging the Anthropocene as it manifests specifically in the wake of the oil wars of the Niger Delta.

Habila recalls, "I grew up in a time of so much injustice, when the politics were just so dysfunctional. I grew up in the decade of military dictatorships [...] all I saw was military rulers and military governors."[117] As a young man he

---

112   Lynn Badia, Marija Cetinić and Jeff Diamanti, "Introduction" in *Climate Realism. The Aesthetics of Weather and Atmosphere in the Anthropocene*, eds. Lynn Badia, Marija Cetinić and Jeff Diamanti (London: Routledge, 2020): 10–11.

113   Philip Aghoghovwia, "Anthropocene Arts: Apocalyptic Realism and the Post-Oil Imaginary in the Niger Delta," *Climate Realism. The Aesthetics of Weather and Atmosphere in the Anthropocene*, eds. Lynn Badia, Marija Cetinić and Jeff Diamanti (London: Routledge, 2020): 33.

114   Aghoghovwia, "Anthropocene Arts," 38.

115   Ismail Einashe, "'It's Time to Decolonize Environmentalism': An Interview with Zina Saro-Wiwa," *Frieze* (September 11, 2018), https://www.frieze.com/article/its-time-decolonize -environmentalism-interview-zina-saro-wiwa.

116   The memorial volume *Ogoni's Agonies: Ken Saro-Wiwa and the Crisis in Nigeria*, ed. Abdul Rasheed Na'Allah (Trenton NJ: Africa World Press, 1998) comprehensively documents their reactions.

117   *Ayiba Magazine* (September 2, 2014), http://ayibamagazine.com/?s=helon+habila.

"THE IMAGINING OF POSSIBILITIES"

experienced the period of the dictatorship of Sani Abacha, which he so harrowingly portrays in his first novel *Waiting for an Angel,* set in 1997, when the execution of Ken Saro-Wiwa was still fresh in people's minds. The novel's narrator, reflecting on the fate of those he regards as "political martyrs," whose deaths he assumes "have to be especially dire and painful,"[118] proceeds in a particularly gruesome passage to describe in detail the process of the hanging which Saro-Wiwa suffered. In the polemical "Afterword" to the novel, Habila writes, "It was a terrible time to be alive. Most intellectuals had only three options: exile, complicity, or dissent."[119] Outspokenly attacking the country's history of military rule, and particularly Abacha's "plain, old-fashioned terror," he observes how the brutal dictator "finally surpassed himself with the hanging of writer and political activist Ken Saro-Wiwa."[120] Anyone following in Saro-Wiwa's footsteps had to be aware of the risks.

Nevertheless, Habila has been vociferous in condemning environmental degradation in Nigeria, brought about by the activities of oil companies and the inaction of successive governments, reluctant to forego the profits they make from those companies. He expresses sympathy with those who "take up arms to fight the government over the lands" and warns that not only the oil companies but also Nigerians generally, who in his view have been too passive on these issues, will "be held accountable [...] by future generations."[121]

Oil on Water is a product of Habila's decision to lend his work a more activist orientation, speaking up against injustice, oppression and exploitation. Originally commissioned as a film script, at a time when Nigeria was going through a kidnapping crisis (2007), the project was abandoned when the author discovered that the film company wanted a sensationalist film in the manner of *Blood Diamonds* (2006), which would take no account of his own environmental concerns. This led him to reconceive the work as a literary thriller in which he could integrate a critique of environmental pollution. Imre Szeman describes the novel as one of the "surprisingly few literary fictions that undertake an exploration of what could well be said to have defined world politics since the discovery of oil in the mid-19th century,"[122] while Graeme

---

118   Helon Habila, *Waiting for an Angel* (London: Hamish Hamilton, 2002): 162.

119   Helon Habila, *Waiting for an Angel,* 228.

120   Helon Habila, *Waiting for an Angel,* 227.

121   Gabrielle Zuckerman, "Nigerian Author Helon Habila Mixes Oil and Water in New Novel," https://www.africanamerica.org/topic/nigerian-author-helon-habila-mixes-oil-and -water-in-new-novel.

122   Imre Szeman, "Conjectures on World Energy Literature: Or, What is Petroculture?" *Journal of Postcolonial Writing* 53.3 (June 2017): 282. The fact that the issue of the *Journal of Postcolonial Writing* referred to is devoted to "Resistant Resources/Resources of

Macdonald categorizes it as an "oil-encounter novel," even as an "oil-extraction text."[123] The novel today is hailed as a "petrofiction," a generic identification that refers to the theory of "petroculture" developed by Amitav Ghosh, who coined both of these terms in his 1992 review of the Jordanian-Saudi writer Abdelrahman Munif's *Cities of Salt* (1992), in which he observed that "the oil encounter" had hitherto produced scarcely "a single work of note."[124] Not surprisingly he had wondered "why, when there is so much to write about, [...] this encounter [has] proved so imaginatively sterile."[125] One reason he advanced for this was that "we do not yet possess the form that can give the Oil Encounter a literary expression"[126]—an assertion which Habila's novel, published some eighteen years later, might be thought to refute.[127]

The novel tells a relatively simple story: two journalists, the one old, experienced and seriously ill, the other a young novice hoping to learn the tricks of the trade on his first big story, are hired by a British expatriate to find his wife, who has been kidnapped by militants opposed to oil exploration in the hope of obtaining a ransom which will finance their campaign. They have since vanished into the myriad waterways of the vast Niger Delta. The pursuit bears characteristics of a thriller and the journey upriver is in some ways reminiscent of Joseph Conrad.

Just how strongly Habila feels about the ongoing pollution of the Niger Delta is evident from a number of unsparing descriptions he incorporates in the text, such as this typical one of the first village encountered on the journey, which heralds what is to come:

---

 resistance: World Literature, World-Ecology and Energetic Materialism" may be regarded as further evidence of the emergence of the "energy humanities".

123 Graeme Macdonald, "'Monstrous Transformer': Petrofiction and World Literature," *Journal of Postcolonial Writing* 53.3 (June 2017): 293. Macdonald also lists Saro-Wiwa's collection of stories *A Forest of Flowers* (1986; Harlow: Longman, 1995) as an 'oil-extraction text' (293). The term hardly seems to apply, however, as there are only two references to gas flares in the whole book (4 and 116) and nowhere any indication of the impact of the oil industry on the local inhabitants.

124 Originally published in *The New Republic* (March 2, 1992) "Petrofiction: The Oil Encounter and the Novel" was reprinted in Ghosh, *The Imam and the Indian: Prose Pieces* (2002: New Delhi, Penguin, 2010): 74–87.

125 Ghosh, "Petrofiction," 75.

126 Ghosh, "Petrofiction," 78.

127 Curiously, as we learn from his blog, Ghosh did not become aware until 2014 that his review had "become a seminal text in a field that is expanding rapidly in the US and Canada." He had "no idea," he writes, that his piece on "Petrofiction" had had this "catalytic effect." Ghosh supplies a partial bibliography of the expanding field in "Petrofiction and Petroculture" (August 27, 2014), https://amitavghosh.com/blog/?p=6441.

"THE IMAGINING OF POSSIBILITIES"   79

The village looked as if a deadly epidemic had swept through it. A square concrete platform dominated the village centre like some sacrificial altar. Abandoned oil-drilling paraphernalia was strewn around. [...] A weather-beaten signboard near the platform said: OIL WELL NO.2 1999. 15,000 METRES. [...] Behind one of the houses we found a chicken pen with about ten chickens inside, all dead and decomposing.[128]

And further on:

Soon we were in a dense mangrove swamp: the water underneath us had turned foul and sulphurous. [...] We followed a bend in the river and in front of us we saw dead birds draped over tree branches, their outstretched wings black and slick with oil; dead fishes bobbed white-bellied between tree roots.[129]

Two memorable passages in the novel are central to Habila's condemnation of the oil companies. The first is Chief Ibiram's emotional account of his people's peaceful existence in harmony with their environment, which has been disrupted by the enticing offers made by oil companies and then destroyed as the villagers prove unable to resist the companies, who together with soldiers evict them from their ancestral lands, leaving them "mere wanderers without a home."[130] The second is the village doctor's distressing account of the effects of environmental pollution on his people's health,[131] in which he tries to explain the dangers from poisoned wells and the impact of the toxin levels from the gas flares[132] to the uncomprehending villagers. Finally, he can only stand by as they die, their community disintegrates, and the whole village, as he puts it, "disappears almost overnight." "Sometimes," he adds, "I wonder what I'm doing here; I tell you there's more need for gravediggers than for a doctor."[133]

---

128   Habila, *Oil on Water* (London: Hamish Hamilton, 2010): 8.
129   Habila, *Oil on Water*, 9.
130   Habila, *Oil on Water*, 41. This passage (38–41) beginning "Once upon a time they lived in paradise ..." is the one Habila chose to read at the Library of Congress.
131   Habila, *Oil on Water*, 91–94.
132   The American Association for the Advancement of Science has published an enlightening text entitled "Eyes on Nigeria: Gas Flaring" which explains the environmental hazards for human habitations caused by the flares, https://www.aaas.org/page/eyes-nigeria-gas -flaring; Cf. the Greenpeace Report "Shell-Shocked: The environmental and social costs of living with Shell in Nigeria" (July 1994): 9–10.
133   Habila, *Oil on Water*, 93.

Habila's background is in journalism, which is surely the reason why he has cast the protagonists of both *Waiting for an Angel* (2002) and *Oil on Water* (2011) as journalists. He admits that "there was a functional element [here] because I know exactly what a journalist does."[134] Both novels reflect on the practice of that profession and on the role of journalists, particularly in establishing accountability in a state like Nigeria where government and oil companies are rarely called to account. As Maximilian Feldner states: *Oil on Water*, "highlighting as it does the role of the journalist as observer and witness, amounts to an act of literary activism, since it provides testimony concerning the destruction of the region."[135]

Or as Rufus puts it, in *Oil on Water*, "I couldn't turn my face away for long. ... my job was to observe, and to write ... [t]o be a witness for posterity."[136] But it is not only journalists, in Habila's view, who should be writing about the crisis of the natural environment. In the face of climate change, all writers should be writing about it:

> Right now we are engaged in a sort of attritional war with the fossil fuel industries, their propaganda machines, and their paid politicians. Climate change is all around us; the science is indisputable. ... In Nigeria, we are already experiencing severe floods and desertification at unprecedented levels. The incessant clashes between nomadic herdsmen, who are being pushed further and further south because of loss of grazing grounds for their cattle, is proof of this. Even the Boko Haram conflict in the northeast can be linked to the shrinking of Lake Chad, which used to be a source of fishing, irrigation, and transportation for people around the lake, but has shrunk by about 90 percent since the 1960s.[137]

The Nigerian government still has no coherent policies in place to address these emergent crises. That is why, Habila believes, *all* writers should be writing about climate change. "We must never let those who run the extractive industries and their propaganda machines tell us what to think."[138]

---

134   Zuckerman, "Nigerian author Helon Habila mixes oil and water in new novel".

135   Maximilian Feldner, "Representing the Neocolonial Destruction of the Niger Delta: Helon Habila's *Oil on Water* (2011)," *Journal of Postcolonial Writing* 54.4 (2018): 515.

136   Habila, *Oil on Water,* 55.

137   Habila, "Wild Authors," *Artists and Climate Change* (June 29, 2020), https://artistsandclimatechange.com/2020/06/29/wild-authors-helon-habila/.

138   Habila, "Wild Authors".

"THE IMAGINING OF POSSIBILITIES" 81

Habila's comment about conflicts between Nigeria's nomadic herdsman is a reference to climate-forced displacement. The terms for this kind of migration vary: climate refugees, environmental refugees, ecological refugees, environmentally displaced persons (EDP), environmental-refugees-to-be (ERTB) and so on. By 2050 it is estimated that climate change will have forced up to three hundred million people to migrate from their homes.[139] In the opening pages of *The Great Derangement: Climate Change and the Unthinkable*,[140] Amitav Ghosh informs us, "My ancestors were ecological refugees long before the term was invented."[141] He relates how they were forced to flee their village on the banks of the Padma River in what is now Bangladesh in the mid-1850s, when it was flooded by the river which "suddenly changed course." "The elemental force that untethered my ancestors from their homeland"[142] he regards as one of the shaping influences in his own life, and he attributes to their experience the fact that "the relationship between humanity and the environment has always been in my mind in some way."[143] This theme was abundantly evident in his fiction long before he embarked on the lectures he gave at the University of Chicago, which were later published as *The Great Derangement.*

An instructive early example, which he takes up in *The Great Derangement*, is his novel *The Hungry Tide* (2004). In fact, Ghosh has dated the beginning of his interest in climate change to when he commenced writing this novel. Set amid the Sundarban archipelago of West Bengal, part of which is a forest reserve for tiger conservation, the novel paints a comprehensive portrait of the natural environment of the tide country—its islands, its mangrove forests, its exposure to shifting currents and extreme climatic conditions, its precarious human settlements and its non-human inhabitants, above all dolphins and tigers. Through the story of an American cetologist who comes to the Sundarbans to research an endangered species of river dolphin (Orcaella), and who dedicates her life's work to their conservation, Ghosh explores a range of ecological and conservation issues. Among these are the conflict between humans and wildlife over territory, the forced removals of population which are implemented to make room for wildlife projects, the spread of environmental

---

139   "Climate Refugees," http://breckclimaterefugees.weebly.com/.
140   The book is based on the Berlin Family Lectures given at the University of Chicago in the autumn of 2015 entitled "The Great Derangement: Literature, History and Politics in the Age of Global Warming." The lectures can be viewed on YouTube.
141   Ghosh, *The Great Derangement*, 4.
142   Ghosh, *The Great Derangement*, 5.
143   J. Daniel Elam, "The Temporal Order of Modernity has Changed: Daniel Elam in Conversation with Amitav Ghosh," *boundary2* (March, 2017).

degradation, and the need to work together with (rather than against) those who have Indigenous knowledge about their environment. Ghosh makes clear that conservation policies must "take into consideration the lives and livelihoods of the people who live within these ecosystems,"[144] showing how it is mainly the poor who suffer the human costs of both conservation projects imposed from outside and of extreme climatic events, such as the storm so graphically captured in the book.[145] Not surprisingly the novel displays a particular sensitivity to the impending effects of climate change, as exemplified for instance in the following observation contained in Nirmal's notebook: "The birds were vanishing, the fish were dwindling and from day to day the land was being reclaimed by the sea. What would it take to submerge the tide country? Not much—a minuscule change in the level of the sea would be enough."[146] And this is of course a theme which resonates in *The Great Derangement*.

By any standards *The Great Derangement* is a powerful activist text, which challenges its readers to confront the issue of climate change and, as its subtitle implies, to think "the unthinkable." It is a work from which the reader cannot fail to learn, as it unflinchingly describes the process by which humankind came to find itself in such a grim predicament and clearly sets out the dimensions of the almost insurmountable climate-induced problems that lie before us. It is a work which, together with the lecture series on which it is based, makes a major contribution to awareness of global warming and has accordingly excited a good deal of comment.

I will focus here on two aspects of the book in particular: Ghosh's discussion of the representation of climate events in literature and his "Asian" perspective.

In the belief that climate change is "perhaps the most important question ever to confront culture,"[147] Ghosh observes that, "considering what climate change actually portends for the future of the earth, it should surely follow that this would be the principal preoccupation of writers the world over—and this, I think, is very far from being the case."[148] The situation has changed somewhat since 2016, when the book was published. At that time, however, the review journals were discussing climate change almost exclusively in the context of

---

144   Sabine Lauret-Taft, "Imagined Topographies of the Sundarbans in Amitav Ghosh's *The Hungry Tide*" in *Literary Location and Dislocation of Myth in the Post/Colonial Anglophone World*, eds. André Dodeman and Élodie Raimbault (Leiden: Brill Rodopi, 2017): 194.

145   In *The Great Derangement* Ghosh confesses that he found this scene "extraordinarily difficult to write," 44.

146   Amitav Ghosh, *The Hungry Tide* (London: HarperCollins, 2004): 215.

147   Ghosh, *The Great Derangement,* 12.

148   Ghosh, *The Great Derangement*, 10.

non-fiction or science fiction.[149] Ghosh found himself "at a loss" trying to think of "writers whose imaginative work communicated a more specific sense of the accelerating changes in our environment."[150] Margaret Atwood and Ian McEwan appear in *The Great Derangement* as notable exceptions. But what, Ghosh asks, has brought about this division of "the imaginative and the scientific,"[151] since the days of Goethe or Bernardin de Saint-Pierre, when no such division existed? And why is it, he asks, taking up the argument of his earlier article on petrofiction, "that we do not yet possess the form that can give the Oil Encounter a literary expression."[152] If the answer he advances in the latter case is that "oil is inscrutable"[153] and that the vocabulary of the subject hardly lends itself to literary expression, his wider response is to argue with John Updike that the contemporary novel has largely focused on "the individual moral adventure" at the cost of representing the kind of collective experience that is to be found in a work like Steinbeck's *Grapes of Wrath* (1939), which he sees as one of the few novels which articulates "a visionary placement within the non-human" and adopts "a form, an approach that grapples with climate change *avant la lettre.*"[154] Such an approach, Ghosh argues, is what is needed in facing up to and representing the kind of collective experience which threatens us in the shape of global warming. This is a particularly important point in relation to what I said earlier about postcolonial activism—that historically its roots are in collective resistance rather than unfettered individualism. Unless literature engages with the climate crisis, Ghosh argues, the "arts and literature of this time will one day be remembered not for their championing of freedom, but rather because of their complicity in the Great Derangement."[155] Further, "artists and writers" will be held "culpable" for not realizing "the imagining of possibilities"[156] which should be their essential function.

---

149   Ghosh, *The Great Derangement,* 9.

150   Ghosh, *The Great Derangement,* 167.

151   Ghosh, *The Great Derangement,* 95.

152   Ghosh, *The Great Derangement*, 102. Critics such as Jennifer Wenzel have disputed that this is the case (cf. her contribution at the MLA session devoted to *The Great Derangement* in New York in January 2018).

153   Ghosh, *The Great Derangement,* 100.

154   Ghosh, *The Great Derangement,* 107. He does credit a number of writers from India with a concern for the non-human and for the representation of collective experience (107). At the MLA session, Amrit Rahul Baishya spoke on literature in Assamese which engaged with the natural environment of Northeast India and which he termed "flood fictions".

155   Ghosh, *The Great Derangement,* 162.

156   I have taken this phrase from Ghosh's *The Great Derangement* where he writes, "The great, irreplaceable potentiality of fiction is that it makes possible the imagining of possibilities," 172, 181.

Although he is wholly in agreement with Naomi Klein's analysis of the responsibility of capitalism in the production of global warming,[157] Ghosh insists that the impact of empire should also be taken into account. He argues further that "to look at the climate crisis through the prism of empire is to recognise, first, that the continent of Asia is conceptually critical to every aspect of global warming."[158] Accordingly, the Asian perspective he adopts in important sections of *The Great Derangement* not only provides essential support for his argument, but also, bearing in mind that the lectures were addressed initially to an audience in the US, enables him to assemble a set of hitherto too little regarded examples both of the historical impact of empire in Asia and of present-day environmental threats to the Asian continent. As Jennifer Wenzel puts it, "he connects the dots between colonial violence and climate justice."[159] Thus, for example, he documents the use of oil in Burma from mediaeval times, claiming that the "first steps towards the creation of a modern oil industry were actually taken in Burma";[160] and he recalls how steam power was put to use to build steamships in Bombay (now Mumbai). It was only the imposition of colonialism through the use of European military force, which in both cases effectively undermined such emerging industries, Ghosh asserts, that prevented them from flourishing, and that served to maintain what he dismisses as "the supposed singularity" of the West.[161]

Asia provides Ghosh with some of his most telling examples of the threats posed by climate change, beginning with an experience of his own when, in 1978, he found himself in the path of an unprecedented tornado which struck parts of Delhi and which confronted him with "a scene of devastation such as [he] had never before beheld."[162] It was an event of such improbability, he later reflects, that he would have been unable to render it convincingly in fiction. Ghosh's repeated recourse to personal experience, as when he visits the remote Nicobar Islands to assess the impact of the 2004 tsunami there, serves to lend authority to his argument.

Ghosh's depiction of the many threats climate change poses to Asia is very unsettling, in spite of the fact that he believes that the strength of community ties there will better equip people to resist them than in the West. He is

---

157   See Naomi Klein, *This Changes Everything: Capitalism vs the Climate* (New York: Simon & Schuster, 2014).

158   Ghosh, *The Great Derangement*, 117.

159   MLA session on *The Great Derangement*, New York, January 2018.

160   Ghosh, *The Great Derangement*, 137.

161   Ghosh, *The Great Derangement*, 138.

162   Ghosh, *The Great Derangement*, 17.

"THE IMAGINING OF POSSIBILITIES" 85

particularly concerned about patterns of settlement which have consistently ignored considerations of climate, for example, in the Nicobars where reckless building along the coasts illustrates how "the bourgeois belief in the regularity of the world had been carried to the point of derangement,"[163] or in Mumbai where building such a city on low-lying islands now constitutes what he terms "an extraordinary, possibly unique, concentration of risk."[164] That risk was catastrophically demonstrated in 2005 when flooding caused by fourteen hours of rain confronted the city's inhabitants with "the costs of three centuries of interference with the ecology of an estuarine location."[165]

Arguing that the discourse of global warming has been all too Eurocentric, Ghosh reminds his Western audience that "the great majority of potential victims are in Asia."[166] He lets the staggering figures speak for themselves: in the Bengal floodplains "rising sea levels could result in the migration of up to 50 million people in India and 75 million in Bangladesh";[167] desertification is already encroaching on 24 percent of arable land in India; the accelerating water crisis in Asia could affect half a billion people. "The consequences are beyond imagining," he warns.[168] And lest his American audience remain all too complacent in their belief that such disasters always take place "far away," he reminds them of the devastation Hurricane Sandy wrought in New York.

Insisting that "the freakish weather events of today, despite their radically non-human nature, are nonetheless animated by cumulative human actions [...] the mysterious work of our own hands returning to haunt us in unthinkable shapes and forms,"[169] Ghosh attacks the phenomenon of "denial," and particularly the funding of climate change denial by vested interests such as Exxon and assorted energy billionaires together with media outlets owned by "climate sceptics like Rupert Murdoch."[170] In contrast to such misguided denialists, Ghosh points to the example of those who do accept the findings of climate science and, in a chapter of the book written after the lectures,

---

163 Ghosh, *The Great Derangement*, 48.
164 Ghosh, *The Great Derangement*, 53.
165 Ghosh, *The Great Derangement*, 60. In an interview with Vidya Venkat in *The Hindu* Ghosh extends his argument about the non-representation of climate change in literature to the film industry and asks, "How is it that a great cultural centre, where much of Bollywood films are made, did not produce any movie or recognisable work of art on the flood disaster" ("Chains of Causality whose ends we cannot see," *The Hindu* (July 17, 2016).
166 Ghosh, *The Great Derangement*, 118.
167 Ghosh, *The Great Derangement*, 120.
168 Ghosh, *The Great Derangement*, 121.
169 Ghosh, *The Great Derangement*, 43.
170 Ghosh, *The Great Derangement*, 184.

he submits the texts of the Paris Agreement (2015) and the papal encyclical *Laudato Si'* (2015) to close analysis. The former he criticises for its invoking of the impossible, by which he means the limitation of the rise in global temperature to 1.5 degrees Celsius, its failure to address the causes of the present crisis, and the overall impression the text gives that "the negotiations had been convened to deal with a minor annoyance."[171] The latter he praises for its acknowledgement of the limitations of growth, its commitment to social equity and its recognition of the "'ecological debt' [that] exists, particularly between the global north and south."[172]

In *The Great Derangement* Ghosh issues a rhetorically powerful call for urgent action. Unfortunately, he refrains from formulating practical solutions to the climate crisis. Rather unexpectedly, however, he highlights the involvement of religious groups, which in his view possess an ability to mobilise people for the cause of climate change which secular organisations lack. This he considers a sign of hope, together with "a spreading sense of urgency among governments and the public; the emergence of realistic alternative energy solutions; widening activism around the world; and even a few signal victories for environmental movements."[173]

Research has shown that protest is a crucial determinant of the kind of social changes that are needed to address the climate crisis.[174] But there is so far no indication that that any single activist strategy will have a guaranteed outcome; and the success of any approach depends on the cultural context, as attitudes to civil disobedience and social disruption (for example) are far from uniform. History tells us that activism can work, raising consciousness and garnering public support for policy change. A key finding of recent research, however, is that tactical diversity is crucial to success.[175] In the broad context of climate change activism, literary activism may be just one tool in the tactical repertoire but literary authors often have at least two relevant skills: they are

---

171   Ghosh, *The Great Derangement,* 207.

172   Ghosh, *The Great Derangement,* 211.

173   Ghosh, *The Great Derangement,* 213.

174   See Kate Aronoff, Alyssa Battistoni, Daniel Aldana Cohen and Thea Riofrancos, *A Planet to Win: Why We Need a Green New Deal* (New York: Verso Books, 2019); John Bellamy Foster, Brett Clark and Richard York, *The Ecological Rift: Capitalism's War on the Earth* (New York: NYU Press, 2011); Richard York, Eugene A. Rosa and Thomas Dietz, "Footprints on the Earth: The Environmental Consequences of Modernity," *American Sociological Review* 68.2 (2003): 279–300.

175   Dylan Bugden, "Does Climate Protest Work? Partisanship, Protest, and Sentiment Pools," *Socius: Sociological Research for a Dynamic World* 6 (May, 2020): 1–13.

"THE IMAGINING OF POSSIBILITIES" 87

able to produce telling counter-narratives to the dominant political paradigm; and they know how to sway sympathy and instil empathy. In other words, the relationship between activism and literature is a valuable resource. In postcolonial contexts, this is particularly the case, because both activism and literature have often partnered in their resistance to the deranged social-material relations produced by colonialism. Postcolonial writers are increasingly drawn to environmental activism. Tim Winton narrates, in *Island Home: A Landscape Memoir* (2015) how, until the 1990s, he had always "avoided joining environmental organizations."[176] But then: "I became aware of a diminution in the ecosystems I knew best, the limestone reefs and islets of the midwest coast. Wherever I swam in a mask and snorkel, I was seeing more and more of less and less."[177] In the end he felt that he "couldn't avoid being involved in environmental matters."[178] He soon found himself "the public face" of a campaign to save "Australia's second great coral reef, the Ningaloo"[179] from the developers who wanted to build a marina there. He did not think they could win—but win they did, and in 2011 Ningaloo became a World Heritage site. This is the kind of "signal victory" that Ghosh acknowledges at the optimistic conclusion of *The Great Derangement*, on the basis of which he states his preferred belief—"that out of this struggle will be born a generation that will be able to transcend the isolation in which humanity was entrapped in the time of its derangement."[180] Based on the projections of the United Nations Intergovernmental Panel on Climate Change, however, unless fossil fuels are phased out and the world acts urgently to address global warming, Ningaloo Reef (indeed, all of the world's coral reefs) will be dead in less than thirty years.

Editors' Note

As indicated in the Introduction, this essay is published posthumously. Present tense references by the author to his own experience need to be understood in this context.

---

176 Tim Winton, *Island Home: A Landscape Memoir* (London: Picador, 2016): 87.
177 Winton, *Island Home,* 86–87.
178 Winton, *Island Home,* 88.
179 Winton, *Island Home,* 88. Winton gives a full account of the campaign to save the reef in "The Battle for Ningaloo Reef" in *The Boy Behind the Curtain: Notes from an Australian Life* (London: Picador, 2017): 153–72.
180 *The Great Derangement,* 217.

Works Cited

Adivasis. Legal Provisions, Languages, Locations. A Reference Document for the Status of Adivasis and Denotified and Nomadic Jatis in India. (Vadodara: Adivasi Academy and Bhasha Research and Publication Centre, 2004).

Aghoghovwia, Philip. "Anthropocene Arts: Apocalyptic Realism and the Post-Oil Imaginary in the Niger Delta." *Climate Realism. The Aesthetics of Weather and Atmosphere in the Anthropocene.* eds. Lynn Badia, Marija Cetinić and Jeff Diamanti (London: Routledge, 2020).

Appiah, Kwame Anthony. "Preface" in *Ogoni's Agonies: Ken Saro-Wiwa and the Crisis in Nigeria*, ed. Abdul Rasheed Na'Allah (Trenton NJ: Africa World Press, 1998): xix–xxi.

Apter, Andrew. "Death and the King's Henchmen: Ken Saro-Wiwa and the Political Ecology of Citizenship in Nigeria" in Na'Allah, *Ogoni's Agonies, Ken Saro-Wiwa and the Crisis in Nigeria*, ed. Abdul Rasheed Na'Allah (Trenton NJ: Africa World Press, 1998): 121–160.

Aronoff, Kate, Battistoni, Alyssa, Cohen Daniel and Riofrancos Thea. *A Planet to Win: Why We Need a Green New Deal.* (New York: Verso Books, 2019).

Badia, Lynn, Cetinić Marija, and Jeff Diamanti eds. "Introduction" in *Climate Realism. The Aesthetics of Weather and Atmosphere in the Anthropocene.* (London: Routledge, 2020).

Birnbaum, Michael QC. *Nigeria: Fundamental Rights Denied. Report of the Trial of Ken Saro-Wiwa and Others.* (London: Article 19, the International Centre against Censorship, June 1995).

Boyd, William. Introduction to Saro-Wiwa, *A Month and a Day. A Detention Diary.* (Harmondsworth: Penguin, 1995): vii–xv.

Bugden, Dylan. "Does Climate Protest Work? Partisanship, Protest, and Sentiment Pools." *Socius: Sociological Research for a Dynamic World* 6, (May, 2020): 1–13.

Chaudhuri, Amit. *Literary Activism: Perspectives.* (New Delhi: Oxford UP, 2017).

Chauhan, Vibha. "Crystallizing Protest into Movement: Adivasi Community in History, Society and Literature" in *Indigeneity: Culture and Representation*, eds. G.N. Devy, Geoffrey V. Davis and K.K. Chakaravarty (New Delhi: Orient BlackSwan, 2009): 55–69.

Coveney, Peter and Highfield, Roger. *Arrow of Time. A Voyage Through Science to Solve Time's Greatest Mystery.* (New York: Fawcett Books, 1991).

Däwes, Birgit and Marc Maufort eds. *Enacting Nature: Ecocritical Perspectives on Indigenous Performance.* (Bruxelles: Peter Lang, 2014).

Devy, G.N. *Painted Words. An Anthology of Tribal Literature.* (New Delhi: Penguin, 2002).

Devy, G. N. "Foreword" to *Adivasis. Legal Provisions, Languages, Locations. A Reference Document for the Status of Adivasis and Denotified and Nomadic Jatis in India.*

(Vadodara: Adivasi Academy and Bhasha Research and Publication Centre, 2004): 3–4.

Devy, G. N. *A Nomad called Thief: Reflections on Adivasi Silence.* (Hyderabad: Orient Longman, 2006).

Devy, G. N. *The G.N. Devy Reader.* (Hyderabad: Orient BlackSwan, 2009).

Devy, G. N., ed. *Tribal Arts in India.* The National Inventory of Tribal Museums Project (Vadodara: Bhasha Publications, 2012).

Devy, G.N. "Forests Now Speak English: The Indigenous at Odds with the State." *Environment and Belief Systems.* (New Delhi: Routledge India, 2020).

Douglassa Kristina and Cooper, Jago. "Archaeology, Environmental Justice, and Climate Change on Islands of the Caribbean and Southwestern Indian Ocean." *Proceedings of the National Academy of Sciences of the United States of America* 117.15 (April 14, 2020).

Einashe, Ismail. "'It's Time to Decolonize Environmentalism': An Interview with Zina Saro-Wiwa." *Frieze* (September 11, 2018), https://www.frieze.com/article/its-time -decolonize-environmentalism-interview-zina-saro-wiwa.

Elam, J. Daniel. "The Temporal Order of Modernity has Changed: Daniel Elam in Conversation with Amitav Ghosh." *boundary2* (March, 2017).

Elwin, Verrier. "Leaves from the Jungle, Foreword to the Second Edition." *The Oxford India Elwin.* (Delhi: Oxford UP, 2009): 1–11.

Feldner Maximilian. "Representing the neocolonial destruction of the Niger Delta: Helon Habila's Oil on Water (2011)." *Journal of Postcolonial Writing* 54.4 (2018): 515–527.

Forsyth Timothy. "Environmental Social Movements in Thailand: How Important is Class?" *Asian Journal of Social Science* 29.1 (2001): 35–51.

Foster, John Bellamy, Clark Brett, and Richard York. *The Ecological Rift: Capitalism's War on the Earth.* (New York: NYU Press, 2011).

Ghosh, Amitav. *The Hungry Tide.* (London: HarperCollins, 2004).

Ghosh, Amitav. "Petrofiction: The Oil Encounter and the Novel" in Ghosh, *The Imam and the Indian: Prose Pieces.* (2002: New Delhi, Penguin, 2010): 74–87.

Ghosh, Amitav. *The Great Derangement: Climate Change and the Unthinkable* (Gurgaon, India: Allen Lane, 2016).

Green, Allyson. "Exceeding the Limits of Reconciliation: 'Decolonial Aesthetic Activism' in the Artwork of Canadian Artist Meryl McMaster." *Cultural Studies Review* 25 (July 2019).

Greenpeace. *Shell-Shocked: The Environmental and Social Costs of Living with Shell in Nigeria* (July 1994).

Habila, Helon. *Waiting for an Angel.* (London: Hamish Hamilton, 2002).

Habila, Helon. *Oil on Water.* (London: Hamish Hamilton, 2010).

Habila, Helon. *Ayiba Magazine.* (September 2, 2014), http://ayibamagazine.com/?s=helon+habila.

Habila, Helon. "Wild Authors." *Artists and Climate Change* (June 29, 2020), https://artistsandclimatechange.com/2020/06/29/wild-authors-helon-habila/.

Hale, Dorothy J. "Fiction as Restriction: Self-Binding in New Ethical Theories of the Novel." *Narrative* 15.2 (2007): 187–206.

Huggan, Graham and Helen Tiffin. *Postcolonial Ecocriticism: Literature, Animals, Environment.* 2nd ed. (Abingdon and New York: Routledge, 2015).

Joyce, Mary C. "Activism Success: A Concept Explication." MA thesis (University of Washington, 2014).

Kelkar, Govind. *Adivasi Women Engaging with Climate Change.* (New Delhi: United Nations Development Fund for Women, 2009).

Klein, Naomi. *This Changes Everything: Capitalism vs the Climate.* (New York: Simon & Schuster, 2014).

Kothari, Ashish. "The Language of Diversity." *India Together* (December 22, 2015), http://www.indiatogether.org/language-of-diversity-op-ed.

Lauret-Taft, Sabine. "Imagined Topographies of the Sundarbans in Amitav Ghosh's *The Hungry Tide*" in *Literary Location and Dislocation of Myth in the Post/Colonial Anglophone World*, eds. André Dodeman and Élodie Raimbault (Leiden: Brill Rodopi, 2017): 195–207.

Lindfors, Bernth. "Ken Saro-Wiwa—in Short, A Giant," reprinted in *Ogoni's Agonies: Ken Saro-Wiwa and the Crisis in Nigeria*, ed. Abdul Rasheed Na'Allah, (Trenton NJ: Africa World Press, 1998): 195–197.

Macdonald, Graeme. "'Monstrous Transformer': Petrofiction and World Literature." *Journal of Postcolonial Writing* 53.3 (June 2017): 289–302.

Miller, D.A. *The Novel and the Police.* (Berkeley: University of California Press, 1988).

Na'Allah, Abdul Rasheed, ed. *Ogoni's Agonies: Ken Saro-Wiwa and the Crisis in Nigeria*, *Ogoni's Agonies: Ken Saro-Wiwa and the Crisis in Nigeria.* Ed., Abdul Rasheed Na'Allah (Trenton NJ: Africa World Press, 1998).

Ndebele, Njabulo S. *Fine Lines from the Box: Further Thoughts About Our Country.* (Roggebaai: Umuzi, 2007).

Nixon, Rob. *Slow Violence and the Environmentalism of the Poor.* (Cambridge MA and London: Harvard UP, 2011).

Platz, Norbert H., Birgit Fiddelke and Anne Unfried, ed. *Sustaining the Earth: An Anthology of Green Poems in English* (Kiel: L&F Verlag, 1998).

Quayson, Ato. "For Ken Saro-Wiwa: African Postcolonial relations through a Prism of Tragedy" in *Ogoni's Agonies, Ken Saro-Wiwa and the Crisis in Nigeria*. Ed. Abdul Rasheed Na'Allah (Trenton NJ: Africa World Press, 1998): 57–80.

Ramnath, Madhu. "Something is Wrong with the Language of Climate Change." *Vikalp Sangam* (October 18, 2020), https://vikalpsangam.org/article/something-is-wrong-with-the-language-of-climate-change/.

Ritter, Harry. *Dictionary of Concepts in History*. (New York, Greenwood Press, 1986).

Roy, Arundhati. *The God of Small Things*. (London: HarperCollins, 1996).

Roy, Arundhati. *The Algebra of Infinite Justice*. rev. and updated edition (New Delhi: Penguin Books India, 2002).

Roy, Arundhati. *The Shape of the Beast: Conversations with Arundhati Roy* (New Delhi: Penguin, 2009).

Roy, Arundhati. "Walking with the Comrades" in *Outlook* (March 29, 2010), https://magazine.outlookindia.com/story/walking-with-the-comrades/264738.

Roy, Arundhati. *The End of Imagination*. (Chicago: Haymarket Books, 2016).

Roy, Arundhati. *The Ministry of Utmost Happiness*. (London: Hamish Hamilton, 2017).

Roy, Arundhati. "The Deadly Flood in Kerala May Be Only A Gentle Warning." *Climate & Capitalism*. (August 23, 2018), https://climateandcapitalism.com/2018/08/23/arundhati-roy-the-deadly-flood-in-kerala-may-be-only-a-gentle-warning/.

Roy, Arundhati. "Capitalism Is a 'Form of Religion' Stopping Solutions to Climate Change & Inequality." *Democracy Now* (May 13, 2019), https://www.democracynow.org/2019/5/13/arundhati_roy_capitalism_is_a_form.

Sargunam, S. Davidson and S. Suja. "Eco-spirituality in the face of climate change: Learning from the Kaani tribe of Kanyakumari District–Tamil Nadu," https://indiantribalheritage.org/?p=18372#gsc.tab=0.

Saro-Wiwa, Ken. *Genocide in Nigeria: The Ogoni Tragedy*. (Port Harcourt: Saros International Publishers, 1992).

Saro-Wiwa, Ken. *A Forest of Flowers*. (Harlow: Longman, 1995).

Saro-Wiwa, Ken. *A Month and a Day: A Detention Diary*. (Harmondsworth: Penguin, 1995).

Saro-Wiwa, Ken. "We Will Defend Our Oil With Our Blood" in *Ogoni's Agonies: Ken Saro-Wiwa and the Crisis in Nigeria*, ed., Abdul Rasheed Na'Allah (Trenton NJ: Africa World Press, 1998): 343–359.

Saro-Wiwa, Ken. "They Are Killing My People," in *Ogoni's Agonies, Ken Saro-Wiwa and the Crisis in Nigeria*, ed. Abdul Rasheed Na'Allah (Trenton NJ: Africa World Press, 1998): 329–342.

Shell International Petroleum Company Limited. *Shell and the Environment* (London: Shell International Petroleum Company Limited, 1995).

Soyinka, Wole. *The Open Sore of a Continent: A Personal Narrative of the Nigerian Crisis*. (New York: Oxford UP, 1996).

Szeman, Imre. "Conjectures on World Energy Literature: Or, What is Petroculture?" *Journal of Postcolonial Writing* 53.3 (June 2017): 277–288.

Taylor, Astra. "Get Out There and Organise." *Le Monde diplomatique*. (July 2016), https://mondediplo.com/2016/07/14activism.

Tribal Arts in India, The National Inventory of Tribal Museums project (Baroda: Bhasha Publications, 2012).

Venkat, Vidya. "Chains of Causality whose ends we cannot see." *The Hindu* (July 17, 2016).

Westra, Laura. *Environmental Justice and the Rights of Indigenous Peoples*. (Abingdon: Earthscan, 2008).

"When Land is Lost, Do We Eat Coal? Coal Mining and Violations of Adivasi Rights in India" (Bangalore: Amnesty International India, 2016).

Winton, Tim. *Island Home: A Landscape Memoir*. (London: Picador, 2016).

Winton, Tim. "The Battle for Ningaloo Reef" in *The Boy behind the Curtain. Notes from an Australian Life*. (London: Picador, 2017): 153–172.

York, Richard, Eugene A., Rosa and Thomas Dietz. "Footprints on the Earth: The Environmental Consequences of Modernity." *American Sociological Review* 68.2 (2003): 279–300.

Zuckerman, Gabrielle. "Nigerian Author Helon Habila Mixes Oil and Water in New Novel," https://www.africanamerica.org/topic/nigerian-author-helon-habila-mixes-oil-and-water-in-new-novel.

CHAPTER 3

River Writing

Culture, Law and Poetics

Chris Prentice

In a context of anthropogenic climate change, any measure that purports to transform the place of humans in a more-than-human world[1] warrants attention, not least in the island and coastal zones of the planetary and political antipodes. Storms and flooding occur with increasing frequency and severity in some regions, alongside persistent drought and loss of waterways in others. Anthropogenic climate change, as a result of human-produced changes to the chemical composition of the atmosphere, brings drastic changes to local ecosystems that sustain lives and livelihoods. At the same time, the scale of the phenomenon is no less than global. As Dipesh Chakrabarty argues, climate change entails both the magnitude of human impact and the limits of the human as an adequate figure for the necessary scale of analysis and address.[2] Climate change is, in this sense, the most obvious manifestation of the current era of the Anthropocene. The Anthropocene, Chakrabarty contends, breaches the long-established distinction between human and natural history,[3] as the human species has become "a force of nature in the geological sense."[4] In short, anthropogenic climate change is a planetary crisis; at the same time, it

---

1   The term 'more-than-human' can be understood in the sense coined by David Abram, *The Spell of the Sensuous: Perception and Language in a More-than-Human World* (New York: Vintage, 1996) to suggest that which includes but also exceeds the human, placing the human in the midst, rather than at the top, of the sensuous world (49). Abram's work addresses the myriad ways modern western civilisation has lost (or suppressed) its reciprocity with a more-than-human world, and contrasts that loss with Indigenous oral cultures in which "language seems to encourage and augment the participatory life of the senses" (71) through which reciprocity with the more-than-human world is experienced. However, Chakrabarty's argument that the Anthropocene entails the need to think beyond the ontological human to encompass the human as a geological force proposes a further orientation to the more-than-human.
2   Dipesh Chakrabarty, "Postcolonial Studies and the Challenge of Climate Change," *New Literary History* 43.1 (Winter 2012): 1–18.
3   Dipesh Chakrabarty, "The Climate of History: Four Theses," *Critical Inquiry* 35.2 (2009): 221.
4   Chakrabarty, "The Climate of History," 207.

is "experienced first and foremost as weather,"[5] that is, at the local level. Like the broader concept of the Anthropocene, it must be thought across various spatio-temporal and conceptual scales at once. Weather, though inescapable, does not disclose the phenomenon in its entirety, but it literally brings the materiality of climate change home.

Australia and New Zealand, as two geographically southern regions, are shaped as much by their status as settler-invader colonies as by their antipodal locations. This confluence of historical and geographical factors generates overdetermined unsettlements at the interface of climate change vulnerabilities and questions of postcolonial justice. Today, the locally-lived instabilities of planetary climate change often exacerbate the effects of colonial displacement for Indigenous peoples who face the longue-durée consequences of colonial capitalism's destructive environmental impacts. However, as discourses of postcolonial historical justice intersect with those of climate change justice, Astrida Neimanis reminds us that colonialism itself is "carried by currents in a weather-and-water world of planetary circulation, where we cannot calculate a politics of location according to stable cartographies or geometries."[6] Anthropogenic climate change and imperial colonialism are historically implicated in one another, both impelled by industrial capitalism, so that responses to climate change impacts are inevitably imbricated with postcolonial politics. But what are the problems of "calculating" a politics or "justice" of location in conditions of planetary instability? And how can our notions of justice account for "the *volatility* of earth processes which reinforce 'the porosity of human bodies to other living things' "?[7] At the same time, are there potentialities to be rediscovered and reanimated in what Ross Gibson identifies as a particularly southern orientation to the aqueous qualities of place and "being"?[8]

To explore some responses to these questions, I begin with a specific New Zealand legal Act of Parliament, the Te Awa Tupua Act (2017), which enshrines the ancestral status of the Whanganui River for the Whanganui *iwi* (people/ tribe), granting legal personhood to the river. The Act represents iwi efforts to redress an instance of colonial (un)settlement, to restore the cultural status of

---

5   Graham Huggan, "Australian Literature, Risk and the Global Climate Change," *Lit: Literature Interpretation Theory* 26.2 (March 25, 2015): 96.

6   Astrida Neimanis, *Bodies of Water: Posthuman Feminist Phenomenology* (London: Bloomsbury, 2017): 36.

7   Huggan, "Australian Literature," 98; citing Nigel Clark, "Volatile Worlds, Vulnerable Bodies: Confronting Abrupt Climate Change," *Theory, Culture & Society* 27.2–3 (March 2010): 47.

8   Ross Gibson, *Changescapes: Complexity Mutability Aesthetics* (Crawley, WA: UWA Publishing, 2015): 34.

the river in terms of *whakapapa*, the Māori extended sense of genealogy placing humans and nonhumans in ties of symbolic obligation reaching back to cosmology. I read this Act alongside literary works that figure rivers within more-than-human worlds: poems by Māori poet Hone Tuwhare, and *Carpentaria* by Indigenous Australian (Waanyi) novelist Alexis Wright.[9] Spanning the discursively polarised registers of law and poetics—language in the services, respectively, of settlement and unsettlement—these writings focus less on recognisable climate change phenomena as such than on how historical, cultural and political factors are enmeshed with questions of human "being" among elemental and environmental "beings" and phenomena—locally lived contexts of climate change. My argument is that to meet the challenge of anthropogenic climate change, it is first necessary to challenge anthropocentrism itself, and the commitment to human exceptionalism brought with colonial Christianity and Enlightenment humanism to the antipodes.

In 2017, the New Zealand parliament passed the Te Awa Tupua Act, "settling" the longest running litigation in the country's history. Since the 1870s, the Whanganui iwi had fought for recognition of their relationship with the Whanganui River.[10] As the lead negotiator for the iwi, Gerrard Albert explains, "We treat the river as a tupuna, as an ancestor, and we needed to find something that would approximate that in law and uphold it."[11] The Act refers to the river as Te Awa Tupua, which is not its geographic name but, eluding translation into English, refers to the river in its fullest significance: both the whole river system taking in mountains and tributaries, banks and beds, to the sea; and embracing metaphysical or spiritual significance, the intrinsic relationship of people with it as "an indivisible and living whole."[12] Māori Party MP Mārama Fox distinguishes the relationship most New Zealanders might feel to rivers, or even a particular river, from that of the Whanganui iwi to this river. She invokes an embodied connection with the river at individual and

---

9   Alexis Wright, *Carpentaria* (Sydney: Giramondo, 2006).

10 Although known and cartographically inscribed as the Whanganui River, Māori did not have one name for the whole river, but named different parts of it according to local significance.

11 Radio New Zealand, "What It Means To Give the Whanganui River the Same Rights as a Person," *The Wireless* (2017), https://www.rnz.co.nz/news/the-wireless/374515/what-it -means-to-give-the-whanganui-river-the-same-rights-as-a-person.

12 Unlike western systems of categorisation, or taxonomic ordering in terms of species, genus, class and so on, whakapapa relation refers to the interconnection of things in given environment/life-world. Further, ancestors are understood by Māori as being intrinsic to their living descendants in the contemporary world. Te Puni Kōkiri, "Te Awa Tupua," *Kōkiri 33* (Raumati/Summer, 2016): 30.

collective levels, declaring, "A river runs through their veins; a river of whaka-papa; of sacred significance"; Te Awa Tupua is "the central artery of their tribal heart." Calling on the whakapepeha (proverbial saying), "ko au te awa, ko te awa ko au" (translated into English as "I am the river, the river is me"),[13] she explains that "The river and the land and its people are inseparable. ... if the Awa dies we die as a people. Ka mate te Awa, ka mate tātou te Iwi."[14] These expressions convey, then, that the river cannot be conceived of as a "thing" or "place" external to the people themselves, *as* a people. Despite references to a "relationship" with the river in the discourse of and around the Act, the whakapepeha suggests that, fundamentally, it is not a matter of the relation of the Whanganui iwi *to* or *with* the river, but of their "being" as inseparable from it. As Gerrard Albert puts it, Māori trace their genealogies to the origins of the universe; rather than masters of the natural world, Māori see themselves as part of it, equal to it, at one with mountains, rivers and sea.[15] I wonder, though, whether the whakapepeha's potentially radical challenge to the dualist sepa-ration of humans and "environment" or "nature"—humans and river—will be animated or constrained by the mechanism and terms of the legal Act, and the postcolonial politics of justice that inform it?

The Act specifies that "Te Awa Tupua is a legal person and has all the rights, power, duties and liabilities of a legal person."[16] Legal "personhood" casts Te Awa Tupua as having certain intrinsic interests and values of its own,[17] encap-sulated in two key principles: one, encompassing an integrated view of the river from the mountains to the sea; and two, understanding that the health and wellbeing of the river are intrinsically interconnected with the health and wellbeing of the people.[18] Judging that the river is not in a position to safeguard its rights, or act on its duties and liabilities, in the sense that the legal framing invokes, then-Minister of Treaty Negotiations, Chris Finlayson explained that

---

13   This translation is given in *The Wireless*, 2017, and in *The Whanganui Chronicle*, 2012. Mārama Fox does not give the literal translation in her speech, but instead glosses the whakapepeha as saying "the health and well-being of the Whanganui River is intrinsically interconnected with the health and well-being of the people." The difference between the translation and the gloss will be significant to my argument.

14   Mārama Fox, "Te Awa Tupua (Whanganui River Claims Settlement) Bill—Second Reading." (December 6, 2016), https://www.parliament.nz/mi/pb/hansard-debates/rhr/document/HansS_20161206_126900000/fox-marama

15   Eleanor Ainge Roy, "New Zealand River Granted Same Legal Rights as Human Being," *Guardian* International edition (March 16, 2017), www.theguardian.com/world/2017/mar/16/new-zealand-river-granted-same-legal-rights-as-human-being.

16   Te Awa Tupua (Whanganui River Claims Settlement) Act of 2017, s. 14[1].

17   Kōkiri, "Te Awa Tupua," 30.

18   Fox, "Te Awa Tupua—Second Reading".

RIVER WRITING 97

two guardians would be appointed to act on the river's behalf: one from the Crown, and one from the Whanganui iwi. Although postcolonial legal settlements have usually entailed restoration of Māori ownership of land, waters and other properties, in the context of this legal settlement nothing changes, in law, regarding ownership of the river. However, the basis of the Act points to a deeper shift in notions of restoration than return of property to Māori or iwi ownership. As Albert explains, the Whanganui iwi do not see their relationship with the river in terms of ownership—if anything, the river "owns" the iwi. The settlement is about recognising the mana[19] of the river, its health and well-being, an aim translated into more secular terms as enabling "better environmental outcomes"[20] in terms of land-use, including run-off into the river. As Minister Finlayson reaffirmed, "The river will own itself."[21] Already, we might see points of tension between the whakapepeha ("ko au te awa") and the legal and political discourse framing the Act that continues to articulate precisely what the whakapepeha challenges: notions of personhood, recognition, rights, property and environment.

In many ways, this legislation does indicate departure from the anthropocentric assumptions of European Enlightenment humanism, contesting colonial settlement's possessive, exploitative, polluting treatment of land and waters. Astrida Neimanis refers to "small glimmers of innovation" in qualifying her view that "regimes of human rights, citizenship, and property" persist as norms and goals that "depend upon individualized, stable, and sovereign bodies—those 'Enlightenment figures of coherent and masterful subjectivity.'"[22] Perhaps the legislation *is* one of those "small glimmers." However, I suggest that there are grounds for considering some less obvious pitfalls of the mechanism through which this innovation has been enacted: settler law. By "settler law", though, I mean not simply the legal structures, systems and their contents, but the very ontological grounds on which that law rests—grounds whose ultimate inability to encompass such a proposition as "ko au te awa, ko te awa ko au" is evident in the translation into "legal personhood." Those involved in bringing the Act into being evince a pragmatic acceptance of terms that will create a space for Māori meanings. When Albert refers to the Act as

---

19 This term has no English equivalent, but is often translated into English as one or more of the following terms: prestige, status, authority, spiritual power, charisma.

20 Kōkiri, "Te Awa Tupua," 30.

21 Kōkiri, "Te Awa Tupua," 30.

22 Neimanis, *Bodies of Water: Posthuman Feminist Phenomenology* (London: Bloomsbury, 2017): 2, citing Donna Haraway, "Anthropocene, Capitalocene, Plantationocene, Chthulucene: Making Kin," *Environmental Humanities* 6 (May 2015): 159–165.

arising from the need to find "something that would approximate" and uphold the Whanganui iwi's ancestral relation to the river "in law," he implies an act of translation, and (re)accommodation. However, when he claims that seeing themselves as part of the natural world "is not an anti-development, or anti-economic use of the river," but rather a matter of considering its future beginning "with the view that it is a living being,"[23] one might ask to whom the development-economics (re)assurance is being given. For whom is the protection of "development" and "economic use" a vital and ongoing stake? Is use of the river in economic development compatible with viewing it as a living being, as a "person"? How, and with what implications, are "persons"—or any living beings, or indeed tūpuna[24]—subject to economic development? And how does the progressive temporality (and the temporalness) of 'development' relate to the layered, cyclical (and cosmological) temporality of whakapapa? Although the Act recognises the river as having "legal" personhood, different in law from being a "natural" person, when Minister Finlayson claims that legal personality for a "natural resource" is "no stranger than family trusts, or companies, or incorporated societies,"[25] can we entirely agree that legal corporate abstractions are comparable to a living body/ecosystem? Is the notion of a "natural resource" consistent with the claim to tupuna status for the river? If there are tensions here, how do we interpret Albert's apparent disavowal of them? If there are not, then what has fundamentally changed, or been challenged?

As the settlement of an Indigenous claim against the settler state,[26] the Act registers the relationship of river and iwi as a "right" rather than as *culture*; the iwi's right to the river, and the river as having rights.[27] In that sense, the justice sought by the Act is haunted by annexation—in this case, annexation by socialisation, drawing the river into the social logic of (western humanist)

---

23 Ainge Roy, "New Zealand River".

24 The macron signifies the word is plural (ancestors).

25 *The Wireless*.

26 The Treaty of Waitangi Amendment Act (1985) empowered the Waitangi Tribunal to hear claims under the terms of the Treaty dating back to 1840 when the Treaty was signed by representatives of the British Crown and Māori chiefs, founding New Zealand as a Crown colony. Certain rights were preserved for Māori under the Treaty, and claims generally relate to Crown breaches of those assurances.

27 Māori film-maker Barry Barclay raises concerns about a similar kind of translation involved in Māori knowledge being encompassed by intellectual property law. He argues that "it is difficult to see how any property concept might be introduced ... which would not do a profound violence to the very foundations of their world view. The violence might be such that the culture collapses and those for whom it has been their only known way of life are made futureless and without hope." Barry Barclay, *Mana Tūturu: Māori Treasures and Intellectual Property Rights* (Auckland: Auckland UP, 2005): 88.

equivalence—intimated, for example, in the suggestion that although the river has not been ascribed a gender, this could happen in future if the human guardians want the river to be referred to by a pronoun other than "it".[28] Rather than confront humanism with the end, through dispersal, of human specificity and exceptionalism, does the fact of being protected with rights in law reaffirm that sovereignty, holding that to be recognised as a "person" is some kind of good, or benefit, to be bestowed (but also potentially rescinded)? The whakapepeha ("ko au te awa") adumbrates a challenge to human sovereignty; but enshrining the legal status of nonhuman bodies and lives as "persons" may *strengthen* the humanist regime of rights by extending it to the more-than-human.

An apparent anthropocentrism underpins "recognition" of the river according to a notion of calculable justice, governed by identity. Perhaps there is another translation, another annexation here, to the postcolonial claims process itself, and its articulation of place and property relations. We might ponder the role of colonial displacement and cultural subsumption in *postcolonial* Indigenous discourses of "place" and "identity"—precisely the terms in which claims are adjudicated by the settler state.[29] That is, what acts of historical and cultural translation have shaped postcolonial Indigenous *discourse*, diverting or deterring its most far-reaching challenge to European imperialist assumptions? How has alterity been captured by the mechanisms of western modernity that are called on to safeguard what that modernity has named and cast as "rights"? Yet this may not be a one-way process that simply annexes and settles Indigenous "meanings"; perhaps there are aspects of the Act—not its positive terms, but its points of *instability* precisely at those junctures of linguistic and cultural translation—that indicate its deeper potential for articulating humans as part of a more-than-human world, reopening settlement in all its manifestations. The legislation thus presents some "undecidables" in its implications for a shift away from European humanism and colonial capitalism, away from the currents of history that have brought us to the Anthropocene.

Referring to another colonial Pacific context, Sudesh Mishra suggests that what colonial history has relegated to the realms of the "archaic" emerges, under pressure of environmental crisis, as being "breathtakingly in advance of the modern," the latter characterised by extraction, property law and exclusivity.[30] As the poles of the "archaic" and the "modern" collapse, perhaps *western*

---

28 Ainge Roy, "New Zealand River".

29 Cf. Stephen Turner, "Anglosphericism," *Journal of New Zealand Literature* 31.2 (October 2013): 15.

30 Sudesh Mishra, "On Seeing a Bull's Skull in a Bicycle Seat: Innovative Archaisms in Oceania," *Contracampo: Brazilian Journal of Communication* 36.3 (2017): 52.

modernity needs to *catch up with* Indigenous ways of being in the world. I refer neither to the lived conditions in which colonised Indigenous peoples find themselves, nor to political and rights discourses through which these conditions are represented and challenged but, rather, to the postulate—or memory—of culture lived as more-than-human. Indigenous cultures have always known, in one way, what posthumanist feminist theorists like Donna Haraway and Rosi Braidotti argue, in another: that "we have never been (only) human."[31] Posthumanist or ecocritical theorists might pursue this insight towards an appreciation of human identification as co-constituted with water, microbes, minerals, other animal and living beings. However, the repudiation of human exceptionalism represented by such perspectives remains susceptible to a pursuit of ever-increasing, finer, deeper knowledge—bringing those others/our otherness into the realms of recognition—in the end to re-affirm human sovereignty. Knowledge in this sense is arguably too deeply enmeshed with mastery, and ultimately property relations, to challenge the empire of anthropocentrism. What else can it mean, then, to say "ko au te awa" or "I am the river"? Surely this enigmatic claim casts that "I" beyond finite identification, beyond familiar ontological grounds, beyond representational systems predicated on equivalence, beyond graspable meaning. Does it not destabilise those very foundations of western thought—meaning, equivalence, representation—and the ontological law that predicates them? I propose that the more radical potential of "ko au te awa, ko te awa ko au"—its enigma—points away from attempts to name or represent who or what "we" (humans), or non-human beings and elements *are*, beyond all our changes, multiplicities and relations to other beings and elements. It points away from identitarianism, to what *happens* beyond ontology.

A gesture beyond ontology might be at least partly intimated in the linguistic composition of the whakapepeha—in its grammatical difference from the translation into English. Just as what is connoted in the name Te Awa Tupua—as given to the river and the Act that "recognises" it—cannot be fully rendered in English, there is the trace of an alterity to be inferred in its expression in te

---

31   Neimanis, *Bodies of Water*, 2. Ecocritical and Indigenous perspectives have challenged both western cultural authority and anthropocentric 'species' thinking, with their associated notions of sovereignty and autonomy. For example, Donna Haraway (2015) proposes the Chthulucene ethic of 'kin-making' with the other beings of the world, beyond genealogical or ancestral relation (though she does offer a range of cosmological figures from different cultural sources as 'proper names' for the Chthulucene timespace). However, I suggest that kin-making ultimately falls within the logic of identity, projecting some principle of sameness, and thus does not constitute a thorough-going challenge to humanist thought.

RIVER WRITING

reo Māori (the Māori language). That expression does not include an equivalent of the English verb "to be." There is no common grammatical equivalent of that verb.[32] *Being* is suggested, *gestured*, in everyday speech by way of particle and definitive: "ko au te awa" might be literally rendered as "I the river," where the "ko" particle places emphasis on what follows it, in this case alternately "au" (I) and "te awa" (the river). In English translation, the verb "to be" might be considered implicit. However, that very assumption of ontological being is also put into question. Words like "am," "is," or "are" constitute the signs they refer to—"I" and "river"—as positive identities articulated in relations of equivalence;[33] their ontological status as identities pre-exists their representation and their "relation". Perhaps the grammatical formulation gestures (back) to an ambivalent orientation to being as more of the nature of an event, of a cyclical process of emergence and reversion. An orientation to "being" that retains its ambivalent quality would not see being and non-being as poles, or oppositions, but rather as always ever-present dimensions. The order of identity is fixated on excluding non-being, or reversion, to hold "being" as a discrete and privileged term. The same opposition of life and death in modern western culture constitutes life as the positive term, dissociated from death. Death in this context becomes the irreversible end, an ever-threatening void that nevertheless haunts life.[34] As Jean Baudrillard has argued, "our whole [modern western] culture is just one huge effort to dissociate life and death, to ward off the ambivalence of death in the interests of life as value."[35] As a result, "the price we pay for the 'reality' of this life, to live it as a positive value, is the ever-present phantasm of death."[36] Indeed, the "separation of life and death constructs life

---

32   There is a rarely used substantive form of the verb 'to be'—'ai' as in "Te ai he aha hei whakaohooho mai, There was nothing to disturb them," Herbert W. Williams, *A Dictionary of the Maori Language* (Wellington, GP Books, 1885): 5. However: "In English, when the predicate is not a verb, the verb 'to be,' commonly called the substantive verb, is used to connect the predicate with its subject. This verb has no equivalent in Maori, but the relation of subject to predicate is indicated by the use of certain particles and by the relative position of the different words in the sentence" (NZETC First Lessons in Maori #35 Substantive Verb). I do not believe my argument is compromised by the fact that there are other languages that do not have an equivalent of the verb 'to be.' I am not arguing for Māori language and culture as exceptional, and if it is plausible that the 'absence' of that verb gestures (back) to a different conception of 'being,' then this could also be the case in other languages and cultures.

33   Cf. Victoria Grace, *Baudrillard's Challenge: A Feminist Reading* (London: Routledge, 2000): 23.

34   Grace, *Baudrillard's Challenge*, 44–45.

35   Jean Baudrillard, *Symbolic Exchange and Death*, trans. Iain Hamilton Grant (London: Sage Publications, 1993): 147.

36   Baudrillard, *Symbolic Exchange and Death*, 133.

in terms of survival, with 'needs' to be met" to sustain it.[37] The paradox is that life (as resource, and as resources) is exploited by whatever violent means are necessary to continue accumulating it—inevitably at the cost of instantiating the very death it attempts to exclude. In other words, in exploiting the world in the name of our sovereign human right to accumulate, we destroy the very conditions of life itself, including our own.

These observations about the (excluded) co-presence of life and death, in the sense of being and not-being, intimated in the whakapepeha and its "lack" of a verb "to be", bring us back to another aspect of the Whanganui iwi's claim: that the river is an ancestor. Could this, too, gesture towards culture founded on the non-exclusion of death from life, the dead from the living? It is uncertain whether the Act, enshrining recognition of the ancestral status of the river, is predicated on an identitarian claim of kinship—the status of the river as ancestral kin—and whether *this* is the postcolonial commitment under which the iwi sought the legislation. Perhaps it is, rather, an inevitable (mis)translation into English language and settler law that misses a deeper challenge to the order of identity that would ward off death and the dead. The Act may indeed harbour a challenge to an order in which the instrumental use of the world in the interests of self-preservation, of accumulating life itself, inevitably destroys it. When Māori Party MP Mārama Fox says "Ka mate te Awa, ka mate tātou te Iwi" ("if the river dies, we die as a people"), I think she encompasses both a recognition of the parlous state of rivers and other waterways under the postcolonial anthropocentric dispensation, and a cultural challenge to the orders of human exceptionalism, identity and property relations.

The Te Awa Tupua Act is arguably an act of cultural translation that attempts to recognise and protect something that is radically other to the Law. Legislating for the protection of a particular river, and a specific iwi relationship to the river, the Act shares some discursive features with modern western cartography as a mode of place-writing. Encoding a particular way of seeing the world as objective, cartography has sought "to produce a 'correct' relational model of the terrain" comprising "objects in the world" that exist "independent of the cartographer" who simply expresses their reality and relations in systematically rendered "truth."[38] The Te Awa Tupua Act, too, seeks to encode a given relation between given parties. After outlining the major terms of the Act, sections and subsections spell out in finer detail the consequential effects of the river's personhood status across other pre-existing interests, obligations

---

37   Grace, *Baudrillard's Challenge*, 68.
38   J.B. Harley, "Deconstructing the Map," *Cartographica* 26.2 (Spring 1989): 4.

RIVER WRITING 103

and relationships. It strives to leave nothing unaccounted for in the abstraction of principle. Though *place* in western terms commonly connotes fixity and stability (connotations that inform postcolonial and environmental politics), Ross Gibson reminds us that place encompasses *dynamics*[39]—process and flow, time. Thus, while a map is therefore in obvious senses static—a "freeze-frame in a restless flow-chart"[40]—it also *enables* particular *actions*. Postcolonial scholars have shown how maps propelled imperial conquest of "territories", drawing them into western possession. On the other hand, when Graham Huggan refers to the map's coherence as "the subject of a proposition rather than a statement of fact,"[41] he indicates its representational authority as contingent, vulnerable to readings that expose its artifactual and rhetorical status—that invoke *poetics*. Activating the instabilities of translation in cross-cultural space may result in contestation between "this"claim to a space and "that", between differently founded claims to priority. But animating the cross-cultural "translation zone"[42] may point further towards space as inaccessible to definitive capture by any representational systems. On the one hand, then, both western cartographic representation and the mechanism of legislation are limited by "blind-spots":[43] they cannot account for what they cannot see (in law, the differend); and what they can see is ontologically and culturally delimited. On the other hand, while unable to *represent* time and being as process and change, both maps and law are formulated to be *enacted* as event. The question becomes whether and how the event of this legislation will challenge and displace the complicity of representation with conquest of space and time in the name of sovereign human being.

While unsettlement is the ever-present potentiality of the settled languages of law and mapping when they are opened to the dynamics of the event,

---

39 Gibson, *Changescapes*, 22.

40 Gibson, *Changescapes*, 27.

41 Graham Huggan, "Decolonizing the Map: Post-Colonialism, Post-Structuralism, and the Cartographic Connection," in *Past the Last Post: Theorizing Post-Colonialism, Post-Structuralism, and the Cartographic Connection,* eds. Ian Adam and Helen Tiffin (New York & London: Harvester Wheatsheaf, 1989): 127.

42 I invoke Mary Louise Pratt's concept of the 'contact zone,' which she defines as those "social spaces where cultures meet, clash, and grapple with each other, often in contexts of highly asymmetrical relations of domination and subordination," such as colonialism, Mary Louise Pratt, *Imperial Eyes: Travel Writing and Transculturation* (London: Routledge,1992): 4. However, I refer to 'translation zone' to specify cultural and linguistic translation as a particular facet or process that the colonial contact zone entails, with just as much asymmetrical meeting, clashing and grappling in language as in political and social arrangements.

43 Huggan, "Decolonizing the Map," 127.

poetic language is inherently more of the order of event than of meaning or representation. Meaning functions differently in poetic language; the concept, governed by reason, is unlocked to the workings of figuration, admitting restlessness, provisionality and dynamics. A poem is a singularity, where language becomes an event that exceeds and escapes circum-*script*-ion by paraphrase or commentary. Speaking of the "curious ontological status" of literature more generally, Pheng Cheah argues that:

> It is not something objective and so cannot be reduced to the subject's rational powers of determination and calculation. Its radical indeterminacy also means that it exceeds the subject's powers of interpretation. Hence literature does not simply map the spatialized world and give it value and meaning. Rather, its formal structures enact the opening of a world by the incalculable gift of time.[44]

Heeding Gayatri Spivak's call for literary studies to "take the [irreducible] 'figure' as its guide,"[45] where the figure connotes language of the order of alterity—irreducible to an equivalent in discourse, to representation—I propose that poetic language animates, rather than fixes, both words and worlds. It gestures beyond finite thought, reopening representational space to recast the world as always in process, always in the making. Indeed, Pheng Cheah points to literature as an "active power of world making,"[46] where "The world is [...] a form of relating, belonging, or being-with."[47] That is to say, the world does not precede such "relating" as in the representational mode, but is brought into being in these very acts. Literature offers not knowledge, but attunement,[48] opening us to the flux of the world perceived within the singular moment of the (literary) encounter or event.

Indigenous literatures often bring to light relegated understandings of more-than-human worlds. Hone Tuwhare's poem, "The River is an Island,"[49] writes waters in dynamic encounter with and among human and more-than-human

---

44   Pheng Cheah, "World against Globe: Toward a Normative Conception of World Literature," *New Literary History* 45.3 (Summer 2014): 323–324.

45   Gayatri Chakravorty Spivak, *Death of a Discipline* (New York: Columbia UP, 2003): 52, 71.

46   Cheah, "World against Globe," 303.

47   Cheah, "World against Globe," 319.

48   Cf. Gibson, *Memoryscopes: Remnants Forensics Aesthetics* (Crawley: UWA Publishing, 2015): 139–40.

49   Hone Tuwhare, "The River is an Island" in *Year of the Dog: Poems New and Selected*, (Dunedin: McIndoe, 1982): 43.

RIVER WRITING 105

forms. Alexis Wright's *Carpentaria* also writes a river in "supervital"[50]/poetic terms that refuse containment by western cartographic knowledge systems: a river that exchanges *materially* with such forces as land, winds, ocean and spirits. Yet precisely because they are produced within postcolonial cultural and linguistic translation zones, the works and their worlds embody forms of contingency that both echo and respond to the unsettled conditions of climate change. As works principally in English by Indigenous writers, they are complexly situated across languages and cultures, and in relation to the social and physical environments they invoke. Like the Te Awa Tupua legislation, these literary works do not specifically address climate change. However, as Graham Huggan notes, "a good climate change novel [or poem] may not be 'about' climate change at all ...; rather, it may take place within the general context of climate change, a context marked by a high degree of uncertainty and contingency, and by a strong ethical awareness of the issues at stake."[51] Accordingly, the poetry and the novel speak to a climate change context to imply links between environmental crisis and the legacies of colonial development, while giving expression to world-making in terms other than those of anthropocentric mastery, identity and the linearity of developmental time.

Much of Hone Tuwhare's work can be characterised by encounters that decentre human sovereignty. For example, in his well-known poem "Rain,"[52] the lyric subject apostrophises Rain, addressing it as "you" through the poem, as he does with "Tree" in "No Ordinary Sun."[53] "Rain" (and rain) animates the world, "making small holes / in the silence" and enlivening it with "the something / special smell of you / when the sun cakes / the ground." Even without the human sensory perception through which he experiences rain, though, the lyric subject would emerge as "me" through the agency of rain:

But if I
should not hear
smell or feel or see
you

---

50   Frances Devlin-Glass, "A Politics of the Dreamtime: Destructive and Regenerative Rainbows in Alexis Wright's *Carpentaria,*" *Australian Literary Studies* 23.4 (2008): 392–407, uses this term to convey the spiritually-imbued form of a vital (living/natural) being.

51   Huggan, "Australian Literature," 87–88.

52   Hone Tuwhare, "Rain" in *Come Rain Hail* (Dunedin: Otago UP, 1970): 6.

53   Hone Tuwhare, "No Ordinary Sun" in *No Ordinary Sun: Poems* (Auckland: Blackwood and Janet Paul, 1964): 15.

you would still
define me
disperse me
wash over me
rain.

The lines "define me" and "disperse me" might invoke whakapapa, connecting in layered and cyclical temporalities of life and death.[54] Rain thus disperses the speaker in time, extending his being into the time of eternity, while he embodies his ancestral whakapapa in the present. However, tracing the form of the speaker's body, while opening the body to its place as part of the more-than-human (more-than-self) world would be consistent with a reading that challenges and displaces anthropocentrism more generally. Although "Rain" is not specifically about a river, neither is it entirely separate from rivers, a notion suggested by the elemental exchange between land, cloud and water figured in "The River is an Island."

"The River is an Island" enacts an elemental dynamism that challenges the limits of imperialist cartography. Here again, the river is not a third person entity but is directly addressed in the second-person: "You are river" (not 'a' river). This formulation hovers between an act of naming or an affirmation of name, an acknowledgement in the mode of address, and recognition of a state of being, all with different possible connotations. The imagery invites human—embodied, sensory—associations evincing the speaker's intimate familiarity with river moods:

A low bank on your left holds
your laughing stitches in. On your right
side skips another hushing your
loud protests.

but there is no assertion that the river is a person. Repeating, "*You are river,*" the lyric subject attributes emotions, again through imagery that evokes, for humans, human constructions—

---

54 Tāne, the offspring of Papatūānuku (Earth mother) and Ranginui (Sky father), trapped with his brothers within the embrace of his parents, stood up between them to separate them into the spheres of earth and sky, bringing "the world of light" (Te Ao Marama) into being. Rain is understood as Ranginui's tears expressing grief at his separation from Papatūānuku.

RIVER WRITING 107

> *…Joy leaping down*
> *a greenstone stairway: anger cradled*
> *in a bed of stones*

but human associations are subsumed by the energies, encounters and transformations of the river:

> You're a harbour; a lake; an island
> only when your banks lock lathered
> arms in battle to confine you: slow-release you.
>
> Go river, go. To ocean seek your
> certain end. Rise again to cloud;
> to a mountain—to a mountain
> drinking from a tiny cup.
> Ah, river
>
> you are ocean: you are island.

The poem thus proposes that what the river "is" emerges in relation to other elements or beings encountered. "You," named or acknowledged as "river," encompasses geophysical forms produced by the interaction of land and water, air and sun: "river" is also a harbour and a lake, and an island, just as Te Awa Tupua includes river banks, beds, mountains and tributaries. The poem, though, describes the river's movement not simply through space but also in time, its constant change and exchange. More than a cartographically representable feature of the landscape, even tracing its path from mountain to sea, the river is in continual process: it does not simply encompass those elements, but becomes them, always transforming. Its "certain end" is only a moment in a new beginning of the cycle of elements, rising as moisture to cloud, falling to mountain as mist or rain, feeding streams that return to river. For all that the poem can be understood as voiced by a human lyric subject, and incorporates imagery suggesting human bodies and structures, there is little to suggest human sovereignty. If anything, it draws the human fully into the dynamic circulation of elements in the world. The final line, "you are ocean: you are island," suggests neither contradiction nor amassing of identity. The proposition is left to stand, unresolved, slightly apart from the apostrophisation, "Ah, river." Perhaps if anything resolves the poem, it is the word "you," less a call to fix what it refers to than to suggest an encounter whose terms emerge as provisional, never definitive. The poem asserts no "I" (or "we") as subject of knowledge or identity.

Further, the poem is in English, and only in English as far as I know, but Tuwhare grew up speaking Māori in his early childhood, his father later helping him learn English by way of the Bible.[55] While the rhetorical features and cadences of his poetry might find their source in these two traditions of oratory, I suggest that the poetry—and specifically this poem—is also an instance of writing in the postcolonial cultural and linguistic translation zone. Even in English language, Tuwhare's poetry tends to invoke a Māori language world. That is, in the translation zone, the shadow of his first language might be adumbrated, unsettling the sovereignty of each language, and figuring worlds in exchange. Thus, the opening line, "You are river," might call up another beginning, as approximately, "He awa koe/Ko koe te awa" (You [the] river), or, in the apostrophising form, "E awa" (O river).[56] Again, the "absence" of the verb to be animates other possible connotations. While we cannot simply overlook that the poem is in English, and the verb "to be" *is* used in the poem, we might recognise the mutual unsettlement effected by each language, each world, in contact and translation; languages invoking and unsettling one other as "transformative agency in the world."[57] This dynamic unsettlement of meaning and reference, an aesthetics of contingency, could also be seen as a political gesture in the context of climate change, in the sense that Rancière envisions political art. Huggan cites Rancière's " 'dream of a suitably political work of art' " as " 'the dream of disrupting the relationship between the visible, the sayable, and the thinkable without having to use the terms of a message as a vehicle. It is the dream of an art that would transmit meanings in the form of a rupture with the very logic of meaningful situations.' "[58]

Tuwhare's poems evince a single lyric voice articulating a more-than-human world within the postcolonial cultural and linguistic contact zone. By contrast, Alexis Wright's *Carpentaria* explicitly portrays a complex and conflictual social order of colonial (un)settlement, dramatising a clash of irreconcilable philosophies and systems of world-making. The contact zone, which I have argued is also a translation zone, is implicit in Tuwhare's poems, but in Wright's novel,

---

55   Anne Collett, "One Tuwhare: At the Interface of Poetic Traditions," *Asiatic* 6.2 (December 2012): 51.

56   The English does not employ an article, and it is this grammatical omission, as a poetic variation on standard English expression (a/the river) that opens the possibilities of meaning. While grammatically, te reo Māori would use a definite or indefinite article ("te" or "he"), it is possible that a Māori poet might make similar grammatical variation for poetic effect.

57   Cheah, "World against Globe," 316.

58   Jacques Rancière, *The Politics of Aesthetics*, trans. G. Rockhill (London: Continuum, 2004): 61 cited in Huggan, "Australian Literature," 91.

linguistic contestation and unsettlement are more explicit. Waanyi language is included in the narrative, alongside frequently defamiliarised English idiom, marking both languages as spoken from a space of cultural translation.[59] Such a space of translation cannot be mapped; the reader must navigate the challenging narrative from within its changeable movements and moods; external reference points cannot be relied on to chart its trajectory.[60] *Carpentaria* decentres human mastery to present an animate, agential riverine world, home to the Indigenous Rainbow Serpent people in the Gulf of Carpentaria. The novel writes a river, named Wangala, in ways that cannot be contained within representational systems. Unamenable to human control,[61] the river exceeds the grasp of colonial law and cartography. Pheng Cheah invokes Heidegger when he distinguishes cartography, as a process that "epistemologically constructs the world by means of discursive representations," from a process of "worlding":

> Cartography reduces the world to a spatial object. In contradistinction, worlding is a force that subtends and exceeds all human calculations that reduce the world as a temporal structure to the sum of objects in space. Imperialist cartography is such a calculation in the sphere of geopolitical economy.[62]

Casting worlding as a "process of temporalization,"[63] a world as "a form of relating, belonging, or being-with,"[64] Cheah begins to suggest something of the incompatibility between western systems based on knowledge and mastery, and the Indigenous orientation to the world featured in Wright's novel. Indeed, Wright specifically satirises the colonial fixation on solidity and stability of place, its disavowal of the displacements that engender settlement. She invokes the map of the colonial nation-state—its charted landscapes and recognised place-names—only to overturn, displace and disorient it. Thus, the fictional town of Desperance, home to the white settlers of this north-eastern region, both echoes and connotatively reverses Esperance, the town located

---

59 Cf. Paul Sharrad, "Beyond *Capricornia*: Ambiguous Promise in Alexis Wright," *Australian Literary Studies* 24.2 (September 2010): 54, 59.

60 Here I invoke the account of contrasting canoe and motorboat navigation methods cited in Ross Gibson, *Changescapes: Complexity Mutability Aesthetics* (Crawley, UWA Publishing, 2015): 28, as a metaphor for reading.

61 Cf Wright, *Carpentaria*, 3.

62 Cheah, "World against Globe," 322.

63 Cheah, "World against Globe," 322.

64 Cheah, "World against Globe," 319.

diagonally across on the south-west coast of the Australian mainland. The fictionalised Gulf country suggests its corresponding extra-fictional region but cannot be mapped directly on to it.[65]

Unlike Wright's third novel, *The Swan Book*,[66] which is set in the aftermath of planetary climate change, *Carpentaria* is not usually considered a climate change novel. However, the fictional world is figured in the midst of environmental, ecological, social and cultural disaster. This multidimensional disaster is the long-term impact of colonial (un)settlement, though it manifests in certain spectacular catastrophes through the course of the narrative.[67] The pivot that articulates these as insinuations of climate change is the multinational mining development that instrumentalises land and water to extract mineral resources for profit. The mine promises an economic "boom" of development for the town, but it cannot defray the immeasurable cost of destruction and pollution of land and the waterways that feed it, and the lives that feed from them both. Frances Devlin-Glass situates the significance of *Carpentaria*'s account of "wildlife and ecosystems [...] contaminated by poisonous tailings from inundated open-cut or deep-shaft mines" in the context of climate change:

> This is the more serious in the driest continent on earth where water is key to survival and the scarcest resource, and likely to become increasingly potent politically as climate change dries out the populous southeast of the continent and the northern rivers are looked to supplement drying southern river systems.[68]

Recognising the interpenetration of spiritual and political dimensions of land as culture, the young spiritual pilgrim and political activist Will Phantom is determined to destroy the mine that is killing the country, but he does not seek justice through the system, still less the Native Title legislation, of settler law. Will recognises that the mine is a "new war on their country," a "war for money,"[69] and he is a guerilla fighter in that war, not a negotiator—it is not a

---

65 Cf. Laura Joseph, "Dreaming of Phantoms and Golems: Elements of Place Beyond Nation in *Carpentaria* and *Dreamhunter*," in "Australian Literature in a Global World," special issue, *Journal of the Association for the Study of Australian Literature* (2009): 2.

66 Alexis Wright, *The Swan Book* (Sydney: Giramondo, 2013).

67 Cf. Rob Nixon's (2011) account of slow violence as distinct from 'spectacular' disasters.

68 Frances Devlin-Glass, "Review Essay: Alexis Wright's *Carpentaria*," *Antipodes* 21.1 (June 2007): 83.

69 Alexis Wright, *Carpentaria*, 378.

RIVER WRITING

matter of negotiation. *Carpentaria* poses questions around the conditions for physical, social and cultural survival. The novel issues a challenge to notions of calculation and equivalence governing climate change management and justice—attempts to balance cost and benefit, to exchange a good for a harm—which subsume the planet within an economic rationale.[70] *Carpentaria* points its own questions of postcolonial and climate change justice away from the premises and mechanisms of settler law. As Kathleen Birrell argues, the novel presents "an antinomic Indigenous Law, a transformative aesthetic to which Australian law is called to respond."[71] This Indigenous Law, she continues, "speaks from the realm of the unpresentable and incalculable [...] which disrupts and displaces colonial law."[72]

The novel opens in postcolonial time, on "translated" and shifting ground/waters: the apocalypse of colonisation has already taken place, while the narrative builds towards a new "Armageddon"[73] of fire and storm for the (post)colonial town of Desperance and the nearby multinational mine. Against all evidence of an animate, changing landscape, the paranoid Desperanians attempt to exclude all otherness, desperate to find and fix the town's identity and materialise it in a giant mascot. But recurring references to the town's clocks running out of time[74] are seemingly borne out when the air, saturated with moisture in the wake of Cyclone Leda, damages their mechanisms. This effect of cyclonic interference with the mechanical measurement of progressive time indicates that time in the novel is more complex than linear conceptions such as build-up or count-down suggest. As Daley argues, "The novel's events are depicted by cyclical (climatic) and generational (remembered) experiences of time rather than by the time of the nation-state measured by clock, calendar, and chronology."[75] Remembered time is also layered time: the past emerging through the present, and the present infusing the past. The narrator—a storyteller—invokes creation cosmology in terms that call on imaginative, figurative vision to draw the reader actively into the moment and movement he depicts:[76]

---

70   Carbon miles are one such 'measure'; or planting trees against fossil fuel consumption.

71   Kathleen Birrell, Review of *Carpentaria* by Alexis Wright, *Law, Culture and the Humanities* 5.1 (February 2009): 156.

72   Birrell, Review of *Carpentaria*, 157.

73   Alexis Wright, *Carpentaria,* 1.

74   Alexis Wright, *Carpentaria,* 12.

75   Linda Daley, "Alexis Wright's Fiction as World Making," *Contemporary Women's Writing* 10.1 (2016): 9.

76   I use the masculine pronoun because Wright has indicated that she has created the storyteller from hearing the conversation between two elderly Indigenous men. See Anne Brewster, "Indigenous Sovereignty and the Crisis of Whiteness in Alexis Wright's *Carpentaria," Australian Literary Studies* 25.4 (November 2010): 89.

> The ancestral serpent, a creature larger than storm clouds, came down from the stars, laden with its own creative enormity. It moved graciously—*if you had been watching with the eyes of a bird* hovering in the sky far above the ground ...
>
> *Picture* the creative serpent, scoring deep into—scouring down through—the slippery underground of the mudflats ... [77]

The reader is invited to "*Imagine* the serpent's breathing rhythms as the tide flows inland [...]. Then with the outward breath, the tide turns, and the serpent flows back to its own circulating mass of shallow waters."[78] This opening chapter, "From Time Immemorial," allows the time of creation of the rivers that snake across the Gulf country to encompass the postcolonial point of narration and reading. After finishing its work of movement back and forth across marine plains, salt flats, past mangrove forests and back out to sea, it continues to live today "deep down under the ground in a vast network of limestone aquifers."[79] Situating himself and his world within this "immemorial" temporality, the storyteller discloses collective cultural knowledge: "*They say its being is porous; it permeates everything. It is all around in the atmosphere and is attached to the lives of the river people like a skin.*"[80] The river therefore emerges from the generative figure of the Rainbow Serpent that inhabits it, which in turn gives rise to the people who live *as* the river people. The inhalations and exhalations of this "tidal river snake of flowing mud"[81] propel the movements of continual exchange with the sea. The Serpent also manifests in the course of the novel as winds, cyclonic storms, monsoonal floods and explosive fire—the mining "Booom!"[82]

Frances Devlin-Glass's observation that "everything is something else" in the "supervital" more-than-human fictional world of *Carpentaria* conveys something of its unmappable quality.[83] However, I suggest that another important dynamic could also be inferred from the transformations; not simply being many things at once, but encompassing reversion. The Gulf is a weather world, where forces meet to produce wind, rain, storm or, conversely, drought, each

---

77   Alexis Wright, *Carpentaria,* 1, my emphasis.
78   Alexis Wright, *Carpentaria,* 2, my emphasis.
79   Alexis Wright, *Carpentaria,* 2.
80   Alexis Wright, *Carpentaria,* 2, my emphasis.
81   Alexis Wright, *Carpentaria,* 2.
82   Alexis Wright, *Carpentaria,* 409.
83   Frances Devlin-Glass, "A Politics of the Dreamtime: Destructive and Regenerative Rainbows in Alexis Wright's *Carpentaria,*" *Australian Literary Studies* 23.4 (2008): 399.

RIVER WRITING 113

dying as those forces disperse and other gatherings form elsewhere. To the extent that these climatic forces are associated by Indigenous tradition with the movements of the Rainbow Serpent, and the river/Serpent connected to the river people themselves, it suggests a similarly non-cumulative quality to their "worlding." When the storyteller describes the Serpent as "attached to the lives of the river people like a skin,"[84] there is an echo with the description of Te Awa Tupua as the central artery of the tribal heart of the Whanganui iwi. Just as "Ko au te awa" is not a claim to *be* the river in an ontological sense, or to merge with it in an undifferentiated plenum,[85] still less to *own* the river, there is something here that evokes a cyclical process of *emerging* through encounter, through alterity. I am gesturing to a non-ontological mode that opens to the incalculable dynamics of the social in a more-than-human world. It is a world not harnessed to "the linearity of time, language, economic exchange, accumulation and power."[86] Instead, life and death, being and non-being, are in communication, as the cyclical reversibility that puts an end to linear accumulation of bounded energies, identities and oppositions. I suggest that *catastrophic* collapse is that which afflicts systems, orders or investments that pursue endless production, growth, value and identity by excluding reversibility. Thus, anthropogenic climate change itself might be understood as the effect of the system of endless production and growth pushed to, and beyond, its limit: "At the peak of value we are closest to ambivalence."[87] Perhaps, like our never having been only human, this is also something Indigenous cultures have always "known".[88]

---

84 Alexis Wright, *Carpentaria*, 2.

85 Cf. Devlin-Glass, "A Politics of the Dreamtime," 404.

86 Baudrillard, *Symbolic Exchange*, 2.

87 Baudrillard, *Symbolic Exchange*, 2.

88 I do not mean either to describe or to impose an interpretation of Indigenous Law and spiritual matters. I acknowledge readings, such as Devlin-Glass's, that position their claim to discuss such matters with reference to working with Indigenous communities. Instead, my argument partly accords with Alison Ravenscroft's point that "Indigenous Law … cannot appear" through Western epistemology; that "at best its traces are translated into English, into modern western discursive frames such as 'ecology' or 'natural history' or 'science'." Alison Ravenscroft, "Dreaming of Others: *Carpentaria* and its Critics," *Cultural Studies Review* 16.2 (September 2010): 214. In referring to the postcolonial 'translation zone' my argument asks whether and how articulations of Indigenous Law might have been 'translated'—not least for fictional purposes—through contact with English language and the European Christian tradition. My questions and suggestions may or may not resonate for Indigenous readers; I do not claim to issue them from a space of knowledge of Indigenous Law, but offer them for what they might generate.

The Indigenous "Pricklebush" people, dwelling amidst "dense Pricklebush scrub on the edge of town" have lived in this "human dumping ground next to the town tip" in "trash humpies made of tin, cloth, and plastic too" since they were "*dumped here by the pastoralists* [who] *refused to pay the blackfella equal wages, even when it came in.*"[89] They build lives on translated postcolonial ground. Many find ways of living creatively off the ideological and material detritus of colonial settlement. Angel Day's entrepreneurial spirit earns her civic recognition as "a prime example of government policies of [blackfella advancement] at work."[90] Joseph Midnight's inventive response to government Native Title legislation requirements[91] secures a measure of recognition and funding. However, such negotiations are presented as limited, pointedly strategic and ultimately subject to the same inevitable collapse towards which Desperance itself is heading.

Norm (short for Normal) Phantom declares himself apolitical. However, it is arguably the civic and state politics of postcolonial negotiation that he refuses, in the same spirit as Will's refusal to regard the land—and its "traditional owners"—as negotiable. The storyteller recounts how "social planners" were "anxious to make deals happen for the impending mining boom. ... including changing the river's name to Normal."[92] This sycophantic and manipulative scheme, culminates in an official ceremony where the river's name is "changed from that of a long dead Imperial Queen, to 'Normal's River.' "[93] The traditional people gathered know that "the river only had one name from the beginning of time. It was called *Wangala*."[94] Although the town has "encumbered" Norm with the title of "leader of the Aboriginal people,"[95] Norm distances himself from multiple acts of colonial appropriation: the naming and renaming of the river, and the attempted political annexation of Norm himself to secure access for mining.

Normal Phantom, whose name signals his acceptance of the co-presence of life and death, is a man of the river and the sea, who can spend years at a time navigating the ocean by way of clouds and his familiar groper companions, reading the weather, the behaviour of fish and storms. He survives by navigating as *part of* his elemental world, neither attempting to master it nor securing

---

89   Alexis Wright, *Carpentaria,* 4, italics original.

90   Alexis Wright, *Carpentaria,* 16.

91   Alexis Wright, *Carpentaria,* 53–53.

92   Alexis Wright, *Carpentaria,* 8.

93   Alexis Wright, *Carpentaria,* 9.

94   Alexis Wright, *Carpentaria,* 10, italics original.

95   Alexis Wright, *Carpentaria,* 37.

RIVER WRITING 115

himself from it. He exemplifies the aqueous orientation that Ross Gibson describes as "understand[ing] how the vectors of yourself and the ocean are indivisible even as you try to determine your own distinct trajectory."[96] Norm says, " 'We are the flesh and blood of the sea and we are what the sea brings the land.' "[97] A storm builds out at sea, heading towards the town. Norm hears the wind playing "ancestor music"[98] all day and night, while Will, who "carrie[s] the tide in his body"—a feeling for the sea inherited from Norm[99]—senses "a mysterious change of great magnitude."[100] While for those who live 'traditionally,' "the very division into [...] body and country [is] undecidable,"[101] the Desperanians are oblivious to the storm's approach, busy ridding themselves of imagined plagues of fruit bats by cutting down all the fruit trees.[102] When the winds and wall of water strike the town, its security gates, bars and fences cannot protect it.[103] Will looks back to see the town obliterated, a "monstrous palace" of wreckage.[104] He eventually washes up on an island of floating rubbish and debris that becomes strangely fertile and bountiful, but he recognises it as a "temporary structure which would break apart in the first storm."[105] Our last image of Will is of him wondering, "What would the discoverers call the sole inhabitant on his sinking oasis: a native?"[106]

Surviving the storm at sea, and rescuing his grandson Bala, they return to find a "flattened landscape."[107] Norm, though, is "already planning the home he would rebuild on the same piece of land where his old house had been, among the spirits in the remains of the ghost town, where the snake slept underneath."[108] The storyteller concludes, "It was a mystery, but there was so much song wafting off the watery land, singing the country afresh as they walked

---

96 Gibson, *Changescapes*, 28.
97 Alexis Wright, *Carpentaria,* 33.
98 Alexis Wright, *Carpentaria,* 458.
99 Alexis Wright, *Carpentaria,* 401.
100 Alexis Wright, *Carpentaria,* 460.
101 Alison Ravenscroft, "Dreaming of Others: *Carpentaria* and its Critics," *Cultural Studies Review* 16.2 (September 2010): 206.
102 Alexis Wright, *Carpentaria,* 462–5.
103 Alexis Wright, *Carpentaria,* 470ff.
104 Alexis Wright, *Carpentaria,* 491–2.
105 Alexis Wright, *Carpentaria,* 499.
106 Alexis Wright, *Carpentaria,* 502. Although there is not space to elaborate on the point here, this episode is one facet of the novel that calls up Serge Latouche's account of the "castaways" of development. Serge Latouche, *In the Wake of the Affluent Society: An Exploration of Post-Development* (London: Zed Books, 1993).
107 Alexis Wright, *Carpentaria,* 516.
108 Alexis Wright, *Carpentaria,* 519.

hand in hand out of town … to home."[109] In view of this ending, Paul Sharrad raises an important point when he argues that *Carpentaria* presents some risks of appropriation to "romanticised wishful thinking":

> Imaginative engagement with the land is a means of tapping into majority Australian interest in ecological sustainability. But faith in the self-sufficient abiding land does not altogether support an activist interventionist politics, and ideas of custodianship can get in the way of claims for land rights.[110]

However, I suggest that the novel's conclusion insinuates that renewal is predicated on the necessary destruction of Desperance, precisely for what it represents. This much has been suggested in the uncertain fates of Angel Day and Joseph Midnight who stake survival, in different ways, on *appropriating* the material and ideological detritus of postcolonial settlement. Similarly, Will's fertile island of storm-amassed debris from the town is but a fragile life-raft from which even rescue may spell entrapment in a repetition of colonial history.

Carpentaria poses unsettling questions about survival and justice at the intersection of postcolonial politics and climate change. While postcolonial politics have typically been articulated around notions of identity, property, recognition and rights, the novel exposes ways in which these terms and goals are complicit with the very problems they seek to redress. *Carpentaria* reopens the question of justice to the incalculable dimension of culture. It does not disavow historical, linguistic and cultural contact zones, but issues its challenge to the reader precisely from that unsettled and unsettling ground. If Ravenscroft is concerned that non-Indigenous readers may reduce Indigenous knowledge to "already a kind of fiction,"[111] I argue that the power of fiction can be described as what Cheah refers to as its "transformative agency."[112]

Reading the Te Awa Tupua Act alongside Hone Tuwhare's poems "Rain" and "The River is an Island," and Alexis Wright's *Carpentaria*, I have explored reading at the interface of law and poetics, meaning and figuration, each *producing* and *challenging* the other to respond. I suggest that the most radical potential of the Act lies in its challenge to law as "settlement." The whakapepeha "ko au te awa, ko te awa ko au" that underpins the Act opens on to something beyond

---

109   Alexis Wright, *Carpentaria,* 519.
110   Sharrad, "Beyond *Capricornia*," 63.
111   Ravenscroft, "Dreaming of Others," 211.
112   Cheah, "World against Globe," 316.

RIVER WRITING 117

what is knowable or contained by the finitude of identity. By way of translated/untranslatable names and phrases, the Act shows the law entering into its own reversion. Both the whakapepeha and the literary works evince, in Birrell's words, "a transformative aesthetic" to which the law is "called to respond."[113] They challenge subjects of the modern west to put aside our investments in who/what "it", "we" or "they" *are*. They ask how far are "we" humans prepared to go to challenge our anthropocentrism, to acknowledge our place in a more-than-human world? How far we are prepared to look to see the connection between the familiar commitments by which we order the world—identity, place, property, mastery—and the contemporary vulnerability of life on the planet?

Works Cited

Abrams, David. *The Spell of the Sensuous: Perception and Language in a More-than-Human World.* (New York: Vintage, 1996).

Ainge Roy, Eleanor. "New Zealand River Granted Same Legal Rights as Human Being." *Guardian* International edition (March 16, 2017), www.theguardian.com/world/2017/mar/16/new-zealand-river-granted-same-legal-rights-as-human-being.

Barclay, Barry. *Mana Tūturu: Māori Treasures and Intellectual Property Rights.* (Auckland: Auckland UP, 2005).

Baudrillard, Jean. *Symbolic Exchange and Death.* trans. Iain Hamilton Grant (London: Sage Publications, 1993).

Birrell, Kathleen. "Review of *Carpentaria* by Alexis Wright." *Law, Culture and the Humanities* 5.1 (February 2009): 156–170.

Brewster, Anne. "Indigenous Sovereignty and the Crisis of Whiteness in Alexis Wright's *Carpentaria*." *Australian Literary Studies* 25.4 (November 2010): 85–100.

Chakrabarty, Dipesh. "The Climate of History: Four Theses." *Critical Inquiry* 35.2 (Winter 2009): 197–222.

Chakrabarty, Dipesh. "Postcolonial Studies and the Challenge of Climate Change." *New Literary History* 43.1 (Winter 2012): 1–18.

Cheah, Pheng. "World against Globe: Toward a Normative Conception of World Literature." *New Literary History* 45.3 (Summer 2014): 303–329.

Clark, Nigel. "Volatile Worlds, Vulnerable Bodies: Confronting Abrupt Climate Change." *Theory, Culture & Society* 27.2–3 (March 2010): 31–53.

---

113 Birrell, Review of *Carpentaria*, 156.

Collett, Anne. "Hone Tuwhare: At the Interface of Poetic Traditions." *Asiatic* 6.2 (December 2012): 45–56.

Daley, Linda. "Alexis Wright's Fiction as World Making." *Contemporary Women's Writing* 10.1 (2016): 8–23.

Devlin-Glass, Frances. "Review Essay: Alexis Wright's *Carpentaria*." *Antipodes* 21.1 (June 2007): 82–84.

Devlin-Glass, Frances. "A Politics of the Dreamtime: Destructive and Regenerative Rainbows in Alexis Wright's *Carpentaria*." *Australian Literary Studies* 23.4 (2008): 392–407.

Fox, Mārama. "Te Awa Tupua (Whanganui River Claims Settlement) Bill—Second Reading." (December 6, 2016), https://www.parliament.nz/mi/pb/hansard-debates/rhr/document/HansS_20161206_126900000/fox-marama.

Gibson, Ross. *Changescapes: Complexity Mutability Aesthetics*. (Crawley, Western Australia: UWA Publishing, 2015).

Gibson, Ross. *Memoryscopes: Remnants Forensics Aesthetics*. (Crawley, Western Australia: UWA Publishing, 2015).

Grace, Victoria. *Baudrillard's Challenge: A Feminist Reading*. (London: Routledge, 2000).

Harley, J.B. "Deconstructing the Map." *Cartographica* 26.2 (Spring 1989): 1–20.

Haraway, Donna. "Anthropocene, Capitalocene, Plantationocene, Chthulucene: Making Kin." *Environmental Humanities* 6 (May 1, 2015): 159–165.

Huggan, Graham. "Decolonizing the Map: Post-Colonialism, Post-Structuralism, and the Cartographic Connection" in *Past the Last Post: Theorizing Post-Colonialism and Post-Modernism*, eds. Ian Adam and Helen Tiffin (New York & London: Harvester Wheatsheaf, 1989): 125–138.

Huggan, Graham. "Australian Literature, Risk, and the Global Climate Challenge." *Lit: Literature Interpretation Theory* 26.2 (March 2015): 85–105.

Joseph, Laura. "Dreaming of Phantoms and Golems: Elements of Place Beyond Nation in *Carpentaria* and *Dreamhunter*," in "Australian Literature in a Global World," special issue, *Journal of the Association for the Study of Australian Literature* (2009): 1–10.

Latouche, Serge. *In the Wake of the Affluent Society: an Exploration of Post-Development*, trans. and Introduction by Martin O'Connor and Rosemary Arnoux (London: Zed Books, 1993).

Mishra, Sudesh. "On Seeing a Bull's Skull in a Bicycle Seat: Innovative Archaisms in Oceania." *Contracampo: Brazilian Journal of Communication* 36.3 (2017): 42–57.

Neimanis, Astrida. *Bodies of Water: Posthuman Feminist Phenomenology*. (London: Bloomsbury, 2017).

New Zealand Electronic Text Collection. First Lessons in Maori, http://nzetc.victoria.ac.nz/tm/scholarly/tei-WilFirs-t1-body1-d1-d1-d7-d2.html.

Nixon, Rob. *Slow Violence and the Environmentalism of the Poor*. (Cambridge, MA: Harvard UP, 2011).

Pratt, Mary Louise. *Imperial Eyes: Travel Writing and Transculturation*. (London: Routledge, 1992).

Radio New Zealand. "What It Means to Give the Whanganui River the Same Rights as a Person." *The Wireless* (March 16, 2017), https://www.rnz.co.nz/news/the-wireless/374515/what-it-means-to-give-the-whanganui-river-the-same-rights-as-a-person.

Rancière, Jacques. *The Politics of Aesthetics*, trans. G. Rockhill (London: Continuum, 2004).

Ravenscroft, Alison. "Dreaming of Others: *Carpentaria* and its Critics." *Cultural Studies Review* 16.2 (September 2010): 194–224.

Sharrad, Paul. "Beyond *Capricornia*: Ambiguous Promise in Alexis Wright." *Australian Literary Studies* 24.1 (May 2009): 52–65.

Spivak, Gayatri Chakravorty. *Death of a Discipline* (New York: Columbia UP, 2003).

Te Awa Tupua (Whanganui River Claims Settlement) Act, 2017.

Te Puni Kōkiri. "Te Awa Tupua." *Kōkiri 33* (Raumati/Summer 2016): 30.

Turner, Stephen. "Anglosphericism." *Journal of New Zealand Literature* 31.2 (October 2013): 15–34.

"Tutohu Whakatupua Explained: Questions and Answers." *Wanganui Chronicle*, http://www.nzherald.co.nz/wanganui-chronicle/news/article.cfm?c_id=1503426&objectid=11073833.

Tuwhare, Hone. "No Ordinary Sun" in *No Ordinary Sun: Poems* 15 (Auckland: Blackwood and Janet Paul, 1964).

Tuwhare, Hone. "Rain" in *Come Rain Hail* 6 (Dunedin: Otago UP, 1970).

Tuwhare, Hone. "The River is an Island" in *Year of the Dog: Poems New and Selected* 43 (Dunedin: McIndoe, 1982).

Walters, Laura. "If the Whanganui River is a Person, Is It Just Like You and Me?" *Stuff* (16 March 2017), https://www.stuff.co.nz/national/90516475/if-the-whanganui-river-is-a-person-is-it-just-like-you-and-me?rm=m.

Williams, Herbert W. *A Dictionary of the Maori Language*, 7th ed. (Wellington: GP Books. 1885).

Wilson, Zaryd. "Te Awa Tupua will Take Time to Manifest." *Whanganui Chronicle* (3 May 2017), http://www.nzherald.co.nz/wanganuichronicle/news/article.cfm?c_id=1503426&objectid=11849380.

Wright, Alexis. *Carpentaria*. (Sydney: Giramondo, 2006).

Wright, Alexis. *The Swan Book*. (Sydney: Giramondo, 2013).

CHAPTER 4

Which Island, What Home?

Plantation Ecologies and Climate Change in Australia and Nauru

Paul Sharrad

The Pacific Ocean has become a focus for critical analysis of climate change and a whole range of environmental concerns. However, when Nauru is mentioned, most Australians at least will think only of a tent city of detained asylum seekers. Discussion of Australia's "Pacific solution" to its "problem" of refugees arriving on unofficial "people smuggler" boats has tended to focus on the legal and moral obligations of Australian politicians on the one hand, and, on the other, the plight of hapless refugees condemned to "inhuman" living conditions in "remote" island isolation and uncomfortable tropical heat. If we concentrate on the "Pacific" as the site for "solving" an Australian problem, we might wonder about the people who live as a matter of course and origin on the same hot island. In doing so, we come up against questions of environmental sustainability, including the effects of climate change. These effects stem from histories of what I call "plantation ecologies" that constitute a transnational— in this case, oceanic—dynamic that challenges constructions of international relations and Australia's relationship to Pacific islands.

The entanglement of climate change and refugee movements has been discussed within many disciplinary frames and by a host of scholars. Daniel Faber and Christine Schlegel survey much of the debate, noting how temperature rises and drought in the Middle East have damaged economies, some also subject to political trade embargoes, thereby leading to conflict and large-scale movements of refugees. They comment that the effects of climate change are most damaging for Small Island Developing States (SIDS), especially in the Pacific, where many populations lack the means to migrate, and where foreign aid has been focused on disaster relief and development assistance has been "militarized" with the effect of "distort[ing] climate and human rights policies."[1] Large movements of asylum seekers have been reconfigured as threats to national security, and refugees have been rebranded under neoliberal

---

1 Daniel Faber and Christine Schlegel, "Give me Shelter from the Storm: Framing the Climate Refugee Crisis in the Context of Neoliberal Capitalism," *Capitalism Nature Socialism* 28.3 (2017): 1–9.

© KONINKLIJKE BRILL NV, LEIDEN, 2022 | DOI:10.1163/9789004514164_005

capitalism as "economic migrants": free agents seeking to improve their lot in life rather than victims of political oppression and the effects of climate change. How this works in Nauru is spelled out in the fieldwork of geographer Anja Kanngieser.[2]

The environmental humanities has regularly taken up the idea of slow violence as expounded by Rob Nixon.[3] In looking at the oceanic Pacific, scholarship under this rubric invoking Nixon's work has tended to take the form of postcolonial critiques of French and American military occupation, nuclear testing and the slow violence of radioactive fallout and forced migration, whether that be in poetry from the Marshall Islands and Hawai'i or fiction from Tahiti or critical studies of the region.[4] In more recent times, attention to climate change and its effects on the low atolls of Kiribati has raised concern. Nauru, as a "high" island, and one not operating in the largely *South* Pacific and Polynesian realms of cultural discussion, has not featured as a site of concern in humanities-based Pacific studies. Nonetheless, it too suffers from slow violence: the same trans-Pacific accumulation of climate change outcomes caused by industrialised urbanisation in developed nations, and the more dramatically visible environmental degradation by colonial mining interests. To these we can add the particular slow violence of detaining asylum seekers for years on the island. All three are interconnected within the international handling of refugee movements, the now faster violence of climate change outcomes for small islands, and the political implications of plantation ecologies.

I am thinking of plantation ecologies in the context of Ann Stoler's notion of "imperial formations": those structures that endure beyond the age of empire, issuing "promissory notes" deferring outcomes, installing trusteeships, that result in the "ruination" of parts of the globe.[5] The plantation was initially a resettlement of one group of people in another location, in particular, the

---

2 Kanngieser, Anja, "Climate Change: Nauru's Life on the Frontlines," *The Conversation* (October 22, 2018) and "Weaponzing Ecocide: Nauru Offshore Incarceration and Environmental Crisis," *The Contemporary Pacific* 32.2 (2020): 492–502.

3 Rob Nixon, *Slow Violence and the Environmentalism of the Poor* (Cambridge MA: Harvard UP, 2010).

4 See Kathy Jetñil-Kijiner, *Iep Jaltok: Poems from a Marshallese Daughter* (Tucson: U of Arizona P, 2017); Wayne Westlake, *Poems by Wayne Kaumali'i Westlake* (Honolulu: U of Hawai'i P, 2009); Chantal Spitz, *L'Isle des rêves écrasés* 1991, trans. Jean Anderson. *Island of Shattered Dreams* (Wellington: Huia, 2007); Teresia Teaiwa, "bikinis and other s/pacific n/oceans" *The Contemporary Pacific* 6.1 (1994): 87–109; Elizabeth DeLoughrey; "Radiation Ecologies and The Wars of Light," *MFS Modern Fiction Studies* 55.3 (2009): 468–498.

5 Ann Stoler, "Imperial Debris: Reflections on Ruin and Ruination," *Cultural Anthropology* 23.2 (2008): 191–219.

colonisation of northern Ireland by Protestant English and Scots as organised by James I and Oliver Cromwell ("Plantations of Ireland"). Plantations under colonial/imperialist regimes became a common strategy for demographic and economic management of global space, with Irish poor shipped as indentured labour to the Caribbean, British convicts transported first to the US and then to Australia, Indians sent as indentured labour to Africa, the Caribbean and Fiji. The African slave trade is but one aspect, albeit the most brutal, of this wider movement of people around the world.[6]

Such "plantations" of people were usually associated with a particular mode of economic production: the large-scale extraction of raw materials to supply Europe's industrial revolution and later First World consumer capitalism. The literal meaning of plantation—the planting of flora often also transported from an original endemic site to "empty" expanses of colonial territory—created large agricultural industries centred on cotton, sugar, wheat, copra, palm oil and so on, depending on the location. Thinking beyond the actual plantings of cash crops, plantation production can be seen to encompass monoculture extractive economies in mining and the harvesting of ocean products: seals and whales, historically; tuna in more recent times. The dynamics are the same: raw materials from colonies or the global South generally, being shipped for processing to imperial centres and the global North. Plantation economies operate on a "boom and bust" cycle swinging from "plenitude to exhaustion," partly because they are controlled by centres of power beyond the control of the producing location.[7]

In Nauru, Germany set up a colonial regime of minimal local impact until it sold mining rights to a British-controlled company that included interests from Australia and New Zealand. In 1906 the Pacific Phosphate Company began digging out extensive guano deposits laid by centuries of nesting Noddy terns. This bird shit was worth its weight in pounds sterling because, as "superphosphate", it could fertilise the depleted ancient soils of Australia to grow wheat and pasture for wool-bearing sheep (or in New Zealand for lamb and dairy cattle) that would supply the mouths and banks of the "mother country". It led to an internal transplanting of Australia's soldiers returned from World War One onto dry acreages that were then cleared of bush and sometimes irrigated from the southern region's few rivers. That war also led to Australia taking over

---

6 Alfred Crosby, *Ecological Imperialism: The Biological Expansion of Europe 900–1900* (Cambridge: Cambridge UP, 1986).

7 Michael Niblett, "Oil on Sugar: Commodity Frontiers and Peripheral Aesthetics," in *Global Ecologies and the Environmental Humanities*, eds. Elizabeth DeLoughrey, Jill Didur and Anthony Carrigan (New York: Routledge 2015): 278, 281.

governance of Nauru as a trust territory. Later, Nauru established a trust fund based on royalties from the three countries that had plundered its soil, making it briefly the richest Pacific nation until bad investments and corruption "harvested" the wealth, leaving a debris of imperial ruin.[8]

Colonies were disparaged by empires for having no ruins (no history, no tradition that might fuel cultural production). Ruins were not thought of, however, in terms of the natural environment.[9] Extractive plantation ecologies have since produced their own (un)natural ruins: the eroded pinnacles of Nauru, the dustbowl of Australia's Mallee region, the collapsed shorelines of both countries. Books like Tim Flannery's *The Weather Makers* and Charles Massy's *The Call of the Reed Warbler* all tell the tale of Australia's environmental degradation resulting from superphosphate's extension of plantation economy farming.[10] Deforestation produced drought; increased herds broke the soil down; half the country blew across the Pacific in storms of dust. Smaller farmers move back to the cities leaving large-scale agribusiness to take over with machine run on fossil fuels. Cycles of climate change were being pushed into larger, more dramatic forms, and spreading more widely in their effects. "Natural disasters" of drought, famine, fire and flood prove to be distinctly unnatural outcomes of climate change.

Empires and plantation economies are closely linked with movements of people, as already noted. Australia's origin as a nation was a "plantation" of convicts and poor British and Irish, that went in tandem with plantation economies of wheat, wool and mining. Distant islands were a convenient place to confine people in and draw labour from. One-thousand-two-hundred Nauruans were transplanted as labourers to Chuuk during Japanese occupation. When phosphate extraction started to reach its limit, the Queensland government, recognising Australia's moral debt and economic profit from Nauru (but also probably seeing the benefits of a new unskilled labour force) proposed relocation of Nauruans to Curtis Island in the state's north. By 1964 this "plantation" failed because Nauruans wanted national autonomy and Australia would not allow an independent country to occupy Australian territory. Nauru's nearest neighbour, Ocean Island, was also stripped of its soil for phosphate and its Banaban inhabitants transplanted to an island in Fiji.[11] So it was partly out of

---

8   "Nauru," *Encyclopedia Britannica*, www.britannica.com. "Nauru" in *The Pacific islands: An Encyclopedia,* eds. Brij Lal and Kate Fortune (Honolulu: U of Hawai'i P, 2000): 588–590.

9   Stoler, 194.

10   Tim Flannery, *The Weather Makers* (Melbourne: Text Publishing, 2008); Charles Massy, *The Call of the Reed Warbler* (St Lucia: U of Queensland P, 2017).

11   Jane McAdam, "The High Cost of Resettlement," *Australian Geographer* 48.1 (2016): 7–16; "Banaba," https://en.wikipedia.org/wiki/Banaba.

historical habit—out of the transnational culture of "the carceral archipelago of empire"[12]—that the boom and bust of a plantation economy at one end of an exchange and the transplanting of people escaping wars and famine at the other end should lead politicians to accept a new plantation of Australia's refugees on Nauru.

We can track the logic of island internment back to the British origins of Australia's first white settlers, and beyond to the literature informing European culture. Gillian Beer notes the tradition of figuring Britain as an island kingdom, and credits air travel with exposing the fiction of "the concept of nationhood which relies upon the cultural idea of the island."[13] If the British Isles were protected from the Continent, they were also provincial in relation to it, leading to artists and aristocrats embarking on overseas adventures. Internally, the "mainland" displaced its marginal citizens to smaller isles: monks to Iona, convicts and political prisoners to the Isle of Wight, and then thousands of their fellows were exported to what was New Holland. That large island further deported its incorrigible felons to Van Diemen's Land and Norfolk Island. Its Aboriginal tribes were sequestered either for punishment or protection—the difference being often hard to discern—on Rottnest Island in the West, Palm Island in the north and Bruny Island in Tasmania. New Zealand sent Maori actively opposing white settler incursion on their lands into captivity on the Chatham Islands. British India confined its rebels on the Andamans; the United States built Alcatraz as an island fortress no one could escape from. France sent its revolutionaries to the Isle of Pines, an island off the larger island of New Caledonia, and its convicts went to Devil's Island in French Guiana, as we see in the novel and film, *Papillon*.[14] Napoleon was exiled to islands: first to Elba, then to Saint Helena.

Islands have been felt as, and thought of as, places of both refuge and confinement: as both paradises and prisons. C.A. Cranston extends Gillian Beer's ideas to think about ecology and islands, particularly about Tasmania, and notes that a "challenge to the reading of islands is that they are reductively constructed as escape from the human population into self-sufficiency and Romantic solitude ... but also, when populated, as parochial cultural prisons."[15] Thomas Keneally's novel *Napoleon's Last Island* shows the great emperor

---

12   Stoler, 194.

13   Gillian Beer, "The Island and the Aeroplane: The Case of Virginia Woolf" in *Nation and Narration*, ed. Homi K. Bhabha (London: Routledge, 1990): 266.

14   Henri Charrière, *Papillon* (London: Hart-Davis, 1970).

15   C.A. Cranston, "Islands," in *The Littoral Zone: Australian Contexts and their Writers*, eds. C.A. Cranston and Robert Zeller (Amsterdam: Rodopi, 2007): 221.

WHICH ISLAND, WHAT HOME? 125

chafing at his confinement, but also freed by his isolation to play children's games with his captors' offspring.[16] R.M. Ballantyne was a Scot who had never visited the Pacific but felt able to write about it on the basis of reading all the images circulating in Europe from novelists, explorers, missionaries and scientists. Three boys are shipwrecked on a Pacific atoll. This is at first a tragic restriction of mobility and freedom, but quickly transmutes into a realisation of Bougainville's Tahitian paradise (itself a realisation of Europe's dream of Cythera as an island paradise). The islands the boys encounter oscillate between being havens of delight and places of danger and imprisonment.[17] This is a habit of representation akin to Said's idea of orientalist discourse, and one that in turn induces a habit of thinking and behaviour. It is, overtly in Ballantyne's case, but less so in Australia's use of Manus Island and Nauru as its solution to a "refugee problem", imbued with historical and contemporary imbalances of power resting on imperialist structures of economy, race and nature. Once labelled Pleasant Island, Nauru has featured in media discussion as a kind of carceral hell on earth, not unlike early Australian depictions of Tasmania such as Marcus Clarke's *For the Term of his Natural Life*.[18] Literature has played a subtle but by no means insignificant role in perpetuating and sometimes critiquing such patterns of representation.

Discussion related to the Pacific in general and Nauru in particular in the context of the environmental humanities has mostly occurred outside of the literary field. The exception—and it shows how even the most isolated island is still part of an oceanic network—is a set of poems by a Samoan academic who worked on Nauru as part of the Fiji-based University of the South Pacific's education outreach. The collection is titled *Pinnacles*.[19]

The title refers to the stony outcrops left as the result of phosphate mining and still waiting on satisfactory land refurbishment. The strange beauty of this abandoned landscape is reflected in the ambivalent language of the book's title poem in which dry barrenness is contrasted to "the blue expanse of the Pacific" but resonating with:

the heavens
hovering
close above
suffocating

---

16 Thomas Keneally, *Napoleon's Last Island* (North Sydney: Random House, 2015).
17 R.M. Ballantyne, *The Coral Island* [1858] (Oxford: Oxford UP, 1990).
18 Marcus Clarke, *For the Term of his Natural Life* [1874] (Hawthorn: Lloyd O'Neil, 1970).
19 Makerita Va'ai, *Pinnacles* (Suva: Mana Publications, 1993).

the admirer
trapped
by the serenity
of destruction. ("Pinnacles")

In this we can detect the old pattern of islands as sites of beauty that are also suffocating in their delimited space and there to be exploited. There is also the intimation of the oppressive climate close to the equator. The pinnacles are both signs of colonial depredation and of embedded "memories of wisdom" that "warm the soul / embrace the spirit / with hope" ("Angam Day").[20] Va'ai's largely inspirational poems hide darker images beneath their celebrations of identity rooted in land and traditions. A sunset poem depicts an idyllic scene of evening fishing, but the coast is "littered with blue cans" (that is, with Fosters beer cans, island drinking being the subject of the poem "Fosters"), and the poet goes to bed dreaming of "fresh cool water" cascading down a waterfall only to wake and "find no water and / wish myself drowned / in the waters of my dream" ("Sunset in Nauru"). The poem reflects the fact that Nauru suffers from drought and has to import fresh water. The EU granted 11.4 million Euros to the Secretariat of the Pacific Community in 2015 to ensure sustainable water supply to Nauru and other islands. This has resulted in the construction of a desalination plant, the rebuilding of a larger reservoir tank in the main town and provision of rainwater tanks to many of the houses across the island.[21]

Other poems point to lung damage from the dust of phosphate mining ("Loading Day") and to indigenous dangers to ecological balance as manifest in the local sport of netting birds ("Black Noddy").[22] "Constitution Day" celebrates a new generation of educated "challengers / of tomorrow" and ends:

Waves from afar
lash against virgin shores
eroding the *vanua*
raping the beauty of her smile.
an intrusion to the spirit of the *earoeni*
intoxicating her soul
eat imin ngen bwain aton
    pollution
    disease

---

20   Va'ai, *Pinnacles*: "Pinnacles," 25; "Angam Day," 18.

21   Secretariat of the Pacific Community, "Securing Safe Drinking Water in Nauru".

22   Va'ai, *Pinnacles*: "Loading Day," 22; "Black Noddy," 23.

WHICH ISLAND, WHAT HOME?

> lies
> destruction.
> in the name of development
> waves from afar
> roll in, armoured with a gospel of
> greed and exploitation.[23]

The waves from afar are symbolic here of colonial exploitation of natural resources, but they also point to real contemporary problems of an ocean affected by climate change. The increasing regularity and intensity of storms and rising sea levels are beginning to erode the coastline, even on this relatively high island.

Pinnacles predates contemporary concerns about climate change, but the collection points to an extractive "plantation" economy that ruins vegetation and soil, leaches chemicals, raises dust, and leads eventually to hotter air and warmer, more acidic oceans. In directing our attention to the environmental degradation of phosphate mining on Nauru, Va'ai's collection points both Nauruans and Australian readers to a history of circuits of plantation ecologies that help explain how it became possible for one large country to dump several hundred foreigners on another country's smaller island territory and how seemingly distant and quite distinct nations are mutually implicated in climate change.

More recently a book about Nauru records the impressions of Mark Isaacs, who worked for some time with the Salvation Army given the impossible task of ensuring the welfare of internees at the Nauru Refugee Processing Centre. Isaacs describes Nauru as "Australia's Pacific island rubbish dump."[24] He means that people have been turned into waste matter, not unlike others sent to concentration camps. However, he also turns the figure of speech into literal meaning when he starts talking to Nauruans. They wonder why people complain about living in a place they themselves call home, when they eat better than islanders do. They point out that no one consulted them about taking in a lot of foreigners and accuse the President of profiteering from the arrangement. The employment of Nauruan guards—even at artificially suppressed wage levels—causes jealousy in a largely subsistence economy, and the camp produces huge amounts of waste: plastic water bottles being a major component.[25] The question of whose island home we are looking at arises, and

---

23   Va'ai, *Pinnacles*: "Fosters," 27; "Sunset in Nauru," 19–20; "Constitution Day," 17.

24   Mark Isaacs, *The Undesirables* (Melbourne: Hardie Grant, 2014): 17.

25   Isaacs, *The Undesirables*, 50–51.

it is clear that the island is caught up in global flows, the waste products of oil-based manufacturing, hotter temperatures and rising oceans. It was Nauru's President, Marcus Stephens, President of the Pacific Small Islands Developing States, who issued a cry for global attention to climate change to the *New York Times* in 2011 and then addressed the UN in 2012, bringing global attention to the particularly pressing dangers facing Pacific Islands as the result of global warming.[26] He specifically labelled Oceania as "the canary in the coalmine" and blamed the major developed economies of the world for excessive use of fossil fuels causing pollution and climate change. It was the same leader who accepted the reopening of the refugee detention centre.

If we Google "Nauru Island Home", we find a YouTube compilation by Candace Detudamo (relation of one of Nauru's ruling chiefs) that provides a visual tour of her island home to the accompaniment of Christine Anu's singing of the Australian hit song "My Island Home."[27] Elizabeth McMahon has teased out the ambiguous imaginary of Australia as an island continent,[28] and we see it reflected in the nation's relationship with the Pacific Islands. In the days of sailing ships, Australia was dependent on, and linked to, the "South Seas" as necessary refuelling stations and suppliers of some raw materials (copra, coir, whales), but since then has mainly dealt with the Islands as places of holiday to be visited briefly by plane or cruise ship. Australia has come to see itself as a large, land-based society. In fact, the song was originally composed by Warumpi Band, and contrasts living in the desert with the singer's island home on Elcho Island, underlining the (unhomely) continental aspect of an Australia, but also pointing to the nation only able to think of itself as a large country providing economic support to small distant islands in need of aid, sometimes providing sources of cheap and transitory labour in return. The same superior continent seeing itself as a player on the world stage turns in its domestic politics into an island protecting its borders to exclude disease, terrorism and selected migrants.

It is telling that a Nauruan would connect with Australia by selecting Christine Anu's version of a song ostensibly located in the Torres Strait, the tropical island home in that version, rather than the desert interior, contrasted with living in the city. This region of small islands is an anomaly in Australia: part of the continent that is not continental, more Pacific culturally,

---

26   Marcus Stephens, "On Nauru: A Sinking Feeling," *New York Times* (July 19, 2011); Al Jazeera, "Nauru Asks UN to Fight Climate Change".

27   Candace Detudamo, "Nauru Island Home," (2013), https://www.youtube.com/watch?v=QHDcTHm6_JA.

28   Elizabeth McMahon, *Islands, Identity and the Literary Imagination* (London: Anthem, 2016).

WHICH ISLAND, WHAT HOME? 129

but through Eddie Mabo a significant part of continental land rights legislation and a rethinking of colonial history. As part of Queensland, with its history of sugar plantations and the transplanting (forced indenture) of Pacific labour, as well as its awareness of "island" issues such as coral reef bleaching and rising sea levels, "My Island Home" of "saltwater people" calls to the Pacific and reminds continental Australia that it too is an island with Pacific ties.

What Detudamo's YouTube clip shows and doesn't show is interesting. We follow a motorbike making a circuit of the island on the coast road. We see a lot of palm trees but also a strip development of concrete shops and houses—and the back of a motorbike. Nauru did rely at one point on the export of coconut products for some of its income, and it is the coconut palm, once part of a colonially constructed plantation economy, that iconically and ironically has come to signify a tropical island, Eden. What we don't see are the "Pinnacles" of phosphate mining detritus. What we don't necessarily realise is that this visual celebration of an island home is made around the time Nauru is trying to develop a tourism industry because income from phosphate mining has been drying up. What we see without it being spelled out is that the motorbike, the petrol fuelling it, the concrete and tin sheets for all the buildings are imported, and mostly imported from Australia, and all contributing to raising the Earth's temperature.

Nauru currently reports problems of drought, salination of soil and water, coastal erosion from increasingly high king tides and rising temperatures.[29] It imports most of its food and fresh water. At the same time, it accepts greater demand on its resources by encouraging Australia to reopen its refugee detention camp in 2012 to pay "rent" of many millions and provide jobs for locals. The government has attempted to diversify its economy by providing a tax haven for international banking and creating a tax-free industrial zone that assembles electrical goods and leather apparel for Asian countries, including the incongruous production on an equatorial island of air conditioners and knitwear destined for other places.[30]

The "weaponising" of development aid by Australia in leveraging Nauru's climate crisis (in part historically caused by Australia) to oblige it to accept a detention camp as a "Pacific solution" to an Australian "problem" of border protection against people fleeing some mix of climate and political violence arguably continues to impose a form of slow violence on the island. It gives the illusion of security in the form of a financial bailout and focuses attention

29　Kanngieser 2001; DFAT. Australian Government, Department of Foreign Affairs and Trade, "Australia's Commitment to Climate Change Action in Nauru," www.dfat.gov.au.

30　"Nauru: Overview of Economy," www. nationsencyclopedia.com.

more on the refugee issue than on environmental crisis. It is in keeping with the one-off "disaster aid" that is the common response to Pacific needs and distracts from the "sustainability" and "development" aid that is really required, allowing some sections of the exchange to continue to see climate change as a process too slow to count as disaster. There is the additional violence of increasing environmental stresses by "planting" a thousand refugees on an island whose habitable 20 percent of land already houses 13,000 Nauruans.

Nauru has no return to a pristine pastoral unless there is major soil remediation, and inhabitants revert to subsistence agriculture. To maintain visibility in the world, a nation state formation is necessary, and that kind of modernity entails reasonable demands from citizens for education, good standards of health care and so on—all continuing the island's immersion in networks of capital. Modes of sustainability that don't succumb to the plantation ecologies related to climate change are required. Shifting from land-based extraction to ocean farming by contracting out fishing rights and the mining of manganese is unlikely to promote island existence in the long term.[31] Reliance on Australian aid that keeps in place thinking settled on distance and difference and international state-to-state solutions is not a solution either. Australia's commitment to climate change action in Nauru, other than shoring up port facilities, seems to consist of meaningless managerialism that is rendered even more useless in the face of refusal by the island continent's government to espouse genuine climate change solutions of its own and break free of pastoral myths and plantation ecologies of large-scale mining.[32]

To return to the environmental humanities and its literary links, Elizabeth DeLoughrey asks, "how might we parochialize the Anthropocene in order to engage the often conflicting narratives of relationship to place, multispecies, and planet?" Following Epeli Hau'ofa's remodelling of the Pacific from Western empty space dotted with tiny isolated islands into the Indigenous conception of a moving network of connections, DeLoughrey joins other scholars turning to oceanic models of environmental thinking in positing "oceanic futures" whose currents and connections break open stable singular entities into newly conceived relationships while noting that the ocean itself is becoming "a renewed space of empire and territories" and conflict over resources.[33] In the

---

31   "Nauru," *Encyclopedia Britannica*, www.britannica.com.

32   DFAT, "Australia's Commitment to Climate Change Action in Nauru".

33   Elizabeth DeLoughrey, "Ordinary Futures: Interspecies Worldings in the Anthropocene" in *Global Ecologies and the Environmental Humanities*, eds. Elizabeth DeLoughrey, Jill Didur and Anthony Carrigan (New York: Routledge 2015): 352, 354; Epeli Hau'ofa, "Our Sea

context of Australia and its ties to the Pacific, we have seen how plantation ecologies have linked the continent with the islands, and it is worth noting the attempt to undo the land-based pastoral habit of mind that underpins industrialised plantation agriculture on the part of John Kinsella, living at the edge of Western Australia's wheat belt.[34] On the other side of the continent, we see how Indigenous and speculative writing from Australia is pushing at the exceptionalism of a continental imaginary and reconnecting to an oceanic sense of flows and circuits including island settings. Alexis Wright's *Carpentaria*, for example, seemingly a land-based epic, resolves several conflicts (including the invasion of territory by a multinational mining company) with a flood and the escape of a young Aboriginal resistance fighter to a floating island of accumulated waste (see also Chapter 3). Ellen Van Neerven's *Heat and Light* allegorises race relations in a human–plant cross species tale of containment and revolt located across mainland and offshore island.[35] The ruins of plantation ecologies (some of them not immediately visible) reconnect continent Australia to its island aspect and thereby link it to its interconnection with the Pacific. A relationship of binary difference turns out to be a transnational network of mutual involvement heavily influenced by histories of plantation ecologies. Seeing this might play some role in rearranging the inequities of exceptionalism and "aid" and might generate more meaningful efforts to reduce climate change across all of the region's islands. "My Island Home" might well return to the airwaves as a national anthem of both Australia and Nauru, but with the purpose of focusing attention on the real violences of plantation ecologies and climate change underlying idyllic images of island life and refusing any notion of an isolated human home.

---

of Islands," in *A New Oceania: Rediscovering Our Sea of Islands*, eds. E. Waddell, V. Naidu and E. Hau'ofa. (Suva: University of the South Pacific, 1993); Sidney I. Dobrin, *Blue Ecocriticism and the Oceanic Imperative* (New York: Routledge, 2021); Melody Jue, *Wild Blue Media: Thinking through Seawater* (Durham NC: Duke UP, 2020).

34   John Kinsella, *Disclosed Poetics: Beyond Landscape and Lyricism,* (Manchester: Manchester UP, 2007); *Polysituatedness: A Poetics of Displacement*, (Manchester: Manchester UP, 2017); Martha Read, "John Kinsella's Anti-Pastoral: A Western Australian Poetics of Place" *Antipodes* 42.1 (2010): 91–96.

35   Alexis Wright, *Carpentaria* (Artarmon: Giramondo, 2006); Ellen Van Neerven, *Heat and Light* (St Lucia: U of Queensland P, 2014).

Works Cited

Al Jazeera. "Nauru asks UN to fight climate change" (2012), https://www.youtube .com/watch?v=6oNmHW-G-ek&index=6&list=PL9My0osnt8Y1rbirZpreP2xL4H GwTZaGH.

Ballantyne, R.M. *The Coral Island.* (Oxford: Oxford UP, 1990). Originally published 1858.

"Banaba." https://en.wikipedia.org/wiki/Banaba.

Beer, Gillian. "The Island and the Aeroplane: The Case of Virginia Woolf" in *Nation and Narration*, ed. Homi K. Bhabha, (London: Routledge, 1990): 265–290.

Chakrabarty, Dipesh. "Postcolonial Studies and the Challenge of Climate Change." *New Literary History* 43.1 (2012): 1–18.

Charrière, Henri. *Papillon* (London: Hart-Davis, 1970).

Clarke, Marcus. *For the Term of His Natural Life* (Hawthorn: Lloyd O'Neil, 1970). Originally published 1874.

Cranston, C. A. "Islands." In *The Littoral Zone: Australian Contexts and their Writers*, eds. C. A. Cranston and Robert Zeller (Amsterdam: Rodopi, 2007): 219–260.

Crosby, Alfred. *Ecological Imperialism: The Biological Expansion of Europe 900–1900* (Cambridge: Cambridge UP, 1986).

DeLoughrey, Elizabeth. *Routes and Roots: Navigating Caribbean and Pacific Island Literatures* (Honolulu: U of Hawai'i P, 2007).

DeLoughrey, Elizabeth. "Radiation Ecologies and The Wars of Light." *MFS Modern Fiction Studies* 55.3 (2009): 468–498.

DeLoughrey, Elizabeth. "Ordinary Futures: Interspecies Worldings in the Anthropocene" in *Global Ecologies and the Environmental Humanities*, eds. Elizabeth DeLoughrey, Jill Didur and Anthony Carrigan (New York: Routledge 2015): 352–372.

Detudamo, Candace. "Nauru Island Home" (2013), https://www.youtube.com/ watch?v=QHDcTHm6_JA.

DFAT. Australian Government, Department of Foreign Affairs and Trade. "Australia's Commitment to Climate Change Action in Nauru," www.dfat.gov.au.

Dobrin, Sidney I. *Blue Ecocriticism and the Oceanic Imperative.* (New York: Routledge, 2021).

Faber, Daniel and Christine Schlegel. "Give me Shelter from the Storm: Framing the Climate Refugee Crisis in the Context of Neoliberal Capitalism." *Capitalism Nature Socialism* 28.3 (2017): 1–17.

Flannery, Tim. *The Weather Makers.* (Melbourne: Text Publishing, 2008).

Hau'ofa, Epeli. "Our Sea of Islands." *A New Oceania: Rediscovering Our Sea of Islands*, eds. E. Waddell, V. Naidu and E. Hau'ofa (Suva: University of the South Pacific, 1993).

Huggan, Graham and Helen Tiffin. *Postcolonial Ecocriticism.* (London: Routledge, 2010).

Isaacs, Mark. *The Undesirables.* (Melbourne: Hardie Grant, 2014).

Jetñil-Kijiner, Kathy. *Iep Jaltok: Poems from a Marshallese Daughter.* (Tucson: U of Arizona P, 2017).

Jue, Melody. *Wild Blue Media: Thinking through Seawater.* (Durham NC: Duke University Press, 2020).

Kanngieser, Anja. "Climate Change:.Nauru's life on the Frontlines." *The Conversation* (October 22, 2018), www.theconversation.com.

Kanngieser, Anja. "Weaponzing Ecocide: Nauru Offshore Incarceration and Environmental Crisis." *The Contemporary Pacific* 32.2 (2020): 492–502.

Keneally, Thomas. *Napoleon's Last Island.* (North Sydney: Random House, 2015).

Kinsella, John. *Disclosed Poetics: Beyond Landscape and Lyricism.* (Manchester: Manchester U P, 2007).

Kinsella, John. *Polysituatedness: A Poetics of Displacement.* (Manchester: Manchester U P, 2017).

Massy, Charles. *The Call of the Reed Warbler.* (St Lucia: U of Queensland P, 2017).

McAdam, Jane. "The High Cost of Resettlement." *Australian Geographer* 48.1 (2016): 7–16.

McMahon, Elizabeth. *Islands, Identity and the Literary Imagination* (London: Anthem, 2016).

"Nauru." In *The Pacific Islands: An Encyclopedia,* eds. Brij Lal and Kate Fortune (Honolulu: U of Hawai'i P, 2000): 588–590.

"Nauru." Encyclopedia Britannica, www.britannica.com.

"Nauru: Overview of Economy," www. nationsencyclopedia.com.

Niblett, Michael. "Oil on Sugar: Commodity Frontiers and Peripheral Aesthetics" in *Global Ecologies and the Environmental Humanities,* eds. Elizabeth DeLoughrey, Jill Didur and Anthony Carrigan, (New York: Routledge 2015): 268–285.

Nixon, Rob. *Slow Violence and the Environmentalism of the Poor.* (Cambridge MA: Harvard UP, 2010).

"Plantations of Ireland," https://en.wikipedia.org/wiki/Plantations_of_Ireland.

Read, Martha. "John Kinsella's Anti-Pastoral: A Western Australian Poetics of Place." *Antipodes* 42.1 (2010): 91–96.

Secretariat of the Pacific Community. "Securing Safe Drinking Water in Nauru" (2015), https://www.youtube.com/watch?v=5SlZTgx8nQM.

Spitz, Chantal. *L'Isle des rêves écrasés* 1991, trans. Jean Anderson. *Island of Shattered Dreams* (Wellington: Huia, 2007).

Stephen, Marcus. "On Nauru: A Sinking Feeling." *New York Times* (July 19, 2011), http://www.nytimes.com/2011/07/19/opinion/19stephen.html?_r=1&ref=opinion.

Stoler, Ann. "Imperial Debris: Reflections on Ruin and Ruination." *Cultural Anthropology* 23.2 (2008): 191–219.

Teaiwa, Teresia. "bikinis and other s/pacific n/oceans." *The Contemporary Pacific* 6.1 (1994): 87–109.

Va'ai, Makerita. *Pinnacles* (Suva: Mana Publications, 1993).

Van Neerven, Ellen. *Heat and Light* (St Lucia: U of Queensland P, 2014).

Westlake, Wayne. *Poems by Wayne Kaumalii Westlake*, ed. Mei-Li M. Siy and Richard Hamasaki (Honolulu: U of Hawai'i P, 2009).

Wright, Alexis. *Carpentaria* (Artarmon: Giramondo, 2006).

CHAPTER 5

Island Life and Wild Time

Crossing into Country in Tim Winton's Island Home

Stephen Harris

The subtitle to Tim Winton's book *Island Home: A Landscape Memoir* announces a conceptual challenge: the idea of a "landscape memoir" immediately contests customary understandings of "life story", calling into question dominant Australian assumptions concerning the relationship between humans and the land. As this chapter will elucidate, Winton seeks to encourage a profound shift in human consciousness, as a necessary response to the pressing environmental challenges that confront humanity at this time. Winton's passionate views about his relationship with place—the idea of Australia as "home" conveys the full weight of his experience—are framed by his insistence on the value of a particular geographical perspective. That is, he writes both as a self-proclaimed "islander", deeply respectful of the manner in which the island continent of Australia imposes a humbling sense of scale upon its human inhabitants, and as a "littoralist,"[1] a dweller of peripheries: a West Australian inhabitant of the underpopulated western edge of the island, and a resident of a small town, north of the metropolis of Perth. The littoralist perspective provides the template for the change in consciousness he advocates. As I will argue, by deploying the literary conceit of "family", Winton compels contemporary non-Indigenous Australians to accept the importance of "learning to see" country—to become collectively more "properly awake and aware of our place,"[2] and so to arrive at a deeper understanding of the human relationship with the land, and more particularly with the subtly distinctive characteristics and elusive temperament of the antipodean island continent. This involves confronting stubborn assumptions and beliefs ingrained over generations, and learning to recognise that the material prosperity (inequitably) distributed across the modern Australian

---

1 Thanks to Melissa Lucashenko for this reference: "Winton jokingly describes himself as a littoralist—meaning someone strongly attached to the margins of the continent"—see "I Pity the Poor Immigrant," *Journal of the Association of the Study of Australian Literature* 17.1 (2017): 5.

2 Tim Winton, *Island Home: A Landscape Memoir* (Melbourne: Hamish Hamilton/Penguin Australia, 2015): 28.

© KONINKLIJKE BRILL NV, LEIDEN, 2022 | DOI:10.1163/9789004514164_006

nation-state induces a self-inhibiting myopia, or at least wilful misperception. Thus, sentimentalised conceptions of the land, long-nurtured and expressed through comfortingly contrived images of landscape and geography, serve to obscure the fact that "country" is still habitually treated primarily as quarry and marketable commodity. In robustly lyrical terms, Winton's story endorses the broader ethical, political and practical imperative placed upon the collective human community in the face of escalating environmental destruction and the effects of climate change. More pivotally, Winton's memoir, in celebrating the unique qualities of "islandness" in language evocatively attuned to localised place and innovative literary form, conjures an instructive response in the face of the pressing urgencies and uncertainties of the present age.

Island Home invites the reader's imaginative response in a manner that affirms a sense of belonging and yet, paradoxically, involves a sense of being put *in* one's place, whereby the "pressure of geography" bears down upon, and so becomes the measure of, human presence.[3] Winton's phrase—"pressure of geography"—evokes the palpable presence of "country," as it shapes the conditions of "island life" as they pertain to dwelling in Australia, where "geography trumps all."[4] For Winton, country is primordial: in *Island Home* the "absence of wildness" in Paris calls him home to his "Australian life [...] and the wild spaces that made it possible."[5] Yet the impress of the land also represents immeasurable scales of time and space, and Winton understands the land as an enigma that eludes the comprehension of contemporary non-Indigenous Australians, even as it beckons for understanding: "the land speaks to so many of us, and like any long-suffering parent it yearns for a little recognition. But not everyone is paying attention."[6] The narrative pivots on the trope of familial connection, which reinforces an ethical imperative and proposes a conceptual challenge concerning the relationship between self and place: "This country leans in on you [...] To my way of thinking, it *is* family [...it] exerts a kind of force on me that is every bit as geological as family."[7] This is the metaphor that presents the central claim of *Island Home*: the land of this immense island continent is the terra firma defining human existence in Australia, as well as an animating "watchful presence,"[8] an all-encompassing complexity that Australians, too often and too readily, see in terms of a boundless commodity—as real estate

---

3 Winton, *Island Home*, 25.
4 Winton, *Island Home*, 17.
5 Winton, *Island Home*, 7.
6 Winton, *Island Home*, 49.
7 Winton, *Island Home*, 10, 23.
8 Winton, *Island Home*, 24.

ISLAND LIFE AND WILD TIME

and resource—and, in doing so, fail to understand the fundamental constitutive relationship between human and land.[9]

While *Island Home* can be read as a "meditation on the centrality of land, place and belonging,"[10] such an appraisal can be counterbalanced by a more contentious assertion. For, through the powerful metaphor of kinship, Winton asserts a land claim through the telling of his story. That is to say that he responds in full candour to a claim *made upon him* by the land. As radical as this idea might be for many readers, both Aboriginal and non-Aboriginal, his story testifies to his acceptance and celebration—both as a literary artist and human being—of this constitutive relationship. In this way, memoir becomes a testament that seeks to persuade Australians to begin to see in the deeper sense that he does—to gain new insight by sharing knowledge acquired through learning to "walk the land" and so to become "more fully present to it," in Australian philosopher Freya Mathews's words.[11] Put differently, he encourages what might be called a resighting of self in relation to land and country so as to initiate a fundamental change in our understanding of human *being*—an ontological reorientation inducing a different experience of being *in* place. In itself, the landscape memoir—an innovative generic hybrid, as will be discussed—aims to encourage readers to learn to see the country as "an organic whole, a web of interdependent relationships."[12] Ultimately, if ideally, readers will undergo a transformative shift in consciousness in response to the "sacramental ache"[13] that presses at the edge of awareness, and so come to experience a profound change in their "bearing in the face of mystery."[14] They

---

9 Except where particular emphasis is required, the terms *land* and *country* are used interchangeably in this chapter, as is consistent with Winton's own use of the terms (along with cognate terms *geography*, *landscape* and, in the more generalised sense, *place*; see pages 16–17 and 92–3, for example). However, the aim is not to disavow the cultural, political and semantic sensitivities surrounding these words, but rather to align with his broader aims in using the familial trope, and as based on his reading of contemporary Australia's changing relation with the land reflected in language: "In my own lifetime Australians have come to use the word 'country' as Aborigines use it, to describe what my great-great-grandparents would surely have called territory. A familial, relational term has supplanted one more objectifying and acquisitive ... [denoting] an emergent admiration and respect for the land we find ourselves in" (28).

10 Lyn McCredden, *The Fiction of Tim Winton: Earthed and Sacred* (Sydney: Sydney UP, 2017): 88.

11 Freya Mathews, "Ontopoetics in Australia," in *Sacred Australia: Post-Secular Considerations*, ed. Makarand Paranjape (Melbourne: Clouds of Magellan, 2009): 261.

12 Winton, *Island Home*, 97.

13 Winton, *Island Home*, 24.

14 The phrase is Wendell Berry's, from "Think Little" in *A Continuous Harmony: Essays Cultural and Agricultural* (Counterpoint Press: Berkeley, 2012): 84–85.

will come to know the privilege of "reverence" before the "earthly mystery,"[15] as Winton proclaims it.

This chapter will consider the manner in which *Island Home* addresses the problem of seeing and its particular relevance to Australians, and as this problem reflects a common human challenge. Equally, however, Winton's approach raises persistent questions, for example, concerning the relation between language and materiality, and between literary texts and political action. Such questions are important in themselves, as the ensuing discussion will demonstrate, yet are to some extent unanswerable, given the social and political complexities prevailing at present. In view of anticipated criticisms—Winton's willingness to be self-critical in his account imbues his argument with added force—he proceeds in the mode of negative capability in the manner described by George B. Handley: "the inherent faith of literature is not that language is adequate but that seeing and exploiting its inadequacy can sustain us."[16] Yet, for all his avowed belief in the powers of the literary imagination, Winton's call to reform human attitudes to the land also agitates politically, for it is a carefully measured protest in the face of the encompassing phenomenon of climate change and the global ecocide presently being enacted by our species. In this respect, Winton is in no way a solitary voice; and while the account offered in *Island Home* makes no direct reference to the now-highly politicised debates around climate change, these are obviously implicated in his deeper concerns with the human experience. Certainly, his persuasive urging of Australians to reassess their sense of place fosters a keener awareness of biospheric values and global environmental conditions; and his effort to inspire an expansion of awareness—an "emotional deepening"[17] as he calls it—encourages Australians to learn to see and know their island home in more environmentally nuanced ways. By extension, the human collective might better know its larger island home (planet Earth). In fact, Winton's call to a richer imaginative engagement with the land attests to his environmental activism through literature.[18] *Island Home*, then, aims to reform contemporary attitudes and practical approaches to the very earth on which all life depends.

---

15   Winton, *Island Home*, 77.

16   George B. Handley, "Climate Change, Cosmology, and Poetry: The Case of Derek Walcott's *Omeros*" in *Global Ecologies and the Environmental Humanities: Postcolonial Approaches*, eds. Elizabeth DeLoughrey, Jill Didur and Anthony Carrigan (New York: Routledge, 2016): 334–335.

17   Winton, *Island Home*, 203.

18   Winton refers to himself as a sea-faring "hunterer and gatherer," conceding that his has been a "slow realisation," "I've lived long enough to witness a diminution in the seas,

ISLAND LIFE AND WILD TIME

Winton writes as a self-declared "islander," as both title and epigraph confirm in alluding to the chorus line of Australian musician Neil Murray's popular song of belonging and return, "My Island Home."[19] Readers will also recall Homer's great story, in which wandering Odysseus insists on the abiding value of land, home and family: "So nothing is as sweet as a man's own country / his own parents."[20] Winton's trope of family knots together the sense of both fealty and belonging. Yet the narrative also works in relation to a greater sense of homelessness, which assumes another kind of meaning in the 21st century. This is the human condition of "solastalgia," denoting the pain arising from the growing sense of homelessness—of being out of place while at home—a condition induced by the broadscale destruction of the natural world.[21] In being "enisled,"[22] then, Winton's story takes on different inflections. Consciousness becomes grounded in a formative understanding of territorial confinement, bound up in the imaginative impulse to be elsewhere: "Moated in by oceans, sharing no borders, they [islanders] become curious, restless, oppressed by the relentless familiarity of their surroundings ... Islanders can't help conjure distant paradises for themselves."[23] That the effects of an increasingly erratic climate have not so far been felt on island Australia in the same precipitous way that they have been on the world's many smaller islands cannot be lost on Winton. The geographical scale and mass of the continent means that the psychology of enislement does not apply so immediately to life in Australia. It is, nevertheless, useful to consider the islandness in Australia in relation to Mark Twain's point concerning the doubleness of islands:

---

and to notice a fragility where once I saw—or assumed—an endless bounty." Winton in "When the Tide Turns," *Sydney Morning Herald* (April 14, 2012): 34–36.

19   The phrase 'island home' appears in Tennyson's poem, "The Lotos-Eaters," in *Victorian Poetry: An Annotated Anthology*, ed. Francis O'Gorman (Oxford: Blackwell Publishing, 2004): 68.

20   Homer, *The Odyssey*, trans. Robert Fagles (New York: Penguin Classics, 1996): 212, lines 38–9. The line becomes more emphatic in the most recent translation by Emily Wilson: "... when a man is far from home/living abroad, there is no sweeter thing/than his own native land and family," *The Odyssey*, trans. Emily Wilson (New York: w.w. Norton & Company, 2018): 241.

21   The neologism is Glenn Albrecht's from his 2004 essay: "solastalgia," a combination of the Latin word *solacium* (comfort) and the Greek root–*algia* (pain), which he defined as "the pain experienced when there is recognition that the place where one resides and that one loves is under immediate assault ... a form of homesickness one gets when one is still at 'home.' " Albrecht quoted in Daniel B Smith, "Is there an Ecological Unconscious?," *New York Times Magazine* (January 27, 2010).

22   The term is Patrick Barkham's, from *Islander: A Journey Around Our Archipelago* (London: Granta, 2017): 4.

23   Winton, *Island Home*, 19–20.

The élan that draws humans toward islands extends the double move-ment that produces islands in themselves. Dreaming of islands—whether with joy or in fear, it doesn't matter—is dreaming of pulling away, of being already separate, far from any continent, of being lost and alone—or it is dreaming of starting from scratch, recreating, beginning anew. Some islands drifted away from the continent, but the island is also that towards which one drifts; other islands originated in the ocean, but the island is also the origin, radical and absolute.[24]

If, in Winton's view, the island continent disorientates in its expansive dis-tances (he use the word "bewilders"), it nonetheless resolves in a comforting paradox: "wildness soon intervenes to disabuse us ... the pressure of geogra-phy reasserts itself palpably and unmistakably to remind us that, of course, we could only be *here*."[25] As the impress of "wildness" dissolves environmental hubris,[26] so the great mass of land brings consciousness to the material ground of awareness and being (as he insists, "we could only be *here*," materially speak-ing);[27] and while the invocation of wildness aligns with ideas popularised by proponents of "rewilding,"—for instance, British writer George Monbiot argues for the revitalising effects of the feral—it is for Winton less a restorative form of primality that we might reach out to experientially (though that is not discounted as such) than it is a means of learning to recognise what is *here*, with and *in* us, and as such demands understanding.

Winton charts the coordinates of personal story onto and *into* geography, the text working as a whole to affirm his sense of an indissoluble bond with the island continent. Equally, in telling his story—*albeit* very selectively, with elements of literary flourish and an insistence upon *inter*relation—he is also always in the land of metaphor, as the phrase "island home" in fact denotes, even as he persuades the reader of the materiality of the country that is beneath his feet. To take a line from Randolph Stow's poem "The Singing Bones," the

---

24 Mark Twain in Philip Mead, "A Barren Place, and Fertile" in *An Introduction to Tasmania in the Literary Imagination* (AustLit: Literature of Tasmania, 2004), https://www-austlit -edu-au.ezproxy.une.edu.au/austlit/page/9674597. In the same place, and on the distinc-tion between island and continent in regard to Australia, see Marc Shell's *Islandology: Geography, Rhetoric, Politics* (Stanford: Stanford UP, 2014): 7. The poet John Mateer con-tends that, "contrary to conventional belief, Australia is not an island—it's an archipelago, culturally porous and edgeless ... the nation consists, in effect, of a handful of islands ..." "Australia is Not an Island," *Meanjin* 65.1 (2006): 89.
25 Winton, *Island Home*, 25.
26 Winton, *Island Home*, 140.
27 Winton, *Island Home*, 25.

ISLAND LIFE AND WILD TIME   141

island home is a place "mainly of the mind" existing in imagination as it does in the external environment. There are further implications to this point, as I will argue below; but another kind of double movement also becomes obvious as the metaphor of land-as-family exerts its gravitational pull on the reader's imagination, insisting on a familial bond with the land, yet simultaneously directing him or her to take up a different *figurative* space, and so to recognise more fully the conceptual frames that determine behaviour. Importantly, the evocation of this other imaginative space emphasises the phenomenological aspect of being more consciously and completely *in* place ("places exert active, unpredictable power, a lively and sometimes fickle agency.")[28] In turn, then, Winton also gestures towards another dimension of time coextensive with the distinct modes of spatial awareness he discerns in Australia. He alludes to what might be called a zone of *wild time* beyond the Western temporal conceptions that correspond to "human dominion"—the "unrelieved enclosure and containment"[29] he encounters in Europe and the "cossetted and manicured and airconditioned"[30] lives of most Australians. As such, he swings the narrative compass beyond the temporal horizon of measurable Western historical time to the deeper temporalities of the land of the "wild world"[31] that is "hatched and laced with ancient story."[32] In these places, the sense of deep time at once inspires a certain mode of reverence and a kind of psychic disturbance among non-Indigenous people. On encountering the Wandjina sites in the Kimberley, for example, "the non-indigenous visitor is likely to be *overcome* by the antiquity of these sites when for those who maintain and are maintained by them they are living places where past, present and future are indistinguishable."[33] Equally, in the same place, he describes conflicting sensations of time in relation to complex (if latent) emotions: on "walking through old mine diggings where land has been laid waste forever," he feels a "queasiness, a sense of reproach so direct it seems to come from the place itself—a feeling of sorrow and agitation ... not so different to the creeping shame and awe you're subject to at the scene of any violent crime. You *feel the dead*, the *afterglow of experience*."[34] A reflexive ethical sensitivity intimates this *other* time in which

---

28   Winton, *Island Home*, 145.
29   Winton, *Island Home*, 13.
30   Winton, *Island Home,* 24.
31   Winton, *Island Home,* 62.
32   Winton, *Island Home*, 15.
33   Winton, *Island Home*, 149, emphasis added.
34   Winton, *Island Home*, 146, emphasis added.

the assumed distinctions between the living and the dead are dissolved, if only temporarily.[35]

Throughout the narrative, Winton repeatedly honours the importance of Aboriginal culture in direct relation to notions of lived time and place, although the wider significance of such mythic time, as it might be called, figures more by implication, since, by definition, it is an *other* time beyond ready (and rational) articulation in contemporary Western terms. Before considering the further implications and effects of the leading conceit of familial relations with place, it is important to understand how the landscape memoir challenges the conventions of memoir as a genre of non-fiction. Readers might in the first instance come to the author's life story for its dramatic variety, intimate exposure or an instructive chronicle of redemption.[36] They will likely have expectations concerning the genre, as it typically describes the lineaments of an individual's identity and revelatory acts of self-discovery (and, unavoidably, self-performance). Contrawise, and as suggested earlier, *Island Home* advances a thesis—"a quietly polemical, and not uncontentious, argument," in Delia Falconer's words.[37] In advocating a "different kind of seeing,"[38] it also presents a kind of well-tempered provocation based on Winton's formative experiences of the land. If it is "not uncontentious," as Falconer says, it is because readers also sense a certain sacerdotal presumption or paternalistic prescriptiveness in the stance. But Winton succeeds in forestalling this criticism for the most part, offering an important contribution to what Mathews calls the "re-valorisation of nature" as part of the "world-wide renegotiation of the human relationship with nature." Despite the priestly tone of the text, one has the sense of being invited along for a kind of life lesson with Winton as trustworthy guide. The lesson is animated by both a deep moral concern and, inseparably, a serious artistic commitment to fostering collective human potential.

---

35   On the poetics of water in Aboriginal culture, Deborah Bird Rose makes this observation: "This abundant life [generated by water] flows into a poetics of oscillating pulses, of call and response, as living beings go rushing to meet each other *across country and across time*" (emphasis added). "Arts of Flow: Poetics of 'Fit' in Aboriginal Australia," *Dialectical Anthropology* 38 (2014): 433.

36   Lyn McCredden reads Winton's fiction in terms of "narratives of redemption," insisting also on the "deeply political" impulse informing his literary vision (McCredden, *The Fiction of Tim Winton*, 48–49).

37   Delia Falconer, review of *Island Home*, "When a Writer Keeps Watch on the Beat of his Heartland," in 'Spectrum', *Sydney Morning Herald* (October 24–5, 2015): 29.

38   Winton, *Island Home*, 203.

ISLAND LIFE AND WILD TIME 143

Clearly, then, Winton is far less concerned with extended introspective efforts at self-discovery (as in most literary memoirs)—with himself as the singular subject—than he is with sharing what he has discovered through sustained and considered reflection on his experience of being *of* country. Indeed, his memoir makes a familiar political call: the personal is political. More particularly, as generic hybrid, the landscape memoir signals a reorientation of the narratorial relation between self and place—what might be thought of as a conceptual re-enactment of self-as-subject. As a landscape memoir, *Island Home* shifts the perceptual axis of self-telling (as it were) from that of seeing the natural world as an object to the apprehension of the constitutive interaction between humans and the more-than-human world. Winton offers his compelling view of the island world to encourage readers to know themselves in deeper relation to country. As he observes more than once, the majority of Australians are conditioned by homogenised, placeless, urbanised enclaves that impoverish the sensory powers in a manner represented by travelling *through* country (cocooned in cars, suspended in a kind of "geographical limbo")[39] rather than into it. Readily acknowledging his own limitations, Winton admits to being an inveterate car traveller, but that only modulates the moral message of his memoir. True to his egalitarian ethos, he also wants to be seen working alongside fellow Australians, committed to a common endeavour. He observes a "palpable outward urge"[40] in the behaviour of millions of Australians that is telling:

> It speaks of an implicit collective understanding that the land is still present at *the corner of our eye*, still out there, but also carried within, as a generic connection ... For despite how cossetted and manicured and airconditioned contemporary life has become, the land remains a tantalizing and watchful presence over our shoulder. We've imbibed it unwittingly; it's in our bones like a sacramental ache.[41]

Eschewing dogmatism, his narrative attains its full strength by working persuasively to challenge the common assumptions by which Australians imagine and understand their place.

Principally, what Winton has learnt through his meditations on landscape is the power of peripheral perception—the power of "vision beyond mere glimpsing," as he puts it in his earlier essay, "Strange Passion: A Landscape

---

39   Winton, *Island Home*, 180.
40   Winton, *Island Home*, 24.
41   Winton, *Island Home*, 24, emphasis added.

Memoir."[42] In that essay, he identifies the challenges surrounding contemporary Australian attitudes to place—"[l]earning to see has been a long, slow and sometimes bitter problem" for non-Indigenous Australians.[43] The essay also introduces Richard Woldendorp's impressive collection of aerial landscape photographs entitled *Down to Earth: Australian Landscapes*; with it, prefatory to *Island Home*, he appeals to the collective human potential for change. Explicitly, Winton aims to foster what he calls in *Island Home* "a mental step forward" in our understanding of our place *in place*: "an emotional deepening ... [that] takes humility and patience to see what truly lies before us."[44] *Island Home* elaborates on, and effectively completes, the earlier exploratory essay.[45] Complementarily, each half (as it were) addresses different ways of seeing: "seeing" denotes both the literal ocular act—in both texts aerial views of the land from 10,000 feet are described and serve as points of critical reflection—and the phenomenological implications of the word (what Winton calls the "other means of seeing.")[46] To *see*, in the precise and nuanced way that he encourages, then, is to nurture an awareness of one's deepest connection to place. Moreover, it is to begin to understand how one's sense of identity and self is always *in-formed* by a very specific place. "To be properly awake and aware of our place" is to know hope; and to learn to *be in place* is to accept and cherish the fact that "this earth is our home, our only home."[47] The intersection between essay and memoir is signified by Winton's use of the same extract from the poem "Land," by Gagudju Elder Bill Neidjie to close both texts ("Big" Bill Neidjie was a senior traditional owner and representative of his father's country, the Bunitj Clan Estate, and the Gagudju language group, Kakadu National Park, Northern Territory).[48] In that poem, Neidjie speaks with expressive humility of the poetic wisdom of animism, describing (through the "working" voice of a tree) the interanimating energy

---

42 Tim Winton, "Strange Passion: A Landscape Memoir" in Richard Woldendorp, *Down to Earth: Australian Landscapes* (North Fremantle: Fremantle Arts Centre Press, 1999): xxvi.

43 Winton, "Strange Passion: A Landscape Memoir," xvi.

44 Winton, *Island Home*, 203.

45 The term *essay* used here in reference to the earlier version of the landscape memoir is primarily descriptive, denoting both the length and exploratory character of the piece, in keeping with the Montaignian notion of *assaying* a subject. Equally, that same experimental approach invites consideration of the formal relation between memoir and the essay, although that entails another line of discussion.

46 Winton, "Strange Passion," xv.

47 Winton, "Strange Passion," xx.

48 Stephen Davis, "Bill Neidjie," *Gagudju Man: Bill Neidjie* (Australia: JB Books, 2002): 13.

ISLAND LIFE AND WILD TIME

of the natural world, a form of mindfulness that Winton calls "practical mysticism."[49]

Of the relation between the phenomenological and literary qualities of *Island Home*, more will be said. In more general literary critical terms, however, Winton's memoir can be seen as consistent with other developments in Australian life writing, particularly regarding the emergence of other "formally diverse and politically charged" auto/biographical narratives.[50] One critic has advanced the term *ecobiography* to encapsulate the ways in which Winton's memoir gives "voice to the landscape's mood, memory, solitude, and wildness, place becomes geographic, created and remembered, formed and forming."[51] *Island Home* is one example of what the critic Timothy Morton calls "ecomimesis," of "reinhabitory" literature, enacting "place-consciousness" in the way of bioregionalism.[52] That is, it strives by an act of imagination to "resacralise" the natural world as a transformative shift in consciousness.[53] It has also been heralded as an example of the "new nature writing", concerned with the "imaginative counter-mapping of the place-imaginary" (which is central to the much wider project of "globally inspired eco-localization.")[54] But Winton's literary compatriot and fellow landscape memoirist, Mark Tredinnick, encapsulates it

---

49 Bill Neidjie, *Gagudju Man: Bill Neidjie* (Australia: JB Books, 2002): xxxi. Calling for "climate justice," the Seed Indigenous Youth Climate Network argues that climate change is already having a disproportionate effect on Aboriginal and Torres Strait Island people; in making their point, they refer directly to Neidjie's teachings at https://www.seedmob.org .au/indigenous_youth_declaration.

50 David McCooey, "Poetry and Non-Fiction from 1950," in *The Literature of Australia; An Anthology*, ed. Nicolas Jose (Sydney: Allen & Unwin, 2009): 47.

51 Melanie Pryor, "Eco-Autobiography: Writing Self through Place," *Auto/biography Studies* 32:3 (April 25, 2017): 391. Pryor makes specific reference to Winton's *Island Home*.

52 Tom Lynch, Cheryll Glotfelty, Karla Armbruster, eds. "Introduction," *The Bioregional Imagination: Literature, Ecology, and Place* (Athens: University of Georgia Press, 2012): 3–4.

53 Paranjape, *Sacred Australia: Post-Secular Considerations* (Clouds of Magellan: Melbourne, 2009): 5.

54 Jos Smith, *The New Nature Writing: Rethinking the Literature of Place* (London: Bloomsbury Academic, 2017): 5–6. Tamsin Kerr refers to "ecoregionalism" as the guiding philosophy in landscape memoir as a broader cultural practice: "Landscape memoir tells of 'tru-stori' connection to place–a mythic archaeology that creatively speaks that which lies at the heart of every geographic community." Tamsin Kerr, "If I Say I Love My Place, What's with the Bags I've Packed?: The Cultural Changes Required by Landscape Memoir and Eco-Regionalism," *Art Monthly Australia* 214 (October 2008): 5–8. Note: the creolised or "composite" mode of "tru-stori" alludes to legends telling of the supernatural beings that created Country and Law; see Stuart Cooke, "The Case for Gularabulu by Paddy Roe," *The Conversation* (April 15, 2014), https://theconversation.com/the-case-for-gularab ulu-by-paddy-roe-25320.

more aptly to my mind: landscape memoir is a "literature of place, ecologically imagined and written in the landscape's own vernacular ... [a] celebration of, [and] an enacted belonging in, the land."[55] It is a literary genre that promotes immersive connection with the natural world, an imaginative (re-) engagement with the materiality of the living environment, directly informing environmental ethics but also, inseparably, developing new environmental understandings of self that are themselves coextensive with the concept of the Anthropocene.

As eloquent as Tredinnick's formulation might be, one might pause over notions such as "ecologically imagined," the "landscape's own vernacular" and the textualised "enactment [of] belonging in the land"—not least because such lyrically neat formulations carry a hint of glibness. As is the case with *Island Home*, this mode of landscape writing has generated critical cross-examination, much of it concerning the role of textuality and language in mediating the encounter with the natural world. Certainly, in a more general sense, Winton anticipates the attention of the more sceptical literary critics in exercising what might best be called an unfussy self-reflexivity, as when he repeatedly acknowledges his own complicity in the misguided treatment of country ("[b]ut I was a boy of my time, the son of a culture still resisting such notions of submission to a greater complexity"),[56] acknowledges the romantic impulses in his reveries ("I know they [excursions into the bush] sound like escapes, but to me they're more like calls answered";[57] and more defensively, "I'm not self-hating utopian,")[58] and recognises the need for careful qualifications and deliberations over semantic meaning ("I'm not saying Australia has no culture or that its cultural life is inconsiderable.")[59] Critically speaking, the views propounded in *Island Home* can also be assessed from an ethically progressive ecocentric perspective. In J. Scott Bryson's account, an ecopoetic ethos (where ecopoetics is understood to incorporate the full spectrum of literary, artistic and creative practices that promote ecological and environmental values) rests on the recognition of a fundamental interdependence among and between all living things, on the "imperative toward humility in relationships

---

55   Mark Tredinnick. *The Land's Wild Music: Encounters with Barry Lopez, Peter Mathiessen, Terry Tempest Williams, and James Galvin* (San Antonio, Texas: Trinity University Press, 2005): 7. Concerning his own explorations in *The Blue Plateau: A Landscape Memoir* (2009), and by way of thanking Tim Winton for the use of the phrase 'landscape memoir,' Tredinnick suggests that the term is Winton's conception.

56   Winton, *Island Home*, 76.

57   Winton, *Island Home*, 22.

58   Winton, *Island Home*, 17.

59   Winton, *Island Home*, 16.

ISLAND LIFE AND WILD TIME

with both human and nonhuman nature" (a humility pressing against the practised assumptions of dominant land practices) and on a determined scepticism towards "an overtechnologized modern world."[60] Winton articulates precisely this ecopoetic ethos by his insistence that, in Australia, one finds oneself in the humbling "presence of wildness,"[61] and also by his stern criticism of the prevailing mindset that the land lacks intrinsic value:

> [...] any status must be conferred by an enterprising human and the only standard he or she will recognize is market price, which, despite sounding rational and authoritative, is based on ephemeral and arbitrary perceptions and therefore subject to fluctuation, or what the market touchingly calls 'wildness'.[62]

But what sharpens Winton's challenge in *Island Home* is his insistence on drawing his readers to the ground, encouraging them to be more attentive to the complexity, particularity and fragility of their surrounds. It is hoped that this will initiate "a mental step forward" into a more responsive understanding of one's place *in place*. In other words, "[l]earning to see this place with an open heart and mind"[63] inheres in a heightened attentiveness and a re-learning of self in relation to land.[64]

David Malouf conveys a sense of what has been lost to sight in his response to the radical landscapes of the Australian painter, William Robinson: "[Robinson takes] a bit of local earth whose vigorous being, and variety and otherness is taken so deeply in by the observing eye, and so lovingly and movingly remade in the creator's consciousness, as to make consciousness and the created world when we enter these painted landscapes, one."[65] Winton *pictures* the experience of "travelling deep into landscape"[66] similarly. As this entails the recognition of one's "smallness," it becomes a lesson in seeing in itself. For Winton,

---

60   J. Scott Bryson, *The West Side of Any Mountain: Place, Space, and Ecopoetry* (Iowa City: U of Iowa P, 2005): 5–6.
61   Winton, *Island Home*, 25.
62   Winton, *Island Home*, 198–99.
63   Winton, *Island Home*, 204.
64   Winton, *Island Home*, 203.
65   David Malouf, "Making Consciousness and the Created World One" in *William Robinson: The Transfigured Landscape* (Brisbane: Queensland University of Technology and Piper P, 2011): 74. Malouf talks of "the experience of being in the landscape and part of its endless process of becoming [which is more] than what we get in more conventional landscape views".
66   Winton, *Island Home*, 225.

one must surrender the assurance of acquired epistemological certainties and the reliance on the deeper drives of will and agency in the face of the "uncompromising landscape:" "the quest for an open-minded engagement with nature is as challenging and uncertain for individuals as it is for corporations and communities. Ingrained habits of mind are tenacious and nature is elusive, enigmatic, at times resistant."[67] Winton stresses the full weight of the natural world's materiality—of the island's commanding material presence infused with our human beingness. Since this is to begin the necessary renegotiation of self in relation to land, it cannot occur in isolation from the willingness to challenge the political controls on perception that influence how land is defined and used as well as what can be seen through the control of information.

As outlined above, the problem of seeing immediately denotes an enduring problem of relationship with and to land. In approaching that problem in *Island Home*, Winton necessarily confronts readers with the fact that the capacity to see and thus know the ground is frustrated by the challenges of broadscale environmental destruction and the mounting effects of climate change. Winton notes climate change in passing, not for the reason that it bears little consequence or concern, but because it confirms an elementary fact about life on the world's largest island—that the human presence has always been at "the mercy of nature:" "climate change [is] what we've always felt [that] geography and weather have never been mere backdrop in this country."[68] In this sense, Australians already *know* climate change, when this is understood in terms of unpredictable weather marked by dramatic extremes. The increase in the unpredictability and climatic extremes as a result of climate change only underscores the imperative that Australians need to learn to accept what they already *know*—the self-evident fact that we are "mere creatures of the earth, vulnerable and dependent."[69] This point permits the author to step around the divisive politics of climate change and to focus instead on encouraging fundamental change in attitudes and understandings. As a genre, the landscape memoir serves his needs most aptly, not least as a writer actively concerned with his immediate world, environmentally and culturally, but also

---

67 Winton, *Island Home*, 225.

68 Winton, *Island Home*, 26; on the veracity of climate change, Winton is self-described conservative: "I don't know if anthropogenic climate change is real or not [...] But in the same way that I'm not sure if anyone's going to drive safely on the road or not, I'll take precautions. I'll err on the side of conservative for the sake of my kids and take whatever measures seem to be prudent." Winton in Matthew Westwood, "Prosperity and a Secure Future for Our Kids Has a Price: Winton," *The Australian*, (May 20, 2011), http://search .proquest.com.ezproxy.une.edu.au/docview/867607991?accountid=17227.

69 Winton, *Island Home*, 225.

ISLAND LIFE AND WILD TIME   149

insofar as the change he advocates must occur on the plane of human imagination. To cite, as he does, the litany of abuses of Australia's "wildness" (as he insistently calls it) in the name of mercantile interests; to register the fact that the dominant narrative of progress relies on an exhausted colonial model speaking only in shop-worn slogans rehearsing a belated triumphalism is to identify stories bereft of imaginative vitality. Instead, and in concert with a growing number of writers and thinkers addressing the manifold problems arising from the disruptive impact of human life on the planet, Winton offers a narrative aligned to a wider generative energy inhering in imaginative activity itself. The memoir encourages Australians to change pace, reorient their perceptual frames and begin to walk *in* country, rather than to insist acquisitively on taking it *over*.

In compelling ethical and political change by reconfiguring ideas governing the human relationship with the earth, Winton does not deliberate over the much-analysed term *landscape* as it has figured in Western cultural history, nor is he concerned with elucidating a new conception of landscape in any formal, theoretical sense. Rather, he works from Australian novelist Liam Davison's observation that "landscaping is about imposing a way of seeing on to the land, a mind-set of ideas that are given expression through the changing relationships between things"[70] to propose in *Island Home* the broadscale rethinking of the self-in-place, not by *imposing a way of seeing* on to the land but rather by changing the *relationship* between self and land, and reimagining the very notion of self as ontologically *involved* in place. Put more directly, by resisting abstraction, Winton draws attention to *being in active relation* to land—a phenomenological relation predicated on shared inhabitation and underlining an egalitarian ethos. His approach is never reductively materialist but a matter of being drawn down to a level of fresh perceptual and existential possibility that offers collective transcendence: "Our future *is* organic [...] The dirt beneath our feet is sacred. Every other consideration springs from this and you don't need to be an archaeologist, geologist or botanist to know it."[71] It is a belief he hears in Neidjie's "practical mysticism," and which he has expressed before, in his earlier memoir, *The Land's Edge: A Coastal Memoir*:

> I think that everything that lives is holy and somehow integrated; and on cloudy days I suspect that these extraordinary phenomena and the

---

70   Liam Davison, "Landscape with Words—Writing about Landscape," *Overland* 134 (1994): 7. On more recent ideas of landscaping, see Paul Carter, *Groundtruthing: Explorations in a Creative Region,* (Crawley, WA: U of Western Australia P, 2014).

71   Winton, *Island Home*, 233, emphasis original.

hundreds of tiny, modest versions no one hears about, are an ocean, an earth, a Creator, something shaking us by the collar, demanding our attention, our fear, our vigilance, our respect, our help.[72]

It is also an idea forcefully dramatised in the earlier novel, *Dirt Music*, through the experiences of the protagonist Luther Fox, who embodies the harmonisation of self and country through the natural language of "dirt music," and so represents a relationship that speaks of a new understanding of the possibilities of self and identity *through* a return to the original bond between humans and the natural world. Yet, such a bond neither derives from imported European symbolic forms nor appropriates sacred Aboriginal rites.[73] It should of course be noted that any argument to renew the relationship between humans and the natural world in Australia invokes the earlier efforts of the literary nationalist Jindyworobak Movement (1930s to 1940s), whose manifesto pronounced the importance of environmental values, which were construed at the time as part of Aboriginal culture. And, so, Jindyworobakan literary practice involved the appropriation of certain aspects of Aboriginal culture as they understood it at the time.[74] Yet Winton does not conform to a nationalist dogma. In openly acknowledging and respecting the contributions of Aboriginal Elders (along with Bill Neidjie, he references the contributions of "visionary Ngarinyin lawman David Banggal Mowaljarlai")[75] and Aboriginal culture in general, he seeks to *work with* such valuable principles and beliefs for the common purpose and collective welfare of land and humans together:

[Mowaljarlai's] project of Two-Way Thinking, a philosophy of mutual respect, mutual curiosity and cultural reciprocity [...] springs from the earth itself. It should apply in the boardrooms of telcos and miners and bankers, be embodied in our personal and collective decision-making, for the ethic acknowledges the organic facts of life that underwrite all human endeavours.[76]

---

72   Tim Winton, *The Land's Edge: A Coastal Memoir* (Camberwell, Vic: Penguin Books, 2010): 47.

73   Tim Winton, *Dirt Music* (Sydney: Picador, 2002).

74   More recently, the poet Les Murray adapts Aboriginal oral narrative in his poem "The Buladelah-Taree Holiday Song Cycle," *Les Murray: Collected Poems,* (Carlton, Vic: Black Inc, 2018): 137–146.

75   Winton, *Island Home*, 230–233.

76   Winton, *Island Home*, 231–232.

ISLAND LIFE AND WILD TIME 151

It is a working principle that is also already *there*, a formative reflex in the form of an inward receptivity to "earthly mystery"[77] that, he suggests, bespeaks a unifying commonality: "I think people everywhere yearn for connection, to be overwhelmed by beauty. Maybe, deep down, people need to feel proper scale. Perhaps in the face of grandeur we silently acknowledge our smallness, our bit-part in majesty."[78]

In this way, Winton's landscaped self (so to speak), emphasising the active, constitutive involvement of the land in human consciousness, is always at the same time a way of seeing the land. The point is made succinctly by British writer, Robert Macfarlane, who, in his quest for wildness, reminds readers that "the land itself, of course, has no desires as to how it should be represented. It is indifferent to its pictures and to its picturers."[79] It is the mind's eye that landscapes country—it is in *how* we see country that meanings are conferred, values adduced and actions initiated. Winton's ease of articulation might appear to obscure the degrees of uncertainty and difficulty inherent in the effort to decolonise the European or Anglo-Australian mind. But author and artist Kim Mahood conveys something of this in her own recent landscape memoir, *Position Doubtful: Mapping Landscapes and Memories,* where the narrative pivots around the destabilisation of seeing: "this country displaces assumptions, resists meanings."[80]

Similarly, and in view of Winton's insistence that the land is emphatically *there*—the irrefutable ground beneath the feet—David Brooks makes the salient point that language exemplifies the fact that the relation between human and nature is mediated by culture. Winton's memoir, as with any act of human expression, cannot avoid fundamental questions concerning the act of writing itself as a gesture towards the materiality of the landscape:

> To think that we are somehow getting closer to some actual 'fact' of the landscape is a little troubling, if not actually paradoxical or absurd, and flies in the face of so much we have come to believe about the impossibility, given the nature of language and all other systems which compose our modes of apprehending anything, of our apprehending anything directly, of any actual, immediate and unmediated seeing or

---

77   Winton, *Island Home*, 77.
78   Winton, *Island Home*, 233.
79   Robert Macfarlane, *The Wild Places* (London: Granta, 2007): 10.
80   Kim Mahood, *Position Doubtful: Mapping Landscapes and Memories* (Brunswick: Scribe Publications, 2016): 36.

knowing. From this perspective, all is—can never be anything other than—gesture.[81]

In her reading of Winton's novel *Eyrie*, Lyn McCredden makes the point that this same challenge is also inextricably bound up in the deeper complications of writing. She suggests that Winton confronts the fragile borders where identity ceases to hold, where "signification and meaning-making—writing, autobiography, plotting, characterisation, ideology, theology, moral declaration, communication with others—are intimately, even irretrievably, entwined with what is—humanly, culturally—intolerable."[82]

Nevertheless, Winton's commitment to the written word—the fact that his memoir affirms the power of the literary imagination—refutes Brooks's argument, or at least his seemingly unforgiving conclusion that contact with the land is irremediably gestural. To that end, the thesis Winton unfolds in his memoir prompts readers to know more completely the experience of the "self-in-place"[83] so as to recognise the deeper formative involvement of place-in-self—to *earth* the self through realigning one's relationship with "the dirt beneath our feet."[84] That same "dirt" is never merely material, instead denoting at once *ground* and *earth*, and as such, always an outward manifestation of spiritualised matter.[85] Such interrelatedness is figured in the familial bond humans might have with the land, were they to begin to understand the relationship in those terms. *Island Home* testifies to the sheer and vital presence of the natural world: recounting a break he takes from driving from east to west across Australia to observe a spring tide coming in across "the vast tidal

---

81 "*If* the land teaches and informs, then it will not be changing its lessons and languages to suit intellectual fashion. Somehow this idea of being in-formed and the idea of finding *new ways of being* don't seem to go too readily together. Even for those who pursue the latter in one or another of its various forms, the problem of language, and the *grip* of language, and the releasing of that grip, will maintain." David Brooks, "Possession, Landscape, the *Unheimlich* and Lionel Fogarty's 'Weather Comes'," *Cordite Poetry Review* 82 (August 1, 2017), http://cordite.org.au/essays/possession-landscape-unheimlic/.

82 Lyn McCredden, " 'Intolerable Significance': Tim Winton's Eyrie," in *Tim Winton: Critical Essays,* eds. Lyn McCredden and Nathanael O'Reilly (Crawley: U of Western Australia P, 2014): 306–329; 239.

83 Neil Evernden, "Beyond Ecology: Self, Place, and the Pathetic Fallacy" in *The Ecocriticism Reader: Landmarks in Literary Ecology,* eds. Harold Fromm and Cheryll Glotfelty (Athens, GA: U of Georgia P, 1996): 93.

84 Winton, *Island Home*, 233.

85 For a discussion of the connotative range of the word *dirt*, see Stephen Harris, "Tim Winton's Dirt Music: Sounding Country/Re-siting Place," *Journal of the Association for the Study of Australian Literature* 15.1 (2015): 4–5.

ISLAND LIFE AND WILD TIME   153

mudscape of King Sound, near Derby," Winton brings the reader into sensory contact with this spectacular phenomenon:

> As slick brown water retreated from the ramparts it seemed to flee the land in a headlong stampede, flaying the trees that flashed olive green and then tawny and silver as they shivered and creaked, clutching at one another to survive the force of it. A million snarls of roots began to show and then canyons of mud, foetid and spidered with runnels and sucking pits. It popped and blurted, fizzing with skippers and the crone fingers of pneumatophores.[86]

The imaginative drive of these observations focuses outwards from the philo-sophical point identified by Brooks; and in seeking to persuade a broad public audience, Winton takes an avowedly political stance that necessarily involves confronting both the "deep-rooted colonizing instinct" that limits the capacity to see the land—"landscape" seen as "open space, a species of vacancy, another form of untapped potential awaiting discovery and exploitation"[87]—and, more pointedly, the political and ideological influences that press upon that same collective *incapacity* to see.

The problem of seeing, as Winton understands it, compounds in complexity when considered in relation to the fractiously politicised debates concerning climate change. Such debates occur in the national and international spheres, and are limited by the human inability (or refusal, as many insist) to apprehend the full scale and complexity of the phenomenon. Referencing (in paraphrase) Rachel Carson's observation that "you can get a sense of the health of an eco-system by how its birds are faring," Winton makes a similar point thinking back on his 2013 novel, *Eyrie,* drawing an analogy between the avian and his central child character: "I was thinking during the writing of *Eyrie* that perhaps you can also tell how a society is travelling by the situation its children find themselves in ... the little boy, Kai, is the canary in the mine."[88] That the "bird song" of chil-dren registers the disharmonies of their worlds is hardly a new observation. But Winton's use of the child as an "agent of grace"[89] to shake adults from their torpor and make them aware of the perils that surround them, and for which they are responsible, sharpens his point about the malaise afflicting Australia

---

86   Winton, *Island Home*, 184.

87   Winton, *Island Home*, 198.

88   Winton quoted in Madeleine Watts, "Contending with a Blank Page: On Writing, Wealth and Being a West Coaster," *Griffith Review* 47 (2015): 108; the boy as "agent of grace," 111.

89   Winton, *Island Home*, 111.

and the global community. As both author and environmental activist, albeit trading in well-thumbed metaphor—canaries in coalmines—Winton here again confirms the political possibilities of the literary imagination. Yet he also acknowledges that, in practical interventionist terms, the telling of yet another story is always to some extent incommensurate with the problem.

Addressing this question of political effect, George B. Handley emphasises the paradoxical manner in which literature encourages insight:

> The question, I would argue, is not whether human imagination takes a short cut by simplifying human diversity or human history in order to get to a worldview whole enough to encompass the globe. Of course, it does. The question is if those efforts are self-consciously fashioned and whether they exploit and ironize their own limitations. The inherent faith of literature is not that language is adequate but that seeing and exploiting its inadequacy can sustain us ... certainly climate change requires believing in and acting on more than what we can see [... but] for this same reason, stories must be imagined as inadequate and contingent. They become metaphors, expressions of hope for wholeness and order in direct response to the dispersing threat of chaos, rupture, and fragmentation.[90]

While Handley's elucidation weighs further on the problem of seeing— principally concerning the role of literature (and the arts more generally) as a means of reconfiguring one's imaginative relationship with the natural world—it also points to the intrinsically political question with which Winton is concerned as writer and activist: the political problem of what *can* and *should* be seen. It is this matter, of what humans wish, choose or are permitted to see, according to whether they align themselves with the politically motivated denialists; whether, as discriminating readers, they work to arrive at a credibly balanced reading of the phenomenon derived from an informed interpretation of competing accounts; or, whether, in more elementary human terms, they possess the constitutional fortitude and moral willingness to look the imminent fact of the extinction of all life on Earth full in the eye.[91] As John

---

90   Handley, "Climate," 334–335.

91   As one author states the case with prophetic insistence, "In just the past six centuries, the bipedal masters of the world have wrought such changes that we are now facing the end of life on this planet, either by choking to death in a smog of greenhouse gases or drowning in acid seas." Fittingly, Maslen concludes his jeremiad by impugning the present Australian Government as "leading a blind Australia stepping confidently into the

ISLAND LIFE AND WILD TIME

Broome argues, while there is a broad consensus among scientists and other observers that "man-made climate change is now in progress [...] and that there is overwhelming evidence that it is harmful," the phenomenon itself is often further obscured by corporate interests:

> The harm done by climate change is insidious. Its progress till now has been slow so that we scarcely notice it, and its biggest harms will not emerge for many decades yet. Voters do not find the benefits of slowing climate change easy to discern, and vested interests, particularly the oil industry, work hard to conceal them.[92]

Contributors to this continuing debate are numerous; and, for some, such as George Marshall, the answer to the refusal to *see* climate change does not concern the issue itself so much as the way it is communicated: "It must be something about the way the story of climate change has been constructed and communicated, the people who tell it, and how it has attached itself to their values."[93] Others respond more combatively. Paul Kingsnorth, in launching the project of "uncivilised art," calls upon concerned citizens to become "uncivilised" as an act of broadscale disobedience in the face of impending ecocide. We need, he argues, "uncivilised writing," for it alone "is determined to shift our worldview, not to feed into it [... It is] writing which unflinchingly stares us down, however uncomfortable that may be ... it is writing for outsiders."[94] As a writer and an environmental activist, Winton might well subscribe in spirit to Kingsnorth's program of literary resistance, at least insofar as this might contribute to new modes of communal understanding. And certainly, as an "islander" he identifies with Kingsnorth's "writing for outsiders," just as he identifies himself with fellow "outliers" such as the pioneering nineteenth-century botanist Georgiana Molloy, whose "most important contribution is a matter of sensibility," bringing to attention "riches" in this "strange new place" that "toiling settlers were to overlook for two centuries."[95] However, while sharing Kingsnorth's scepticism towards present-day environmentalism, Winton

---

abyss." Geoffrey Maslen, *Too Late: How We Lost the Battle With Climate Change* (Richmond, Vic: Hardie Grant Books, 2017): 105, 109.

92   John Broome, *Climate Matters: Ethics in a Warming World* (New York: w.w. Norton & Company, 2012): 6–7.

93   George Marshall, *Don't Even Think About It: Why Our Brains Are Wired to Ignore Climate Change* (New York: Bloomsbury, 2014): 21.

94   Paul Kingsnorth, *Confessions of a Recovering Environmentalist,* (London: Faber & Faber, 2017): 272–274.

95   Winton, *Island Home*, 205–206.

eschews more strident attitudes (Kingsnorth advocates a form of political anarchism), insisting that he is no "eco-warrior,"[96] in the same manner that he adopts a measuredly conservative stance concerning the phenomenon of climate change ("I don't know if anthropogenic climate change is real or not.")[97] Where such tempered scepticism might be construed as ineffectual by those who insist on more radical action in response to a broad-scale planetary emergency, Winton's continued commitment to the defence of the Ningaloo Reef in Western Australia countermands such views.[98]

Such activism is not so much secondary to, as an extension of, his principal manner of addressing environmental problems—his dedication to the use of the written word to appeal to readers' imaginations. If, as he contends, "to many of us country is no longer just real estate,"[99] such changes in perception, attitude and behaviour arrive as much through the persuasive powers of literature as through the more explicit activities of political protest. The governing conceit identified at the beginning of this chapter amply illustrates the point: "This country leans in on you. It weighs down hard. Like family. To my way of thinking, it *is* family."[100] In employing this governing metaphor of family as the rhetorical axis on which his argument and story turns, Winton renders, in his own imaginative and expressive terms the "profound lesson to be learnt from Aboriginal lawmen and women [which] is that the relationship to country is corporeal and familial. We need a more intimate acquaintance with the facts. We need to feel them in our bodies and claim them and belong to them as if they were kin."[101]

For some, this acknowledgement will be seen as a questionable Jindyworobak-like claim to white indigeneity, while others will see it as a gesture towards a transcendentalist parable of mystical rapture, or a primitivist's ode to animistic authenticity. For many Australian readers too, seasoned over generations to life on the long-settled eastern seaboard, Winton's insistence that Australia is "wild" might rankle, as when he writes: "for most of the twentieth century you could have argued that amongst peoples of developed nations this felt pressure [of geography]—the presence of wildness—was a default

---

96   Winton, *Island Home*, 106.

97   Westwood, "Prosperity," 4.

98   For a recent report on Winton's activism, see Adam Morton, "Exmouth Split Over Pipeline Factory Proposed for Gulf That Supports Ningaloo Reef," *Guardian* (October 14, 2018), https://www.theguardian.com/australia-news/2018/oct/14/exmouth-split-over-pipeline -factory-proposed-for-gulf-that-supports-ningaloo-reef.

99   Winton, *Island Home*, 206.

100   Winton, *Island Home*, 23.

101   Winton, *Island Home*, 229.

ISLAND LIFE AND WILD TIME

experience unique to Australians."[102] As well, some readers might question his confidence in speaking for all, or at least, the majority of Australians.

Still, the essential challenge to the reader remains. To see the land in familial terms is to understand one's relationship with country as one of profound responsibility: it "weighs down hard" for the very reason that the land supports us, and that *we* therefore rely on *it* in the most fundamental, mutually supportive sense. We are, it might be said, bound in belonging, fully and actively coextensive with country, for the environment makes claims upon us "that perhaps only family can,"[103] and from which a "new communal understanding" evolves.[104] The trope also generates further associations—of home, of kin, of intergenerational continuity; the family as source and sanctuary. Equally, since the great majority of humans are directly acquainted with families, the relationship is not self-evidently simple: *going home* is not necessarily comfortable or a matter of being welcomed—homecomings, as he puts it, very often entail "submitting to the uncomfortably familiar,"[105] but also to a regime of imposed obligation and expectation. Indeed, family dynamics can be a tormenting puzzle, and, unavoidably, involve dynamics of power: "like a hapless adult child," he reports submitting himself to this relationship—a necessary, even constitutive form of subordination to the larger organism or force. As well, "the land, like any parent, is large and strange and hard to read." It might be the home that the "songman Neil Murray reminds us [of]"[106]—Winton's reference to the second of the epigraphs he chooses—yet it will not admit of complacent inhabitants: "it's a mistake to equate familiarity with intimacy."[107] But the conceit is also arresting in more immediate sense as regards prevailing notions of identity—readers are compelled to reflect on the limits of the possessive individualism that so profoundly shapes life in the 21st century.

Nevertheless, the problem of seeing—of wanting and being able to really know what one sees—persists in all its intransigence, particularly in view of the continuing graphic reports of the attenuating ice-lands of the polar regions, and the corresponding, empirically verifiable inundation of numerous islands through rising sea levels. Why, then, in view of the undeniable evidence of climate change on the local and global scale, is decisive action commensurate with the scale of the problem seemingly impossible, most obviously

---

102   Winton, *Island Home*, 25.
103   Winton, *Island Home*, 110.
104   Winton, *Island Home*, 110.
105   Winton, *Island Home*, 23.
106   Winton, *Island Home*, 227.
107   Winton, *Island Home*, 167.

concerning the current Australian government's determined inaction on climate change policy? Certainly, the discerning observer might point to the high levels of communicative *activity* around the topic of climate change—witness at once the earnest and vocal protests from growing numbers of citizens networked across space and time, the rhetorical prevarications by many in positions of political power, and, most conspicuously, the active and determined chorus of denialism by influential others. This same observer might also add that the contribution of one more story to this congested field of globalised communication, be it a memoir from Tim Winton or another narrative by any number of other notable writers, simply inflames the irritation. And yet, that is precisely the challenge Winton meets in *Island Home*—the challenge of creating for the reader an imaginative space apart from the hyperactive din of contemporary communication, and through which one might be afforded other perspectives.

Winton's effort to call Australians home through the telling of his own story addresses the sense of psychic dispossession and disconnection that afflicts not only Australians but human beings at large. In urging all Australians to *be possessed of* country—to take the Earth more completely and reciprocally into their beings—he proposes less a solution in itself than a place, literally and figuratively, from which to work towards such a solution. As he argues in *Island Home*, it requires learning to see and thus know differently; to commence the process of outgrowing the legacy of early explorers and settlers as "possessive seers"—a legacy by which today so many are habituated to seeing "landscape as property, territory, tenement,"[108] and in doing so, to begin to look over and around habituated modes of knowing, and so beyond the accustomed categories by which humans place themselves presumptuously *on* the land. To insist that "[t]he encounter between ourselves and the land is a live concern"[109] is to insist we pay attention and be attentive: "our life in nature remains an open question and how we answer it will define not just our culture and politics but our very survival."[110] To begin to see, in the way that Winton wants us to see, is not only to nurture a deeper understanding of land and place but also to endorse the human potential for change. Not all readers will assent to his pantheistic belief in a sacred immanence; and not all will agree with his revisionist concept of patriotism by which one is now "as likely to revere the web of ecosystems that make a society possible [...] a true patriot is passionate about defending this—from threats within as much as without—as if the land were

---

108   Winton, *Island Home*, 198.
109   Winton, *Island Home*, 21.
110   Winton, *Island Home*, 21.

ISLAND LIFE AND WILD TIME

kith and kin."[111] Yet, in its finely tuned literary modulations, *Island Home* manages to avoid becoming a jeremiadic complaint against the collective state of habituated purblindness, and instead issues a persuasive appeal to the collective human capacity for greater imaginative possibility.

Works Cited

Barkham, Patrick. *Islander: A Journey Around Our Archipelago.* (London: Granta, 2018).

Berry, Wendell. "Think Little" in *A Continuous Harmony: Essays Cultural and Agricultural.* (Berkeley: Counterpoint Press, 2012).

Brooks, David. "Possession, Landscape, the *Unheimlich* and Lionel Fogarty's 'Weather Comes'." *Cordite Poetry Review* 87 (2017): 1–6, http://cordite.org.au/essays/possession-landscape-unheimlic/.

Broome, John. *Climate Matters: Ethics in a Warming World.* (New York: W.W. Norton, 2012).

Bryson, J. Scott. *The West Side of Any Mountain: Place, Space, and Ecopoetry.* (Iowa City: U of Iowa P, 2005).

Carter, Paul. *Groundtruthing: Explorations in A Creative Region.* (Crawley, WA: U of Western Australia P, 2014).

Cooke, Stuart. "The Case for Gularabulu by Paddy Roe." *The Conversation* (April 15, 2014), https://theconversation.com/the-case-for-gularabulu-by-paddy-roe-25320.

Davis, Stephen. "Bill Neidjie." *Gagudju Man: Bill Neidjie.* (Australia, JB Books, 2002): 6–12.

Davison, Liam. "Landscape with Words—Writing about Landscape." *Overland* 134 (1994): 6–10.

Evernden, Neil. "Beyond Ecology: Self, Place, and the Pathetic Fallacy" in *The Ecocriticsm Reader: Landmarks in Literary Ecology*, eds. Harold Fromm and Cheryll Glotfelty (Athens, GA: U of Georgia P, 1996): 92–105.

Falconer, Delia. "When a writer keeps watch on the beat of his heartland" in 'Spectrum', *Sydney Morning Herald* (October 24–5, 2015): 29.

Handley, George B. "Climate Change, Cosmology, and Poetry: The Case of Derek Walcott's *Omeros*" in *Global Ecologies and the Environmental Humanities: Postcolonial Approaches* eds. Elizabeth DeLoughrey, Jill Didur and Anthony Carrigan (New York: Routledge, 2016): 331–351.

Harris, Stephen. "Tim Winton's Dirt Music: Sounding Country/Re-siting Place." *Journal of the Association for the Study of Australian Literature*, 'Critical Soundings' 15.1 (2015): 1–13.

---

111   Winton, *Island Home*, 29.

Homer. *The Odyssey*, trans. Robert Fagles (New York: Penguin Classics, 1996).

Homer. *The Odyssey*, trans. Emily Wilson (New York: w.w. Norton & Company, 2018).

Kerr, Tamsin. "If I Say I Love My Place, What's with the Bags I've Packed?: The Cultural Changes Required by Landscape Memoir and Eco-Regionalism." *Art Monthly Australia* 214 (October 2008): 5–8.

Kerr, Tamsin. "An Ecoregional Story: Ross Annels's Regional Crafting of Landscape Memoir [online]." *Art Monthly Australia* 236 (December 2010–February 2011): 50–52, https://search-informit-com-au.ezproxy.une.edu.au/documentSummary;dn=6360 93354426452;res=IELLCC.

Kingsnorth, Paul. *Confessions of a Recovering Environmentalist* (London: Faber & Faber, 2017).

Lucashenko, Melissa. "I Pity the Poor Immigrant." *Journal of the Association of the Study of Australian Literature* 17.1 (2017): 1–10.

Lynch, Tom, Cheryll Glotfelty and Karla Armbruster, ed. *The Bioregional Imagination: Literature, Ecology, and Place*. (Athens: The University of Georgia Press, 2012).

Macfarlane, Robert. *The Wild Places*. (London: Granta, 2007).

Mahood, Kim. *Position Doubtful: Mapping Landscapes and Memories*. (Brunswick: Scribe Publications, 2016).

Malouf, David. "Making Consciousness and the created world one" in *William Robinson: The Transfigured Landscape*. (Brisbane: Queensland University of Technology and Piper Press, 2011).

Marshall, George. *Don't Even Think About It: Why our brains are wired to ignore climate change* (New York: Bloomsbury, 2014).

Maslen, Geoffrey. *Too Late: How We Lost the Battle With Climate Change* (Richmond, Vic: Hardie Grant Books, 2017).

Mateer, John. "Australia is not an Island." *Meanjin* 65.1 (2006): 89–93.

Mathews, Freya. "Ontopoetics in Australia" in *Sacred Australia: Post-Secular Considerations* ed. Makarand Paranjape (Melbourne: Clouds of Magellan, 2009): 253–270.

McCooey, David. "Poetry and Non-Fiction from 1950" in *The Literature of Australia; An Anthology* ed. Nicolas Jose. (Sydney: Allen & Unwin, 2009): 45–50.

McCredden, Lyn. "Intolerable significance: Tim Winton's Eyrie" in *Tim Winton: Critical Essays* eds. Lyn McCredden and Nathanael O'Reilly (Crawley: UWA Publishing, 2014, 306–329).

McCredden, Lyn. *The Fiction of Tim Winton: Earthed and Sacred*. (Sydney: Sydney UP, 2017).

Mead, Philip. (Mark Twain quoted in) "A Barren Place, and Fertile" in *An Introduction to Tasmania in the Literary Imagination*. (AustLit: Literature of Tasmania), https://www-austlit-edu-au.ezproxy.une.edu.au/austlit/page/9674597.

Morton, Adam. "Exmouth split over pipeline factory proposed for gulf that supports Ningaloo Reef." *Guardian* (October 14, 2018), https://www.theguardian.com/austra lia-news/2018/oct/14/exmouth-split-over-pipeline-factory-proposed-for-gulf-that -supports-ningaloo-reef.

Murray, Les. *Les Murray: Collected Poems.* (Carlton VIC: Black Inc Publishing, 2018).

Neidjie, Bill. *Gagudju Man: Bill Neidjie.* (Marleston, Australia: JB Books, 2002).

Paranjape, Makarand, ed. *Sacred Australia: Post-Secular Considerations.* (Thornbury, Vic: Clouds of Magellan, 2009).

Pryor, Melanie. "Eco-Autobiography: Writing Self through Place" in *Auto/biography Studies* 32:3 (25 April 2017): 391–393.

Rose, Deborah Bird. "Arts of Flow: Poetics of 'fit' in Aboriginal Australia," in *Dialectical Anthropology* 38 (2014): 431–445.

Shell, Marc. *Islandology: Geography, Rhetoric, Politics* (Stanford: Stanford UP, 2014).

Smith, Daniel B. (Glenn Albrecht quoted in) "Is there an Ecological Unconscious?" *New York Times Magazine* (January 27, 2010).

Smith, Jos. *The New Nature Writing: Rethinking the Literature of Place* (London: Bloomsbury Academic, 2017).

Tennyson, Alfred Lord. "The Lotos-Eaters," in *Victorian Poetry: An Annotated Anthology*, ed. Francis O'Gorman (Oxford: Blackwell Publishing, 2004).

Tredinnick, Mark. *The Land's Wild Music: Encounters with Barry Lopez, Peter Mathiessen, Terry Tempest Williams, and James Galvin* (San Antonio, Texas: Trinity University, 2005).

Tredinnick, Mark. *The Blue Plateau: A Landscape Memoir* (St Lucia: U of Queensland P, 2009).

Watts, Madeleine. "Contending with a Blank Page: On Writing, Wealth and Being a West Coaster." *Griffith Review* 47 (2015): 105–115.

Westwood, Matthew. "Prosperity and a Secure Future for Our Kids Has a Price: Winton." *The Australian* (May 20, 2011), http://search.proquest.com.ezproxy.une.edu.au/docv iew/867607991?accountid=17.

Winton, Tim. "Strange Passion: A Landscape Memoir" in *Down to Earth: Australian Landscapes*, ed. Richard Woldendorp, VII–XXXII. (North Fremantle: Fremantle Arts Centre Press, 1999).

Winton, Tim. *Dirt Music.* (Sydney: Picador, 2002).

Winton, Tim. *The Land's Edge: A Coastal Memoir.* (Camberwell (Vic.): Hamish Hamilton Penguin Books, 2010).

Winton, Tim. "When the Tide Turns." *Sydney Morning Herald* (April 14, 2012): 34–36.

Winton, Tim. *Island Home: A Landscape Memoir.* (Penguin Australia: Hamish Hamilton, 2015).

CHAPTER 6

Islands Within Islands

Climate Change and the Deep Time Narratives of the Southern Beech

John C. Ryan

The southland beech sleeps alone,
very vertical, very poor, very frazzled,
very decisive in the pure meadow
with its shabby down-and-outer's suit
and its head full of solemn stars.

from "Botany," PABLO NERUDA[1]

∴

From Point Lookout, ridges shrouded in shadow direct my gaze towards the Pacific Ocean glinting fifty miles to the east. This is New England National Park at the edge of the Northern Tablelands plateau of New South Wales. The park lies within the Gondwana Rainforests of Australia—a World Heritage-listed area preserving vestiges of the rainforest that blanketed the landscape more than eighty-million years ago.[2] I'm here to see the Antarctic beeches of the escarpment just below the five-thousand-foot summit. Bearing an extensive fossil and pollen record, the species emerged during the Late Cretaceous when Antarctica, South America, New Zealand and Australia formed a supercontinent.[3] In the 1950s, conservationist Phillip Wright characterised these very trees as "an anachronism" and understood that "some of a similar species remain in

---

1 Pablo Neruda, *The Poetry of Pablo Neruda*, ed. Ilan Stavans (New York: Farrar, Straus and Giroux, 2003): 254, ll. 49–53. The poem was translated by Jack Schmitt and originally published in *Canto General* in 1950.

2 See, for example, Roger Kitching, Richard Braithwaite and Janet Cavanaugh, eds., *Remnants of Gondwana: A Natural and Social History of the Gondwana Rainforests of Australia* (Baulkham Hills, NSW: Surrey Beatty & Sons, 2010).

3 Robert Hill and Gregory Jordan, "The Evolutionary History of *Nothofagus* (Nothofagaceae)," *Australian Systematic Botany* 6.2 (1993): 111–126. The genus *Nothofagus* appeared 83-million years ago, but individual trees can be 500–1000 years old.

© KONINKLIJKE BRILL NV, LEIDEN, 2022 | DOI:10.1163/9789004514164_007

Patagonia."[4] Following the walking track, I drop into an island-like habitat of gnarled beeches cloaked thickly in mosses, lichen and orchids. Undisturbed by human presence, a lyrebird struts in my direction then swerves upslope. At Weeping Rock, rainwater trickles from a boulder crevice and collects in a small, opaque pool. The temperature dips, and dusk light suffuses the primeval forest canopy. The place feels like an island within an island—the Tablelands—within the "island continent" of Australia.[5]

Aesthetic enchantment, however, is only one mode of encountering the Gondwanan relics at Point Lookout. As scholars in the postcolonial environmental humanities suggest—especially those concerned with climate change—deep time is inherently complex in its affective dimensions and historical registers.[6] Intersectional temporalities—human and more-than-human; of evolutionary, geological, cultural and organismic *times*—constitute place and our perception of it. My experience of time at Point Lookout indeed was "productive, homely and wondrous as well as unsettling, uncanny and dangerous."[7] Literary narratives, moreover, mediated this experience, allowing me to become aware in advance of Point Lookout and, specifically, the colonial violence enacted against Aboriginal people there. Phillip Wright's daughter, poet-activist Judith Wright, spent her early years at nearby Wallamumbi Station. Her family often camped at Point Lookout.[8] In *Born of the Conquerors*, she refers to an escarpment across the valley from the Point where "long ago," her father told her, "the white settlers of that region of the tableland had driven the Aborigines over its cliffs, as reprisal for the spearing of their cattle."[9]

---

4   Phillip A. Wright, "More Amenities for Visitors to New England National Park," *The Armidale Express* (October 14, 1959): 1.

5   Writers often characterise Australia as an "island continent" as, for instance, in geographer Grenfell Price's study *Island Continent: Aspects of the Historical Geography of Australia and Its Territories* (Sydney: Angus and Robertson, 1972).

6   Dipesh Chakrabarty, "Anthropocene Time," *History and Theory* 57.1 (2018): 5–32; Elizabeth DeLoughrey, Jill Didur and Anthony Carrigan, "Introduction: A Postcolonial Environmental Humanities" in *Global Ecologies and the Environmental Humanities: Postcolonial Approaches*, eds. Elizabeth DeLoughrey, Jill Didur and Anthony Carrigan (New York: Routledge, 2015): 1–32; Franklin Ginn, Michelle Bastian, David Farrier and Jeremy Kidwell, "Introduction: Unexpected Encounters with Deep Time," *Environmental Humanities* 10.1 (2018): 213–225; and Ariel Salleh, "The Anthropocene: Thinking in 'Deep Geological Time' or Deep Libidinal Time?," *International Critical Thought* 6.3 (2016): 422–433.

7   Ginn et al., "Introduction," 223.

8   Veronica Brady, *South of My Days: A Biography of Judith Wright* (Pymble, NSW: Angus & Robertson, 1998).

9   Judith Wright, *Born of the Conquerors: Selected Essays* (Canberra: Aboriginal Studies Press, 1991): 30.

Although an enchanting place for Judith Wright, there remained "a darkness in it apart from the depths of the rainforest."[10] Her poem "Nigger's Leap: New England" confronts the trauma that time, history and perception can conceal: "Night floods us suddenly as history / that has sunk many islands in its good time."[11]

Orienting myself from Point Lookout, I develop in this chapter a Gondwanan approach to the postcolonial environmental humanities through the deep time narratives of the southern beech (botanical genus *Nothofagus*).[12] Of increasing interest to scholars of climate change, deep time narratives "engage the different registers of deep time as it presents itself" in places, things and lives.[13] These kinds of texts construe deep time "not as distant and abstract but as an intimate and compelling element woven into our everyday lives."[14] Inflected by the Anthropocene, my reading of beech narratives pivots on a dual sense of vulnerability and resilience—of the trees as enduring survivors of past climatic disruptions and potential casualties of anthropogenic climate change. On the one hand, significant climatic perturbations associated with the break-up of Gondwana during the Cenozoic era fractured the distribution of nothofagus.[15] The occurrence of living members of the genus in Argentina, Chile, New Zealand, Australia, New Caledonia and New Guinea—along with the discovery of beech fossils in Antarctica[16]—puzzled early biogeographers, including Charles Darwin and Joseph Hooker,[17] and led to the theorisation of a "land connection" between South America and Oceania.[18] On the other hand, ecologists predict that, in response to climate disturbance, the extent

---

10 Wright, *Born of the Conquerors*, 30.

11 Judith Wright, *The Moving Image: Poems* (Melbourne: Meanjin Press, 1946): 23, ll. 26–27. Graham Huggan and Helen Tiffin discuss Wright's poem in *Postcolonial Ecocriticism: Literature, Animals, Environment* (London: Routledge, 2010): 92.

12 I will refer to the tree as either "beech," "southern beech" or "nothofagus."

13 Ginn et al., "Introduction," 216.

14 Ginn et al., "Introduction," 223.

15 Thomas Veblen, Robert Hill and Jennifer Read, "Introduction: Themes and Concepts in the Study of *Nothofagus* Forests" in *The Ecology and Biogeography of Nothofagus Forests*, eds. Thomas Veblen, Robert Hill and Jennifer Read (New Haven, CT: Yale UP, 1996): 6.

16 Nothofagus fossils have been located at McMurdo Sound in the Ross Sea and the Antarctic Peninsula (Wardle 1984): 24.

17 Charles Darwin, *Narrative of the Surveying Voyages of His Majesty's Ships Adventure and Beagle, Between the Years 1826 and 1836: Volume 3*, ed. Robert Fitzroy (London: Henry Colburn, 1839); Joseph Hooker, *The Botany of the Antarctic Voyage of H.M. Discovery Ships Erebus and Terror in the Years 1839–1843* (London: Reeve Brothers, 1844).

18 Leonard Rodway, "Botanic Evidence in Favour of Land Connection Between Fuegia and Tasmania During the Present Floristic Epoch," *Papers and Proceedings of the Royal Society of Tasmania* (1914): 32.

of cool-temperate beech rainforest will continue to decline in Australia and elsewhere.[19]

Nothofagus narratives call upon readers to consider deep time not as an abstract and homogenous designation but, instead, as an embodied and plural phenomenon encompassing deep evolutionary (species), deep geological (Gondwanan), deep cultural (Indigenous), deep organismic (arboreal) and other temporalities. Grasping deep time as a heterogeneity through literary narratives, I maintain, is essential to approaching the Anthropocene from interdisciplinary perspectives. As scholars point out, literature has the potential to intervene in climate change metanarratives—often dominated by scientist or techno-rationalist discourses—by restoring attention to the affective, corporeal, relational and more-than-human elements of environmental catastrophe.[20] Ecocritic Ursula Heise suggests that "the aesthetic transformation of the real has a particular potential for reshaping the individual and collective ecosocial imaginary."[21] Framing climate change according to its temporal registers, I focus on poetry that narrativises nothofagus. Poets as diverse as James K. Baxter and Ruth Dallas (New Zealand), Pablo Neruda and Gabriela Mistral (Chile) and Peter Kama Kerpi and Steven Edmund Winduo (Papua New Guinea) have written about the beeches of their respective parts of the old supercontinent. Placing nothofagus at the centre of my analysis, furthermore, prompts Gondwanan consciousness—or what could be called "thinking [super]continental"[22]—as a framework for the postcolonial environmental humanities. This arboreal instantiation of "comparative environmental

---

19   See, for example, Claudia Mansilla, Robert McCulloch and Flavia Morello, "The Vulnerability of the *Nothofagus* Forest-Steppe Ecotone to Climate Change: Palaeoecological Evidence from Tierra del Fuego (~53°S)," *Palaeogeography, Palaeoclimatology, Palaeoecology* 508 (2018): 59–70.

20   DeLoughrey et al., "Introduction"; Elizabeth DeLoughrey and George B. Handley, "Introduction: Toward an Aesthetics of the Earth" in *Postcolonial Ecologies: Literatures of the Environment*, eds. Elizabeth DeLoughrey and George B. Handley (New York: Oxford UP, 2011): 3–41; George B. Handley, "Climate Change, Cosmology, and Poetry: The Case of Derek Walcott's Omeros" in *Global Ecologies and the Environmental Humanities: Postcolonial Approaches*, eds. Elizabeth DeLoughrey, Jill Didur and Anthony Carrigan (New York: Routledge, 2015): 333–351; and Bonnie Roos and Alex Hunt, "Introduction: Narratives of Survival, Sustainability, and Justice" in *Postcolonial Green: Environmental Politics and World Narratives*, eds. Bonnie Roos and Alex Hunt (Charlottesville, VA: U of Virgina P, 2010): 1–13.

21   Ursula Heise, "Afterword: Postcolonial Ecocriticism and the Question of Literature" in *Postcolonial Green: Environmental Politics and World Narratives*, eds. Bonnie Roos and Alex Hunt (Charlottesville, VA: U of Virginia P, 2010): 258.

22   Tom Lynch, Susan Naramore Maher, Drucilla Wall and O. Alan Weltzien, eds., *Thinking Continental: Writing the Planet One Place at a Time* (Lincoln, NB: U of Nebraska P, 2017).

criticism" aims to decentre the primacy of geopolitics—of states, districts, territories, nations—by provoking "a better understanding of the transnational and transtemporal processes" of the Anthropocene.[23] Before proceeding, however, it is crucial to consider the interconnections between southern beech trees, deep time, climate change, the environmental humanities and the poets—legibly postcolonial and otherwise—who have taken an interest in these "Gondwanan relics."[24]

1 The Southern Beech, Deep Time and Climate Change

Coveted, cleared, collected, cultivated, classified, named and renamed, plants—from herbs and orchids to shrubs and trees—are the more-than-human subjects of the (neo)colonialist drive to order the natural world for reasons of intellectual advance, economic aggrandisement and imperial growth. Historians have developed critiques of botanical science as an instrument of colonisation in which the procurement of plant specimens paralleled the spread of empire.[25] As with other plants that galvanised colonial desire and were transformed into global commodities, the southern beech became an imperial subject, in part, through the process of its naming. The term *beech* itself is a catachresis inscribing the imposition of northern botanical ideas on the southern flora. In the early-nineteenth century, naturalists assigned the tree to the Fagaceae family due to its resemblance to the beeches of the Northern Hemisphere. In the 1850s, however, botanist Carl Ludwig Blume proposed the genus name *Nothofagus*—or "false beech"—to indicate those trees with a disjunctive distribution from the New Guinea Highlands and New Caledonia to Southeastern Australia and Tierra del Fuego.[26] Around this time, conflicting theories regarding the scattered occurrence of nothofagus coincided with the postulation of the Gondwana supercontinent by geologists. In the 1850s, the botanist-explorer Joseph Hooker speculated about "the possibility of the

---

23 Karen Thornber, "Literature, Asia, and the Anthropocene: Possibilities for Asian Studies and the Environmental Humanities," *Journal of Asian Studies* 73.4 (2014): 998.

24 Quentin Chester, "Early Warning (Antarctic Beech Trees at Mount Warning, New South Wales)," *Australian Geographic* 91 (Jul–Sep 2008): 47.

25 See, for example, David Philip Miller and Peter Hanns Reill, eds., *Visions of Empire: Voyages, Botany and Representations of Nature* (Cambridge, UK: Cambridge UP, 1996).

26 Veblen et al., "Introduction," 1. Of the thirty-four species of nothofagus, nine occur in Chile and Argentina, three in New Zealand, three in Australia, and nineteen in New Guinea and New Caledonia. See Martyn Rix and Andy Jackson, "Plate 489. *Nothofagus moorei* Fagaceae," *Curtis's Botanical Magazine* 21.1 (2004): 65.

ISLANDS WITHIN ISLANDS

plants of the Southern Ocean being the remains of a flora that had once spread over a *larger and more continuous tract of land* than now exists in that ocean."[27]

The southern beech has been implicated with deep time almost since the emergence of the concept. In other words, nothofagus is a deep time agent; it helps us to think about, and come into contact with, the phenomenon of deep time. In 1785, at a meeting of the Royal Society of Edinburgh, geologist James Hutton proposed deep, or geological, time after observing soil erosion patterns in Scotland.[28] Hutton determined that spatial arrangements between rock layers "translated into *temporal relations* and implied a long Earth history."[29] Although a controversial notion that defied the geo-theological norms of the late-eighteenth century, deep time was embraced by Charles Lyell. The geologist chastised traditionalists who would claim that "Calabria 'rose like an exhalation' from the deep, after the manner of Milton's Pandemonium."[30] Such an antiquated perspective on Earth history, for Lyell, dismissed "that peculiar removing force required to form a regular system of deep and wide valleys; for *time*, which they are so unwilling to assume, is essential to the operation."[31] In the early 1980s, the American writer John McPhee popularised the phrase in *Basin and Range*. McPhee acknowledges the incomprehensibility of deep time—its "obscure dimensions"—constituted by geological periods so vast that "each has acquired its own internal time scale."[32] More recently, with regard to the Anthropocene as the proposed epoch in which humankind has become a planetary agent, palaeobiologist Jan Zalasiewicz has pointed to "a peculiarity of geological time, which is that, at heart, it is simply time—albeit in very large amounts."[33] According to writers since Hutton, then, deep time is peculiar, obscure, unfathomable and implicated with the geological.

---

27   Joseph Hooker, "Introductory Essay" in *The Botany of the Antarctic Voyage of H.M. Discovery Ships, Erebus and Terror, in the Years 1853–55. II. Flora Novae Zelandiae* (London: Reeve Bros, 1853): 21, emphasis added.

28   Michael Northcott, "Eschatology in the Anthropocene: From the *Chronos* of Deep Time to the *Kairos* of the Age of the Humans" in *The Anthropocene and the Global Environmental Crisis: Rethinking Modernity in a New Epoch*, eds. Clive Hamilton, Christophe Bonneuil and François Gemenne (London: Routledge, 2015): 100.

29   E-an Zen, "What Is Deep Time and Why Should Anyone Care?" *Journal of Geoscience Education* 49.1 (2001): 5, italics original.

30   Charles Lyell, *Principles of Geology; or, The Modern Changes of the Earth and its Inhabitants Considered as Illustrative of Geology*, 7th ed (London: John Murray, 1847): 467.

31   Lyell, *Principles of Geology*, 467, emphasis original.

32   John McPhee, *Basin and Range* (New York: Farrar, Straus and Giroux, 1982): 231.

33   Jan Zalasiewicz, "The Extraordinary Strata of the Anthropocene" in *Environmental Humanities: Voices from the Anthropocene*, eds. Serpil Oppermann and Serenella Iovino (London: Rowman & Littlefield, 2017): 124.

Nonetheless, the consideration of geological time is essential to thinking critically about "the depth of the predicament that confronts humans today."[34] Spatiotemporally far-reaching, climate change and the Anthropocene are much more than the calamitous, decorporealised, capitalism-derived "hyperobjects" of post-nineteenth-century industrial provenance.[35] They impact everyday lives. The problem is that the radically extensive nature of deep temporality flummoxes the capacity of most people to cognise—and, indeed, to feel and sense—time through immense stretches of tens of thousands of years. Despite its contested standing in the scientific community, alongside numerous calls by scholars for alternate names, such as the Capitalocene, the Anthropocene does signify the challenge of "confronting vast timescales"[36] and "conceiving of the immemorial plotting of geology and life as intermingled with human activities over time spans that transcend the limited scope of our mind's eye."[37] The effect of the Anthropocene frame can be at once consciousness-expanding and mind-boggling as it "puts the present in contact with distant times beyond the scope of human experience or even imagining," and accordingly confounds one's temporal orientation.[38] Recognising that the Anthropocene involves temporal awareness yet, paradoxically, stymies human agency with its immense abstractedness, sociologist Ariel Salleh proposes "thinking in deep affective time" as a means "to articulate flows—between ideas and feelings, ecosystems and bodies."[39] Salleh articulates an ecofeminist stance that values the "embodied libidinal energies" situating humans *as* nature and, hence, resisting the subject-object, mind-body and people-environment binaries underlying the global climate crisis.[40]

Deep time resonates for scholars in the postcolonial environmental humanities interested in "setting environmental change in its deep-time context."[41] The field seeks to recuperate "the alterity of both history *and* nature, without reducing either to the other."[42] Scholars concur that anthropogenic climate

---

34 Chakrabarty, "Anthropocene Time," 6.

35 Tim Morton, *Hyperobjects: Philosophy and Ecology After the End of the World* (Minneapolis, MN: U of Minnesota P, 2013).

36 Ginn et al., "Introduction," 216.

37 Serpil Oppermann and Serenella Iovino, "Introduction: The Environmental Humanities and the Challenges of the Anthropocene" in *Environmental Humanities: Voices from the Anthropocene*, eds. Serpil Oppermann and Serenella Iovino (London: Rowman & Littlefield, 2017): 13.

38 Ginn et al., "Introduction," 214.

39 Salleh, "The Anthropocene," 423.

40 Salleh, "The Anthropocene," 422.

41 Jeremy Davies, *The Birth of the Anthropocene* (Oakland, CA: U of California P, 2016): 23.

42 DeLoughrey and Handley, "Introduction," 4, emphasis original.

change reconfigures conceptions of time.[43] Dipesh Chakrabarty contends that "to call human beings geological agents is to *scale up* our imagination of the human."[44] In a subsequent essay, moreover, Chakrabarty stresses the need to embrace two divergent time scales, Earth history and world history, or "tens of millions of years" in contrast to "five hundred years at most that can be said to constitute the history of capitalism."[45] Deep temporal events "outscale our very human sense of time" and remain "vast and incomprehensible in terms of the concerns of human history."[46] Nevertheless, Chakrabarty concedes, geological time is "available to our cognitive and affective faculties" and the current epoch occasions the possibility of "inhabiting these two presents at the same time."[47] Absent from his relatively sanguine account of Anthropocene temporality, however, is an elaboration of precisely *how*—through what means—deep time becomes accessible.

Envisioning time beyond the human purview and scaling up our imagination require the language for doing so. Poetic narratives, I maintain, offer one medium for negotiating Chakrabarty's "two presents"—or, apropos multiple temporal scales, more than two—and for rendering deep time *sensible*. Indeed, attention to narrative facilitates understanding of climate crisis.[48] The field of postcolonial environmental humanities interprets ecological change through "narratives, histories and material practices of colonialism and globalization."[49] Deep time narratives intersect directly or indirectly—in material-embodied and metaphorical-symbolic ways—with (neo)colonial legacies.[50] Such narratives place critiques of imperialism in contexts "of planetary history and futures" while disclosing the limits of language, representation and subjectivity.[51] Notwithstanding its uncanniness and enormity, deep time can pull "at us as it manifests through places, objects or affective atmospheres."[52] Although theorists like Chakrabarty and Zalasiewicz privilege geological forces, deep time can be encountered cognitively and affectively through the living

---

43   DeLoughrey et al., "Introduction," 12.

44   Dipesh Chakrabarty, "The Climate of History: Four Theses," *Critical Inquiry* 35.2 (2009): 206.

45   Chakrabarty, "Anthropocene Time," 6.

46   Chakrabarty, "Anthropocene Time," 6, 25.

47   Chakrabarty, "Anthropocene Time," 25, 30.

48   DeLoughrey et al., "Introduction," 13.

49   DeLoughrey et al., "Introduction," 2.

50   DeLoughrey et al., "Introduction," 5. I use the term "(neo)colonial" to denote a continuum of imperialist practices from colonial to postcolonial times.

51   Ginn et al., "Introduction," 217.

52   Ginn et al., "Introduction," 217.

arboreal relics of Gondwana. Yet the deep time of nothofagus, I put forward, is a "hetero-temporality" constituted by the evolutionary time of its genus, the geological time of Gondwana, the cultural time(s) of Indigenous peoples and the organismic time of long-lived individual tree-subjects themselves.[53]

Poetic narratives of the beech set the hetero-temporality of the tree in sharp relief to the short-lived histories of capitalism, imperialism, technocracy and globalisation. Inhering within these narratives and my interpretation of them, moreover, is a sense of nothofagus as both a survivor of past climatic disturbance and a potential casualty of anthropogenic climate change. The dual inflection—of nothofagus as Gondwanan endurer and Anthropocene fatality—underlies my approach to the poetic narratives of these trees. Although serving as buffers,[54] forests weakened by ecological disturbance become acutely susceptible to climate change. This is so for the beech, affected by logging, grazing, pollution, fire and disease in combination with genetic isolation and myriad other factors that have over time compromised its resilience.[55] Drawn from different literary traditions, the beech poems I trace here indicate a grappling with the seemingly unplumbable scale of deep time. Yet, in its embodiment of multiple temporalities—evolutionary, geological, cultural, organismic—the tree renders deep time palpable or "available to our cognitive and affective faculties."[56] The hetero-temporality of the beech supplies a counterforce to the (neo)colonial histories that drive the subjugation of the tree, its ecological community and the Indigenous cultures associated with both.

A caveat: some of the poets I have selected are not typically characterised by literary critics as "postcolonial"—except, for instance, Pablo Neruda in Chile and Steven Edmund Winduo in Papua New Guinea. What's more, most texts address neither climate change nor the Anthropocene explicitly. Nearly all of the poems were written well before climate change entered public discourse. The evocation of nothofagus in these works, nevertheless, proffers a means for thinking about the increasingly complex relationship between deep time, climate change, more-than-human life and postcolonial concerns. Indeed, the postcolonial environmental humanities responds "to ongoing political and

---

53   I borrow the term "hetero-temporal" from Michael Marder to refer to the temporalities of plant life and to argue against a view of time as a monologic phenomenon. See, *Plant-Thinking: A Philosophy of Vegetal Life* (New York: Columbia UP, 2013): 95.

54   The "carbon sink" metaphor is often invoked in the scientific literature. See, for example, Colin A.G. Hunt, *Carbon Sinks and Climate Change: Forests in the Fight Against Global Warming* (Cheltenham, UK: Edward Elgar, 2009).

55   Veblen et al., "Introduction," 8.

56   Chakrabarty, "Anthropocene Time," 25.

ISLANDS WITHIN ISLANDS

ecological problems and to diverse kinds of texts."[57] In my curation of narratives, I follow Bonnie Roos and Alex Hunt who claim that any text "can profitably be read from a postcolonial green perspective."[58]

2 "To Have Been Born Among Them:" New Zealand Beech Narratives

In the opening line of a poem drafted in 1949, Dunedin-born poet James K. Baxter (1926–72) alludes to the beech trees that form a significant part of Aotearoa/New Zealand forests, especially in subalpine areas.[59] Much of Baxter's early verse responds to the South Island, including its nothofagus-dominated environments.[60] "Poem in the Matukituki Valley" thus begins:

> Some few yards from the hut the standing beeches
> Let fall their dead limbs, overgrown
> With feathered moss and filigree of bracken.
> The rotted wood splits clean and hard
> Close-grained to the driven axe, with sound of water
> Sibilant falling and high nested birds.[61]

Embodied in the moss and bracken overgrowth, the deep organismic time of the "standing beeches" imbricates with the geological time of Matukituki yet abrades against the (neo)colonial temporalities of the "driven axe" and, in the second stanza, the "wild scrub cattle" that have "acclimatized" to Aotearoa.[62] The depiction of Anglo-European settlers, or Pākehā, as estranged from the Gondwanan landscape underscores, as Trevor James observes, "the limitations of language against the vast scale of the natural order."[63]

---

57   Roos and Hunt, "Introduction," 9.
58   Roos and Hunt, "Introduction," 9.
59   Tall forests of silver, mountain and red beech dominate the glacier-fed Matukituki River Valley connecting Mount Aspiring and Lake Wanaka. John Wardle, *The New Zealand Beeches: Ecology, Utilisation and Management* (Christchurch, NZ: New Zealand Forest Service, 1984): 21, 435.
60   Trevor James, " 'Pitched at the Farthest Edge': Religious Presence and the Landscape in Contemporary New Zealand Poetry" in *Mapping the Sacred: Religion, Geography and Postcolonial Literatures*, eds. Jamie Scott and Paul Simpson-Housley (Amsterdam: Rodopi, 2001): 140.
61   James K. Baxter, *Collected Poems of James K. Baxter*, ed. J.E. Weir (Wellington, NZ: Oxford UP, 1979): 86, ll., 1–6.
62   Baxter, *Collected*, l., 10.
63   James, "Pitched," 142.

This friction between language and timescales—those of the terrain, the beech trees and the settlers—intensifies as the final lines of the narrative shift awareness from the "eternal" valley towards those urbanised settings:

Where man may live, and no wild trespass
Of what's eternal shake his grave of time.[64]

To apprehend deep time as hetero-temporality in Baxter's poem, however, is to understand Matukituki as *ipukarea* (ancestral homeland) and the "standing beeches" as ontologically salient for Māori people. Despite the manifestation— the "grave"—of colonial time that conflicts with, and obscures, other temporalities, the valley endures as a Māori space—as *ipukarea*.[65] Yet the Indigeneity of Matukituki is rendered opaque to Pākehā, in part, by the pre-European names of peaks recast in "a sailor's language and a mountaineer's" as Stargazer and Moonraker.[66] Mediated by intersecting temporalities the postcolonial-environmental inflections of Baxter's narrative become more exigent when we consider the role of climate change in diminishing the glaciers of New Zealand, altering the ecological character of the Matukituki and fracturing the Indigenous traditions attached to place.[67]

Baxter's poem suggests that decolonising Aotearoa and its Gondwanan forests begins with enhanced attention to Māori names, practices and ways of being. Ethnographer Elsdon Best's *Forest Lore of the Māori* lists *tawai* as the "generic name for several species of *Fagus* [*Nothofagus*]" and, moreover, *kiore tawai* for the now-extinct native rats that fed on beech mast and, in turn, were consumed by people as a staple food.[68] Māori ascribed remarkable

---

64   Baxter, *Collected*, 87, ll. 53–54.
65   Shortly before his death in 1972, Baxter founded a commune, based on Māori and Catholic beliefs, in the settlement of Jerusalem, or Hiruhārama, near the Whanganui River on the North Island. The river figures prominently in his late poetry as a spirit or *taniwha*. See, Gregory O'Brien, "Some Remarks on Poetry and the Environment in Aotearoa/New Zealand," *Poetry* 211.5 (2018): 476–477, 480.
66   Baxter, *Collected*, 86, l., 30.
67   David Gawith, Daniel Kingston and Hilary McMillan, "The Effects of Climate Change on Runoff in the Lindis and Matukituki Catchments, Otago, New Zealand," *Journal of Hydrology* (NZ) 51.2 (2012): 121–135.
68   Elsdon Best, *Forest Lore of the Maori: With Methods of Snaring, Trapping and Preserving Birds and Rats, Uses of Berries, Roots, Fern-Root and Forest Products, with Mythological Notes on Origins, Karakia Used Etc.* (Wellington, NZ: E.C. Keating, Government Printer, 1977): 360, original edition 1942. Early botanists differentiated between *tawai* (*N. fusca* and *N. menziesii*) and *tawairauriki* (*N. solandri*). See, Thomas Frederic Cheeseman, *Manual of the New Zealand Flora* (Wellington, NZ: John Mackay, Government Printer, 1906): 1107.

ISLANDS WITHIN ISLANDS

swimming powers to the rats because of their fondness for beech pollen or *nehu*. In the 1890s, Hori Ropiha, a Māori leader from Waipawa on the North Island, explained that, when beech flowers and nuts were profuse, rats were also abundant:

> When the *tawai* blossomed in such a manner then the pollen of the blossoms was carried by streams to the ocean, and drifted far across the great ocean, even to Hawaiki [the traditional Māori place of origin]. It was then that the multitude of rats of that land swam hither across the Great Ocean of Kiwa, even so that the ocean was covered with their myriads, and, as they swam hitherward, they fed on the pollen of the beech, even until they arrived on these shores, and so, on that account, they were in good condition when they so arrived.[69]

In Hori Ropiha's account, deep cultural memory synchronises the ecological transactions of the beech—pollination, flowering, fruiting—with the movement of the mammal between material and immaterial islands. Old, gnarled beech trees, moreover, offered sources of water during long overland trips. In 1862, with the help of his Māori guide Taru, missionary Basil Taylor secured water in the cavity of a tree on the Taumatamahoe Track or *Taumata Mahoe*. Taru "pointed to a wide spreading beech tree called Onerua and said 'There is water' [...] it is a well-known drinking place for the thirsty wayfarer."[70]

The procurement of water from the beech embodies the entanglement of temporal agents and scales: of the human who drinks, of the tree that sequesters water in limbs sculpted by time, of the culture that holds the memory of Onerua and of the Gondwanan landscape through which the wayfarers pass and which articulates its own story. The hetero-temporal approach to narrative I am pointing to here—one which resists the colonial appropriation of time—can unveil the complex effects of climatic disturbance on place, culture, communities and more-than-human life. Nevertheless, the instrumentalisation of the tree—predicated partly on the homogenisation of time—renders these temporal depths opaque. Published by Thomas Frederic Cheeseman in 1906, one year before New Zealand's independence from the Crown, *Manual of New Zealand Flora* is indicative of the reductionism that characterises colonial-era responses to southern beeches. He described the wood of the endemic

---

69   Quoted in Best, *Forest Lore*, 361–362.

70   Quoted in Pete McDonald, *Foot-tracks in New Zealand: Origins, Access Issues and Recent Developments* (2011), https://petemcdonald.co/ft.pdf.

silver beech as "not durable when exposed to the weather. It has been recommended for furniture, tubs and buckets, wine-casks, &c., but is not largely used at the present time."[71] During the 1970s, however, the commoditisation of old-growth beech signalled by Cheeseman began to change with the signing of the Maruia Declaration that phased out the clear-felling of South Island native forests.[72]

Hetero-temporality also offers a framework for thinking about nothofagus and climate change in two poems by Ruth Dallas. A novelist and poet, Dallas was born in Invercargill in 1919 and lived in Dunedin until her passing in 2008. As with the verse of Baxter, her poetry displays an affinity for the South Island environment and its primordial trees.[73] "Entering Beech Forest" and "Under Beech Trees" come from her 1953 collection *Country Road*. The opening stanzas of the first poem filiate narrator and forest through intercorporeal alignments of roots, leaves, hands and fingers. An immersive sense of consanguinity allows deep time to become "available to our cognitive and affective faculties"[74] through human-tree correspondences:

> So much has happened here in root and sap
> The space between the veins of hands and leaves
> Has widened; trees from childhood only hinder.
> To have been born among them, to have known
> No other trees perhaps; coming with blossoms
> Breaking from your fingers it is not easy.[75]

Filiation with the beeches—the speaker was "born among them"—prompts somatic apprehension of "the silence that waits for you to go."[76] The speechless presence of the beech forest, nevertheless, speaks of a remembrance of Gondwana and prehistoric climate changes. These temporal threads coalesce in the image of the leaf, notably smaller in nothofagus than in its northern counterparts:

---

71   Cheeseman, *Manual*, 641.

72   Theodore Catton, "A Short History of the New Zealand National Park System" in *National Parks Beyond the Nation: Global Perspectives on 'America's Best Idea'*, eds. Adrian Howkins, Jared Orsi and Mark Fiege (Norman, OK: U of Oklahoma P, 2016): 80.

73   Betty Gilderdale, "Dallas, Ruth (1919–)" in *Encyclopedia of Post-Colonial Literatures in English*, eds. Eugene Benson and L.W. Conolly (London: Routledge, 2005): 331.

74   Chakrabarty, "Anthropocene Time," 25.

75   Ruth Dallas, *Collected Poems* (Dunedin, NZ: U of Otago P, 1987): 24, ll., 1–6.

76   Dallas, *Collected Poems*, l. 12.

ISLANDS WITHIN ISLANDS

> All they have endured seems changed to strength,
> Simplicity, to have gone to perfect the leaf—
> We have forgotten something, or come too soon.[77]

The poem positions the speaker's lapsed memory in contradistinction to the evolutionary memory of the beeches themselves. Immersion in the forest grants Pākehā a glimpse into the strange knottedness of deep time.

The poems of Baxter and Dallas can be understood as postcolonial narratives of belonging in/to place. Their early work in particular implies that learning to inhabit the South Island as a recent Anglo-European arrival necessitates engaging with the temporal alterity of the forests there. What's more, a postcolonial eco-humanities perspective elicits the potential for climate change to alter these habitats as well as the human relation to time in such places. Their poems imply that one of the risks of the Anthropocene is profound cultural memory loss. In Dallas's "Under Beech Trees," human-forest filiation breaks down as the beeches are rendered sinister with "long-haired and humped dead boughs" and "moss as thick as sheepskins."[78] Rather than a locus of somatic interrelation, the forest is where "beast and bird / Slept in a century's dead leaves" and where creatures crouch "swathed as if spellbound / In lichen and moss."[79] No longer a time-plenum—of evolutionary, Gondwanan, cultural and organismic *times*—the place is dangerous, repellent, *unheimlich*. In Dallas's verse, mosses and lichen signify the venerability of nothofagus forests. The poem, nonetheless, presents the epiphytes as emblems of deep-time strangeness. In the 1830s, a young Charles Darwin seized upon similar figures of uncanny dread during his visit to South America whereas, one-hundred years later, Pablo Neruda resisted (neo)colonial tropes of beech forests as dark and threatening in his epic poem *Canto General*.

3 "Solitary in Your Rainy Kingdom:" Chilean Beech Narratives

Comprising 231 poems over fifteen sections and released originally in Mexico in 1950 as an illustrated book, *Canto General* by Pablo Neruda (1904–1973) is considered one of the greatest epic poems of the twentieth century. The work represents Neruda's ambitious attempt to rewrite the imperialist version of

---

77 Dallas, *Collected Poems*, ll., 13–15.
78 Dallas, *Collected Poems*, 32, ll., 3, 5.
79 Dallas, *Collected Poems*, 32, ll., 7–8, 11–12.

Latin American history through the deep, pre-Columbian histories of Chilean culture and environment.[80] Some critics have characterised *Canto General* as a "lyricised defense of oppressed and subjugated peoples throughout Latin America"[81] whereas others have emphasised its critique of "capitalism's proclivity for environmental despoliation."[82] Patrick D. Murphy examines ecoregional affinities in the narrative apropos a "dyadic counterpoint of land and people" where nature is not a political metaphor but a material agent of temporal otherness.[83] Like Dallas and Baxter, Neruda grew up among nothofagus and, consequently, the trees figure into his sense of an ancestral homeland predating colonisation. In "The Frontier," he relates being "raised amid the southland beeches // I went, a slender child whose pale form / was impregnated with pristine forests."[84] Section III, "The Conquistadors," comprises poems about the ecosystems of Araucanía, a region of Chile known for its extensive *coigüe* (*N. dombeyi*), *raulí* (*N. alpina*), *ñirre* (*N. antarctica*), *guindo* (*N. betuloides*), *lenga* (*N. pumilio*) and *roble* forests. In Spanish, *roble* refers to oaks but, in a Chilean context, the word denotes the common pellín (*N. obliqua*).[85]

In "Land and Man Unite," the roble beech serves as a metonymy for Araucanía and, by extension, its Indigenous people, such as the Yaghan, Pehuenche and Mapuche, who subsisted from the forests well before Spanish conquistadors arrived in the sixteenth century. The opening lines convey affection for the tree as ancestral—as a part of extended genealogy that encompasses more-than-humans:

> Araucanía, cluster of torrential southland beech,
> O merciless Homeland, my dark love,
> solitary in your rainy kingdom.[86]

---

80 Jason Wilson, *A Companion to Pablo Neruda: Evaluating Neruda's Poetry* (Woodbridge, UK: Boydell & Brewer, 2014): 174.

81 Mark Mascia, "Redefining Civilization: Historical Polarities and Mythologizing in *Los Conquistadores* of Pablo Neruda's *Canto General*," *Atenea* 27.2 (2007): 137.

82 Patrick Murphy, "The Poetic Politics of Ecological Inhabitation in Neruda's *Canto General* and Cardenal's *Cosmic Canticle*" in *Postcolonial Green: Environmental Politics and World Narratives*, eds. Bonnie Roos and Alex Hunt (Charlottesville, VA: U of Virginia P, 2010): 215.

83 Murphy, "The Poetic Politics," 219.

84 Neruda, *The Poetry*, 312, ll., 27, 33–34.

85 Jack Schmitt, "Notes to the *Canto General*" in *Canto General*, ed. Jack Schmitt (Berkeley, CA: U of California P, 2000): 403.

86 Pablo Neruda, *Canto General*, trans. Jack Schmitt (Berkeley, CA: U of California P, 2000): 61, ll., 1–3.

ISLANDS WITHIN ISLANDS 177

Araucanía is a "dark love" even though the beech is "torrential" and the terrain "merciless." Deep time consciousness mediates this constellation of narrator, homeland and trees:

> The forefathers of stone became shadows,
> they were bound to the forest, the natural
> darkness, they became icy light.[87]

Neruda lyrically repudiates colonial commentators, namely Darwin, who disparaged the familial trees, for instance, as "the gloomy beech of the southern shores."[88] To be sure, the lack of light in many nothofagus forests results from dense entanglements of leaves, limbs, epiphytes and other plants. But rather than uncanny and melancholic—or filled with the ersatz illumination of imperial ideologies—Araucanía in the narrative is suffused with a "natural darkness" that emanates from the filiation of ancestors and land.

One of the forebears narrativised by Neruda is Caupolicán who, in the 1500s, led the Mapuche fight against the Spanish. In Section IV of *Canto General*, "The Liberators," the poem "Chief Caupolicán" imagines how the leader:

> [...] grew, torso and tempest,
> from the southland beech's secret stock,
> and when he aimed his people
> at the invading firearms,
> the tree walked,
> the homeland's hard tree walked.
> The invaders saw foliage
> moving amid the green mist,
> heavy branches clothed
> in countless leaves and threats,
> the terrestrial trunk becoming people,
> the territory's roots emerging.[89]

Ancestral association with the beech forest—including with its all-consuming darkness, heavy branches and harsh foliage—fortified resistance to colonial invasion historically and, additionally, advances "liberation from neocolonial

---

87   Neruda, *Canto General*, 61, ll., 22–24.
88   Darwin, *Narrative*, 333.
89   Neruda, *Canto*, 79, ll., 1–14.

political domination" in the present.[90] What's more, Neruda represents Caupolicán as a tree-person hybrid, thus decentring the human as arbiter of ecological value. The verse affirms that forests do not need to be pleasing to impart strength of body, spirit and identity; moreover, in the Anthropocene, they are indispensable for the survival of all life. Although written in the first half of the twentieth century, the deep time narratives of *Canto General* presage climate change as a neocolonial threat to Indigenous people who are disproportionately susceptible to its impacts. Their homelands—mountain regions, coastal areas and small islands—on which they depend for basic livelihoods are often acutely vulnerable to climatic disturbance.[91] Significant for the Mapuche of the Andean Patagonian forests, nothofagus forests contain sacred sites inhabited by supernatural entities, supply a range of medicinal substances for community use and ensure the continuity of the knowledge linked to them.[92] Nonetheless, climate change has already triggered water scarcity, weakened agricultural productivity, impacted alpine ecosystems and fragmented certain traditions and practices of the Mapuche.[93]

Notwithstanding their vulnerability to climate change, Indigenous cultures are exemplars of environmental adaptation. So too are the beech forests that the people have depended on and conserved for millennia. Joseph Hooker recognised the resilience of the beech in *The Botany of the Antarctic Voyage*, his account of the voyages of *Erebus* and *Terror* in the Southern Hemisphere between 1839 and 1843. On *ñirre* (*N. antarctica*) and *guindo* (*N. betuloides*) of the southernmost tip of South America, Tierra del Fuego, visited by the expedition in 1842, Hooker wrote: "We see, too, how the adaptation of particular forms of vegetation to certain climates, even in this remote quarter of the globe, is exemplified in these trees."[94] He extolled *ñirre* as "the most distinguishing botanical production of this country" and noted that *guindo* "forms the prevailing feature in the scenery."[95] Indeed, the leafing and budding of

---

90   Murphy, "The Poetic Politics," 214.

91   Ameyali Ramos-Castillo, Edwin Castellanos and Kirsty Galloway McLean, "Indigenous Peoples, Local Communities and Climate Change Mitigation," *Climatic Change* 140.1 (2017): 2.

92   Soledad Molares and Ana Ladio, "Mapuche Perceptions and Conservation of Andean *Nothofagus* Forests and Their Medicinal Plants: A Case Study from a Rural Community in Patagonia, Argentina," *Biodiversity and Conservation* 21.4 (2012): 1079–1093.

93   Elvis Parraguez-Vergara, Jonathan Barton and Gabriela Raposo-Quintana, "Impacts of Climate Change in the Andean Foothills of Chile: Economic and Cultural Vulnerability of Indigenous Mapuche Livelihoods," *Journal of Developing Societies* 32.4 (2016): 454–483.

94   Hooker, *The Botany*, 347.

95   Hooker, *The Botany*, 212, 346.

ISLANDS WITHIN ISLANDS

deciduous beeches, "when a delightfully fragrant odour pervades the woods," inspired euphoric remembrance of the English spring.[96] Counter to Hooker's reverie, Darwin, who arrived in Patagonia ten years earlier, in 1832, perceived only gloom, obscureness and melancholy. After witnessing the brown and yellow hues of *guindo*, he brooded: "As the whole landscape is thus coloured, it has a sombre, dull appearance; nor is it often enlivened by the rays of the sun."[97] Upon encountering the *Cyttaria* fungus that parasitises nothofagus, Darwin further saw the forest as a theatre of the grotesque: "In the beech forests the trees are much diseased; on the rough excrescences grow vast numbers of yellow balls."[98]

Although a preternatural excrescence, the mushroom was consumed by *Fuegians*, a term referring originally to the Yaghan of Tierra del Fuego. Darwin observed that the *Cyttaria* constituted "a very essential article of food for the Fuegian."[99] Displaying a cautious interest in the people, the naturalist nevertheless remained essentially dismissive of them. And, lamentably, his characterisations of Indigenous Chileans as savages and cannibals would hold sway for decades to come.[100] From Darwin's vantage point, the Fuegians were inseparable from the forest and its highly adaptive organisms, epitomised by the uncanny globular fungus that occurs only on these beech trees. Thus, on arriving in Tierra del Fuego, he notices "a group of Fuegians partly concealed by *the entangled forest* [...] perched on a wild point overhanging the sea."[101] However, in their imposition of a colonial European time framework on the environment and people they encountered, Darwin and Hooker failed to conceive of the nothofagus forest as a time-knot of relations linking Indigenous people and a community of beings to an ancient land. A dangerous essentialisation of culture and nature—of the human and non-human as similarly barren of voice—lurks as a spectre within Darwin's image of the entangled Fuegians. Yet an alternate interpretation of that moment—one informed by the Anthropocene—foregrounds the role of Indigenous agencies in climate change adaptation today. In the 1950s, Neruda signalled the transnational

---

96 Hooker, *The Botany*, 348.

97 Darwin, *Narrative*, 232.

98 Darwin quoted in M.J. Berkeley, "On an Edible Fungus from Tierra del Fuego, and an Allied Chilian Species" in *The Phytologist: A Popular Botanical Miscellany*, ed. George Luxford (London: John Van Voorst, 1844): 486.

99 Darwin quoted in M.J. Berkeley, "On an Edible Fungus from Tierra del Fuego, and an Allied Chilian Species," 486.

100 William Edmundson, *A History of the British Presence in Chile: From Bloody Mary to Charles Darwin and the Decline of British Influence* (New York: Palgrave Macmillan, 2009): 199.

101 Darwin, *Narrative*, 227, emphasis added.

spatiotemporal consciousness required to confront the urgencies that overwhelm twenty-first century life. *Canto General* prompts an appreciation of deep time as a plurality weaving between evolutionary (the deep memory of the species), geological, cultural, organismic and other modes. Not an abstraction but a felt reality, the deep time of the forest, for Neruda, instigates topophilia, a "dark love" that counters capitalist exploitation of place.[102]

Murphy contends that the effect of *Canto General* is one of "ennaturing the subalterns in an inhabitory relationship" to the Earth and each other.[103] The poem's subaltern figures include Indigenes and other subjugated people as well as nothofagus trees and the organisms—mosses, lichen, orchids and fungi—adapted to them. In this context, the subaltern denotes the community of beings—the Earth household—repressed by the (neo)colonial appropriation of time. In the poem "Moss" from the collection *Poem of Chile* published posthumously in 1967, Chilean poet Gabriela Mistral (1889–1957), the first Latin American recipient of a Nobel Prize in Literature, considers the deep time of subaltern organisms—in this case, epiphytic moss—in "an inhabitory relationship" with the beech. In the original Spanish version of the poem, Mistral invokes the term *coihue,* derived from the Mapuche language, in reference to Dombey's beech (*N. dombeyi*). The moss occupy their own time position within a domestic space becoming evermore time-plural in character as the wild encroaches:

> They sleep, sleep, sleep,
> and stubbornly say nothing,
> lords of the beech-trunk,
> of the empty house
> and the abandoned garden.[104]

In symbiotic interrelation fostered over a vast timescale, *coihue* and moss reign over the empty house and abandoned garden, bringing their own time modalities to bear on the place.

As such, the scene Mistral depicts can be read as an assemblage of temporal actants. In this way, it becomes possible to approach poetic narratives in the Anthropocene not only for their aesthetic, symbolic and ethical dimensions but also for how temporal alterities coalesce through material agents of deep

---

102 Neruda, *Canto*, 61, l., 2.

103 Murphy, "The Poetic Politics," 217.

104 Gabriela Mistral, *Selected Poems of Gabriela Mistral*, trans. Ursula K. Le Guin (Albuquerque, NM: U of New Mexico P, 2003): 365, ll., 13–17.

ISLANDS WITHIN ISLANDS 181

time: the beech-trunk, moss epiphytes and fungal parasites. Most powerfully, Mistral's poem exhibits empathic identification with the otherness of the epiphytes (or, more precisely, saprophytes) that "grow with great fervor / where the dead lie sleeping."[105] Accordingly, her temporalised ecopoetics refuses Darwin's instantiation of beeches as dull, sombre, disease-ridden and populated by ghastly things. An affective regard for nothofagus, moreover, is evident in poems by Peter Kama Kerpi and Steven Edmund Winduo of Papua New Guinea (PNG) where the Gondwanan trees dominate the Highlands and embody resistance to neo-imperial ruination of ancestral homelands.

4 "Sacred Forest's Mysteries": Papua New Guinean Beech Narratives

Eighty kilometres north of Bougainville, the low-lying Carteret Atoll has received international media coverage as the imperiled homeland of the world's first climate refugees.[106] In 2003, the PNG government authorised the total evacuation of the atoll and, in 2009, three-thousand residents were relocated. Carteret underscores PNG's vulnerability to climatic disturbance not only in coastal areas but also in the Highlands, a cordilleran region where deforestation intensifies weather extremes, weakens the capacity of forests to absorb carbon and precipitates widespread biodiversity decline.[107] An altered climate endangers the 80 percent of Papuans who draw their livelihood directly from the land.[108] When, in 2007, then-Prime Minister of PNG, Michael Somare, proclaimed that "if we lose the world's forests we lose the fight against climate change"[109] he neglected to emphasise the contribution of Indigenous Papuans to the struggle. In the PNG cordillera, anthropogenic climate change exacerbated by the ecological abuses of mining conglomerates continues to fracture

---

105   Mistral, *Selected Poems*, ll., 21–22.
106   Darren James, "Lost at Sea: The Race Against Time to Save the Carteret Islands from Climate Change," *ABC News* (August 4, 2018), https://www.abc.net.au/news/2018-08-04/the-race-against-time-to-save-the-carteret-islanders/10066958. Reports of the "world's first climate refugees" have also focused on other Pacific nations, such as Vanuatu, Kiribati and Tuvalu.
107   Amand Lang, Matthew Omena, Mohammad Abdad and Rebecca Ford, "Climate Change in Papua New Guinea: Impact on Disease Dynamics," *Papua New Guinea Medical Journal* 58.1–4 (2015): 1.
108   Martin Bush, *Climate Change Adaptation in Small Island Developing States* (Hoboken, NJ: John Wiley & Sons, 2018): 203.
109   Somare quoted in Marion Struck-Garbe, "Reflections on Climate Change by Contemporary Artists in Papua New Guinea," *Pacific Geographies* 21.38 (2012): 29.

longstanding biocultural linkages to a nothofagus terrain.[110] Disseminated by global capitalism, climate malaise has become a neocolonial juggernaut—a new colonising force—threatening Papuan traditions in Gondwanan forests.

Paul Sharrad characterises PNG literature, especially work published after independence from Australia in 1975, as distinctively "vernacular in voice," anti-colonial in sentiment and marked by "post-independence unease."[111] Part of this unease, I argue, derives from the uncertainty of an ecopolitically viable future in a postcolonial sovereignty ever more impacted by climate change. Born in 1952 "on a ridge (Kaling)" in the Chimbu Province of the Central Highlands, Peter Kama Kerpi is the first Highlander to publish a poetry collection, *Call of Midnight Bird*.[112] Shortly after, he published the play *Voices from the Ridge* and numerous short stories.[113] Incorporating chant structures and celebrating tribal life outside of urban Port Moresby, his writing challenges denigrative imperialist attitudes towards Highlander cultures as primitive, peripheral and exploitable.[114] While lacking the overt references to nothofagus found in the work of the writers discussed previously, Kerpi's verse nevertheless evokes the affinities between cordilleran people and forests. Given the broad geographical distribution and cultural importance of nothofagus in the Highlands, we can infer that some of the trees he poeticises are beeches. Kerpi closes "Prayer at the Graveyard" with:

> And winds kissing giant trees,
> Howling down river beds
> Have stopped.
> And sun has gone down,
> Swallows have retired home,
> Darkness setting in.[115]

The first two lines of the sestet provide a chorus that sets the cadence of the poem throughout. This is representative of the rootedness of modern Papuan prosody in songs and incantations thematising the friction between the

---

110   Wardle, *The New Zealand Beeches*, 23.

111   Paul Sharrad, " 'Ghem Pona Wai?': Vernacular Imaginations in Contemporary Papua New Guinea Fiction," *Cross / Cultures* 181 (2015): 123–124.

112   Peter Kama Kerpi, *Call of Midnight Bird* (Port Moresby: Papua Pocket Poets, 1973): 35.

113   Peter Kama Kerpi, *Voices from the Ridge* (Port Moresby: Centre for Creative Arts, 1974).

114   Nigel Krauth, "Contemporary Literature from the South Pacific," *Journal of Postcolonial Writing* 17.2 (1978): 611.

115   Kerpi, *Call*, 6, ll., 70–75.

ISLANDS WITHIN ISLANDS　　　　　　　　　　　　　　　　　183

vernacular (local) and the cosmopolitan (global).[116] In the Anthropocene, climate change is an inexorable part of both.

The defiant recuperation of local knowledge—of "mother's midnight stories"—in spite of upheaval in the nation state, recurs in Kerpi's poem "Moments of Initiation."[117] Emplaced traditions vastly predate the myopic temporality of imperialism. The process of recovery centres on deep listening to the land's ancestral voices:

> The solemn march.
> Only the winds
> Whistling through giant trees
> Accompany murmurs of encouragement
> From dead fathers.[118]

This final stanza of the poem is redolent of *Canto General* and, specifically, Neruda's genealogisation of trees and forebears as a source of subaltern agency. And, as in Neruda's narratives, the subaltern is a situated and filiated community of human and more-than-human beings. "Song of Lament," moreover, makes extensive use of vernacularisms. The names Uchimakona (for place) and Ochimakona (for forebear) act as refrains that affirm nature-culture solidarity across temporalities, prompting memory retrieval:

> Uchimakona.
> White bear whispers song of departure,
> Decaying tree trunk of Ochimakona.
> Memories of our days lie
> Rusting in the most forgotten corner of my house.[119]

Kerpi's narrative is elegiac, but hope is clarion in the potential to restore ancestral relations to a land sundered by colonialism. In its hybridisation of oral and print-based textualities, PNG poetry mediates this process of restoration, remembering and healing.

The poetry of Kama Kerpi signifies Highlanders' traditional affinities for Gondwanan forests. The Wola of the Southern Highlands, for instance, refer to beech as *pel* and distinguish between four types, including *pel-kelkel* or

---

116　Krauth, "Contemporary Literature"; Sharrad, " 'Ghem Pona Wai?' ".
117　Kerpi, *Call*, 7, l., 17.
118　Kerpi, ll. 21–25.
119　Kerpi, 20, ll., 56–60.

N. grandis.[120] In the 1950s, the Dutch botanist Cornelis van Steenis recorded the names *ufoiya*, *ifoya*, *gripe*, *sama* and *unuza* for Eastern Highlands species.[121] Summarising the observations of Leonard Brass, who led the 1953 Archbold Expedition to PNG, van Steenis observed the influence of nothofagus on human livelihoods:

> *Nothofagus* forest appears to be valuable to man. In Mr. Brass' opinion Upland Papuans have mainly made their fields on the soils bearing fagaceous [*sic*] forests: *man has followed the beeches*, he says [...] the trees are well known to Papuans, partly on account of their suitability as timber-producing plants.[122]

Though serving practical ends, interactions with nothofagus were not predicated on a nature-culture opposition that, in Western ontology, constructs the wild as firmly separate from the domestic. On this note, van Steenis relates that Eastern Highlands people:

> [...] plant *Nothofagus* in their homesteads, along tracks and around their garden lands, it is said for ornamental purpose. This is reported of *N. grandis*, *N. perryi* and *N. pullei*. But they do not raise them from seed, but invariably transplant seedlings from the forest.[123]

Accordingly, the "decaying tree trunk of Ochimakona" Kerpi mentions could very well be a beech.

This brings our discussion to the work of Steven Edmund Winduo, a poet-scholar born in East Sepik in 1964 who maintains an ongoing interest in Indigenous knowledge systems.[124] In a manner comparable to Kerpi's *Call of Midnight Bird*, Winduo's collections *Lomo'ha I Am, In Spirits' Voice I Call*[125] and

---

120 Paul Sillitoe, "An Ethnobotanical Account of the Plant Resources of the Wola Region, Southern Highlands Province, Papua New Guinea," *Journal of Ethnobiology* 15.2 (1995): 206, 211.

121 C.G.G.J. van Steenis, "Results of the Archbold Expeditions: Papuan *Nothofagus*," *Journal of the Arnold Arbortetum* 34.4 (1953): 316.

122 van Steenis, "Results," emphasis added.

123 C.G.G.J. van Steenis, "*Nothofagus*, Key Genus of Plant Geography, in Time and Space, Living and Fossil, Ecology and Phylogeny," *Blumea: Biodiversity, Evolution and Biogeography of Plants* 19.1 (1971): 73–74.

124 Sharrad, " 'Ghem Pona Wai?'," 135.

125 Steven Edmund Winduo, *Lomo'ha I Am, In Spirits' Voice I Call: 1984–1991* (Suva: South Pacific Creative Arts Society, 1991).

Hembemba: Rivers of the Forest[126] attend to the recovery of ancestral heritage through the reterritorialisation of "English as New Guinean, even as the vernacular is itself deterritorialised in the process."[127] Winduo's mediating figure is Lomo'ha, a heroic spirit in the Nagum Bokien culture of East Sepik.[128] Many poems in *Hembemba* take place in the province, where nothofagus forests occur at higher elevations. In "Seeds and Roots," Winduo emphasises consanguinity between forebears, community and forests:

Blood of roots so ancient
Roots becoming of seeds
Early passionate moments
Textured clay masks
Sacred forest's mysteries
Valley of thousand tribes
Ponds where animals visit.[129]

The alternation between nature and culture reinforces the entanglement of both. An object neither of scientific conquest nor of capitalistic appropriation, the mysterious forest is a sacred locus of Lomo'ha. As with many other postcolonial writers, Winduo occupies a hybridic position both as a scholar-poet and as an East Sepik writer relocated to Port Moresby.[130] Such a perspective, I suggest, is vital for bringing Papuan knowledge of ecological sustainability to bear on global Anthropocene concerns.

Reading the poetry of Kerpi and Winduo vis-à-vis the context of climate change lends new urgency to their late-colonial- and postcolonial-era assertions for robust national identity predicated on the recuperation of biocultural systems. In particular, their poetry counterweighs the rhetoric of nothofagus as a vestige of a bygone supercontinent. For instance, van Steenis mused: "Among the larger continental islands, New Guinea occupies a predominant place as *a refuge of these relics* [...] One wonders why these distributions, accepted as very ancient, are still limited to the Southern hemisphere theatre."[131] The botanist

---

126 Steven Edmund Winduo, *Hembemba: Rivers of the Forest* (Suva and Port Moresby: Institute of Pacific Studies and University of Papua New Guinea, 2000).

127 Sharrad, " 'Ghem Pona Wai?'," 141.

128 Rob Wilson, "Postcolonial Pacific Poetries: Becoming Oceania" in *The Cambridge Companion to Postcolonial Poetry*, ed. Jahan Ramazani (Cambridge, UK: Cambridge UP, 2017): 66.

129 Winduo, *Hembemba*, 12, ll., 1–7.

130 Sharrad, " 'Ghem Pona Wai?'," 141.

131 van Steenis, "Results," 304, emphasis added.

saw the tree as "a living fossil."[132] Indeed, Time (capitalised)—in conjunction with the metaphors associated with it (fossils, relics, vestiges)—constitutes an instrument of othering. In this respect, anthropologist Johannes Fabian stresses that the "use of Time almost invariably is made for the purpose of distancing those who are observed from the Time of the observer."[133] Regarding nothofagus, figurations of Time can negate the hetero-temporality of the tree. Poetic narratives can intervene by providing a counterpoint to "fossilising" rhetoric and, thus, contributing to the decolonisation of Time.

This chapter has suggested that poetic narratives help us to appreciate the thingness of time and, in doing so, invite us to imagine possibilities for responding to a climate-disturbed future. To this effect, I have examined representations of nothofagus in the contemporary poetries of New Zealand, Chile and Papua New Guinea. My approach points to a distinction between, on the one hand, the reading of texts dealing explicitly with climate change and, on the other, the use of a climate-oriented framework for critiquing environmental texts written before the popularisation of the terms *climate change* and *climate disturbance*. As with its postcolonial and ecocritical counterparts, critical climatic theory offers an optic for appraising narratives across histories and cultures. Graham Huggan and Helen Tiffin assert that "one of the central tasks of postcolonial ecocriticism as an emergent field has been to contest— also to provide alternatives to—western ideologies of development."[134] As the coalescence of these ideologies, climate change renders all life exceedingly vulnerable. Materialising deep temporalities in their arboreal bodies, southern beeches occupy islands (isolated, higher-elevation habitats) within islands (cool-temperate regions) within islands (Australia, New Zealand and New Guinea) within the Earth island. Reminding us of our embeddedness in islands of differing kinds, forms and scales, nothofagus narratives call urgent attention to the effects of climate change on spatiotemporally nested biocultural systems. Foregrounding the contribution of literature to the climate change debate, deep time poetic narratives remind us that reading— and rereading—are crucial tasks for the postcolonial eco-humanities in the Anthropocene.

---

132 van Steenis, "Results," 307.

133 Johannes Fabian, *Time and the Other: How Anthropology Makes Its Object* (New York: Columbia UP, 2014, original edition, 1983): 25.

134 Graham Huggan and Helen Tiffin, *Postcolonial Ecocriticism: Literature, Animals, Environment* (London: Routledge, 2010): 27.

Works Cited

Baxter, James K. *Collected Poems of James K. Baxter*, ed. J.E. Weir (Wellington, NZ: Oxford UP, 1979).

Berkeley, M.J. "On an Edible Fungus from Tierra del Fuego, and an Allied Chilian Species" in *The Phytologist: A Popular Botanical Miscellany*, ed. George Luxford (London: John Van Voorst, 1844): 486–487.

Best, Elsdon. *Forest Lore of the Maori: With Methods of Snaring, Trapping and Preserving Birds and Rats, Uses of Berries, Roots, Fern-Root and Forest Products, with Mythological Notes on Origins, Karakia Used Etc.* (Wellington, NZ: E.C. Keating, Government Printer, 1977. Original edition, 1942).

Brady, Veronica. *South of My Days: A Biography of Judith Wright.* (Pymble, NSW: Angus & Robertson, 1998).

Bush, Martin. *Climate Change Adaptation in Small Island Developing States.* (Hoboken, NJ: John Wiley & Sons, 2018).

Catton, Theodore. "A Short History of the New Zealand National Park System" in *National Parks Beyond the Nation: Global Perspectives on 'America's Best Idea,'* eds. Adrian Howkins, Jared Orsi and Mark Fiege (Norman, OK: U of Oklahoma P, 2016): 68–90.

Chakrabarty, Dipesh. "The Climate of History: Four Theses." *Critical Inquiry* 35.2 (2009): 197–222.

Chakrabarty, Dipesh. "Anthropocene Time." *History and Theory* 57.1 (2018): 5–32.

Cheeseman, Thomas Frederic. *Manual of the New Zealand Flora.* (Wellington, NZ: John Mackay, Government Printer, 1906).

Chester, Quentin. "Early Warning (Antarctic Beech Trees at Mount Warning, New South Wales)." *Australian Geographic* 91 (Jul–Sep 2008): 46–57.

Dallas, Ruth. *Collected Poems.* (Dunedin, NZ: U of Otago P, 1987).

Darwin, Charles. *Narrative of the Surveying Voyages of His Majesty's Ships Adventure and Beagle, Between the Years 1826 and 1836.* vol 3, ed. Robert Fitzroy (London: Henry Colburn, 1839).

Davies, Jeremy. *The Birth of the Anthropocene.* (Oakland, CA: U of California P, 2016).

DeLoughrey, Elizabeth and George B. Handley. "Introduction: Toward an Aesthetics of the Earth" in *Postcolonial Ecologies: Literatures of the Environment*, eds. Elizabeth DeLoughrey and George B. Handley (New York: Oxford UP, 2011): 3–41.

DeLoughrey, Elizabeth, Jill Didur and Anthony Carrigan. "Introduction: A Postcolonial Environmental Humanities" in *Global Ecologies and the Environmental Humanities: Postcolonial Approaches*, eds. Elizabeth DeLoughrey, Jill Didur and Anthony Carrigan. (New York: Routledge, 2015): 1–32.

Edmundson, William. *A History of the British Presence in Chile: From Bloody Mary to Charles Darwin and the Decline of British Influence.* (New York: Palgrave Macmillan, 2009).

Fabian, Johannes. *Time and the Other: How Anthropology Makes Its Object.* (New York: Columbia UP, 2014. Original edition, 1983).

Gawith, David, Daniel Kingston and Hilary McMillan. "The Effects of Climate Change on Runoff in the Lindis and Matukituki Catchments, Otago, New Zealand." *Journal of Hydrology (NZ)* 51.2 (2012): 121–135.

Gilderdale, Betty. "Dallas, Ruth (1919–)" in *Encyclopedia of Post-Colonial Literatures in English*, eds. Eugene Benson and L.W. Conolly (London: Routledge, 2005): 331–332.

Ginn, Franklin, Michelle Bastian, David Farrier and Jeremy Kidwell. "Introduction: Unexpected Encounters with Deep Time." *Environmental Humanities* 10.1 (2018): 213–225.

Handley, George B. "Climate Change, Cosmology and Poetry: The Case of Derek Walcott's Omeros" in *Global Ecologies and the Environmental Humanities: Postcolonial Approaches*, eds. Elizabeth DeLoughrey, Jill Didur and Anthony Carrigan (New York: Routledge, 2015): 333–351.

Heise, Ursula K. 2010. "Afterword: Postcolonial Ecocriticism and the Question of Literature" in *Postcolonial Green: Environmental Politics and World Narratives,* eds. Bonnie Roos and Alex Hunt (Charlottesville, VA: U of Virginia P): 251–258.

Hill, Robert and Gregory Jordan. "The Evolutionary History of *Nothofagus* (Nothofagaceae)." *Australian Systematic Botany* 6.2 (1993): 111–126.

Hooker, Joseph. *The Botany of the Antarctic Voyage of H.M. Discovery Ships* Erebus *and* Terror *in the Years 1839–1843.* (London: Reeve Brothers, 1844).

Hooker, Joseph. "Introductory Essay" in *The Botany of the Antarctic Voyage of H.M. Discovery Ships,* Erebus *and* Terror*, in the Years 1853–55. II. Flora Novae Zelandiae* (London: Reeve Bros, 1853): 1–34.

Huggan, Graham and Helen Tiffin. *Postcolonial Ecocriticism: Literature, Animals, Environment.* (London: Routledge, 2010).

Hunt, Colin A.G. *Carbon Sinks and Climate Change: Forests in the Fight Against Global Warming.* (Cheltenham, UK: Edward Elgar, 2009).

James, Darren. "Lost at Sea: The Race Against Time to Save the Carteret Islands from Climate Change." *ABC News* (August 4, 2018), https://www.abc.net.au/news/2018-08-04/the-race-against-time-to-save-the-carteret-islanders/10066958.

James, Trevor. " 'Pitched at the Farthest Edge': Religious Presence and the Landscape in Contemporary New Zealand Poetry" in *Mapping the Sacred: Religion, Geography and Postcolonial Literatures*, eds. Jamie Scott and Paul Simpson-Housley (Amsterdam: Rodopi, 2001): 131–152.

Kerpi, Peter Kama. *Call of Midnight Bird.* (Port Moresby: Papua Pocket Poets, 1973).

Kerpi, Peter Kama. *Voices from the Ridge.* (Port Moresby: Centre for Creative Arts, 1974).

Kitching, Roger, Richard Braithwaite and Janet Cavanaugh, eds. *Remnants of Gondwana: A Natural and Social History of the Gondwana Rainforests of Australia* (Baulkham Hills, NSW: Surrey Beatty, 2010).

Krauth, Nigel. "Contemporary Literature from the South Pacific." *Journal of Postcolonial Writing* 17.2 (1978): 604–645.

Lang, Amanda, Matthew Omena, Mohammad Abdad and Rebecca Ford. "Climate Change in Papua New Guinea: Impact on Disease Dynamics." *Papua New Guinea Medical Journal* 58.1–4 (2015): 1–10.

Lyell, Charles. *Principles of Geology; or, The Modern Changes of the Earth and its Inhabitants Considered as Illustrative of Geology*. 7th ed. (London: John Murray, 1847. Original edition, 1833).

Lynch, Tom, Susan Naramore Maher, Drucilla Wall and O. Alan Weltzien, eds. *Thinking Continental: Writing the Planet One Place at a Time*. (Lincoln, NB: U of Nebraska P, 2017).

Mansilla, Claudia, Robert McCulloch and Flavia Morello. "The Vulnerability of the *Nothofagus* Forest-Steppe Ecotone to Climate Change: Palaeoecological Evidence from Tierra del Fuego (~53°S)." *Palaeogeography, Palaeoclimatology, Palaeoecology* 508 (2018): 59–70.

Marder, Michael. *Plant-Thinking: A Philosophy of Vegetal Life* (New York: Columbia UP, 2013).

Mascia, Mark. "Redefining Civilization: Historical Polarities and Mythologizing in *Los Conquistadores of Pablo Neruda's Canto General*." *Atenea* 27.2 (2007): 137–157.

McDonald, Pete. *Foot-tracks in New Zealand: Origins, Access Issues and Recent Developments*. (2011), https://petemcdonald.co/ft.pdf.

McPhee, John. *Basin and Range*. (New York: Farrar, Straus and Giroux, 1982).

Miller, David Philip and Peter Hanns Reill, eds. *Visions of Empire: Voyages, Botany, and Representations of Nature*. (Cambridge, UK: Cambridge UP, 1996).

Mistral, Gabriela. *Selected Poems of Gabriela Mistral*, trans. Ursula K. Le Guin. (Albuquerque, NM: U of New Mexico P, 2003).

Molares, Soledad and Ana Ladio. "Mapuche Perceptions and Conservation of Andean *Nothofagus* Forests and Their Medicinal Plants: A Case Study from a Rural Community in Patagonia, Argentina." *Biodiversity and Conservation* 21.4 (2012): 1079–1093.

Morton, Tim. *Hyperobjects: Philosophy and Ecology After the End of the World*. (Minneapolis, MN: U of Minnesota P, 2013).

Murphy, Patrick D. "The Poetic Politics of Ecological Inhabitation in Neruda's *Canto General* and Cardenal's *Cosmic Canticle*" in *Postcolonial Green: Environmental Politics and World Narratives*, eds. Bonnie Roos and Alex Hunt (Charlottesville, VA: U of Virginia P, 2010): 213–228.

Neruda, Pablo. *Canto General*, trans. Jack Schmitt (Berkeley, CA: U of California P, 2000).

Neruda, Pablo. *The Poetry of Pablo Neruda*, ed. Ilan Stavans. (New York: Farrar, Straus and Giroux, 2003).

Northcott, Michael. "Eschatology in the Anthropocene: From the *Chronos* of Deep Time to the *Kairos* of the Age of the Humans" in *The Anthropocene and the Global*

Environmental Crisis: Rethinking Modernity in a New Epoch, eds. Clive Hamilton, Christophe Bonneuil and François Gemenne. (London: Routledge, 2015): 100–111.

O'Brien, Gregory. "Some Remarks on Poetry and the Environment in Aotearoa/New Zealand." *Poetry* 211.5 (2018): 475–484.

Oppermann, Serpil and Serenella Iovino. "Introduction: The Environmental Humanities and the Challenges of the Anthropocene" in *Environmental Humanities: Voices from the Anthropocene* eds. Serpil Oppermann and Serenella Iovino. (London: Rowman and Littlefield, 2017): 1–21.

Parraguez-Vergara, Elvis, Jonathan Barton and Gabriela Raposo-Quintana. "Impacts of Climate Change in the Andean Foothills of Chile: Economic and Cultural Vulnerability of Indigenous Mapuche Livelihoods." *Journal of Developing Societies* 32.4 (2016): 454–483.

Price, A. Grenfell. *Island Continent: Aspects of the Historical Geography of Australia and Its Territories.* (Sydney: Angus and Robertson, 1972).

Ramos-Castillo, Ameyali, Edwin Castellanos and Kirsty Galloway McLean. "Indigenous Peoples, Local Communities and Climate Change Mitigation." *Climatic Change* 140.1 (2017): 1–4.

Rix, Martyn, and Andy Jackson. "Plate 489. *Nothofagus moorei* Fagaceae." *Curtis's Botanical Magazine* 21.1 (2004): 65–69.

Rodway, Leonard. "Botanic Evidence in Favour of Land Connection Between Fuegia and Tasmania During the Present Floristic Epoch." *Papers and Proceedings of the Royal Society of Tasmania* (1914): 32–34.

Roos, Bonnie and Alex Hunt. "Introduction: Narratives of Survival, Sustainability and Justice" in *Postcolonial Green: Environmental Politics and World Narratives*, eds. Bonnie Roos and Alex Hunt. (Charlottesville, VA: U of Virginia P, 2010): 1–13.

Salleh, Ariel. "The Anthropocene: Thinking in 'Deep Geological Time' or Deep Libidinal Time?" *International Critical Thought* 6.3 (2016): 422–433.

Schmitt, Jack. "Notes to the *Canto General*" in *Canto General*, ed. Jack Schmitt (Berkeley, CA: U of California P, 2000): 403–413.

Sharrad, Paul. "'Ghem Pona Wai?': Vernacular Imaginations in Contemporary Papua New Guinea Fiction." *Cross / Cultures* 181 (2015): 121–144.

Sillitoe, Paul. "An Ethnobotanical Account of the Plant Resources of the Wola Region, Southern Highlands Province, Papua New Guinea." *Journal of Ethnobiology* 15.2 (1995): 201–235.

Struck-Garbe, Marion. "Reflections on Climate Change by Contemporary Artists in Papua New Guinea." *Pacific Geographies* 21.38 (2012): 26–31.

Thornber, Karen. "Literature, Asia and the Anthropocene: Possibilities for Asian Studies and the Environmental Humanities." *Journal of Asian Studies* 73.4 (2014): 989–1000.

van Steenis, C.G.G.J. "Results of the Archbold Expeditions: Papuan *Nothofagus*." *Journal of the Arnold Arbortetum* 34.4 (1953): 301–374.

van Steenis, C.G.G.J. *"Nothofagus,* Key Genus of Plant Geography, in Time and Space, Living and Fossil, Ecology and Phylogeny." *Blumea: Biodiversity, Evolution and Biogeography of Plants* 19.1 (1971): 65–98.

Veblen, Thomas, Robert Hill and Jennifer Read. "Introduction: Themes and Concepts in the Study of *Nothofagus* Forests" in *The Ecology and Biogeography of Nothofagus Forests,* eds. Thomas Veblen, Robert Hill and Jennifer Read (New Haven, CT: Yale UP, 1996): 1–10.

Wardle, John A. *The New Zealand Beeches: Ecology, Utilisation and Management.* (Christchurch, NZ: New Zealand Forest Service, 1984).

Wardle, Peter. "Distribution of Native Forest in the Upper Clutha District, Otago, New Zealand." *New Zealand Journal of Botany* 39.3 (2001): 435–446.

Wilson, Jason. *A Companion to Pablo Neruda: Evaluating Neruda's Poetry.* (Woodbridge, UK: Boydell and Brewer, 2014).

Wilson, Rob. "Postcolonial Pacific Poetries: Becoming Oceania" in *The Cambridge Companion to Postcolonial Poetry,* ed. Jahan Ramazani (Cambridge, UK: Cambridge UP, 2017): 58–71.

Winduo, Steven Edmund. *Lomo'ha I Am, In Spirits' Voice I Call: 1984–1991.* (Suva: South Pacific Creative Arts Society, 1991).

Winduo, Steven Edmund. *Hembemba: Rivers of the Forest.* (Suva and Port Moresby: Institute of Pacific Studies and University of Papua New Guinea, 2000).

Wright, Judith. *The Moving Image: Poems.* (Melbourne: Meanjin Press, 1946).

Wright, Judith. *Born of the Conquerors: Selected Essays.* (Canberra: Aboriginal Studies Press, 1991).

Wright, Phillip A. "More Amenities for Visitors to New England National Park." *The Armidale Express* (October 14, 1959): 1.

Zalasiewicz, Jan. "The Extraordinary Strata of the Anthropocene" in *Environmental Humanities: Voices from the Anthropocene,* eds. Serpil Oppermann and Serenella Iovino (London: Rowman and Littlefield, 2017): 115–131.

Zen, E-an. "What Is Deep Time and Why Should Anyone Care?" *Journal of Geoscience Education* 49.1 (2001): 5–9.

CHAPTER 7

Refashioning Futures with Sargassum

A Caribbean Poetics of Hope

Kasia Mika and Sally Stainier

Driftwood served on a bed of seaweed (Fig. 7.1): a Caribbean classic, elevated by sargassum patches seemingly coming out of nowhere to pervade the archipelago's pristine waters and idyllic beaches.[1] Pelagic brown algae have swarmed across the region in "island-like masses"[2] since 2011, but 2018 stands out as the worst year yet,[3] with massive strandings recorded all the way up to Florida. The genus responsible for these surges is now thought to originate from the South American coast—rather than the Sargasso Sea located in the North Atlantic and baptised by fifteenth-century Portuguese voyageurs after the ubiquitous and ominous presence of the seaweed.[4] The whirlwind of speculation triggered by the recent proliferation has produced few answers as to the questions "why" and "how," leaving little (if any) room for certainty in the construal of sustainable contingency plans.[5]

---

1 Glissant defines the *archipelago* as "situated between the solitary confines of the islands that constitute it and the expansive territory of the mainland toward which it points, relating the one to the other while retaining its own indeterminately distinct identity." Edouard Glissant, *Traité du Tout-Monde* (Paris: Gallimard, 1997).

2 "What is *Sargassum*?" National Oceanic and Atmospheric Administration, https://oceane xplorer.noaa.gov/facts/sargassum.html.

3 Philippa Fogarty, "Sargassum: The Seaweed Deluge Hitting Caribbean Shores," *BBC News*, August 6, 2018, https://www.bbc.com/news/world-latin-america-45044513; *Research Development and Innovation Joint Call on Sargassum Seaweed,* Conseil Régional de la Guadeloupe, https://www.regionguadeloupe.fr/fileadmin/Site_Region_Guadeloupe/actus/appels_a_proj ets/APP_sargasse_Call_for_Sargassum_final_version.pdf.

4 Unlike any other sea, the Sargasso Sea has no land boundary and is mostly defined by its eponymous algae. "What is the Sargasso Sea?" https://oceanservice.noaa.gov/facts/sargassosea.html.

5 For instance, the Call for Projects issued in February 2019 by Guadeloupe's local government implicated "Amazon nutrients in relation with deforestation and agricultural intensification ... along with shifts in hydrodynamic and wind drift patterns associated with climate change." But the white paper released in October 2018 by the United Nations Environment Programme stated that, while satellite images captured in 2013 had showed concentrations of sargassum 600 km off the mouth of the Amazon River, there was "no evidence that river discharge and nutrients from rivers has stimulated new growth of Sargassum"; *Research Development and Innovation Joint Call on Sargassum Seaweed*, Conseil Régional de la Guadeloupe; United Nations Environment Programme, *Sargassum White Paper—Sargassum Outbreak in the Caribbean: Challenges, Opportunities and Regional Situation* (Panama City, 2018).

© KONINKLIJKE BRILL NV, LEIDEN, 2022 | DOI:10.1163/9789004514164_008

FIGURE 7.1 Sainte-Anne, Guadeloupe—2018.
© SALLY STAINIER, 2018

FIGURE 7.2 Saint-François, Guadeloupe—2018.
© SALLY STAINIER, 2018

At first sight, the image (Fig. 7.2) above presages doom, with man's perennial best friend lying lifeless, nose buried in the algal dune covering the usually white sand. As no autopsy was performed, there is no way of pinpointing the cause of death of this otherwise healthy-looking canine—yet this harrowing image contains a disturbing prophecy: the ocean will keep on delivering death to Carribbean shores. In the Caribbean, disasters are conveniently (and often erroneously) deemed "natural," disregarding the social, geopolitical or structural factors embedded in colonial history and the myriad of consequent vulnerabilities underlying the impact of "natural" disasters on human communities and broader ecosystems. In other words, events are natural but disasters are human: a single Category 5 hurricane will hit several communities differently depending on their governance style, preparedness levels, health infrastructures, housing regulations and environmental health.

Caribbean authorities have recognised sargassum as an increasing threat to Caribbean economies and peoples, no matter how resilient they are (or are expected to be).[6] Can we get rid of it? Make something (profitable) of it? Meanwhile, people have had to abandon their homes, plagued with respiratory ailments,[7] sulphurous pestilence and heavy financial losses caused by the corrosion of all electronics as a result of gas emanations from stranded algae decomposing.[8] Since May 2018 several Guadeloupean schools have had to close periodically because of the stench and the allergenic effects of the rotting sargassum.[9] The entire island of Désirade was stranded by tangled masses of sargassum and sand blocking the harbour channel, in January 2019,[10] and again in 2020, and 2021.[11] Fighting sargassum has proven costly

---

6   *Research development and innovation joint call on Sargassum seaweed*, Conseil Régional de la Guadeloupe; "Communities innovate to address Sargassum seaweed on coasts of Saint Lucia," Organisation of Eastern Caribbean States, https://pressroom.oecs.org/comm unities-innovate-to-address-sargassum-seaweed-on-coasts-of-saint-lucia.

7   Valentino Resiere, et al. "Sargassum Seaweed on Caribbean Islands: An International Public Health Concern," *The Lancet* 392.10165 (2018): 2691, https://www.thelancet.com/journals/lancet/article/PIIS0140-6736(18)32777-6/fulltext.

8   Juliet Lamb, "The Great Seaweed Invasion," *JSTOR Daily* (October 24, 2018), https://daily.jstor.org/great-seaweed-invasion/.

9   E. Golabkan and E. Gire, "Huit établissements scolaires de Petit-Bourg fermés sur décision du maire," Franceinfo à la une des Outre-mer, Guadeloupe 1ère, (May 30, 2018), https://la1 ere.francetvinfo.fr/guadeloupe/neuf-etablissements-scolaires-petit-bourg-fermes-decis ion-du-maire-594217.html.

10   Olivia Losbar, "Un bateau réquisitionné pour désenclaver la Désirade," RCI 96.5FM Radio (January 1, 2019), https://www.rci.fm/infos/risques-naturels/un-bateau-requisitionne -pour-desenclaver-la-desirade.

11   Alejandro Castro, "Sargassum: Brown Tide Threatens the Caribbean," *St. Thomas Source* (April 16, 2021), https://stthomassource.com/content/2021/04/16/sargassum-brown-tide -threatens-the-caribbean/. Inès Tresident, "Le littoral Caraïbe de la Martinique menacé

and stressful for governments and citizens alike, also diminishing tourism, a major industry in the whole area.[12] Attempts have been made to intercept the algae at sea and to collect it from beaches, but often at a great environmental cost.[13] The possibilities of using sargassum in agriculture, construction, cosmetics and even food preparation has been widely discussed,[14] with varying degrees of official endorsement at the local and inter-Caribbean level.[15] It is clear, however, that the sargassum must either be prevented or turned to advantage.

This chapter seeks to challenge the prevailing negative framings of sargassum in popular and political discourse, drawing on anthropological, philosophical and literary texts—by Édouard Glissant, Kamau Brathwaite, Sylvia Wynter, Louis-Philippe Dalembert—in order to propose a new analytical vocabulary for thinking about the intertwined human/non-human vulnerabilities of the climate change era. Taking account of a variety of relational understandings of oceans and archipelagoes, the chapter proposes the idea of "coiled temporality" as a means to address the disjointed and asynchronous ecological present, and to consider possible futures with non-human others on non-hegemonic terms. How does sargassum fit with the hopes and futures expressed by Caribbean communities in the light of their internal and interregional inequalities, exacerbated by the unequal distribution of climate change impacts? To what extent does it echo, encompass or transcend historically known hazards? How does seaweed, currently construed as a (natural, non-human but seemingly human-related) threat, challenge future-making in the Caribbean? Our analysis springs from these questions, seeking to craft an imaginative, conceptual and ethical orientation around the notion of coiled temporality. Our aim is to resist both dialectical and linear narratives of Caribbean futures as an

---

par un important banc d'algues sargasses," Franceinfo à la une des Outre-mer: *Martinique la 1ère* (April 28, 2021), https://la1ere.francetvinfo.fr/martinique/le-littoral-caraibe-de-la -martinique-menace-par-un-important-banc-d-algues-sargasses-994981.html.

12 Philippa Fogarty, "Sargassum: The Seaweed Deluge Hitting Caribbean Shores".

13 See "Evaluation des méthodes de collecte des sargasses"– ADEME (Agency for the Environment and Energy Management), SAFEGE Ingénieurs Conseils, DEAL Guadeloupe, http://www.guadeloupe.developpement-durable.gouv.fr/evaluation-des-methodes-de -collecte-des-sargasses-r1084.html.

14 Jérôme Tirolien, "Valorisation agronomique des algues sargasses," Préfet de la Région Guadeloupe, http://www.guadeloupe.gouv.fr/Politiques-publiques/Risques-naturels-tec hnologiques-et-sanitaires/Dossier-Sargasses/Des-projets-innovants-pour-collecter-et -valoriser-les-sargasses/Valorisation-agronomique-des-algues-sargasses.

15 These differences in official responses to the sargassum situation typically result from diverging quality and safety standards, especially between sovereign territories and the Outermost Regions of Europe, such as the French Antilles.

opportunity (lost). Coiled temporality opens unexpected, non-linear moments and interactions: when time crumbles in on itself, or suddenly strikes, so that the "sting of experience" burns with hope.[16]

The chapter goes on to argue for the sargassum's right to opacity (after Édouard Glissant). Opacity, as Glissant understands it, is both an ethical and political claim. It resists reductionism and homogenisation of difference, by an act of comprehension (a play on the French *com-prendre*, signalling appropriation). For Glissant: "Widespread consent to specific opacities is the most straightforward equivalent of nonbarbarism. We clamor for the right to opacity for everyone."[17] This recognition of sargassum's opacity disrupts its depiction as an invasive force and calls for a more-than-human understanding of our place in the environment, one that accounts for multi-scalar temporalities that mirror the region's multi-scalar vulnerabilities. Building on Michael Marder's analysis of vegetal life and plant-thinking, we ask: how is it possible for us to *encounter* sargassum?[18] We take the repetition and recurrence of sargassum, the openings and foreclosures that it seems to herald, as a way of spiraling into an open mode of thinking through the intertwined, though often unrecognised, human/non-human vulnerabilities of the many lives of (and with) sargassum. With sargassum as a starting knot, then, the chapter crafts a poetics of hope amidst the overlapping times and scales of human/non-human lives, their exigencies and the realities of complex environmental crises and climate change challenges.

1   The Region Has a Problem: Multi-Scalar Vulnerability

In his *History of the Voice: The Development of Nation Language in Anglophone Caribbean,* Edward Kamau Brathwaite famously claimed that a *"hurricane does not roar in pentameter."*[19] In an effort to forge new forms capable of "writing the

---

16   Veena Das and Arthur Kleinman, eds. "Introduction" in *Remaking a World: Violence, Social Suffering and Recovery* (Berkeley: U of California P, 2001): 20.

17   Édouard Glissant, *Poetics of Relation*, trans. Betsy Wing (Ann Arbor, MI, Michigan UP, 2006): 194.

18   Where Marder's guiding questions—how is possible for us to encounter plants? how can we maintain and nurture them, without fetishising, their otherness in the course of the encounter?—anchor the inquiry in key philosophical debates, Glissant's notion of opacity adds a distinctly archipelagic dimension to the analysis of living with sargassum in the Caribbean. Michael Marder, *Plant-Thinking: A Philosophy of Vegetal Life* (New York: Columbia UP, 2013): 3.

19   Edward Kamau Brathwaite, *History of the Voice: The Development of Nation Language in Anglophone Caribbean Poetry* (London: New Beacon, 1984): 265.

Caribbean," the Barbadian poet insisted on the need to find a new radical aesthetic, rooted in histories of imperialism, that might reflect the ecologies and histories of the Caribbean region. Brathwaite poignantly captured the lived experience and complex cadence of Caribbean ecologies, the regularity of seasonal change that entails recurring environmental risks and hazards, such as the annual tropical storms. Still, the seeming predictability of the hurricane season, from early June to late November, does not lessen the uncertainty of their impact, their potential to become disastrous, violently disrupting community and island lives. Louis-Philippe Dalembert's multi-layered novel *The Other Side of the Sea* (1998) interweaves the varied forms of violence and exile that have long shaped life on Caribbean islands, and which often determine the decision to leave, or the ability to stay and survive. The text is a "meditation on the multiple meanings of the Haitian expression *lótbòdlo*—the other side of the water—which refers not only to the lands or countries located across the Atlantic Ocean but also to the divide between life and death."[20] The region's intrinsic vulnerabilities, the recurring hazards and invasions of living space—first, by waste and predatory land acquisition practices and, now, by seaweed—all directly shape the sense of what lives are possible and imaginable for island communities. As one of the main characters and narrative voices in Dalembert's novel admits:

> [...] you don't have to have exhausted your brain and your eyes in interminable study at elite universities to understand that this region has a problem. One day, it's a storm that ushers the ocean and squalls of rain into your home, without asking your permission, uproots hundred-year-old mapou trees that, until then, had known how to resist the destructive power of men. Another day, a volcano spews its lava in your face. Then an earthquake comes like a thief at night and surprises you when you're sound asleep, shaking even a monumental fortress like an ordinary coconut tree.[21]

The "problem" captured here is one of multi-scalar vulnerability,[22] a knot of processes, practices, history and politics, omission and neglect, which amplify

---

20 Toni Pressley-Sanon, "Review of: The Other Side of the Sea by Louis-Philippe Dalembert, Robert H. McCormick Jr., Edwidge Danticat; Memory at Bay by Évelyne Trouillot, Paul Curtis Daw, Jason Herbeck," *Journal of Haitian Studies* 22.1 (2016): 205.

21 Louis-Philippe Dalembert, *The Other Side of the Sea*, trans. Robert H. McCormick Jr. (Charlottesville and London: U of Virginia P, 2014): 16.

22 Kasia Mika, *Disasters, Vulnerability, and Narratives: Writing Haiti's Futures* (London: Routledge, 2019): 3–52.

the force of geological tremors or seasonal storms, and now also amplifies the impact of the unprecedented sargassum blooms. This multi-scalar vulnerability is what enables environmental hazards to become deadly and disastrous, year after year, season after season. Equally, the Caribbean's history of hazards—as Dalembert's novel explores across its three primary voices—is one that joins with the political and environmental processes of the past, which continue to mould the region: the remembering of slavery "when Africans were imported ... as enslaved workers" and the "twentieth-century exodus that drives the narrative."[23] The shift seemingly forecast by the uncanny spread of sargassum seems increasingly likely to signify a transition from "problem" to "dead end:" from the sense of hazard to the reality of uninhabitable island environments and ever-increasing pressures to move *lótbòdlo*.

In the context of climate change, multi-scalar vulnerability, as depicted by Dalembert (above), builds on the view of disaster *as a process*[24] rather than *an event*. It is a concept that captures the compound factors embedded within and contributing to the overlapping dynamics of regional, hemispheric and global politics and histories. Multi-scalar vulnerability exists, manifests and cuts across multiple, non-exclusive levels and timescales. Multi-scalar vulnerability is a combination of long-term processes (including environmental degradation and socio-cultural marginalisation) unfolding on the global level. As such, it articulates the region's uneven connectedness and its susceptibility to environmental hazards and phenomena that often originate well beyond imagined/geographical borders or the Caribbean Sea.

Whereas seasonal storms might offer some warning, prompting often last-minute preparations and evacuations, earthquakes "come like a thief at night,"[25] thrusting all within its reverberating reach into a new, cracked time. Climate change, for its part, which has to be considered along with disasters and within the frame of disaster risk reduction, comes without prior notice: it is always there, and it never leaves, rendering adaptation all the more difficult and individual lives all the less liveable. In the terms of Ann Laura Stoler's theorization of "duress,"[26] these hazards-turned-disasters are at once daily,

---

23   Toni Pressley-Sanon, "Review of *The Other Side of the Sea*," 205.
24   For discussion of the relationship between vulnerability and disasters, see for example: Lowell Juilliard Carr, "Disaster and the Sequence-Pattern Concept of Social Change," *American Journal of Sociology* 38 (1932): 211; Kasia Mika, "*Disasters, Vulnerability, and Narratives*".
25   Louis-Philippe Dalembert, *The Other Side of the Sea*, 16.
26   Ann Laura Stoler, *Duress: Imperial Durabilities in Our Times* (Durham: Duke UP, 2016); Ann Laura Stoler, "Imperial Debris: Reflections on Ruin and Ruination," *Cultural Anthropology* 23.2 (May 2018): 191–219.

commonplace occurrences and unique events. The 2010 Haiti earthquake, for example, and the 2017 hurricanes, Irma and Maria, had an immediate impact but also long-term consequences for those affected, for whom life will never be the same. It is the same with the increasing malignant algal bloom, which is one of the Caribbean's quietest creeping catastrophes.

Sargassum has become the "new natural disaster."[27] While the more recognisable "natural" hazards—earthquakes, hurricanes, floods—are still often seen as devastating but fundamentally short-lived events, the seaweed appears more subtle, eating away at the region's ever more tenuous tourism-based economies. The seaweed "invasions" have changed the timeline yet again, pushing the Caribbean archipelago to reassess its response times and envision different futures. Despite the lack of clear consensus on the exact origins and specific reasons for the sudden sargassum inflow of the past few years, marine scholars attribute it to a combination of anthropogenic and environmental factors. In particular, they argue that "high anomalously unprecedented positive sea surface temperature observed in the tropical Atlantic in 2010–2011 could have induced favorable temperature conditions for Sargassum blooms"—favorable conditions fostered by "additional continental nutrients inputs, principally from the Amazon River"[28] resulting from "deforestation, agro-industrial and urban activities in the Amazonian forest" that contribute directly to the algal proliferation while also fuelling climate change.

Inadequate wastewater and human sewage infrastructure are also contributors,[29] as sargassum "infestations are fed by all land-based nutrient pollution."[30] No immediate resolution is available or clearly discernible for these times of sargassum that have suddenly struck, and which continue to strike, changing the temporality of the Caribbean region.[31] To quote Katie Langin,

---

27 Emily Atkin, "Humans Have Created a New Natural Disaster," *New Republic* (August 29, 2018), https://newrepublic.com/article/150775/humans-created-new-natural-disaster.

28 Sandrine Djakouré, Moacyr Araujo, Aubains Hounsou-Gbo, Carlos Noriega, Bernard Bourlès. On the potential causes of the recent Pelagic Sargassum blooms events in the tropical North Atlantic Ocean. *Biogeosciences Discussions* (European Geosciences Union, 2017): 1–20.

29 Atkin, "Humans Have Created a New Natural Disaster."

30 Atkin, "Humans Have Created a New Natural Disaster."

31 The recent edited volume by Kyrre Kverndokk, Marit Ruge Bjærke, and Anne Eriksen adds to the growing scholarly interest in the relationship between multiple temporalities and climate change discourses. See: Kyrre Kverndokk, Marit Ruge Bjærke, and Anne Eriksen, *Climate Change Temporalities: Explorations in Vernacular, Popular, and Scientific Discourse* (London, New York: Routledge, 2021).

"in retrospect, 2011 was just the first wave."[32] Also, as Jean-Philippe Maréchal, Claire Hellio and Chuanmin Hu note, "the [e]vents of washing ashore of pelagic Sargassum occurred in 2011, 2012, 2014, 2015 and 2016 in the Lesser Antilles and Caribbean region,"[33] leading some even to rename the Caribbean Sea as the "Sea of Trouble,"[34] and others, motivated by the search for "[the] commercial exploration of this biomass," to see the swathes of sargassum as potential "golden tides."[35]

In effect, the stranded algae seem to enact a double foreclosure. First, it materially dominates islands and shorelines, making lives on the coast unlivable. Second, its overpowering presence embodies the symbolic impoundment of an "imaginative horizon."[36] Alternatives beyond the toxic shores seem almost unimaginable, reminding islanders that they are stranded between the draining flows of global tourist capital and sargassum-full seas, with each tide marking a potential loss of income and livelihood. In this context of multiscalar vulnerability and the urgent pressures facing each territory, and indeed the entire region, what does it mean to forge a Caribbean poetics of hope with sargassum? What is at stake in an attempt to reinvigorate the notion of hope as an analytical, experiential and political category?[37] What is the place of hope within the coiled timescales of environmental change, vulnerability and uncertain—but certainly threatened—futures?

2   Coiled Temporality

In the exploration of the "coiled temporality" of sargassum, we draw on recent scholarship in the blue humanities, emerging from the "oceanic turn" as well as the "archipelagic turn", and addressing also some of the concerns of Island Studies. Together, these analytical frames call for a rethinking of archipelagic

---

32   Katie Langin, "Seaweed Masses Assault Caribbean Islands," *Science* 360.6394 (June 2018): 1157–1158.

33   Jean-Phillipe Maréchal, et al. "A Simple, Fast, and Reliable Method to Predict Sargassum Washing Ashore in the Lesser Antilles," *Remote Sensing Applications: Society and Environment* 5 (2017): 54.

34   Langin, "Seaweed Masses Assault Caribbean Islands," 1157–1158.

35   John J. Milledge and Patricia J. Harvey, "Golden Tides: Problem or Golden Opportunity? The Valorisation of Sargassum from Beach Inundations," *Journal of Marine Science and Engineering* 4.3 (2016): 1.

36   Vincent Crapanzano, *Imaginative Horizons: An Essay in Literary-Philosophical Anthropology* (Chicago: U of Chicago P, 2004): 15–17.

37   Crapanzano, *Imaginative Horizons*, 98.

and oceanic space. The oceanic turn places, at the fore, the conceptual-scholarly transition, in Elizabeth DeLoughrey's words, "from a long-term concern with mobility across transoceanic surfaces to theorizing oceanic submersion, thus rendering vast oceanic space into ontological place."[38] Equally, to think with the archipelago affords a dynamically shifting epistemology. In Jonathan Pugh's terms, "thinking *with* the archipelago foregrounds how island movements are generative and inter-connective spaces of metamorphosis, of material practices, culture and politics."[39] Speaking against overly metaphorical and detached analyses of the ocean, in his discussion of ocean ontologies, Philipe Steinberg warns precisely against reproducing the potential failure of "the bulk of ocean-themed literature [...] to incorporate the sea as a real, experienced, social arena." Steinberg turns to the notion of 'ocean assemblage'— that is ' "more-than-human" assemblages, reproduced by scientists, sailors, fishers, surfers, divers, passengers and even pirate broadcasters as they interact with, and are co-constituted by, all the mobile non-human elements that inhabit the depths: including ships, fish, water molecules" and plastic waste, as many would add.[40] In effect, the idea of *ocean assemblage* moves away from the emphasis on a geological phenomenon or single species as a key frame to think about oceanic spaces, instead suggesting the possibility of multiple, unpredictable and dynamic sets of interrelationships happening across all four dimensions of the sea.[41]

The Caribbean Archipelago is such a unique nexus. Always ahead of time, the world's first capitalist region[42] shows and anticipates our global ecological futures. The small island states of the Caribbean are the globe's barometers of environmental change,[43] exposing the violence, complexity and asynchronicity of the Anthropocene in relation to the long histories of colonialism and imperialism that have shaped the lives of human and non-human others in the Caribbean basin. Speaking directly from this specificity of the Caribbean

---

38   Elizabeth DeLoughrey, "Submarine Futures of the Anthropocene," *Comparative Literature* 69.1 (2017): 32.

39   Jonathan Pugh, "Island Movements: Thinking with the Archipelago," *Island Studies Journal* 8.1 (2013): 10.

40   Philip E. Steinberg, "Of Other Seas: Metaphors and Materialities in Maritime Regions," *Atlantic Studies* 10.2 (2013): 159. See also Hester Blum, "The Prospect of Oceanic Studies," *PMLA* 125.3 (2010): 670.

41   Steinberg explains: "The four dimensions referred to here are depth and time, as well as the two dimensions of area".

42   Sidney Mintz, "The Caribbean Region," *Slavery, Colonialism, and Racism* 103 (1974): 45–71.

43   Ilan Kelman and Jennifer West, "Climate Change and Small Island Developing States: A Critical Review," *Ecological and Environmental Anthropology* 5 (2009): 1–16.

experience and the violent histories of colonialism that have moulded the archipelago, Brathwaite's idea of the "tidalectic" connects and further enriches this archipelagic understanding of "the heavy waters of Atlantic modernity" (in Elizabeth DeLoughrey's words),[44] and the past that is not past of the Middle Passage[45] as discussed by Michel-Rolph Trouillot and, more recently, Christina Sharpe in her evocative meditation on the meanings of "the wake" and the conditions of Blackness and being in the ongoing aftermath of transatlantic slavery.[46] In simple terms, Brathwaite's tidalectic marks an anti-progressive approach and "the rejection of the notion of dialectic, which is three—the resolution in the third, [with] 'tide-alectic' which is the ripple and the two tide movement."[47] Tidalectic allows for a *decolonial* conception of "ocean times" that responds critically to the violence and brutality that fills oceanic spaces.[48] For Brathwaite, the "original explosion of the Middle Passage" is "an ongoing catastrophe,"[49] central to tidalectics—and to the human and non-human histories of the Atlantic.[50]

In his meditation on island topographies and their natural histories, Nicholas Laughin interweaves discussions of Caribbean poetry, art, thought and history to offer a poetic consideration of "facts, fictions, names, etymologies, lyrics

---

44   Elizabeth DeLoughrey, "Heavy Waters: Waste and Atlantic Modernity," *PMLA* 125.3 (2010): 703–712.

45   The Middle Passage refers to "the journey from Africa to the Americas," and more specifically to the transatlantic slave trade which began in the 16th century. Henry Louis Gates Jr, *Black Imagination and the Middle Passage* (Oxford: Oxford UP, 1999): 6.

46   Michel-Rolph Trouillot, *Silencing the Past: Power and the Production of History* (Boston, MA: Beacon Press, 2015); Christina Sharpe, *In the Wake: On Blackness and Being* (Durham: Duke UP, 2016).

47   Paul Naylor, *Poetic Investigations: Singing the Holes in History* (Evanston, IL: Northwestern UP, 1999) in Anna Reckin (2003) "Tidalectic Lectures: Kamau Brathwaite's Prose/Poetry as Sound-Space," *Anthurium: A Caribbean Studies Journal* 1.1 Article 5, 145.

48   We understand *decoloniality* as an emancipatory praxis that involves leaving behind the imaginaries underlying the modern relation between peoples and civilisations, as well as self-abolishing the construction of self-as-other imposed by the colonial imaginary of race. Adler Camilus, "La révolution haïtienne de 1804 entre les études postcoloniales et les études décoloniales latino-américaines," *Revue d'études décoloniales* (October 1, 2017), http://reseaudecolonial.org/2017/10/01/la-revolution-haitienne-de-1804-entre-les-etu des-postcoloniales-et-les-etudes-decoloniales-latino-americaines/.

49   Joyelle McSweeney, "Poetics, Revelations, and Catastrophes: An Interview with Kamau Brathwaite," *Rain Taxi* (Fall 2005), http://www.raintaxi.com/poetics-revelations-and -catastrophes-an-interview-with-kamau-brathwaite/.

50   Elizabeth DeLoughrey, "Toward a Critical Ocean Studies for the Anthropocene," *English Language Notes* 57.1 (2019): 21–36.

and questions"[51] that come together in "the form of a broken-up archipelago."[52] Stories of sugar cane and sargassum contribute to the braided fabric of his essay, joining fragments of poetry, news coverage, anecdote and archival material. Reflecting on the botanical histories of the broken-up archipelago, Laughin asks, "What are the flora most typical of these islands? The coconut palms that fringe our beaches? The mango tree, whose fruit inspires love poems? [...] Or the plant that, more than any other species, has shaped the destiny of the Caribbean, the sugar cane?"[53] Or, following the trace of journalists reporting in the *Trinidad Express* and their warning that "*The Seaweed is Coming*":[54] is sargassum the islands' new "typical" flora, shaping the destiny of the region in times of increasingly violent environmental injustices and climate change? It is a plant that invades shorelines, issuing threats and inspiring a sense of "*new*" times—times *with* sargassum?

Coiled temporality, as we propose it, incorporates these non-linear and interconnected approaches that join the ocean and the archipelago and put them in dialogue with Édouard Glissant's "poetics of relation" as a way of incorporating the non-human other—sargassum—to its oceanic and archipelagic histories. For Glissant, "rhizomatic thought" is the principle behind a "Poetics of Relation, in which each and every identity is extended through a relationship with the Other."[55] Thinking with sargassum and through its various narratives—from its symbolic portrayal as a ghostly menace threatening the course of colonisation, as recorded in Columbus's diary,[56] to the exponential blooms fuelled today by rising temperatures and nitrogen imbalance (as in contemporary scientific framings)—radically extends Glissant's formulation of "poetics of relation" and "rhizomatic thought." Sargassum's errantry, first as a rich living ecosystem and habitat, then as a menace, and finally as a

---

51 Nicholas Laughin, "There Are No Islands Without the Sea: Being a Compendium of Facts, Fictions, Names, Etymologies, Lyrics, and Questions in the Form of a Broken-Up Archipelago" in *Relational Undercurrents: Contemporary Art of the Caribbean Archipelago*, eds. Tatiana Flores and Michelle Ann Stephens (Durham: Duke UP, 2017): 261.

52 Nicholas Laughin, "There Are No Islands Without the Sea," 261.

53 Laughin, "There Are No Islands Without the Sea," 265.

54 "The Seaweed is Coming ... Tobago Braces," *Trinidad Express* (September 7, 2019), https://www.trinidadexpress.com/news/local/the-seaweed-is-coming/article_b849b240-3cc0-5042-8021-68b23b6dad82.html.

55 Édouard Glissant, *Poetics of Relation*, trans. Betsy Wing (Ann Arbor: U of Michigan P, 2010): 11.

56 John M. Kingsbury, "Christopher Columbus as a Botanist," *Arnoldia* 52. 2 (Summer 1992): 12.

toxic nuisance, calls for a decolonial, multi-species consideration of ecological threats, hopes and futures.

The algae's many functions and lives, as habitat and shelter, beneath and above the water surface, are often completely overshadowed in discussion, and forgotten once this unique open ocean ecosystem hits the shore with its "seaweed deluge,"[57] submerging wildlife and destroying sea-dependent economies. Similarly, in a further translation of the logic of capital and production, the only relation envisaged with the algae is one of commodification, converting it from ecological threat to a desirable source of fuel. For the Barbadian Minister of Maritime Affairs and the Blue Economy, the diagnostic is clear: "Sargassum: A National Emergency and Energy Source."[58] This paradoxical joining of threat and fuel, crisis and capital, which completely overlooks the aforementioned correlation between harmful algae blooms and rising sea temperatures, is an archipelagic variation of disaster capitalism. The frame of radical reduction and extraction, "rendering [sargassum] amenable for appropriation and exchange,"[59] proposes only one desirable and possible relation: the other as fuel.

A relational tidalectic of the times with sargassum challenges this kind of commodifying logic. It acknowledges sargassum as a material in and of itself as well as a conceptual figure for interweaving human/non-human lives and the histories underpinning them. Sargassum, as Aaron Pinnix argues, challenges us to reconsider what it means to live with the seaweed, the histories it indexes and the futures it might herald. In his attempt to rethink Atlantic histories of colonialism and exploitation, and to reconceptualise "[the] transoceanic connections" of the Black Atlantic,[60] Pinnix first turns to Glissant's rhizome concept. Observing its "terrestrial" character, however, its fixedness (which makes it a trope inadequate for aquatic contexts), he replaces it with sargassum as "a figure of relation,"[61] one capable of making the ocean "material critically present, while also refusing to ever be attached to one location."[62] For

---

57   Philippa Fogarty, "Sargassum: The Seaweed Deluge Hitting Caribbean Shores".

58   Julia Rawlins-Bentham, "Sargassum: A National Emergency and Energy Source," *Barbados Government Information Service* (June 10, 2018), https://gisbarbados.gov.bb/blog/sargassum-a-national-emergency-energy-source/#:~:text=Sargassum%3A%20A%20National%20Emergency%20%26%20Energy%20Source%20by,being%20treated%20as%20a%20national%20emergency%20by%20Government.

59   Maan Barua, "Lively Commodities and Encounter Value," *Environment and Planning D: Society and Space* 34.4 (August 2016): 736.

60   Aaron Pinnix, "Sargassum in the Black Atlantic: Entanglement and the Abyss in Bearden, Walcott, and Philip," *Atlantic Studies* 16. 4 (2019): 1.

61   Pinnix, "Sargassum in the Black Atlantic," 4.

62   Pinnix, "Sargassum in the Black Atlantic," 4.

Pinnix, the "rhizome falters as a model for transoceanic connection because as a terrestrial figure the rhizome relies on an environmental milieu that is unmoving and stable."[63] By contrast, the seaweed's entangled materiality and the conceptual repositioning that it affords "can be understood as symbolically interconnecting various Atlantic cultures and histories, including Africa, the Mediterranean, Europe and the Americas, while also allowing for gaps in knowledge and interconnection."[64]

In dismissing the "terrestrial" rhizome as a trope too fixed for Caribbean environment, however, Pinnix fails to take account of the shifting, dynamic and unpredictably eruptive nature of Caribbean geologies. The 1902 Mount Pelée volcanic eruption in Martinique (the deadliest of the twentieth century), the 1995 eruption in Montserrat and the 2021 eruption of La Soufrière in St. Vincent (to name but a few) demonstrate that there is nothing stable about the archipelago's geology.[65] Pinnix's emphasis on connectivity-as-entanglement also risks equalizing the many distinctions, not least those determined by issues of class, national sovereignty and varying degrees of dependence on global economy, that expand and elongate, on a vertical plane, the connections between the varying Caribbean islands,[66] the nations and kingdoms of which they are still part, and the wider regional and global dynamics that define and change the Caribbean every day.

This sense of non-analogous, disparate connections is central to the notion of coiled temporality and is particularly important when considering sargassum in the context of the multi-scalar vulnerability of the islands, where potentially deadly tremors meet ever more extreme climate events. The intertwined histories of ecology, environmental hazard, capital and political interests unfolding on a macro-level are experienced by those thrown in their midst (on the

---

63   Pinnix, "Sargassum in the Black Atlantic," 3.
64   Pinnix, "Sargassum in the Black Atlantic," 3.
65   See Keith H. James, "A Simple Synthesis of Caribbean Geology," Transactions of the 16th Caribbean Geological Conference, Barbados. *Caribbean Journal of Earth Science* 39 (2005): 69–82.
66   The reality of uneven connectedness, compound vulnerabilities and asymmetrical exposure put to the fore the tensions between capital, sovereignty and aid—within regions; indeed, for each and every island in the Caribbean. This became clear following the 2017 hurricane season in the Atlantic. For example, St. Kitts and Nevis and British Overseas Territories including Anguilla, the British Virgin Islands and Turks and Caicos, according to OECD guidelines, were not eligible for assistance. The gross national income per capita of these islands was deemed to too high for them to have access to aid and recovery budgets. See, for example, Guy Hewitt, "Our Hurricane-Hit Islands Deserve Aid: The Rules That Block It Are Wrong," *Guardian* (September 19, 2017), https://www.theguardian.com/commentisfree/2017/sep/19/hurricane-maria-caribbean-oecd-aid-rules-assistance.

micro-level) as daily deprivation and inequality, and as an ongoing, embodied experience of crisis—from being unable to open a window, or pursue a livelihood, or attend school. In this "powerful state of 'routinized ruptures,'"[67] everyday crisis becomes ordinary. This violent politico-environmental experience of the everyday is precisely what the speaker in Kamau Brathwaite's poem "Negus" protests against. The notion of "enough"—as an expression of desire, of scarcity (not enough), of protest and agency (enough!)—unites these varying scales of crisis. In an insistent rhythm of resistance and aspiration, the speaker asserts:

> it is not
> it is not
> it is not enough
> it is not enough to be free
> of malarial fevers, fear of the hurricane,
> fear of invasions, crops' drought, fire's
> blisters upon the cane
> [...]
> It is not
> it is not
> it is not enough
> to be pause, to be hole
> to be void, to be silent
> to be semicolon, to be semicolony;[68]

Here, repetition is not a stutter, by any means. Rather, "it is," repeated as a refrain, is an affirmation of resolve and an attempt to carve out an opening, a space of "more", where sufficiency and sovereignty conjoin. While clearly critical of the halted present, the speaker affirms that, with the punctuation mark as a political category, the semicolon(y) is only "intermediate in value."[69] It signals a break, a temporary separation of what is, from what will be. The confined present, the silence of the semicolony, is not all that there is. In their

---

67 Erica Caple James, "Ruptures, Rights, and Repair: The Political Economy of Trauma in Haiti," *Social Science & Medicine* 70.1 (January 2010): 107. For an extended discussion of *ensekirite* see James, "Haunting Ghosts: Madness, Gender, and Ensekirite in Haiti in the Democratic Era" in *Postcolonial Disorders*, eds. Mary-Jo Delvecchio Good, Sandra Teresa Hyde, Sarah Pinto and Byron J. Good (Berkley: U of California P, 2008): 132–156.

68 Kamau Brathwaite, "VI Negus," *Islands* (London, New York, and Toronto: Oxford UP, 1969): 66–67.

69 "semicolon, n." *OED Online* (Oxford UP, September 2019), www.oed.com/view/Entry/175618.

REFASHIONING FUTURES WITH SARGASSUM 207

coiled movement, these verses turn from repetition to a different mode of positioning in the world. They reach towards a new political imaginary, the imaginative horizon of a future that is neither foreclosed nor asphyxiated.

As Brathwaite's "Negus" makes clear, this foretold and foreseen imaginative horizon, in the context of the Caribbean, must entail the undoing of exploitative hierarchies, moving (as Sylvia Wynter urged) "Towards the Human, After Man";[70] or towards the human/non-human, after Man. Joining the words and worlds of human/non-human exploitation, in order to devise an alternative set of liberating relations, the poem's speaker exclaims:

> I
> must be given words to shape my name
> to the syllables of trees
>
> I must be given words to refashion futures
> like a healer's hand[71]

Calling for "new words to refashion futures / like a healer's hand," the poem does not conjure any idealised vision of an easily achievable or recoverable better tomorrow. Neither is it is possible to "go back" to less threatening times devoid of earthquakes, storms or sargassum strandings. Rather, the refashioning of futures—which we inevitably share—with non-human others involves moving away from the antithetical, binary and exploitative positioning of the Caribbean as either "paradise" or "paradise lost," always at "your service", and rarely anything in between.

After the halt of the semicolon in Brathwaite's poem—a short pause, a moment to breathe in—comes the breathing out, or exhalation, which is a determined, future-oriented action that breaks the silence and the void of the earlier stanza:

> fling me the stone
> that will confound the void
> find me the rage
> and I will raze the colony
> fill me with words

---

70 Sylvia Wynter, "Unsettling the Coloniality of Being/Power/Truth/Freedom: Towards the Human, After Man, Its Overrepresentation—An Argument," CR: The New Centennial Review 3.3 (Fall 2003): 288.

71 Brathwaite, "VI Negus," 67.

and I will blind your God.

Att
Att
Attibon

Attibon Legba
Attibon Legba
Ouvri bayi pou'moi
Ouvir bayi pou'moi[72]

The hole turns to a stone; the rage fills the void; words counter silence, and the hesitation of the semicolon gives way to the decisive fling of the stone, one that echoes the Biblical struggle of David and Goliath (1 Samuel 17) in which David "took out a stone, slung it, and struck the Philistine on his forehead; the stone sank into his forehead, and he fell face down on the ground" (1 Sam 17; 49).[73] The poem's speaker wishes for and, in some ways, anticipates the righteous anger of David's hurling of the stone, which manifests in a future to come, starting at *kalfou/kafou* (the crossroads in Haitian Kreyòl).

The Vodou chant for Papa Legba with which the poem concludes calls out: "Attibon Legba, open the gate for me! / You see, Attibon Legba, open the gate for me!"[74] In the Haitian Vodou cosmology, Papa Legba is the "Spirit of rituals, keeper of the gates and guardian of the crossroads between the sacred and the mortal worlds."[75] He is the "*lwa* [spirit] of the thresholds."[76] Usually sung at the beginning of ceremonies, the ritual call to Legba echoes the poem's earlier visions of an "opened-up," freed future: beyond the bond, the bounds, and the halt of the semicolon(y). Culminating in an ellipsis, these lines signal, in formal terms, a thought-pause and point towards the unknown, which comes once the gates are opened and the threshold crossed.

At the same time, these words, usually accompanied by the beat of the Vodou drum, echo and recall the Middle Passage and the beginnings of Creole

---

72   Brathwaite, "VI Negus," 67.

73   *The Bible* (New Revised Standard Edition), https://bible.usccb.org/bible/1samuel/17.

74   Yvonne Daniel, *Dancing Wisdom: Embodied Knowledge in Haitian Vodou, Cuban Yoruba, and Bahian Candomblé* (Urbana, IL: U of Illinois P, 2005): 70.

75   Alex Farquharson and Leah Gordon "Characteristics of the Spirits (lwa)," *Kafou: Haiti, Art and Vodou* (Nottingham: Nottingham Contemporary, 2012): 50.

76   Donald J. Cosentino, "Gede Rising," in *Extremis: Death and Life in 21st-Century Haitian Art* (Los Angeles: Fowler Museum at UCLA, 2012): 44.

literature, with "[a] sudden *cry* arising from the ship's hold."[77] The chant calls out to all the spirits and ancestors in Guiné, inaugurating a hoped-for opening up, "an appreciation of historical contingency: that things might have been and so might yet still be, otherwise."[78] Indexed here, the future starts with the idiosyncratic vocabulary of Vodou, each syllable joining, in Derek Walcott's gloss, "our shattered histories, our shards of vocabulary [...] whose restoration shows its white scars,"[79] and hoping to create new words, a new vocabulary for a convalescent world—with sargassum one among the many species on this trajectory. Extending the philosophical project of the preceding stanzas, the invocation embedded in Brathwaite's poem indexes the transition between the halted present of the semicolon(y), which is predicated upon the exploitation of the Caribbean human/non-human others, and a decolonial future, hopefully imagined outside of these confines.

The anticipatory affirmation of "Negus" and the vision that the poem charts is in stark contrast to the reversely predictive imaginary that sees the present and the future of the Caribbean, in Martin Munro's words, as a "tropical apocalypse" and "a presage of a broader catastrophic collapse, a window onto all of our apocalyptic futures."[80] Or "the algae apocalypse," as another commentator calls it.[81] While giving voice to both the sense of urgency and the need to look to long-term histories of disasters, the paradoxical evocation of apocalyptic decline and solidarity risks ignoring the reality of uneven, non-analogous ecological connections and situations with and within which some communities are forced to live, while others are protected by distance and capital. Brathwaite challenges the ethical and political limitations of any envisioned future that does not embrace more-than-human participants and that does not address climate change and the likelihood of recurring hazzards. In this sense "Negus" might be read as an anticipation of the humanities "after Man," as Kandice Chuh puts it, "generating and proliferating imaginaries disidentified from the

---

77 'Un *cri* surgissant de la cale. Celui d'un Africain quelconque.' Patrick Chamoiseau and Raphaël Confiant, *Lettres créoles: Tracées antillaises et continentales de la littérature Haïti, Guadeloupe, Martinique, Guyane 1635–1975* (Paris: Hatier, 1991): 32.

78 Thom van Dooren, "Care," *Environmental Humanities* 5.1 (2014): 293.

79 Derek Walcott, "Nobel Lecture: The Antilles: Fragments of Epic Memory," *Nobelprize.org* (Nobel Media AB: 2014), http://www.nobelprize.org/nobel_prizes/literature/laureates/1992/walcott-lecture.html.

80 Martin Munro, *Tropical Apocalypse: Haiti and the Caribbean End Times* (Charlottesville: U of Virginia P, 2015): 199.

81 Rick Spillman, "Algae Apocalypse—Sargassum Spreads Across the Caribbean & Florida," *The Old Salt Blog*, (October 12, 2018), http://www.oldsaltblog.com/2018/10/algae-apocaly pse-sargassum-spreads-across-the-caribbean-florida/.

ideologies and logics of liberalism and derived instead from attention to the entangled histories of and ongoing connection among the impoverishment of peoples and worlds, enslaved and gendered labor, Indigenous dispossession, developmentalism, and knowledge work."[82] These "times to come" might well start with the symbolic invocation of Legba at the crossroads. Yet they carry into the unknown: whatever the ellipsis and the ocean hold.

3   Opaque Hopes

With news reports portraying the Caribbean as a semi-permanent disaster zone, it is easy to give into foreclosed visions of the region as one of ongoing crisis where the "sargassum invasion" figures as a just another recurring threat of environmental collapse—unless, of course, it can be commodified. Yet the seaweed's plasticity eludes this binary positioning. Its fundamental opacity— and the opacity of the many forms of life and debris entangled with it—is "a fundamental prerequisite for the constitution of the Other, just as uncircumventable difference is the basis for relations between all things."[83] For Glissant, opacity is "an epistemological notion that gives everyone the right to hold on to their thicker shadow, that is their psycho-cultural depth."[84] Applying Glissant's theorisation of alterity to human/non-human relations brings the opacity of sargassum (which ties together diverse life forms and things from shrimp to plastic detritus) to be seen as a "fundamental prerequisite" for rethinking ecological relations in the Caribbean archipelago. Even if we take Pinnix's view of sargassum, as a "form of interrelation through entanglement,"[85] it appears as neither "a confused or stagnant mass"[86] nor simply a resource for exploitation. Conceding to this "thickness" is equally a gesture of giving up and of relinquishing at least some mastery over non-human others—which means making a first step toward a nonhegemonic ecological vocabulary.

Acknowledgement of the opacity and complex connectivity of archipelagic ecologies is central to Brathwaite's horizon of "refashioned futures," and to our

---

82   Kandice Chuh, *The Difference Aesthetics Makes: On the Humanities 'After Man'* (Durham: Duke UP, 2019): 6.

83   Ulrich Loock. "Opacity," *Frieze* 7 (Winter 2012), https://frieze.com/article/opacity.

84   Clément Mbom, "Édouard Glissant, de l'opacité à la relation," in *Poétiques d'Edouard Glissant*, ed. Jacques Chevrier (Presses Paris Sorbonne, 1999): 248.

85   Pinnix, "Sargassum in the Black Atlantic," 10.

86   DeLoughrey, *Routes and Roots: Navigating Caribbean and Pacific Island Literatures* (Honolulu: U of Hawai'i P, 2010): 70.

REFASHIONING FUTURES WITH SARGASSUM

own conceptualisation of coiled temporality. Extending the call for "words [...] like healer's hands," the speaker of "Negus" declares:

> I must be given words so that the bees
> in my blood's buzzing brain of memory
>
> will make flowers, will make flocks of birds,
> will make sky, will make heaven,
> the heaven open to the thunder-stone and the volcano and the un-
> folding land.[87]

The image of the "bees / in my blood's buzzing brain of memory," followed by the accumulation of botanical, atmospheric and geological references, paints a vision of an ecologically relational subjectivity, where the different parts connect to each other without ever losing their distinct characteristics. Also, the repetition of the future tense ("will make") creates a resolute and generative cadence whereby each verse affirms new words and worlds to come. Finally, the paradoxical pairing of memory (pointing to the past) and prophetic future times to come suggests, here and elsewhere in the poem, that the imaginative horizon of individual and collective sovereignty is a direct overturning of exploitative ecological relations, as indicated in earlier lines by the "United-Fruit-Company-imported / hard sell"[88] and the speaker's repeated criticism of the relentless exploitation of Caribbean communities and environments.

Indeed the poem's invocation of the sovereign hope of a more-than-human future is best seen as "a reality that goes beyond temporality and any political, cultural, or technological idea of progress or of any further commodification and exhaustion of the environment that this notion implies."[89] In times of sargassum, that nonlinear hope calls for a more-than-human positioning of "us" in the environment, beyond the militaristic discourse of "war against Sargassum."[90] It involves asking after more-than-human vulnerabilities and recognising, first and foremost, the ways in which anthropogenic activities— that cause global climate change and the associated warming of ocean surface temperatures as well as the increased nutrient loads in the water and marine

---

87 Brathwaite, "VI Negus," 67.
88 Brathwaite, "VI Negus," 66.
89 Vincent Wargo, "Festivity, Tradition, and Hope: Josef Pieper and the Historical Meaning of Human Praxis," *Logos: A Journal of Catholic Thought and Culture* 21.4 (2018): 69.
90 Kory Leslie, "The War against Sargassum," *Amandala* (June 22, 2019), http://amandala .com.bz/news/war-sargassum/.

litter[91]—contribute to the anomalous quantities of sargassum in the region, and to the force with which it hits the shore. This perceptual shift is key to formulating a more radical climate change politics, one that resists techno-cratic quick-fixes or looking at sargassum in isolation from its histories and entanglements. In other words, the coiled temporality and materiality of sar-gassum, from the timelines of the species it supports to those of the debris and litter it carries, demonstrate the suffocating telos and dead-end of linear pro-gress as well as the illusion of mastery and control that it suggests. Sargassum escapes both.

This chapter's opening images, upon first viewing, might well seem to suggest a story of sargassum's aggressive invasion and loss of economic opportunity, affective relations and open horizons; a story embedded in the disturbing por-trait of non-human and more-than-human bodies decomposing, intertwined in death. Yet these images also challenge the ways in which some species are con-strued as loss and others as nuisance. They confront the viewer with the multi-ple facets of excess and entanglement where the overabundance of seaweed— its overwhelming volume and threatening proximity—seems to foretell what the ecological times to come might look like. Still, the moment of arrest that the sargassum seems to enact, like the semicolon(y) in Brathwaite's "Negus," is not all that there is. In other words, to extend the poem's call: it is not enough to be free of sargassum, or to remove sargassum from Caribbean resort beaches.

Motion and movement define oceanic and archipelagic ecologies, creating the possibility of a re-encounter with sargassum on different terms, as neither foe nor fuel. According to Maan Barua, to encounter is "to become-worldly, to open up contingencies and processes of life, rather than cutting up the world into inert natures and static societies."[92] Such unmoored reposition-ing allows for a future-making anchored *in relation*, after Glissant, not in the often-alleged resilience of the Caribbean and its communities. Ultimately, the photos, as well as "Negus's" insistent call, serve as stark reminders and visual arguments (for those in doubt) that we can neither disconnect nor disentangle ourselves from "other" life forms and the processes that define our respective being and becoming in the world. As Crapanzano puts it: sharing "the same direction as expectation," hope "penetrates further into the future than expec-tation."[93] Ecological hope, with the ocean, the archipelago, climate change and

---

91   See Dutch Caribbean Nature Alliance, *Prevention and Clean-up of Sargassum in the Dutch Caribbean* (2019), https://www.dcnanature.org/wp-content/uploads/2019/02/DCNA -Sargassum-Brief.pdf.

92   Maan Barua, "Encounter," *Environmental Humanities* 7.1 (2016): 265–270.

93   Crapanzano, *Imaginative Horizons*, 104.

sargassum—that is relational tidalectics at its core—folds, loops and spirals without assuming a linear, teleological movement of hegemonic commodification of the environment and non-human others. Such an urgent reconfiguration of human/non-human relations in the Caribbean starts at the crossroads of crisis and entails recognising, as distinct from impenetrability, the opacity of both the ecological other and of our ecological selves.

Works Cited

Atkin, Emily. "Humans Have Created a New Natural Disaster." *New Republic* (August 29, 2018), https://newrepublic.com/article/150775/humans-created-new-natural-disaster.

Barua, Maan. "Encounter." *Environmental Humanities* 7.1 (May 1, 2016): 265–270.

Barua, Maan. "Lively Commodities and Encounter Value." *Environment and Planning D: Society and Space* 34.4 (August 2016): 725–744.

Bible. New Revised Standard Edition, https://www.biblegateway.com/passage/?search=1%20Samuel+17&version=NRSV.

Blum Hester. "The Prospect of Oceanic Studies." *PMLA* 125.3 (2010): 670–677.

Brathwaite, Edward Kamau. "VI Negus." *Islands* (London, New York, and Toronto: Oxford UP, 1969).

Brathwaite, Edward Kamau. *History of the Voice: The Development of Nation Language in Anglophone Caribbean Poetry.* (London: New Beacon, 1984).

Camilus, Adler. "La révolution haïtienne de 1804 entre les études postcoloniales et les études décoloniales latino-américaines," *Revue d'études décoloniales* (October 1, 2017), https://hal.archives-ouvertes.fr/hal-01712977/document.

Carr, Lowell Juilliard. "Disaster and the Sequence-Pattern Concept of Social Change." *American Journal of Sociology* 38 (1932): 207–218.

Castro, Alejandro. "Sargassum: Brown Tide Threatens the Caribbean." *St. Thomas Source* (April 16, 2021), https://stthomassource.com/content/2021/04/16/sargassum-brown-tide-threatens-the-caribbean/.

Chamoiseau, Patrick and Raphaël Confiant. *Lettres créoles: Tracées antillaises et continentales de la littérature Haïti, Guadeloupe, Martinique, Guyane 1635–1975.* (Paris: Hatier, 1991).

Chuh, Kandice. *The Difference Aesthetics Makes: On the Humanities 'After Man'.* (Durham: Duke UP, 2019).

Conseil Régional de la Guadeloupe. *Research Development and Innovation Joint Call on Sargassum Seaweed,* https://www.regionguadeloupe.fr/fileadmin/Site_Region_Guadeloupe/actus/appels_a_projets/APP_sargasse_Call_for_Sargassum_final_version.pdf.

Cosentino, Donald J. "Gede Rising" in *Extremis: Death and Life in 21st-Century Haitian Art*.(Los Angeles: Fowler Museum at UCLA, 2012): 25–76.

Crapanzano, Vincent. *Imaginative Horizons: An Essay in Literary-Philosophical Anthropology* (Chicago: U of Chicago P, 2004).

Dalembert, Louis-Philippe. *The Other Side of the Sea*, trans. by Robert H. McCormick Jr (Charlottesville and London: U of Virginia P, 2014).

Daniel, Yvonne. *Dancing Wisdom: Embodied Knowledge in Haitian Vodou, Cuban Yoruba, and Bahian Candomblé*. (Urbana, IL: U of Illinois P, 2005).

Das, Veena, and Arthur Kleinman. "Introduction" in *Remaking a World: Violence, Social Suffering and Recovery,* eds. Arthur Kleinman, Mamphela Ramphele, Margaret M. Lock, Pamela Reynolds and Veena Das (Berkeley: U of California P, 2001): 1–31.

DeLoughrey, Elizabeth. *Routes and Roots: Navigating Caribbean and Pacific Island Literatures.* (Honolulu: U of Hawai'i P, 2010).

DeLoughrey, Elizabeth. "Toward a Critical Ocean Studies for the Anthropocene." *English Language Notes* 57.1 (2019): 21–36.

Deloughrey, Elizabeth. "Submarine Futures of the Anthropocene." *Comparative Literature* 69.1 (2017): 32–44.

Deloughrey, Elizabeth. "Heavy Waters: Waste and Atlantic Modernity." *PMLA* 125.3 (2010): 703–712.

Djakouré, Sandrine, Moacyr Araujo, Aubains Hounsou-Gbo, Carlos Noriega and Bernard Bourlès. "On the Potential Causes of the Recent Pelagic Sargassum Blooms Events in the Tropical North Atlantic Ocean." *Biogeosciences Discussions* (European Geosciences Union, 2017): 1–20.

Dutch Caribbean Nature Alliance, *Prevention and Clean-up of Sargassum in the Dutch Caribbean*(2019),https://www.dcnanature.org/wp-content/uploads/2019/02/DCNA -Sargassum-Brief.pdf.

"Evaluation des méthodes de collecte des sargasses—ADEME," (Agency for the Environment and Energy Management), SAFEGE Ingénieurs Conseils, DEAL Guadeloupe, http://www.guadeloupe.developpement-durable.gouv.fr/evaluation -des-methodes-de-collecte-des-sargasses-r1084.html.

Farquharson, Alex and Leah Gordon. "Characteristics of the Spirits (lwa)." *Kafou: Haiti, Art and Vodou*. (Nottingham: Nottingham Contemporary, 2012).

Flores, Tatiana and Michelle Ann Stephens, eds. *Relational Undercurrents: Contemporary Art of the Caribbean Archipelago*. (Durham: Duke UP, 2017).

Fogarty, Philippa. "Sargassum: The Seaweed Deluge Hitting Caribbean Shores." *BBC News* (August 6, 2018), https://www.bbc.com/news/world-latin-america-45044513.

Gates, Henry Louis Jr. *Black Imagination and the Middle Passage.* (Oxford: Oxford UP, 1999).

Glissant, Edouard. *Traité du Tout-Monde*. (Paris: Gallimard, 1997).

Glissant, Édouard. *Poetics of Relation* trans. Betsy Wing (Ann Arbor, MI: U of Michigan P, 2010).

Golabkan, E. and E. Gire. "Huit établissements scolaires de Petit-Bourg fermés sur décision du maire." *Guadeloupe 1ère* (May 30, 2018), https://la1ere.francetvinfo.fr/guadeloupe/neuf-etablissements-scolaires-petit-bourg-fermes-decision-du-maire-594217.html.

Hewitt, Guy. "Our Hurricane-Hit Islands Deserve Aid. The Rules That Block It Are Wrong." *Guardian* (September 19, 2017), https://www.theguardian.com/commentisfree/2017/sep/19/hurricane-maria-caribbean-oecd-aid-rules-assistance.

James, Erica Caple. "Haunting Ghosts: Madness, Gender, and Ensekirite in Haiti in the Democratic Era" in *Postcolonial Disorders*, eds. Mary-Jo Delvecchio Good, Sandra Teresa Hyde, Sarah Pinto and Byron J. Good (Berkley: U of California P, 2008): 132–156.

James, Erica Caple. "Ruptures, Rights, and Repair: The Political Economy of Trauma in Haiti." *Social Science & Medicine* 70.1 (2010): 106–113.

James, Keith H. "A Simple Synthesis of Caribbean Geology," Transactions of the 16th Caribbean Geological Conference, Barbados. *Caribbean Journal of Earth Science* 39 (2005): 69–82.

Kelman, Ilan, Jessica Mercer and JC Gaillardal. "Editorial Introduction to this Handbook: Why Act on Disaster Risk Reduction Including Climate Change Adaptation?" in *The Routledge Handbook of Disaster Risk Reduction Including Climate Change Adaptation* (Routledge: London, 2017): 3–9.

Kelman, Ilan and Jennifer West. "Climate Change and Small Island Developing States: A Critical Review." *Ecological and Environmental Anthropology* 5 (2009): 1–16.

Kingsbury, John M. "Christopher Columbus as a Botanist." *Arnoldia* 52. 2 (Summer 1992): 12.

Kyrre, Kverndokk, Marit Ruge Bjærke and Anne Eriksen. *Climate Change Temporalities: Explorations in Vernacular, Popular, and Scientific Discourse.* (London, New York: Routledge, 2021).

Lamb, Juliet. "The Great Seaweed Invasion." *JSTOR Daily* (October 24, 2018) https://daily.jstor.org/great-seaweed-invasion/.

Langin, Katie. "Seaweed Masses Assault Caribbean islands." *Science* 360.6394 (June 2018): 1157–1158.

Laughin, Nicholas. "There Are No Islands Without the Sea: Being a Compendium of Facts, Fictions, Names, Etymologies, Lyrics, and Questions in the Form of a Broken-Up Archipelago" in *Relational Undercurrents: Contemporary Art of the Caribbean Archipelago*, eds. Tatiana Flores and Michelle Ann Stephens (Durham: Duke UP, 2017).

Leslie, Kory. "The War against Sargassum." *Amandala,* (June 22, 2019), http://amandala.com.bz/news/war-sargassum/.

Loock, Ulrich. "Opacity." *Frieze* 7 (Winter 2012), https://www.frieze.com/article/opazität.

Losbar, Olivia. "Un bateau réquisitionné pour désenclaver la Désirade." RCI 96.5FM Radio, (January 1, 2019), https://www.rci.fm/infos/risques-naturels/un-bateau-requisitionne-pour-desenclaver-la-desirade.

Marder, Michael. *Plant-Thinking: A Philosophy of Vegetal Life* (New York: Columbia UP, 2013).

Maréchal, Jean-Phillipe, Claire Hellio and Chuanmin Hu. "A Simple, Fast, and Reliable Method to Predict Sargassum Washing Ashore in the Lesser Antilles." *Remote Sensing Applications: Society and Environment* 5 (2017): 54–63.

Mbom, Clément. "Édouard Glissant, de l'opacité à la relation" in *Poétiques d'Edouard Glissant*, ed. Jacques Chevrier (Presses Paris Sorbonne, 1999).

McSweeney, Joyelle. "Poetics, Revelations, and Catastrophes: an Interview with Kamau Brathwaite." *Rain Taxi* (Fall 2005), http://www.raintaxi.com/poetics-revelations-and-catastrophes-an-interview-with-kamau-brathwaite/.

Mika, Kasia. *Disasters, Vulnerability, and Narratives: Writing Haiti's Futures.* (London: Routledge, 2019): 3–52.

Milledge, John J. and Patricia J Harvey. "Golden Tides: Problem or Golden Opportunity? The Valorisation of Sargassum from Beach Inundations." *Journal of Marine Science and Engineering* 4.3 (2016).

Mintz, Sidney. "The Caribbean Region." *Slavery, Colonialism, and Racism* 103 (1974): 45–71.

Munro, Martin. *Tropical Apocalypse: Haiti and the Caribbean End Times.* (Charlottesville: U of Virginia P, 2015).

Naylor, Paul. *Poetic Investigations: Singing the Holes in History.* (Evanston, Il: Northwestern UP, 1999) in Anna Reckin (2003) "Tidalectic Lectures: Kamau Brathwaite's Prose/Poetry as Sound-Space." *Anthurium: A Caribbean Studies Journal* 1.1 Article 5.

Organisation of Eastern Caribbean States. "Communities innovate to address Sargassum seaweed on coasts of Saint Lucia," (May 24, 2018), https://pressroom.oecs.org/communities-innovate-to-address-sargassum-seaweed-on-coasts-of-saint-lucia.

Pinnix, Aaron. "Sargassum in the Black Atlantic: Entanglement and the Abyss in Bearden, Walcott, and Philip." *Atlantic Studies* (2019): 1–29.

Pressley-Sanon, Toni. "Review of: The Other Side of the Sea by Louis-Philippe Dalembert, Robert H. McCormick Jr., Edwidge Danticat; Memory at Bay by Évelyne Trouillot, Paul Curtis Daw, Jason Herbeck." *Journal of Haitian Studies* 22.1 (2016): 204–208.

Pugh, Jonathan. "Island Movements: Thinking with the Archipelago." *Island Studies Journal* 8.1 (2013): 9–24.

Resiere, Dabor, Ruddy Valentino, Rémi Nevière, Rishika Banydeen, Papa Gueye, Jonathan Florentin, André Cabié, Thierry Lebrun, Bruno Mégarbane, Gilles

Guerrier and Hossein Mehdaoui. "Sargassum Seaweed on Caribbean Islands: An International Public Health Concern." *The Lancet* 392.10165 (2018): 2691, https://www.thelancet.com/journals/lancet/article/PIIS0140-6736(18)32777-6/fulltext.

Rawlins-Bentham, Julia. "Sargassum: a National Emergency and Energy Source." *Barbados Government Information Service* (June 10, 2018), https://gisbarbados.gov.bb/blog/sargassum-a-national-emergency-energy-source/#:~:text=Sargassum%3A%20A%20National%20Emergency%20%26%20Energy%20Source%20by,being%20treated%20as%20a%20national%20emergency%20by%20Government.

"Semicolon, n.". *OED Online.* (London: Oxford UP, 2019), https://www.oed.com/view/Entry/175618.

Sharpe, Christina. *In the Wake: On Blackness and Being* (Durham: Duke UP, 2016).

Spillman, Rick. "Algae Apocalypse—Sargassum Spreads Across the Caribbean & Florida." *The Old Salt Blog* (October 12, 2018), http://www.oldsaltblog.com/2018/10/algae-apocalypse-sargassum-spreads-across-the-caribbean-florida/.

Steinberg, Philip E. "Of Other Seas: Metaphors and Materialities in Maritime Regions." *Atlantic Studies* 10.2 (2013): 156–169.

Stoler, Ann Laura. "Imperial Debris: Reflections on Ruin and Ruination." *Cultural Anthropology* 23.2 (May 2018): 191–219.

Stoler, Ann Laura. *Duress: Imperial Durabilities in Our Times.* (Durham: Duke UP, 2016).

"The Seaweed is Coming, Tobago Braces." *Trinidad Express* (September 7, 2019), https://www.trinidadexpress.com/news/local/the-seaweed-is-coming/article_b849b240-3cc0-5042-8021-68b23b6dad82.html.

Trouillot, Michel-Rolph. *Silencing the Past: Power and the Production of History* (Boston, MA: Beacon Press, 2015).

Tresident, Inès. "Le littoral Caraïbe de la Martinique menacé par un important banc d'algues sargasses." *Franceinfo à la une des Outre-mer*: *Martinique la 1ère* (April 28, 2021), https://la1ere.francetvinfo.fr/martinique/le-littoral-caraibe-de-la-martinique-menace-par-un-important-banc-d-algues-sargasses-994981.html.

Tirolien Jérôme. "Valorisation agronomique des algues sargasses," Préfet de la Région Guadeloupe, http://www.guadeloupe.gouv.fr/Politiques-publiques/Risques-naturels-technologiques-et-sanitaires/Dossier-Sargasses/Des-projets-innovants-pour-collecter-et-valoriser-les-sargasses/Valorisation-agronomique-des-algues-sargasses.

United Nations Environment Programme. *Sargassum White Paper—Sargassum Outbreak in the Caribbean: Challenges, Opportunities and Regional Situation.* (Panama City, 2018).

Van Dooren, Thom. "Care." *Environmental Humanities* 5.1 (2014): 291–294.

Walcott, Derek. "Nobel Lecture: The Antilles: Fragments of Epic Memory." *Nobelprize.org* (Nobel Media AB: 2014), http://www.nobelprize.org/nobel_prizes/literature/laureates/1992/walcott-lecture.html.

Wargo, Vincent. "Festivity, Tradition, and Hope: Josef Pieper and the Historical Meaning of Human Praxis." *Logos: A Journal of Catholic Thought and Culture* 21.4 (2018): 60–79.

"What is Sargassum?" National Oceanic and Atmospheric Administration, https://oceanexplorer.noaa.gov/facts/sargassum.html.

"What is the Sargasso Sea?" National Oceanic and Atmospheric Administration, https://oceanservice.noaa.gov/facts/sargassosea.html.

Wynter, Sylvia. "Unsettling the Coloniality of Being/Power/Truth/Freedom: Towards the Human, After Man, Its Overrepresentation—An Argument." CR: *The New Centennial Review* 3.3 (Fall 2003): 257–337.

CHAPTER 8

"Kāne and Kanaloa Are Coming"

Contemporary Hawaiian Poetry and Climate Change

Craig Santos Perez

> *As an indigenous Chamorro from the Pacific Island of Guåhan currently living in Hawaiʻi, I acknowledge the unceded, ongoing sovereignty of the Hawaiian Kingdom, and I offer my respect and solidarity to the Kānaka Maoli in their struggle for decolonization, demilitarization, and self-determination.*

∵

1 Introduction

The global focus on climate change has brought unprecedented attention to the Pacific Islands in recent years. Media reports of low-lying islands and atolls threatened by rising sea levels have appeared in national and international newspapers, magazines, television news broadcasts and documentaries. Climate change movement leaders and celebrities (such as Naomi Klein, Bill McKibben and Leonardo DiCaprio) have visited the Pacific, and they often reference the region in their writing and speeches. Indigenous Pacific Islanders, like the late Marshallese politician Tony de Brum and former I-Kiribati President Anote Tong, have become prominent figures as well. In 2014, Marshallese author and environmentalist Kathy Jetñil-Kijiner was chosen from over five hundred applicants to represent civil society and give the opening plenary at the United Nations Climate Summit, during which she performed her poem, "Dear Matafele Peinem," and received a standing ovation.[1] In 2017, Fiji presided over the 23rd Conference of the Parties (COP) to the United Nations Framework Conventions on Climate Change in Bonn, Germany. There is now

---

1 For a video of the performance and the text of the poem see, https://www.kathyjetnilkijiner .com/united-nations-climate-summit-opening-ceremony-my-poem-to-my-daughter/.

© KONINKLIJKE BRILL NV, LEIDEN, 2022 | DOI:10.1163/9789004514164_009

a global awareness of the impacts of climate change in the Pacific (rising sea levels, ocean acidification, coral bleaching, extreme storms and drought), the legacy of environmental imperialism (militarism, nuclear testing and waste, natural resource extraction and species extinction), and the plight of Pacific islanders (disease, poverty and migration).

This new visibility has created an assemblage of representations of the Pacific and its Indigenous peoples. Historically, the Pacific Islands have been imagined as *both* paradises, utopias, exotic destinations and biodiversity hotspots *and* as dystopias, plantations, military bases, nuclear testing grounds and extinction capitals. Pacific Islanders have been imagined as *both* noble savages, environmental sages, dusky maidens, proud warriors, natural athletes, disciplined soldiers and hospitable hula dancers *and* as primitive cannibals, sexual predators, lazy natives, violent criminals and even the fattest people on Earth.[2] New depictions have emerged in the climate change era. For example, the Pacific Islands are now depicted as *both* "disappearing islands" threatened by rising sea levels *and* as "sustainable islands" at the forefront of "green" and "blue" technologies and policies. In turn, Pacific Islanders are depicted as *both* harbingers of climate change and vulnerable, "drowning" victims *and* as resilient "climate warriors" who are "fighting" and "rising" to save their islands and "thrive." With the global circulation of these representations, the Pacific islands and native islanders have become emblematic places and charismatic faces of the climate change movement.[3]

Despite the global attention, some islands in the Pacific have remained marginalised in the climate change conversation because they are neither low-lying islands nor sovereign nation states (and thus without representation or a vote in the United Nations).[4] In this essay, I draw attention to one of these

---

2   For further reading on historical representations of the Pacific, see Paul Lyons, *American Pacificism: Oceania in the U.S. Imagination* (New York: Routledge, 2006) and Rob Wilson and Vilsoni Hereniko, eds. *Inside Out: Literature, Cultural Politics, and Identity in the New Pacific* (Lanham: Rowman, 1999).

3   For climate change era representations of the Pacific, see Elizabeth DeLoughrey, "The Sea is Rising: Visualising Climate Change in the Pacific islands" in *Meteorologies of modernity: Weather and climate discourses in the Anthropocene*, eds. Fekadu et al. (Tübingen: Narr Francke Attempto, 2017): 237–253; Candice Elenna Steiner, "A Sea of Warriors: Performing an Identity of Resilience and Empowerment in the Face of Climate Change in the Pacific," *The Contemporary Pacific* 27.1 (2015): 147–180; and Rebecca Hogue, "I Kū Mau Mau (Stand Together): Pacific Islander Solidarity in the March for Real Climate Leadership," *The Contemporary Pacific*, forthcoming.

4   Independent Pacific Island nations are classified under the United Nations category of Small Island Developing States (SIDS). In 2014, the UN declared the "International Year of SIDS" and held a summit in Samoa that focused on issues, like climate change, affecting SIDS.

places: Hawai'i, a mountainous archipelago and an incorporated territory (or "state") of the United States of America. First, I will highlight the impacts of climate change in Hawai'i through a reading of the *Hawai'i Sea Level Rise Vulnerability and Adaptation Report*, published by the Hawai'i Climate Change Mitigation and Adaptation Commission in 2017. I will then analyse how the *Report* represents Kānaka Maoli (Native Hawaiian)[5] culture and 'ike 'āina (environmental knowledge). Lastly, I will close-read three poems by Kānaka Maoli authors (Keali'i Mackenzie, Joe Balaz and Brandy Nālani McDougall) to show how they articulate a Hawaiian climate change poetics ("cli-po") that foregrounds the deep connection between Hawaiian identity, culture, genealogy and the environment; critiques the history and ongoing impacts of environmental injustice, climate change and "carbon colonialism"[6]; and expresses a range of emotional responses (fear, resignation and hope) to the changing climate.

2   Climate Change Impacts in Hawai'i

The first study on the impacts of climate change in Hawai'i was *Effects on Hawai'i of a Worldwide Rise in Sea Level Induced by the Greenhouse Effect*, requested by the Hawai'i State Senate and released in 1985. The first Hawai'i Climate Change Action Plan was completed in 1998, and the first sustainability plan in 2008, which was titled, *Hawai'i 2050 Sustainability Plan*. In 2009, a Framework for Climate Change Adaptation in Hawai'i was developed. In 2011, the Hawai'i State Planning Act was amended to include "Sustainability Priority Guidelines and Principles," and amended once again the following year to add "Climate Change Adaptation Priority Guidelines." In 2013, Hawai'i became a signatory to the International Majuro Declaration for Climate Leadership, and the then Governor of Hawai'i, Neil Abercrombie, was appointed to the U.S. President's *State, Local, and Tribal Leaders Task Force on Climate Preparedness and Resilience*. The Hawai'i State Legislature formally established *The Hawai'i*

---

5 In 'ōlelo Hawai'i, or Hawaiian language, kānaka/kanaka means people/person and maoli means native, real, and true. In Hawaiian studies scholarship, Kānaka/Kanaka 'Ōiwi is also used to refer to the Indigenous people of the Hawaiian Islands. 'Ōiwi means native but also refers to bones.

6 For readings on "carbon colonialism," see Anil Agarwal and Sunita Narain, *Global Warming in an Unequal World: A Case of Environmental Colonialism* (New Delhi: Centre for Science and the Environment, 1991) and Michael Ziser and Julie Sze, "Climate Change, Environmental Aesthetics, and Global Environmental Justice Cultural Studies," *Discourse: Journal for Theoretical Studies in Media and Culture* 29.2 (2007): 384–410.

Climate Adaptation Initiative and the coordinating body, the Interagency Climate Adaptation Committee, in 2014, which was expanded into the Hawai'i Climate Change Mitigation and Adaptation Commission in 2017. That same year, the commission released its most important study to date: the *Hawai'i Sea Level Rise Vulnerability and Adaptation Report.*[7]

This 300-page *Report* contains over a hundred photographs, maps, figures, images, data tables, boxes, charts and graphs. The introduction provides detailed information about Hawai'i's climate change policy and the climate initiative commission's tasks, responsibilities, framework, guidelines and sustainable development goals. The first main chapter discusses global and local sea level rise projections, while the second chapter describes the methodology of the *Report*. The third chapter, titled "Results," details the impacts, challenges and opportunities of sea level rise on the Hawaiian archipelago as a whole, and then separate sub-chapters detailing sea level rise impacts on each individual island. The last chapter of the *Report* lists nine recommendations for the state to mitigate the risks and adapt to these changes.

According to the *Report*, the predicted global sea level rise will be 3.2 feet by the end of the century, with the possibility that this level will be reached in the Pacific decades sooner. Across the archipelago, the *Report* estimates that periodic flooding, permanent inundation and coastal erosion due to sea level rise will damage more than 6,500 structures (hotels, shopping malls, small businesses, schools, community centers, churches, houses and apartments), 25,000 acres of nearshore land (urban, agricultural and conservation), 500 Hawaiian cultural sites (Hawaiian homestead lands, burial grounds, ancestral settlements, fishponds and other places of cultural significance), forty miles of major roads and highways (and the public utilities which run parallel or underneath roadways), natural resources and habitats (iconic beaches, wildlife habitats, native species), heightened exposure to marine hazards and saltwater intrusion to surface and groundwater systems, loss of commerce, loss of access to emergency services, increased traffic as well as damage to harbor and airport facilities, often on low-lying coastal areas. This would result in the displacement of over 20,000 residents and cause over $20 billion in damage. Billions more would be lost from the reverberating impact on the economy––in particular, the tourism industry, the state's main economic driver and

---

7   This history is documented in the *Report* itself: Hawai'i Climate Change Mitigation and Adaptation Commission, *Hawai'i Sea Level Rise Vulnerability and Adaptation Report* (2017). Prepared by Tetra Tech, Inc. and the State of Hawai'i Department of Land and Natural Resources, Office of Conservation and Coastal Lands, under the State of Hawai'i Department of Land and Natural Resources Contract No: 64064.

employer. The recommendations in the *Report* include supporting sustainable land use, prioritising smart urban development, incentivising improved flood risk management, enabling legacy beaches to persist, preserving Native Hawaiian culture and communities, protecting nearshore water quality, developing innovative and sustainable financing to support adaptation, supporting research on adaptation and promoting collaboration and accountability.[8]

Even though the *Report* focuses on the sea level rising, it mentions other impacts of climate change in Hawai'i. The archipelago is expected to face rising temperatures and incidence of heat waves (affecting water supplies and human health such as increased respiratory and mosquito-borne diseases); changing rainfall patterns (affecting agriculture and ecosystems); increased risk of extreme drought; increased ocean temperatures and acidity; coral bleaching (resulting in fewer fish and less coastal protection); more frequent natural disasters such as hurricanes and tsunamis; and the extinction of endemic species.[9] As one journalist put it, "The future isn't forecast to look like all the pretty postcards."[10]

While the *Report* is mostly data-driven, there are moments throughout the text in which Hawaiian culture is represented. The main form through which this occurs is the 'ōlelo no'eau, or Hawaiian proverb.[11] The introduction begins with a passage that connects a well-known 'ōlelo no'eau to climate change:

> There is an 'ōlelo no'eau, a Hawaiian proverb, that speaks of humans' relationship to the 'āina, the land. *He ali'i ka 'āina; he kauwā ke kanaka.* 'The land is chief; man is its servant'. ... To Hawaiians, land provides everything that is needed for man to survive. It is our responsibility to care for the land so that it continues to provide the necessary resources for survival such as food, water, and shelter. However, if we neglect the 'āina, then the 'āina will neglect us.

---

8   *Hawai'i Sea Level Rise Report.*

9   While not as comprehensive in relation to Hawai'i, there is a chapter on "Hawai'i and U.S.-Affiliated Pacific Islands," in the U.S. National Climate Assessment, 2018.

10   Nathan Eagle, "Hawai'i 2040: Climate Change Is Already Here. And We're Running Out of Time," *Honolulu Civil Beat* (January 14, 2019): np., https://www.civilbeat.org/2019/01/hawaii-2040-climate-change-is-already-here-and-were-running-out-of-time/. Throughout 2019, an online magazine, *Honolulu Civil Beat,* is producing a series of articles, "Hawai'i 2040: Climate Change." The title, "Hawai'i 2040," refers to the year when Hawai'i is predicted to experience the worst effects of climate change.

11   To explore this form further, see Mary Kawena Pukui, *'Ōlelo No'eau: Hawaiian Proverbs and Poetical Sayings* (Honolulu: Bishop Museum Press, 1986).

We are now facing the consequences of what happens when we neglect the 'āina on a global scale. Global anthropogenic impacts on the climate have potentially done irreparable harm to ecosystems around the world and now the earth is responding, showing us who truly is the chief.[12]

While 'āina is defined simply as "land," it actually has much more complex significations, as Hawaiian literary scholar ku'ualoha ho'omanawanui notes in her essay, " 'This Land Is Your Land, This Land Was My Land': Kanaka Maoli versus Settler Representations of 'Āina in Contemporary Literature of Hawai'i."[13] For one dimension of 'āina, she quotes from *Native Planters of Old Hawaii: Their Life, Lore and Environment*:

> 'āina also conveys the sense of arable land. It is essentially a term coined by an agricultural people, deriving as it does from the noun or verb 'ai, meaning food or to eat, with the substantive *na* added, so that it may be rendered either 'that which feeds' or 'the feeder'. *āina* thus has connotations in relation to people as conveying the sense of 'feeder,' birthplace, and homeland. In this sense it entered also into the compound *maka'āinana,* meaning the common people or country folk in general as distinguished from the ali'i and their entourage. The broad social concept contained in [maka'ainana] was for the Hawaiian derived from *'āina,* meaning land, which in its turn is a derivative of the word meaning food, primarily cultivated food, and specifically in many uses, taro.[14]

She then points to the *Hawaiian Dictionary* for the root word of 'āina; " 'ai" means "food, esp. fruits and vegetables; to rule, as over land or people; to eat," which is related to the words "ai" (sexual reproduction), "aina" (sexual intercourse) and " 'aina" (meal).[15] She also writes how "the value of the 'āina is not monetary; it is familial,"[16] as demonstrated in the following Hawaiian creation story:

---

12   *Hawai'i Sea Level Rise Report*, 1.

13   ku'ualoha ho'omanawanui, " 'This Land Is Your Land, This Land Was My Land': Kanaka Maoli versus Settler Representations of 'Āina in Contemporary Literature of Hawai'i" in *Asian Settler Colonialism: From Local Governance to the Habits of Everyday Life in Hawai'i,* eds. Candace Fujikane and Jonathan Y. Okamura (Honolulu: U of Hawai'i P, 2008).

14   E.S. Craighill Handy, Elizabeth Green Handy, and Mary Kawena Pukui, *Native Planters of Old Hawaii: Their Life, Lore, and Environment.* (Honolulu: Bishop Museum Press, 1972): 45. Quoted in ho'omanawanui, "This Land," 150.

15   Samuel Elbert and Mary Kawena Pukui, *Hawaiian Dictionary,* rev. ed. (Honolulu: U of Hawai'i P, 1986): 58. Quoted in ho'omanawanui, "This Land," 150.

16   ho'omanawanui, "This Land," 124.

In one creation story of Papahānaumoku and Wākea (Sky Father), a keiki alualu (miscarried fetus) is born to them. After the child is buried outside the home, a kalo plant, which they name Hāloa-naka, 'quivering stalk with long breath,' grows from the spot. The next child born to them is also named Hāloa and is said to be the progenitor of Kanaka Maoli people. Thus Kānaka Maoli aren't masters over the land, as in the Judeo-Christian tradition set forth in the book of Genesis in the Bible, but are the sub-servient younger siblings of the 'āina and the mea 'ai, 'fruits' of the land, most directly, the kalo plant Hāloa-naka, our elder sibling.[17]

ho'omanawanui also shows that Hawaiian words for people are related to land, such as "maka'āinana" (steward of the land) and "kama'āina" (child born on the land). Two fundamental Hawaiian values emerge from this relationship between the environment and the people: "aloha 'āina" (love for the land) and "mālama 'āina" (caring for the land)."[18] While these phrases are often used when promoting environmentalism in Hawai'i, ho'omanawanui reminds us:

> [M]ālama 'āina does not equate to 'environmentalism' because the man-date to the 'āina is the same as mālama/aloha 'ohana (care for, cherish the family): we care for/love the land in the same way we care for our elders, our siblings, our spouses, and our children, and by doing so, we maintain our relationship with those we are caring for, whether it be our human family, earthly family (Papahānaumoku, Hāloa the taro), or spiritual family (through the presence of our 'aumākua, or spirit guardi-ans who physically manifest themselves in nature).[19]

The interconnection between Hawaiians and the 'āina is bodily, familial, gene-alogical, spiritual, intellectual, cultural, social, political, historical and environ-mental. From this interconnection, Hawaiians have cultivated an ecological consciousness and an ethics of sustainability, humility, respect, reverence and mutual care.[20]

---

17 ho'omanawanui, "This Land," 125.
18 ho'omanawanui, "This Land," 124–125.
19 ho'omanawanui, "This Land," 128.
20 For more on the relationship between Hawaiians and 'āina, see Lilikalā Kame'eleihiwa, *Native land and foreign desires: Pehea lā e pono ai?* (Honolulu: Bishop Museum Press, 1992); George Kanahele, *Kū kanaka—Stand tall: A search for Hawaiian values* (Honolulu: U of Hawai'i P, 1986); and Shawn Malia Kana'iaupuni and Nolan Malone, "This land is my land: The role of place in Native Hawaiian identity," *Hūlili: Multidisciplinary Research on Hawaiian Well-Being* 3 (2006): 281–307.

Other 'ōlelo no'eau are included in the *Report* as epigraphs to several of the chapters, appended with a translation and very brief interpretation. The proverbs all relate, in some way, to the environment or to working together and solving problems:

'A'ohe pu'u ki'eki'e ke ho'ā'o 'ia e pi'i.
No cliff is so tall that it cannot be scaled.
No problem is too great when one tries hard to solve it.
Pua a'e la ka uwahi o ka moe.
The smoke seen in the dream now rises.
The trouble of which we were forewarned is here.
E nānā ana i ka 'ōpua o ka 'āina.
Observing the horizon clouds of the land.
Seeking to discover future events by observing the cloud omens.
Ka manu ka'upu hālō 'ale o ka moana.
The ka'upu, the bird that observes the ocean.
Said of a careful observer.
'A'ohe hana nui ke alu 'ia.
No task is too big when done together by all.[21]

The next time we encounter a more sustained engagement with a 'ōlelo no'eau is towards the end of the *Report*, in the "Recommendations":

There is an 'ōlelo no'eau, a Hawaiian proverb, that gives insight into a clever method that the ancient Hawaiians once used in response to flooding—Mānā, i ka pu'e kalo ho'one'ene'e a ka wai. Translated, it means 'Mānā, where the mounded taro moves in the water'. The story behind the proverb takes place in Mānā, Kaua'i, which was once home to deep water kalo (taro) patches that flooded for several weeks during the rainy season. To save their crops, the mahi'ai kalo (taro farmers) would construct rafts and paddle out to the kalo patches where they would dive down and carefully wiggle the roots of the kalo free from the soil, bringing the kalo to the surface one by one. Once the plants were at the surface, they would secure the stalks to the rafts so that their leaves could continue to grow above water. Eventually, the entire patch became a floating network

---

21   These five proverbs appear in the *Hawai'i Sea Level Rise Report* on these respective pages: 1, 15, 32, 61, and 213.

of rafts and kalo plants, thus saving the crops. We must endeavor to be as clever and resilient as the mahiʻai kalo.[22]

This ʻōlelo noʻeau, like the others, illustrates Hawaiian ecological wisdom and practices. They function as inspirational quotes to teach us how we can become "clever and resilient" in response to climate change.

Besides ʻōlelo noʻeau, the other reference to Hawaiian culture in the *Report* is through a discussion of the "ahupuaʻa system" in a short section of the introduction titled, "Our Kuleana as Stewards of the Future." To understand the word, "kuleana," I once again turn to hoʻomanawanui: "One of the fundamental aspects of Polynesian culture is the idea of communal responsibility, which Hawaiians call kuleana. Kuleana (rights, privilege, responsibility, and authority) includes the many ways these principles are present in our lives: individually, socially, professionally, and culturally."[23] Besides alluding to kuleana, this section explains the ahupuaʻa system, which is a Hawaiian method of resource management:

> Our Native Hawaiian community has taught us how to apply traditional cultural knowledge to solve problems of resource management. This includes the revitalization of the ahupuaʻa land system which was a section of land that ran from mauka (inland) to makai (seaward) and the size of the ahupuaʻa was dependent on the resources of the area. The ahupuaʻa was thought of as the basic self-sustaining unit and emphasized the interrelationship of the elements (nature) and beings (humans).[24]

In depictions of the extraordinarily productive ahupuaʻa system, waterfalls and streams flow from mauka (the inland mountain) to makai (the sea). Hawaiians planted fields of kalo (taro) and ʻuala (sweet potato) along the stream, as well as other crops (such as sugarcane), breadfruit, and coconut. They also built fishponds near the muliwai, or the estuary where the stream mixed with the ocean. The ahupuaʻa system is the most emblematic symbol of Hawaiian environmental management and values because it embodies sustainability, biodiversity and interconnection and inspires people to remember our kuleana to steward the ʻāina for future generations.[25]

---

22 *Hawaiʻi Sea Level Rise Report*, 213.

23 hoʻomanawanui, "This Land," 139.

24 *Hawaiʻi Sea Level Rise Report*, 3.

25 For a more scientific description of the ahupuʻa system, see Aurora K. Kagawa and Peter M. Vitousek, "The Ahupuaʻa of Puanui: A Resource for Understanding Hawaiian Rain-Fed

The authors of the *Report* claim that Hawai'i's "unique cultural heritage provides us a broader spectrum of ideas and possible solutions which makes us stronger and more resilient to face all crisis and challenges together."[26] While it seems positive that the *Report* honours Hawaiian culture and discusses 'ōlelo no'eau and the ahupua'a system, the fact that Hawaiian culture is only engaged as pithy epigraphs or in brief passages makes the engagement feel ornamental and superficial. Moreover, I argue that these depictions traffic in "imperialist nostalgia" and "salvage environmentalism." Renato Rosaldo defined "imperialist nostalgia" as the feeling that emerges when "agents of colonialism long for the very forms of life they intentionally altered or destroyed." He goes on to explicate this contradictory emotion:

> Imperialist nostalgia revolves around a paradox: a person kills somebody, and then mourns the victim. In more attenuated form, someone deliberately alters a form of life, and then regrets that things have not remained as they were prior to the intervention. At one more remove, people destroy their environment, and then they worship nature. In any of its versions, imperialist nostalgia uses a pose of 'innocent yearning' both to capture people's imaginations and to conceal its complicity with often brutal domination ... 'We' (who believe in progress) valorize innovation and then yearn for more stable worlds, whether these reside in our own past, in other cultures, or in the conflation of the two.[27]

Clearly, the *Report* innocently yearns for and mourns the loss of the ahupua'a system and of Hawaiian environmental values, while at the same time concealing the state's complicity with the history the U.S. empire that overthrew the Hawaiian Kingdom in 1893, illegally annexed the archipelago in 1898, and incorporated Hawai'i as the 50th state in 1959.[28] Not to mention the actual displacement of Hawaiian people from their 'āina, the suppression of Hawaiian culture and identity through assimilationist policies, and the destruction of

---

Agriculture," *Pacific Science* 66.2 (Apr 2012): 161–172; and Dieter Mueller-Dombois, "The Hawaiian Ahupua'a Land Use System: Its Biological Resource Zones and the Challenge for Silvicultural Restoration," *Bishop Museum Bulletin in Cultural and Environmental Studies* 3 (2007): 23–33.

26   *Hawai'i Sea Level Rise Report*, 3.

27   Renato Rosaldo, *Culture and truth: The Remaking of Social Analysis* (Boston: Beacon, 1989): 108.

28   For a political history of Hawai'i, see Noenoe Silva, *Aloha Betrayed: Native Hawaiian Resistance to American Colonialism* (Durham: Duke University, 2004) and Dean Saranillio, *Unsustainable Empire: Alternative Histories of Hawai'i Statehood.* (Durham: Duke UP, 2018).

the ahupuaʻa system through land theft and capitalist development. Indeed, the *Report* also conflates its own "cultural heritage" with the Hawaiian culture that the state itself has suppressed for over a century.

The idea of imperialist nostalgia is connected to what Elizabeth DeLoughrey terms "salvage environmentalism." In her analysis of climate change film and media, she argues:

> Problematically, the figure of the indigenous islander––who is associated with lost culture––is represented in atemporal terms akin to the logic of what Renato Rosaldo has termed 'imperialist nostalgia' ... By bracketing out empire, capitalism, and carbon colonialism, these films trade on a *salvage environmentalism* that recuperates a historic and nostalgic nature by detemporalizing the Pacific Islander, while suppressing the issue of the viewer's complicity.[29]

The *Report* depicts Hawaiian culture ahistorically (as merely "ancient" and "traditional") and its environmental wisdom as lost and forgotten, waiting to be reclaimed by the state. The *Report* brackets out the state's complicity in the maintenance of plantation agriculture, a massive tourism industry, and the development of urban/suburban sprawl. The *Report* also brackets out the state's historical and ongoing militarization of the islands, which includes occupying massive amounts of land, testing and storing weapons and fuel, and contaminating the land and water with military waste and toxins, making once fertile lands and waters into "Superfund" sites.[30] Furthermore, the *Report* brackets out the fact that the Department of Defense is "the world's largest institutional user of petroleum and correspondingly, the single largest producer of greenhouse gases in the world."[31] While the *Hawaiʻi Sea Level Report* provides a scientific analysis of the major impacts of climate change in Hawaiʻi, it does not deeply engage with Hawaiian cultural and environmental knowledge, nor does

---

29   DeLoughrey, "The Sea is Rising," 190.

30   For a history of militarism in Hawaiʻi, see Kyle Kajihiro, "Resisting Militarization in Hawaiʻi," in *Bases of Empire: The Global Struggle against U.S. Military Posts*, ed. Cathering Lutz (New York: New York UP, 2009): 299–332. While the *Hawaiʻi Sea Level Rise Report* does not examine militarism in any detail, it does mention that many Superfund sites, including the Pearl Harbor Naval Complex, is within the sea level rise zone and could become flooded and release contaminants into nearshore waters, 172.

31   Neta Crawford, "Pentagon Fuel Use, Climate Change, the Costs of War," *Costs of War Project* (June 12, 2019), https://watson.brown.edu/costsofwar/files/cow/imce/papers/2019/Pentagon%20Fuel%20Use%2C%20Climate%20Change%20and%20the%20Costs%20of%20War%20Final.pdf.

it confront the legacy and impacts of U.S. empire, colonialism, militarism and capitalism. This leads to its problematic replication of imperialist nostalgia and salvage environmentalism. In order to truly enact our kuleana to steward the future, we must confront these issues as well as the issues of Hawaiian decolonisation, demilitarisation, self-determination and sovereignty.

3 Indigenous Ecopoetics and Contemporary Hawaiian Climate Change Poetry

Before diving into Hawaiian climate change poetry, I want to first contextualize my analysis within a wider literary genealogy (or literary ecology) of Pacific Islander, Native American, Indigenous, post/decolonial and Trans-Pacific ecopoetics. Scholars of these fields have examined how eco-literature articulates the beliefs that the Earth is an ancestor, all life is interconnected and sacred, and human beings should act according to the values of reciprocity, sustainability and mutual care. Scholars have foregrounded how the primary themes in native texts express the idea of interconnection and interrelatedness of humans and nature; the centrality of land and water in the conception of Indigenous genealogy, identity and community; and the importance of knowing the Indigenous histories of a place. They illustrate how native writers employ ecological images, metaphors and symbols to critique colonial and Western views of nature as an empty, separate object that exists for men to control and from which to profit.[32] In *Blood Narrative: Indigenous Identity in American Indian and Maori Literary and Activist Texts*, Chadwick Allen names a "blood/land/memory complex" to describe the "central role that land plays both in the specific project of defining indigenous minority personal, familial, and communal identities (blood) and in the larger project of reclaiming and

---

32 See, for example, Donelle N. Dreese, *Ecocriticism: Creating Self and Place in Environmental and American Indian Literatures* (New York: Peter Lang, 2002); John Elder and Hertha D. Wong, eds. *Family of Earth & Sky: Indigenous Tales of Nature from around the World* (Boston: Beacon Press, 1996); Hsinya Huang, "Toward Transpacific Ecopoetics: Three Indigenous Texts," *Comparative Literature Studies* 50.1 (2013): 120–147; Dennis Kawaharada, *Storied Landscapes: Hawaiian Literature and Place* (Honolulu: Kalamaku Press, 1999); J. McLaren, *New Pacific Literatures: Culture and Environment in the European Pacific* (New York: Garland, 1993); Robert Nelson, *Place and Vision: The Function of Landscape in Native American Fiction* (New York: Peter Lang, 1993); Lee Schweninger, *Listening to the Land: Native American Literary Responses to the Landscape* (Athens, GA: U of Georgia P, 2008); Norma Wilson, *The Nature of Native American Poetry* (Albuquerque: U of New Mexico P, 2001).

reimagining indigenous minority histories (memory)."[33] Literature as critique of colonial views of nature is a key point in the critical anthology, *Postcolonial Ecologies: Literature and the Environment,* edited by Elizabeth DeLoughrey and George B. Handley. Their introduction, "Towards an Aesthetics of the Earth," argues that postcolonial literature reckons with the devastations of "ecological imperialism," such as the displacement of Indigenous peoples from ancestral lands; the establishment of plantation, industrial and chemical agriculture; the development of tourism and urbanism; the contamination from militarism and nuclearism; rapid deforestation and desertification; the extraction of natural resources and Indigenous remains; and species extinction and endangerment. In addition, they foreground how "precolonial epistemologies of place ... survive and are transformed and translated through narrative."[34] These transformed and transformative stories assert that the environment is a "primary site of postcolonial recuperation, sustainability, and dignity," reinforcing the idea that the ecopoetic imagination is "vital to liberating land from the restrictions of colonialism and ... from neocolonial forms of globalization."[35] The "Trans-Pacific" turn in ecocriticism complements the Indigenous and postcolonial turns in the field. Rob Wilson, in "Oceania as Peril and Promise: Towards Theorizing a Worlded Vision of Trans-Pacific Ecopoetics," insists that the perils of ecological degradation demand a new, politically and culturally committed ecological world view: "Oceania means not only having a sense of history and cultivating a set of attitudes and beliefs, it means cultivating a sense of belonging to the earth and ocean as a bioregional horizon of care."[36] This movement articulates "a vision of altered transnational belonging, ecological confederation, and trans-racial solidarity."[37] Literature is crucial to nurturing this world view because "stories, images, art, dance, and legend give a deeper sense of Pacific belonging; long-woven networks of interconnected reciprocity prove crucial to this formation, as islands and oceans are connected, linked, and would counter the late-capitalist world from before, within, and after it."[38]

---

33   Chadwick Allen, *Narrative: Indigenous Identity in American Indian and Maori Literary and Activist Texts* (Minneapolis: U of Minnesota P, 2012): 16.

34   Elizabeth DeLoughrey and George Handley, "Introduction" in *Postcolonial Ecologies: Literature and the Environment,* eds. Elizabeth DeLoughrey and George B. Handley (Oxford: Oxford UP, 2011): 24.

35   DeLoughrey and Handley, "Introduction," 3.

36   Rob Wilson, "Oceania as Peril and Promise: Towards Theorizing a Worlded Vision of Trans-Pacific Ecopoetics," Paper presented at the Oceanic Archives and Transnational American Studies Conference, Hong Kong University (June 4–6, 2012): 12.

37   Wilson, 5.

38   Wilson, 8.

The Pacific ecopoetic region of care is extended in Hsinya Huang's "Toward Transpacific Ecopoetics: Three Indigenous Texts," to include a "multispecies ecopoetics rooted in the Indigenous stories and myths of the Pacific."[39] Within an imperial ecological framework, animals exist to benefit human beings; however, the "indigenous imagination in the transpacific context breaks down the division between human and nonhuman."[40] Through literature, Pacific writers narrate the environment as "a site of cobelonging and cohistory across species boundaries and racial/ethnic and cultural borders."[41] In "'Healing, Belonging, Resistance, and Mutual Care': Reading Indigenous Ecopoetics and Climate Narratives," Eric Magrane discusses how Indigenous climate change poetry "fosters alternative subjectivities in the face of climate change," "complicates climate narratives, both ontologically and epistemologically," "recalibrates climate change narratives by embodying Indigenous themes and frameworks," and exhibits "the interconnections, interdependence and interrelationship of Indigenous and Native science."[42] It is this literary genealogy that forms the theoretical foundation of my understanding of Indigenous ecopoetics, of which Hawaiian climate change poetry is interrelated.[43]

When describing Hawaiian literature, hoʻomanawanui employs an ecological metaphor: the haku lei, or braided flower garland. She offers an interpretation of the haku lei's three layers and its symbolism:

> First is the overlapping meanings found in the terms: The verb *haku* means 'to compose, invent, put in order, arrange; to braid, as a lei.' Haku refers both to lei making and poetry, as haku mele are poets or composers of song or chant, or those who speak in proverbs. Both lei and mele are composed, with the mea haku (one who composes) selecting, arranging, and putting in order the pua—literally, the flowers; in poetry, the metaphors and symbolic imagery that evoke kaona.
>
> Second is the importance of the base that gives structure to the lei or mele. In Hawaiian, the word for form is *kino,* which also means "body." Without the braided ti-leaf cords to hold it together, the lei would not be

---

39   Hsinya Huang's "Toward Transpacific Ecopoetics: Three Indigenous Texts," *Comparative Literature Studies* 50.1 (2013): 122.

40   Huang, 144.

41   Huang, 123.

42   Eric Magrane, "'Healing, Belonging, Resistance, and Mutual Care': Reading Indigenous Ecopoetics and Climate Narratives," *Literary Geographies* 4.2 (2018): 158–9, 167.

43   As an aside, it is worth citing that hoʻomanawanui wrote the afterword to the *Oxford Handbook of Indigenous American Literatures*, eds. Daniel Heath Justice and James H. Cox (Oxford: Oxford UP, 2014).

a lei ... Likewise, without a general acknowledgement of form, Hawaiian mele would not be poetry ... Both lei pua (flower lei) and lei mele (poetic composition) highlight the pua (flowers/metaphors); without the underlying structure to organize and hold them in the shape of lei and poem, they would still be beautiful, but they would not be lei.

Third is the interweaving of traditions, represented by the braided strands. Contemporary Hawaiian poetry descends from at least two traditions, one native and the other foreign, which, like the different interwoven strands of the haku lei, are combined to hold fast, giving both shape and beauty to the lei (poem).[44]

This image of the haku lei offers a beautiful and complex metaphor through which to understand Hawaiian literature. Scholars usually categorize the history of Hawaiian literature into different historical strands, waves or generations. The first is the millennia old tradition of "precontact" Hawaiian-language orature, including moʻolelo (stories), mele (songs/poems), oli (chant) and moʻokūʻauhau (genealogy), wahi pana (place stories) and ʻōlelo noʻeau. The second strand of Hawaiian literature emerges "post-contact" with the introduction of writing and the printing press to Hawaiʻi in the 19th century. Hawaiians began writing their orature and publishing in Hawaiian-language newspapers and books. After the overthrow of the Hawaiian kingdom and the beginning of U.S. colonialism, the Hawaiian language was banned, so writers of the early 20th century began to compose in English and Western literary forms. The contemporary period is dated from the 1960s to the present. The 1960s marks the beginning of the "Hawaiian Renaissance," when Hawaiians began reclaiming their traditional arts, culture and language and becoming more involved in social, political and decolonial activism. Today, there is a diverse and vibrant archive of contemporary Hawaiian literature (poetry, plays, novels, short stories, anthologies, spoken word, orature and more) written about Hawaiian cultural and political issues composed in English, Hawaiian and Hawaiʻi Creole English (Pidgin).[45]

---

44   kuʻualoha hoʻomanawanui, "He Lei Hoʻoheno no nā Kau a Kau: Language, Performance, and Form in Hawaiian Poetry," *The Contemporary Pacific* 17.1 (2005): 32–33.

45   In addition to the work of hoʻomanawanui, see: Rubellite Kawena Johnson, *Kukini ʻAhaʻilono, To Carry on the News: Over a Century of Native Hawaiian Life and Thought from the Hawaiian Language Newspapers of 1834 to 1948* (Honolulu: Topgallant, 1976); Richard Hamasaki, "Singing in their genealogical trees: the emergence of contemporary Hawaiian poetry in English," MA Thesis (University of Hawaiʻi, Mānoa, 1989); Monica Kaʻimipono Kaiwi, "I Ulu no nā Lālā i ke Kumu: An Epistemological Examination of Native Hawaiian Literature", MA Thesis (University of Auckland, 2000); Brandy Nālani McDougall, *Finding*

One of the most prominent subjects of traditional and contemporary Hawaiian literature is the genealogical, cultural, spiritual, historical and political connections between Kānaki Maoli and the environment. hoʻomanawanui affirms:

> The vast majority of Kanaka Maoli moʻolelo and mele are called pana; storied or legendary places are called wahi pana, the songs composed for them mele pana. By far this is one of the largest categories of moʻolelo and mele: thousands upon thousands of these moʻolelo and mele have been catalogued and published over the years.[46]

This vast archive is a major source of "ʻike ʻāina," or "knowledge from/about the land," which is more than just geography or geology as it includes oral traditions, cultural memories and experiences of wahi pana, or storied places, all of which demonstrate "the relationship of our ancestors to place, their worldview developed from living on that ʻāina, and the poetic, intellectual, and philosophical epistemologies that result."[47] This literature formed the curriculum of Indigenous, environmental and decolonising literacies.[48] Throughout her scholarship, hoʻomanawanui shows that the ʻike ʻāina of Hawaiian literature "often contradicts or refutes the colonial perspectives taught in schools that ignore, demean, and/or suppress our pilina (connections) and kuleana (responsibilities) to the ʻāina (land) and each other." She provides two powerful examples of ʻāina literature to illustrate her point:

> For example, Western science teaches that the formation of the earth and the evolution of humans were separate occurrences, while the Kumulipo, a foundational Hawaiian creation epic, recounts the birth of the universe, earth, and all living creatures, including Kanaka Maoli, who are thus genealogically related to the land. In addition, the moʻolelo of Papahānaumoku, our Earth Mother, and Wākea, our Sky Father, reminds

---

    Meaning: Kaona and Contemporary Hawaiian Literature (U of Arizona P, 2016); David Kealiʻi Mackenzie, "In Words There is Life: Kanaka ʻŌiwi Participation in Slam Poetry," MA Thesis (University of Hawaiʻi, Mānoa, 2016).

46   hoʻomanawanui, "This Land," 146.

47   kuʻualoha hoʻomanawanui, "ʻIke ʻāina: Native Hawaiian Culturally Based Indigenous Literacy," *Hūlili: Multidisciplinary Research on Hawaiian Well-Being* 5 (2008): 204, 229.

48   hoʻomananui discusses her personal experiences researching, writing, and teaching ʻāina based literature to students as an effective tool for teaching Indigenous and environmental literacy in "Hanohano Wailuanuiahoʻāno: Remembering, Recovering, and Writing Place," *Hūlili: Multidisciplinary Research on Hawaiian Well-Being* 8 (2012): 187–243.

us that the kalo plant is our elder sibling, and it is our responsibility to cultivate and care for it, as it feeds and sustains us in return.[49]

Hawaiian literature teaches us that the Earth is sacred, that there are genealogical connections to the land and water, and that all beings are interconnected. It also teaches us that we live surrounded by wahi pana, or storied places, that contain layers of memories, histories, politics and spirits. If closely read/listened to, we can learn 'ike 'āina; indigenous, environmental and decolonial literacies; and the values/ethics of malama 'āina and aloha 'āina.

In recent years, a new strand of Hawaiian literature has slowly begun to emerge: climate change poetry (or what we might call "cli-po," after the more popular genre of climate fiction, or "cli-fi"). For the remainder of this essay, I will examine three poems by respected Hawaiian writers, Keali'i Mackenzie, Joe Balaz and Brandy Nālani McDougall. I will argue that their poems foreground the connection between Hawaiian culture and the environment, critique the legacy and ongoing impacts of environmental colonialism, and articulate how climate change is radically shifting human relationships to the land and water.

Hawaiian poet David Keali'i Mackenzie is the author of the chapbook, *From Hunger to Prayer*,[50] and his work has appeared in *Storyboard Journal, Assaracus: A Journal of Gay Poetry* and *Hawai'i Review*, among others. He holds an MLISc and an MA in Pacific Islands Studies from the University of Hawai'i at Mānoa. He has worked as a poet-facilitator with the Honolulu-based non-profit Pacific Tongues, and he has performed his poetry throughout the Pacific and the United States.

Mackenzie's poem, "Kanaloa 'Ai Moku," is a powerful example of Hawaiian climate change poetry. The invocation of "Kanaloa," the Hawaiian god of the ocean, in the title immediately signals the interconnection between Hawaiian genealogy, spirituality and the environment. Formally, the poem is composed of many short stanzas (between 1–5 lines), some of which are left justified and others that are indented. This arrangement creates a sense of movement, but also resembles the shape of an archipelago of small islands stanzas with the white space of the page embodying oceanic space. The poem begins:

---

49   ku'ualoha ho'omanawanui, "Hā, Mana, Leo (Breath, Spirit, Voice): Kanaka Maoli Empowerment through Literature," *The American Indian Quarterly* 28.1–2 (Winter/Spring 2004): 88.

50   David Keali'i Mackenzie, *From Hunger to Prayer* (Silver Needle Press, 2019), https://thesilverneedle.wordpress.com/.

When I approach
the ocean I pray
    to Kanaloa
    ka heʻe
    master of salt water
    and ʻawa drinking companion of Kāne
for permission to enter
to swim free
that I may not be swept
into deep unfurling
currents.[51]

Praying to Kanaloa when the speaker approaches the ocean shows that the speaker is knowledgeable about Hawaiian culture since the act of asking permission to enter the ocean is an important Indigenous protocol that shows respect to the environment and seeks consent from the spirit that guards that particular realm. Moreover, the speaker is knowledgeable about Kanaloa's many forms: as "master" of the sea, companion of Kāne, the Hawaiian god of procreation, with whom he shares ʻawa, a ceremonial drink, and as the "heʻe," or octopus. The speaker asks for safe passage as he knows that Kanaloa once "ushered waʻa of all kinds across / the Pacific," referring to the waʻa, or seafaring canoes. Also, the speaker asks for Kanaloa to grant him "the joy of water / open sky / salt kissed skin." Taken together, Kanaloa is viewed as welcoming, protective and a source of pleasure. In the next part of the poem, the speaker travels to Aotearoa (New Zealand), yet still displays the same reverence for the environment:

Even in Aotearoa,
at the other end of
Moana nui ākea
I ask Tangaroa
permission to touch
the waters at Piha,
feet cold from ocean
stained mud.

---

51   Mackenzie, "Kanaloa ʻAi Moku," *Pacific Islander Eco-Literature Anthology* (Honolulu: U of Hawaiʻi P, forthcoming): np.

This trans-Polynesian moment, when the speaker travels across Moana nui ākea, the Pacific Ocean, he asks Tangaroa, the Māori god of the sea, for permission. Whereas other visitors may go to the beach and only see a beach and swim without second thought, Mackenzie shows us how an Indigenous perspective views the environment as a sacred place protected by the gods, who should be treated with reverence and respect.

While the first half of the poem depicts a kind of Indigenous ecopoetic sublime, the second half of the poem takes a turn towards climate change. A stark, single-line stanza announces this tectonic shift: "But my God has changed." The poem then pivots into a series of questions addressed to Kanaloa:

> What does it mean
> when foreigners change you?
>   When you become a terror.
>
>   ʻAi moku—eater of land—
> How many islands
> will you devour?
>
> How many
>   prayers must we crash
>   into unending waves?

The use of the word "change" suggests how carbon colonialism has changed Kanaloa from a protective God to a terrifying god. The "foreigners" refers to people from imperial, industrial nations who have changed the climate through carbon emissions. Because of rising sea levels, Kanaloa has now become ʻai moku, or eater of land, figuratively alluding the fact that rising sea levels will "devour," or in the more common rhetoric, "drown" low lying islands and atolls, as well as erode the coastlines of mountainous, volcanic islands like Hawaiʻi. It is at this point in the poem when we realize the deeper meaning of the title, and confront a new image for Kanaloa. The series of questions the speaker asks embody the "unending waves" of climate anxiety. This emotion is poignantly captured in the final scene of the poem:

> Now at the shore,
> before the advance
> of you, uliuli walls,
> a new prayer goes out:
> ʻE Kanaloa ...

my God
my God ...

what will become of us
when your appetite is satiated'?

The speaker is once again at the shore, harkening us back to the beginning of the poem. Yet, as opposed to the speaker approaching the ocean with relative calm, as he does in the first half of the poem, now he stands fearful at the "uli-uli walls," or stone seawalls, as Kanaloa advances. Instead of seeking to swim, freely and joyously like he did at the beginning of the poem, the speaker sends out a new prayer, repeats "my God," as if trembling, and asks about the fate of Hawaiians and Pacific Islanders when the seas rise and Kanaloa devours our islands. The poem ends in this frightening moment of precarity and impending climate catastrophe.

This powerful poem articulates a Hawaiian ecological worldview in which spirituality and the environment are interwoven in the figures of Kanaloa and the sea. The poem enacts Indigenous protocols and values of respect, reverence and consent when engaging with the natural world. The poem, then, expresses the connection between climate colonialism and climate change by highlighting how foreigners have changed the ocean. The poem doesn't end with any political polemic or critique, but instead leaves us trembling at the shore, praying and terrified of the "unending waves" and the swelling appetite of the devouring sea.

The next poem I will discuss, "Moa Space Foa Ramble,"[52] by Joe Balaz, picks up where Mackenzie's poem leaves off in the sense that it imagines what will happen to Hawai'i when Kanaloa rises. Joe Balaz is the author of multiple chapbooks and books of poetry, most recently *Pidgin Eye*, and the editor of *Ho'omānoa: An Anthology of Contemporary Hawaiian Literature*.[53] This poem is written in Hawai'i Creole English, also known as Pidgin, which first developed as a means of communications between Hawaiians and foreigners after the arrival of Captain Cook in 1778, and later as a means of communication in the sugar plantations between the 1880s and 1920s, when English speakers, Hawaiians, and Chinese, Japanese, Korean, Filipino, Puerto Rican and Portuguese immigrants all worked in the same sugar plantations. The colonial

---

52   Joe Balaz, "Moa Space Foa Ramble," *Juked* (November, 2015): np.

53   Joe Balaz, *Pidgin Eye* (Honolulu: Ala Press, 2019) and *Ho'omānoa: An Anthology of Contemporary Hawaiian Literature* (Honolulu: Ku Pa'a, 1989).

elites stigmatise Pidgin as a substandard, local, mongrel and working class talk. As hoʻomanawanui notes,

> The tension between Hawaiʻi Creole English and so-called 'standard' English is ongoing, although in the past few decades, it has taken a twist: seen as a form of resistance to haole [foreign] dominance, as well as a fierce expression of 'local' identity, Hawaiʻi Creole English has become one of the important markers of Hawaiʻi-based literature, taken up by Hawaiian and other writers in the contemporary period as an important aspect of self-expression and identity in their craft.[54]

Through his use of pidgin, the speaker in "Moa Space Foa Ramble" expresses himself as a "local" who is critical of foreign colonisation. The poem is written in the second person, which gives it a conversational, talk-story tone. Formally, the poem is composed of free verse couplets and single line stanzas, all left justified. Like Mackenzie, Balaz centers a Hawaiian ecological worldview by depicting the ocean as Kanaloa. Instead of wondering about the terrifying impact of rising sea levels, Balaz teaches the reader about climate change and its impacts in both serious and humorous ways, while offering advice on how to respond and adapt.

The poem begins with the speaker's first piece of advice: "Sell dat beachfront property now / and get as much as you can foa da house." The next stanza uses humour to explain rising sea levels: "Wheah you got your plumeria tree / and nice green lawn // going be wun playground foa da fishes." Even though flooding is usually figured in apocalyptic terms, Balaz tempers the catastrophe by describing it as becoming a "playground" for fish. The next four lines continues this juxtaposition of the grim with the humourous:

> Methane from da tundra
> and CO_2 from smoke stacks and exhaust pipes
>
> going turn all dat melted ice from da poles
> into moa watah foa da lobsters and da eels.

Balaz manages to explain aspects of global warming in a few lines while also maintaining the image of the melting ice as "moa watah" (more water) for sea

---

54   hoʻomanawanui, "He Lei Hoʻoheno no nā Kau a Kau," 50–51.

life. In the next section of the poem, the speaker becomes resigned about the situation:

> Middle of da island
> dats da place to go.
>
> Dere's no getting around it
> cause da coastline going sink.
>
> Take wun good look at da airport
> and da brand new rail—
>
> all of it is moving inland, brah.
>
> Waikiki going be real different too.
>
> Might as well just give it up
> cause wun surrounding wall not going help.

At this point, Balaz soberly faces the realities of climate change in Hawai'i, and a future in which people may have no choice but to move to the "middle of da island." When discussing rising sea levels in Hawai'i, Waikīkī is often highlighted because it is a coastal area that will become inundated, severely impacting the tourism industry––the main economic industry in the state. One of the strategies to save Waikīkī is to build seawalls. But as the speaker says: "wun surrounding wall not going help." The final lines of the poem reflect on the failure to act on climate change sooner:

> Global warming—
>
> Foa da longest time
> plenty people wen blow it off as wun myth.
>
> Now Kanaloa going have moa space foa ramble.

"Global warming" is invoked on its own line to give it a mythic tone since, as the speaker points out, it has been continually dismissed by many people as "wun myth." This climate denial has, indeed, been one of the main reasons for the continued lack of governmental policy and action on climate change. The final line is reminiscent of Mackenzie's ending, in which the rising sea is

"KĀNE AND KANALOA ARE COMING" 241

figured as Kanaloa. Yet Kanaloa is not depicted as a devourer of islands, but instead as a god who will now have more space to ramble around his watery playground. In Balaz's poem, the speaker does not express fear or terror, but a resigned acceptance of our adaptation as nature—in this case, the ocean and its creatures—claims its new domain.

The final poem I will discuss, "Water Remembers" by Brandy Nālani McDougall, focuses specifically on the legacy of environmental injustice and the impacts of climate change in Waikīkī. Whereas Balaz is resigned to the fact that Waikīkī is "going be real different" and we might as well give it up, McDougall actually sees the flooding of Waikīkī as a decolonising act.

McDougall is the author of a poetry collection, *The Salt-Wind, Ka Makani Pa'akai* and an academic book, *Finding Meaning: Kaona and Contemporary Hawaiian Literature*, as well as the co-editor of several anthologies, including *Huihui: Navigating Art and Literature in the Pacific*.[55] She is an Associate Professor of American Studies (specialising in Indigenous studies) at the University of Hawai'i at Mānoa.

"Water Remembers" is a narrative poem composed of four stanzas with a third person, omniscient speaker. The first stanza begins in the ancient past by describing the pre-colonial environment of Waikīkī:

> Waikīkī was once a fertile marshland
> ahupua'a, mountain water gushing
> from the valleys of Makiki, Mānoa,
> Pālolo, Wai'alae, and Wailupe
> to meet ocean water. Seeing such
> wealth, Kānaka planted hundreds
> of fields of kalo, 'uala, 'ulu in the uka,
> built fishponds in the muliwai.
> Waikīkī fed O'ahu people for generations
> so easily that its ocean raised surfers,
> hailed the highest of ali'i to its shores.[56]

---

55 Brandy Nālani McDougall, *The Salt Wind: Ka Makani Pa'akai* (Honolulu: Kuleana 'Ōiwi Press, 2008), *Finding Meaning: Kaona and Contemporary Hawaiian Literature* (Tucson: U of Arizona P, 2016); *Huihui: Navigating Art and Literature in the Pacific* (Honolulu: U of Hawai'i P, 2014).

56 Brandy Nālani McDougall, "Water Remembers," *Slate Magazine: Special feature on Pacific Islander Climate Change Poetry* (2017), http://journal.themissingslate.com/2017/10/01/water-remembers/.

McDougall sets the scene by immediately noting what Waikīkī once was "a fertile marshland ahupua'a," in which water flows freely from the mauka to makai. She foregrounds how Hawaiians studied the environment and intentionally planted "hundreds of fields" of traditional Hawaiian crops—kalo (taro), 'uala (sweet potato), 'ulu (breadfruit)—and built fishponds in the estuary. This abundance fed the people for generations and was the beacon of Hawaiian surfers and ali'i (chiefs). The figuration of water as "wealth" speaks to how Hawaiians valued water. This Indigenous pastoral is an awe-inspiring image of Hawaiian agricultural practices, embodying Hawaiian environmental values and the ethics of sustainability.

The second stanza, which is twice as long as the first stanza, moves forward to present-day Waikīkī, a world-famous tourist destination. I quote the stanza in its entirety to show the full potency of its imagery:

> Waikīkī is now a miasma of concrete
> and asphalt, its waters drained
> into a canal dividing tourist from resident.
> The mountain's springs and waterfalls,
> trickle where they are allowed to flow,
> and left stagnant elsewhere, pullulate
> with staphylococcus. In the uplands,
> the fields and have long been dismantled,
> their rock terraces and heiau looted
> to build the walls of multi-million dollar
> houses with panoramic Diamond Head
> and/or ocean views. Closer to the ocean,
> hotels fester like pustules, the sand
> stolen from other 'āina to manufacture
> the beaches, seawalls maintained
> to keep the sand in, so suntan-oiled
> tourists can laze on what never was,
> what never should have been. No one
> is fed plants and fish from this 'āina now—
> its land value has grown so that nothing
> but money *can* be grown—its waters unpotable, polluted.

McDougall exposes how decades of tourism and urban development have destroyed the once productive ahupua'a system. She notes how the waters were drained into what is the Ala Wai canal, itself polluted. The once flowing streams are now contaminated by bacteria. The heiau, or sacred stone structures, have been replaced by multi-million-dollar houses. Native surfers and

"KĀNE AND KANALOA ARE COMING" 243

ali'i are replaced by "suntan-oiled tourists." The hotels are metaphorized as "pustules," and even the sand is imported from elsewhere. Tourism and urban development are diseases upon the once healthy land and water.[57] The environment no longer feeds people as it once did, and the only thing that can be grown is money. Water was once a source of wealth and life, but it is now "unpotable, polluted" in this colonial necropastoral.

The next stanza, which is substantially shorter, stays in the present and addresses the impacts of climate change in Waikīkī, which include heavier rainfall and rising sea levels:

> Each year as heavy rainfalls flood the valleys,
> spill over gulches, slide the foundations
> of overpriced houses, invade sewage pipes
> and send brown water runoff to the ocean,
> the king tides roll in, higher in its warming,
> lingering longer and breaking through
> sandbags and barricades, eroding the resorts.

The heavier rainfalls regularly flood the valleys and overcome the city sewage system, spewing waste into the streets of Waikīkī. At the same time, the higher king tides erode the shoreline, pulling the imported sand out to sea—no doubt ruining many tourists' vacations (and perceptions of a postcard paradise). In the past, healthy waters flowing from mauka to makai created an idyllic environment; today, however, water from the mountain valleys and from the sea are creating a health crisis.

In the final stanza, McDougall offers a different interpretation of climate change in Hawai'i than Mackenzie and Balaz. Instead of seeing the impacts as devouring and destructive, she sees these changes as decolonial:

> This is not the end of civilization, but
> a return to one. Only the water insisting
> on what it should always have, spreading
> its liniment over infected wounds. Only
> the water rising above us, reteaching us
> wealth and remembering its name.

---

57 McDougall, also a literary scholar, expands on the depiction of colonialism as disease in her essay, "Christianity, Civilization, Colonialism, and Other Diseases: The Poetry of Haunani-Kay Trask," *Jacket2 Magazine* (2011): np, https://jacket2.org/article/christianity -civilization-colonialism-and-other-diseases.

McDougall subverts the common narrative that climate change is an apocalyptic "end of civilization," and instead insists that the water will heal the diseased wounds of colonialism and return us to a more sustainable way of living. As the water rises to wash away the tourism industry of Waikīkī, it can re-teach us that the true meaning of "wealth" is not how much money the land can generate, but how much we can sustain, nurture and care for the environment and each other. The last line also contains a moment of "kaona," which deserves explication. In her essay, "Putting Feathers on Our Words: Kaona as a Decolonial Aesthetic Practice in Hawaiian Literature," McDougall describes the complexity of kaona:

> Kaona is an intellectual practice (one that is literary, rhetorical, pedagogical, and compositional) in Hawaiian Literature, often defined as 'hidden meaning;' however, it is more exact to say that kaona refers to meaning hidden out in the open, with a range of both the 'hiddenness' and 'openness' of meaning engaged. That is, the practice of kaona allows for meaning to be hidden in such a way as to seem ornamental, trivial, or merely imagistic—with seemingly innocent meaning—to those unfamiliar with [the language of symbols] ... Inclusive of allusion, symbolism, punning, and metaphor, kaona draws on the collective knowledges and experiences of Hawaiians ...[58]

The key piece of knowledge that a reader needs to have in order to find the "hidden meaning" in the last line is that the Hawaiian word for "wealth" is "waiwai," which comes from the Hawaiian word for "water," "wai" (it should be noted as well that "wai" forms the base for several of the place names at the beginning of the poem: Waikīkī, Waiʻalae, and Wailupe). While the last line seems simple at first, with this knowledge of Hawaiian language, the deeper meaning of the ending and the title opens up as water remembers that its name means wealth, and as it rises, it will teach us that true wealth is measured by the presence of clean water and ecological abundance. Instead of imagining climate change as a devouring terror or as an impending, unmitigated disaster that will force people inland, McDougall re-imagines the rising waters as a decolonial opportunity to wash away "civilization" so that we can relearn and remember the true meaning of wealth.

---

58   Brandy Nālani McDougall, "Putting Feathers on Our Words: Kaona as a Decolonial Aesthetic Practice in Hawaiian Literature," *Decolonization: Indigeneity, Education & Society* 3.1 (2014): 3.

4 Conclusion

In 2019, the Hawai'i Conservation Conference, the largest annual environmental event in the state, was themed "He 'A'ali'i Kū Makani Au: Resilience in the Face of Change." Its opening plenary panel was titled: "Kāne and Kanaloa Are Coming: How Will We Receive Them? A Kānaka Take on Climate Change and Indigenous Resilience," and featured six Hawaiian women scientists and scholars: Aurora Kagawa-Viviani, Haunani Kane, Kalei Nu'uhiwa, Noelani Puniwai, Rosie Alegado, and Kealoha Fox. This was the first time in the conference's 26-year history that the opening plenary featured all Hawaiian scientists. Their panel focused on their perceptions of climate change and adaptation from a Hawaiian perspective, such as understanding that everything is interconnected and thus, we must focus on restoring entire ecosystems as opposed to individual issues. They also focused on Indigenous survival and resilience in the face of change: "Water will always be here but maybe not in a drinkable form, [Nu'uhiwa said]. The ocean will be here but maybe it will occupy more space, she said, which might mean having to migrate as her ancestors did." For Puniwai, "the underlying solution to the climate crisis is aloha for the places and people, as Native Hawaiians had for their land and country ... 'We'll only make a difference in climate change if we love these places,' she said, adding that adaptation and mitigation can't just be based on data and science." Alegado made a pointed comment about how Indigenous people are experiencing a "third wave of colonialism": "The first was geographic displacement— think Waikiki. The second was social and psychocultural—think illegal occupation, forced assimilation and militarism in Hawai'i. And the third is climate change, she said, driven by a consumer capitalist economy."[59] Alegado also proclaimed "We're not scared," due to her people's history of survival and resilience, and their respect for the environment—hence the title of their plenary not focusing on apocalypse but asking how we will receive the coming changes to Kāne and Kanaloa.

I conclude with this historic plenary panel to emphasise the importance of deeply engaging with Hawaiian knowledge, culture, history and communities when discussing the impacts, risks and opportunities of climate change in Hawai'i. Moreover, we can't begin to confront climate change unless we also confront the legacy and ongoing environmental injustice of U.S. colonialism,

---

59   Quoted in Nathan Eagle, "'We're Not Scared': Hawai'i Confronts Next Wave of Climate Change," *Honolulu Civil Beat: Hawaii 2040* (July 9, 2019): np, https://www.civilbeat.org/2019/07/were-not-scared-hawaii-confronts-next-wave-of-climate-change/.

capitalism and militarism that have all contributed to ecological precarity and climate change in Hawai'i, across the Pacific islands, and globally. Also, if we don't address the denial of Hawaiian sovereignty and self-determination, we deny the Indigenous rights of Hawaiians to steward the future of these islands.

I hope this chapter will also bring much needed attention to climate change in Hawai'i, a place that has often been ignored in global media coverage. I turn to Hawaiian scholars to underscore the significance of 'ike 'āina, wahi pana, malama 'āina, aloha āina, and Indigenous, decolonial and environmental literacies. I listen closely to Hawaiian literature and how it represents the sacredness of the environment, the interconnection of all beings, the genealogical and cultural relationship between people and the world, powerful critiques of ecological imperialism and carbon colonialism, symbolic sites of revitalization, resilience, and healing, and visions of decolonial and sustainable futures. I turn to Hawaiian poets who are addressing climate change so that we can witness a range of aesthetic, emotional and political responses. ho'omanawanui poignantly describes Hawaiian literature as "a lei ho'oheno no nā kau a kau, a lei to be cherished for all seasons,"[60] and perhaps even more cherished when the seasons are themselves dramatically changing.

Works Cited

Agarwal, Anil, and Sunita Narain. *Global Warming in an Unequal World: A Case of Environmental Colonialism.* (New Delhi: Centre for Science and the Environment, 1991).

Allen, Chadwick. *Narrative: Indigenous Identity in American Indian and Maori Literary and Activist Texts.* (Minneapolis: U of Minnesota P, 2012).

Balaz, Joe. *Ho'omānoa: An Anthology of Contemporary Hawaiian Literature.* (Honolulu: Ku Pa'a Inc., 1989).

Balaz, Joe. "Moa Space foa Ramble." *Juked* (November, 2015).

Balaz, Joe. *Pidgin Eye.* (Honolulu: Ala Press, 2019).

Crawford, Neta. "Pentagon Fuel Use, Climate Change, the Costs of War." *Costs of War Project.* (June 12, 2019), https://watson.brown.edu/costsofwar/files/cow/imce/papers/2019/Pentagon%20Fuel%20Use%2C%20Climate%20Change%20and%20the%20Costs%20of%20War%20Final.pdf.

Department of Planning and Economic Development, Hawaii. *Effects on Hawaii of a Worldwide Rise in Sea Level Induced by the Greenhouse Effect* (January 1985),

---

60   ho'omanawanui, "He Lei Ho'oheno," 73.

https://planning.hawaii.gov/wp-content/uploads/2013/04/Sea-Level-Rise-Effects-on-Hawaii-1985.pdf.

DeLoughrey, Elizabeth. "The Sea is Rising: Visualising Climate Change in the Pacific Islands" in *Meteorologies of modernity: Weather and climate discourses in the Anthropocene*, ed. Fekadu et al. (Tübingen: Narr Francke Attempto, 2017): 237–253.

DeLoughrey Elizabeth and Handley, George. "Introduction" in *Postcolonial Ecologies: Literature and the Environment*, eds. Elizabeth DeLoughrey and George B. Handley (Oxford: Oxford UP, 2011): 3–42.

Dreese, Donelle N. *Ecocriticism: Creating Self and Place in Environmental and American Indian Literatures.* (New York: Peter Lang, 2002).

Eagle, Nathan. "Hawai'i 2040: Climate Change Is Already Here. And We're Running Out Of Time." *Honolulu Civil Beat* (January 14, 2019).

Elbert, Samuel, and Mary Kawena Pukui. *Hawaiian Dictionary*, revised edition (Honolulu: U of Hawai'i P, 1986).

Elder, John, and Hertha D. Wong, eds. *Family of Earth & Sky: Indigenous Tales of Nature from around the World.* (Boston: Beacon Press, 1996).

Hamasaki, Richard. "Singing in Their Genealogical Trees: The Emergence of Contemporary Hawaiian Poetry in English." MA Thesis (University of Hawai'i, Mānoa, 1989).

Handy, E.S. Craighill, Elizabeth Green Handy and Mary Kawena Pukui. *Native Planters of Old Hawaii: Their Life, Lore, and Environment* (Honolulu: Bishop Museum, 1972).

Hawai'i Climate Change Mitigation and Adaptation Commission. *Hawai'i Sea Level Rise Vulnerability and Adaptation Report.* Prepared by Tetra Tech, Inc. and the State of Hawai'i Department of Land and Natural Resources, Office of Conservation and Coastal Lands, under the State of Hawai'i Department of Land and Natural Resources Contract (No: 64064), 2017.

Hogue, Rebecca. "I Kū Mau Mau (Stand Together): Pacific Islander Solidarity in the March for Real Climate Leadership." *The Contemporary Pacific*, (forthcoming).

ho'omanawanui, ku'ualoha. "Hā, Mana, Leo (Breath, Spirit, Voice): Kanaka Maoli Empowerment through Literature." *The American Indian Quarterly* 28.1.2 (Winter/Spring 2004): 77–100.

ho'omanawanui, ku'ualoha. "He Lei Ho'oheno no nā Kau a Kau: Language, Performance, and Form in Hawaiian Poetry." *The Contemporary Pacific* 17.1 (2005): 30–55.

ho'omanawanui, ku'ualoha. " 'This Land Is Your Land, This Land Was My Land': Kanaka Maoli versus Settler Representations of 'Āina in Contemporary Literature of Hawai'i" in *Asian Settler Colonialism: From Local Governance to the Habits of Everyday Life in Hawai'i*, eds. Candace Fujikane and Jonathan Y. Okamura (Honolulu: U of Hawai'i P, 2008): 116–154.

ho'omanawanui, ku'ualoha. "'Ike 'āina: Native Hawaiian culturally based indigenous literacy." *Hūlili: Multidisciplinary Research on Hawaiian Well-Being* 5 (2008): 204–229.

hoʻomanawanui, kuʻualoha. "Hanohano Wailuanuiahoʻāno: Remembering, Recovering, and Writing Place." *Hūlili: Multidisciplinary Research on Hawaiian Well-Being* 8 (2012): 187–243.

Huang, Hsinya. "Toward Transpacific Ecopoetics: Three Indigenous Texts." *Comparative Literature Studies* 50.1 (2013): 120–130.

Johnson, Rubellite Kawena. *Kukini ʻAhaʻilono, To Carry on the News: Over a Century of Native Hawaiian Life and Thought from the Hawaiian Language Newspapers of 1834 to 1948.* (Honolulu: Topgallant, 1976).

Justice, Daniel Heath and James H. Cox, eds. *Oxford Handbook of Indigenous American Literatures.* (Oxford: Oxford UP, 2014).

Kagawa, Aurora K., and Peter M. Vitousek. "The Ahupuaʻa of Puanui: A Resource for Understanding Hawaiian Rain-Fed Agriculture." *Pacific Science* 66.2 (Apr 2012): 161–172.

Kaiwi, Monica Kaʻimipono. "I Ulu no nā Lālā i ke Kumu: An Epistemological Examination of Native Hawaiian Literature." MA Thesis (University of Auckland, 2000).

Kajihiro, Kyle. "Resisting Militarization in Hawaiʻi" in *Bases of Empire: The Global Struggle against U.S. Military Posts*, ed. Cathering Lutz (New York: New York UP, 2009): 299–332.

Kameʻeleihiwa, Lilikalā. *Native land and foreign desires: Pehea lā e pono ai?* (Honolulu: Bishop Museum, 1992).

Kanahele, George. *Kū kanaka—Stand tall: A search for Hawaiian values* (Honolulu: U of Hawaiʻi P, 1986).

Kanaʻiaupuni, Shawn Malia, and Nolan Malone. "This land is my land: The role of place in Native Hawaiian identity." *Hūlili: Multidisciplinary Research on Hawaiian Well-Being* 3 (2006): 281–307.

Kawaharada, Dennis. *Storied Landscapes: Hawaiian Literature and Place.* (Honolulu: Kalamaku Press, 1999).

Lyons, Paul. *American Pacificism: Oceania in the U.S. Imagination.* (New York: Routledge, 2006).

Mackenzie, David Kealiʻi. "In Words There is Life: Kanaka ʻŌiwi Participation in Slam Poetry." MA Thesis (University of Hawaiʻi, Mānoa, 2016).

Mackenzie, David Kealiʻi. *From Hunger to Prayer.* (Silver Needle, 2019), https://thesilverneedle.wordpress.com/.

Mackenzie, David Kealiʻi. "Kanaloa ʻAi Moku." *Pacific Islander Eco-Literature Anthology* (Honolulu: U of Hawaiʻi P, forthcoming).

Magrane, Eric. "'Healing, Belonging, Resistance, and Mutual Care': Reading Indigenous Ecopoetics and Climate Narratives." *Literary Geographies* 4.2 (2018) 158–167.

McDougall, Brandy Nālani. *The Salt Wind: Ka Makani Paʻakai.* (Honolulu: Kuleana ʻŌiwi, 2008).

McDougall, Brandy Nālani. "Christianity, Civilization, Colonialism, and Other Diseases: The Poetry of Haunani-Kay Trask." *Jacket2 Magazine* (2011), https://jacket2.org/article/christianity-civilization-colonialism-and-other-diseases.

McDougall, Brandy Nālani. *Huihui: Navigating Art and Literature in the Pacific.* (Honolulu: U of Hawai'i P, 2014).

McDougall, Brandy Nālani. "Putting feathers on our words: Kaona as a decolonial aesthetic practice in Hawaiian Literature." *Decolonization: Indigeneity, Education & Society* 3.1 (2014): 3–30.

McDougall, Brandy Nālani. *Finding Meaning: Kaona and Contemporary Hawaiian Literature* (Tucson: U of Arizona P, 2016).

McDougall, Brandy Nālani. "Water Remembers." *Slate Magazine: Special feature on Pacific Islander Climate Change Poetry* (2017), http://journal.themissingslate.com/2017/10/01/water-remembers/.

McLaren, J. *New Pacific Literatures: Culture and Environment in the European Pacific.* (New York: Garland, 1993).

Mueller-Dombois, Dieter. "The Hawaiian Ahupua'a Land Use System: Its Biological Resource Zones and the Challenge for Silvicultural Restoration." *Bishop Museum Bulletin in Cultural and Environmental Studies* 3 (2007): 23–33.

Nelson, Robert. *Place and Vision: The Function of Landscape in Native American Fiction.* (New York: Peter Lang, 1993).

Pukui, Mary Kawena. *'Ōlelo No'eau: Hawaiian Proverbs and Poetical Sayings.* (Honolulu: Bishop Museum, 1986).

Rosaldo, Renato. *Culture and Truth: The Remaking of Social Analysis.* (Boston: Beacon, 1989).

Saranillio, Dean. *Unsustainable Empire: Alternative Histories of Hawai'i Statehood.* (Durhan: Duke UP, 2018).

Schweninger, Lee. *Listening to the Land: Native American Literary Responses to the Landscape.* (Athens, GA: U of Georgia P, 2008).

Silva, Noenoe. *Aloha Betrayed: Native Hawaiian Resistance to American Colonialism.* (Durham: Duke UP, 2004).

Steiner, Candice Elanna. "A Sea of Warriors: Performing an Identity of Resilience and Empowerment in the Face of Climate Change in the Pacific." *The Contemporary Pacific* 27.1 (2015): 147–180.

Wilson, Norma. *The Nature of Native American Poetry.* (Albuquerque: U of New Mexico P, 2001).

Wilson, Rob. "Oceania as Peril and Promise: Towards Theorizing a Worlded Vision of Trans-Pacific Ecopoetics." Paper presented at the Oceanic Archives and Transnational American Studies Conference, Hong Kong University (June 4–6, 2012).

Wilson, Rob, and Vilsoni Hereniko, eds. *Inside Out: Literature, Cultural Politics, and Identity in the New Pacific.* (Lanham: Rowman, 1999).

Ziser, Michael, and Julie Sze. "Climate Change, Environmental Aesthetics, and Global Environmental Justice Cultural Studies." *Discourse: Journal for Theoretical Studies in Media and Culture* 29.2 (2007): 384–410.

CHAPTER 9

Monsoonal Memories and "the Reliable Water"

Reading Climate Change in Selected Malaysian Literature

Agnes S. K. Yeow

In Malaysia, public and policy discourse on climate change is erratic at best, often making headlines only after irreversible damage has been done. This is surprising, given the backdrop of the country's clear environmental protection laws and ratification of multiple United Nations-sponsored conventions on greenhouse gas emission mitigation. As part of the landmark Paris Agreement of 2015, Malaysia pledged to reduce its greenhouse gas emissions by 45 percent by 2030 and to cut 32 million tonnes of carbon emissions by 2020. Notably, for the first time in the nation's history, climate change was tagged on to a list of interrelated concerns handled by the Ministry of Energy, Science, Technology, Environment and Climate Change in 2018. Despite the presence of various agencies and departments overseeing matters ranging from deforestation to transborder haze, challenges such as the country's "catch-up" development agenda and dogged push for industrialised nation status threaten to undo any positive measures to decarbonise. This chapter seeks to unearth evidence of climate change awareness in a selection of contemporary Malaysian literary works and to trace how this consciousness is translated into writings about the weather, rivers and land as well as the communities and places that are the most at risk in a warming world. I show how the selected writers, namely Shirley Geok-lin Lim, Muhammad Haji Salleh and K. S. Maniam—knowingly or otherwise—have addressed changing climatic conditions in their works even before the spectre of climate change gained wide recognition and understanding as the unprecedented environmental crisis of our times. I explore how climate disturbance destabilises social equilibrium and transforms places, identities and communities—entities that express topographical and meteorological realities—and examine the implications of their transformation. Before I turn to the works—a cluster of poems and a short story—to probe their underlying climatological themes, a brief sketch of the country's vulnerability and response to climate change, as well as the conceptual framework of my study, is in order.

Malaysia is often criticised for its dismal environmental track record by both the international community and its own citizens. In terms of energy policy,

---

© KONINKLIJKE BRILL NV, LEIDEN, 2022 | DOI:10.1163/9789004514164_010

for instance, Malaysia is lacking on many fronts. In his hard-hitting criticism of the country's obsession with mega-dams, social activist Kua Kia Soong notes that Malaysia seems bent on generating more power than is actually needed and then "[hopes] that energy guzzling industries such as aluminium smelters will come and take up this surplus of energy" when ironically, "[t]here is vast potential for renewable energy resources in Malaysia."[1] Kua denounces these huge, expensive projects as "environmentally disastrous, socially disruptive and economically misconceived"[2] and describes the suffering of forest-dwelling Indigenous communities displaced by mega-dams as nothing less than ethnocide. As of 2013, 94 percent of the country's electricity is generated through the burning of imported coal—a staggering 1.7 million tonnes a month—and 26 percent of the country's total CO_2 emissions come from the energy sector. Despite the bleak picture, over the years, the government has taken positive steps to confront climate change especially since the effects of global warming on agriculture—an economic mainstay—have far-reaching consequences on livelihoods and food security.

Indeed, the impact of climate change in Malaysia has been the subject of extensive empirical study and analysis. One such study conducted in 2013 concluded that on the East Coast of peninsular Malaysia—where a large proportion of the nation's fishery industry is located—the temperature has risen by an average of 1.5 degrees Celsius from 1950 to the first decade of this century with a significant increase in the number of warmer days and nights. Other studies point to the fact that, throughout the country, climate change has resulted in higher variability of rainfall, longer and more extreme wind and thunderstorm events, abnormally severe floods and the erosion of 30 percent of the country's 4,809 kilometres of coastline.[3] Studies on climate impacts in the Asia-Pacific region—which includes Malaysia—have highlighted the adverse effects of rising temperatures between 1961–2003:

> Societal and environmental temperature-related impacts under greenhouse-gas-induced warming in the Asia–Pacific region could include [...] increased heat mortality, reduction in cold-temperature morbidity, increased tropical vector-borne diseases (such as dengue

---

1 Kua Kia Soong, *Damned Dams and Noxious Nukes: Questioning Malaysia's Energy Policy* (Petaling Jaya, Selangor, Malaysia: Suara Inisiatif, 2013): 19, 20.

2 Kua, *Damned Dams and Noxious Nukes*, 19.

3 Hayrol Azri Mohamed Shaffril, Bahaman Abu Samah, Jeffrey Lawrence D'Silva and Sulaiman Md. Yassin, "The Process of Social Adaptation Towards Climate Change Among Malaysian Fishermen," *International Journal of Climate Change Strategies and Management* 5.1 (2013): 39.

fever and malaria), increased fire risks, coral bleaching, increased urban pollution-related respiratory problems (related to hotter weather), and mixed impacts on agricultural and water resources.[4]

Based on tidal data from 1984–2013, mean sea levels in Malaysian waters have been rising at a rate higher than the projected global rate "due to local climate and topographical conditions."[5] Tropical Malaysia—comprising peninsular West Malaysia and Bornean East Malaysia and bounded by the Malaccan Straits, the South China Sea and the Sulu Sea—has an equatorial climate with hot and humid weather for much of the year and two major monsoon seasons (April–September and October–March), which affect annual climate variability. It has also "experienced warming and rainfall irregularities particularly in the last two decades [2000s]."[6] The risk is exacerbated by a shrinking rainforest—a direct consequence of timber extraction and the clearing of vast tracts of land for palm oil plantations. In the Malaysian state of Sabah in north Borneo, the major cause of degradation of the lowland forests from the 1970s to 2010 has been logging, including premature re-logging of previously once-logged forests and the large-scale conversion of natural forest to agricultural plantations.[7]

Climate change reports and analyses—like the ones cited above—circulate mainly in the form of what Antonia Mehnert describes as "lifeless modes of description," which not only attests to the privileging of scientific over human testimony but also "[suppresses] other perceptions of global warming."[8] She notes that "[i]n order to understand this unprecedented phenomenon not only in its scientific, but also cultural complexity, it is important to consider it within a broader context of discourses and narratives, which implies an awareness of social and cultural spheres through which climatic changes are brought to the fore."[9] The socio-cultural expressions of climate change are

---

4   G. M. Griffiths et al., "Change in Mean Temperature as a Predictor of Extreme Temperature Change in the Asia–Pacific Region," *International Journal of Climatology* 25 (2005): 1303.
5   Kuok Ho Daniel Tang, "Climate Change in Malaysia: Trends, Contributors, Impacts, Mitigation and Adaptations," *Science of the Total Environment* 650 (2019): 1861.
6   Tang, "Climate Change in Malaysia," 1859.
7   Glen Reynolds et al., "Changes in Forest Land Use and Management in Sabah, Malaysia Borneo, 1990–2010, with a Focus on the Danum Valley Region," *Philosophical Transactions of the Royal Society B* 366 (2011): 3168–73, https://www.jstor.org/stable/23076285.
8   Antonia Mehnert, *Climate Change Fictions: Representations of Global Warming in American Literature.* (New York: Palgrave Macmillan, 2016): 3.
9   Mehnert, *Climate Change Fictions: Representations of Global Warming in American Literature*, 3–4.

understandably complex. Emphasising the discordant social perceptions and diverse rhetoric of climate change, Mike Hulme asserts: "Not only is climate change altering our physical world, but the idea of climate change is altering our social worlds."[10] He argues that climate change as an idea "possesses a certain plasticity"[11] and that it can be framed in different ways making it "a carrier of ideology."[12] The premise that climate change has become a medium for a host of social concerns is aptly summed up by Bronislaw Szerszynski and John Urry: "Climate change is always already social; the social does not need to be added to it, just to be revealed."[13]

The intrinsic nexus between climate change and society throws a key question into relief: how has climate change altered literary expression and vice versa? In discussing the climate change "pretrauma"—anxiety about future catastrophic climate-related events—triggered by dystopian film and fiction in her book *Climate Trauma*, E. Ann Kaplan argues:

> By definition, genres change as the social context changes. In this case, part of the critic's job is to lay bare such dual contexts of society and genre. The pretrauma genre emerges as Eurocentric cultures become newly aware of the uncertainty of human futurity. Genres shape how we think about our lived worlds by establishing certain kinds of story, certain repeated narratives and situations, that lead to well-defined expectations.[14]

Kaplan's argument raises the important point of Eurocentrism as a determining factor in the creation of dystopian narratives set in a climate-change ravaged future. This begs the question, however, of whether such genres have also germinated in postcolonial environments, where Eurocentric histories, contexts and values are consciously resisted. It is safe to say that representations of climate trauma and injustice by writers from industrialised economies will differ in context, perspective and substance from those by writers from the global South. Critics need to avoid universalising the perception of climate

---

10   Mike Hulme, *Why We Disagree About Climate Change: Understanding Controversy, Inaction and Opportunity* (Cambridge UP, 2009): xviii.

11   Hulme, *Why We Disagree About Climate Change*, xviii.

12   Hulme, *Why We Disagree About Climate Change*, 217.

13   Bronislaw Szerszynski and John Urry, "Changing Climates: Introduction," *Theory, Culture & Society* 27.2–3 (2010): 4.

14   E. Ann Kaplan, *Climate Trauma: Foreseeing the Future in Dystopian Film and Fiction* (New Brunswick, New Jersey: Rutgers UP, 2016): 28.

change or making it fit the analytical frameworks—predominantly Western in orientation—that are employed to evaluate climate-oriented literature. Ironically, although climate change may be the ultimate trans-border atmospheric phenomenon that is truly planetary in scale, Ramachandra Guha's cautionary "Third World Critique" of American environmentalism and wilderness preservation[15]—highlighting the incompatibility between American/First World and Indian/Third World environmental ethics—remains particularly relevant to considerations of climate change criticism and the universal yardstick used in measuring processes like climate adaptability and mitigation. As Laura Wright points out, "in postcolonial cultures, the factors that shape environmental concerns, strategies for dealing with environmental issues, and, in fact, the very reasons for an individual's environmentalist identification are vastly different from those in the West."[16] As the imposition of an undifferentiated environmental philosophy and ethics across the board is problematic and untenable, so too is the sweeping attribution of blame for the crisis on the rich nations of the first world. Dipesh Chakrabarty asserts that both economics and human actions have contributed to the crisis:

> Climate change, refracted through global capital, will no doubt accentuate the logic of inequality that runs through the rule of capital; some people will no doubt gain temporarily at the expense of others. But the whole crisis cannot be reduced to a story of capitalism … Climate change is an unintended consequence of human actions and shows, only through scientific analysis, the effects of our actions as a species.[17]

Acknowledging the immense and historical proportions of the crisis, the editors of the volume *Whose Anthropocene?*—a response to Chakrabarty's seminal essay—suggest a practical approach to grasping the colossal phenomenon: "Understanding the near-future consequences of global warming depends on the artfulness with which we imagine and render the often quotidian experiences of climate change."[18] These daily experiences are necessarily

---

15 Ramachandra Guha, "Radical American Environmentalism and Wilderness Preservation: A Third World Critique," *Environmental Ethics* 11.1 (Spring 1989): 71–83.

16 Laura Wright, *Wilderness into Civilized Shapes: Reading the Postcolonial Environment* (Athens, GA: U of Georgia P, 2010): 10.

17 Dipesh Chakrabarty, "The Climate of History: Four Theses," *Critical Inquiry* 35 (Winter 2009): 221.

18 Robert Emmett and Thomas Lekan, "Foreword" and "Introduction" to *Whose Anthropocene? Revisiting Dipesh Chakrabarty's "Four Theses,"* eds. Robert Emmett and Thomas Lekan (Munich: Rachel Carson Centre for Environment and Society, 2016): 11.

construed in light of the crucial difference in timescale between weather and climate. Weather denotes short-term atmospheric events and changes over a particular hour, day, week or month at a particular location while climate refers to what the weather is like over a long period of time in a particular place. Climate, if stable, suggests predictability and what the weather would typically be like for a specific time and place. The fact that climate has *changed* suggests that weather is no longer what people expect in a specific time and place. A climate-changed world means that weather patterns have changed significantly. As such, given the reality of fluctuating weather patterns, any experience of short-term weather—no matter how brief, slight or seemingly negligible—deserves closer scrutiny. Bronislaw Szerszynski points out that reading the weather in terms of seasons "involves being alert to its new, unstable temporality, as the coiled cycles of annual weather patterns unravel into the irreversible time of the *longue durée*, and each storm and drought becomes unseasonable, unique, historical."[19] In recent years, climate change has begun to set the tone for literary criticism. Matthew Griffiths, for instance, encourages the ecocritic to "emphasise the adaptability of the literary to changing climates, whether literal or figurative, so that we regard it as much as a series of dynamic processes as the environment is."[20] He goes on to prescribe a bold approach to climate change criticism:

> If criticism is to be informed by climate change, our critical practice must be as pervasive and connective as the phenomena of climate change themselves.[21]

Griffiths advocates a more integrative way of reading that does not "read environmental crisis in the texts of environmental crisis"[22] alone but in any text which is read for its representation of nature. Certainly, climate change has been front and centre in ecocritical discourse and is the fundamental basis for the epochal narratives of the Anthropocene. As a geohistorical event, the Anthropocene has invigorated environmental studies in general and opened the world's eyes to the destructive effects of human tampering with the Earth system. It has also prompted literary critics to read literary texts innovatively

---

19   Bronislaw Szerszynski, "Reading and Writing the Weather: Climate Technics and the Moment of Responsibility," *Theory, Culture & Society* 27.2–3 (2010): 23–24.

20   Matthew Griffiths, *The New Poetics of Climate Change: Modernist Aesthetics for a Warming World* (London: Bloomsbury Academic, 2017): 15.

21   Griffiths, *The New Poetics of Climate Change*, 15.

22   Griffiths, *The New Poetics of Climate Change*, 15–16.

and improvisationally with the understanding that such readings can only be partial and provisional—a reflection of "the limits of knowledge and the inexpressible qualities of the Anthropocene."[23]

In fact, this turn to a more climate-conscious literary arts and criticism is almost superfluous in the Malaysian literary context because, to a large extent, Malaysian literature has always been informed by climate and—by extension—climate change. In my examination of selected Malaysian works, I return to the assertion, "Climate change is always already social; the social does not need to be added to it, just to be revealed."[24] I argue that Malaysian society has always been living with climate change—it is the rate of change that needs to be revealed and the societal response that needs to be amplified. In this chapter, I seek to situate contemporary Malaysian literature within this literary-critical arc of climate change discourse and to draw out the implications of doing so.

This chapter focuses mainly on writings from the 1950s through the 1990s—the decades immediately following Independence from the British in 1957—which address the social, political, economic and spiritual concerns of post-colonial Malaysian society. This period of Malaysian history saw increased economic activity of the extract-consume-pollute economic model inherited from the colonial state, with commodities like tin, rubber and palm oil still yielding handsome revenues for the young country. Development was, and still is, the top priority for the government, and in the manic pursuit of economic prosperity, environmental protection became a problematic, albeit peripheral, concern, underscoring the intractable tensions between human needs and environmental wellbeing. Post-1957, Malaysian writers focussed their thoughts on nationhood and national identity in a multicultural country struggling to find its place in the world, while drawing imagery and symbols freely from the natural world, including climate. A retrospective reading of this literature sheds new light on the varying extent to which writers were aware of climate change when writing poems and stories about devastating monsoons or extended droughts and heatwaves, and about the attendant anxieties and hardships created by these events. That Malaysian writers have long been preoccupied by the weather and bodies of water is an unsurprising fact considering the country's topographical and meteorological realities—peninsular, insular, archipelagic, riverine, maritime, tidal and littoral—with alternating

---

23   Tobias Menely and Jesse Oak Taylor, "Introduction" to *Anthropocene Reading: Literary History in Geologic Times*, eds. Menely and Taylor (PA: Pennsylvania State UP, 2017): 13.

24   Szerszynski and Urry, "Changing Climates: Introduction," 4.

wet and dry seasons, as well as perpetual heat and humidity. In the words of poet Shirley Geok-lin Lim, it is a conjunction of:

> Storm and heat, sun and rain
> horizon drenched: lightning stares
> and thundering voices. Early morning
> warm and morning to noon glares;
> afternoon oven-blast; sticky evening;
> sweaty nights: equatorial
> living on the fat zero line ...[25]

Historically, the Malay peninsula's strategic geographical location in the Malay Archipelago and its characteristic weather patterns enabled commercial and cultural flows, which in turn played a key role in shaping the region from the precolonial to the postcolonial periods. The fluid nature of this tropical environment (defined by rain, drought, rivers, seas, coastlines, beaches, swamps and mangrove forests) explains the local term for homeland, *tanahair,* which literally translates as "landwater." The underlying question, then, is how do Malaysian writers represent water in all its iterations in a climate-changed world? Although literary representations of water in the tropics vary according to the writers' attitudes, circumstances and ideologies, it is fair to say that the figure of the river or "reliable water" found in the poem "prologue"[26] by Muhammad Haji Salleh reverberates in Malaysian climate ecopoetics. "Reliable water" is the foundation of civilisation and life itself. It is a metonym for the river basins, the littoral and surrounding seas and a trope for the social, political and environmental integrity of the country. In Muhammad's imaginative rendering of the *Sejarah Melayu* or *Malay Annals*[27]—a quasi-historical text narrating the genealogy of the sultans of Malacca and describing life in the realm during the precolonial era—the poet-persona exhorts the court's prime minister-cum-royal bard to:

---

25 Shirley Geok-lin Lim, "No Seasons," in *Do You Live In?* (Singapore: Ethos Books 2015): 40.

26 Muhammad Haji Salleh, "prologue," in *Rowing Down Two Rivers* (Bangi Selangor, Malaysia: Penerbit Universiti Kebangsaan Malaysia, 2000): 73–76. Muhammad uses lower case letters for proper nouns and poem titles.

27 This literary-historical text was commissioned by the Malaccan court and composed between the 15th and 16th centuries. A blend of legend, myth and facts, its function was to chronicle the origin and sanctity of the Malay rulers and the traditions of the court and its subjects. The text became an important source of instruction and legitimation for successive Malay kings who traced their lineage to Malacca. The stories within the text are also widely regarded as exemplifying Malay ethos and identity.

MONSOONAL MEMORIES AND "THE RELIABLE WATER" 259

write us our history,
of the malays and all their islands,
[…]
fill the straits with water,
that scours the boundaries of the state,
celebrate the seas
that have ferried us here,
initiating and filling the bazaars,
drawing junks and barges from china,
making space for indians and their cloths,
so that the portuguese are in awe of malaccan life.[28]

In this poem, water imagery is employed to underscore how pristine waters epitomise the prestige of the court of a great maritime empire and the wellbeing of the court's subjects. Water is also synonymous with equality and justice and its pollution with corruption, greed and vanity:

speak of the justice
of the raja, prince and minister
offer the evidence of
how dignity, greatness and majesty
grew from the waters of equality,
and the waters desecrated by slander,
or darkened by shadows
of the kings or ministers
who stand before mirrors,
will kill all,
rot the palace floors,
overturn the thrones,
and flow into the people's wells,
in the city or distant villages.
[…]
paint pictures of how power is more like mist
quickly fading and vanishing.
What is essential is a river, the reliable water,
Love of the people
And a responsibility that flows
Within the conscience.[29]

---

28 Muhammad Haji Salleh, "prologue," 74.
29 Muhammad Haji Salleh, "prologue," 75–76.

In the context of the Anthropocene, "the reliable water" has a far broader significance. For the remainder of this chapter, I will identify moments in Malaysian literature when—in contrast to a time when the weather was dependable and nurturing even in its more destructive aspects—the 'water' is no longer reliable but has become unruly in a climate-changed world. I will also highlight some of the complications that arise when climate is represented through a postcolonial lens in the context of Malaysia where issues of race, place and indigeneity reflect the socio-political dynamics between the majority Malays and the minority others. In unpacking the trope of the reliable water, there is a sense that the river mirrors society so that its degradation reflects disharmony within society itself. The reliable, equalising waters may yet be the antidote not only to the ravages of climate change but also to social injustices. In this regard, works which highlight the imbrication of climate in society and society in climate— what I would call socio-climatic literature—may also potentially offer a vital corrective to damaging environmental attitudes and behaviours.

Writers Shirley Geok-lin Lim, Muhammad Haji Salleh and K. S. Maniam have each engaged creatively with the vicissitudes of the Malaysian climate in contemplating issues of identity, belonging, exile, loss, memory, nostalgia, love and despair, as well as what they portend in a climate-changed world. Lim—who left Malaysia in the 1980s for the USA and subsequently made it her home—was born in the historical port city of Malacca. Her works dwell on memories of the homeland and the "complexities and contradictions of being a diasporic writer, for whom the question of home is fraught with ambiguity and ambivalence."[30] The childhood and communal memories indelibly etched in her consciousness include those of the weather, the shorelines and the sea. In her signature weather poems "Monsoon History"[31] and "Crossing the Peninsula"[32] she stakes her claim to the ancestral homeland via the memories of the elements, the Malacca Straits, the Straits Chinese[33] forebears, the fishers and the ways that the human and nonhuman realms interpenetrate to create a spatial and temporal dwelling and history that is saturated and shaped by the monsoons:

---

30 Boey Kim Cheng, "Foreword" in *Ars Poetica for the Day,* Shirley Geok-lin Lim (Singapore: Ethos Books, 2015): 13.

31 Shirley Geok-lin Lim, "Monsoon History" in *Monsoon History: Selected Poems* (London: Skoob Books Publishing, 1994): 17–18.

32 Shirley Geok-lin Lim, "Crossing the Peninsula" in *Monsoon History: Selected Poems* (London: Skoob Books Publishing, 1994): 20.

33 The Straits Chinese—a group which Lim identifies with—derives its name from the Straits Settlements, a former British crown colony established in 1867. The Straits Settlements— composed of Singapore, Malacca and Penang—were strategically located along the Straits of Malacca which formed part of the important shipping route between China and the West. In the colonial period (and perhaps even before that), Chinese immigrants to

MONSOONAL MEMORIES AND "THE RELIABLE WATER"   261

The air is wet, soak
Into mattresses, and curls
In apparitions of smoke.
Like fat white slugs furled
Among the timber,
Or silver fish tunnelling
The damp linen covers
Of schoolbooks, or walking
Quietly like centipedes,
The air walking everywhere
On its hundred feet
Is filled with the glare
Of tropical water.

Again we are taken over
By clouds and rolling darkness.
[...]
Nonya and baba sit at home.
This was forty years ago.
 [...]
Listening to down-pour-
ing rain: the air ticks
With gnats, black spiders fly,
Moths sweep out of our rooms
Where termites built
Their hills of eggs and queens zoom
In heat. We wash our feet
For bed, watch mother uncoil
Her snake hair, unbuckle
The silver mesh around her waist,
Waiting for father pacing
The sand as fishers pull
From the Straits after monsoon[34]

---

the colony intermarried with local Malays and created a distinct creole culture and community known as *peranakan*, meaning 'local-born.' The British recognised these colonial subjects as the Straits-born or Straits Chinese. In the *peranakan* community, the men are referred to as *Baba* and the women as *Nyonya*.

34   Shirley Geok-lin Lim, *Monsoon History: Selected Poems* (London: Skoob Books Publishing, 1994): 17–18.

Lim's hydropoetics depicts precipitation and moisture as an intrinsic feature of dwelling and being. In the essay "Living with the Weather" from his landmark book *Romantic Ecology*, Jonathan Bate states that the "weather is the primary sign of the inextricability of culture and nature."[35] This culture-nature entanglement is very clearly delineated in "Monsoon History" where we are presented with living arrangements in which water is all-pervasive and where human inhabitants and the teeming insect and gastropods coinhabit and are in their element, as it were. The monsoons highlight the reciprocal relationship between the weather and the human realm as well as the clearly demarcated gender roles of father and mother. Crucially, it also establishes the centrality of weather patterns for the fishers whose livelihoods depend on the regularity of the monsoons. There is also the tacit recognition that like the diasporic self—in the poet-persona's case, a double dispersal as she transitions from Malaysian-Chinese to Asian-American—the weather is neither the timeless, knowable nor stable phenomenon that guarantees a good catch or even a secure homespace. Father is tellingly "pacing / The sand" and although "The air is still, silent / Like sleepers rocked in the pantun, / Sheltered by Malacca," this relative safety is "forty years ago."[36]

In Lim's "Crossing the Peninsula," the same nostalgia for the tropical weather is evident but, this time, the poet foregrounds the timescale:

> First, the sea, blue heart pulsing,
> Spilling stars, nuts, and sand
> On Tanjung Bunga. ...
> ... Then sky
> With swift light changing to rain.
> The humming breakers push by,
> Recede, run in again
> Through days, through years. It is *monsoon*
> *Climate*, the migrating season
> When nets and boats come home to shelter.
> And all night the water beats heavily.[37]

In Tanjung Bunga, a promontory facing the Straits which is the setting for this flashback, the ebb and flow of waves agitated by monsoonal storms mark the

---

35 Jonathan Bate, "Living with the Weather," *Studies in Romanticism* 35.3 (Fall 1996): 439, http://www.jstor.org/stable/25601183.

36 Shirley Geok-lin Lim, *Monsoon History*, 18.

37 Shirley Geok-lin Lim, *Monsoon History*, 20, italics added.

passage of time as weather—short-term atmospheric variations—becomes climate. Enough time has passed to reveal weather patterns and trends. Once again, the promise of shelter for the fishers—also serving as a figure for those who have left Malaysian shores—is fragile as "all night the water beats heavily," foreshadowing the more turbulent storms of the near-future. Here, monsoon climate is linked to the notion of migration or diaspora and the impossibility of a homecoming as expressed in the concluding lines suggesting that the peninsular home is only accessible in dreams, memories and occasional physical and spiritual 'crossings': We dream like grey gulls blown inland, / Or as one-eyed ships, blown, espying / The bright-shelled peninsula."[38]

Reading "Monsoon History" and "Crossing the Peninsula" from a climate perspective brings out the ways in which personal and communal histories are predicated on and influenced by the history of the monsoon; at the same time, it sheds light on the poems' more nuanced expressions of global warming. Lim's preoccupation with the weather influences her construction of diasporic identity: a self that is clearly contingent on memories of Southeast Asian monsoons and the coastal contours of childhood. Almost two decades later, when the unseasonal heat of an American city triggers the remembrance of the ancestral home, the unusual equatorial conditions lead to a transparent reflection on global warming in "Greenhouse Effect in New York:"[39]

> Today I wake up and it's
> already eighty-two in the shade.
> The weathercable bleats:
> humidity is near tropical;
> dew point set at seventy-eight.
> [...]
> My coffee is instant. Its vapor
> rises saturated with berries
> from Sumatra, whose mountains lie
> visible on the sharply strung
> horizon of the Malacca Straits:
> my Malacca Straits where
> it is always eighty-two
> and childhood's a fermented
> dew point of denials

---

38 Shirley Geok-lin Lim, *Monsoon History,* 20.

39 Lim, "Greenhouse Effect in New York" in *What the Fortune Teller Didn't Say* (Albuquerque, NM: West End Press, 1998): 54–55.

and tears. I breathe the roasted
berry smog. It covers my cheeks
with the sweat of plantations,
a brown aroma from Southeast
Asia like sun-dried anchovies
Just this side of rotten.
[...]
This is
my usual heat. I am my
usual self—husbandless for
two weeks—returned to normalcy,
to rain-forest torpor
whose water swells and swells
in cumulus clumps. The sky
rumbles all day and night, like
vague threats a child overhears.[40]

The heat and humidity in the eastern seaboard of North America bear ironic comparison with the Malaccan/Southeast Asian heat and humidity. Here, global warming recalls the tropical weather of the Malaccan home. The unusually high temperatures in New York provide the sensory triggers for memories of a former climate where oppressive heat and humidity are normal: "This is / my usual heat. I am my / usual self [...] returned to normalcy." The greenhouse effect in this poem is homesickness or the nostalgia for the childhood home as tropical conditions evoke memories—both bad and good—of childhood and the lost home. Here, too, global warming relates to diasporic identity. Past and present, the child and the grown-up, the old home and the new, are linked by the weather. Yet this weather in temperate New York is uncanny, *unheimlich*. Bate asserts, "Weather is a prime means of linking spatiality and temporality,"[41] but when space and time become displaced in a warming world, the effect is far from assuring. The irony is that the poet-persona's return "to normalcy," her "usual self" and "[her] Malacca Straits" is enabled by a phenomenon which is far from normal. It is not farfetched to argue that by aligning the diasporic condition with global warming—itself a form of "diasporic," dislocated weather—Lim seems to equate climate change with a sense of irretrievable loss. Her nostalgia for tropical climes is not characterised by an uncritical longing for home

---

40   Lim, "Greenhouse Effect in New York," 54–55.
41   Bate, "Living with the Weather," 444.

MONSOONAL MEMORIES AND "THE RELIABLE WATER"

but by the implicit recognition that the equatorial conditions of the Malaccan home are out of place in the American context of the poem. The extremely hot and humid New York weather that enabled the nostalgic "return" spells endangerment and disaster. The poet-persona ends by "[drinking] / the bitter brew. Sugar / is no good for someone like me / who hoards sullen solitudes / against the approaching front."[42] It can be argued that the approaching front referred to here is potentially the extremely cold air mass that will replace the extremely hot, "near tropical" one. The contrast between intense heat and cold—a significant detail in the poem—is evoked through references to the husband who "is away in Finland" and who "will grow / even more Caucasian cool, / a Slav from remote winters / with a meaty manly texture / evolved for frigid conditions."[43] The poet-persona's feelings of dread and gloom for extreme fronts suggest tension and contradictory emotions rather than a straightforward or complacent longing to re-connect with her personal monsoonal history.

Like Shirley Lim, poet Muhammad Haji Salleh is preoccupied by the monsoons and the hydro-centric geography of the Malay Archipelago as well as by the memories that are encoded and stored within them. His literary focus, however, lies firmly on the ethnic Malays and their evolution as the dominant community in Malaysia. As such, his works—especially given his status as poet-laureate—can be read as espousing a Malay nationalist agenda and cementing the Malays' legitimacy in terms of race, place-belonging and identity. "Ancient" Malays in their village dwellings are depicted as being rooted to the landscape and possessing a timeless wisdom of the natural world that comes with a long and close relationship with the world around them. For example, in the poem "story,"[44] the storyteller with his "ancient mouth" is "rooted to earth," "implanted [...] in the marshes," "chosen / elder to land and river, / children and grandchildren / to sand or water that he dug and diverted / with his dark hands," recounting his story to "this young man who has lost his place."

While such a communal rhetoric of natural piety tends to marginalise the other communities in culturally plural Malaysia, there is an aspect of Muhammad's vision that transcends this race-inflected representation of the Malays and their real or imagined links with nature, namely his empathy for the victims of environmental injustice including climate injustice. The poems containing "the most scathing indictment of capitalist oppression make use of the ancestral village trope to highlight the injustice so that the whole idea of a

---

42   Lim, "Greenhouse Effect in New York," 55.
43   Lim, "Greenhouse Effect in New York," 54.
44   Muhammad Haji Salleh, "story" in *Rowing Down Two Rivers* (Bangi, Selangor, Malaysia: Penerbit Universiti Kebangsaan Malaysia, 2000): 237–238.

return to roots becomes strategic rather than thematic."[45] In "quiet village,"[46] Muhammad portrays the plight of impoverished rubber smallholders at the mercy of middlemen and the fluctuating price of the commodity:

> the inhabitants are too poor,
> [...]
> industry is only a mark
> of the satiated,
> and the rubber tree is no factory,
> prices come from businessmen.
> when you are poor
> you can't borrow from the poor

And so the smallholders "[feel] the force of the new grip / around their stomach / [...] killing them one by one / before their own eyes."[47] This desperate scene is a far cry from the prosperity of the ancient Malays in the thriving Malacca Sultanate as depicted in "chapter thirty-two (ii)"[48] of the *Malay Annals*:

> all morning traders flow in surrounding hamlets
> northern towns and creeks that drain brown hills,
> bringing honey from forest trees, coconut sugar,
> cloths from a thousand malay islands,
> all taken from the earth, sea and air.[49]

Muhammad plays up the stark contrast between this romanticised, exoticised history and the reality faced by present-day rural Malays who eke out a living as rice farmers and fishermen and whose survival depends on the elements as well as the climate. If the alternating rain and drought defy their usual patterns, the consequences are dire to say the least. In "leaf fall,"[50] the dry season is "stretched among" the tantalising "familiar clouds," and becomes a ruthless harbinger of death:

---

45 Agnes S. K. Yeow, "Place, Race and Environment in the Poetry of Muhammad Haji Salleh," *Textual Practice* 29.1 (2015): 179–180.

46 Muhammad Haji Salleh, "quiet village" in *The Second Tongue: An Anthology of Poetry from Malaysia and Singapore*, ed. Edwin Thumboo (Singapore: Heinemann, 1976): 96–97.

47 Muhammad Haji Salleh, "quiet village," 97.

48 Muhammad Haji Salleh, "chapter thirty-two (ii)" in *Rowing Down Two Rivers* (Bangi, Selangor, Malaysia: Penerbit Universiti Kebangsaan Malaysia, 2000): 103–108.

49 Muhammad Haji Salleh, "chapter thirty-two (ii)," 107–108.

50 Muhammad Haji Salleh, "leaf fall" in *Rowing Down Two Rivers* (Bangi, Selangor, Malaysia: Penerbit Universiti Kebangsaan Malaysia, 2000): 200.

Between the monsoons
And the green mountain of the peninsula
The season's draughty skeletons
Are stretched among the familiar clouds.
Rubber leaves burn themselves bronze
On their copper stalks.
The wind moves in and detaches
The brown tissue from their brittle fingers,
Letting them fly like Kelantan moon kites
To the bright graveyard.

It can be argued that Muhammad's 'return' to roots is marked not so much by nostalgia as by solastalgia as defined by Glenn Albrecht: "Solastalgia is not about looking back to some golden past, nor is it about seeking another place as 'home.' It is the 'lived experience' of the loss of the present as manifest in a feeling of dislocation; of being undermined by forces that destroy the potential for solace to be derived from the present. In short, solastalgia is a form of homesickness one gets when one is still at 'home.' "[51] In the poem "return,"[52] the returnee[53] speaks of "the flaring present" and bemoans how "the earth is / changed in its essence," for "man has declared war / on nature."[54] His past and present selves "must live as neighbours, / with the change, / or break without solutions."[55] Traditional rural values and modern city sensibilities collide and must reconcile with each other, for there is no return to any glorified pastoralism. It is the poet-persona's *present* sense of place and belonging that is under assault, transformed by changing environmental attitudes and providing little solace, if any. The returnee laments the loss of equality— "many are rich / in the country of the poor"—and the commodification of the environment: "nature and earth / are for sale."[56] It can be argued that what he bemoans is the absence of the essential river— "the reliable water."

---

51   Glenn Albrecht, " 'Solastalgia' A New Concept in Health and Identity," *PAN: Philosophy, Activism, Nature* 3 (2005): 48.

52   Muhammad Haji Salleh, "return" in *Rowing Down Two Rivers* (Bangi, Selangor, Malaysia: Penerbit Universiti Kebangsaan Malaysia, 2000): 239–245.

53   The persona is a reflection of the poet himself who had spent many years abroad as an academic and who embodies both Malay and Western cultural sensibilities.

54   Muhammad, "return," 239.

55   Muhammad, "return," 239.

56   Muhammad Haji Salleh, "return," 243, 241.

It is important to stress that this indispensable river, the lifeblood of the community, is both symbolic and literal in meaning. Edwin Thumboo has noted that Muhammad's poetic sensibility "collapses the boundaries separating the literal and the metaphorical," achieving a "verbal freedom" that "allows him to project the quality and shape of life, in particular the real intimacy which exists between the individual and creation."[57] The poetry itself is strikingly amenable to climate change or Anthropocene readings for this very reason. Menely and Taylor point out that "[t]he Anthropocene provides an opportunity for literary studies to test and transform its methods by examining how the symbolic domain might, or might not, index a historicity that exceeds the human social relation and encompasses planetary flows of energy and matter."[58]

Muhammad's symbolism dovetails with such an approach to reading. As such, the imagery of death, barrenness and vulnerability in Muhammad's socio-climatic poems are particularly brutal and visceral. In a later version of "quiet village"[59]—a poem with intertextual links to Rachel Carson's "A Fable for Tomorrow" in *Silent Spring*—the village is "quiet / behind a lalang weed fence / asleep through the long heat, / birds are muted / by the new harshness."[60] The "long heat" is potentially an important subtext for climate change where extreme and prolonged weather events exacerbate the fraught and ambivalent relationship between humans and the elements.

In Muhammad's climate imaginary, the villagers seem to alternate between waiting and praying for rain, and when the storms do come, grappling with the floodwaters, then finally enduring the harsh droughts all over again. They seem invariably suspended between two extreme weather conditions: extended periods of aridity and violent, destructive storms. In "prayer,"[61] the supplicants are "in a dry desert / waiting for the same rumble of thunder / that stopped over the sea" [...] "once comfortable, / deserted by the river. / beyond this

---

57   Edwin Thumboo, introduction to *Time and Its People*, Muhammad Haji Salleh (Kuala Lumpur: Heinemann Educational Books [Asia] Ltd, 1978): xix.

58   Tobias Menely and Jesse Oak Taylor, "Introduction" in *Anthropocene Reading: Literary History in Geologic Times*, eds. Menely and Taylor (PA: Pennsylvania State UP, 2017): 5.

59   The poem "quiet village" is anthologised in *The Second Tongue: An Anthology of Poetry from Malaysia and Singapore*, ed. Edwin Thumboo (Singapore: Heinemann, 1976), and its later, abbreviated version entitled "the quiet village" is collected in *Rowing Down Two Rivers*, 193.

60   Muhammad Haji Salleh, "the quiet village," 193.

61   Muhammad, "prayer" in *Rowing Down Two Rivers* (Bangi, Selangor, Malaysia: Penerbit Universiti Kebangsaan Malaysia, 2000): 141.

MONSOONAL MEMORIES AND "THE RELIABLE WATER" 269

nothing matters. / my eyes are seared by the red dust, / it's night / and the rain has not come." In "flooded,"[62] the persona expresses an ironic familiarity with floodwaters: "we are no longer afraid of the rain / ... ropes of water are lashing / the stilts of our hut. / at last we have arrived in the garden, / leaves and flowers floating, / and there's neither house nor home."

In Muhammad's poetry, apart from the catastrophic effects of severe flooding, storms and droughts, the community's difficult and ambiguous relationship with climate is effectively a barometer of climate change, as illustrated in the poem "villagers:"[63]

> villagers are patient readers
> of the lessons of earth sky and water.
>
> earth dries in drought
> breaks the tapioca or corn.
> [...]
> make way for eager padi roots.
> the same earth.
> [...]
> the sky often drives them to prayer
> realisation of a past death by lightning
> or houses turned into wood heaps.
>
> winds cool their night
> and blow their boats to fishing grounds.
> monsoon rush into villages,
> seasonal reservoirs
> of water or fate
> that pour down into fields.
> rain freshens age,
> fertilises frog eggs on withering grasses.
>
> the lessons swim
> in their eyes, arteries
> or words.

---

62   Muhammad, "flooded" in *Rowing Down Two Rivers*, 184–185.
63   Muhammad, "villagers" in *Rowing Down Two Rivers*, 178–179.

Despite the lessons learnt and patient attempts to "read" the climate over the ages, there is a tacit acknowledgement that the climate is unknowable or unreadable in the end, bringing both life and death in its wake. The villagers' intimate knowledge of the climate which "swims" in their bodies and words—an apt image given the preponderance of rainfall and water all around them—suggests fatalistic resignation and unease rather than assurance and comfort: the lessons which "swim / in their eyes" being tears and in "arteries" being death from drowning, as well as in "words" suggesting their vain attempts to learn or read the weather. It is possible to imagine that as conditions worsen incrementally with time and climate change, other new, futile lessons are learnt in which the only certainties are hardship and mortality. Bronislaw Szerszynski asserts that weather, time and history are inexorably connected:

> Weather was—and is—experienced as an aspect of time perceived not chronologically but kairologically, as the quality of particular periods of time, typically a season. Yet traditional seasonal 'weatherwising' no longer works, for the simple reason that the weather is no longer sufficiently stable from one year to the next, let alone from one generation to the next. To read our own weather kairologically involves being alert to its new, unstable temporality, as the coiled cycles of annual weather patterns unravel into the irreversible time of the *longue durée*, and each storm and drought becomes unseasonable, unique, historical. [...] Once again, we are oriented not so much to the regularities of nature but to its 'wanderings': droughts, storms, floods, and extremes of heat and cold.[64]

He argues that signs of the weather can no longer be read as signs of stable climates, and that "[w]e are also being drawn to forms of mitigation that presume to calculate the weather and promise to make it stable."[65] It is noteworthy that Muhammad's villagers—both "ancient" and present-day Malays—are confronted with "seasonal reservoirs / of water or fate"[66] but ironically remain at the mercy of the weather. "Traditional seasonal 'weatherwising'," as Szerszynski puts it, offers little certainty and fate takes over. It is also notable that this poem about reading the weather was originally collected in a volume titled *Time and its People*—an acknowledgement that time is synonymous

---

64 Bronislaw Szerszynski, "Reading and Writing the Weather: Climate Technics and the Moment of Responsibility," *Theory, Culture & Society* 27.2–3 (2010): 23–24.

65 Szerszynski, "Reading and Writing the Weather," 23.

66 Muhammad, "villagers," 178.

with weather for the poet imagines the Malays' historical interaction with the weather as a longstanding and gradually changing one.

Muhammad focuses more on the climate culture of the rural Malays because these communities are the most dependent on climate and therefore the most vulnerable to climate-related threats of desertification, flooding and violent storms impacting food security, traditional livelihoods, cultural heritage, and social equilibrium. Nevertheless, cities are also the subject of his climate poetry. A toxic "river of acid"[67]—of the kind found in the city—is clearly the antithesis of the essential, dependable, life-supporting river that civilisations can be built upon. Commerce, overconsumption and industrialism as well as the insatiable appetite for natural resources—all anthropogenic contributors to greenhouse emissions—are the focus of Muhammad's environmental critique. Global warming is also directly linked to the loss of forest cover (not to mention wildlife habitat) caused by the voracious timber and palm oil industries: a theme treated with dystopian undertones in "the forest's last day."[68] Muhammad's grim vision applies not only to polluted and polluting cities but also to eerily silenced villages (as in "quiet village"). Muhammad draws parallels between the present-day urban-rural divide and the precolonial court and kampung (village) dichotomy represented in his *Sejarah Melayu* poems; however, in both worlds, it is the same ethical trope of the essential river and "reliable water"—a conceivable corrective to climate change—that reverberates in his environmental poetry.

Not unlike Muhammad, Malaysian-Indian writer K. S. Maniam's literary vision is underscored by the desire of the deracinated figure to "return" to the homeland—as the native returnee in Muhammad's case and as the descendant of Tamil immigrants in Maniam's. For Maniam's fictional characters, however, the ironic return to the "new" adopted homeland is fraught with challenges on many fronts, spiritual, cultural, emotional and physical. Bernard Wilson notes that Maniam's first novel *The Return*[69] "functions primarily as nomadic narrative(s)" where "journey, arrival and departure motifs are predominant in the text and form the cyclical structure of the novel" and that for the characters, "flux and transition are, oxymoronically, permanent states."[70] Survival in the "new" country entails:

---

67 Muhammad, "this too is my earth" (2000): 124–125.
68 Muhammad, "the forest's last day" (2000): 49–51.
69 K.S. Maniam, *The Return* (London: Skoob Books Publishing, 1993).
70 Bernard Wilson, "Memory, Myth, Exile: The Desire for Malaysian Belonging in K.S. Maniam's *The Return*," "Haunting the Tiger," and "In a Far Country," *Textual Practice* 17.2 (2003): 397.

the creation of new hybrid-polyglot, transcultural myths without the rejection of an ancestral base: a weaving of the fabric of cultures and discourses to make sense of this permanent state of transition and to combat the political discourses of colonialism and neocolonialism.[71]

Much of this weaving and combat takes place in the rubber plantations of Maniam's fictional post-independent Malaysia as well as the urban centres where money can be made in capitalist enterprises like real estate, namely the buying and selling of land and property. Maniam's environmental ethos is discernible in the recurring trope of the land and the spiritual desire for communion or kinship with land which is often thwarted by the commodification of land itself. In his second novel *In a Far Country*,[72] the protagonist Rajan becomes a realtor: a job in which " '[y]ou divide the land and sell the lots like pieces of cloth' " to people who " 'don't use the land properly' "[73] and one which ultimately alienates him from the "far" country.

Mastery over the land as economic resource is also the theme of "Removal in Pasir Panjang,"[74] a complex and enigmatic short story about a river, a road, a housing estate and human greed in a fictionalised coastal town of Pasir Panjang—a place name that translated from the Malay means "Long Sands." The story does not allude explicitly to climate change but, because Maniam's engagement with the conventional postcolonial issues of transcultural diasporic identity, belonging and exile is almost always underlaid with notions of the land and uses put to the land, the story warrants a closer inspection from a climate change perspective.

In this narrative, the contrapuntal mode of storytelling—the human story developing in tandem with the environmental story and commenting on each other—is a strategy blurring the boundaries of human and natural histories while shedding light on the writer's environmental consciousness. As a third-generation Malaysian-Indian with a lifelong preoccupation with the diasporic condition, Maniam often counters the state's discriminatory migrancy narrative through his writings. Sharmani P. Gabriel argues that Maniam effectively subverts the state's myths of diaspora and indigeneity that claim diasporic groups—like Malaysian Indians—feel displaced and estranged from their surroundings and are therefore constantly looking back nostalgically at

---

71   Wilson, "Memory, Myth, Exile," 397–398.

72   K.S. Maniam, *In a Far Country* (London: Skoob Books Publishing, 1993).

73   K.S. Maniam, *In a Far Country*, 92, 81.

74   K.S. Maniam, "Removal In Pasir Panjang" in *Haunting the Tiger and Other Stories* (London: Skoob Books Publishing, 1996): 68–88.

the Indian motherland. She argues that Maniam's works "reject essentialist notions of national and ethnic identity for more processual and historically contextualized definitions from a perspective in diaspora."[75] In his poem "The Truly Privileged,"[76] the speaker debunks these racial-political constructs of the migrant and the native as well as the latter's claims of special earth privileges,[77] by emphasising the land's generosity and equal treatment of all:

> The rare enlightened among you calling us migrants,
> go tell the rest we're all migrants come from asteroids
> or simply from out there, as dark particles of matter.
> [...]
> We lay absorbing the absorbed earth in our mother's wombs,
> becoming indigenous to the land we were born in, soil
> the chrysanthemum grew in, soil the orchid flourished in,
> soil life awakened in, soil intelligence waited in to grow,
> I dare you, the few enlightened to go tell those persistent
> we're not indigenous that earth has already indigenised us.

The poet-persona speaks of the "intelligence of this all-accommodating earth, our only home,"[78] its agency as well as its vast capacity for justice. Maniam's environmental critique is often targeted at the ways land is exploited in the name of development in his fictionalised Malaysia, especially when marginalised and dispossessed segments of society become the victims of purportedly beneficial economic development in the form of housing projects and the construction of roads and other infrastructure to support industrial growth. "Removal in Pasir Panjang" revolves around the quiet town and community of Pasir Panjang—a nondescript town not unlike other small towns in 1970s and '80s Malaysia. Key narrative events are the death of a mute girl Leng Leng who is run over by a carbon-emitting vehicle on the very day that a new main road was opened with much fanfare as well as the construction of new houses on reclaimed land, which saw the town's river filled in with rubbish.

---

75   Sharmani Patricia Gabriel, "Nation and Contestation in Malaysia: Diaspora and Myths of Belonging in the Narratives of K.S. Maniam," *Journal of Southeast Asian Studies* 36.2 (June 2005): 238.

76   K.S. Maniam, "The Truly Privileged" in *Selected Works* (Petaling Jaya, Selangor, Malaysia: Maya Press, 2019): 284–285.

77   Under the Malaysian constitution, the majority Malays who are defined as *bumiputera* meaning 'sons of the soil' are accorded special rights and privileges.

78   K.S. Maniam, "The Truly Privileged," 285.

The climate change element in this story is implied in the setting—an unseasonably long drought—and the environmental risk precipitated by development such as better road connectivity, transportation and housing. When the story begins, the protagonist Nathan notes that the dry season has been longer than usual:

> The drought had gone beyond the three-month limit and cows wandered into the main street to chew off the grass growing in the cracks of the drains. Opposite Ah Seng's coffee-shop stood the courthouse, an old wooden building, the paintwork flaking off under the leafless trees surrounding it. Waves of heat piled upon the cars and bicycles in the street. The town needed planning, he thought.[79]

The general opinion among some of the townspeople is that the sterile, sluggish town needed better infrastructure to stimulate economic growth. This tragic tale which involves the death of the beloved disabled girl Leng Leng in a traffic accident has a companion story in Maniam's speculative, post-catastrophe short story "Parablames."[80] In that story, a narrator from a future time studies the "pre-Holocaust civilisation" that had been destroyed by a nuclear disaster and discovers that the people then had been the victims of the "Oil Crisis," a dependence on a depleting resource that did nothing to curb their desire for cars and factories: "Fuel was needed for factories, buses, lorries, trains and cars [...] Property, house and land became scarce commodities.[...] The decades before the Holocaust were running down because they depended on the depletive fuel, petroleum. The belief, following the tenets of deception, was current that petroleum was inexhaustible."[81] A headline of the day proclaims casually "Eight Deaths a Day on the Roads" as "the murderous, iron quality" of "the roaring stream of cars"[82] endangered the community. In "Removal in Pasir Panjang," it is the victims of gruesome vehicle accidents that are ominously "removed." Ah Seng tells Nathan of other victims dispatched in the same manner: " 'Three died at the corner. One in front of my shop [...] And then the schoolgirl. Her dress red ...' "[83] It can be argued that these deaths—similar to the ones in the other story—are deliberately linked to the oil crisis

---

79   K.S. Maniam, "Removal in Pasir Panjang," 68.

80   K.S. Maniam, "Parablames" in *Haunting the Tiger and Other Stories* (London: Skoob Books Publishing, 1996): 143–161.

81   K.S. Maniam, "Parablames," 153, 154, 151–152.

82   K.S. Maniam, "Parablames," 154, 155.

83   K.S. Maniam, "Removal in Pasir Panjang," 71.

MONSOONAL MEMORIES AND "THE RELIABLE WATER"   275

(and the denial that oil was a finite resource), which had ironically led to the exponential proliferation of vehicles, roads and factories. Malaysia is rich in fossil fuels like natural gas, coal and oil and its government-linked petroleum company PETRONAS has contributed significantly to the country's industrial growth. Energy researchers, however, have determined that the oilfields are drying up; more alarmingly, "even after more than a decade since renewable energy (RE) was introduced and numerous relevant programmes instigated, RE only manages to garner a measly 1–2 percent in the total energy mix."[84] In Maniam's stories, the addiction to oil exacts a heavy toll on society and climate.

The blessings of a resource-rich country are also its curse, as ecocritic Rob Nixon asserts:

> What are the repercussions of having mineral belongings that literally undermine a community or society's capacity to belong? And what forces turn belongings—those goods, in a material and an ethical sense—into evil powers that alienate people from the very elements that have sustained them, environmentally and culturally, as all that seemed solid melts into liquid tailings, oil spills, and plumes of toxic air? The notion of the resource curse hinges on the paradox of plenty, whereby nation-states blessed with abundant mineral wealth are too often concomitantly blighted.[85]

The resource curse in "Removal in Pasir Panjang" is oil, but ironically it is also land. In the short story, the town councillor "Big mouth Ramasamy" is the proverbial villain. As Ah Seng notes, " 'He brought death to this town. And dust.' "[86] The tractors and bulldozers outside his window had not ceased working for five years—the "machines wailed indifferently in their destruction"—and the blame for that is placed squarely on Ramasamy, "A bad man intent on making Pasir Panjang more than a dot on the map."[87] He represents the manic scramble for socio-economic growth in developing economies, which sometimes brings no advantage to the locals but enriches the unscrupulous and greedy.

---

84 Oh Tick Hui et al., "Energy Policy and Alternative Energy in Malaysia: Issues and Challenges for Sustainable Growth—An Update," *Renewable and Sustainable Energy Reviews* 81 (2018): 3022.

85 Rob Nixon, *Slow Violence and the Environmentalism of the Poor* (Cambridge, Massachusetts: Harvard UP, 2011): 69.

86 K.S. Maniam, "Removal in Pasir Panjang," 69.

87 K.S. Maniam, "Removal in Pasir Panjang," 80, 69.

The new road was built to increase the volume of traffic passing through the town " 'so the land rent will go up.' "[88] Amidst talk about a new residential project, Nathan points out that new houses could not possibly be built because the town is located between a mountain and a river—" 'There's no more land.' "[89] Ah Seng retorts, " 'Ramasamy will grow the land, [...] Always making mountains flat, making water into land.' "[90] That is exactly what unfolds as the river is filled in with truckloads of rubbish and levelled to form a site on which new houses will be built, effectively turning the river into profitable real estate. The curse of land in this instance lies in its shortage and not abundance. The river is effectively obliterated along with its historical and ecological heritage— the crumbling jetty and neglected customs shed are a reminder of what was once a lively river port. The significance of this event from a climate change perspective can be derived from the blatant " 'stopping [of] the river' "[91] with mountains of rubbish and the potentially disastrous effects this could have on the ecology of Pasir Panjang such as desertification, contamination and loss of fish leading to food shortage. If rivers are prevented from joining the sea, climate will also be impacted due to the disruption of the water cycle, resulting in severe droughts and floods.

Crucially, the victims of this slow violence and alienation are those pushed to the fringes of society such as the mute boy who is literally voiceless, the Public Works Department labourers who live in squalid, dilapidated quarters near the river, and Nathan himself who feels out of place in the town as well as in his vocation as a teacher. In one of his long evening walks, he meets a mysterious Malay man Yahaya at the secluded riverbank and jetty—a familiar allegorical motif in Maniam's oeuvre where the migrant or descendant of migrants encounters the native Malay who is comfortable in his own skin. The migrant seeks help from the Malay to guide him towards the indigenous spirit of the land so that he can forge a sense of belonging to the new country—a process fraught with spiritual conflict and tensions. Yahaya "guides" Nathan in two ways: by pointing out the destruction of the river and by cryptically advising him to be wary of the new development. However, these lessons are unheeded by Nathan. While Yahaya laments the loss of the river, its history, and its 'ghosts', Nathan has a positive reaction to it:

---

88 K.S. Maniam, "Removal in Pasir Panjang," 69.

89 K.S. Maniam, "Removal in Pasir Panjang," 71.

90 K.S. Maniam, "Removal in Pasir Panjang," 78.

91 K.S. Maniam, "Removal in Pasir Panjang," 78.

'That rubbish you can see? In a year it will fill the river. No more boats will come here.[...] Children will come and chase the ghosts away[...]'

The man [Yahaya] spoke nostalgically and Nathan was saddened. But the thought of children scampering on the banks, of houses finally resting on the tamped down rubbish mound, cheered him. He might even find a friend among them; he saw himself entering a household beside the swamp.[92]

Yahaya's wariness of the new houses and their occupants is justified when Nathan is attacked as he rides his bicycle past the row of new houses late one night. He had attempted to befriend a young girl from the new neighbourhood and was assaulted probably by her jealous boyfriend. The new community of residents had rejected him; one of the residents had even mistaken him for a rag man. The story ends with Nathan coming to terms with his life in Pasir Panjang and feeling a sense of belonging to the old, familiar community despite the difficulties he faced at work, the general sense of alienation and the tenuous ties that he held with the land. In his initial indirect endorsement of the artificial land, Nathan's complicity with the town's developers is a factor in his awakening to the realisation that the commoditisation of land and water devalues human life, including that of the "native" inhabitants. Yahaya himself feels dispossessed and robbed of his entitlement. As the houses were built, he had spoken to Nathan "with the bitterness of a man who had lost the power over the land he thought was his."[93] In this example, Maniam's stance towards development is informed by concerns of environmental justice and not by a categorical aversion to progress. The schism between the newly arrived residents and the rest of the townspeople is clearly founded on economic disparity and racial prejudice. The townspeople must now endure the environmental degradation caused by development. The outlook for the near future is best expressed in Nathan's previously cynical and bleak assessment of his life in the town. In ironic contrast to the new reservoir that is nearing completion—prompting Nathan to declare " 'Now there will be water all the time' "—is his desolate image brooding on the banks of the dying river: "He had his life—an empty gazing into a murky, drying river."[94]

In the poems and short story examined above, the treatment of weather, rivers, water and land offers a glimpse into the environmental imagination of

---

92   K.S. Maniam, "Removal in Pasir Panjang," 78.
93   K.S. Maniam, "Removal in Pasir Panjang," 79.
94   K.S. Maniam, "Removal in Pasir Panjang," 86–87.

Malaysian writers and demonstrates that considerations of climate change are part and parcel of their environmental worldviews. More accurately, it is anthropogenic water and land degradation that is emphasised in the works. For the *tanahair* where land and sea—the peninsula and the surrounding archipelago—merge to form the homeland, any rise in sea level or temperature will have devastating effects on livelihoods, habitats, place-attachments, place memories and eco-social harmony. In this hydro-centric and climate-dependent world, the trope of the river—"the reliable water"—conveys the fundamental truth that stable, regular waters support life, enhance sustainability and hold the key to society's future. The writers and works discussed here resonate with the premise forwarded in this chapter that climatological issues are inexorably embedded in society and that a reliable climate is essential to live and remember by.

Lim, Muhammad and Maniam began their literary careers in the last century which was a time marked by post-Independence aspirations as the country ramped up economic development and the impetus for nation-building intensified. They remained active as the new millennium took hold and are still writing today, except for Maniam who passed away in 2020. Through their implicitly cautionary writings, these writers laid the groundwork for a new generation of climate-conscious Malaysian writers who, like them, understand how the environment—and climate itself—is intertwined with culture, identity, belonging and home. The environmental realities encoded in literature underscore the importance of reading and interpreting texts in ways that reveal the representation of multi-scalar, climatic phenomena be it in the form of a rise in temperature, a deluge or a drying river.

Works Cited

Albrecht, Glenn. "'Solastalgia' A New Concept in Health and Identity." *PAN: Philosophy, Activism, Nature* 3 (2005): 44–59.

Bate, Jonathan. "Living with the Weather." *Studies in Romanticism* 35.3 (Fall 1996): 431–447.

Boey, Kim Cheng. Foreword to *Ars Poetica for the Day,* Shirley Geok-lin Lim (Singapore: Ethos Books, 2015): 9–19.

Chakrabarty, Dipesh. "The Climate of History: Four Theses." *Critical Inquiry* 35 (Winter 2009): 197–222.

Emmett, Robert, and Thomas Lekan. "Foreword" and "Introduction" to *Whose Anthropocene? Revisiting Dipesh Chakrabarty's "Four Theses,"* eds. Robert Emmett and Thomas Lekan (Munich: Rachel Carson Centre for Environment and Society, 2016): 5–11.

Gabriel, Sharmani Patricia. "Nation and Contestation in Malaysia: Diaspora and Myths of Belonging in the Narratives of K.S. Maniam." *Journal of Southeast Asian Studies* 36.2 (June 2005): 235–248.

Griffiths, G.M., L.E. Chambers, M.R. Haylock, M.J. Manton, N. Nicholls, H.-J. Baek, Y. Choi, P.M. Della-Marta, A. Gosai, N. Iga, V. Laurent, L. Maitrepierre, H. Nagamigawa, N. Ouprasitwong, D. Solofa, L. Tahani, D.T. Thuy, L. Tibig, B. Trewin, K. Vediapan and P. Zhai. "Change in Mean Temperature as a Predictor of Extreme Temperature Change in the Asia–Pacific Region." *International Journal of Climatology* 25 (2005): 1301–1330.

Griffiths, Matthew. *The New Poetics of Climate Change: Modernist Aesthetics for a Warming World.* (London: Bloomsbury Academic, 2017).

Guha, Ramachandra. "Radical American Environmentalism and Wilderness Preservation: A Third World Critique." *Environmental Ethics* 11.1 (Spring 1989): 71–83.

Haji Salleh, Muhammad. *Rowing Down Two Rivers.* (Bangi, Selangor, Malaysia: Penerbit Universiti Kebangsaan Malaysia, 2000).

Hulme, Mike. *Why We Disagree About Climate Change: Understanding Controversy, Inaction and Opportunity.* (Cambridge UK: Cambridge UP, 2009).

Kaplan, E. Ann. *Climate Trauma: Foreseeing the Future in Dystopian Film and Fiction.* (New Brunswick, New Jersey: Rutgers UP, 2016).

Kua, Kia Soong. *Damned Dams and Noxious Nukes: Questioning Malaysia's Energy Policy.* (Petaling Jaya, Selangor, Malaysia: Suara Inisiatif, 2013).

Lim, Shirley Geok-lin. *Monsoon History: Selected Poems.* (London: Skoob Books Publishing, 1994).

Lim, Shirley Geok-lin. *What the Fortune Teller Didn't Say* (Albuquerque, NM: West End Press, 1998).

Lim, Shirley Geok-lin. *Ars Poetica for the Day.* (Singapore: Ethos Books, 2015).

Lim, Shirley Geok-lin. *Do You Live In?* (Singapore: Ethos Books, 2015).

Maniam, K.S. *In a Far Country.* (London: Skoob Books Publishing, 1993).

Maniam, K.S. *The Return.* (London: Skoob Books Publishing, 1993).

Maniam, K.S. *Selected Works.* (Petaling Jaya, Selangor, Malaysia: Maya Press, 1996).

Maniam, K.S. *Haunting the Tiger and Other Stories.* (London: Skoob Books Publishing, 1996).

Mehnert, Antonia. *Climate Change Fictions: Representations of Global Warming in American Literature.* (New York: Palgrave Macmillan, 2016).

Menely, Tobias, & Jesse Oak Taylor. "Introduction" to *Anthropocene Reading: Literary History in Geologic Times,* eds. Menely and Taylor (University Park: Pennsylvania State UP, 2017).

Nixon, Rob. *Slow Violence and the Environmentalism of the Poor.* (Cambridge, MA: Harvard UP, 2011).

Oh, Tick Hui, Md Hasanuzzaman, Jeyraj Selvaraj, Siew Chein Teo and Shing Chyi Chua. "Energy Policy and Alternative Energy in Malaysia: Issues and Challenges for Sustainable Growth—An Update." *Renewable and Sustainable Energy Reviews* 81 (2018): 3021–3031.

Reynolds, Glen, Junaidi Payne, Waidi Sinun, Gregory Mosigil and Rory P.D. Walsh. "Changes in Forest Land Use and Management in Sabah, Malaysia Borneo, 1990–2010, with a Focus on the Danum Valley Region." *Philosophical Transactions of the Royal Society B* 366 (2011): 3168–3176.

Shaffril, Hayrol Azri Mohamed, Bahaman Abu Samah, Jeffrey Lawrence D'Silva, and Sulaiman Md. Yassin. "The Process of Social Adaptation Towards Climate Change Among Malaysian Fishermen." *International Journal of Climate Change Strategies and Management* 5.1 (2013): 38–53.

Szerszynski, Bronislaw. "Reading and Writing the Weather: Climate Technics and the Moment of Responsibility." *Theory, Culture & Society* 27.2–3 (2010): 9–30.

Szerszynski, Bronislaw, and John Urry. "Changing Climates: Introduction." *Theory, Culture & Society* 27.2–3 (2010): 1–8.

Tang, Kuok Ho Daniel. "Climate Change in Malaysia: Trends, Contributors, Impacts, Mitigation and Adaptations." *Science of the Total Environment* 650 (2019): 1858–1871.

Thumboo, Edwin, ed. *The Second Tongue: An Anthology of Poetry from Malaysia and Singapore.* (Singapore: Heinemann, 1976).

Thumboo, Edwin. "Introduction" to *Time and Its People*, Muhammad Haji Salleh, (Kuala Lumpur: Heinemann Educational Books (Asia) Ltd, 1978): xi–xx.

Wilson, Bernard. "Memory, Myth, Exile: The Desire for Malaysian Belonging in K.S. Maniam's *The Return*, 'Haunting the Tiger,' and *In a Far Country.*" *Textual Practice* 17.2 (2003): 391–412.

Wright, Laura. *"Wilderness into Civilized Shapes:" Reading the Postcolonial Environment* (Athens, GA: U of Georgia P, 2010).

Yeow, Agnes S.K. "Place, Race and Environment in the Poetry of Muhammad Haji Salleh." *Textual Practice* 29.1 (2015): 173–199.

CHAPTER 10

Aswan High Dam and Haggag Oddoul's *Stories from Old Nubia*

Redefining the Line between Immediate Catastrophe and Slow Violence

Amany Dahab

The ancient land of Nubia stretched along the Nile Valley from the first cataract south of Aswan, where a series of rock formations that cut across the riverbed provided a natural border with Egypt, to the fourth cataract in Sudan. Despite the overlapping cultures and common racial origins of the region, the Nubians maintained their distinct languages (Kenuzi and Mahasi) and culture. Throughout their history, which can be traced back to 11,000 BC, they experienced periods of prosperity and decline, driven by the Nile's alternately peaceful and destructive flood cycles and climate changes, on the one hand, and tensions with their northern and southern neighbours, on the other.[1] The Nile's unpredictability "became a transcendental preoccupation with ancient Egypt, the focus of myth and ceremony,"[2] as Robert Fernea puts it. Egypt without the Nile is unthinkable. But Sudan and Ethiopia also depend upon it; and several other upstream African nations are also affected by the ongoing Nile River geopolitics. As Fernea also points out, despite the influence of Christianity and Islam over the centuries, "the Nile remained an important element in Nubian beliefs and ceremonialism."[3] Yet modern technology, "in providing the means to conquer the Nile, has removed the ancient homelands of the Nubians themselves from the river."[4]

Between 1898 and 1902, the Aswan Dam, designed by the British engineer Sir William Willcocks, was built across the first cataract. It was the largest dam in the world at that time. After the subsequent heightening of the dam, its reservoir submerged an area that extended from Aswan in southern Egypt to Wadi Halfa in northern Sudan.[5] As the reservoir engulfed a great part of the

---

1   Jocelyn Gohary, *Guide to the Nubian Monuments on Lake Nasser* (Cairo: American U in Cairo P, 1998): 1.

2   Robert A. Fernea, *Nubian Ceremonial Life: Studies in Islamic Syncretism and Cultural Change* (Cairo: American U in Cairo P, 1978): xi.

3   Fernea, *Nubian Ceremonial Life*, xi.

4   Fernea, *Nubian Ceremonial Life*, xi.

5   Gohary, *Guide to the Nubian Monuments on Lake Nasser*, 21–22.

© KONINKLIJKE BRILL NV, LEIDEN, 2022 | DOI:10.1163/9789004514164_011

Nubians' lands, some relocated north and south, but the great majority chose to rebuild their homes on higher elevations around its new banks and to stay on their land despite the harsh conditions. The rise of the water level south of the dam—from 87 to 121 metres—left the ancient monuments of lower Nubia partially submerged for most of the year.[6]

After the 1952 Revolution ended the Egyptian monarchy and eliminated the British military presence from Egypt, the second President Gamal, Abd El Nasser, decided to build the Aswan High Dam. This dam aimed to serve three main purposes: to regulate the Nile water so as to avoid the threat of severe floods and droughts; to "save" the flood water for perennial (instead of basin) irrigation, thereby increasing the amount of arable land; and to generate more hydroelectric power to support the emerging industrial sector. The High Dam built seven kilometres south of the first dam was 3.6 kilometres long and 111 metres high. Its reservoir submerged an area stretching southward over 510 kilometres, one third of which is in Sudan.[7]

With the anticipated submersion of Nubia, over one-hundred thousand Nubians were displaced to newly reclaimed lands during the 1960s.[8] Fifty thousand Egyptian Nubians were re-housed in new villages that the Egyptian government built near Kom Ombo, to the north of Aswan. Fifty-three thousand Sudanese Nubians were displaced from Wadi Halfa over 1000 kilometres south to near Khashm al Girba, on the Atbara River.[9] From 1960 to 1980, UNESCO sponsored a campaign to rescue the Nubian archaeological sites, which the reservoir threatened with permanent inundation. Many monuments, like the temples of Abu Simbel and Isis, were cut from the rock or dismantled and reassembled at new sites in Egypt and Sudan.[10] The original Nubian villages, however, with their intricately nestled mud-brick vaulted dwellings, were consigned to oblivion. With them the long tradition of building with mud-brick disappeared, opening the way for a proliferation of reinforced concrete buildings across the Nile Valley and Delta.

The submersion of Nubia was the most evident and immediate consequence of building the dam, a problem that Nasser's regime "solved" by the relocation of the Nubian people and monuments. It was thought that the benefits of the dam outweighed these considerations. In a speech on July 23, 1970

---

6   Gohary, *Guide to the Nubian Monuments on Lake Nasser*, 22.

7   Gohary, *Guide to the Nubian Monuments on Lake Nasser*, 23.

8   Ahmed Belal, John Briggs, Johan Sharp and Irina Springuel, *Bedouins by the Lake: Environment Change and Sustainability in Southern Egypt* (Cairo: The American U in Cairo P, 2009): 4.

9   Gohary, *Guide to the Nubian Monuments on Lake Nasser*, 25.

10   Belal et al., *Bedouins by the Lake*, 4.

announcing the completion of the Aswan High Dam, Nasser stated: "We do not need on this precious day of our struggle but to look between two lines on the land of our country so that we know the essence of this struggle, the goals of this struggle, and the forces that move and drive this struggle."[11] The "struggle" at the heart of Nasser's discourse was the struggle against imperialism, capitalism and colonialism. As one of the Free Officers whose rule had been legitimised by opposition to the British occupation of Egypt, Nasser was keen to emphasise the ongoing nature of the "struggle." The first of the two "border" lines referred to here is "a line at the south by the width of the Great Nile, the High Dam," a line that Nasser marked as red as the blood that had been shed on the second line—that is, "the line at the north, along the Suez Canal, the line of fighting," where the Egyptian people and the national army were "fighting the most honorable of their battles, the greatest of their battles, the fiercest of their battles."[12] When Nasser decided to build the dam, most of its financing was to be provided by Western powers. In 1956, however, the Western financial offer was withdrawn as a reaction to Nasser's arms purchase from the Eastern bloc. He responded by nationalising the Suez Canal in July 1956, to secure finance for the dam. In October 1956, Israel, Britain and France commenced to invade Egypt to regain control over the Suez Canal and to overthrow Nasser.[13] However, contrary to expectations, Nasser gained more power, and the "struggle" along the two aforementioned lines became the centre of a hegemonic discourse that forced dissidents into silence or jails. Furthermore, the tripartite aggression made Nasser a leader of the Pan Arab movement and of the liberation movement in Africa.

The hegemony of Nasser's nationalist discourse rendered marginal everything south of the line demarcated by the Aswan High Dam, including the Nubians in Egypt and Sudan, for whom it embodies an immediate and attritional catastrophe. The cultural heritage the dam threatened to submerge, and the ecological balance of the "Great Nile" and its valley that the dam destroyed by interrupting the natural flooding cycles, were absent from his discourse. The displacement of the Nubians received a great deal of international press coverage at the time, as did the temples threatened by the dam. But the significance of the other attending "attritional catastrophes" has been blurred by temporal, geographical and rhetorical displacements that have masked their violence. Such displacements, according to Rob Nixon, "smooth the way

---

11   Gamal Abdel Nasser, Speech on the Completion of the construction of Aswan High Dam that coincides with the 18th Anniversary of the July Revolution in 1970, my translation.
12   Nasser, Speech on the Completion of the Construction of Aswan High Dam.
13   Michael S. Mayer, *The Eisenhower Years* (City: Infobase Publishing, 2010): 44.

for amnesia, as places are rendered irretrievable to those who once inhabited them, places that ordinarily pass unmourned in the corporate media,"[14] or (in the case of Nubia) in the Egyptian national media.

Attritional catastrophes usually affect marginalised communities. Devalued as political agents, they are often the long-term casualties of what Nixon calls "slow violence." The violence affects their environments, as well as their cultures, and erodes their ecological traditions. Addressing attritional catastrophes entails rethinking our commonly accepted definitions of violence to include this kind of "slow" violence. It means changing conventional assumptions about "violence as a highly visible act that is newsworthy because it is event focused, time bound, and body bound."[15] It is essential to understand how the temporal dispersal of slow violence affects the way it is perceived, delaying and reducing, if not blocking, responses to its catastrophic social and environmental consequences.

It is not until the counter-discourse of the Nubian writers, Muhammad Khalil Qassem (1912–68) and Zakī Murād (1927–79), started to challenge the nationalist discourse that Egyptians began to see the other side of the story. Qassem, a Communist activist imprisoned from 1948 to 1964, published the novel al-*Shamandoura* (*The River Gauge*) in 1968,[16] a few months before his early death.[17] The following year, Murād, also a Communist, published an important collection of poetry called *Sirb Al Balshun* (*Flock of Pelicans*)[18] with other Nubian poets.[19] A gap of twenty years separates these works from *Nights of Musk: Stories from Old Nubia* (1989)[20] by Haggag Oddoul (born 1944). In *Nights of Musk,* Oddoul moves between realism in "Adila Grandmother," mythical realism in "Nights of Musk" and "The People of the River,"[21] and magical realism in "Zeinab Uburty," relying on the mythological richness of the Nubian culture, and the long tradition of storytelling in Nubia and Egypt. When *Nights*

---

14   Rob Nixon, *Slow Violence and the Environmentalism of the Poor* (Cambridge, MA: Harvard UP, 2011): 7.

15   Nixon, *Slow Violence*, 2.

16   Muhammad Khalil Qassem, *al-Shamandūrah: Awwal Riwāyah Nūbīyah fī Tārīkh al-Adab al-'Arabī,* (Cairo: Dār al-Kātib al-'Arabī, 1968).

17   Richard Jacquemond, *Conscience of the Nation: Writers, State, and Society in Modern Egypt*, trans. David Tresilian (Cairo: The American U in Cairo P, 2008): 181.

18   Zakī Murād, *Sirb al-balashūn ash'ār min al-Nūbah* (Cairo: Dār al-Kātib al-'Arabi, 1969).

19   "Haggag, Hassan Adoul: Nubia's Human Aspirations." Interview conducted by Hosam Aboul-Ela, *The Nubian*, http://thenubian.net/haggag/enterview.doc.

20   Haggag, Oddoul, *Nights of Musk: Stories from Old Nubia*, trans. Anthony Calderbank (Cairo & New York: American U in Cairo P, 2008).

21   Jacquemond, *Conscience of the Nation*, 182.

of Musk won the National Literature Award in 1990, it brought back into focus the work of Qassem and Murād, and encouraged new works like Idris Ali's *Poor*[22] and *Dongola*,[23] which draw heavily on Ali's personal experience of marginalisation as a displaced Nubian. Oddoul is an Egyptian activist and writer of Nubian descent. His early years as a young man were spent working as a construction worker on the Aswan High Dam and serving in the Egyptian army on Suez Canal, experiences that shaped his writing.

Nubian literature, according to Richard Jacquemond, was born of the urge "to save the heritage of the Nubian communities from oblivion and to preserve Nubian collective memory."[24] However, its importance exceeds this role. The portrayal of the displaced Nubians' declining living conditions in Nubian literature characterises them, in Thayer Scudder's words, as "developmental refugees";[25] and by portraying the precarity of being a developmental refugee in a postcolonial state, Nubian literature exposes the hypocrisy of Nasser's nationalist discourse. The contrast between the images of the lost Nubia that they mourn and the industrial Egypt that Nasser promised reveals the paradoxicality of mega-dams as indicators of immense industrial power and as the erasers of some of the earliest human civilisations.

Alternating between realism, mythical realism and magical realism, Oddoul intricately connects the immediate catastrophe of Nubia's submersion behind the Aswan High Dam with the attritional catastrophes that followed its construction. Most importantly, for my purpose in this chapter, Oddoul renders visible the connection between the High Dam and climate change, the slowest evolving and most underestimated of mega-dams' ecological consequences. Climate change is the embodiment of slow violence, a violence that is "neither spectacular nor instantaneous, but rather incremental and accretive."[26]

Mega-dams' contribution to climate change was not visible when Oddoul published "Zeinab Uburty," the third story of *Nights of Musk*. In retrospect, however, the story is suggestive of mega-dams' contribution to climate change. The word *uburty* (the Nubian word for "soot") conveys the meaning of pollution caused by carbon emissions. It was almost two decades after the construction of the Aswan High Dam before researchers revealed the under-accounting

---

22   Idris Ali, *Poor*, trans. Elliott Colla (Cairo: American U in Cairo P, 2007).

23   Idris Ali, *Dongola: A Novel of Nubia*, trans. Peter Theroux (Fayetteville: U of Arkansas P, 1998).

24   Jacquemond, *Conscience of the Nation*, 181.

25   Quoted in Jacques Leslie, *Deep Water: The Epic Struggle over Dams, Displaced People, and the Environment* (New York: Farrar, Straus and Giroux, 2005): 156.

26   Nixon, *Slow Violence*, 2.

of the climate impacts of mega-dams' release of greenhouse gases from the stratification of reservoir water, the decay of submerged organisms and emissions from hydropower stations.[27] This research, which usually does not attract the attention of policy-makers, enables a new reading of Oddoul's stories of "the people of the river" and the palm trees trapped under the reservoir. The radicality of Oddoul's discourse and literary devices make visible the demonic pacts that connect policy-makers with industry and allow them to "break the barriers" that maintain ecological balance, thus triggering climate change. The promoters of mega-dams present them as locomotives of development, symbols of resistance in postcolonial states, and even as solutions to control climate change. In the light of new scientific findings, however, Oddoul's stories appear as an early warning of how mega-dams in fact help cause, rather than resist, climate change. In order to read Oddoul's stories through the interpretative optic of climate change, I will start by analysing the colonialist and nationalist discourses around the building of the dam to which the stories respond. My analysis aims to identify the causes of the absence of environmental concerns from nationalist discourse, and to reveal the relevance of texts written before climate change became evident.

In the case of Aswan High Dam, as with most mega-dams in the developing world, the nationalist discourse presented the construction of the dam as a symbol of resistance *against* colonialism, imperialism and capitalism. Ironically, the High Dam in fact compromised the political and economic independence of Egypt. Between 1953 and 1956, Egypt negotiated the financing of the High Dam with three major icons of capitalism: the World Bank, the United States and Britain. When the British-American offer was withdrawn, Egypt became financially and technologically dependent on the Soviet Union.[28] However, Nasser's "Speech on the Nationalisation of Suez Canal" (1956) reveals the motivation for building the Aswan High Dam:

> When we build the High Dam, we build the dam of glory, freedom and dignity, and destroy the dams of humiliation and shame. We will not allow the merchants of wars to control us, will not allow the colonisers to control us, will not allow the traders of humans to control us. [...] We move towards political independence, economic independence, we move towards a national economy for the common good of the people. [...] We will build industry in Egypt and compete against them. They do

---

27   "Greenhouse Gas Emissions from Dams," *International River Network* (2007).

28   Gohary, *Guide to the Nubian Monuments on Lake Nasser*, 23.

not want us to be an industrialised country because our country is a market for their products. One nation, we pledged to commit ourselves to a sacred march towards construction and towards industrialisation.[29]

The High Dam became the temple of Egypt's new religion—industry—while the rising water of the suffocated river upstream threatened to drown the temples of the old gods and dissolve the old villages of Nubia. Turning Egypt into an industrial country to compete against the capitalist industrial West was central to Nasser's socialist program, culminating in the founding of the Arab Socialist Union in Egypt in December 1962 as the country's sole political party.[30]

In *The Politics of the Earth: Environmental Discourses,* John Dryzek writes that "industrial societies have of course featured many competing ideologies [...] But whatever their differences, all these ideologies are committed to industrialism."[31] Gamal Abdel Nasser, Kwame Nkrumah and Jawaharlal Nehru feverishly rushed to erect mega-dams as national symbols of political and economic independence. They made their recently decolonised countries arenas for the industrialists' competing powers and ideologies, allowing them to exploit resources, disturb the ecological balance and destroy cultural and social fabrics that had evolved over millennia.

The Cold War rivalry for technological supremacy between the United States and the Soviet Union, or what Nixon calls "dam wars," was manipulated by the Egyptian government to present the High Dam as an expression of political sovereignty. Mega-dams in the newly decolonised nations, as Nixon suggests, "served as highly visible, spectacular statements that new nations were literally soaring toward development by mastering rivers and reaching for the sky."[32] Aswan High Dam was one of these spectacular statements. The dam dwarfed the Old Aswan Dam that the British colonial administration had erected. For the British, the old dam had made a different statement, one of colonial mastery. Changing history, dominating the ecology of the colonised territory, enables control over both people and resources, but it also presents the colonising power as culturally and technologically superior to its subjects. In "Harnessing the Nile," published in 1899, American diplomat in Cairo Frederic Courtland Penfield wrote:

---

29   Gamal Abdel Nasser, "Speech on the Nationalization of Suez Canal" (Alexandria, 1956), my translation, https://www.youtube.com/watch?v=YFyIVC6bmzk.

30   Rami Ginat, *Egypt's Incomplete Revolution: Lutfi Al-Khuli and Nasser's Socialism in the 1960s* (London: Frank Cass, 1997): 149.

31   John S. Dryzek, *The Politics of the Earth* (Oxford: Oxford UP, 2013): 13.

32   Nixon, *Slow Violence*, 166.

> The Pyramids and the Sphinx have borne testimony through the centuries to the grandeur and power of execution which dwelt within the Nile valley; and what more fitting now than that the same valley be the theater of a gigantic engineering exploit, audacious perhaps, but certain of success, and ministering to man's necessities, rather than to his vanity?[33]

But the building of the mega-dam also added a redemptive credibility to Egyptian nationalism, in accordance with which Nasser promoted it as a locomotive of development moving towards a national economy for the common good.

Securing finance for such enormous projects added to their symbolism. Britain had initially proposed £2,000,000, to be provided by banker Ernest Cassel, to guarantee the production of Egyptian cotton for British trade and industry and as an act of goodwill towards the Egyptians, who would repay the loan in annual instalments over three decades.[34] On the other hand, Nasser's nationalisation of the Suez Canal, to secure the construction cost of the High Dam, made him the redeemer of lost dignity for those who had dug the canal by corvée. However, some of the costs of development remain absent from both the British and the Egyptian discourse. The greater the dam, the greater the tacit costs, beginning with displaced populations, or "developmental refugees,"[35] and extending to the ecological destablisation of the river.

"Developmental refugee" is a paradoxical term. Development implies growth and ascent towards a higher goal, whereas the refugee phenomenon "implies flight from a grave threat—in this case, the threat of development inflicted destitution or even, when it comes to mega-dams, of drowning,"[36] as Nixon puts it. As an icon of national ascent, the mega-dam "becomes coupled to the descending prospects of communities that have become ecologically unmoored, cut off from drowned commons that, however modestly or precariously, had offered a diverse diet and an identity."[37] Such communities are, "in the most literal sense, inundated by development."[38]

The notion of the developmental refugee "holds in tension an official, centripetal logic of national development on the one hand, and on the other a

---

33 Frederic Courtland Penfield, "Harnessing the Nile," *Century Magazine* 57.4 (1899), https://en.wikisource.org/wiki/Century_Magazine/Volume_57/Issue_4/Harnessing_the_Nile.

34 Sidney Peel, *The Binding of the Nile and the New Sudan* (London: Edward Arnold, 1904): 79.

35 Leslie, *Deep Water*, 156.

36 Nixon, *Slow Violence*, 152.

37 Nixon, *Slow Violence*, 152.

38 Nixon, *Slow Violence*, 152.

terrifying, centrifugal narrative of displacement, dispossession, and exodus."[39] But in the absence of a discourse that could expose such a terrifying narrative of displacement, this tension is removed, smoothing the way for the national media to erase the Nubians from the collective memory of Egypt. A 1997 report published by the Egyptian authors M. Abu-Zeid and F. El-Shibini reveals how the rhetoric of nationalist discourse continued to marginalise the Nubians, presenting their tragic displacement as a positive development deserving gratitude, even decades after Nasser:

> Because the [Aswan High Dam] reservoir was expected to rise gradually to higher elevations, it was decided to resettle the Nubians to a new area downstream of the dam. The new settlement area was not far from the areas they used to live in, where 28,000 acres of fertile land was reclaimed, and infrastructures and other services were supplied. Some 25,000 houses were built among 33 villages which were given the same names as the old Nubian villages. The villages were built in the same order as beforehand. After about 30 years, the social impact on the migrants has been viewed remarkably positively by the population concerned.[40]

Identifying Egyptian Nubians as Nubians is not so much an act of discrimination as it is an identification of which they are proud. However, identifying Egyptian emigrants by their ethnicity, in some contexts, has different connotations. In "Before the Flood," Arundhati Roy writes that "the ethnic 'otherness' of the victims takes some of the strain off the nation-builders."[41] Describing the life of the Nubians before the Aswan High Dam as "very hard" is a justificatory way to focus their life after its construction "remarkably positively."[42]

---

39   Nixon, *Slow Violence*, 152.

40   M.A. Abu-Zeid and F.Z. El-Shibini, "Egypt's High Aswan Dam," *Water Resources Development* 13.2 (1997): 213.

41   Arundhati Roy, "Before the Flood," *The Amicus Journal* (2000): 17. Roy bases the conclusion on her observation that "about 60 per cent of those displaced by development [in India] are either Dalit or Adivasi." Considering that Dalits account for 15 percent and Adivasis only 8 per cent of India's population, would open up a whole other dimension to the story. The number of Nubians who have been resettled away from southern Egypt since the 1960s, when the Aswan High Dam was built on the Nile is estimated at 50,000 people according to Robert Fernea. As large as this number would be, especially in relation to the whole population of the Nubian, it presents less than 3 percent of the Egyptian population at the 1960s.

42   Arundhati Roy, "Before the Flood," 17.

Another tacit cost of mega-dams is the change to land cover and the interruption of river flows from uplands to sea, which consequently changes biogeochemical cycles, disturbing the terrestrial water cycle and altering the water vapor flow from land to atmosphere.[43] Thus, mega-dams are connected to most of the anthropogenic causes behind climate change. As in most North African countries, temperature is Egypt are increasing, and global warming has intensified the severity and frequency of sandstorms and fog.[44] Climate change also has a negative impact on coastal zones, due to storm surges in the short term and sea levels rising in the long term. In the case of the Nile Delta erosion of the shoreline was initiated, as Hisham Elsafti explains, "by the construction of the High Aswan Dam that prevented the nourishment of the Nile Delta with fresh Nile siltation."[45] The erosion today is accelerating because of climate change.

When the British built the first dam in Aswan, the water and silt carried on the flood tides were not halted. Sidney Peel cites an observation made by F. Vansleb, a Dutchman who visited Egypt around 1670: "The fertility of the Nile flood is caused, [Vansleb] says, by the fall of dew, which usually takes place on June 17, just after the appearance of 'green' water. This dew purifies the foul water, and makes it swell by fermentation."[46] Taking into consideration the "green water" rich with algae, and the dew rich with silt, the dam was designed so that "during the months of the flood every gate will be up, and the 'red' water, carrying all its heavy burden of silt, will pass through without impediment."[47] Relying on the annual cycle of the river, the dam "provide[d] its own remedy: every year the force of the flood will act like a gigantic broom sweeping the floor of the reservoir."[48] This "remedy" emerged from a pragmatic industrial concern, namely "to avoid the danger of large silt deposits, which could soon diminish the capacity of the reservoir and, if allowed to accumulate, render it in long time entirely useless."[49] Thus, the first dam mitigated the ecological

---

43 Will Steffen et al., "The Anthropocene: Conceptual and Historical Perspectives," *Philosophical Transactions: Mathematical, Physical and Engineering Sciences* 369.1938 (2011): 843.

44 "Climate Change Information Fact Sheet Egypt," *Climate Links*, https://www.climatelinks .org/sites/default/files/asset/document/Egypt%20Climate%20Info%20Fact%20Sheet _FINAL.pdf.

45 Mohammed El-Said, "How Climate Change Threatens Egypt's Coasts, Agriculture," *Daily News Egypt* (January 24, 2018), https://dailynewsegypt.com/2018/01/24/climate-change -threatens-egypts-coasts-agriculture/.

46 Peel, *The Binding*, 71.

47 Peel, *The Binding*, 74.

48 Peel, *The Binding*, 75.

49 Peel, *The Binding*, 72.

consequences of accumulating sediments, allowing silt to pass through to the valley and delta, and to the Mediterranean as well. But the second dam, built during Nasser's presidency, sought to recuperate the thirty-billion cubic metres that the first dam had allowed downstream.

Nasser's "sacred march towards industrialisation" made his socialism merely an ideological variation of industrialism, which habitually ignores or suppresses environmental concerns. Within such a context, the absence of environmental concern in Nasser's thinking comes as no surprise, as the dominance of a Promethean discourse becomes inevitable. The Promethean discourse, according to Dryzek, "comes close to denying the very existence of nature, which is at most seen in inert, passive terms."[50] Relations with nature are governed by "a hierarchy in which humans (and in particular, human minds) dominate everything else."[51]

This Promethean discourse, as it focused on the Nile, was born in imperial Britain more than fifty years before Nasser. Penfield's essay, "Harnessing the Nile" (1899) and Peel's book, *The Binding of the Nile and the New Sudan* (1904), are examples. In Egypt, however, the attitude towards the natural world that the national anticolonial discourse conveyed during Nasser's rule amplified the Promethean discourse, so that it persisted for decades after his death in 1970. Abu-Zeid and El-Shibini, perhaps without even realising that they are echoing their former colonisers, start their 1997 report by writing: "History tells us that Egypt's fertile land is the gift of the Nile. However, for the first time in history, full control of the Nile water was achieved in 1970 after the construction of the High Aswan Dam."[52] In a Foucauldian sense, Abu-Zeid and El-Shibini's affirmation of the "full control" of the Nile water twenty-seven years after Nasser's death, is evidence of the lasting influence of Nasser's discourse. But reading this report in parallel with Penfield and Peel's earlier writings, one wonders if it is not evidence of the greater power of colonialist discourse to condition the perception even of decolonised subjects after a century?

Against the colonialist and the nationalist discourses of development, Oddoul's *Stories* give voice to the Nubians displaced by the dams of Aswan, who have been silenced for decades. The realism of "Adila, Grandmother," the first of the four stories of *Nights of Musk* expose the precarity of being a developmental refugee. The Nubian word in the title means "farewell"; and the story opens with the narrator, Mohammed, sitting beside the tombstone of his recently deceased grandmother. In the background are the "tiny houses of the

---

50   Dryzek, *The Politics of the Earth,* 13.
51   Dryzek, *The Politics of the Earth,* 58.
52   Abu-Zeid and Shibini, "Egypt's High Aswan Dam," 209.

exiles' village,"[53] which, in reality, were situated on desert land near Kom Ombo that the national media described as fertile. In a flashback, Mohammed—who is born of a Nubian father and an Alexandrian mother—remembers the first cold encounter with his grandmother. He expresses the feelings of the people living in this arid land of exile: "The men were angry, discussing this new village of theirs and the desert land that so far had yielded only rocks and stones. They wondered about the water, and when it would arrive to wet the cement channels, which had cracked from the lack of moisture."[54] Oddoul contrasts their misery to the life of old Nubia. "Where is our Nile?" the agonised grandmother asks. "Where are our palm trees and our spacious houses? And the waterwheels? And the wedding parties full of food and drink and the beat of tambourine? Where are the days of the flood and the days of the harvest? Where's our old village [...] the village of Bahjurah?"[55] The villages of the new Nubia were given the same names as the old villages, but the names are the only things left from Old Nubia. The Nubians' new land did not compensate for the loss of harmony in their lives, which had been tied to the natural flood cycle of the Nile, despite its unpredictability, for millennia.

After displacement, Nubian communities were torn apart by subsequent waves of migration as the men moved north to find employment, leaving their families behind.[56] In the voice of the grandmother: "Everybody in the village relied on their children who worked in the north. Whoever had no support in the north reared chicken and sold eggs, or ate alone with no one to ask after them. It was a challenge for those people just to find the price of a spoon of sugar to put in their cup of tea."[57] They had to choose between starvation on lands they could not cultivate and migration to the cities, where their lack of formal education often prevented them from earning a decent living. With migration came another challenge. An escalating feeling of otherness alienated the Nubians, and not only from other Egyptians. It also drove a wedge between old and new generations, between those who grew up in Old Nubia and those born away from their communities. Inevitably some married *gorbatiya* (the Nubian word for the people of the north). One can feel the bitterness

---

53 Oddoul, *Nights of Musk*, 1.

54 Oddoul, *Nights of Musk*, 11.

55 Oddoul, *Nights of Musk*, 13.

56 The studies and documents Nicholas Hopkins and Sohair Mehanna collected in *Nubian Encounters: The Story of the Nubian Ethnological Survey 1961–1964*, convey an image similar to that Oddoul draw of the New Nubia, which makes his style more of a realist in the first story entitled Adila, Grandmother!

57 Oddoul, *Nights of Musk*, 13.

of the grandmother who screams at her grandson: "Your mother *gorbatiya*. She took your father from his People."[58]

As the narrative advances, however, Mohammed's feeling of otherness turns to a deep feeling of belonging. Even his grandmother's bitterness towards his mother fades, though her resentment of her new village remains. In the last lines of the story, she returns to her native tongue, speaking in Nubian to her daughter, Awada: "Wo nor ... wo nor. Awada, can you see our palm trees standing row upon row? The date season, Awada, and the village of Bahjurah in the feast ... Wo nor ... wo nor. Our Nile is sweet and kind. The buoy is dancing."[59] Yearning for her lost homeland, she envisions the "village ancestors" sitting under her grandfather's doum tree. "Is that a boat's sail?" she wonders. "Is it coming for me?"[60] The yearning, according to Oddoul, is a characteristic of Nubian literature arising from the forced migration of the Nubians in 1964, when a splinter [was] planted in each Nubian's heart. "The yearning for the deluged environment has become an essential part" of Nubian being, "individually and communally, and with it the sense of depression at having been thrown into an artificial environment that neither accepted them nor was accepted by them."[61] Central to Oddoul's cause as an activist is the right of Nubians to return to the lands south of the High Dam. But the yearning for homeland is also integral to his own perception of the natural environment, so that he is able to anticipate and describe the ecological impacts of development as clearly as he sees its social drawbacks.

Reading through the interpretative lens of climate change entails maintaining an active interrogation of the connections between the social implications of violence against the environment and its attritional exacerbation of climate change. In that sense, one must ask: How much cement was needed to build those "tiny houses of the exiles' village[s]" in Egypt and Sudan? How much more has been needed to replace mud-brick vernacular architecture of the Nile Valley and Delta since the building of High Dam? How much fertiliser has been needed to cultivate the desert land, "that so far had yielded only rocks and stones"?[62] How much more has been needed to maintain the lands of the valley and delta since the dam deprived them of silt? How much nitrous acid

---

58 Oddoul, *Nights of Musk*, 7.

59 In Nubian, "Wo nor" is an exclamation of praise to, or fear of, God.

60 Oddoul, *Nights of Musk*, 25–26.

61 Oddoul, Interview.

62 Robert Sanders, "Fertilizer Use Responsible for Increase in Nitrous Oxide in Atmosphere," University of California Berkeley, http://news.berkeley.edu/2012/04/02/fertilizer-use-responsible-for-increase-in-nitrous-oxide-in-atmosphere/.

has been used in the manufacture of fertilisers contributing to greenhouse gases?[63]

Slow violence, according to Nixon, "is often not just attritional but also exponential, operating as a major threat multiplier; it can fuel long-term, proliferating conflicts in situations where the conditions for sustaining life become increasingly but gradually degraded."[64] It is crucial to emphasise the exponential nature of slow violence in addressing attritional catastrophes, such as the social degradation and cultural loss associated with displacements, as well as the ecological impacts of interrupted natural cycles. Representing attritional catastrophes poses a major challenge for writers: that is, as Nixon puts it, "how to devise arresting stories, images, and symbols adequate to the pervasive but elusive violence of delayed effects."[65]

Oddoul deals with this challenge not only by the imagery and symbolism he devises but also by the interconnectivity of his storying. "Nights of Musk," the second story of *Stories from Old Nubia*, moves farther back in time: "Long long ago, south of the rapid, the nights exuded incense and oozed musk."[66] The story returns to the lost environments of Old Nubia, "watered by the Celestial majesty of the Nile and nourished by the green strip of life that lined its banks. Their sky was pure and their air invigorating."[67] The "Celestial majesty of the Nile" is not just a figure of speech. It reflects the Ancient Egyptian belief that the Nile is the course along which the sun god, Ra, travels during the day,[68] and which by night is visible as the Milky Way.[69] The terrestrial path of the Nile mirrors its flow through heaven.[70] The terrestrial Nile is simply "the river" (*itrw*), but the beginning of the flood season, when the river swells with silt and water and bestows its fertility upon the fields, marks the "Arrival of Hapy."[71] Ancient Egyptian mythology presents Hapy, by virtue of the cyclic rhythm of flood, as a maintainer of the cosmic balance, a creator god with life-giving ability. The

---

63   Sanders, "Fertilizer Use Responsible for Increase in Nitrous Oxide in Atmosphere".
64   Nixon, *Slow Violence*, 3.
65   Nixon, *Slow Violence*, 3.
66   Oddoul, *Nights of Musk*, 29.
67   Oddoul, *Nights of Musk*, 29.
68   Veronica Ions, *Egyptian Mythology* (Middlesex: Paul Hamlyn, 1965): 42.
69   R.O. Faulkner, *The Ancient Egyptian Book of the Dead* (London: British Museum Publications, 1985): 90.
70   According to hymn to the sun-disk (itn) from the tomb of Huy at Amarna, composed during the reign of Amenhotep IV Akhenaten (1379–1362 B.C.) as quoted by R. Drew Griffith in "Homeric ΔΙΙΠΕΤΕΟΣ ΠΟΤΑΜΟΙΟ and the Celestial Nile," *The American Journal of Philology* 118.3 (Autumn 1997): 357.
71   Richard H. Wilkinson, *The Complete Gods and Goddesses of Ancient Egypt* (London: Thames and Hudson, 2003): 107.

story revives Ancient Egyptian beliefs, intricately connected to the natural world, and emphasises the delicate balance between the Nile cycles and the climate. In Old Nubia the nights are "watered" by the river, "nourished by the green strip of life that lines its banks," the sky is "pure" and the air "invigorating." Generation after generation. The language underlines the climate change that comes in the wake of the High Dam's construction, with the "putrid" air and the "dead crops" that "bring rats and lice and blood."

The flood that dominates the Nubian belief system inspires Oddoul's allegory. The narrator describes his beloved wife, Salha, as "a whirlpool raging in the flood season, a lavish wave of giving."[72] He recalls:

> In the darkness before dawn, we jumped into the celestial Nile to perform our ablutions in its pure and holy water. It flows from the springs of Salsabeel in Paradise. The rippling water has its effect. It passes over our bodies and we absorb its silt and fertile mud. My pores draw it into my bones, into my marrow and it kisses the water of life and gives it its dark color. It embraces your sweet body slowly and, deliberately and seeps inside until it rests in the womb, enfolding the tiny beginning, giving it color.

There it grows and curls up. And outside, the belly looks like a soft round sand dune.[73] The flooding Nile connects heaven and earth in harmony, and man and woman become one with the river, creating new life. But there can be no reclamation of the lost paradise, as the next story in the volume makes very clear.

The apocalyptic allegory of the third story, "Zeinab Uberty," could be read as a response to the Promethean discourse of Penfield's "Harnessing the Nile" and Peel's "Binding the Nile," which reached its zenith in the nationalist discourse affirming the full control of Nile's water. Oddoul builds his allegory on "the magic and binding of males,"[74] depriving the village people of "that sweet cursed thing that joins man and woman together" and bringing to an "abrupt halt the production of the new generation, and the gift of procreation that [the] Lord has bestowed upon most creatures."[75] Oddoul bases his allegory upon the traditional and still prevalent Egyptian belief that magic can be bind or block a man so that he is unable to make love to a woman, making

---

72 Oddoul, *Nights of Musk*, 39.
73 Oddoul, *Nights of Musk*, 39–40.
74 Oddoul, *Nights of Musk*, 49. "The magic of binding the males" is a sort of magic that Egyptians believe to prevent males from having intimate relationship with females.
75 Oddoul, *Nights of Musk*, 49.

procreation impossible. Thus, in "Zeinab Uberty," a spell prevents all the men of the village from making love with their wives, at the same time preventing both the flow and the flooding of the Nile. This is a theme deeply related to the absence of the flood season, which according to Oddoul, "is nothing more than the long, broad river's manhood overflowing his banks with the water of life. [When] it mounts the land, and plants are born, and udders grow fat."[76] Without the flood, without the procreation, "colors grow pale, and life's fire goes out."[77]

The stories that "took place in the land of Nubia, land of gold [...] between the first and second rapids on the mighty river of the world, the River Nile," the narrator tells us, were related to him by "the late Hulla, who witnessed them as a small child. [And] God granted him a long age through one hundred and ten floods."[78] They started when Zeinab Uburty, "the foolish woman, sought the help of the perfidious devil Kakoky" [and] "uncovered a most unholy book, a book of magic."[79] Like the other stories in *Nights of Musk*, "Zeinab Uberty" is narrated in the first person (in the voice of Hulla). This is something of a tradition of Nubian storytelling. Indeed, first-person voicings are used extensively by Indigenous writers. In "Zeinab Uberty" Oddoul's use of the first person assists the creation of a magical realist world, blending Uberty's "native" magic with the existential realities of the High Dam's impact on Nubia. Uburty is not the only person to use the book of magic. Her grandfather also made a pact with the devil. Oddoul associates Uburty with the second dam, rather than the first, and he emphasises the kinship of those who use the unholy "book of magic." But kinship in this context is ironic because it refers also to the colonisers who commissioned the first dam and the nationalists who commissioned the second. Both of which harnessed the supernatural powers of industrial magic to subjugate the Nile which, as Hulla indicates, had catastrophic consequences:

> Like every year, Touba followed Kiyahk [names of months according to the ancient Egyptian calendar]. That's when strange events started to take place that made my hair turn white even though I was only a child. That Touba, boys, was colder than cold itself. We huddled inside our houses around braziers and ovens, for the sun had left us and had moved away to

---

76 Oddoul, *Nights of Musk*, 49.
77 Oddoul, *Nights of Musk*, 49.
78 Oddoul, *Nights of Musk*, 42–43. Oddoul uses the Ancient Egyptian calendar that starts with flood season to count Hulla's years and used the Egyptian names of its months (Kiyahk, Touba), which are still used by Egyptian peasants today.
79 Oddoul, *Nights of Musk*, 46–47.

the farthest reach of the sky's dome and let through dark northern clouds that didn't normally appear. They veiled the blueness of the sky and only little light reached us. Our entire day was gray. Imagine, every morning we would find the water in the pots and jugs and metal pans covered was an extremely cold glass like layer. 'We had to break it to let the water flow out from underneath. [...] The Nile itself, until well after dawn, was clothed in that translucent glass layer, which we have neither seen nor heard of before or since. With our very own eyes we saw dead fish, goggle-eyed in terror, motionless except for the motion of that layer.[80]

The slow violence of this transformation challenges the reader to connect the abstract scientific theory that led to the dam being built on the Nile in the late 1960s (in order to increase the salinity of the Mediterranean by depriving it of fresh water) with other actions that have led to the "shifting climatic patterns throughout the world that may cause high-latitude areas in Canada to glaciate within the next century."[81] In other words, what literary intervention can render visible the connection between human activity and climate change?

Reading the text today through the optic of climate change gives its narrative new meaning. Oddoul's recall of a winter "colder than cold," juxtaposed with the "scorching summer" that follows, captures what Katharine Hayhoe calls a "dipole" pattern,[82] which, according to recent studies, climate change may trigger.[83] Juxtaposition is just one of Oddoul's literary tools that renders visible the otherwise invisible symptoms of climate change. "To render slow violence visible, entails among other things redefining speed," Nixon states.[84] With accelerating climate change, environmental metaphors acquire inverse implications. For instance, " 'glacial'—once a dead metaphor for 'slow'— [becomes] a rousing, iconic image of unacceptably fast loss."[85] The swift shift in Oddoul's story, from a freezing winter to a scorching summer in the month of Barmhaat, can be read as an attempt to redefine speed, a concept that Oddoul touches on when he writes: "The day which had passed so slowly in

---

80   Oddoul, *Nights of Musk*, 44.
81   R.G. Johnson, "Climate Control Requires a Dam at the Strait of Gibraltar," *EOS, Transactions, American Geophysical Union* 78 (1997): 277–281.
82   Michael Mann, "A 'Perfect Storm': Extreme Winter Weather, Bitter Cold, and Climate Change," *The Climate Change Reality Project* (January 4, 2018), https://www.climatereality project.org/blog/perfect-storm-extreme-winter-weather-bitter-cold-and-climate-change.
83   Mann, "A 'Perfect Storm' ".
84   Nixon, *Slow Violence*, 13.
85   Oddoul, *Nights of Musk*, 13.

the months of cold, now raced past with devilish speed."[86] Oddoul shortens the temporal span of long-term environmental catastrophe so that his reader can visualise its effects.

> The sun came down so low that in the mornings as it appeared above the horizon, its bloody halo collided with the summit of the eastern mountain. The mountain shuddered and bellowed before the horror that assailed it and flaming rocks flew off and crashed down into the river which passed directly below: We heard the sound of the water hissing from the fire: tshshshsh tshshshsh tshshshsh. At the same time, the earth rumbled in our village and the houses shook. [...] The birds flew frantically west and bumped into one another! shrieking and calling for their little ones, who had fallen in shock from their nests to the ground. Our animals ran west too, and the lads followed them to stop them reaching the ravine. Then the sun leapt across the wide course of the river and passed over our heads, its halo transformed into a massive ball of dazzling silver fire, whose flames licked the air above us: wshshshsh wshshshsh. The bottom of its halo, which had regained its bloody color, struck the top of Mount 'Wawaat and caused a second, stronger tremor. [...] It was our good fortune that the blazing rocks that were falling landed far from the village. Otherwise, we'd have all been incinerated like the people of Sodom and Gomorra.[87]

The misery associated with the metaphorical movement of the sun can be read as an apocalyptic allegory of the global warming that began with the Industrial Revolution, and more generally of anthropogenic climate change. The river, the terrestrial reflection of the celestial Nile that reveals the course of the sun god, Ra, across the sky in *Nights of Musk*, is interrupted by the High Dam, and this prevents the arrival of the fertility god, Hapy. This blockage of the celestial Nile, throwing the sun off its course, triggers the anger of the gods Ra and Hapy. The image of Uburty's house invites a symbolic reading as the image of the High Dam. The location of the house, between the First and Second Cataract, its height (dwarfing the Palace of Ibreem), the heat it radiates and the giants who build it are all aspects that recall the High Dam.

Oddoul writes of the building of Uburty's house: "We were astonished when we saw on a hill in the distance tall, broad workmen, bare-chested in

---

86 Oddoul, *Nights of Musk*, 37.
87 Oddoul, *Nights of Musk*, 44–45.

the freezing cold, building a strange-looking house with incredible speed. And where exactly? On the top of a hill that was difficult to climb, and well away from the village."[88] The image of the bare-chested workers in the freezing cold suggests the heat emissions that the building process itself entails. But ignorance or indifference prevails, as "no man made the effort to ride over to the hill and find out what was happening," or because the locals were "terrified of the giant builders."[89]

The image Oddoul draws of the giant builders, as magical as it may seem, conveys a perfect sense of reality. The giant builders might symbolise the colonial powers, the nationalist autocracies or the global corporations that control the construction of mega-dams. This dam-building industry is a giant contributor to climate change. Research shows that anthropogenic emissions of carbon dioxide to the atmosphere come from three main sources: (a) oxidation of fossil fuels; (b) deforestation and associated land clearance; and (c) carbonate decomposition, of which the cement industry is the largest source of emissions.[90] Among these three main sources of carbon dioxide emission, the last two are mainly triggered by the building industry. The construction of thousands of mega-dams across the world has contributed to the increase of global cement production thirty-fold since 1950, and almost four-fold since 1990.[91] One wonders how much carbon must have been released into the atmosphere in the construction of the Aswan High Dam.[92] How much carbon must have been emitted to produce the cement needed for building new villages in Egypt and Sudan for the displaced populations?

The "mass of writhing, hissing snakes," as Oddoul imagines the wall of the "great fortress, taller and stronger than the castle of Ibreem,"[93] clearly symbolises the movement of the turbines of the High Dam. The "hissing snakes" along with the "hissing water"[94] can be read anew in the light of scientific findings

---

88   Oddoul, *Nights of Musk*, 56.

89   Oddoul, *Nights of Musk*, 56.

90   Robbie M. Andrew, "Global CO2 Emissions from Cement Production," CICERO *Center for International Climate Research* (Norway, January 26, 2018), https://www.earth-syst-sci -data.net/10/195/2018/essd-10-195-2018.pdf.

91   Andrew, "Global CO2 Emissions from Cement Production".

92   The Aswan High Dam is 3,830 metres (12,570 ft) long, 980 m (3,220 ft) wide at the base, 40 m (130 ft) wide at the crest and 111 m (364 ft) tall. It contains 43,000,000 cubic metres (56,000,000 cu yd) of material.

93   Oddoul, *Nights of Musk,* 67.

94   Oddoul, *Nights of Musk*, 44–45.

that refute the claim that mega-dams produce clean energy.[95] Emitting over 100 million metric tonnes of methane annually from reservoir surfaces, turbines, spillways and rivers downstream, mega-dams are the largest single anthropogenic source of methane, accounting for around one quarter of all anthropogenic methane emissions.[96] While carbon dioxide lasts longer in the atmosphere, methane's capacity for heat trapping is exponentially higher, with a warming impact seventy-two times that of carbon dioxide when measured over twenty years, and twenty times higher over one hundred years.[97] The decay of drowned plantations (mainly palm trees and corn), the erosion of formerly fertile soils, and entrapped organisms (such as plankton and algae) that flow with the silt into reservoirs is responsible for the mega-dams continuing over their entire lifespan to emit methane, carbon dioxide and nitrous oxide.[98] While methane is produced at the reservoir bottom, most of the emissions take place at spillways, turbines and downstream. Reading through the lens of the climate changes that have become more evident since the time when Oddoul was writing, it is possible to see the image of the "hissing snakes," with "darting tongues over a yard long," as an attempt to make visible these otherwise invisible emissions.

Oddoul's chosen mode of magical realism enables him to create alternative worlds, where the geographically, socially and economically marginalised can revise the reality created by established powers. It allows him a vehicle for political criticism of colonialist and nationalist bodies perhaps not possible in other literary modes. Stephen Slemon argues that, "by conveying the binary, and often dominating, oppositions of real social conditions through the 'speaking mirror' of their literary language, magic realist texts implicitly suggest that enabling strategies for the future require revisioning the seemingly tyrannical units of the past in a complex and imaginative double-think of 'remembering the future.'"[99] Accordingly, Oddoul's text can be read as testimony to the colonialist and nationalist violence perpetrated against the Nubians and their

---

95 Gary Wockner, "Dams Cause Climate Change, They Are Not Clean Energy," *Echo Watch* (August 14, 2014), https://www.ecowatch.com/dams-cause-climate-change-they-are-not-clean-energy-1881943019.html.

96 Ivan B.T. Lima et al, "Methane Emissions from Large Dams as Renewable Energy Resources: A Developing Nation Perspective," *Mitigation and Adaptation Strategies for Global Change* 13 (2008): 193–206.

97 "Greenhouse Gas Emissions from Dams," *International Rivers* (May 2007), https://www.internationalrivers.org/sites/default/files/attached-files/globalresghgsfaq.pdf.

98 "Greenhouse Gas Emissions from Dams".

99 Stephen Slemon, "Magic Realism as Post-Colonial Discourse," *Magic & Other Realisms. Special issue of Canadian Literature* 116 (Spring 1988): 9–24.

ASWAN HIGH DAM AND HAGGAG ODDOUL'S *STORIES FROM OLD NUBIA*   301

environment, and as contributing to the discourse of climate change *avant la lettre*.[100]

The tragic impact of the dam's construction relates directly to its halting of "the yearly flood that came slowly, pouring gently into the sprawling water course," carrying "brown goodness with a touch of red, full of fertile silt, seeping into the life-giving earth."[101] Oddoul emphasises this tragic impact in two contrasting images, representing the two sides of the High Dam. The first image portrays the reservoir's swift inundation of Old Nubia through the despairing voice of Asha Ashry as she speaks to the river and its people: "I stopped by the last hanging house. I looked at the drowned valley below me, eaten up by flood. What have they done to you, our river? They made you devour our plantations!"[102] The second portrays the slow violence of escalating deprivation as it spreads along the Nile Valley and Delta, this time in the voice of Hulla, who sees it as a consequence of "the anger of the river, the anger of the mighty Nile," in response to its becoming "as emaciated as one of the shallow irrigation canals of the north."[103] The slow violence has many faces: the drought, that affects the river and the land; the putrified air, reflecting climatic degradation; the withered crops that bring the "rats and lice and blood," underscoring the disturbed balance of things. All of this has its basis in reality, even the soaring rat population, which the annual flood used to keep under control, submerging the many nooks, crannies and caves where they lived and multiplied.[104]

Against the hegemony of Egypt's nationalist discourse, Oddoul raises a cry of resistance in the voice of Asha Ashry, who speaks directly to the river, and to the "people of the river:"

---

100   The First Assessment Report (FAR) of the Intergovernmental Panel on Climate Change (IPCC) was not issued until 1990. In it, scientists stated confidently the existence and cause of climate change. It served as the basis of the United Nations Framework Convention on Climate Change (UNFCCC), which argues: there was a natural greenhouse effect that keeps the Earth warmer than it would otherwise be; and that emissions resulting from human activities were substantially increasing the atmospheric concentrations of the greenhouse gases: carbon dioxide, methane, chlorofluorocarbons (CFCs) and nitrous oxide. These increases will only enhance the greenhouse effect, warming the Earth's surface further. The main greenhouse gas, water vapour, will increase in response to global warming and further enhance it. J.T. Houghton, G.J. Jenkins, J.J. Ephraums, Intergovernmental Panel on Climate Change, Working Group I, *Climate Change: The IPCC Scientific Assessment* (Cambridge & New York: Cambridge UP, 1990): xi.

101   Oddoul, *Nights of Musk*, 100.

102   Oddoul, *Nights of Musk*, 115.

103   Oddoul, *Nights of Musk*, 75.

104   Chris Maser, *Ecological Diversity in Sustainable Development: The Vital and Forgotten Dimension* (Boca Raton, Fla: Lewis, 1999): 282.

They have hurled the dam into your vast body and bruised it. They have raised it up over your solemn timeless melody. Be strong, mighty meandering river, for I am like you. The dam has destroyed my life. I was born the year it was built, and what an evil omen that was [...] Smash the dam to pieces. Flex your muscles in anger. Bring forth an invincible flood, not around the sides but headlong into the high wall.[105]

As Oddoul shows, the "sacred march towards industrialisation" by which Nasser hoped to unite the nation in fact caused the earliest crack in its foundations. He exposes the emptiness and fragility of the nationalists' discourse, as Fanon had anticipated:

[N]ational consciousness, instead of being the all-embracing crystallization of the innermost hopes of the whole people, instead of being the immediate and most obvious result of the mobilisation of the people, will be in any case only an empty shell, a crude and fragile travesty of what it might have been.[106]

The incapacity of the nationalist middle class (which rose to power after decolonisation) to acknowledge the dissatisfactions of the lower classes is a weakness "almost congenital to the national consciousness of underdeveloped countries."[107] This, Fanon argues, was not solely a result of the mutilations inflicted on colonised people by their oppressors; it was also a consequence "of the intellectual laziness of the national middle class, of its spiritual penury, and of the profoundly cosmopolitan mold that its mind is set in."[108]

In India in 1958, Jawaharlal Nehru, who had previously placed mega-dams such as the Bhakra Dam in Himachal Pradesh among the "new temples of India,"[109] came to recognise the effect of what he called "the disease of gigantism."[110] This gigantism, according to Nehru, is a "dangerous outlook," which developed in India after the Raj with the idea of " having big undertakings and

---

105   Oddoul, *Nights of Musk*, 105.
106   Frantz Fanon, *The Wretched of the Earth*, trans. Constance Farrington (New York: Grove Press, 1963): 148.
107   Fanon, *The Wretched of the Earth*, 149.
108   Fanon, *The Wretched of the Earth,*149.
109   "When the Big Dams Came Up," *The Hindu* (March 20, 2015), https://www.thehindu.com/todays-paper/tp-national/when-the-big-dams-came-up/article7013509.ece.
110   "When the Big Dams Came Up".

doing big things for the sake of showing that we can do big things."[111] Eventually Nehru came to realise that "the small irrigation projects, the small industries and the small plants for electric power" offered a better outlook for a sustainable future.[112] Nasser did not live to see the social and ecological consequences of the construction of the High Dam. However, the rhetoric of his rule remains pervasive, reverberating all over Africa, Asia and South America, even though the mega-dams have proved more potent in serving the interests of the developed world than the needs of people in the developing world. As Arundhati Roy wrote in "The Greater Common Good" in 2001, "the dam-building industry in the first world is in trouble and out of work, so it is exported to the third world in the name of development aid [... but] aid is just another practorian interprise, like colonialism was. It has destroyed most of Africa."[113] That statment remains valid today.

While the major powers of the developed world have been decommissioning thousands of dams to liberate their rivers since the 1990s,[114] their agents are still active in commissioning new ones in the developing world. In 2017, the French government decided to remove the Vezins Dam (almost one hundred years old and thirty-five metres high) and La Roche Qui Boit Dam (fifteen metres high) from the Selune River in Normandy.[115] The decommissioning of European dams marks a shift in Europe's approach to rivers that aims at "bringing life back" to these rivers. As Roy predicted, however, this puts the dam-building industry in the developed world. But does this decommissioning recognise the role of the mega-dams in boosting climate change? No, for the developed world, the reputation of mega-dams as sources of clean energy must be maintained, so that the dams-building industry can continue in the developing world. In 2013 the French company Alstom signed a major contract to supply turbines and

---

111   C.V.J. Sharma, *Modern Temples of India: Selected Speeches of Jawaharlal Nehru at Irrigation and Power Projects* (New Delhi: Central Board of Irrigation and Power, 1989): 40.

112   Nixon, *Slow Violence*, 168.

113   Arundhati Roy, "The Greater Common Good," *Liberating the Rivers,* Echo Watch (January/February 2001): 34.

114   According to Pao Fernández Garrido of Dam Removal Europe, "Europe is actually leading the world when it comes to the demolition of dams. It has previously been thought that the USA was ahead of the pack, with more than 1,300 documented dams removed. However, Europe has managed to demolish over 4,500 barriers. According to their records, France has removed more than 2,300 barriers, naturally or artificially." Garrido, Pao Fernández, "Interview with Dam Removal Europe," *Sustain Europe* at http://www.sustaineurope.com/interview-with-dam-removal-europe-20180224.html.

115   "River revolution in Europe as France launches largest dam removal project on the continent," *Panda,* http://wwf.panda.org/?317031/River-revolution-in-Europe-as-France-lacnhes-largest-dam-removal-project-on-the-continent.

generators for the hydropower plant of the Grand Renaissance Dam, located on the Blue Nile in Ethiopia.[116] Jérome Pécresse, President of Alstom Renewable Power, stated: "This contract strengthens Alstom's prominent position in the African hydropower market."[117] Alstom has been active for eighty years in Mozambique, Angola, Ghana, South Africa and Sudan and, more recently, in Uganda, Zambia and the Democratic Republic of Congo.[118] France is not the only European country involved in the construction of mega-dams in Africa.[119] With Sinohydro, probably the world's largest hydropower company, China also has entered the competition for African dam construction.[120]

More alarming, though, is the competition between authoritarian regimes with long records of human rights violations—China and Saudi Arabia for instance—to finance new dams in Africa. In 2010, the Sudanese government awarded a $705 million five-year contract for the Kajbar Dam to the Chinese company Sinohydro.[121] The finance for this was mostly provided as a loan from China. Africa's huge Chinese debt threatens to lock it in a debt trap that could lead to a new form of colonialism.[122] The Kajbar Dam and the proposed Dal Dam are both to be built on ancestral Nubian land. These dams will displace more than 15,000 people, and their reservoirs will submerge five hundred archaeological sites. The Nubians are resisting. But the Sudanese government has reacted to the Nubians' peaceful demonstrations with extreme violence. The Nubians thought that the Kajbar project had been abandoned after the affected communities called upon Sinohydro to withdraw from the

---

116   Alstom, "Alstom to supply hydroelectric equipment for the Grand Renaissance dam in Ethiopia" (January 7, 2013), https://www.alstom.com/press-releases-news/2013/1/alstom-to-supply-hydroelectric-equipment-for-the-grand-renaissance-dam-in-ethiopia.

117   Alstom, "Alstom to supply hydroelectric equipment".

118   Alstom, "Alstom to supply hydroelectric equipment".

119   Companies from across Europe are involved in the construction of other mega-dams such as the Katse Dam (1996), the Merowe Dam (2009), the Tekezé Dam (2009) and Gilgel Gibe III Dam (2015). The Italian company Salini Impregilo, the French Bouygues, the German Hochtief and the British Kier are a few examples.

120   "China's Biggest Bank to Support Africa's Most Destructive Dam," *International Rivers* (May 13, 2010), https://www.internationalrivers.org/resources/china%E2%80%99s-biggest-bank-to-support-africa%E2%80%99s-most-destructive-dam-3758; "Chinese dams in Africa," *International Rivers*, https://www.internationalrivers.org/campaigns/chinese-dams-in-africa.

121   "Kajbar Dam, Sudan," *International Rivers*, https://www.internationalrivers.org/campaigns/kajbar-dam-sudan.

122   François Picard, "Debt trap? The allure of Chinese money in Africa," *France 24* (September 4, 2018): https://www.france24.com/en/20180903-debate-china-xi-jinping-investment-africa-construction.

contract.[123] But in November 2015 the Sudanese government announced that Saudi Arabia had committed to invest 1.7 billion U.S dollars in the construction of three dams: the Kajbar, the Dal and Shereik.[124] The announcement came a few months after "Sudan joined the Saudi-led military coalition against Houthi rebels," who were accused by Riyadh of being "a proxy to Iran in the region,"[125] raising concerns over extending the conflict in the Middle East to Africa. However, the climatological threat posed by the dams is barely addressed; on the contrary, they are presented as a solution to halting climate change. According to a 1 Gigaton Coalition report published in November 2017 by the United Nations, hydropower is categorised among the renewable energy technologies recommended to mitigate global warming (along with solar, wind, biomass/waste and geothermal technologies).[126]

As Geoff Davis demonstrated earlier in this volume, postcolonial writers like Roy in India and Ken Saro-Wiwa in Nigeria have sought to reveal to their readers the links between the old imperialism and the new transnational agents of development. Oddoul belongs in their company. He shows beyond doubt that social injustice and ecological violence (from which climate change is inseparable) are deeply rooted in the colonial ideology of development, widely incorporated into the nationalist agendas of formerly colonised nations, and incarnated in globalisation. Embedded in the project of modernisation, this colonialist ideology is born of a conception of "nature" that, as Bruno Latour argues, "has allowed the Moderns to occupy the Earth in such a way that it forbids others to occupy their own territories differently."[127] To change the politics, one needs agents with ecological interests matched by a capacity for action. But it is not possible to make alliances between "political actors and objects that are external to society and deprived of the power to act,"[128] Latour explains. The dilemma, as Latour sees it, is well expressed by the French Zadists: "We are not defending nature, we are nature defending itself."[129] In any case, the modern ideology of progress and development, and the conception

---

123   "Kajbar Dam," *International Rivers*.

124   "Saudi Arabia to Provide 1.7 Billion Dollars for Sudan's Dam Projects," *Sudan Tribune* (November 6, 2015), http://www.sudantribune.com/spip.php?article56960.

125   "Saudia Arabia to Provide 1.7 Billion Dollars".

126   1 Gigaton Coalition, *Renewable Energy and Energy Efficiency in Developing Countries: Contributions to Reducing Global Emissions* (United Nations Environment Programme, 2017): 78.

127   Bruno Latour, *Down to Earth: Politics in the New Climatic Regime* (Cambridge: Polity Press, 2018): 64.

128   Latour, *Down to Earth*, 64.

129   Latour, *Down to Earth*, 64.

of "nature" that comes with it, alienates the human-animal from its natural environment, the social from the ecological, and eventually the global from the terrestrial. Oddoul's *Nights of Musk* conveys the same message as the Zadists— "we are nature." The violence against the river is reflected in the agonies of its people.

As Lawrence Smith writes, rivers have served human civilisations "ever since our first great societies rose along the banks of the Tigris-Euphrates, Indus, Nile, and Yellow Rivers in present-day Iraq, India-Pakistan, Egypt and China."[130] In many ways, history begins on the banks of the rivers where human-animals wisely integrated their lives with the water cycle. The Promethean proponents of mega-dams see these rivers as resources to exploit, without any consideration of the societies that are rooted in their ecology. *Nights of Musk* renders scientific warnings about the climatological impact of mega-dams' visible and audible. Oddoul's stories show how mega-dams like the Aswan High Dam enforce the separation of culture and nature, societies and their ecological habitats. Many postcolonial writers now seek to expose the social and ecological shortcomings of the developments that exploit their homelands. Oddoul was an early exponent of the evolving environmental consciousness of postcolonial literatures. With climate change as an optic, enabling readers to re-vision the past imaginatively through the lens of the present, we may yet evolve strategies for a future that avoids the climate catastrophe we are otherwise facing.

Acknowledgements

In memory of Geoffrey V. Davis. No words can describe your graceful soul. I am thankful to Prof. Russell McDougall, Dr. John Ryan and Dr. Pauline Reynolds for their intellectual contribution and all the help they offered me. This chapter would not be possible without their kindness and support.

Works Cited

Abu-Zeid. M.A., F.Z. El-Shibini. "Egypt's High Aswan Dam." *Water Resources Development* 13.2 (1997): 209–217.

---

130   Lawrence Smith, *Rivers of Power: How a Natural Force Raised Kingdoms, Destroyed Civilizations, and Shapes Our World* (London, Penguin, 2020): 6.

Andrew, Robbie M. "Global CO2 emissions from cement production." *CICERO Center for International Climate Research*, Norway (January 26, 2018).

Alstom. "Alstom to Supply Hydroelectric Equipment for the Grand Renaissance Dam in Ethiopia" (January 7, 2013), https://www.alstom.com/press-releases-news/2013/1/alstom-to-supply-hydroelectric-equipment-for-the-grand-renaissance-dam-in-ethiopia.

Ali, Idris. *Dongola: A Novel of Nubia*, trans. Peter Theroux (Fayetteville: U of Arkansas P, 1998).

Ali, Idris. *Poor,* trans. Elliott Colla (Cairo: The American U In Cairo P, 2007).

Belal, Ahmed, John Briggs, Johan Sharp and Irina Springuel. *Bedouins by the Lake: Environment Change, and Sustainability in Southern Egypt.* (Cairo: The American U in Cairo P, 2009).

Climate Links. "Climate Change Information Fact Sheet Egypt." https://www.climatelinks.org/sites/default/files/asset/document/Egypt%20Climate%20Info%20Fact%20Sheet_FINAL.pdf.

Dryzek, John S. *The Politics of the Earth: Environmental Discourses*, 3rd ed. (Oxford: Oxford UP, 2013).

El-Said, Mohammed. "How Climate Change Threatens Egypt's Coasts, Agriculture." *Daily News Egypt* (January 24, 2018), https://dailynewsegypt.com/2018/01/24/climate-change-threatens-egypts-coasts-agriculture/.

Fanon, Frantz. *The Wretched of the Earth*, trans. Constance Farrington (New York: Grove Press, 1963).

Fernea, Robert A. *Nubian Ceremonial Life: Studies in Islamic Syncretism and Cultural Change* (Cairo: American U in Cairo P, 1978).

Faulkner, R.O. *The Ancient Egyptian Book of the Dead*, 2nd ed. (London: British Museum Publications, 1985).

"Fertilizer use responsible for increase in nitrous oxide in atmosphere." University of California Berkeley, http://news.berkeley.edu/2012/04/02/fertilizer-use-responsible-for-increase-in-nitrous-oxide-in-atmosphere/.

Garrido, Pao Fernández. "Interview with Dam Removal Europe", http://www.sustaineurope.com/interview-with-dam-removal-europe-20180224.html.

Ginat, Rami. *Egypt's Incomplete Revolution: Lutfi Al-Khuli and Nasser's Socialism in the 1960s* (London: Frank Cass, 1997).

Gohary, Jocelyn. *Guide to the Nubian Monuments on Lake Nasser* (Cairo: The American U in Cairo P, 1998).

Griffith, R. Drew. "Homeric ΔΙΙΠΕΤΕΟΣ ΠΟΤΑΜΟΙΟ and the Celestial Nile." *The American Journal of Philology* 118.3 (Autumn, 1997): 353–362.

Hopkins, Nicholas and Sohair Mehanna. *Nubian Encounters: The Story of the Nubian Ethnological Survey 1961–1964.* (New York: The American U in Cairo P, 2010).

Houghton, J.T., G.J. Jenkins, J.J. Ephraums. Intergovernmental Panel on Climate Change, Working Group I. *Climate Change: The IPCC Scientific Assessment* (Cambridge and New York: Cambridge UP, 1990).

Ions, Veronica. *Egyptian Mythology.* (Middlesex: Paul Hamlyn, 1965).

International Rivers. "Greenhouse Gas Emissions from Dams." (May 2007), https://www.internationalrivers.org/sites/default/files/attached-files/globalresghgsfaq.pdf.

International Rivers. "China's Biggest Bank to Support Africa's Most Destructive Dam." (May 13, 2010), https://www.internationalrivers.org/resources/china%E2%80%99s-biggest-bank-to-support-africa%E2%80%99s-most-destructive-dam-3758.

International Rivers. "Chinese Dams in Africa," https://www.internationalrivers.org/campaigns/chinese-dams-in-africa.

International Rivers. "Kajbar Dam, Sudan," https://www.internationalrivers.org/campaigns/kajbar-dam-sudan.

Jacquemond, Richard. *Conscience of the Nation: Writers, State, and Society in Modern Egypt*, trans. from French by David Tresilian (Cairo & New York: The American U in Cairo P, 2008).

Johnson, R.G. "Climate Control Requires a Dam at the Strait of Gibraltar." *EOS, Transactions, American Geophysical Union* 78 (1997): 277–281.

Latour, Bruno. *Down to Earth: Politics in the New Climatic Regime* (Cambridge: Polity Press, 2018): 64–67.

Leslie, Jacques. *Deep Water: The Epic Struggle over Dams, Displaced People, and the Environment*, 1st ed. (New York: Farrar, Straus and Giroux, 2005).

Lima, Ivan, B.T. Lima, Ivan, Fernando Ramos, Luis Bambace and Reinaldo Rosa. "Methane Emissions from Large Dams as Renewable Energy Resources: A Developing Nation Perspective." *Mitigation and Adaptation Strategies for Global Change* 13 (2008): 193–206.

Mann, Michael. *A 'Perfect Storm': Extreme Winter Weather, Bitter Cold, and Climate Change*, The Climate Reality Project. (January 4, 2018), https://www.climatereality project.org/blog/perfect-storm-extreme-winter-weather-bitter-cold-and-climate-change.

Maser, Chris. *Ecological Diversity in Sustainable Development: The Vital and Forgotten Dimension* (Boca Raton, Fla: Lewis, 1999).

Mayer, Michael S. *The Eisenhower Years.* (New York: Infobase Publishing, 2010).

Murād, Zakī. *Sirb al-balashūn: ashʿār min al-Nūbah* (Cairo: Dār al-Kātib al-ʿArabi, 1969).

Nasser, Gamal Abdel. Speech on the Nationalization of Sueze Canal, Mansheya Square, Alexandria (July 26, 1956), https://www.youtube.com/watch?v=YFyIVC6bmzk.

Nasser, Gamal Abdel. Speech on the Completion of the Construction of Aswan High Dam. (July 23, 1970), https://www.youtube.com/watch?v=bMcOi9i0PtM.

Nixon, Rob. *Slow Violence and the Environmentalism of the Poor.* (Cambridge, MA.: Harvard UP, 2011).

Oddoul, Haggag. *Nights of Musk: Stories from Old Nubia*, trans. Anthony Calderbank (Cairo and New York: The American U in Cairo P, 2008).

Oddoul, Haggag. "Haggag Hassan Adoul: Nubia's Human Aspirations." Interview conducted by Hosam Aboul-Ela, http://thenubian.net/haggag/enterview.doc.

"River Revolution in Europe as France Launches Largest Dam Removal Project on the Continent," http://wwf.panda.org/?317031/River-revolution-in-Europe-as-France-launches-largest-dam-removal-project-on-the-continent.

Peel, Sidney. *The Binding of the Nile and the New Sudan*. (London: Edward Arnold, 1904).

Penfield, Frederic Courtland. "Harnessing the Nile." *Century Magazine* 57.4 (February 1899), https://en.wikisource.org/wiki/Century_Magazine/Volume_57/Issue_4/Harnessing_the_Nile.

Picard, François. "Debt Trap? The Allure of Chinese Money in Africa," (September 4, 2018), https://www.france24.com/en/20180903-debate-china-xi-jinping-investment-africa-construction.

Qassem, Muhammad Khalil. *al-Shamandūrah: Awwal Riwāyah Nūbīyah fī Tārīkh al-Adab al-ʿArabī* (Cairo: Dār al-Kātib al-ʿArabī, 1968).

Roy, Arundhati. "Before the Flood," *The Amicus Journal* (Fall 2000): 12–18.

Roy, Arundhati. "The Greater Common Good," *Liberating the Rivers*, Echo Watch (January/February 2001): 33–36.

Sanders, Robert, "Fertilizer Use Responsible for Increase in Nitrous Oxide in Atmosphere." *Berkley News* (April 2, 2012), http://news.berkeley.edu/2012/04/02/fertilizer-use-responsible-for-increase-in-nitrous-oxide-in-atmosphere/.

"Saudi Arabia to Provide 1.7 billion Dollars for Sudan's Dam Projects." *Sudan Tribune* (November 6, 2015), http://www.sudantribune.com/spip.php?article56960.

Sharma, C. V. J. ed. *Modern Temples of India: Selected Speeches of Jawaharlal Nehru at Irrigation and Power Projects*. (New Delhi: Central Board of Irrigation and Power, 1989).

Smith, Lawrence. *Rivers of Power: How a Natural Force Raised Kingdoms, Destroyed Civilizations, and Shapes Our World*. (London, Penguin, 2020).

Steffen, Will, Jacques Grinevald, Paul Crutzen, John McNeill. "The Anthropocene: Conceptual and Historical Perspectives." *Philosophical Transactions: Mathematical, Physical and Engineering Sciences* 369.1938 (2011): 842–867.

Slemon, Stephen. "Magic Realism as Post-Colonial Discourse." *Magic & Other Realisms. Spec. issue of Canadian Literature* 116 (Spring 1988): 9–24.

The 1 Gigaton Coalition. *Renewable Energy and Energy Efficiency in Developing Countries: Contributions to Reducing Global Emissions* (United Nations Environment Programme, 2017), https://wedocs.unep.org/bitstream/handle/20.500.11822/22149/1_Gigaton_Third%20Report_EN.pdf?sequence=1.

"When the Big Dams Came Up," (March 20, 2015), https://www.thehindu.com/todays-paper/tp-national/when-the-big-dams-came-up/article7013509.ece.

Wilkinson, Richard H. *The Complete Gods and Goddesses of Ancient Egypt* (London: Thames and Hudson, 2003).

Wockner, Gary. "Dams Cause Climate Change, They Are Not Clean Energy." *Echo Watch* (August 14, 2014), https://www.ecowatch.com/dams-cause-climate-change-they -are-not-clean-energy-1881943019.html.

CHAPTER 11

Caring for the Future

Climate Change, Kinship and Inuit Knowledge

Renée Hulan

In *The Great Derangement*, Amitav Ghosh observes that "we need only glance through the pages of a few highly regarded literary journals and book reviews" to confirm that "climate change casts a much smaller shadow within the landscape of literary fiction than it does even in the public arena."[1] A similar glance at the lists of winners and nominees for the major literary prizes in Canada leads to the same conclusion. Likewise, perusing the yearly roundup of new work in the "Letters in Canada" section of the *University of Toronto Quarterly* reveals no sharp turn towards the environment in the past twenty years, though stories and poems that engage with nature, landscape, region and place have been a core part of Canadian literature throughout its history. While the non-fiction shelves are laden with books about the environment, global warming and climate change, fiction devoted to the theme remains scarce. Instead, Canadian literary fiction explores the themes of what Ghosh calls "moral adventure" that characterize the human experience of a contemporary multicultural society: exile, arrival, self-discovery, family. The new genre of cli-fi only seems to accentuate Ghosh's point that global warming has been banished from the "mansion of literature" to the "outhouses" of genre fiction. At the end of his essay, Ghosh imagines a future generation capable of seeing differently, and he hopes "that they will be able to transcend the isolation in which humanity was entrapped in the time of its derangement; that they will rediscover their kinship with other beings, and that this vision, at once new and ancient, will find expression in a transformed and renewed art and literature."[2]

The privileged position of literary fiction was illustrated in the 2017 CBC Canada Reads competition when Sheila Watt-Cloutier's *The Right to be Cold* was nominated for selection as the book everyone should read. *The Right to Be Cold* documents the role Indigenous peoples are playing in bringing attention to climate change and negotiating measures to deal with it at the international

---

1 Amitav Ghosh, *The Great Derangement: Climate Change and the Unthinkable* (Chicago: U of Chicago P, 2016): 7.
2 Ghosh, *The Great,* 162.

© KONINKLIJKE BRILL NV, LEIDEN, 2022 | DOI:10.1163/9789004514164_012

level. In it, Watt-Cloutier argues that the right to be cold is a human right and that "the future of Inuit is the future of the rest of the world—our home is a barometer for what is happening to our entire planet."[3] Despite the urgency of the book's subject, *The Right to Be Cold* was eliminated early in the competition which clearly favoured literary fiction. Discussing these events in *Climate Change and Writing the Canadian Arctic*, I argued that we need to look beyond literary fiction to genres like the memoir in order to escape the state of derangement Ghosh describes.[4] Broadening the frame of reference and abandoning the categories that demarcate genres and media, might also lead to giving up the distinction between human and nonhuman; indeed, we might abandon the notions of "human" and "nonhuman" altogether as we stop making ourselves the point of reference for everything else.

Even though climate change denial is not prominent in Canadian public discourse, there is a tendency to want to look away from what thoughtful observers are calling "Arcticide."[5] In "The Endangered Arctic, the Arctic as Resource Frontier: Canadian News Media Narratives of Climate Change and the North," Mark Stoddart and Jillian Smith found not only that the Arctic is "not central to Canadian news about climate change" but also that the "nationalization" of the issue by Canadian media presents change in the Arctic as having both costs and benefits. Given that the stark division in the discourse between ecological costs and economic opportunity, it is not surprising that "climate justice framing is marginal"; instead, coverage in Canadian media offers a mixed message concerning the Arctic's fate: "Three main issue categories frame climate change and the Arctic. In order of prevalence, these are the broad theme that global climate change is rapidly and substantially transforming the Arctic; climate change harms polar bear populations; and melting sea ice offers new shipping routes in the Arctic."[6] The ambivalence towards changes in the Arctic that the study found may account, in part, for the apparent preference for literary fiction that turns away from the crisis.

As if to illustrate Ghosh's point, climate change stories are often categorised as, and feature prominently in, genre fiction such as the recent anthology

---

3   Sheila Watt-Cloutier, *The Right to Be Cold: One Woman's Story of Protecting her Culture, the Arctic, and the Whole Planet* (Toronto: Allen Lane, 2015): xi.

4   For the full analysis of Watt-Cloutier's work, see Renée Hulan, *Climate Change and Writing the Canadian Arctic* (New York: Palgrave, 2018): 52–81.

5   John McCannon, *A History of the Arctic: Nature, Exploration and Exploitation* (London: Reaktion, 2012).

6   Mark C. J. Stoddart and Jillian Smith, "The Endangered Arctic, the Arctic as Resource Frontier: Canadian News Media Narratives of Climate Change and the North," *Canadian Sociological Association/La Société canadienne de sociologie* 53.3 (2016): 326.

CLI-FI: Canadian Tales of Climate Change, Margaret Atwood's MaddAddam series and Cherie Dimaline's *The Marrow Thieves*. In *The Marrow Thieves*, the narrator, Frenchie, joins up with other Indigenous people fleeing north. Each night they listen to their leader Miigwans tell the story of the Water Wars and the Melt, the events that have brought them together. As Miigwans carefully spins out his tale, leaving the ending for another day, Frenchie, pressed by the young girl RiRi, paraphrases:

> After the rains started and the lands shifted so that some cities fell right into the oceans, people had to move around. Diseases spread like crazy. With all this sickness and movement and death, people got sad. One of the ways the sadness came out was when they slept. They stopped being able to dream.[7]

Because Indigenous people in the novel still possess the power to dream in their bone marrow, they are being hunted for it and incarcerated in centres where their marrow is extracted. In a post-apocalyptic world typical of cli-fi, the action resonates with the history of removing Indigenous children to residential schools in Canada as *The Marrow Thieves* powerfully evokes the strength of Indigenous beliefs in the aftermath of environmental destruction.

Contemporary literature written in English and French by Indigenous writers such as Dimaline and theory like Stó:lō professor Jo-ann Archibald/Q'um Q'um Xiiem's storywork, which is based on seven principles that articulate Indigenous values, highlight the potential of Indigenous knowledge to contribute to the fight against climate change.[8] As Margery Fee notes in *Literary Land Claims*, "The decolonization of Canadian literature will require a new genre of academic writing, one that signals its acknowledgement not only of emerging from Indigenous land, but also of learning from Indigenous storied thinking."[9] While Indigenous knowledge has yet to be accepted in academic institutions as expertise with the same authority as university education, Indigenous scholars and their allies are transforming methodologies and disciplines according to Indigenous principles and values. In this chapter, I read the healing literary and visual culture created and produced by Inuit artists Tanya Tagaq and Zacharias Kunuk. This work is crucial to collective knowledge

---

7   Cherie Dimaline, *The Marrow Thieves* (Toronto: Cormorant Books, 2017): 29.

8   Jo-Ann Archibald/Q'um Q'um Xiiem, *Indigenous Storywork: Educating the Heart, Mind and Spirit* (Vancouver: U of British Columbia P, 2008).

9   Margery Fee, *Literary Land Claims: The "Indian Land Question" from Pontiac's War to Attiwapiskat* (Waterloo: Wilfrid Laurier UP, 2015): 223.

and understanding of the consequences of environmental degradation, and, as I argue, care needs to be taken with it so as not to perpetuate the colonialism that has led us to this place.

While there is relatively little Canadian literary fiction that tackles climate change as a problem in the way Ghosh does in *The Hungry Tide*, literary and cultural theorists are approaching the subject by expanding their frame of reference beyond literary fiction and by reading contemporary culture through the lens of climate change and through the lived experience of those most affected by it, including Inuit communities experiencing its profound impact on traditional lifeways. As Nancy Wachowich has shown in her study of Isuma Productions, Inuit tradition has never been static. What is understood as Inuit traditional knowledge, Inuit *Quajimajatuqangit*, today has been shaped over centuries and in relation to others: "Since the early contact period, southerners have reinforced idealized and exoticized notions of the remote and pristine arctic environment and the authentic Inuit who inhabit that landscape," and Inuit "use these iconic categories in their own cultural productions as a way to communicate social agendas."[10] According to Wachowich, the "hunt for tradition" has been incorporated into economic activities, even the hunt itself, creating a "new Inuit cultural capital" to be consumed in the first instance by the youth who are learning how to navigate the social and political landscape inhabited by granting agencies, government departments, and charitable organizations and by "secondary consumers" such as journalists, scholars, and other outsiders, including tourists.[11] Indeed, before tradition became a form of cultural capital, it would not have been labelled "tradition" but how things are done, and Wachowich acknowledges the considerable role of outsiders in shaping how tradition is being reimagined:

> Arctic anthropology's development as a discipline has helped to transform the tundra, the Inuit, and their material culture into objects of investigation for science. In the face of this cultural intrusion, Inuit creatively transformed these symbolically laden traits into politically effectual emblems of the contrast between Inuit and qalunaat worlds.[12]

---

10   Nancy Wachowich, "Cultural Survival and the Trade in Iglulingmiut Traditions," *Critical Inuit Studies: An Anthology of Contemporary Arctic Ethnography* (Lincoln: U of Nebraska P, 2006): 121.

11   Wachowich, "Cultural Survival and the Trade in Iglulingmiut Traditions," 129–131.

12   "Cultural Survival and the Trade in Iglulingmiut Traditions," 127.

CARING FOR THE FUTURE

The representation of Inuit "walking the border between two worlds," as in the title of Alootook Ipellie's poem,[13] emerges from resistance to being rendered artifacts for western science. The constant "hunt for tradition" Wachowich observes shows the adaptability of Inuit knowledge in the constant evolution of hunting.

Isuma's 2010 film *Qapirangajuq: Inuit Knowledge and Climate Change* by award-winning director Zacharias Kunuk in collaboration with environmental scientist Ian Mauro combines classic techniques of both documentary film making and Inuit storytelling.[14] Interviews with Elders from Igloolik, Iqaluit, Pangnirtung and other communities are edited together with long shots of the land and water in the Arctic that illustrate the stories being told. The ethnographic approach by which the people are filmed in the environment is interspersed with indoor shots of Elders speaking to an interviewer just off camera. These techniques ground the film in the "detailed knowledge of local practices and power relations on the ground" that Julie Cruikshank calls for in *Do Glaciers Listen?* As she argues, the detailed, situated knowledge of practices and relationships must be found in the stories of lived experience because "the aftermaths of colonialism are always local."[15] The stories told in *Qapirangajuq* are firmly and precisely located. As Faye Ginsburg observes, "the film challenges western conventions for understanding climate change by offering an Inuit angle."[16] The Elders tell that it is no longer possible to predict the weather by looking at the sky, the first thing every Inuit child is taught to do each morning. The Elders describe how the river running through Pangnirtung suddenly changed course in 2008 and tell of the disappearance of glaciers and the multiyear ice as well as icebergs. In each case, they explain the occurrence in terms of the difference from what was known of the land in the past. The change in the behaviour of animals reveals the new climate: for example, seals move differently, diving into their breathing holes on an angle if the ice is thin, and animals are appearing in different times and places.

---

13   Alootook Ipellie, "Walking Both Sides of an Invisible Border," *An Anthology of Canadian Native Literature in English*, eds. Daniel David Moses and Terry Goldie (Toronto: Oxford UP, 1992): 333.

14   *Qapirangajuq: Inuit Knowledge and Climate Change*, directed by Zacharias Kunuk and Ian Mauro, 2009. isuma.tv/inuit-knowledge-and-climate-change.

15   Julie Cruikshank, *Do Glaciers Listen? Local Knowledge, Colonial Encounters, and Social Imagination* (Vancouver: U of British Columbia P, 2005): 9.

16   Faye Ginsberg, "Isuma TV, Visual Sovereignty, and the Arctic Media World" in *Arctic Cinemas and the Documentary Ethos*, eds. Lilya Kaganovsky, Scott MacKenzie and Anna Westerstahl Stenport (Bloomington: Indiana UP, 2019): 264.

In "Materializing Climate Change: Images of Exposure, States of Exception," Nicole Shukin observes "a distributed agency" in "the rich visual and aural text of *Qapirangajuq*": "Ice, wind, and animals are attributed a kind of agency that, again, counters modern liberal-humanist traditions that reify agency in the willing, autonomous subject."[17] Shukin's discussion of the film is used to contrast "a salvage paradigm that frames both Indigenous peoples and wildlife as doomed to disappear in the face of technological modernity" which she establishes in a fulsome account of artworks created by British artists on the Cape Farewell expedition. In contrast to the tourists' view, the Inuit interviewed in the film, according to Shukin, resist the salvage paradigm with their own experiences. For example, in climate crisis literature, "polar bears are mourned in the future anterior tense as animals that soon will have disappeared with vanishing ice formations" but "several Inuit comment that polar bears are superb swimmers more than capable of surviving warming oceans and thinning ice sheets."[18] "We never saw bears," says Evie Anilnilliak from Pangnirtung. Inookie Adamie from Iqaluit confirms this, and Joanasie Karpik tells how there were no bears when he was a young man but that bears and ravens are more plentiful on land now that the amount of floating ice has decreased. As Mauro explained, "The stories of those interviewed also helped scientists better understand the range of unique and dramatic climate impacts taking place"; for example, atmospheric scientists were able to "confirm a hypothesis about global warming's ability to produce visual distortions" based on the Elders' "observations of how the sun, moon and stars were shifting."[19]

As climate change creates new forms of Inuit knowledge, Inuit leaders and artists are working to bring Inuit perspectives to a world still in the grip of climate change denial and skepticism. Inuit have been observing and adapting to the changes in the environment as they grapple with what it means. The role film has taken on as a new form of storytelling reveals how artificial the stark separation of tradition and modernity is, especially as it concerns life in the Anthropocene, and how knowledge and ways of knowing are continuing to change over time. In alliances forged to combat the environmental and social

---

17 Nicole Shukin, "Materializing Climate Change: Images of Exposure, States of Exception," *Material Cultures in Canada*, eds. Thomas Allen and Jennifer Blair (Waterloo, ON: Wilfrid-Laurier UP, 2015): 203.

18 Shukin, "Materializing Climate Change," 202.

19 *Qapirangajuq: Inuit Knowledge and Climate Change* campaign material, https://climat eaccess.org/campaign/qapirangajuq-inuit-knowledge-and-climate-change. See also Jane George, "Inuit Elders Speak through Climate Change Film," *Nunatsiaq News* (December 16, 2010).

CARING FOR THE FUTURE 317

consequences of climate change, Indigenous knowledge exerts agency when it occupies a central space as it does in *Qapirangajuq*.[20]

The relationship between Inuit, the land, and the animals they eat is beautifully rendered in *Tungijuq*, a short film with Zacharias Kunuk and music written and performed by Tanya Tagaq and Jesse Zubot.[21] In her perceptive analysis of the film, Keavy Martin concludes that "the film provides an entryway into the cycles of kinship and responsibility that have existed in the Arctic for thousands of years."[22] Martin notes that *Tungiyuq* was released in 2009, the same year that then Governor General Michaëlle Jean drew criticism for eating a piece of raw seal while on a visit to Rankin Inlet. As Martin observes, animal rights groups condemned Jean's actions, and the mainstream media lingered over the description using language that had the double effect of presenting both Canada's first black Governor General and her Inuit hosts as "barbaric."[23] Martin's reading of the film provides the necessary "corrective" to the story by explaining how it depicts "the love for and even intimacy with animals" and "affirms the parallel and deeply interconnected personhood of animal beings" whereby animals and humans exist as "different peoples" who "rely deeply on one another."[24]

The film combines choreographed scenes and computer-generated graphics to celebrate the deep connections Inuit living in what is now called the Canadian North share with the animals they eat, including seals. The film opens with the image of an all-white landscape of clouds, ice and falling flakes of snow. In the distance, a human figure dressed in fur stands on a plateau in the distance, before a close up of Tanya Tagaq's face, her eyes a startling whiteblue and her mouth smeared with red: the human and animal form merged to show their intimate, existential relationship. In what follows, she plays both the predator and prey. After the animated wolf chases down a caribou, its deep

---

20 Michael Bravo, "Voices from the Sea Ice," *Journal of Historical Geography* 35.2 (2009): 256–278; Cameron, Emilie, Rebecca Mearns and Janet Tamalik McGrath. "Translating Climate Change: Adaptation, Resilience, and Climate Politics in Nunavut, Canada," *Annals of the Association of American Geographers* 105.2 (2015): 274–283. See also Frank Sejersen, *Rethinking Greenland and the Arctic in the Era of Climate Change* (London: Routledge, 2015).

21 *Tungijuq (What We Eat)*, directed by Félix Lajeunesse and Paul Raphaël, 2009, www.isuma,tv/en/tungijuq/tungijuq720p.

22 Keavy Martin, "The Hunting and Harvesting of Inuit Literature," *Learn, Teach, Challenge: Approaching Indigenous Literatures,* eds. Deanna Reder and Linda M. Morra (Waterloo: Wilfrid Laurier UP, 2016): 452. See also Martin's *Stories in a New Skin: Approaches to Inuit Literature* (Winnipeg: U of Manitoba P, 2012).

23 Martin, "The Hunting," 449.

24 Martin, "The Hunting," 451. See also Keavy Martin, *Stories in a New Skin: Approaches to Inuit Literature.* (Winnipeg: U of Manitoba P, 2012).

red blood the only colour in the white landscape, Tagaq appears in the guise of the dying caribou. The camera closes in on bloody tracks in the snow which turn into bare human feet. Tagaq's face peers from beneath antlers; her brown eyes slowly close, and she crumples to the ground. In the next shot, her naked body clutches a piece of dark red meat to her chest and writhes on the snow before the camera rises to an aerial view of her body lying at the end of a trail of blood on the edge of the ice. As her naked body plunges into the water, dark red billows around her swimming form, and she is transformed into a seal deep below the ice. As the seal surfaces towards the light of its breathing hole, a red cloud suddenly bursts from its head. An aerial shot shows a man and a woman dressed in Inuit clothing kneeling, a rifle and hook laid next to them close by on the ground, as the hunter slices the length of the seal's belly. They begin to eat. A close up of the open belly showing all the seal's richly colourful and beautifully arranged internal organs fills the screen and the woman's hand reaches out to caress it gently. The camera shifts to the face of the woman played by Tagaq as she eats a small piece. Her soft bangs blow around her face and her brown eyes look straight into the camera as a slight smile passes over her lips. Martin interprets this last look as one of defiance and pleasure, interpreting the film's sensual imagery in sexual terms. On this reading, the film offers as "a wonderful twist on the tradition of busty blond bombshells cuddling up enticingly to seals on the ice."[25] The familiar photo of Brigitte Bardot capitalises on her sex appeal as it simultaneously speaks to the responsibility human beings have to care for the natural world. While Tagaq's gaze invites viewers to the feast, Bardot's seems to ask them to share the maternal duty of protecting the vulnerable young. The scene also challenges the rhetoric of care manipulated by animal rights groups in images in which the caring role is played by humans.

Tungijuq is a modern animal transformation story that demonstrates the persistence of Inuit traditional knowledge in daily life. Across the circumpolar world, "Inuit tell stories of human beings transformed into seals and of seals being transformed into human beings. So too a seal could become a caribou or a fox. All creatures were equal in this regard, including humans."[26] In the mid-twentieth century, Inuit stories were collected by editors who sought to preserve Inuit culture during the rapid acculturation brought about by the incursion of the Canadian government and its exertion of control over Inuit life. In such collections of oral tradition, animal-spouse and animal transformation stories stand in isolation from daily life. At the time, Inuit culture was

---

25   Martin, "The Hunting," 450.

26   David Pelly, *Sacred Hunt: A Portrait of the Relationship between Seals and Inuit* (Seattle: U of Washington P, 2001): 12.

CARING FOR THE FUTURE

perceived as a "stone age" remnant entering into the modern world, and stories were recorded, translated and gathered as anthropological artifacts. Removed from their context and appearing in textualised and illustrated form, these stories present the complex worldview of the Inuit in deceptively simple English. As the early work of Robin McGrath revealed, Inuit stories were for a long time treated as children's literature within Canadian literature.[27] For example, many collections offer a version of the story of the most powerful figure in Inuit tradition, Nuliajuk (or Sedna), the mother of the sea beasts. The creation of the sea mammals from Sedna's body is more than a lively and imaginative story. Like the animal spouse and transformation stories, it articulates the connection between human and animal that informs Inuit life. In *Tungijuq*, this interdependence is represented in the image of the woman's body turning into caribou, wolf and seal, then celebrated in the final feast.

Since the famous photo of Brigitte Bardot cuddling a baby seal appeared on the cover of *Paris Match* in 1977, the anti-seal hunt protest has generated a constant flow of images capturing the conservationist premise that human beings have a responsibility to care for the natural world. In the photo, the human actress assumes the role of seal mother by lying beside the pup just as its mother would, and viewers are invited to join this surrogate mother in protecting the vulnerable young. This image made Bardot a star of the animal rights movement, but, when singer and artist Tanya Tagaq, an actual Inuit mother, posted a photo of her baby lying next to the body of an adult seal, there was a backlash. What happened next features in Alethea Arnaquq-Baril's brilliant film *Angry Inuk*, a documentary about the impact of the European ban on seal products on Inuit communities.[28]

As the winner of the Polaris Prize in 2014, Tanya Tagaq is one of Canada's most visible artists: her televised performances have millions of views, and her music has been featured everywhere from primetime television to festivals around the world. When she raised her voice in defence of the Inuit seal hunt, it did not go unnoticed. In "Sealfies, Seals and Celebs: Expressions of Inuit Resilience in the Twitter Era,"[29] Kathleen Rodgers and Willow Scobie reconstruct the episode, using text and images from the most significant tweets, within the history of the anti-sealing movement from the "Save the

---

27   Robin McGrath, *Canadian Inuit Literature: The Development of a Tradition* (Ottawa: National Museums of Canada, 1984), *passim.*

28   Alethea Arnaquq-Baril, *Angry Inuk* (2016), https://www.nfb.ca/film/angry_inuk/.

29   Kathleen Rodgers and Willow Scobie, "Sealfies, Seals and Celebs: Expressions of Inuit Resilience in the Twitter Era," *Interface: A Journal For and About Social Movements* 7.1 (2015): 70–71.

Seals" campaign in the 1960s and 1970s and the EU's ban seal products in 1983 and 2009. The "#sealfie" movement began in 2014 when Samsung decided to donate $1 for every retweet of the selfie staged by Ellen de Generes at the Oscars that year. At the request of de Generes, the total $3 million was shared between St. Jude Children's Research Hospital and the Humane Society of the United States, an organization that opposes the seal hunt. Northern residents responded by posting photos of themselves wearing sealskin or hunting seals, using the hashtag #sealfie: "On March 28, 2014, Tagaq joined the #sealfie efforts and posted an old photo of her infant daughter lying next to a dead seal."[30] What happened next was widely covered in the media, and Tagaq has spoken frequently about it. The backlash was violent; Tagaq's life was threatened, her fitness as a mother was questioned, and someone posted a photoshopped image of her baby daughter being skinned. If the response of animal rights activists to Tagaq's tweet to #sealfie shows anything, it is the shocking capacity of some activists to advocate harm to human beings in the name of their cause.

Tagaq has not been deterred. "Though the offending posts were removed following cyberbullying charges, Tagaq experienced an almost daily barrage of tweets and messages that were abusive ... The media attention Tagaq received from the events reinforced her commitment to her activism, effectively appointing her as a key spokesperson for the movement."[31] In 2017, she once again defended the seal hunt when a petition circulated protesting the serving of seal meat by chef Joseph Shawana of Toronto's Kukum Kitchen, and she has been a vocal social media presence, from calling for the name of the Edmonton Eskimos to be changed to calling out a professor who defended the indefensible comments made by Lynn Beyak in the Senate of Canada. In both her art and her activism, Tanya Tagaq works towards finding common cause with others: "We are scarring the entire earth" she told *Nunatsiaq News* in 2013, "and if people are stupid enough not to realize we are all living on it and all part of it and all the same minerals, then what hope is there for humanity at all." "Maybe," added Tagaq, "If people were more interested in amalgamating good parts of other cultures instead of destroying them and taking them over in the name of progress we wouldn't be in this situation."[32]

---

30 Alexa Woloshyn, " 'Welcome to the Tundra': Tanya Tagaq's Creative and Communicative Agency as Political Strategy," *Journal of Popular Music Studies* 29 (2017): 7.

31 Rogers and Scobie, 91–92.

32 Justin Nobel, "From Nunavut, Tanya Tagaq's energy flows out into the world," *Nunatsiaq News* (April 12, 2013), http://nunatsiaq.com/stories/article/65674nunavuts_tanya_tagak_f lows_out_into_the_world/.

CARING FOR THE FUTURE

After the ban on seal products, seal populations exploded. Although Inuit hunters were not the target of the protest, the trade in sealskins that supported their subsistence livelihoods was perhaps the most affected by it, and their experience reveals how the representation of the environment as the subject of care and protection created by conservation and environmental movements can have unintended consequences for Indigenous people.[33] Along with the loss of livelihood, Inuit suffered a loss of agency that is now being reclaimed. In the tradition of the Inuit hunt, seals are kin: "the seal hunt, for Inuit, was never just a matter of harvesting food."[34] The seal hunt embodies the spiritual and material connections between Inuit and the animals they eat, and its defense by the community, including prominent figures like Tagaq, is an expression of who they are.

Tanya Tagaq's art, like her activism in support of Inuit hunters, is strongly rooted in her Inuit identity. As she has often recounted, Tagaq began singing while she was a student at the Nova Scotia College of Art and Design living far from home. Singing along to the recordings of throat singing her mother sent her, she developed her own style: "My singing is really based in improvisation and freedom from choruses and licks—it's about feeling connected"[35] Songs such as "Sila" featuring Björk and "Breather" from her 2005 album *Sinaa* evoke the sounds and rhythms practiced by throat-singers within an original score.[36] Vocals in the throat-singing style are prominent on *Animism* in "Uja," "Rabbit" and the repetition of "Umingmak" through that song.[37] On "Rabbit," for example, the vocals seem to beckon and call before collapsing into sounds of surrender. While the later albums *Animism* and *Retribution* also evoke the practice, the musical arrangements of original songs and the inclusion of covers of songs by the Pixies and Nirvana create her unique expression. Every concert is an improvisation that includes experimentation with many forms, including musical traditions from around the world.

By collaborating with musicians and artists from many different backgrounds, Tagaq creates original works that nevertheless retain a strong sense

---

33 According to David Pelly, the price of a sealskin dropped from \$23 in 1976 to \$4 in the years following the Bardot cover, and the number of pelts sold dropped by 97% by the mid-1980s. As hunters modernised, the sale of sealskins helped defray the increased cost of hunting. Once the market collapsed, hunting was no longer sustainable. See David Pelley, *Sacred Hunt: A Portrait of the Relationship between Seals and Inuit* (Seattle: U of Washington P, 2001): 110; 113.

34 David Pelly, *Sacred Hunt*, 113.

35 Cindy Filipinko, "Outspoken," *Herizons* 28.3 (2015): 24–27, 3.

36 Tagaq, *Sinaa* (Jericho Beach Music, 2005).

37 Tagaq, *Animism* (Six Shooter Records, 2014).

of who she is and where she comes from.[38] In musical collaborations, artists form bonds of common purpose that build trust, and Tagaq is well known for working with a diverse array of musicians from Kronos Quartet on "Nunavut" and other projects to recording "Sila" with A Tribe Called Red (now called The Halluci Nation) and more recently, singing "Scream" with Jasmyn Burk on Weave's album *Wide Open*. She first came to international prominence when she joined Björk on tour and collaborated with the Icelandic star on the song "Ancestors." In 2017, she recorded a remake of "You Gotta Run (Spirit of the Wind)" with Buffy Sainte-Marie, a song originally recorded for the 1979 film "Spirit of the Wind" about dog sledding champion George Attla. The new version blends the distinctive styles of the two artists, and Tagaq's interpretation of the song's message that "you can't let things bring you down" has become part of her effort to raise awareness about high rates of suicide.[39] Although she is often described as an Inuit throat singer in the media, Tagaq has repeatedly explained that her music is not traditional though grounded in who she is as an Inuk: "What I'm doing is following an emotion that drives me. I am not trying to represent the North. I'm from Nunavut, so it's a big part of me."[40] Whether Tagaq's visibility is due to her virtuosity, activism, social media presence or award-winning music and performances, hers is one of the strongest and most influential Indigenous voices in the world today.

With her success as a recording artist comes a platform on social and mainstream media that she uses to educate and advocate, and where she has defended her integrity against attack from online trolls and traditionalists alike. With each of her six albums, the connection of human life and the life of the planet has become more explicit: from the celebration of Inuit life and culture in *Sinaa* to the interconnectedness of life evoked in *Animism* and the link between the degradation of the earth and violence against Indigenous women drawn in *Retribution*. Although best known as an improvisational vocalist, Tagaq is also an accomplished visual artist and writer. *Split Tooth* is her first book. As in her music, Tagaq's fiction makes explicit the relationship between the abuse of Indigenous women and girls and the destruction of the Earth.

---

38   Laura Stanley, Tanya Tagaq (July 11, 2019), https://www.thecanadianencyclopedia.ca/en/article/tanya-tagaq/.

39   "Buffy Sainte-Marie delivers new song collaboration with Tanya Tagaq," *Canadian Press* (February 22, 2017), https://www.ctvnews.ca/entertainment/buffy-sainte-marie-delivers-new-song-collaboration-with-tanya-tagaq-1.3296093.

40   Liisa Ladouceur, "Transforming the Past," *Words & Music* 13.4 (2006): 20–22.

CARING FOR THE FUTURE

Tanya Tagaq's *Split Tooth* is a rare example of literary fiction that directly confronts the dilemma of living in the Anthropocene. The narrator, a young girl growing up in the Arctic, acknowledges the threat by naming it:

> The freeze traps life and stops time. The thaw releases it. We can smell the footprints of last fall and the new decomposition of all who perished in the grips of winter. Global warming will release the deeper smells and coax stories out of the permafrost. Who knows what memories lie deep in the ice? Who knows what curses? Earth's whispers released back into the atmosphere can only wreak havoc.[41]

The land is sentient, holding secrets and memories: "We are the land, same molecules, and same atoms. The land is our salvation. Save our Souls."[42] These lines conclude the story of going out with her father to shoot foxes. When there is too much rain, there are too many foxes and something has to be done: "Empathy is for those who can afford it. Empathy is for the privileged. Empathy is not for Nature":

> No choice, only action. These foxes will die of starvation; better to put them out of their misery. These foxes will harm schoolchildren; better to put them out of their misery. These humans will destroy the earth; better to put them out of their misery. Right now we are Earth Eaters, but I want to be a blood lover, an oil spewer, someone with a great wingspan, a spirit sipper, a flesh licker. I want it all.[43]

As in her song lyrics, human arrogance is no match for Nature, grown angry, will act and "retribution will be swift."[44]

While the reception of *Split Tooth* has been overwhelmingly positive, reviewers struggle to describe its form. As *Quill and Quire* reviewer Carleigh Baker noted, *Split Tooth* "defies categorization": though "formally identified as fiction, it is in fact a thick braid of lived experience, philosophy, poetry, and traditional knowledge."[45] The *Kirkus Review* calls the book a "shamanic coming-of-age journey" whose "raw, powerful voice breathes fresh air into traditional

---

41   Tanya Tagaq, *Split Tooth* (Toronto: Viking, 2018), 6.
42   Tagaq, *Split Tooth*, 62.
43   Tagaq, *Split Tooth*, 61.
44   Tagaq, *Retribution*, 2016.
45   Carleigh Baker, Review of *Split Tooth* by Tanya Tagaq, *Quill & Quire*, https://quillandquire
       .com/review/split-tooth.

Inuit folklore to create a modern tale of mythological proportions," yet while recognizing that her "astral flights are a reclaiming if her spiritual heritage," it unfortunately confines the spiritual to a way of coping with the social problems.[46] It is true that the narrator realises that her experiences have readied her to leave her body: "I realize only once my spirit is leaving that all those nights my bedroom door got opened taught me how to be numb, to shut off, to go to the Lonely Place. I was forced out of my body. I was forced to pretend I was a shadow. Those nights gave me the pain that has guided me to death."[47]

Norma Dunning, reviewing the book for *Inuit Art Quarterly*, focuses on Tagaq's innovative style of writing, which she sees as shaking up both western and Inuit literary conventions, but gently criticises what she sees as the depiction of "Inuit as dead and desperate" and cautions that "as Inuit, we must remember that when we speak, especially to a broad public audience, we speak for all of us."[48] It is risky for an Inuit writer to describe the violence and violation experienced by the heroine and to open herself to charges of exploitation and negative stereotyping, but Tagaq renders the emotional experience of the narrator without realism. Instead, she evokes such experiences in poetic passages or in lyrics like "Sternum," a free verse poem that follows the story in which the girls strip "one of the cocky boys" of his pants and his dignity. The narrator is exhilarated as she and her friend run through the streets in the midnight sunshine, feeling their temporary victory, but in the end, the narrator recalls that it "is not the last time he will get himself into trouble with bravado that cannot be backed up" and that he "ends up dying that way."[49] The poem follows, meditating on the role the sternum plays as a protective shield and a cage for the heart and diaphragm, and ends with the devastating lines: "Even when it smothers a little girl's face / As the bedsprings squeak."[50]

Split Tooth resists the expectations of literary fiction by creating a fiction in which the everyday and the eternal, the mundane and the spiritual, cannot be separated. As Ghosh observes, the novel as a genre "was midwifed around the world, through the banishing the improbable and the insertion of the everyday,"[51] and this tendency towards verifiable realism explains why climate change is not a common subject of literary fiction. In *Split Tooth*, the

---

46   Norma Dunning, Review of *Split Tooth* by Tanya Tagaq, *Inuit Art Quarterly* (April 5, 2019), https://iaq.inuitartfoundation.org/review-split-tooth-by-tanya-tagaq/.

47   Tagaq, *Split Tooth*, 182–183.

48   Dunning, Review of *Split Tooth*.

49   Tagaq, *Split Tooth*, 16.

50   Tagaq, *Split Tooth*, 17.

51   Ghosh, *The Great*, 17.

CARING FOR THE FUTURE   325

everyday world of science class and solvent parties, junk food and drunks at
the door, is not separate from the world in which the heroine is impregnated
by the Northern Lights and has sex with a man-like Fox. As Dunning notes,
perhaps the thing that is most original about *Split Tooth* is the absence of the
two worlds trope that always casts Inuit reality in terms of a transition from
traditional to modern life forced by colonisation. Instead, *Split Tooth* fits into
oral traditions inhabited by figures like Sedna and stories of shamans and animal spouses.[52] Out in a whiteout, in "spirit flesh form," the narrator is stranded
on an ice floe that is breaking up:

> The ocean is eating the ice, licking and chewing on it. Large cracks form
> in the floe and the water is calling my name. I will die in the frozen ocean.
> Humans cannot survive in the frigid water, even in spirit form (most
> times).[53]

As she sinks, a polar bear swims beside her, warming the waters, and she
mounts him: "We are lovers. We are married ... I am invincible. Bear mother,
rabbit daughter, seal eater. Bear lover, human lover, ice pleaser. I will live
another year."[54] Like the shaman in the story of Sedna, the narrator travels in
spirit form, gaining the strength and knowledge that comes from her culture,
and the reader learns to imagine worlds in which living beings exist in relation
to one another.

   As Dana Mount and Susie O'Brien observe, "colonialism and its legacies,
nationalism and globalization, may have ruptured patterns of Indigenous
environmentalism" but in recent years, Indigenous groups have "reinvigorated
decolonization on a global scale."[55] Yet, as they acknowledge, citing Diana
Brydon's insight, postcolonial criticism has had less to do with Indigenous
scholarship than one might expect. If postcolonialism has a role to play in

---

52   Removed from the storytelling context, Nuliajuk is an Inuit creation story. First, she is
     punished for refusing to marry by being married to one of her father's dogs, and later she
     is tricked into marrying a deceitful fulmar who tries to capsize the boat her father has
     used to rescue her. As she clutches the side of the boat, her father cuts off all of her fingers,
     and she sinks to the bottom of the ocean. Each finger becomes one of the sea mammals
     the Inuit hunt. The story of Sedna has been retold many times in print. It is beautifully
     told by Ruben Komangapik at: https://www.youtube.com/watch?v=dL2g8SjojRQ.
53   Tagaq, *Split Tooth*, 92.
54   Tagaq, *Split Tooth*, 93.
55   Dana Mount and Susie O'Brien, "Postcolonialism and the Environment," 521–539. *The
     Oxford Handbook of Postcolonial Studies*, ed. Graham Huggan (Oxford: Oxford UP,
     2013): 522.

restoring a sense of the collective, as these scholars think it should, then learning from Indigenous cultures, not appropriating them, will be crucial, and the challenge will be to embrace local, situated, Indigenous knowledge without generalizing or generating universalizing theories.[56] The challenge is illustrated by references to Tanya Tagaq found in ecocritical theory.

In *Staying with the Trouble*, Donna J. Haraway, one of the most influential theorists of the Anthropocene, invokes Tagaq's *Animism* to support her theory of "kin-making": "The task is to make kin in lines of inventive connection as a practice of learning to live and die well with each other in a thick present."[57] Tagaq features in the final chapter of the book, "The Camille Stories: Children of Compost," which Haraway calls a "speculative fabulation" of a future world in which kin-making sustains life and multispecies collaboration protects it. In this future world, each generation passes on knowledge of the first Camille who, it is said, "had studied with Native American, First Nation, and Métis teachers, who explained and performed diverse practices and knowledges for conjoined human and other-than-human becoming and exchange."[58] Within this narrative, Tagaq is remembered as "the Canadian-Nunavut, non-traditional, young Inuk woman throat singer" whose album *Animism* "had been so powerful in strengthening Inuit and also other situated resurgence in the 21st century ... Hunting, eating, living-with, dying-with, and moving-with in the turbulent folds and eddies of a situated earth: these were the affirmations and controversies of Tagaq's singing and website texts and interviews ... She wore seal fur cuffs during her Polaris performance; she affirmed the natural world and hunting by her people."[59] While this interpretation serves Haraway's speculative theory well, the lack of engagement with the material and cultural context for Tagaq's work also raises ethical concerns about how Indigeneity is being cast in discussions of the Anthropocene.

As provocative as Haraway's theoretical language, formal experiments and imaginative arrangements of ideas are, these passages rely on an appropriation of, not an engagement with, Indigenous cultures. Such abstraction, which reflects Cruikshank's critique of postcolonial universalism, can marginalize

---

56   A good example of criticism that takes these issues up by closely reading non-fiction is Graham Huggan's "From Arctic Dreams to Nightmares (and back again): Apocalyptic Thought and Planetary Consciousness in Three Contemporary American Environmentalist Texts," *ISLE: Interdisciplinary Studies in Literature and Environment* 23.1 (2016): 71–91.

57   Donna J. Haraway, *Staying with the Trouble: Making Kin in the Chthulucene* (Durham, NC: Duke UP, 2016): 1.

58   Haraway, *Staying*, 153.

59   Haraway, *Staying*, 164–165.

CARING FOR THE FUTURE

and distract from the particular knowledge and specific lessons Inuit writers contribute to the climate change crisis. It suits Haraway's purpose to focus on what can be interpreted as "traditional" in Tagaq's performance and to ignore the punk aesthetic and musical influences evident in the cover of the Pixie's "Caribou," for example, raising the spectre of the binary opposition of tradition and modernity that Tagaq's work deliberately troubles. This framing of Indigenous knowledge as "traditional" marginalises Inuit knowledge of climate change. Although Haraway concludes that "It matters who eats whom and how," there is no discussion of Tagaq's activism and efforts to educate about her people's relationship with what they eat.[60] Nor does she mention Tagaq's famous acceptance speech at the Polaris Prize gala when she gestured towards her seal fur cuffs and said: "People should wear and eat seal as much as possible because if you imagine an Indigenous culture thriving and surviving on a sustainable resource (points to seal fur wrist cuff). Wearing seal and eating it. It's delicious, and there's lots of them, and fuck PETA."[61]

Elsewhere in *Staying with the Trouble*, Haraway criticises PETA's protest against PigeonBlog, yet she never mentions Tagaq's speech at the Polaris award ceremony or the #sealfie movement. Although Indigenous knowledge, including the rich field of Indigenous feminism, has much to offer ecocritical and posthumanist discussions of climate change, it is only beginning to be heard over the voices of groups like PETA whose well-funded, corporate infrastructure is exposed in *Angry Inuk*. Instead of referencing Indigenous scholars, Haraway uses Tagaq's performance at the Polaris Prize ceremony as proof that kinship is possible. Despite acknowledging the "situated" nature of the performance, Haraway's speculations ignore the details surrounding it; instead, she tends to collapse the situated and particular into the category of geo-political "zones" in need of ecological protection: "Madagascar, the Inuit Arctic, and the Navajo-Hopi Black Mesa" are all the same.[62] The Camille stories adopt an omniscient narrative perspective to tell the story of our present: this speculative fictional mode is Haraway's self-conscious conceit. Like everyone reading *Staying with the Trouble*, Tanya Tagaq is imagined as dead matter creating the compost for future worlds, and her art is part of that future's heritage. Making a spectacle of any living being's future death is morally questionable; in the

---

60   Haraway, *Staying*, 165.
61   Quoted in Woloshyn. See also Patch, N. "Tagaq wins Polaris, swears at PETA, urges crowd to 'wear and eat seal'," *Canadian Press* (September, 2014), https://www.ctvnews.ca/entertainment/throat-singer-wins-polaris-swears-at-peta-urges-crowd-to-wear-and-eat-seal-1.2018610.
62   Haraway, *Staying*, 202n79.

context of the high mortality rate of Indigenous women and the MMIWG inquiry, the choice is a particularly troubling one. The narrator uses the past tense to describe both the artist and her work. "Camille 1," the narrator tells us, "invoked Tanya Tagaq to share her power more than two hundred years after her death."[63] After introducing Tanya Tagaq as a "young Inuk woman" in the past tense, the narrator tells no more, leaving the reader wondering what kind of fictional death has the writer imagined for her? Did it come moments or decades later? If she was an Elder, an ancient great-grandmother, then why describe her as "young"? In the fictional world Haraway creates, Tagaq vanishes like the murdered and missing Indigenous women and girls, victims of what has recently been termed an ongoing genocide, whose names scrolled continuously on screen during Tagaq's Polaris performance and the "Missing and Murdered Indigenous Women and Girls and survivors of residential schools" to whom she dedicates *Split Tooth*.

There is no denying that this portrayal of a living Inuit artist does a great deal of harm in the name of caring for the future. As such, it does not conform to the principles of a feminist ethics of care that envisions a social world in which care for the other structures our moral lives. "An ethic of justice proceeds from the premise of equality" concludes Carol Gilligan in her pathmaking psychological theory, "an ethic of care rests on the premise of nonviolence—that no one should be hurt."[64] It may be true that Haraway's goal is not to explain the complex worldview underlying Tagaq's representation of humans and animals in her music and videos, but to imagine possible solutions to the climate crisis by imagining worlds in which the interdependence of species is as meaningful to everyone as it is to Inuit; yet, it is an argument made through the imagined disappearance of an Indigenous woman.

Indigenous feminists have challenged exclusion by producing feminist analysis that engages with the material realities Indigenous women face, such as Cheryl Suzack's study of the new forms of emotional harm caused by legislation around the Indian Act. Haraway's project of troubling the categories that have separated the human and non-human world contributes to ecofeminist thinking that aims to find connections between ecology and feminism in order to liberate women and nonhuman nature; however, when nonhuman nature is constructed within feminist theory, it is often, and admittedly, within the narrowly defined parameters of western thought. Until recently, these parameters

---

63   Haraway, *Staying*, 165.

64   Carol Gilligan, *In a Different Voice: Psychological Theory and Women's Development* (Cambridge, MA: Harvard UP, 2003): 174.

CARING FOR THE FUTURE 329

rarely encompassed Indigenous perspectives. The critical insight of ecofeminism has been to point out how environmental issues affect women even though not all women have been included in its practice. As long as Indigenous voices remain marginalised, the inclusion of Indigenous examples risks serving as mere decoration. In addition to respecting the rights of Indigenous people and promoting social justice, the feminist ethics of care calls on everyone engaged in social and political action to address the potential for these various forms of harm.

For the artists discussed in this chapter, the colonisation of their homeland is within living memory and the ongoing fight for political sovereignty is lived experience. Indeed, the northern territories were first described as "Canada's colonies" by historians in the 1970s. Dana Mount and Susie O'Brien acknowledge that groundbreaking scholarship on literature and the environment has developed independently of both postcolonial criticism and ecocriticism, citing Cruikshank's work as an example.[65] In *Postcolonial Ecocriticism*, Graham Huggan and Helen Tiffin also map the recent convergence of postcolonial studies and ecocriticism which they interpret as a response to "the need for a broadly materialist understanding of the changing relationship between people, animals and environment."[66] For the artists discussed in this chapter, that understanding is ancient and alive. With their success, the many long years of struggle by Indigenous people to be heard seem to be yielding results as interest in Indigenous culture is growing. Nevertheless, efforts by postcolonial literary scholars to think through these matters are confronted with the problem Ghosh describes: the limitations of literature itself.

In this chapter, I have tried to read selected works by Tanya Tagaq and Zacharias Kunuk from the inside out, as advocated by Indigenous literary scholars, to pay respect to the eternal relationship of Inuit to the land, and to learn from it. As Emilie Cameron argues in *Far Off Metal River*, telling different stories will not change the material realities affecting people's lives; instead, she suggests the Inuit term *pilimmaksaq*, meaning "to commit ourselves to becoming more competent" as an alternative to appropriation and mastery:

> In the face of uncertainty and confusion, as we confront the limits and stakes of what we know and the necessity of knowing differently, we must

---

65 Dana Mount and Susie O'Brien, "Postcolonialism and the Environment," *The Oxford Handbook of Postcolonial Studies*, ed. Graham Huggan (Oxford: Oxford UP, 2013): 525.

66 Graham Huggan and Helen Tiffin, *Postcolonial Ecocriticism: Literature, Animals, Environment* (New York: Routledge, 2010): 12.

be actively attentive, practiced and wise. And continually turn toward worlds worth living in.[67]

The work of Tanya Tagaq and Zacharias Kunuk represents the kinship of all living beings in the kind of the "transformed and renewed art and literature"[68] that Ghosh hopes for in *The Great Derangement*. It challenges us all to accept the shared plight of life on the Earth facing the environmental crisis of climate change and exemplifies the potential of artistic expression and collaboration to model an ethics of care in the Anthropocene.

Works Cited

Angry Inuk, directed by Alethea Arnaquq-Baril (2016), https://www.nfb.ca/film/angry _inuk/.

Archibald, Jo-ann/Q'um Q'um Xiiem. *Indigenous Storywork: Educating the Heart, Mind and Spirit*. (Vancouver: U of British Columbia P, 2008).

Atwood, Margaret. *MaddAddam*. (London: Virago, 2013).

Baker, Carleigh. Review of *Split Tooth* by Tanya Tagaq, *Quill & Quire*, https://quillandqu ire.com/review/split-tooth.

Bravo, Michael. "Voices from the Sea Ice." *Journal of Historical Geography* 35.2 (2009): 256–278.

"Buffy Sainte-Marie delivers new song collaboration with Tanya Tagaq." *Canadian Press* (February 22, 2017), https://www.ctvnews.ca/entertainment/buffy-sainte-marie -delivers-new-song-collaboration-with-tanya-tagaq-1.3296093.

Cameron, Emilie. *Far Off Metal River: Inuit Lands, Settler Stories, and the Making of the Contemporary Arctic*. (Vancouver: U of British Columbia P, 2015).

Cameron, Emilie, Rebecca Mearns and Janet Tamalik McGrath. "Translating Climate Change Adaptation, Resilience, and Climate Politics in Nunavut, Canada." *Annals of the Association of American Geographers* 105.2 (2015): 274–283.

Cruikshank, Julie. *Do Glaciers Listen? Local Knowledge, Colonial Encounters, and Social Imagination* (Vancouver: U of British Columbia P, 2005).

Dimaline, Cherie. *The Marrow Thieves* (Toronto: Cormorant Books, 2017).

Dunning, Norma. Review of *Split Tooth* by Tanya Tagaq, *Inuit Art Quarterly* (April 5, 2019): 70–71.

---

67   Emilie Cameron, *Far Off Metal River: Inuit Lands, Settler Stories, and the Making of the Contemporary Arctic* (Vancouver: U of British Columbia P, 2015): 191.

68   Ghosh, *The Great Derangement*, 162.

Fee, Margery. *Literary Land Claims: The "Indian Land Question" from Pontiac's War to Attiwapiskat* (Waterloo, ON: Wilfrid Laurier UP, 2015).

Filipinko, Cindy. "Outspoken." *Herizons* 28.3 (2015): 24–27, 3.

George, Jane. "Inuit Elders Speak through Climate Change Film." *Nunatsiaq News* (December 10, 2010).

Ghosh, Amitav. *The Great Derangement: Climate Change and the Unthinkable.* (Chicago: U of Chicago P, 2016).

Gilligan, Carol. *In a Different Voice: Psychological Theory and Women's Development.* (Cambridge, MA: Harvard UP, 2003).

Ginsberg, Faye. "Isuma TV, Visual Sovereignty, and the Arctic Media World." In *Arctic Cinemas and the Documentary Ethos*, eds. Lilya Kaganovsky, Scott MacKenzie and Anna Westerstahl Stenport (Bloomington: Indiana UP, 2019): 254–274.

Haraway, Donna J. *Staying with the Trouble: Making Kin in the Chthulucene.* (Durham, NC: Duke UP, 2016).

Huggan, Graham and Helen Tiffin. *Postcolonial Ecocriticism: Literature, Animals, Environment.* (New York: Routledge, 2010).

Huggan, Graham. "From Arctic Dreams to Nightmares (and Back Again): Apocalyptic Thought and Planetary Consciousness in Three Contemporary American Environmentalist Texts." *ISLE: Interdisciplinary Studies in Literature and Environment* 23.1 (2016): 71–91.

Hulan, Renée. *Climate Change and Writing the Canadian Arctic.* (New York: Palgrave, 2018).

Ipellie, Alootook. "Walking Both Sides of an Invisible Border." *An Anthology of Canadian Native Literature in English*, 3rd ed, eds. Daniel David Moses and Terry Goldie (Toronto: Oxford UP, 1992): 333.

Jaggar, Alison M. *Living With Contradictions: Controversies in Feminist Social Ethics* (Boulder, Co: Westview Press, 1994).

Jensen, Lars and Graham Huggan, eds. "New Narratives of the Arctic." [Special Issue] *Studies in Travel Writing* 20.3 (2016): 223–322.

Komangapik, Ruben. *Nuliajuk*, https://www.youtube.com/watch?v=dL2g8SjojRQ.

Ladouceur, Liisa. "Transforming the Past." *Words & Music* 13.4 (2006): 20–22.

Martin, Keavy. *Stories in a New Skin: Approaches to Inuit Literature.* (Winnipeg: U of Manitoba P, 2012).

Martin, Keavy. "The Hunting and Harvesting of Inuit Literature." *Learn, Teach, Challenge: Approaching Indigenous Literatures*, eds. Deanna Reder and Linda M. Morra (Waterloo, ON: Wilfrid Laurier UP, 2016): 445–458.

McCannon, John. *A History of the Arctic: Nature, Exploration and Exploitation.* (London: Reaktion, 2012).

McGrath, Robin. *Canadian Inuit Literature: The Development of a Tradition.* (Ottawa: National Museums of Canada, 1984).

Meyer, Bruce, ed. "CLI-FI: Canadian Tales of Climate Change." (Toronto: Exile Editions, 2017).

Mount, Dana, and Susie O'Brien. "Postcolonialism and the Environment." *The Oxford Handbook of Postcolonial Studies*, ed. Graham Huggan (Oxford: Oxford UP, 2013): 521–539.

Nobel, Justin. "From Nunavut, Tanya Tagaq's energy flows out into the world." *Nunatsiaq News* (April 12, 2013), https://nunatsiaq.com/stories/article/65674nunavuts_tanya _tagak_flows_out_into_the_world/.

Patch, Nick. "Tagaq wins Polaris, swears at PETA, urges crowd to 'wear and eat seal'." *Canadian Press* (September, 2014), https://www.ctvnews.ca/entertainment/throat -singer-wins-polaris-swears-at-peta-urges-crowd-to-wear-and-eat-seal-1.2018610.

Pelly, David. *Sacred Hunt: A Portrait of the Relationship between Seals and Inuit.* (Seattle: U of Washington P, 2001).

Qapirangajuq: Inuit Knowledge and Climate Change, directed by Zacharias Kunuk and Ian Mauro (2009), isuma.tv/inuit-knowledge-and-climate-change/movie.

Review of *Split Tooth*. *Kirkus Reviews* (September 25, 2018), https://www.kirkusreviews .com/book-reviews/tanya-tagaq/split-tooth/.

Rodgers, Kathleen and Willow Scobie. "Sealfies, Seals and Celebs: Expressions of Inuit Resilience in the Twitter Era." *Interface: A Journal For and About Social Movements* 7.1 (2015): 70–97.

Sejersen, Frank. *Rethinking Greenland and the Arctic in the Era of Climate Change.* (London: Routledge, 2015).

Shukin, Nicole. "Materializing Climate Change: Images of Exposure, States of Exception." *Material Cultures in Canada*, eds. Thomas Allen and Jennifer Blair (Waterloo, ON: Wilfrid Laurier UP, 2015): 189–207.

Stanley, Laura. "Tanya Tagaq" (January 11, 2019), *The Canadian Encyclopedia*, https:// www.thecanadianencyclopedia.ca/en/article/tanya-tagaq/.

Stoddart, Mark C. J. and Jillian Smith. "The Endangered Arctic, the Arctic as Resource Frontier: Canadian News Media Narratives of Climate Change and the North." *Canadian Sociological Association/La Société canadienne de sociologie* 53.3 (2016): 316–336.

Suzack, Cheryl. *Indigenous Women's Writing and the Cultural Study of the Law* (Toronto: U of Toronto P, 2017).

Tagaq, Tanya. *Sinaa* (Jericho Beach Music, 2005).

Tagaq, Tanya. *Animism* (Six Shooter Records, 2014).

Tagaq, Tanya. *Retribution* (Six Shooter Records, 2016).

Tagaq, Tanya. *Split Tooth* (Toronto: Viking, 2018).

Tungijuq (What We Eat), directed by Félix Lajeunesse and Paul Raphaël (2009), http:// www.isuma.tv/en/tungijuq/tungijuq720p.

Wachowich, Nancy. "Cultural Survival and the Trade in Iglulingmiut Traditions." *Critical Inuit Studies: An Anthology of Contemporary Arctic Ethnography* (Lincoln: U of Nebraska P, 2006): 119–138.

Watt-Cloutier, Sheila. *The Right to Be Cold: One Woman's Story of Protecting her Culture, the Arctic, and the Whole Planet.* (Toronto: Allen Lane, 2015).

Woloshyn, Alexa. "'Welcome to the Tundra': Tanya Tagaq's Creative and Communicative Agency as Political Strategy." *Journal of Popular Music Studies* 29 (2017).

CHAPTER 12

Fictional Representations of Antarctic Tourism and Climate Change

To the Ends of the World

Hanne E.F. Nielsen

Antarctica is sliced off the bottom of most Mercator maps, with the southern latitudes banished beyond the margins. Yet the continent is home to a thriving tourism industry, with over 74,000 people heading south for leisure during the 2019/2020 summer season.[1] As Elizabeth Leane puts it, "Antarctica, which for centuries has for most people functioned primarily as a symbol, is now an expensive but nonetheless feasible travel destination."[2] Promoted through tourism, Antarctica has become a commodity in its own right. And yet, when it comes to climate change, Antarctic tourism raises a paradox: by carrying people to view the regions that are affected by anthropogenic warming, ships actively contribute to further greenhouse gas emissions.[3] These emissions in turn have global effects, leading to ocean acidification, warming average temperatures, disruption of sea ice formation and sea level rise.[4] In seeking to experience untouched wilderness, then, tourists can hasten its demise.[5] Authors such as Bulgarian-German writer and translator Ilija Trojanow (born 1965) have explored these complex relationships between humans, ice and travel in their fiction. Trojanow's novel *The Lamentations of Zeno* (2011) re-centres Antarctica.

---

1 IAATO (International Association of Antarctica Tour Operators) (2021a). IAATO Antarctic visitor figures 2019–2020, (July 2020), https://iaato.org/wp-content/uploads/2020/07/IAATO -on-Antarctic-visitor-figures-2019-20-FINAL.pdf.

2 Elizabeth Leane, "Antarctic Travel Writing and the Problematics of the Pristine: Two Australian Novelists' Narratives of Tourist Voyages to Antarctica" in *Travel Writing*, eds. T Youngs and C Forsdick (London: Routledge, 2012): 247.

3 Ramon Farreny, Jordi Oliver-Solà, Machiel Lamers, Bas Amelung, Xavier Gabarrell, Joan Rieradevall, Martí Boada and Javier Benayas, "Carbon Dioxide Emissions of Antarctic Tourism," *Antarctic Science* 23.6 (2011): 556.

4 Intergovernmental Panel on Climate Change, "Global Warming of 1.5 Degrees: Summary for Policy Makers," *Intergovernmental Panel on Climate Change* (2018), http://ipcc.ch/sr15.

5 It should be noted that any kind of air or cruise travel contributes CO_2 to the atmosphere— those who travel in more temperate regions also contribute to environmental issues that affect the far south.

© KONINKLIJKE BRILL NV, LEIDEN, 2022 | DOI:10.1163/9789004514164_013

It invites readers to see the continent as part of wider global systems of labour, power and climate, and to reflect ecocritically on their own relationship with the ice at the ends of the Earth.

1 Imagining Antarctica

Although most people will never visit Antarctica, most of us carry versions of the far south in our imaginations. These have been shaped by a range of cultural inputs, such as photographs, films, diaries, advertisements and media narratives. Lack of access is not a barrier to understanding, or to imagining, Antarctica. Indeed, as David Walton writes, "the very idea of this polar place has excited the imagination for centuries."[6] As artist Anne Noble explains, what examining these imagined versions of Antarctica have manifested and evolved "can tell us is a lot more about our culture of imagining than of Antarctica itself."[7] It is noteworthy that Antarctica is regularly represented in the media as a fragile environment, threatened by anthropogenic climate change, to the point that the continent and its ice have come to stand in for fragile environments across the globe. Judith Williamson highlighted in 2010 that "we have a very specific and limited repertoire of imagery currently at our command to signify 'climate change' "[8]—this includes penguins, polar bears, glaciers, icescapes and calving ice. Antarctica's ice can be understood as shorthand for a global climate system that is under threat.[9] With this in mind, any novel that represents Antarctica is implicated in climate change critique. In an age of climate crisis when local actions have global impacts, Antarctica is also implicated in a web of postcolonial and globalised connections, and must therefore be considered in relation to wider global systems.

---

6 David W.H. Walton, "Discovering the Unknown Continent" in *Antarctica: Global Science from a Frozen Continent*, ed. David Walton (Cambridge, UK: Cambridge UP, 2013): 25.

7 Anne Noble, "*Antarctica Nullius*" in *Now Future: Dialogues with Tomorrow 2010 Series*, eds. Sophie Jerram and Dugal McKinnon (2010), https://web.archive.org/web/20130207235036/http://dialogues.org.nz/2010/index.php?/01/anne-noble/.

8 Judith Williamson, "Unfreezing the Truth: Knowledge and Denial in Climate Change Imagery" in *Now Future: Dialogues with Tomorrow 2010 Series*, eds. Sophie Jerram and Dugal McKinnon (2010), https://web.archive.org/web/20130208052553/http://dialogues.org.nz/2010/index.php?/06/judith-williamson/.

9 Hanne Nielsen, "Brand Antarctica: Selling Representations of the South from the 'Heroic Era' to the Present," unpublished PhD Thesis (University of Tasmania, 2017): 259.

Antarctic literature contributes to the wider genre of climate change fiction, defined by Adeline Johns-Putra as "fiction concerned with anthropogenic climate change."[10] This climate change is both scientifically and culturally complex,[11] so fiction offers an ideal way of interrogating human relationships with the more-than-human world. Kathryn Yusoff and Jennifer Gabrys emphasise how climate change "is being reimagined as an ethical, societal, and cultural problem that poses new questions and reconfigures the geographic imaginaries of the world."[12] For Antarctica—a land that exists for most only in the imagination—this is particularly important. This chapter asks how the Antarctic imaginary is constructed; how the commercial activity of tourism has been depicted in and has informed the writing of contemporary Antarctic literature; and how climate change is depicted in case studies of Antarctic fiction. It first provides an overview of the phenomenon of Antarctic tourism, before turning to fictional representations. The chapter takes as a case study Ilija Trojanow's *The Lamentations of Zeno*, as the novel explicitly addresses the interface between climate change and Antarctic tourism. While Trojanow's novel is not the only example to feature Antarctica, tourism and climate change, it self-consciously interrogates all three themes. *The Lamentations of Zeno* therefore serves as an ideal text to interrogate the representation of south polar tourism in narrative and the implications of presenting the human/ice relationship in fiction.

2   Postcolonial Contexts

Although Antarctica has a short human history, and no permanent or Indigenous human population, it is implicated in the cultural legacy of colonialism and imperialism. The explorers of the "Heroic Era" headed south to claim territory for their home nations; this overt performance of imperialism has parallels in the modern-day practice of establishing scientific research stations. In order to gain Consultative Party status, Antarctic Treaty Parties have until recently been "expected to replicate (or mimic as some postcolonial critics would contend) the colonising behaviour of earlier parties" by establishing

---

10   Adeline Johns-Putra, "Climate Change in Literature and Literary Studies: From Cli-fi, Climate Change Theatre and Ecopoetry to Ecocriticism and Climate Change Criticism," *WIRES Climate Change* 7 (2016): 267.

11   Adam Trexler and Adeline Johns-Putra, "Climate Change in Literature and Literary Criticism," *WIRES Climate Change* 2 (2011): 185.

12   Kathryn Yusoff and Jennifer Gabrys, "Climate Change and the Imagination," *WIRES Climate Change* 2 (2011): 517.

bases of their own.[13] Antarctic tourism is also implicated in the legacy of colonialism. Diane Erceg writes how "the idea that Western tourists cast a 'colonial gaze' over non-Western cultures became a commonplace in tourism literature"[14] and argues that "colonial imaginaries are just as valid in Antarctic tourism as in other postcolonial spaces."[15] Applying a postcolonial lens to Antarctica can be helpful, as it highlights the ways that systems of colonial domination—from production of knowledge to the prevailing international order—continue to persist today, and to impact upon the ways humans conceptualise and interact with the southern continent.[16] As Klaus Dodds argues, "postcolonial and ontological investigation of Antarctica's representation in imperial and post-imperial terms as the white continent deserves further reflection."[17] In the twenty-first century, the "world is locked in a dance of cultural, economic, and ecological interdependence,"[18] as Dipesh Chakrabarty puts it, and "globalization and global warming are born of overlapping processes."[19] The current climate crisis reveals how deeply interconnected the injustices of the world are, and demands an approach that does not see postcolonial contexts in isolation; rather, any approach must recognise that global connections also include the far-flung corners of the planet, such as Antarctica.

The Bulgarian-German author Ilija Trojanow takes Antarctica as a setting to explore the wide-ranging social and ecological implications of human beings becoming geological agents. Trojanow has inhabited many different corners of the Earth, and has been described as a "transcultural writer."[20] Born in Bulgaria in 1965, he moved to Germany with his family in 1971 as a political refugee; the following year the family moved to Kenya. Trojanow later studied back in Germany, and has also lived in India and South Africa.[21] He has

---

13   Klaus Dodds, "Post-colonial Antarctica: An Emerging Engagement," *Polar Record* 42 (2006): 63.

14   Diane Erceg, "Explorers of a Different Kind A History of Antarctic Tourism 1966–2016," unpublished PhD thesis (Australian National University, 2017): 11.

15   Erceg, *Explorers of a Different Kind*, 12.

16   Nicoletta Brazzelli, "Postcolonial Antarctica and the Memory of the Empire of Ice," *Le Simplegadi*, XII, 12 (2014): 135.

17   Dodds, "Post-colonial Antarctica," 66.

18   Bonnie Roos and Alex Hunt, "Introduction Narratives of Survival, Sustainability, and Justice," in *Postcolonial Green: Environmental Politics and World Narratives,* eds. Bonnie Roos and Alex Hunt (Virginia: U of Virginia P, 2010): 3.

19   Dipesh Chakrabarty, "The Climate of History: Four Theses," *Critical Enquiry* 35.2 (2009): 200.

20   Arianna Dagnino, "Global Mobility, Transcultural Literature, and Multiple Modes of Modernity," *Transcultural Studies* 2 (2013): 131.

21   Dirk Göttsche, *Remembering Africa: The Rediscovery of Colonialism in Contemporary German Literature* (Woodbridge, Suffolk: Camden House, 2013): 197.

written a number of non-fiction and travel books about Africa, and edited an anthology of contemporary African literature. Although much of his oeuvre is published in languages other than English, it often deals with postcolonial questions; Trojanow's work has, as Dirk Göttsche explains, engaged "in implicit dialogue with postcolonial theory and related critical debate."[22] Most notably, Trojanow's 2006 best seller *Der Weltsammler* (*The Collector of Worlds*) offers a fictive meditation on the life of explorer Sir Richard Burton. *The Lamentations of Zeno* builds on postcolonial concerns about the legacy of colonisation and empire, and extrapolates these impacts to a global scale. Such an approach is timely in the age of the Anthropocene when, as Dipesh Chakrabarty argues, "to call human beings geological agents is to scale up our imagination of the human."[23] Trojanow explores questions of commercialisation, globalisation, agency, alienation and connection to place in the face of a shifting global climate, and, in doing so, offers readers a new perspective on how "the wall between human and natural history has been breached."[24]

Ilija Trojanow's *The Lamentations of Zeno* was originally published in German in 2011, with the title *EisTau* (literally "IceThaw"). The novel functions on several levels. Sabine Wilke characterises it as being like an iceberg, with "a significant deep structure that lies beneath the surface."[25] When it was translated to English in 2016, the translator Philip Boehm commented on the difficulty of choosing a title:

> A literal 'IceThaw' not only lacks the 'aura' of the original *EisTau,* it also fails to convey the layers of meaning lurking in the German. 'Melting Ice' seemed a bit lacklustre, while 'Meltdown' was more appropriate for any number of TV movies.[26]

The book does deal with a number of meltdowns, however, including both the literal melting of Zeno's glacier, and the subsequent meltdown Zeno suffers within his own life. The change in title shifts the focus from the nonhuman ice to the very human protagonist, but it is the relationship between Zeno and the landscapes he encounters that is the most important element. Coordinates at the start of each chapter help to situate the action at specific geographic locations.

---

22 Göttsche, *Remembering Africa*, 197.
23 Chakrabarty, "The Climate of History," 206.
24 Chakrabarty, "The Climate of History," 221.
25 Sabine Wilke, "Performances in the Anthropocene: Embodiment and Environment(s) in Ilija Trojanow's Climate Change Novel" in *Presence of the Body: Awareness in and Beyond Experience*, eds. Gert Hofmann and Snježana Zorić (Leiden: Brill Rodopi, 2016): 181.
26 Ilija Trojanow, *The Lamentations of Zeno* (London: Verso, 2016): vii.

FIGURE 12.1 Antarctic tourists in a zodiac craft, Antarctic Peninsula.
© HANNE NIELSEN, 2016

Meanwhile, each chapter ends with a mix of garbled radio voices, highlighting both the pervasiveness of commerce and the breakdown of meaningful communication. *The Lamentations of Zeno* is set firmly in the Anthropocene, and foregrounds themes of human impacts, changing climate, and the despair and futility that can be experienced in the face of issues of such a global scale. Antarctic tourism serves as a vehicle bringing these themes to the fore.

3   Tourism in Antarctica

Commercial Antarctic tourism began in 1956, and is largely managed by an industry body known as the International Association of Antarctica Tour Operators (IAATO). Its mission is "to advocate and promote the practice of safe and environmentally responsible private-sector travel to the Antarctic."[27] Although the Antarctic continent is governed by the Antarctic Treaty System (ATS) of fifty-four nations who meet annually,[28] IAATO influences decisions made in this forum. The organisation tables papers every year at the Antarctic

---

27   IAATO, "IAATO Reports Latest Antarctic Tourism Figures".
28   Secretariat of the Antarctic Treaty, "Parties," www.ats.aq/devAS/ats_parties.aspx?lang=e.

Treaty Consultative Meeting (ATCM), and many of its recommendations and guidelines have been officially adopted by the Treaty Parties.

IAATO also backs the creation of "Antarctic Ambassadors," arguing that travel to Antarctica is one way of creating advocates for the frozen continent who will "champion this unique environment in a global context."[29] This includes championing initiatives to reduce carbon emissions and promoting ways for tourists to mitigate their own environmental footprints. Companies employ naturalists and offer on-board lecture programmes to cater to tourists' curiosity and to enrich their experience of the Far South (Figure 12.1). Operators hope that those who visit Antarctica will learn from their expedition leaders, discuss their experiences with others and garner support for the ongoing protection of the continent. As American author Midge Raymond's main character Deb puts it in the 2016 novel *My Last Continent*, "what people learn down here might actually make a difference if they go home thinking about how much their actions up north affect the creatures down here."[30]

Despite this optimistic outlook, tourism does not always affect ongoing change. In their 2008 study, Robert Powell and his colleagues noted that, while Antarctic Ambassadors potentially might have a positive impact, there are many challenges involved in educating tourists and altering behaviours.[31] Trojanow's protagonist Zeno voices a cynical approach to long-term change in tourist behaviour:

> I know from experience that the insights they will gain during the next few days will put them in a more reverent mood, but does that mean I should ignore the fact that this reverence will dissipate as soon as they're back home, that they aren't about to renounce their comfortable lifestyle, despite all the harm it causes?[32]

This view accords with a 2010 survey finding that Antarctic tourists returned home with little change to their environmental attitudes.[33] Antarctic tourism

---

29 IAATO, "Climate Change in Antarctica ... Understanding the Facts," https://uploads-ssl .webflow.com/5e5ddc55e1c897c329044bd5/5ea41352dddc5f9b6a85f84a_Climate%20Cha nge%20In%20Antarctica.pdf.

30 Midge Raymond, *My Last Continent* (New York: Scribner, 2016): 87.

31 Robert B. Powell, Stephen R. Kellert and Sam H. Ham, "Antarctic Tourists: Ambassadors or Consumers?" *Polar Record* 44.230 (2008): 239.

32 Trojanow, *The Lamentations of Zeno*, 32.

33 Eke Eijgelaar, Carla Thaper and Paul Peeters, "Antarctic Cruise Tourism: The Paradoxes of Ambassadorship, 'Last Chance Tourism' and Greenhouse Gas Emissions," *Journal of Sustainable Tourism* 3 (2010): 337.

and its long-term impacts can therefore be viewed in very different ways; as a catalyst for environmental change, or as yet another manifestation of consumerism and human greed.

4 Antarctica as Exceptional

Tourists have a range of motivations for visiting Antarctica, including to view the scenery and wildlife, experience the remoteness, and to gain status amongst their peers.[34] Advertisements for Antarctic tours reflect these motivations,[35] casting the continent as a place for heroes,[36] a place of extremity,[37] a place of untouched wilderness[38] and a place of transformation. The idea of Antarctica as an untouched wilderness is problematic, as the continent plays a vital role in global climate and ocean systems,[39] and has long been bound up with human activity in the rest of the world. This chapter argues against so-called "Antarctic exceptionalism," which sees the continent as existing independent from the human history and structures of other parts of the world.[40] This can lead to problems, creating a gap for instance between global best-practice in terms of policy approaches and what happens in Antarctica. As Alan Hemmings puts it, "globalisation now denies us the capacity to treat anywhere differently and thereby disables the principle of Antarctic exceptionalism."[41]

Human activity in other distant locations can have an impact upon Antarctica, as evidenced by the discovery in ice cores of traces of nuclear

---

34 Patrick T. Maher, Margaret E. Johnston, Jackie P. Dawson and Jamie Noakes, "Risk and a Changing Environment for Antarctic Tourism," *Current Issues in Tourism* 14.4 (2011): 393.

35 Hanne Nielsen "Selling the South: Commercialisation and Marketing of Antarctica," in *The Handbook of Polar Politics*, eds. K. Dodds, A.D. Hemmings and P. Roberts (Cheltenham: Edward Elgar Publishing, 2017): 188.

36 Lindblad Expeditions/ National Geographic, "Antarctica: Once in a Lifetime, One in a Century," Brochure, (2014).

37 Antarctic Logistics and Expeditions, "Ready to Jump?," https://antarctic-logistics.com/.

38 Chimu Adventures, "Antarctica the last frontier," *Jetsetter* (Spring 2015): 75.

39 R.P. Abernathey, I. Cerovecki, P.R. Holland, E. Newsom, M. Mazloff and L.D. Talley, "Water-mass Transformation by Sea Ice in the Upper Branch of the Southern Ocean Overturning," *Nature Geoscience* 9.27 (2016): 596.

40 Glasberg outlines the similarities between American exceptionalism and Antarctic exceptionalism. Elena Glasberg, "Scott's Shadow: 'Proto Territory' in Contemporary Antarctica" in *Antarctica and the Humanities,* eds. Peder Roberts, Adrian Howkins and Lize-Marié Van der Watt (London: Palgrave Macmillan, 2016): 210.

41 Alan Hemmings, "From the New Geopolitics of Resources to Nanotechnology: Emerging Challenges of Globalism in Antarctica," *Yearbook of Polar Law* 1 (2009): 55.

explosions[42] and the Industrial Revolution. Activities undertaken in Antarctica also have impacts elsewhere; as Ramon Farreny et al. note, the "increase of tourism to the Antarctic continent may entail not only local but also global environmental impacts."[43] It is not just the physical footprints of individual scientists and tourists but also the species-level influence of humans in distant locations that must be taken into account when considering human impacts upon Antarctica, and vice versa.

The question of how tourists ought to conceive of and experience the Antarctic landscape is linked to both their motivations and expectations. Anxiety over the motivations people have for visiting Antarctica emerges when Midge Raymond's character, the guide Keller, laments:

> [...] there's a whole new breed of so-called adventurers who don't care one bit about the continent. They just want to skydive or paraglide or water-ski in the coldest place on earth so they have something to brag about at the next cocktail party.[44]

Antarctica is a draw card because of its associations with superlatives and extremity, but Keller is concerned these tourists do not see it in a wider global context. In Trojanow's novel, the title character Zeno raises other concerns. Visitors do not experience the place with the same passion he feels for the frozen regions of the planet. He writes that:

> They drift through this place just as they do through all the other places that have been defiled, all our ports of call (what pretentious phrase from some liturgy of advertising), seeming not to touch the ground when they go ashore.[45]

This brings the question of Antarctic exceptionalism to the fore—should we treat Antarctica differently to other places in the world? And what is the appropriate response to the Antarctic landscape? Encounters with new landscapes are primed by tourists' previous cultural inputs, and by their cultural imaginary.[46]

---

42 R.J. Delmas, J. Beer, H.-A. Synal, R. Muscheler, J.-R. Petit and M. Pourchet, "Bomb-test ^{36}Cl Measurements in Vostok Snow (Antarctica) and the Use of ^{36}Cl as a Dating Tool for Deep Ice Cores," *Tellus B.* 56.5 (December 2011): 492.

43 Farreny et al, "Carbon dioxide emissions of Antarctic tourism," 556.

44 Raymond, *My Last Continent,* 186.

45 Trojanow, *The Lamentations of Zeno,* 2.

46 Hanne Nielsen and Cyril Jaksic, "Recruitment Advertising for Antarctic Personnel: Between Adventure and Routine," *Polar Record* 54.1 (2018): 66.

FICTIONAL REPRESENTATIONS OF ANTARCTIC TOURISM   343

The types of responses and level of engagement are as varied as the people who visit.

5   Antarctica in Cultural Production

Few literary texts substantially engage with the issue of Antarctic tourism. Those that do engage often anticipate disaster, using tourism as an engine to drive the plot and to invoke a sense of suspense as the tourists head for catastrophe. Raymond's *My Last Continent,* for instance, features an accident inspired by the 2007 sinking of the tour vessel *Explorer* in Antarctica's Bransfield Strait. Although all passengers were rescued, the sinking made concrete anxieties about the risks of operating in remote regions, and sparked discussion and change across the cruise industry.[47] This is a prime example of how "environmental fears seep into popular fiction."[48] Further themes that emerge when Antarctica appears in fiction include transformation, ecological fear, vulnerability or futility, and the contrast of human relationships and actions with the harsh environment. Tourism can play a small or a large role in bringing these themes to the fore. In British novelist Geraldine McCaughrean's young adult novel *White Darkness* (2005) a tour vessel provides the vehicle for the main characters to reach Antarctica; tourism itself is not at the heart of the story.[49] Similarly, the title character in American author Maria Semple's *Where'd You Go, Bernadette* uses a tourist vessel to get to Antarctica, but the novel concentrates on the continent as a remote location for self-discovery and transformation rather than interrogating tourism as a practice. In American adventure writer Clive Cussler's thriller *Shockwave*, Antarctic tourism features as a way to mark the hero's love interest—a tour guide—as someone who is passionate about the environment; the novel works on the assumption that those who make their careers in Antarctic tourism have a relationship with the continent where they work.

---

47   E.J. Stewart and D. Draper, "The Sinking of the MS *Explorer*: Implications for Cruise Tourism in Arctic Canada," *InfoNorth* 61.2 (June 2008): 224–228. Changes include the requirement for lifeboats to be covered, rather than open.

48   Miyase Christensen, Anna Åberg, Susanna Lidström and Katarina Larsen, "Environmental Themes in Popular Narratives," *Environmental Communication* 12.1 (2018): 4.

49   For analysis of Antarctica in young adult fiction, see Caroline Campbell, "Between the Ice Floes: Imaging Gender, Fear and Safety in Antarctic Literature for Young Adults," *International Research in Children's Literature* 5.2 (2012): 151–166.

Other texts, such as J.M. Coetzee's *Elizabeth Costello*, include Antarctic cruise scenes to undermine notions of Antarctic exceptionalism by painting the continent as being intimately tied up with the actions and preoccupations of the rest of the world, including postcolonial concerns. The fictional tourists Shirley and Steve label themselves as "ecotourists" due to their travels in exotic and wildlife-heavy destinations: "Last year the Amazon, this year the Southern Ocean."[50] This framing places Antarctica on a level footing with any other tourist destination around the globe, further challenging the conceptualisation of Antarctica as exceptional and unique. Coetzee's entire Antarctic chapter takes place on a cruise ship; entitled "The African Novel," it is focused more on the question of what constitutes African literature than any preoccupation with what lies just out the portholes. Elizabeth Leane has written how the juxtaposition of characters Elizabeth Costello (a white Australian writer) and Emmanuel Egudu (a black Nigerian novelist) raises questions of exoticism and "succinctly summarizes the racial politics of many far southern novels."[51] Antarctica is not immune to racialised discourse; Lize-Marié van der Watt and Sandra Swart have argued that Antarctica invites analogies between the whiteness of the ice and notions of purity, and write how "in apartheid South Africa, Antarctica was constructed as a white continent, particularly a white continent of and for men."[52] By focusing on literary arguments, Coetzee's chapter decentres the gendered and racialised heroic discourse of Antarctica.

These titles, which provide fruitful material for further studies, all use Antarctic tourism as a narrative device, but their main focus is on other major themes. Like so much literature, even though they use Antarctica as a setting, the majority of "Antarctic" texts come back to examine the question: what does it mean to be human? More specifically, they ask what it means to be human in the Anthropocene. This is a central concern in Trojanow's *The Lamentations of Zeno*, which brings ecological fears and the spectre of catastrophe to the fore and uses Antarctic tourism as a setting to address human-ice relationships, environmental impacts, questions of possession and agency, and the politics of the tourist gaze.

6   Zeno and Paradox

The Lamentations of Zeno centres on frozen landscapes and the ways in which humans interact with the wider cryosphere. The protagonist, Zeno Hintermeier,

---

50   J.M. Coetzee, *Elizabeth Costello* (London: Secker and Warburg, 2003): 49.
51   Elizabeth Leane, *Antarctica in Fiction* (Cambridge: Cambridge UP, 2012): 104.
52   Leane, *Antarctica in Fiction*, 126.

FICTIONAL REPRESENTATIONS OF ANTARCTIC TOURISM

is a disillusioned glaciologist who has watched his glacier in the European Alps melt away as a result of anthropogenic climate change, and now guides visitors to the Antarctic Peninsula. Zeno is deeply misanthropic, but experiences a strong relationship with the natural world, which he seeks to protect. For Thomas Hobbes "appetite, with an opinion of obtaining, is called HOPE. The same without such opinion, DESPAIR."[53] Zeno experiences that Hobbesian despair first with the death of the Swiss glacier and then with his anticipation of the melting Antarctic ice sheets. He feels like no one is listening to any of the warnings and he struggles with inertia. The protagonist's namesake, Zeno of Elea (490–430 BC), famously saw motion as illusory, and is remembered for a series of paradoxes that continue to provoke philosophical response.[54] Trojanow's Zeno also brings paradox to the fore—he participates in Antarctic tourism despite being aware of its attendant environmental impacts, and he struggles with questions of human agency on personal and species levels. Zeno raises the question of what is ethically acceptable behaviour, remarking that knowing the state of the world's climate, for one "to go on giving lectures undeterred seemed as grotesque as teaching veterinary medicine to palaeontologists."[55] This fatalist view casts the ice of the South in an irreversible state of meltdown.

Trojanow foreshadows the theme of human impact prior to Zeno's voyage, when Zeno's colleague Hölbl first shows him photographs of the Antarctic Peninsula. Zeno recounts how "I picked up one of the photos as carefully as I could but still left a fingerprint on one of the icebergs."[56] Even the most ecologically-minded tourists leave an impact on the places they visit—the question raised here is what kinds of impacts are acceptable. Zeno's concern about human impacts on the planet is articulated prior to the Antarctic voyage, with a visit to the National Park near Ushuaia. He remarks upon the guide's boots: "They left deep prints, and some name or other, probably that of the manufacturer, got stamped into the earth with every step he took."[57] This observation makes literal the human footprint upon the environment; whether fingerprints or footprints, the imprint is a matter of depth and scale. A metaphorical "footprint" is a concept commonly used in Antarctic environmental

---

53 Leane, *Antarctica in Fiction*, 126.
  Hobbes, quoted in Bernard Gert "Hobbe's Psychology" in *The Cambridge Companion to Hobbes*, ed. Tom Sorrell (Cambridge: Cambridge UP, 2006): 161.
54 Niko Strobach, "Zeno's Paradoxes," in *A Companion to the Philosophy of Time*, eds. Heather Dyke and Adrian Bardon (West Sussex: John Wiley & Sons, 2013): 31.
55 Trojanow, *The Lamentations of Zeno*, 89.
56 *The Lamentations of Zeno*, 25.
57 *The Lamentations of Zeno*, 7.

management, where it refers to both the spatial extent and the overall intensity of a disturbance.[58] Trojanow's physical boot print, complete with branding, also introduces the theme of consumerism, which is tightly woven throughout the book. Taken together, these elements highlight that, when it comes to Antarctic tourism, the continent is the product, and the delivery of the experience comes at a cost.

7 Identifying with Ice

In articulating their concept of the "cryoscape," Marcus Nüsser and Ravi Baghel explain how "[g]laciers stand at the intersection of multiple strands of environmental knowledge: scientific, cultural, temporal, spatial and political"[59]— they are not just ice, but ice that is dynamic and imbued with social, cultural and symbolic meanings. The cryoscape lens complements postcolonial analysis methods, as it encourages the reader to critically engage with what Klaus Dodds terms "the varied geographies of colonialism."[60] Zeno addresses multiple strands of knowledge throughout the novel, responding to changes in both alpine glaciers and the Antarctic region with frustration, anger, disgust and feelings of futility. The motif of melting and destruction appears in a recurrent nightmare, which Zeno narrates in a way that highlights his sense of futility:

> Anything would be better than sitting on a cliff with a clump of ice melting in my hands, leaking water that trickles down my arms and into my shirt and over my thighs, dripping and dripping into a puddle between my legs. No matter how carefully I cradle the ice in my hands it continues to melt.[61]

Bringing the theme of fragility to the fore, this excerpt illustrates how a desire to protect a loved environment, combined with a lack of agency to achieve that outcome, can result in a powerful feeling of loss. It also raises questions about

---

58   Shaun Brooks, Julia Jabour and Dana M. Bergstrom, "What is 'Footprint' in Antarctica: Proposing a Set of Definitions," *Antarctic Science* 30.4 (2018): 227.

59   Marcus Nüsser and Ravi Baghel, "The Emergence of the Cryoscape: Contested Narratives of Himalayan Glacier Dynamics and Climate Change" in *Environmental and Climate Change in South and Southeast Asia: How are Local Cultures Coping?* ed. Barbara Schuler (Boston: Brill, 2014): 142.

60   Dodds, "Post-colonial Antarctica," 59.

61   Trojanow, *The Lamentations of Zeno,* 37.

FICTIONAL REPRESENTATIONS OF ANTARCTIC TOURISM

agency on a planetary scale: while Zeno is powerless to stop the meltdown at a local level, it is human action on a global level that instigates the melting in the first place.

Zeno identifies strongly with the glacier he has studied throughout his working life, and personifies the ice, explaining that "every glacier has its own voice."[62] Not only does this ice have a voice, it also has a life, and is cast as very mortal; as Zeno puts it, "we were aging together, the glacier and I, but the glacier was well ahead of me when it came to dying."[63] In their proposal for a feminist glaciology framework, Mark Carey and colleagues examine "human-glacier dynamics, glacier narratives and discourse"[64] and foreground the ways in which glaciers come to be meaningful for a range of people. Trojanow explores similar questions throughout his novel. For example, although Zeno is a scientist, it is the emotional connection with the ice that so profoundly affects him. The death of the Swiss glacier is the catalyst not only for the breakdown of his marriage but also for his subsequent trip to the Antarctic, where he experiences ice on a whole new scale. Reflecting on her own voyage, author Helen Garner mused: "they say that tourist ships to Antarctica, even more than ordinary human conveyances, are loaded down with aching hearts."[65] In Zeno's case, the grief he feels for his glacier influences the way he sees the Far South; Trojanow has Zeno claim that "Anyone who only knows ice as a caged animal in closed valleys is bound to be overwhelmed by the radical freedom of the white south."[66] This ice is alive, wild and dynamic, and must not go the same way as his beloved glacier.

The articulation of the deeply personal relationship between ice and Zeno also raises wider questions, such as how humans grieve for the nonhuman,[67] what it means to be embodied in a particular landscape and what the appropriate response might be to the loss of that landscape. Faced with feelings of loss and inertia, Zeno takes drastic action to bring the plight of the ice to the attention of the wider world. He hijacks the cruise ship while all the tourists are on shore spelling out S-O-S as part of an art installation. The artwork was

---

62   Trojanow, *The Lamentations of Zeno*, 44.

63   Trojanow, *The Lamentations of Zeno,* 45.

64   Mark Carey H Jackson, Alessandro Antonello and Jaclyn Rushing, "Glaciers, Gender and Science: A Feminist Glaciology Framework for Global Environmental Research," *Progress in Human Geography* (2016): 2.

65   Helen Garner, *Regions of Thick Ribbed Ice* (Collingwood, Vic: Black Inc. Books, 2015): 1.

66   Trojanow, *The Lamentations of Zeno,* 27.

67   Lesley Head, *Hope and Grief in the Anthropocene: Re-conceptualising Human–Nature Relations* (London: Routledge, 2016).

348 NIELSEN

intended to draw attention to the climate crisis and to give voice to the silent ice beneath the tourists' feet. By leaving humans abandoned on the ice, and vulnerable to the hostile conditions, Zeno imbues the S-O-S with a new sense of urgency, taking it out of the realm of the symbolic and into the personal. The hijacking turns the S-O-S, which would have gone largely ignored, into prime time news while also highlighting the twin vulnerabilities of the stranded humans, and the icy continent beneath their feet.

8 The Agency of the Anti-Hero

Trojanow's protagonist is the ultimate anti-hero: unlikeable, selfish and, faced with seemingly intractable environmental damage, bent on self-destruction. The novel's Antarctic setting is therefore an interesting choice, given the long association of Antarctica with heroes. The period of exploration that took place between the late 1890s and 1922 is even known as "The Heroic Era." This was the time of staking claims to the ice and planting flags. In the translator's foreword, Philip Boehm notes that Trojanow "contrasts the majestic stillness of the Antarctic with the clamour of human 'civilization'."[68] Antarctica is cast as a place where humans should not be, rather than as a place to conquer. Trojanow also provides comment on the explorers of the Heroic Era, using Zeno to present a view that pulls Heroic Era figures down from their historic pedestals:

> I see them less as pioneers and more as avaricious parvenus seeking to take possession of the Antarctic as if she were a virgin who after the first night was theirs by right for all other nights, and so they despised all competitors as thieving rivals, while they themselves sought to conceal their own lust so as not to endanger their spotless reputation as impeccable gentlemen.[69]

This excerpt also contains echoes of the language of early explorers themselves. When describing the South Pole in 1911, Amundsen wrote, "Beauty is still sleeping, but the kiss is coming, the kiss that shall wake her!"[70] Elizabeth Leane analyses how Antarctica has been characterised in expedition accounts

---

68   Trojanow, *The Lamentations of Zeno*, vii.
69   *The Lamentations of Zeno*, 61.
70   Roald Amundsen, *The South Pole: An Account of the Norwegian Antarctic Expedition in the 'Fram' 1910–1912*, vol. 2. (London: J. Murray, 1912): 194.

FICTIONAL REPRESENTATIONS OF ANTARCTIC TOURISM 349

as "an aloof, virginal woman to be won through chivalrous deeds."[71] Painting the continent as female was useful for early explorers as they sought to stake a claim to the "virgin" ice. The tendency to feminise landscapes is common across Western history. Patricia Price argues that this rendered it "open to the advances of male protagonists,"[72] so that they could claim and conquer territory.[73] In the case of Trojanow's novel, Wilke highlights the colonial mindset that allows visitors to the far south to "take possession of the fragile polar environment."[74] These heroic attitudes that seek to take possession of landscapes are implicated in the current climate crisis. The uncritical claiming of territory which is cast as there for the taking has an analogue in the contemporary sense of entitlement that sees developed countries emit CO_2 and pollutants into the atmosphere, impacting systems in far off places.[75]

Throughout *The Lamentations of Zeno* descriptions of the landscape and of human relationships are tightly bound up with the desire to possess, and with the language of commerce. Although Zeno attempts to set himself apart from those who hunger after the landscape, his partner Paulina points out the hypocrisy of this position: "You're really just like they are, you want to determine what happens to the Antarctic."[76] Jeffrey Jerome Cohen and Lowell Duckert argue that "to think that the world is ours to ruin or to save are two expressions of the same hubris."[77] Both views frame humans as the only beings with agency over the future of the planet Earth. It is within this framework that Zeno struggles to find a way to undertake meaningful action. Zeno's ultimate response to this situation is to hijack a ship and ensure his own demise, explaining his thought process thus: "One human being is an enigma, a few billion human beings organized in a parasitic system are a catastrophe. Under these circumstances I'm just tired of being human."[78] What does it actually mean to be human in the Anthropocene? Zeno's definition is intimately tied

---

71   Elizabeth Leane, "Placing Women in the Antarctic Literary Landscape," *Signs: Journal of Women in Culture and Society* 34.3 (2009): 511.

72   Patricia Price, *Dry Place: Landscapes of Belonging and Exclusion* (Minneapolis, MN: U of Minnesota P 2004): 51.

73   This framing also has strong racial overtones, and is linked to the theft of native lands in many places with a colonial history.

74   Wilke, "Performances in the Anthropocene," 180.

75   IPCC, "Summary for Policy Makers," 25.

76   Trojanow, *The Lamentations of Zeno*, 61.

77   Jeffrey Jerome Cohen and Lowell Duckert, "Introduction: Eleven Principles of the Elements" in *Elemental Ecocriticism: Thinking with Earth, Air, Water, and Fire,* eds. Jeffrey Jerome Cohen and Lowell Duckert (Minneapolis, MN: U of Minnesota P, 2015): 5.

78   Trojanow, *The Lamentations of Zeno*, 157.

FIGURE 12.2 The remains of boilers from whaling days, Whaler's Bay, South Shetland Islands, Antarctica.
© HANNE NIELSEN, 2017

up with loss and destruction, both personal and environmental. This passage raises questions about how the term "human" should be understood in an age of climate crisis. Dipesh Chakrabarty writes how, with humankind acting as a geophysical force at a planetary scale, it is necessary "to think of the two figures of the human simultaneously: the human-human and the nonhuman-human."[79] Zeno represents a human-human who is all too aware of how his species is implicated in global anthropogenic changes. To be tired of being human can also be understood as being tired of being human in the present era of ecological catastrophe. This links the novel to the wider concerns of climate fiction. As Adeline Johns-Putra puts it, "literature is concerned not just with climate change's representational and existentialist challenges but with its emotional and psychological dilemmas."[80] Trojanow's novel raises the question of what risks humans are willing to take, in the light of the impacts our actions will have on other creatures, and also on the environment—the ice.

79 Dipesh Chakrabarty, "Postcolonial Studies and the Challenge of Climate Change," *New Literary History*, 43.1 (2012): 11.
80 Johns-Putra, "Climate Change in Literature," 276.

9 Humans in Antarctica

In 2002 Mark Meister and Phyllis Japp asserted that "when nature is defined as a commodity for consumption it becomes, in a capitalist society, culturally significant."[81] While Antarctic tourism turns the landscapes of the Far South into a commodity, they were of interest to investors well before the first ships offered sightseeing voyages. Antarctica's industrial history is not often foregrounded in discussions of the continent, or in tourism marketing material. Nevertheless, the human history of Antarctica is a commercial history, characterised by early sealing and whaling activity, as well as the exploitation of other resources, including ice (see Chapter 13 of this volume).[82] At Grytviken, on the Island of South Georgia, Zeno observes that the "diesel tanks are lined up as neatly as the graves—a reminder of how much blubber was processed in this cove."[83] As he explains to a nearby passenger: "Everything was put to use—humans are always so eager to show Nature more efficient ways to manage her resources."[84] Later, at the shore-based whaling station of Whalers Bay, in the South Shetland Islands (Figure 12.2), the cynicism returns: "What a wondrous innovation to make explosives out of whales, what a vibrant symbol of progress: destroying the essential to create the superfluous."[85] The Anthropocene has been alternatively characterised as the Capitalocene: "a multispecies assemblage, a world-ecology of capital, power and nature,"[86] where capitalism is a way of organising nature. This recognises that many of the human impacts on the planet are the result of consumer behaviour, and a drive for growth on a planetary scale. The inclusion of industrial scenes in the novel unsettles the reader's pre-existing notions about the Far South as a place of peace, science and wilderness, rather than profit, implicating the region in a global web of capitalist commerce, and inviting analysis through a postcolonial lens.

The Lamentations of Zeno presents a negative view of the human presence in the Antarctic, with Zeno complaining that the "landscape is infested with research stations."[87] The human presence is contrasted with the non-human

---

81 Mark Meister and Phyllis M. Japp, "Introduction" in *Enviropop: Studies in Environmental Rhetoric and Popular Culture*, eds. Mark Meister and Phyllis Japp (London: Praeger. 2002): 2.

82 Nielsen, "Selling the South," 193.

83 Trojanow, *The Lamentations of Zeno*, 74.

84 Trojanow, *The Lamentations of Zeno*, 75.

85 Trojanow, *The Lamentations of Zeno*, 124.

86 Jason W. Moore, *Anthropocene or Capitalocene? Nature, History, and the Crisis of Capitalism* (Oakland: Sociology Faculty Scholarship, 2016): xi.

87 Trojanow, *The Lamentations of Zeno*, 104.

life forms. Zeno explains, for example, that while "the stations are a few decades old, the [penguin] colonies have been there for 30,000 years."[88] The question of who belongs in Antarctica brings together geopolitical histories and value judgements, as well as questions of power and access. The construction of bases is closely associated with territorial claims and with polar colonialism,[89] and is informed by politics in distant places. The Antarctic Treaty (1959) established science as the currency of the continent, and research stations legitimate the human presence. Modern-day activities are subject to environmental impact assessments, and sites of past activity must be cleaned up (fuel drums, buildings and machinery must be removed unless doing so would cause more disturbance to the environment than leaving them in place). Nevertheless, the question of definition arises: what is garbage and should be removed to protect the environment; and what is a historic artefact and should therefore be preserved as heritage.[90] The residues of human activity are highlighted in Trojanow's novel by Zeno's description of how locations are curated for tourism: "[...] we're avoiding the Russian station Bellingshausen on account of the many derelict oil drums, the wreckage and scrap iron that litter the shore, exposing the true legacy of the human race: garbage."[91] Bellingshausen is located on King George Island, along with eleven other nearby stations belonging to different nations, making it the busiest island in the peninsula region in terms of human activity. Supply ships generally remove litter once per year. As it is piled near the docks for easy loading, the waste can be confronting for tourists coming ashore for the first time. This image of garbage in the Antarctic is particularly relevant in the Anthropocene, as it contradicts the image of Antarctica as a place that is "untouched," graphically illustrating how it is affected by human activity—like the rest of the world. For Zeno, this is degradation; for tourists it often makes the place seem inauthentic. But it is also the reality of the human presence, and a microcosm of the wider situation: both in the local Antarctic setting and on a global climatic scale humans are "directly or indirectly responsible for changing the "nature" of our planet to our detriment"[92] and to the detriment of non-human creatures and ecosystems.

---

88 *The Lamentations of Zeno,* 104.

89 Dodds, "Post-colonial Antarctica," 59.

90 Dag Avango, "Acting Artifacts: On the Meanings of Material Culture in Antarctica" in *Antarctica and the Humanities,* eds. Peder Roberts, Adrian Howkins and Lize-Marié Van der Watt (London: Palgrave Macmillan, 2016): 159.

91 Trojanow, *The Lamentations of Zeno,* 105.

92 Roos and Hunt, "Introduction," 1.

FICTIONAL REPRESENTATIONS OF ANTARCTIC TOURISM

10 Curating Antarctica

Characters who are Antarctic tour guides and expedition leaders serve as a useful device for novelists to share information about local wildlife, history and ice. Characterising his role as a naturalist, Zeno remarks: "by all means permit me to influence your vision of the unknown."[93] Just as the naturalist shapes tourists' views of the Far South through targeted narration, the novelist shapes the readers' view by their representation of that process. For instance, in *My Last Continent* Raymond's character Deb tells her passengers "we have less than half the number of Adelie colonies that we had thirty years ago,"[94] opening the door for them to ask if there is any way to save the birds from extinction. Her response to that question is aimed as much at the reader of the novel as it is at the novel's shipboard audience: "Deal with the climate, which is complicating the weather patterns that affect the penguins' breeding. Stop eating fish, which is like taking food from their mouths."[95] This dogmatic device allows Raymond to bring contemporary environmental issues such climate change denial and sustainable seafood practices to the fore. But it also raises questions of perspective and authority, drawing attention to what is left unsaid. The character Keller has been warned already "not to lecture the passengers"[96] following his taking a passenger to task for using a krill oil supplement. By trying to convince a passenger that anthropogenic climate change is a real issue with global consequences, he jeopardises his own presence in Antarctica. Guides on Antarctic tourism vessels have a great deal of power to shape the perceptions of the tourists on board, but they must also take care to avoid confrontation. They are employed to deliver the Antarctic as a touristic product, not to interrogate the personal values of those who pay to be on board. The inclusion of tour guides as characters in Antarctic novels allows for exploration of the human impacts in Antarctica, and what it means to narrate and curate these on a daily basis.

What is the right way of looking? Who gets to look? And in Antarctica, how directed is the viewing? Zeno acknowledges the tourist gaze early on in Trojanow's novel, when he recalls his own experiences as a tourist: "when I am a tourist I appreciate what is staged for tourists."[97] In Antarctica the tourist experience is highly curated. Voyages are planned to match the expectations

---

93   Trojanow, *The Lamentations of Zeno*, 25.
94   Raymond, *My Last Continent*, 183.
95   Raymond, *My Last Continent*, 184.
96   Raymond, *My Last Continent*, 184.
97   Trojanow, *The Lamentations of Zeno*, 114.

set out in the travel brochures. Whales, penguins and icebergs are all part of the itinerary and expedition leaders orchestrate landings to provide the best range of opportunities to view both wildlife and landscapes. IAATO coordinates tourist activity in the Far South and runs a ship schedule to ensure sites are not overloaded in order to minimise environmental impacts and maximise the experience of remoteness. Zeno explains:

> We stay out of each other's way, after all we don't want the sight of another ship to ruin the illusion that we're all on our own here in the Antarctic, far removed from any regulated traffic, alone at the end of the world.[98]

IAATO's 2007 "Wilderness Etiquette"—to which Zeno alludes here—recognises the desire of tourists to experience a remote place, far from other people. And yet, Antarctica is implicated in global systems. The exceptionalist narrative that sees the continent as apart from the rest of the world is damaging in an era of climate crisis. When the Southern Ocean acts as a carbon sink for the CO_2 that the developed world pumps into the atmosphere, the framing of Antarctica as pristine, remote and untouched must be challenged, both in practice and in representations.

The theme of reality versus representation emerges early in *The Lamentations of Zeno*, when Zeno's colleague Hölbl shows him images from a previous Antarctic season. Zeno remarks: "Hölbl was too stingy to print real photos, he'd run off some cheap copies on regular paper, the color looked very artificial."[99] This comment brings to the fore the question of how stay-at-home readers and viewers experience Antarctica vicariously, yet still make judgements about its authenticity or otherwise. Zeno is disparaging of the desire to photograph and capture Antarctic landscapes: "once again out come the camcorders and once again nature is diminished in the zoom of their lenses."[100] Helen Garner expressed a similar sentiment when she headed south aboard *Professor Molchanov* in the early 1990s: "I'm lonely because everyone else is hiding behind a camera."[101] Caroline Scarles explains how "photography and the visual have long been understood as fundamental to tourism"[102]—they link ways of looking and perceived authenticity with the "creation of place

---

98   Trojanow, *The Lamentations of Zeno*, 88.
99   Trojanow, *The Lamentations of Zeno*, 25.
100   Trojanow, *The Lamentations of Zeno*, 12.
101   Garner, *Regions of Thick-Ribbed Ice*, 16.
102   Caroline Scarles, "Becoming Tourist: Renegotiating the Visual in the Tourist Experience," *Environment and Plannings D: Society and Space* 27 (2009): 465.

and experience."[103] But novels, like cameras, are mediating devices and this is particularly pertinent in novels about Antarctic tourism. The novel, like the photograph, acts as a portal to imagining the Far South.

11 Future Directions

Tom Griffiths writes how "the relationship between culture and nature is now high on the Western scholarly agenda."[104] Literature offers a prime avenue for exploring this relationship and rethinking human engagement with the non-human world[105]—including the ice of Antarctica. Attitudes towards Antarctic tourism have been reflected in fiction, and other forms of cultural production. Common themes that have been present in representations of Antarctic tourism to date include ecological fear—often linked to disaster narratives—as well as human transformation and love.

The tourist experience of Antarctica is accompanied by complex human/nonhuman interactions. It is intractably imbedded within climate change, and is interwoven with very personal human experiences. Ilija Trojanow's *The Lamentations of Zeno* brings several of these issues to the fore. Trojanow uses the Antarctic setting to tell a tale of grief, of feeling powerless, a tale of commerce, and of change on a colossal scale, and translates these large emotions into the local, through Zeno's marriage breakdown and the hijacking of the ship. He uses Antarctic tourism as a way to challenge readers to think about their own relationship with the natural world, and in doing so, highlights the way "ecology does not always work within the frames of human time and political interest."[106] Franklin Ginn and colleagues have written how "alienation is perhaps the most logical reaction to sublime, inhuman timescales"[107]—Trojanow makes this alienation tangible, and opens a starting point for further discussions on the role of the human across all of this planet. Trojanow's novel is but one example of fiction that deals with Antarctic tourism, and we should

---

103   Scarles, "Becoming Tourist," 465.
104   Tom Griffiths, "The Humanities and an Environmentally Sustainable Australia," *Australian Humanities Review* 43 (2007).
105   Melina Pereira Savi, "The Anthropocene (and) (in) the Humanities: Possibilities for Literary Studies," *Estudos Feministas, Florianópolis* 25.2 (2017): 953.
106   Elizabeth DeLoughrey and George B. Handley, "Introduction: Towards an Aesthetics of the Earth" in *Postcolonial Ecologies: Literatures of the Environment* eds. DeLoughrey and Handley (Oxford: Oxford UP, 2011): 4.
107   Franklin Ginn, Michelle Bastian, David Farrier and Jeremy Kidwell, "Unexpected Encounters with Deep Time," *Environmental Humanities* 10.1 (2018): 214.

continue to watch this space. As the Antarctic continent becomes more accessible, and tourism becomes a more viable option for a range of creative people, more representations can be expected to emerge. As long as humans continue heading to the ends of the world, Antarctica will keep stretching our imaginations in unexpected ways.

Although as Coetzee's Elizabeth Costello points out "we do not possess a shared story of the future,"[108] such narratives offer a way to explore the possibilities for tomorrow. As Melina Savi puts it, books hold "not only words, but worlds, the possibility of worlds"[109]—they offer a way to examine the values and priorities humans bring to their views on the far south, and to open conversations about global climate challenges. Dipesh Chakrabarty writes that "the crisis of climate should produce anxieties precisely around futures that we cannot visualise."[110] Novels such as *The Lamentations of Zeno* help to articulate those anxieties, and to link human impacts—colonial, environmental and climate—across a range of scales. They give voice to the alienation, grief and solastalgia that can be felt when known places (such as glacial valleys) are altered beyond recognition, and can therefore have an impact upon the wider ecosocial imaginary of readers. In an age of climate crisis, when environmental impacts are experienced on a global, rather than a local scale, this is more important than ever.

Works Cited

Abernathey, R.P., I. Cerovecki, P.R. Holland, E. Newsom, M. Mazloff and L.D. Talley. "Water-mass Transformation by Sea Ice in the Upper Branch of the Southern Ocean Overturning." *Nature Geoscience* 9.27 (2016): 596–601.

Amundsen, Roald. *The South Pole: An Account of the Norwegian Antarctic Expedition in the 'Fram' 1910–1912*, Vol. 2 (London: J. Murray, 1912).

Antarctic Logistics and Expeditions. "Ready to Jump?" https://antarctic-logistics.com/.

Avango, Dag. "Acting Artifacts: On the Meanings of Material Culture in Antarctica" in *Antarctica and the Humanities*, eds. Peder Roberts, Adrian Howkins and Lize-Marié Van der Watt (London: Palgrave Macmillan, 2016): 159–179.

Brazzelli, Nicoletta. Postcolonial Antarctica and the Memory of the Empire of Ice. *Le Simplegadi* XII.12 (2014): 127–141.

108　J.M. Coetzee, *Elizabeth Costello* (London: Secker and Warburg, 2003): 38.
109　Savi, "The Anthropocene," 955.
110　Chakrabarty, "The Climate of History," 211.

Brooks S.T., J. Jabour and D.M. Bergstrom. "What is 'Footprint' in Antarctica: Proposing a Set of Definitions." *Antarctic Science* 30.4 (2018): 227–235.

Campbell, Caroline. "Between the Ice Floes: Imaging Gender, Fear and Safety in Antarctic Literature for Young Adults." *International Research in Children's Literature* 5.2 (2012): 151–166.

Carey, Mark, H Jackson, Alessandro Antonello and Jaclyn Rushing. "Glaciers, Gender and Science: A Feminist Glaciology Framework for Global Environmental Research." *Progress in Human Geography* (2016): 1–24.

Chimu Adventures, "Antarctica the Last Frontier." *Jetsetter* (Spring 2015): 75.

Chakrabarty, Dipesh. "The Climate of History: Four Theses." *Critical Enquiry* 35.2 (2009): 197–222.

Chakrabarty, Dipesh. "Postcolonial Studies and the Challenge of Climate Change." *New Literary History* 43.1 (Winter 2012): 1–18.

Christensen, Miyase, Anna Åberg, Susanna Lidström and Katarina Larsen. "Environmental Themes in Popular Narratives." *Environmental Communication* 12.1 (2018): 1–6.

Coetzee, J.M. *Elizabeth Costello.* (London: Secker and Warburg, 2003).

Cohen, Jeffrey Jerome and Lowell Duckert. "Introduction: Eleven Principles of the Elements." *Elemental Ecocriticism: Thinking with Earth, Air, Water, and Fire*, eds. Jeffrey Jerome Cohen and Lowell Duckert (Minneapolis, MN: U of Minnesota P, 2015): 1–26.

Cussler, Clive. *Shockwave.* (New York: Pocket Star Books, 1996).

Dagnino, Arianna. "Global Mobility, Transcultural Literature, and Multiple Modes of Modernity." *Transcultural Studies* 2 (2013): 130–160.

Delmas, R.J., J. Beer, H.-A. Synal, R. Muscheler, J.-R. Petit and M. Pourchet. "Bomb-test ^{36}Cl Measurements in Vostok Snow (Antarctica) and the Use of ^{36}Cl as a Dating Tool for Deep Ice Cores." *Tellus B.* 56.5 (December 2011): 492–498.

DeLoughrey, Elizabeth and George B. Handley. "Introduction: Towards an Aesthetics of the Earth" in *Postcolonial Ecologies: Literatures of the Environment,* eds. DeLoughrey and Handley (Oxford: Oxford UP, 2011): 3–39.

Dodds, Klaus. "Post-colonial Antarctica: An Emerging Engagement." *Polar Record* 42 (2006): 59–70.

Eijgelaar, Eke, Carla Thaper and Paul Peeters. "Antarctic Cruise Tourism: The Paradoxes of Ambassadorship, 'Last Chance Tourism' and Greenhouse Gas Emissions." *Journal of Sustainable Tourism* 3 (2010): 337–354.

Erceg, Diane. "Explorers of a Different Kind: A History of Antarctic Tourism 1966–2016," unpublished PhD Thesis. (Australian National University, 2017).

Farreny, Ramon, Jordi Oliver-Solà, Machiel Lamers, Bas Amelung, Xavier Gabarrell, Joan Rieradevall, Martí Boada and Javier Benayas. "Carbon dioxide emissions of Antarctic tourism." *Antarctic Science* 23.6 (November 2011): 556–566.

Garner, Helen. *Regions of Thick-Ribbed Ice*. (Collingwood, Victoria: Black Inc. Books, 2015).

Gert, Bernard. "Hobbe's Psychology" in *The Cambridge Companion to Hobbes,* ed. Tom Sorrell (Cambridge: Cambridge UP, 2006): 157–174.

Ginn, Franklin, Michelle Bastian, David Farrier and Jeremy Kidwell. "Unexpected Encounters with Deep Time." *Environmental Humanities* 10.1 (2018): 213–225.

Glasberg, Elena. "Scott's Shadow: 'Proto Territory'" in Contemporary Antarctica" in *Antarctica and the Humanities*, eds. Peder Roberts, Adrian Howkins and Lize-Marié Van der Watt (London: Palgrave Macmillan, 2016): 205–227.

Göttsche, Dirk. *Remembering Africa: The Rediscovery of Colonialism in Contemporary German Literature* (Woodbridge, Suffolk: Camden House, 2013).

Griffiths, Tom. "The Humanities and an Environmentally Sustainable Australia." *Australian Humanities Review* 43 (2007).

Head, Lesley. *Hope and Grief in the Anthropocene: Re-conceptualising Human–Nature Relations*. (London: Routledge, 2016).

Hemmings, Alan. "From the New Geopolitics of Resources to Nanotechnology: Emerging Challenges of Globalism in Antarctica." *Yearbook of Polar Law* 1 (2009): 55–72.

Hobbes, Thomas. *Leviathan or the Matter, Forme, & Power of a Comon-wealth Ecclesiastical and Civill* 1651, https://www.gutenberg.org/files/3207/3207-h/3207-h.htm.

Intergovernmental Panel on Climate Change. "Global Warming of 1.5 Degrees: Summary for Policy Makers." *Intergovernmental Panel on Climate Change* (2018), http://ipcc .ch/sr15.

International Association of Antarctica Tour Operators (2021a). IAATO Antarctic visitor figures 2019–2020. (July 2020), https://iaato.org/wp-content/uploads/2020/07/ IAATO-on-Antarctic-visitor-figures-2019-20-FINAL.pdf.

International Association of Antarctica Tour Operators. "Climate Change in Antarctica ... Understanding the Facts." https://uploads-ssl.webflow.com/5e5ddc55e1c89 7c329044bd5/5ea41352dddc5f9b6a85f84a_Climate%20Change%20In%20Antarct ica.pdf.

Johns-Putra, Adeline. "Climate Change in Literature and Literary Studies: From Cli-fi, Climate Change Theatre and Ecopoetry to Ecocriticism and Climate Change Criticism." *WIRES Climate Change* 7 (2016): 266–281.

Leane, Elizabeth. *Antarctica in Fiction*. (Cambridge: Cambridge UP, 2012).

Leane, Elizabeth. "Antarctic Travel Writing and the Problematics of the Pristine: Two Australian Novelists' Narratives of Tourist Voyages to Antarctica" in *Travel Writing*, eds. T. Youngs and C. Forsdick (UK: Routledge, 2012): 247–257.

Leane, Elizabeth. "Placing Women in the Antarctic Literary Landscape." *Signs: Journal of Women in Culture and Society* 34.3 (2009): 509–514.

Lindblad Expeditions / National Geographic. "Antarctica: Once in a Lifetime, One in a Century," brochure. (2014).

Maher, Patrick T., Margaret E. Johnston, Jackie P. Dawson and Jamie Noakes. "Risk and a Changing Environment for Antarctic Tourism." *Current Issues in Tourism* 14.4 (2011): 387–399.

Meister, Mark and Phyllis M. Japp. "Introduction." *Enviropop: Studies in Environmental Rhetoric and Popular Culture*, eds. Mark Meister and Phyllis Japp (London: Praeger. 2002): 1–13.

Moore, Jason W. *Anthropocene or Capitalocene? Nature, History, and the Crisis of Capitalism.* (Oakland: Sociology Faculty Scholarship, 2016).

Nielsen, Hanne and Cyril Jaksic. "Recruitment advertising for Antarctic personnel: between adventure and routine." *Polar Record* 54.1 (2018): 65–75.

Nielsen, Hanne. "Brand Antarctica: Selling Representations of the South from the 'Heroic Era' to the Present," unpublished PhD Thesis. (University of Tasmania, 2017).

Nielsen, Hanne. "Selling the South: Commercialisation and Marketing of Antarctica" in *The Handbook of Polar Politics*, eds. K. Dodds, A.D. Hemmings and P. Roberts (Cheltenham: Edward Elgar Publishing, 2017): 183–198.

Noble, Anne. *Antarctica Nullius*, Now Future: Dialogues with Tomorrow 2010, Series eds. Sophie Jerram and Dugal McKinnon (2010), https://web.archive.org/web/201 30207235036/http://dialogues.org.nz/2010/index.php/01/anne-noble/.

Nüsser, Marcus and Ravi Baghel. "The Emergence of the Cryoscape: Contested Narratives of Himalayan Glacier Dynamics and Climate Change" in *Environmental and Climate Change in South and Southeast Asia: How are Local Cultures Coping?* ed. Barbara Schuler (Boston: Brill, 2014): 138–157.

Powell, Robert B., Stephen R. Kellert and Sam H. Ham. "Antarctic Tourists: Ambassadors or Consumers?" *Polar Record* 44.230 (2008): 233–241.

Price, Patricia. *Dry Place: Landscapes of Belonging and Exclusion.* (Minneapolis, MN: U of Minnesota P, 2004).

Raymond, Midge. *My Last Continent.* (New York: Scribner, 2016).

Roos, Bonnie and Alex Hunt, "Introduction Narratives of Survival, Sustainability, and Justice" in *Postcolonial Green: Environmental Politics and World Narratives,* eds. Bonnie Roos and Alex Hunt (Virginia: U of Virginia P, 2010): 1–13.

Savi, Melina Pereira. "The Anthropocene (and) (in) the Humanities: Possibilities for Literary Studies." *Estudos Feministas, Florianópolis* 25.2 (2017): 945–959.

Scarles, Caroline. "Becoming Tourist: Renegotiating the Visual in the Tourist Experience." *Environment and Plannings D: Society and Space* 27 (2009): 465–488.

Secretariat of the Antarctic Treaty. "The Protocol on Environmental Protection to the Antarctic Treaty," https://www.ats.aq/e/ep.htm.

Secretariat of the Antarctic Treaty. "Parties," at www.ats.aq/devAS/ats_parties.aspx? lang=e.

Semple, Maria. *Where'd You Go, Bernadette.* (New York: Little, Brown and Company, 2012).

Sorrell, Tom. *The Cambridge Companion to Hobbes.* (Cambridge: Cambridge UP, 2006).

Stewart, E.J. and D. Draper. "The Sinking of the MS Explorer: Implications for Cruise Tourism in Arctic Canada." *InfoNorth* 61.2 (June 2008): 224–228.

Strobach, Niko. "Zeno's Paradoxes" in *A Companion to the Philosophy of Time*, eds. Heather Dyke and Adrian Bardon (West Sussex: John Wiley & Sons, 2013): 30–46.

Trexler, Adam and Adeline Johns-Putra. "Climate Change in Literature and Literary Criticism." *WIRE s Climate Change* 2 (April 2011): 185–200.

Trojanow, Ilija. *The Collector of Worlds* trans. William Hobson (London: Faber & Faber, 2008).

Trojanow, Ilija. *Eistau* (Munich: Carl Hanser Verlag, 2011).

Trojanow, Ilija. *The Lamentations of Zeno* (London: Verso, 2016).

Walton, David W.H. "Discovering the Unknown Continent" in *Antarctica: Global Science from a Frozen Continent*, ed. David Walton (Cambridge: Cambridge UP, 2013): 1–34.

Wilke, Sabine. "Performances in the Anthropocene: Embodiment and Environment(s) in Ilija Trojanow's Climate Change Novel" in *Presence of the Body: Awareness in and Beyond Experience*, ed. Gert Hofmann and Snježana Zorić (Leiden: Brill Rodopi, 2016): 174–189.

Williamson, Judith. "Unfreezing the Truth: Knowledge and Denial in Climate Change Imagery" in *Now Future: Dialogues with Tomorrow 2010 Series,* ed. Sophie Jerram and Dugal McKinnon (2010), https://web.archive.org/web/20130208052553/http://dialogues.org.nz/2010/index.php?/06/judith-williamson/.

Yusoff, Kathryn and Jennifer Gabrys. "Climate Change and the Imagination." *WIRE s Climate Change* 2 (2011): 516–534.

CHAPTER 13

Ice Islands of the Anthropocene

The Cultural Meanings of Antarctic Bergs

Elizabeth Leane

A journey to Antarctica—previously considered glamorously intrepid, adventurous and exotic—takes on new meanings in the Anthropocene. This came home to me following a fieldtrip I undertook in early 2018 as an instructor on the University of Canterbury's Postgraduate Certificate in Antarctic Studies. This unique interdisciplinary course immerses a small group of students in all forms of Antarctic knowledge—scientific, historical, cultural, political— before taking them down to Ross Island in East Antarctica for almost two weeks, where they stay at New Zealand's Scott Base and then camp out on an ice shelf at Windless Bight, carrying out a variety of research projects. After the fieldwork was over and I returned to low latitudes, I experienced a sense of obligation unique to the polar traveller in the Anthropocene. First, there was the need to justify the journey: the carbon footprint of a voyage to the ice, although no greater than other long-distance trips, seems particularly questionable in a time of global warming. But more strongly I felt the expectation to act as an eyewitness to humanity's broader impact on the region: to provide direct testimony on "the state of the ice."

Such an expectation is problematic in a number of ways. First, it bestows upon the traveller, who in most cases has experienced a very specific part of Antarctica as well as a particular mode of travel and form of inhabitation, authority over an entire continent. We tend to homogenise the Antarctic region, to flatten its differences, physical and geopolitical, under the all-encompassing idea of "The Ice." The complex dynamics of the Antarctic cryosphere are lost in the urge to collapse regional differences. This false homogeneity has polarised arguments around climate change, fuelling both denialist claims and apocalyptic visions, as sea ice extent and snowfall increases in East Antarctica and collapsing ice sheets and runaway glaciers on the Antarctic Peninsula battle for airtime.

Another reason I'm reluctant to provide an eyewitness report is that a stay on the ice is just that: a stay *on* the ice. The idea that such an activity provides immediate insight into the state of the Antarctic icescape ignores its three-dimensionality. Camping at Windless Bight provides something of a visual

© KONINKLIJKE BRILL NV, LEIDEN, 2022 | DOI:10.1163/9789004514164_014

sense of the seemingly endless extent of the Ross Ice Shelf, but its depths—around 100 metres at our campsite and, in other places, significantly more—are much more of a mystery. Looking at faint horizontal shadows in the distance, which you know are enormous crevasses, makes you uncomfortably aware that you are living on a moving, shifting substance; and digging a snow pit—even one that is only a few metres deep—allows you some feeling for the information available in the ice shelf's vertical layers. But the ice shelf's underbelly (so to speak), where the impact of a warming ocean is most likely to be felt, can only be seen indirectly, through automated underwater vehicles and cameras sent down through drill holes.

Even if I could see under, over, around and through the ice, my vision would of course be constrained by my disciplinary training. The role of literary studies, and of the humanities more generally, is not to witness the state of the ice so much as to make us aware of the limitations, contingencies and possibilities of our vision—in literary studies, the stories we tell, and those we don't, the tropes we automatically reach for, and those we don't. Humanities researchers have been late to arrive at the polar regions, and particularly Antarctica, but our presence there—both physically and intellectually—has been increasing rapidly in the last decade or so. A recent collection made a cautious argument for the arrival of an "Antarctic humanities;"[1] perhaps there is also a case for an emerging "cryohumanities" less interested in geography than materiality, and sharing more in common with the "blue humanities" than the "geohumanities."[2] These kinds of labels, proliferating at the moment, tend to act as academic marketing tools; nonetheless the insights being produced within these subfields are worth bringing to wider notice. They involve—to speak very broadly—paying greater attention to the concept of place and locality;[3] "thinking volumetrically" about ice, as scientists have done for many years, and

---

1 Peder Roberts, Lize-Marié van der Watt and Adrian Howkins, eds, *Antarctica and the Humanities* (London: Palgrave Macmillan, 2016).

2 Since I first wrote this, geographer Klaus Dodds has put forward the term "ice humanities" to describe this very thing, a "new field of the humanities" that is "appreciative of the scholarship on blue humanities and critical ocean studies," and in which "Ice's composition, volume and the multiple relationships that sustain with human and non-human actors are essential ingredients." "Geopolitics and the Ice Humanities: Elemental, Metaphorical and Volumetric Reverberations," *Geopolitics* (2019): 2, 21. For a collection of essays on the topic, seeKlaus Dodds and Sverker Sörlin, *Ice Humanities: Materiality, Ontology and Representation* (Manchester: Manchester UP,2022).

3 See e.g., Alessandro Antonello, "Finding Place in Antarctica" in Roberts, van der Watt and Howkins, eds *Antarctica and the Humanities*; and Adrian Howkins, "Placing the Past: The McMurdo Dry Valleys and the Problem of Geographical Specificity in Antarctic History" in Leane and McGee, eds *Anthropocene Antarctica* (London: Routledge, 2019).

ICE ISLANDS OF THE ANTHROPOCENE   363

as humanities researchers have begun to do more recently in relation to the oceans and the atmosphere;[4] understanding Antarctica not as politically "frozen" but as a postcolonial space where geopolitics are actively playing out;[5] rethinking questions of Indigeneity in relation to the Antarctic continent;[6] and coming to grips with the variety of human and nonhuman actors on—or, rather, including—the ice.[7]

If climate change has made us particularly alert to the state of the planet's ice, it has likewise focused attention on islands. Paradoxically, Antarctica is a continent of islands and ice. Reduced to its bedrock—as parts of it may be in centuries to come—Antarctica looks very different; it is only the ice, once more, that unifies and homogenises it, turning the archipelago of West Antarctica into (to use John Donne's famous phrase) "a peece of the Continent." And the Antarctic, like the Arctic, constantly confuses the relationship between islands and ice, and between land and water. Historically, explorers had difficulty distinguishing between the two, especially when islands (like Ross Island, the base for the fieldtrip described above) were sutured to the ice shelves. On the Antarctic plateau, ice kilometres thick is punctured by nunataks—the rocky tips of mountains also known as "glacial islands," a term that is only semi-metaphorical as it does, after all, describe land surrounded by water.

I am making my glacial way here to icebergs—the objects originally known—and still known in some contexts—as "ice islands." While this metaphor has its limitations, icebergs—particularly the large tabular bergs typical of the Antarctic region that can, in theory at least, be walked on, landed on, even built on—have many material features in common with islands.[8]

---

4   Klaus Dodds and Mark Nuttall, *The Scramble for the Poles: The Geopolitics of the Arctic and Antarctic* (Cambridge, UK, and Malden, MA: Polity, 2016): 61–64.

5   See, for example, Klaus Dodds and Christy Collis, "Post-colonial Antarctica" in Klaus Dodds, Alan Hemmings and Peder Roberts, eds, *Handbook on the Politics of Antarctica* (Cheltenham: Edward Elgar, 2017).

6   For example, Priscilla M. Wehi, Nigel J. Scott, Jacinta Beckwith, Rata Pryor Rodgers, Tasman Gillies, Vincent Van Uitregt and Krushil Watene, "A Short Scan of Māori Journeys to Antarctica," *Journal of the Royal Society of New Zealand* (2021), https://doi.org/10.1080/03036758.2021.1917633.

7   For example, Lill Rastad Bjørst, "The Tip of the Iceberg: Ice as a Non-Human Actor in the Climate Change Debate," *Études/Inuit/Studies* 34.1 (2010).

8   While more typical of the Antarctic, large tabular bergs can occur in both polar regions. Researchers sometimes deploy instruments on Antarctic bergs, but the most prominent example of building on a tabular iceberg is in the Arctic: the US military established a research base on the berg known as "Fletcher's Island" or "T-3" for over two decades. See Mariana Gosnell, *Ice: The Nature, the History, and the Uses of an Astonishing Substance* (New York: Knopf, 2005): 161, 207.

Icebergs can offer the solidity and extensiveness of land, even while they share and are driven by the material medium of the ocean. While icebergs differ from islands most obviously in their degree of changeability, both spatially and temporally, some can be remarkably durable. Isolated by the southern circumpolar current, large tabular Antarctic bergs can last for many decades. Occasionally their remnants sneak north, to reach more temperate latitudes. The Antarctic accounts for over 90 percent of icebergs, by mass.[9] The rest issue from the Arctic: the Greenland glaciers and, to a much lesser extent, islands such as Svalbard. They tend to be much smaller and are not normally tabular. Several hundred drift far enough south every year to be a danger to North Atlantic shipping lanes. For Inuit and other far northern communities, bergs have always been a taken-for-granted part of daily existence. In the Southern Hemisphere, contact is far rarer, although there are Māori and Pacific Islander traditions of iceberg encounter going back many centuries.[10] But for most lower-latitude cultures, bergs are exotic, dangerous, beautiful objects encountered primarily through visual and written texts.

The Anthropocene has moved icebergs to the centre of public consciousness, their ephemerality and mutability reminding us ominously of the mobile and impermanent nature of the icecaps and of our own impact on the planet's possible future. Beginning with two events that featured prominently in the media in mid-2017, and segueing into an analysis of three postcolonial novels, I want to explore some of the ways in which we talk, write and tell stories about icebergs—Antarctic icebergs particularly—and what the consequences of our habits of thinking about these glacial remnants might be in this epoch we are calling the Anthropocene.

1   A68: A Cryohistorical Moment?

My first point of departure is the media sensation that surrounded the calving of a very large berg from the Antarctic coast in July 2017. Earlier in that year, reports had begun appearing of a rapidly extending rift in an ice shelf in the Antarctic Peninsula.[11] The scientific community had been monitoring the

---

9   Christopher C. Joyner, "The Status of Ice in International Law" in Alex G. Oude Elferink and Donald R. Rothwell, eds. *The Law of the Sea and Polar Maritime Delimitation and Jurisdiction* (The Hague: Martinus Nijhoff-Kluwer Law International, 2001): 35–36.

10   Wehi, "A Short Scan."

11   Jugal K. Patel, "A Crack in an Antarctic Ice Shelf Grew 17 Miles in the Last Two Months," *New York Times* (February 7, 2017), https://www.nytimes.com/interactive/2017/02/07/science/earth/antarctic-crack.html.

ICE ISLANDS OF THE ANTHROPOCENE 365

fracture for years, but now it began to draw wider attention. Over the next few months, the world watched in slow suspense as the spectacular crack in the Larsen C ice shelf made its inexorable way towards the coast. By early June the proto-berg was, according to the *Guardian,* "hanging by a thread"—if that is the right metaphor to apply to a trillion-tonne block of floating ice.[12] Reports on its progress began to appear daily in the international news, until in mid-July the inevitable creation of the giant berg made global headlines.

By this time, initial worries about sea-level rise had been corrected: already displacing its mass in seawater in its former life as a floating ice shelf, the freshwater berg would affect sea level only to the extent that it decreased ocean salinity and density—a comparatively minor effect. Nonetheless, the event was worrying: the neighbouring Larsen A and B shelves had already collapsed unusually quickly, and there was fear that the event might affect the Larsen C's stability. The iceberg's creation was widely framed as an ominous indication of things to come. *Time* magazine predicted the berg "Won't Be the Last to Go"; *National Geographic* announced the event was "Just the Beginning—Antarctica is Melting"; and *WIRED* magazine mused on "Giant Antarctic Icebergs and Crushing Existential Dread."[13] The iceberg became, to use a phase that critic Elena Glasberg applies to Antarctica itself, an object of "anthropocentric panic."[14] Onto its vast whiteness were projected fears as to what its unthinkable bulk suggested about the planet's future; guilt over human complicity in the instability of the Antarctic ice; and anger at the climate inaction of industry and government. Activist group 350.org petitioned the US National Ice Center to have the new berg named "#Exxonknew," a reference to their ongoing campaign to highlight the oil company's contribution to the climate crisis.[15] The media preferred the moniker of "white

---

12   Nicola Davis, "Giant Antarctic Iceberg 'Hanging by a Thread', say Scientists," *Guardian* (June 2, 2017), https://www.theguardian.com/world/2017/jun/02/giant-antarctic-iceberg -hanging-by-a-thread-say-scientists.

13   Justin Worland, "The Enormous Ice Sheet that Broke Off of Antarctica Won't be the Last to Go," *Time* (July 13, 2017), http://time.com/4855567/antarctic-iceberg-glacier-larsen-c -climate-change/; Douglas Fox, "The Larsen C Ice Shelf Collapse Is Just the Beginning– Antarctica Is Melting," *National Geographic* (July 12, 2017), https://www.nationalgeograp hic.com/magazine/2017/07/antarctica-sea-level-rise-climate-change/; Adam Rogers, "Giant Antarctic Icebergs and Crushing Existential Dread," *WIRED* (July 13, 2017), https:// www.wired.com/story/giant-antarctic-icebergs-and-crushing-existential-dread/.

14   Elena Glasberg, *Antarctica as Cultural Critique: The Gendered Politics of Scientific Exploration and Climate Change* (New York: Palgrave Macmillan, 2012): 110.

15   "The #ExxonKnew Iceberg has Broken Free," *350.org,* n.d., http://act.350.org/letter/exxonk new-iceberg/.

wanderer."[16] Both less political and less romantic in its nomenclature, the National Ice Center stuck to its decades-long convention of naming large Antarctic bergs according to geographical quadrant and chronological order, and the berg became A68.

The coming into being of A68 can be understood as an instantiation of the "cryo-historical moment." The term was coined in 2015 by environmental historian Sverker Sörlin, who argues that as the "powers of human forces in the Anthropocene" have made themselves apparent in the cryosphere—the frozen water parts of the Earth—"ice has become historical." The "fate of ice," he observes, is taken as a sign of "the fate of our societies."[17] Sörlin's announcement of a new "cryo-history" echoes Marcus Nüsser and Ravi Baghel's identification, a year earlier, of an emerging "cryoscape," a term they use to describe the coming together of "the physical phenomena that constitute the cryosphere" with "human epistemic practices."[18] However, Sörlin's cryohistory is focused on the Arctic (indeed, he talks of a "rising Arctic humanities"[19]), and Nüsser and Baghel are interested in the glaciers of the Himalaya—both places where humans and ice have been in an entangled coexistence for many millennia. Their scant acknowledgement of the Antarctic—by far the greatest store of ice on the planet—reinforces the widespread idea that this, at least, is one part of our world that asks to be understood through science alone. Yet humanity's actions and interactions are an inescapable part of the Antarctic—something manifest not only through many tens of thousands of annual tourist visitors (pre-COVID-19), the 80-odd stations and facilities, the dozens of runways and skiways, the CO_2, DDT, radioactive debris, heavy metals and other chemicals in the ice, and the microplastics in the surrounding oceans—but also, albeit less straightforwardly, in the behaviour of its ice sheets and ice shelves.

If, as Sörlin asserts, part of our job as humanities researchers is to "[reinterpet] the role of ice," to "see it more clearly as a key element in cultures,

---

16   Jonathan Amos, "Antarctic Iceberg: Giant 'White Wanderer' Poised to Break Free," *BBC News* (July 5, 2017), https://www.bbc.com/news/science-environment-40492957.

17   Sverker Sörlin, "Cryo-History: Narratives of Ice and the Emerging Arctic Humanities" in *The New Arctic*, eds. Birgitta Evengård, Joan Nymand Larsen and Øyvind Paasche (Cham: Springer, 2015): 327, 328.

18   Marcus Nüsser and Ravi Baghel, "The Emergence of the Cryoscape: Contested Narratives of Himalayan Glacier Dynamics and Climate Change" in *Environmental and Climate Change in South and Southeast Asia: How are Local Cultures Coping?*, ed. Barbara Schuler (Leiden and Boston: Brill, 2014): 150.

19   Sörlin, "Cryo-History," 336.

ICE ISLANDS OF THE ANTHROPOCENE 367

communities and economies," to understand its part in "new narratives of the planetary," then what can we make of A68?[20]

The most obvious aspect of the berg's media reception is the contestation of its origins. Like most tabular bergs, A68 was a long time in the making: the fracture that produced it had been forming since the 1960s[21] and the ice that comprises it had been making its way to the coast for far longer. But its transformation into a berg raised the inevitable question of humanity's contribution to its coming into being. Although some scientists linked the event to climate change, others suggested that this particular calving was not unusual. Adrian Luckman in *The Conversation* argued that the berg's relationship with climate change was "far from straightforward," with no direct evidence linking it with either atmospheric or ocean warming; Helen Fricker wrote in the *Guardian* that "while there is plenty going on to merit concern ... large calving events like this are normal processes of a healthy ice sheet."[22] More worrying are runaway glaciers such as the Thwaites or Pine Island, which have grounding lines on retrograde slopes and are thus subject to a positive feedback process resulting, at a certain point, in irreversible retreat; or collapse events, such as the neighbouring Larsen B, triggered by meltwater on top of the ice shelf caused by warmer air temperatures. (In the case of Larsen B, the collapse produced not a giant berg but thousands of comparatively small fragments.) Neither of these concerns applied to the creation of A68. What drew the world's attention was not a general scientific consensus around the causes of the calving or the vulnerability of the Larsen C ice shelf, but rather the size of the berg it produced.

Studying Antarctica inures you to superlatives, but by any measure A68 was big. As the media reports constantly repeated, it was almost 6,000 square kilometres in area and weighed about a trillion tonnes. Although not the biggest recorded berg—B15, which calved from the Ross Ice Shelf in the year 2000, was almost twice its size—A68 was still the largest mobile object on Earth at the time of its appearance.

---

20   Sörlin, "Cryo-History," 336.

21   Ellen Powell, "Can Scientists Crack the Case of an Antarctic Ice Shelf's Growing Rift?" *Christian Science Monitor* (January 16, 2017), https://www.csmonitor.com/Science/2017/0116/Can-scientists-crack-the-case-of-an-Antarctic-ice-shelf-s-growing-rift.

22   Adrian Luckman, "I've Studied Larsen C and Its Giant Iceberg for Years—It's Not a Simple Story of Climate Change," *The Conversation* (July 12, 2017), https://theconversation.com/ive-studied-larsen-c-and-its-giant-iceberg-for-years-its-not-a-simple-story-of-climate-change-80529; Helen Amanda Fricker, "Melting and Cracking—Is Antarctica Falling Apart?" *Guardian* (June 23, 2017), https://www.theguardian.com/science/2017/jun/23/melting-and-cracking-is-antarctica-falling-apart-climate-change.

While the berg's gargantuan size was its drawcard for the media, it also posed a quandary: the difficulty of representing, visualizing, imagining and conceiving of it. The problem was exacerbated by the timing of A68's birth, during the Southern Hemisphere winter. The berg calved very close to mid-winter, when the region south of the Antarctic Circle is in darkness, so photographs were unavailable. Old images of the fracture, taken in daylight the previous summer, had to suffice. Satellite radar images existed, but showed the berg two-dimensionally from above. With no comparator except the ice shelf itself, the images gave no sense of the berg's scale. Media commentators were reduced to words, and inevitably reached for terrestrial comparisons to convey some measure of the iceberg's size. The variety of these gives a sense of the global nature of media interest: the berg was the size of the Australian Capital Territory; the size of Delaware; the size of Prince Edward Island; the size of Crete; almost the size of Bali; one and a half times the size of Goa; twice the size of Luxembourg; twice the size of Samoa; three times the size of Maui; four times the size of Taiwan; half the size of Flanders; a quarter of the size of Wales; a sixth of the size of Istanbul.[23] There are many further examples, but, as the list seems in danger of turning into an icy version of Zeno's paradox, I'll stop there.

This reaching for land analogues to describe a large chunk of ice is of course nothing new—at least for those who live in lower latitudes. Inherent in the term "iceberg" itself, terrestrial comparisons are constantly apparent in polar exploration literature. In an essay in *The Paris Review* on the poetry of icebergs, Marissa Grunes writes that "the language used to describe massive ice forms reflects—and strives to tame—their ambiguities. Metaphoric terms ... ground the protean, imitative fantasias of frozen water in recognizable land features ... these ice forms are metaphoric through and through."[24] However, land features are only one of a series of metaphors that humans reach for to couch the strange in terms of the familiar—jewels, architectural forms and facial features also recur. Helen Garner, in an essay on her experience of an Antarctic cruise, describes her own frustration at this constant reaching for metaphor:

---

23   Most of these examples are collected in Zoë Schlanger, Jennifer Brown and Katherine Ellen Foley, "Two Luxembourgs, 10 Madrids and One Delaware: How a Giant Iceberg is Described Around the World," *Quartz* (July 13, 2017), https://qz.com/1027701/two-luxembourgs-10-madrids-one-delaware-how-a-giant-iceberg-in-antarctica-is-described-around-the-world/.

24   Marissa Grunes, "Masses of Beautiful Alabaster," *The Paris Review* (July 20, 2017), https://www.theparisreview.org/blog/2017/07/20/masses-of-beautiful-alabaster/.

... somebody begins to liken the iceberg to a face. It's got a sad eye. See its nose? On and on people go: it's like a sphinx, a Peke's face, an Indian head with its mouth open. Again I am secretly enraged by this, and by my own urgent desire to do the same. I stare at the iceberg as it looms two hundred metres away on our port side. It gleams with a pearly purity. It's faceted: creamy on the left, whiter on the right. It looks stable, like an island rather than something floating. Water riffles around its foot. I strain and fail to see it only in abstract terms. I don't want to keep going 'like, like, like.' But I can't stop myself.[25]

This reliance on the figurative when it comes to icebergs seems inescapable. When they are not the tenor of metaphors—being understood in terms of their likeness to something else—iceberg are the vehicles, themselves used to explain something else. Google "icebergs and literature" and you are less likely to find any reference to literary engagement with actual bergs than descriptions of the way in which literary writing is *like* a berg. Most prominent is Ernest Hemingway's "Iceberg Theory" of writing: just as, according to Hemingway, "the dignity of movement of an iceberg is due to only one-eighth of it being above water," so the majority of a narrative should be below its surface, implicit rather than stated.[26] For writers, it seems, icebergs are about writing.

Icebergs—and particularly their tips—are such useful metaphors that it is difficult to get past them. Philosopher Timothy Morton, outlining his theory of hyperobjects—things that are "impossible to see on a regular three-dimensional human scale" but can only be apprehended in "pieces ... at a time"[27]—regularly reaches for the metaphor of the iceberg, both the generic object and the specific berg that collided with the *Titanic*; indeed, an iceberg adorns his cover. Arguably it is not this typically Arctic iceberg that best illustrates Morton's idea, but rather a massive tabular berg such as A68, which would make a terrible cover image precisely because it cannot be visually represented in any familiar way—it doesn't even have a tip. The larger point is that, for theorists, icebergs are about theory. In a similar way, we can understand the media construction of and public scientific reaction to A68 in terms of metaphor. While glaciologists argue that the berg's calving cannot at this stage be directly associated with climate change, they readily concede its value

---

25   Helen Garner, "Regions of Thick-Ribbed Ice," *The Feel of Steel* (Sydney: Picador-Pan Macmillan, 2001): 17.

26   Ernest Hemingway, *Death in the Afternoon* (New York: Scribner's, 1932): 192.

27   Timothy Morton, *Hyperobjects: Philosophy and Ecology after the End of the World* (Minneapolis: U of Minnesota P, 2013): 70.

as a powerful symbol of collapsing ice to come. Its relationship with climate change, then, is metaphoric rather than metonymic. Hence the importance of its size: in its massiveness, the berg represents the magnitude of collective fears and distributed guilt, the magnitude of future changes.

This ubiquitousness of metaphor suggests that, to understand the current meaning of A68 and its counterparts, we need to look further than the contemporary media reaction. Icebergs come to us laden with the associations of past tropes, narratives and events. The framing of A68 as a symbol of future climate catastrophe is so powerful partly because it draws on an established cultural framing of bergs in terms of threat. Until recently, when icebergs made headlines, the reason was usually a collision with a ship, with the *Titanic* disaster by far the best known of these. The same applies to fictional treatments: the *Titanic* alone has produced dozens of titles,[28] but imagined iceberg collisions or near-collisions also recur in both popular and literary fiction set in or near the polar regions. Examples include Hammond Innes's *The White South* (1949), Patrick O'Brian's *Desolation Island* (1978) and William Golding's *Fire Down Below* (1989). Adventure thrillers and ecothrillers have produced new forms of the iceberg-threat narrative, with villains deliberately blasting icebergs off shelves to produce global havoc.[29] The iceberg here becomes simultaneously threat, victim and weapon. A68, taken as a symbol of climate catastrophe to come, fits into this narrative arc, its threat not erased but complicated—corrupted—by our possible complicity in the situation that produced it.

The power of the iceberg-as-threat image makes it easy to overlook alternatives. But I want to turn now to another event that garnered media attention at the same time that the fissure in the Larsen C was heading unstoppably for the coast: one that framed tabular bergs as a solution to, rather than a harbinger of, climate challenges ahead.

2   Frozen Resources: Iceberg-Towing Speculations

The drama of the Larsen C fissure in the global media overshadowed reports, in May 2017, that the United Arab Emirates planned "to tow a giant iceberg over 9,000km from Antarctica to the Arabian Peninsula and then break it

---

28   Imaginative works make up fifty pages of D. Brian Anderson's book-length annotated guide to *The Titanic in Print and Screen* (Jefferson, MC: McFarland, 2005).

29   Examples of iceberg-based thrillers include James Follett's *Ice* (1978) and Judith and Garfield Reeves-Stevens' *Icefire* (1998).

ICE ISLANDS OF THE ANTHROPOCENE

down to use as drinking water."[30] While the scheme was greeted in the Western media as an absurdity, it too drew on well-established narratives. The idea of icebergs as a potential resource has a surprisingly long and almost entirely textual history.[31] Although the transport of chippings from glaciers and icebergs for drinking water goes back centuries, and modern commercial operations based on the same idea have also existed for decades, the wholesale towing of bergs is far less common. Arctic oil companies tow bergs small distances to put them out of the way of rigs—diverting a potential threat—but only once has a scheme to move them long distances to use as resources seemingly been actualized: a late nineteenth-century operation in which icebergs were apparently towed and sometimes sailed up the coast of Chile to provide refrigeration for breweries. As all accounts of this operation rely on only one letter written a half-century after the event, it is hard to judge the accuracy of this report.[32] However, as speculation—scientific, economic and literary—the idea of iceberg-towing has a far richer and better substantiated pedigree.

The first mention (to my knowledge) of such a scheme, in English language sources at least, comes from a literary text, and occurs in a context of climate crisis that speaks in surprising ways to our own moment. British naturalist Erasmus Darwin in his 1792 poem-cum-science-popularisation "The Economy of Vegetation" (Part I of his poem *The Botanic Garden*) imagines nymphs fixing sails to Arctic icebergs and steering them to low latitudes, where the "swarthy nations" would benefit as the "arctic snows" cool the "tropic year."[33] In a footnote to the poem, Darwin more prosaically advocates Northern Hemisphere nations putting their military powers to this project rather than fighting wars. Writing during the "Little Ice Age," and believing that an ice build-up at the poles was creating a cooling of temperate regions, Darwin hoped through this idea not only to benefit the tropics but also, by the removal of ice from

---

30   See for example: Lara Pearce, "UAE Company Wants to Tow an Iceberg from Antarctica for Drinking Water," *Huffington Post* (May 19, 2017), https://www.huffingtonpost.com .au/2017/05/18/uae-company-wants-to-tow-an-iceberg-from-antarctica-for-drinking_a_2 2086611/. A year later, the company was still mooting the idea, although there was little sign of it being actualised. In the meantime, a similar scheme was proposed as a solution to the water shortage in Cape Town, South Africa.

31   A useful popular summary is Alexis C. Madrigal's "The Many Failures and Few Successes of Zany Iceberg Towing Schemes," *The Atlantic* (August 10, 2011), https://www.theatlantic .com/technology/archive/2011/08/the-many-failures-and-few-successes-of-zany-iceberg -towing-schemes/243364/.

32   See: W.F. Weeks and W.J. Campbell, "Icebergs as a Fresh-Water Source: An Appraisal," *Journal of Glaciology* 12.65 (1973): 209.

33   Erasmus Darwin, *The Botanic Garden: A Poem in Two Parts* (New York: T & J Swords, 1798): 31–32.

the Arctic, to make winters milder in the latitudes of Britain. As literary critic Siobhan Carroll notes, the idea is an example of "geoengineering"—one that, in its imperial confidence in Britain's right to determine the climate of the "swarthy nations," shows "the kinds of thinking [currently] challenged in climate change critiques mounted by and regarding the Global South."[34]

Although there was no chance of Darwin's suggestion being put into action, it nonetheless "lingered in the popular imagination," becoming a touchstone of hare-brained schemes but occasionally resurrected in seriousness.[35] During the nineteenth century, several similar ideas were raised. An 1863 *Scientific American* article mentions a plan to tow bergs to sell to India and another to fit a propeller to a berg itself.[36] By the mid-twentieth century, the idea was receiving serious scientific attention as an energy-efficient alternative to desalinisation, with various dry locations in the southern USA, Australia, South America, Africa and the Middle East identified as possible beneficiaries.[37] By now the Antarctic was the focus of attention, due to the plentifulness of stable, tabular bergs, although this raised some interesting legal issues. Under the Antarctic Treaty System, ice is not a mineral and theoretically can be harvested, but the status of a drifting iceberg quickly becomes quite complex.[38]

This growing interest came to a head in the 1970s. In 1973 the US National Science Foundation—which administers the nation's Antarctic program—commissioned a hundred-page study of icebergs as resources by the RAND Corporation.[39] This was followed in 1977 by the first of two conferences sponsored by the Saudi royal Mohommad Al-Faisal, who was President of a company entitled "Iceberg Transport International." Held in 1977 at Iowa State University, the first conference featured as its centrepiece a one-tonne iceberg, brought from Alaska by helicopter, plane and refrigerated truck.[40] Both the RAND report and the 1977 conference proceedings make for fascinating

---

34 Siobhan Carroll, "On Erasmus Darwin's *The Botanic Garden*, 1791–1792," BRANCH: Britain, Representation, and Nineteenth-Century History, ed. Dino Franco Felluga. Extension of Romanticism and Victorianism, http://www.branchcollective.org/?ps_articles=siobhan-carroll-on-erasmus-darwins-the-botanic-garden-1791-1792.

35 Carroll, "On Erasmus Darwin's *The Botanic Garden*".

36 See Madrigal, "The Many Failures".

37 J.L Hult and N.C. Ostrander, *Antarctic Icebergs as a Global Fresh Water Resource* (Santa Monica: Rand Corporation, 1973): v.

38 Joyner, "The Status of Ice," 36–40.

39 Hult and Ostrander, *Antarctic Icebergs*.

40 See Brian Mackley, "The Tale of an Iceberg at Iowa State," *Iowa State Daily* (November 15, 2017), http://www.iowastatedaily.com/app_content/article_a862fd50-ca84-11e7-ac5a-f75457213aaf.html; and Rafico Ruiz, "Saudi Dreams: Icebergs in Iowa," *Arcadia* 19 (Summer 2017), http://www.environmentandsociety.org/arcadia/saudi-dreams-icebergs-iowa.

ICE ISLANDS OF THE ANTHROPOCENE
373

reading. While from an environmental perspective some of the ideas seem laughably awful—spraying bergs with polyurethane foam so that they are, effectively, wrapped in plastic; powering a berg caravan by a nuclear reactor—others seem prescient in their engagement with renewables: floating solar collectors could be used to process the water; differences in ocean temperatures could generate the energy to transport the berg. Conference-goers raised the question of whether ice was, in fact, a renewable. The greenhouse effect is mentioned early in the conference proceedings, with one paper pointing to possible sea-level rise and arguing that Southern Hemisphere ice "must be viewed as a diminishing, not an incessantly renewed, resource."[41]

One of the unexpected consequences of the 1977 discussions was Australia's best-known April Fools' Day joke, in which entrepreneur Dick Smith, having heard of the Saudi plans, sailed a barge covered in sheets and white foam into Sydney Harbour, with crowds looking on. On exactly the same day, the state of California gave its "stamp of approval" to a serious Antarctic iceberg-towing scheme.[42] Nonetheless, the idea remained on paper only. It has been resuscitated periodically by Australia, South Africa and several other nations; the UAE scheme is merely one recent example.[43]

Unsurprisingly, given its largely fictive nature, iceberg-towing has inspired novelistic treatment, including several postcolonial literary texts. For the remainder of this chapter, I'd like to briefly consider how these narratives help us think about icebergs. While the three examples examined here have markedly different settings and thematic focuses, they all represent towing or capturing schemes as a fantasy of human control over pure nature, before allowing this idea to upend itself.

The first is *The Nanny and the Iceberg*, published in 1999 by Ariel Dorfman, a Chilean-American novelist who writes in both Spanish and English. Dorfman's

---

41 Lowell Ponte, "Alien Ice: An Evaluation of Some Subsidiary Effects and Concomitant Problems in Iceberg Utilization" in *Iceberg Utilization: Proceedings of the First International Conference Held at Iowa State University, Ames, Iowa*, ed. A.A. Husseiny, Iowa (Elmsford, NY: Pergamon, 1978): 16.

42 "California Legislature Endorses Plan to Tow Iceberg from Antarctica," *Toledo Blade* (April 1, 1978): A.14. I learned of this coincidence via Anthony Fordham, "Could We Actually Tow an Iceberg to Make Drinking Water," *Australian Popular Science* (June 23, 2014), https://www.popsci.com.au/make/could-we-actually-tow-an-iceberg-to-make-drinking-water_388725/.

43 For a historical analysis of Australian iceberg-towing proposals, see Ruth A. Morgan, "Dry Continent Dreaming: Australian Visions of using Antarctic Icebergs for Water Supplies," *International Review of Environmental History* 4.1 (2018), http://press-files.anu.edu.au/downloads/press/n4203/html/09_morgan.xhtml.

novel gives a fictional account of an actual cryohistorical event in 1992, when iceberg fragments from the Antarctic Peninsula—a region claimed by Chile—were assembled into a 28-foot iceberg sculpture in the Chilean pavilion of the World Expo in Seville.[44] The Western media at the time recognised a "magic realist ... impulse" in the venture: "At least in the literary sense," the *New York Times* opined, "the plan was emphatically Latin American."[45] Dorfman uses that iceberg to explore relationships between both a father and a son, and a colonising and colonised people. The novel centres on Gabriel, a young Chilean expatriate who, at the start of the story, is living in New York City in the late 1970s with his activist mother. Heartily sick of her involvement in the Chilean resistance movement, he exits a political meeting and walks the street, becoming enthralled by an image of icebergs playing on a bank of television screens in a shop window. Retelling the story years later, the older Gabriel reflects on its irony: "the very night I declared my unilateral independence from my country I was waylaid by images of a silent crystal continent that was part of the territory of that country."[46] Before long Gabriel finds himself back in Chile with his father and involved in harvesting an iceberg for the Expo.

From this point the iceberg begins to accrete a series of contested and contradictory meanings as the characters project their own personal and political concerns onto its seeming blankness. For those behind the scheme, ice is associated with Chilean modernity and technological mastery. "[A]ll power starts and ends with ice," explains one of the proponents to Gabriel, noting how Spanish invaders of Chile in the sixteenth century survived by preserving their food in the Andean snow.[47] But the berg, part of Chilean Antarctic Territory, represents the colonised as much as the coloniser. Gabriel's half-sister, a feminist film-maker, believes the Selk'nam, Indigenous inhabitants of Patagonia, to be "the owners of the Antarctica" and hence the berg.[48] This speaks back to the novel's title, as the eponymous nanny—Mercedes, Gabriel's childhood caregiver—is, it becomes evident, a Selk'nam descendent. Gabriel determines to explode the berg as a means of suicidal revenge against "the men who had stolen her clan from her and who had, for good measure, stolen Antarctica as well."[49] Yet, speaking from the grave, Mercedes reveals that the berg at the

---

44   The original plan was to tow a whole iceberg; as usual, it had to be abandoned for a more pragmatic solution.

45   "Chile's Chilly Idea," *New York Times* (November 8, 1991), http://www.nytimes.com/1991/11/08/opinion/chile-s-chilly-idea.html.

46   Ariel Dorfman, *The Nanny and the Iceberg* (New York: Seven Stories, 2003): 56.

47   Dorfman, *The Nanny and the Iceberg*, 119.

48   Dorfman, *The Nanny and the Iceberg*, 229.

49   Dorfman, *The Nanny and the Iceberg*, 236.

ICE ISLANDS OF THE ANTHROPOCENE

Expo is not even Antarctic, having melted prematurely because of a broken refrigeration system and been supplemented by Norwegian and Spanish ice. The berg becomes a multinational product. In some ways it already was: the region from which the Antarctic ice was taken is claimed by both Britain and Argentina, and simultaneously governed by an international Treaty suspending sovereignty.

Where the iceberg of Dorfman's title is brought to low latitudes for touristic and nationalistic purposes, Nowra's novel *Ice*, published in 2008, relates an entrepreneurial venture that has, ostensibly at least, more in common with the historical speculations I outlined earlier. The novel opens with a colonial version of Dick Smith's comic fantasy—an Antarctic iceberg towed into nineteenth-century Sydney harbour to cheering crowds. At the centre of the narrative is one of the berg's captors, a businessman who makes his name by fulfilling the "insatiable craving for ice" of the "colonial outpost."[50] As in Dorfman's novel, initial impressions of the iceberg as something "pure and unadulterated" rapidly become complicated by commodification, class and history. "Luminous," "radiant," almost angelically beautiful as it is brought up against the dock, the berg is quickly set upon by labourers with "ropes, chains, saws, axes, spikes and sledgehammers" who cut it into pieces for immediate sale.[51] Within hours, the ice has been fragmented, distributed and transformed into sorbets and ice-creams; ice cubes in glasses of whiskey in bars; a sculpted swan at a fine dinner party; a refrigerant in butchers' carts and—when the quality and price drops enough—a palliative for fevered patients in hospitals.[52]

As the reader continues, a series of revelations gives the berg sinister overtones. The perfectly preserved body of a long-dead sailor is found inside it; the businessman who orchestrates its capture, mourning his dead wife, becomes obsessed with ice as a means to seemingly postpone death; the story itself, it becomes clear, is the product of a similar obsession—that of the twenty-first century narrator, whose wife is in prolonged coma—a form of living death—resulting from an attack by a man addicted to methamphetamine, or "ice." Anything but pure, the iceberg becomes inexorably entangled with love, death and the past. As the increasingly unhinged narrator draws the story towards an inconclusive close, he sees ice wherever he looks: "Ice," he observes, "is everywhere. Not a day goes past when there aren't newspaper articles about global

---

50   Louis Nowra, *Ice: A Love Story* (Crows Nest, NSW: Allen & Unwin, 2009): 11.
51   Nowra, *Ice*, 19, 3, 5.
52   Nowra, *Ice*, 15, 21–3, 26.

warming, melting ice caps, hundreds of icebergs moving relentlessly towards New Zealand ....”[53]

It is from exactly this kind of scenario that Witi Ihimaera's "The Purity of Ice," from his 2012 collection *The Thrill of Falling*, takes its cue. Quite different in setting, style and character, "The Purity of Ice" nonetheless has many commonalities with Nowra's novel: a man grieving the death of loved ones; a seemingly pure berg that yields unexpected meaning. Set in a post-apocalyptic world so devasted by climate change that the middle latitudes are only barely inhabitable, it centres on a Māori-owned conglomerate that harvests Antarctic bergs for international sale, towing them into a fiord in the south of New Zealand to be processed. The central protagonist, a Māori man named Drake, having lost his family in one of the now-frequent solar storms, lives a reckless life as a helicopter pilot, harpooning bergs from the air and dodging attacks from rival corporations and berg-poachers. But his cowboy existence is haunted by the enigmatic berg known as "Moby Dick"—a huge, ancient, whale-shaped berg made of ice of unprecedented purity, but so full of cavities that it turns, descends and ascends unpredictably, evading capture and destroying those who attempt to tackle it as if motivated by an internal wilfulness.[54] Towards the end of the tale, after Drake has finally managed to bring the giant berg home, his pleasure is foreshortened by the discovery of a dark shape within its mass. Ihimaera's description of the slow revelation of this object playfully runs the gamut of Antarctic fiction clichés: "The shape within morphed from one image to another: a giant mosquito from an antediluvian age; a *Tyrannosaurus rex*; an ancient artefact from some sunken Antarctic Atlantis; a legendary waka that missed Aotearoa and ended up girdled in ice. An ancient spaceship with its navigator, a thing from outer space, trapped inside."[55] But what is revealed is not the past but the future: a helicopter like Drake's with people inside; the berg has captured its captors. The apparently successful containment of the nonhuman through technology reveals only the futility of this enterprise, humanity's own containment within the environment it tries to control.

---

53   Nowra, *Ice*, 320.

54   While Ihimaera's conceit of a replacing Melville's white whale with an iceberg seems a playful spin on the canonical tale, the substitution is actually a literalisation of a metaphor that is quite explicit in the original text. When Moby Dick surfaces towards the end of the Melville's novel, the waters part "as if sideways sliding from a submerged berg of ice, swiftly rising to the surface." Herman Melville, *Moby Dick* (London: Dent; New York: E.P. Dutton, 1907): 487.

55   Witi Ihimaera, *The Thrill of Falling: Stories* (Auckland: Vintage-Penguin, 2012): 176.

ICE ISLANDS OF THE ANTHROPOCENE

3   Stories of Ice in the Anthropocene

While these literary narratives all deal with iceberg encounters, they nonetheless follow human characters. What would a story look like if it followed an iceberg? By way of conclusion, I'd like to briefly speculate on the kind of story a writer might tell if A68 were the protagonist. A story a little like this has already been attempted, in marine biologist Richard Brown's *Voyage of the Iceberg*, first published in 1983. The berg of Brown's title is unnamed because, he argues, there is "only one iceberg"—the one that collided with the *Titanic*. But Brown's book is far from a standard iceberg-as-threat narrative. Rather than rehearse a tale of a "capricious, icy demon lying in wait in the dark Atlantic," he looks beyond the "small fraction of the Iceberg's own history" that was the collision. This is not to diminish the scale of the human tragedy, but rather to tell a story different from the other few hundred accounts. In Brown's book, the iceberg is front and centre, and the *Titanic* "only a supporting character in a cast of ships, seals and whales, bears and seabirds, and men as well." The last include not only the passengers on the *Titanic*, but also the earlier explorers who visit and the Inuit who live in the region the berg passes through. Inasmuch as Brown could not know the exact provenance and path of the iceberg, his book is a work of imagination as well as science. In the sense that it speaks of an individual, historical berg rather than an imagined version or generic class of objects, you might term it a semi-fictional cryobiography.[56]

A "cryobiography" of A68, as an early twenty-first century Antarctic tabular berg, would be rather different. For one thing, its protagonist would have a name (admittedly, one that makes it sound like a highway, and that changes as it fragments). Less imagination would be required in describing its journey. Where Brown had to guess his iceberg's route, A68's path—like those of all very large bergs—was tracked by satellite. Between its calving in mid-2017 and its eventual disintegration in 2021, A68 travelled well over four thousand kilometres.[57] Its trajectory was not surprising: the berg spent a year doing "little more than shuffl[ing] back and forth on the spot,"[58] before rotating out through

---

56   Richard Brown, *Voyage of the Iceberg: The Story of the Iceberg that Sank the Titanic* (Toronto, ON: Lorimer, 2012): 10.

57   Jan L. Lieser, "Ice Bulletin: Iceberg A-68A" in Ice Bulletins for the Antarctic Shipping Season 2021–2022, (Hobart, Tasmania: Australian Government Bureau of Meteorology, 2022). By this time, A68 was technically A-68A—the biggest fragment of the remaining berg.

58   Jonathan Amos, "Monster Iceberg's Pivot and Turn," *BBC News* (September 5, 2018), para. 1, https://www.bbc.com/news/science-environment-45421315.

the Weddell Sea and travelling in a broadly predictable north-easterly route through "Iceberg Alley"[59]—named so because so many icebergs journey this way—before finally disintegrating to the west of the island of South Georgia.

During its lifetime, A68 experienced multiple virtual and material interactions with humans and nonhumans. Carefully tracked and much too big to be a contender for harvesting, it was never in danger of collisions and towing schemes, but at least one tourist vessel reported sailing along its edge. The berg contained enough ice, the cruise ship's blog stated, "to make 8,818,490,000,000,000 frozen margaritas!"[60] The various stages of its journey were reported periodically in the press, even as other large icebergs—some much more closely connected to anthropogenic melt—began to steal its limelight.[61] As the iceberg approached South Georgia—an island comparable to its size—the media reported concern about its possible interference with seal and penguin foraging routes. By April 2021, however, it had broken into pieces too small to warrant tracking. Surviving as a reportable iceberg for a little less than four years, A68 (or A68A as it had now become), which was thin compared to its area, had a comparatively short lifetime. Other bergs of comparable size can last for decades: B09B, for example, has been travelling (with long periods of grounded rest) since the late 1980s.

A cryobiography of A68 or any of its counterparts would of course bring home the degree to which icebergs are always interconnected with human lives; the range of disciplinary perspectives needed to understand their journeys; and the repertoire of desires and anxieties that are incessantly projected on them—a repertoire complex and contradictory, but not infinite, as it is constrained both by icebergs' own materiality and the previous narratives attached to them.[62] Ihimaera's references to Melville's novel warn us not to expect an iceberg to yield a single meaning. Rather, like the white whale, like a

---

59 Kathryn Hansen, "Iceberg A-68A nears South Georgia," National Space and Aeronautical Administration Earth Observatory (November 16, 2020), https://earthobservatory.nasa .gov/images/147535/iceberg-a-68a-nears-south-georgia?linkId=104616459.

60 Sheri Bluestein, "Paulet Island and tabular iceberg A-68-A," Lindblad Expeditions-National Geographic (December 14, 2019), https://au.expeditions.com/daily-expedition -reports/191475/.

61 Jonathan Amos. "Antarctica's big new iceberg: Up close with B49," BBC News (February 12, 2020), https://www.bbc.com/news/science-environment-51479329. Not long after A68's disintegration, headlines appeared in the global media of a new arrival, as A76 calved from the Ronne Ice Shelf to become the world's largest iceberg (Fahy 2021).

62 For one attempt at a "cryobiography" see Elizabeth Leane and Ben Maddison, "A Biography of Iceberg B09B," Australian Humanities Review 64 (December 2018), http://australianh umanitiesreview.org/.

hyperobject, a berg reveals how much escapes our attempts to make meaning. In the Anthropocene, it should be no surprise that icebergs signify the paradoxes of our times: material and symbol; threat and resource; 'pure nature' and sinister holders of hidden secrets. Icebergs are victims of humanity's destructiveness and omens of its coming doom, but also speculative sites of its ingenuity, its enterprise, its aspiration to mastery over the planet. We can try to see icebergs shorn of metaphors and previous narratives; we can try, like Helen Garner, to resist going "like, like, like"; but until we manage this, we must try to understand how we tell their stories, and continue to look for new ways to do so.

Works Cited

Amos, Jonathan. "Antarctica's Big New Iceberg: Up Close with B49." *BBC News* (February 12, 2020), https://www.bbc.com/news/science-environment-51479329.

Amos, Jonathan. "Antarctic Iceberg: Giant 'White Wanderer' Poised to Break Free." *BBC News* (July 5, 2017), https://www.bbc.com/news/science-environment-40492957.

Amos, Jonathan. "Monster Iceberg's Pivot and Turn." *BBC News* (September 5, 2018), https://www.bbc.com/news/science-environment-45421315.

Amos, Jonathan. "The 'Monster' Iceberg: What Happened Next?" *BBC News* (July 9, 2018), https://www.bbc.com/news/science-environment-44745734.

Anderson, D. Brian. *The Titanic in Print and Screen* (Jefferson, MC: McFarland, 2005).

Antonello, Alessandro. "Finding Place in Antarctica" in *Antarctica and the Humanities*, eds. Peder Roberts, Lize-Marié van der Watt and Adrian Howkins (London: Palgrave Macmillan, 2016): 181–203.

Bjørst, Lill Rastad. "The Tip of the Iceberg: Ice as a Non-Human Actor in the Climate Change Debate." *Études/Inuit/Studies* 34.1 (2010): 133–150.

Bluestein, Sheri. "Paulet Island and Tabular Iceberg A-68-A." Lindblad Expeditions-National Geographic. (December 14, 2019), https://au.expeditions.com/daily-exp edition-reports/191475/.

Brown, Richard. *Voyage of the Iceberg: The Story of the Iceberg that Sank the Titanic.* (Toronto, ON: Lorimer, 2012).

"California Legislature Endorses Plan to Tow Iceberg from Antarctica." *Toledo* Blade (April 1, 1978): A.14.

Carroll, Siobhan. "On Erasmus Darwin's *The Botanic Garden*, 1791–1792." BRANCH: Britain, Representation, and Nineteenth-Century History, ed. Dino Franco Felluga. Extension of Romanticism and Victorianism on the Net, http://www.branchcol lective.org/?ps_articles=siobhan-carroll-on-erasmus-darwins-the-botanic-gar den-1791-1792.

"Chile's Chilly Idea." *New York Times* (November 8, 1991), http://www.nytimes.com/1991/11/08/opinion/chile-s-chilly-idea.html.

Darwin, Erasmus. *The Botanic Garden: A Poem in Two Parts* (New York: T & J Swords, 1798).

Davis, Nicola. "Giant Antarctic Iceberg 'Hanging by a Thread', say Scientists." *Guardian* (June 2, 2017), https://www.theguardian.com/world/2017/jun/02/giant-antarctic-iceberg-hanging-by-a-thread-say-scientists.

Dodds, Klaus. "Geopolitics and the Ice Humanities: Elemental, Metaphorical and Volumetric Reverberations." *Geopolitics* (2019): 1–29.

Dodds, Klaus, and Mark Nuttall. *The Scramble for the Poles: The Geopolitics of the Arctic and Antarctic.* (Cambridge, UK, and Malden, MA: Polity, 2016).

Dodds, Klaus, and Christy Collis. "Post-colonial Antarctica" in *Handbook on the Politics of Antarctica*, eds. Klaus Dodds, Alan Hemmings and Peder Roberts (Cheltenham: Edward Elgar, 2017): 50–68.

Dodds, Klaus, and Sverker Sörlin. *Ice Humanities: Materiality, Ontology and Representation.* (Manchester: Manchester UP, 2022).

Dorfman, Ariel. *The Nanny and the Iceberg.* (New York: Seven Stories, 2003).

"The #ExxonKnew Iceberg has Broken Free." *350.org*, (n.d.), http://act.350.org/letter/exxonknew-iceberg/.

Fahy, Claire. "Iceberg Splits from Antarctica, Becoming World's Largest." *New York Times* (May 20, 2021), https://www.nytimes.com/2021/05/20/world/iceberg-antarctica-ronne-a76.html.

Fox, Douglas. "The Larsen C Ice Shelf Collapse is Just the Beginning—Antarctica is Melting." *National Geographic* (July 12, 2017), https://www.nationalgeographic.com/magazine/2017/07/antarctica-sea-level-rise-climate-change/.

Fordham, Anthony. "Could We Actually Tow an Iceberg to Make Drinking Water." *Australian Popular Science.* (June 23, 2014), https://www.popsci.com.au/make/could-we-actually-tow-an-iceberg-to-make-drinking-water_388725/.

Fricker, Helen Amanda. "Melting and Cracking—Is Antarctica Falling Apart?" *Guardian* (June 23, 2017), https://www.theguardian.com/science/2017/jun/23/melting-and-cracking-is-antarctica-falling-apart-climate-change.

Garner, Helen. "Regions of Thick-Ribbed Ice." *The Feel of Steel.* (Sydney: Picador-Pan Macmillan, 2001): 13–24.

Glasberg, Elena. *Antarctica as Cultural Critique: The Gendered Politics of Scientific Exploration and Climate Change.* (New York: Palgrave Macmillan, 2012).

Gosnell, Mariana. *Ice: The Nature, the History, and the Uses of an Astonishing Substance.* (New York: Knopf, 2005).

Grunes, Marissa. "Masses of Beautiful Alabaster." *The Paris Review* (July 20, 2017), https://www.theparisreview.org/blog/2017/07/20/masses-of-beautiful-alabaster/.

ICE ISLANDS OF THE ANTHROPOCENE 381

Hansen, Kathryn. "Iceberg A-68A Nears South Georgia." National Space and Aeronautical Administration Earth Observatory (November 16, 2020), https://earth observatory.nasa.gov/images/147535/iceberg-a-68a-nears-south-georgia?linkId= 104616459.

Hemingway, Ernest. *Death in the Afternoon.* (New York: Scribner's, 1932).

Howkins, Adrian. "Placing the Past: The McMurdo Dry Valleys and the Problem of Geographical Specificity in Antarctic History." *Anthropocene Antarctica: Perspectives from the Humanities, Law and Social Sciences*, eds. Elizabeth Leane and Jeffrey McGee (London: Routledge, 2019): 172–184.

Hult, J.L, and N.C. Ostrander. *Antarctic Icebergs as a Global Fresh Water Resource.* (Santa Monica: Rand Corporation, 1973).

Ihimaera, Witi. *The Thrill of Falling: Stories.* Auckland: Vintage-Penguin, 2012.

Joyner, Christopher C. "The Status of Ice in International Law" in *The Law of the Sea and Polar Maritime Delimitation and Jurisdiction*, eds. Alex G. Oude Elferink and Donald R. Rothwell. The Hague: Martinus Nijhoff-Kluwer Law International, 200, 23–47.

Leane, Elizabeth, and Ben Maddison. "A Biography of Iceberg B-9B." *Australian Humanities Review* 64 (December 2018), http://www.australianhumanitiesreview .org/.

Lieser, Jan L. "Ice Bulletin: Iceberg A-68A" in *Ice Bulletins for the Antarctic Shipping Season 2021–2022* (Hobart, Tasmania: Australian Government Bureau of Meteorology, forthcoming 2022).

Luckman, Adrian. "I've Studied Larsen C and its Giant Iceberg for Years—It's not a Simple Story of Climate Change." *The Conversation.* (July 12, 2017), https://theconve rsation.com/ive-studied-larsen-c-and-its-giant-iceberg-for-years-its-not-a-simple -story-of-climate-change-80529.

Mackley, Brian. "The Tale of an Iceberg at Iowa State." *Iowa State Daily* (November 15, 2017), http://www.iowastatedaily.com/app_content/article_a862fd50-ca84-11e7 -ac5a-f75457213aaf.html.

Madrigal, Alexis C. "The Many Failures and Few Successes of Zany Iceberg Schemes." *The Atlantic* (August 10, 2011), https://www.theatlantic.com/technology/archive/2011/08/ the-many-failures-and-few-successes-of-zany-iceberg-towing-schemes/243364/.

Melville, Herman. *Moby Dick.* (London: Dent; New York: E.P. Dutton, 1907).

Morgan, Ruth A. "Dry Continent Dreaming: Australian Visions of using Antarctic Icebergs for Water Supplies." *International Review of Environmental History* 4.1 (2018), http://press-files.anu.edu.au/downloads/press/n4203/html/09_morgan.xhtml.

Morton, Timothy. *Hyperobjects: Philosophy and Ecology after the End of the World.* (Minneapolis: U of Minnesota P, 2013).

Nowra, Louis. *Ice: A Love Story.* (Crows Nest, NSW: Allen & Unwin, 2009).

Nüsser, Marcus, and Ravi Baghel. "The Emergence of the Cryoscape: Contested Narratives of Himalayan Glacier Dynamics and Climate Change" in *Environmental and Climate Change in South and Southeast Asia: How are Local Cultures Coping?* ed. Barbara Schuler (Leiden and Boston: Brill, 2014): 138–156.

Patel, Jugal K. "A Crack in an Antarctic Ice Shelf Grew 17 Miles in the Last Two Months." *New York Times* (February 7, 2017), https://www.nytimes.com/interactive/2017/02/07/science/earth/antarctic-crack.html.

Pearce, Lara. "UAE Company Wants to Tow an Iceberg from Antarctica for Drinking Water." *Huffington Post* (May 19, 2017), https://www.huffingtonpost.com.au/2017/05/18/uae-company-wants-to-tow-an-iceberg-from-antarctica-for-drinking_a_2 2086611/.

Ponte, Lowell. "Alien Ice: An Evaluation of Some Subsidiary Effects and Concomitant Problems in Iceberg Utilization" in *Iceberg Utilization: Proceedings of the First International Conference Held at Ames, Iowa,* ed. A.A. Husseiny (Elmsford, NY: Pergamon, 1978): 11–19.

Powell, Ellen. "Can Scientists Crack the Case of an Antarctic Ice shelf's Growing Rift?" *Christian Science Monitor* (January 16, 2017), https://www.csmonitor.com/Science/2017/0116/Can-scientists-crack-the-case-of-an-Antarctic-ice-shelf-s-growing-rift.

Roberts, Peder, Lize-Marié van der Watt and Adrian Howkins, eds. *Antarctica and the Humanities.* (London: Palgrave Macmillan, 2016).

Rogers, Adam. "Giant Antarctic Icebergs and Crushing Existential Dread." *WIRED* (July 13, 2017), https://www.wired.com/story/giant-antarctic-icebergs-and-crushing-existential-dread/.

Schlanger, Zoë, Jennifer Brown and Katherine Ellen Foley. "Two Luxembourgs, 10 Madrids and One Delaware: How a Giant Iceberg is Described Around the World." *Quartz* (July 12, 2017), https://qz.com/1027701/two-luxembourgs-10-madrids-one-delaware-how-a-giant-iceberg-in-antarctica-is-described-around-the-world/.

Sörlin, Sverker. "Cryo-History: Narratives of Ice and the Emerging Arctic Humanities" in *The New Arctic*, eds. Birgitta Evengård, Joan Nymand Larsen and Øyvind Paasche (Cham: Springer, 2015): 327–339.

Weeks, W.F., and W.J. Campbell. "Icebergs as a Fresh-Water Source: An Appraisal." *Journal of Glaciology* 12.65 (1973): 207–233.

Wehi, Priscilla M., Nigel J. Scott, Jacinta Beckwith, Rata Pryor Rodgers, Tasman Gillies, Vincent Van Uitregt and Krushil Watene. "A Short Scan of Māori Journeys to Antarctica." *Journal of the Royal Society of New Zealand* (2021), https://doi.org/10.1080/03036758.2021.1917633

Worland, Justin. "The Enormous Ice Sheet that Broke off of Antarctica Won't be the Last to Go." *Time* (July 13, 2017), http://time.com/4855567/antarctic-iceberg-glacier-larsen-c-climate-change/.

Index

A68 (iceberg)   38, 364–70, 377–78
A76 (iceberg)   378n62
Aachen (Germany)   72, 73
Abacha, Sani   77
Abercrombie, Neil   221
Aboriginal literature (Australia)   5, 9
Aboriginal peoples (Australia)   9–10, 114, 124, 131, 142, 142n35, 145n49, 150, 156, 163. *See also* Indigenous peoples
Abram, David   93n1
abstraction   30, 34, 149, 164, 168, 326, 369. *See also* deep time
Abu-Zeid, M.   289, 291
academia   58n16, 60, 69–70, 313, 362
access   33, 169, 205n66, 222, 263, 335, 352, 356
accumulation   102, 113, 121, 131, 290–91
Achebe, Chinua   59
activism   14–15, 233, 305–6
  climate change discourses and   31–32, 33, 155
  definition and context   57–58
  of Devy   60–64, 65–66
  of Ghosh   81–86
  of Habila   76–81
  Indigenous peoples and   18–19
  literature and   4–7, 12–13, 56–60, 86–87, 138
  postcolonialism and   16–17, 29
  of Roy   66–71
  of Saro-Wiwa   71–76
  of Tagaq   320, 321, 327
  of Winduo   185
  of Winton   138, 143, 154, 155–56
Adamie, Inookie   316
adaptation   23, 61, 256
  climate change and   29, 30, 198, 255
  in Hawaiʻi   221–23, 239, 241, 245
  Indigenous peoples and   8–9, 178, 179, 180, 315, 316
"Adila, Grandmother" (Oddoul)   284, 291–93
Adivasi Academy   65–66
Adivasis   33, 60–64, 65–66, 68–69, 70, 71, 289n40. *See also* Indigenous peoples
affect   163, 165, 168, 169, 170, 174, 181, 212
affective ecocriticism   22. *See also* ecocriticism

Africa   3, 4, 40, 122, 202n45, 205, 281, 283, 290, 303–5. *See also specific countries*
African literature   56, 338, 344
agency   75, 108, 116, 168, 183, 206, 316, 337, 338
  of adivasis   61, 63–64, 69
  Antarctica and   344, 345, 348–50
  Indigenous   33, 317, 321
  land and   148, 273, 346
  postcolonial studies and   16, 21, 25
Aghoghovwia, Philip   76
agriculture   xviii, 65, 130, 192n5, 195, 224, 231
  ahupuaʻa system   227–28, 229, 241–43
  climate change and   12, 40, 178, 222, 223, 252–53, 266
  plantation   122, 123, 131, 229
ahupuaʻa system   227–28, 229, 241–43
ʻāina   224–26, 228–29, 234–35, 242–43. *See also* land
air pollution   3, 15
Albert, Gerrard   95, 96, 97–98
Albrecht, Glenn   139n21, 267
Alegado, Rosie   245
Alegría, Claribel   7
algae.   *See* sargassum
The Algebra of Infinite Justice (Roy)   68, 69–70
Ali, Idris   285
alienation   61, 272, 275, 276, 277, 292, 306, 338, 355, 356
Allen, Chadwick   230–31
allergies   194. *See also* sargassum
aloha ʻāina   35, 225, 235, 245, 246
Alstom Renewable Power (French company)   304
alterity   21, 99, 100, 104, 113, 168, 175, 180, 210
Amazon rainforest   39, 40, 192n5, 199. *See also* rainforests
Amazon River   192n5, 199
amnesia   5, 284, 289
Amnesty International   63, 73
Amundsen, Roald   348
ancestors   100n31, 115, 209, 293
  displacement and   81, 245
  land and   11, 177, 183, 230, 234
  rivers as   33, 94, 95, 98, 102

Ancient Egypt 294–95. *See also* Egypt
"Angam Day" (Va'ai) 126
Angry Inuk (Baril-Araquq) 319, 327
Anilnilliak, Evie 316
animal rights groups 317, 318, 319–20, 327
animism 144
Animism (Tagaq) 321, 322, 326
annexation 98–99, 114, 228
Antarctica 40
  agency and 348–50
  in cultural production 343–44
  curation of 353–55
  human-ice relationship and 346–48
  human impact on 350–52
  human/non-human relations and 355
  ice and 361–62, 363
  icebergs and 364–76
  imagined concept of 335–36
  in *Lamentations of Zeno* 344–46
  literary studies and 362–63
  postcolonial context of 336–39
  tourism in 38, 334, 339–42
Antarctic humanities 362
Antarctic Peninsula 2–3, 164n16, 339, 345, 352, 361, 364, 374
Antarctic Treaty (1959) 352
Antarctic Treaty Consultative Meeting (ATCM) 340
Antarctic Treaty Parties 336–37, 340
Antarctic Treaty System (ATS) 339, 372
Anthropocene 24, 99, 130, 175, 201, 256–57, 260, 316, 350
  Antarctica and 338–39, 339, 344, 361
  beech trees and 164, 170, 178
  climate change and 1, 4, 11, 12, 15–16, 19, 22, 33, 76, 93, 183
  deep time and 165–66, 167–68, 180–81, 186
  ice/icebergs and 364, 365, 366–67, 378, 379
  indigeneity and 37, 326
  literature and 12, 25–30, 32, 146, 268, 323, 330
anthropocentrism 22, 365
  challenges to 95, 100, 105, 106, 117
  climate change and 11, 23, 25
  rivers and 97, 99, 102
anthropology 22, 35, 42, 186, 195, 314, 319
anti-heroism 348

antipodes 93, 94, 95, 135
Anu, Christine 128
Aotearoa/New Zealand 28, 122, 124, 186, 361, 376
  beech trees and 35, 162, 164, 166n26, 171–75
  in cli-po 236–37
  Whanganui River and 33, 94–95
apartheid 5, 59, 344
apocalypse 30, 76, 111, 209, 239, 244, 245
  Antarctica and 361, 376
  cli-fi and 26, 313
  Nubia and 295, 298
apocalyptic realism 76
Appiah, Kwame Anthony 72
appropriation 12, 114, 116, 150, 173, 180, 185, 196, 326–28, 329
Apter, Andrew 75
Arab Socialist Union 287
Araucanía (Chile) 176–77
archaeology 145n54, 282, 283, 304–5
Archbold Expedition (1935) 184
Archibald, Jo-ann (Q'um Q'um Xiiem) 313
archipelagos 35, 192, 195, 199–203, 205, 210, 212, 236. *See also* islands
Arctic 20, 37–38, 312, 314–15, 317, 327, 363, 364, 366, 371–72. *See also* Antarctica
Arctic Circle 2
Arctic Cycle group 13
Arctic humanities 366
Arcticide 37, 312
Argentina 164, 166n26, 375
Ashcroft, Bill 6
Asia 4, 82, 84–85, 129, 303
Asia-Pacific region 252–53
assemblage, ocean 201
Aswan Dam 281–82, 287, 290–91, 296
Aswan High Dam 36–37, 282–83, 285–88, 290–91, 293–303, 299n91, 306
asylum seekers. *See* refugees
Atlantic Meridional Overturning Circulation (AMOC) 40
Atlantic Ocean 39, 40, 197, 199, 202, 204–5, 364
Attla, George 322
Attridge, Derek 57
attritional catastrophes 283–84, 285, 293, 294. *See also* slow violence
Atwood, Margaret 8, 30, 83, 313

INDEX 385

Australia 5, 40, 124, 131, 182, 373
  climate change and 11, 28, 94, 148–49,
    153–54, 154–55n91, 157–58
  fires in 1–2, 28, 38
  islandness and 139–40
  Nauru and 120, 122–24, 125, 127, 129–30
  Pacific Islands and 128–29
  wild time and 141–42
  Winton and 135–36, 137, 138, 143–44,
    149, 156–57
autonomy 75, 100n31, 123, 316. See
  also agency

B09B (iceberg) 378
B15 (iceberg) 367
Baghel, Ravi 346, 366
Baker, Carleigh 323
Balaz, Joe 35, 221, 235, 238–41
Ballantyne, R.M. 125
Bangladesh 39, 81, 85
Barclay, Barry 98n27
Bardot, Brigitte 318, 319
Baril-Arnaquq, Alethea 319
Barkham, Patrick 139n22
Barua, Maan 212
Basin and Range (McPhee) 167
Bate, Jonathan 262, 264
Baudrillard, Jean 101
Baxter, James K. 34, 165, 171–72, 174, 175
Bay of Bengal 39
beech trees. See southern beech trees
"Under Beech Trees" (Dallas) 174, 175
Beer, Gillian 124
Bellingshausen (Antarctica) 352
Bennde Mutale Threatre Group 13
bergs. See icebergs
Berkoff, Stephen 45
Best, Elsdon 172
Beyak, Lynn 320
Bhakra Dam 302. See also mega-dams
Bharatiya Janata Party (BJP) 69–70
Bhasha (Research and Publication
  Centre) 64, 65–66
The Big Swim (Saxifrage) 27
Bilodeau, Chantal 13
The Binding of the Nile (Peel) 291, 295
biodiversity 11, 42, 62, 181, 220, 227
BirdLife 12
Bird Rose, Deborah 9–10, 23–24, 142n35

birds 79, 82, 122, 126, 153, 226, 298. See also
  penguins
Birnbaum, Michael 73
Birrell, Kathleen 111, 117
Bjærke, Marit Ruge 199n31
Björk 321, 322
Black Atlantic 204
Blackness 202. See also race
Black Summer 1–2, 38–39
blindness 8, 103, 159. See also denialism
Blood Diamonds (film) 77
blood/land/memory complex 230
Blood Narrative (Allen) 230–31
Bloom, Dan 7
blue humanities 200–201, 362, 362n2
Blue Mountains World Heritage Area 1
Blue Nile 304
Blume, Carl Ludwig 166
Boehm, Philip 338, 348
Boko Haram conflict 80
Born of the Conquerors (Wright) 163
botanical science 166. See also colonialism
The Botanic Garden (E. Darwin) 371
"Botany" (Neruda) 162
The Botany of the Antarctic Voyage
  (Hooker) 178–79
Boyd, William 72, 73
braided flower garlands 232–33
Braidotti, Rosi 100
Brass, Leonard 184
Brathwaite, Edward Kamau 195, 196–97,
  202, 206–8, 209, 210–11, 212
Brazil 38, 39
Breitinger, Eckhard 56
Britain 13, 32, 124, 283, 286, 287–88, 290, 291,
  372, 375
Brontë, Charlotte 59
Brooks, David 151–52, 153
Broome, John 154–55
Brown, Jennifer 368n23
Brown, Richard 377
Brutus, Dennis 6
Brydon, Diana 325
Bryson, J. Scott 146–47
buffers 170. See also southern beech trees
building industry 68, 70, 85, 129, 299, 303–4,
  303n115
Burk, Jasmyn 322
Burma 84

Burton, Richard 338
bushfire season 1–2, 28, 38–39
Byron, George Gordon (Lord) 15

California (US) 373
Call of Midnight Bird (Kerpi) 182–83, 184
The Call of the Reed Warbler (Massy) 123
Cameron, Emilie 329–30
Campbell, Melissa Colleen 14–15
Camus, Albert 45
Canada 78n127, 297, 311, 312, 313, 317, 318, 320, 329
Canadian literature 27, 37, 312–14, 318–19
Cann, Heather W. 27–28
Canto General (Neruda) 175–78, 180, 183
Cape Farewell expedition 316
capitalism
    Antarctica and 351
    Aswan High Dam and 283, 286–87
    Caribbean and 201, 205, 205n66
    climate change and 10, 15, 18, 23, 29, 32, 41, 43, 66, 71, 84, 121, 168, 182, 255
    colonial 8, 18, 94, 99
    deep time and 169, 170, 180
    disaster 204
    Hawai'i and 229, 230, 242–43, 245–46
    literature and 6, 176, 185, 231
    Malaysia and 265, 272
    plantations and 122, 130
    public health and 45
Capitalocene 350
carbon colonialism 36, 221, 229, 237–38, 246
carbon dioxide (CO_2) 2, 39, 239, 252, 299–300, 301n99, 334n5, 349, 354, 366
carbon sinks 170n54, 354
carceral archipelago 124. *See also* archipelagos
care, ethics/rhetoric of 38, 318, 319, 321, 328, 329, 330
Carey, Mark 347
Caribbean 5, 11, 58, 122
    coiled temporality and 35, 195–96
    future-making and 207–9
    history and context of 201–2
    and hope, poetics of 210–13
    multi-scalar vulnerabilities of 196–200, 205–6
    sargassum and 192, 194–95, 199–200

Caribbean Sea 198, 200
"Caribou" (Tagaq) 327
Carpentaria (Wright) 33, 95, 105, 108–16, 131
Carrigan, Anthony 21, 22
Carrington, Damian 40
Carroll, Siobhan 372
Carson, Rachel 6, 17, 153, 268
Carteret Atoll 181
cartography 14, 94, 95n10, 102–5, 106, 107, 109, 334
cash crops 122. *See also* plantation ecologies
Cassel, Ernest 288
catachresis 166
Caupolicán (chief) 177
cement industry 293, 299. *See also* dams
Cenozoic era 164
Central America 4, 39
Chakrabarty, Dipesh 25, 93, 169, 255, 337, 338, 350, 356
Chamorro 219
chants 182–83, 208–9, 233
Chaudhuri, Amit 57
Chauhan, Vibha 60–61
Cheah, Pheng 104, 109, 116
Cheeseman, Thomas Frederic 173–74
Chevron (oil company) 75
children's literature 319
Chile 35, 164, 166n26, 170, 175–81, 186, 371, 374
China 39, 40, 63, 259, 260–61n33, 304, 306
chlorofluorocarbons (CFCs) 301n99
Christianity 69, 95, 113n88, 225, 281
Chthuluecene 100n31
Chuh, Kandice 209–10
Cilano, Cara 21
Cities of Salt (Munif) 78
Clark, Nigel 44, 94
Clarke, Marcus 125
class 28, 31, 205, 239, 302, 375
classification 166
CLI-FI: Canadian Tales of Climate Change 313
Climate Change and Writing in the Canadian Arctic (Hulan) 312
climate change poetry (cli-po) 12–13, 26–27, 35–36, 221, 235–45. *See also* ecopoetry/poetics
Climate Change Theatre Action 13

INDEX

climate colonialism 32, 43–44, 238
climate fiction (cli-fi) 7–8, 12, 25–26, 29–30, 235, 311, 313, 336, 350
climate grief 42
climate justice 10, 42, 44, 84, 111, 145n49, 277, 312
  eco-theatre and 14
  poetry and 36
  postcolonialism and 20, 22–23
  Saro-Wiwa and 72, 75
Climate Trauma (Kaplan) 254
cli-po (climate change poetry) 12–13, 26–27, 35–36, 221, 235–45. *See also* ecopoetry/poetics
coal xviii, 32, 63, 252, 275
coconut products 129, 266
Coetzee, J. M. 344, 356
Cohen, Jeffrey Jerome 349
Cohen, Tom 29
coihue (*N. dombeyi*) 180. *See also* southern beech trees
coiled temporality 35, 195, 196, 200–205, 207–13. *See also* deep time
Cold War 287
collectivism 42
The Collector of Worlds (Trojanow) 338
Collett, Anne 19
collisions (with icebergs) 370
colonialism 37, 45, 58, 63, 87, 166, 228, 231, 233, 349n73
  Antarctica and 38, 336–37, 346, 348–49, 352
  beech trees and 171–72, 173–74, 176–77, 178–79, 181
  capitalism and 8, 18, 94, 99
  carbon 36, 221, 229, 237–38, 246
  Caribbean and 201–3, 205
  climate change and 18, 22–24, 29, 32, 42–44, 58, 84, 94, 105, 245, 305
  cli-po and 235, 242–44
  dams and 286–87, 291, 299, 303–5
  deep time and 169, 170, 173, 180
  ecological impact of 62, 74, 75
  Egypt and 283, 300–301, 302
  human-land relationship and 153, 158
  icebergs and 371–72, 374–75
  Inuit and 314–15, 325, 329
  Malaysia and 257, 260–61n33, 272

  maps and 103, 109
  plantations and 121–22, 123–24, 127
  postcolonial studies and 5–6, 16, 18, 21
  tourism and 336–37
Columbus, Christopher 203
commodification 23, 375
  of Antarctica 334, 349, 351
  and hope, poetics of 211, 213
  of land 136, 272, 277
  in Malaysia 257, 266, 267
  postcolonialism and 6, 16
  sargassum and 200, 204, 210
  of southern beech 166, 174
comprehension 136, 167, 169, 196
concrete 129, 242, 282. *See also* dams
Conference of the Parties (COP) 13, 20, 219–20
Conrad, Joseph 78
consciousness, climate 165
  climate 4–5, 12–13, 15, 16–27, 37, 44–45, 251, 256–57, 278, 306
  Winton and 135, 137, 138, 143, 144, 145, 148–49, 158–59
conservation 19, 43, 81–82, 162, 222, 245, 319, 321
"Constitution Day" (Va'ai) 126–27
consumption/consumerism 21, 122, 136–37, 257, 314
  Antarctica and 341, 346, 351
  climate change and 32, 245, 271
  See also commodification
contact zones 103n42, 108, 116
contrapuntal storytelling 272–73
Cook, James (captain) 238
Cooper, Jago 58
Cooper's Hill (Denham) 15
Copernicus Atmosphere Monitoring Service (CAMS) 2
coral reefs 87, 129, 156, 223
corruption 76–77, 123, 259
cosmology 100n31, 111–12, 208–9, 294–95
  Hawaiian 225, 235
  Inuit 319, 325n52
  Māori 95, 173
  Whanganui iwi 98, 106n54
cotton 122, 288
country, concept of 9–10, 34, 135–37, 143, 146, 149–51, 156–57

Country Road (Dallas) 174–75
Coveney, Peter 65
Covid-19 40–42, 44
Cranston, C.A. 124
Crapanzano, Vincent 212
Creole English, Hawaiian 233, 238, 239
Creole literature 208–9
Crichton, Michael 7
Criminal Tribes Act (India) 63
Cromwell, Oliver 122
"Crossing the Peninsula" (Lim) 260, 262–63
Cruikshank, Julie 315, 326, 329
cruises 128, 334n5, 343–44, 347, 368, 378
Cry, the Beloved Country (Paton) 59
cryobiography 38, 377–79, 378n62
cryohistory 38, 366, 374
cryoscape 346, 366
cryosphere 344, 361, 366
cultural time 163, 165, 170, 175, 180. *See also* deep time
Curry, Judith 7
Cussler, Clive 343
Cyclone Ampha 39
Cyttaria (fungus) 179

Dahab, Amany 36–37
Dal Dam 304, 305. *See also* dams
Dalembert, Louis-Philippe 195, 197, 198
Daley, Linda 111
Dalits 289n40. *See also* Indigenous Indians
Dallas, Ruth 34, 165, 174
dams 63, 68–69, 71, 252, 286–88, 299–300, 303–5. *See also* Aswan Dam; Aswan High Dam
Darwin, Charles 164, 175, 177, 179, 181
Darwin, Erasmus 371–72
David and Goliath 208
Davidson Sargunam, S. 62
Davis, Geoffrey V. 32–33, 305
Davison, Liam 149
The Day After Tomorrow (Emmerich) 7
dead land 11. *See also* land
"Dear Matafele Pienam" (Jetñil-Kijiner) xvi–xix, 219
death vs. life 101–2, 197
de Beauvoir, Simone 6
de Brum, Tony 219
decolonisation 6, 24, 58, 76, 151, 186, 202, 202n48

of Canadian literature 313–14
Caribbean and 209
cli-po and 241, 243–44, 246
in Hawai'i 233
Indigenous peoples and 325
mega-dams and 287
postcolonialism and 23, 33
decomposition 194, 212, 299, 323
deep time 141, 179
in Baxter 171–72
beech trees and 165, 166–67, 170, 173, 186
Chilean narratives of 175–81
climate change and 15, 22, 34, 168–69, 179–80
in Dallas 174–75
New Zealand narratives of 171–75
Papua New Guinean narratives of 181–86
theory of 163, 164, 167
deforestation 123, 174, 231, 299
climate change and 41, 43, 181
in India 62, 63, 71
in Malaysia 251, 253, 271
sargassum and 192n5, 199
de Generes, Ellen 320
DeLoughrey, Elizabeth 19, 21, 22, 130, 201, 202, 229, 231
Denham, John 15
denialism 37, 85–86, 274–75, 291, 361
climate change 4, 7, 27–28, 65, 154–55, 158, 241
postcolonialism and 29, 32
Denotified and Nomadic Tribes (DNT) 32–33
desalinisation 126, 372
desertification 3, 9, 80, 85, 231, 271, 276
Désirade (Caribbean) 194
Desolation Island (O'Brian) 370
detention camps 128, 129
Detudamo, Candace 128, 129
development 87, 110, 210, 302
climate change and 32, 44, 105, 349, 354
dams and 286, 287–89, 303–4
Hawai'i and 222, 223, 229, 242–43
in India 61, 63, 64, 65, 71
in Malaysia 251, 257, 273–74, 276–78
Nauru and 121, 127, 128, 129–30
in Nubian literature 285, 291, 293, 305–6
postcolonialism and 6, 16, 19, 56, 186, 231
rivers and 98

INDEX

development aid 120, 129–30, 303
developmental refugees 115n106, 285, 288–89, 291. *See also* refugees
Devi, Mahasweta 60, 62
Devlin-Glass, Frances 110, 112
Devy, Ganesh 32, 59, 60–64, 65–66, 69
Dias, Keila Mcfarland 42–43
diaspora 22, 36, 260, 262–65, 272–73
dictatorships 72, 76–77
Didur, Jill 21, 22
Dimaline, Cherie 9, 313
dipole pattern 297
Dirt Music (Winton) 150
disasters
    in Caribbean 194, 198, 205–6, 209, 210
    climate change and 28, 37, 38–39, 85, 110, 123, 265
    in Hawai'i 223, 244
    islands and 120, 130
    narratives of 343, 355, 370
    sargassum and 199, 204
discourse analysis 44
displacement 17–18, 21, 79, 99, 228, 231, 272, 294
    of Adivasis 63, 68–69
    climate change and 24, 81–82, 94, 222
    dams and 282, 283–84, 288–89, 291–93, 304
dispossession 8, 22, 70, 158, 210, 273, 277, 289
documentaries 315, 319
Dodds, Klaus 337, 346, 362n2
Do Glaciers Listen? (Cruikshank) 315
domestication 26
domination 23, 28, 103n42, 165, 178, 228, 239, 287, 291, 337
    postcolonialism and 18, 19, 26, 29, 32
Dongola (Ali) 285
Donne, John 363
Dorfman, Ariel 373–75
Douglassa, Kristina 58
Douo, Myriam 43
Down to Earth (Woldendorp) 144
drama 13–15, 18, 44, 59n22
dreams 9, 10, 108, 126, 140, 226, 263, 313. *See also* imagination
drinking water 68, 370–71
drought 61, 112, 206, 223
    in Australia 1, 28
    climate change and 93, 120, 220, 256

in Egypt 282, 301
in Malaysia 257, 258, 266, 268–69, 270, 274, 276
in Nauru 123, 126, 129
Dryzek, John 287, 291
Duckert, Lowell 349
Dunning, Norma 324, 325
duress 198–99
dystopias 9, 26, 45, 220, 254, 271

earthquakes xviii, 197, 198–99, 207
East Sepik 184, 185
Eat Like a Fish (Smith) 27
Eckstein, Barbara 5, 15
ecobiography 27, 145
ecocide 29, 33, 74–75, 138, 155
ecocriticism 59n22, 100, 165, 231, 326, 335
    climate change and 256, 327
    postcolonialism and 17–18, 19–23, 56, 66, 186, 329
eco-drama 14–15
ecofeminism 6, 22, 168, 328–29
ecology 36, 116, 124, 146, 195, 276, 327, 328
    Antarctica and 337, 343, 344, 345, 350, 355
    beech trees and 170, 173, 178, 181
    Caribbean 197, 201, 205, 209, 212–13
    climate change and 4, 12, 14–15, 32, 85–86, 164–65, 172, 312, 351
    dams and 283, 285, 286, 287, 288, 290–91, 293, 303, 305–6
    Hawaiian 225, 227, 230, 232, 238–39, 244, 246
    Indigenous peoples and 62, 185
    Nigeria and 72, 75
    of plantations 33, 120, 121–24, 127–31, 229
    postcolonialism and 17, 19–22, 26, 28, 56, 71, 169, 231
    sargassum and 204, 210–11
    slow violence and 284, 294
economic growth 274, 275. *See also* development
eco- or climate anxiety 42, 237, 254
ecopoetry/poetics 26, 146–47, 181, 230–32, 234, 237, 258
ecoregionalism 145n54
eco-spirituality 62
education 13, 33, 62, 63–64, 65–66, 125, 130, 292, 313

Effects on Hawaii of a Worldwide Rise in Seal Level (1985) 221

Egypt 36–37, 281–83, 284, 285–91, 293–95, 301, 306

EisTau (Trojanow). See *The Lamentations of Zeno*

Elba, Emad 37

Elders 144, 150, 225, 315, 316, 328

electricity 63, 252

Elizabeth Costello (Coetzee) 344, 356

Elsafti, Hisham 290

El-Shibini, F. 289, 291

Elwin, Verrier 60

embodiment 95, 106, 150, 165, 168, 169–71, 173, 206, 347

empire. *See* colonialism

"The Endangered Arctic" (Stoddart and Smith) 312

"The End of Imagination" (Roy) 69

energy humanities 77–78n122

energy policy 27, 251–52, 275

Enlightenment 95, 97

enough, concept of 206

"Entering Beech Forest" (Dallas) 174–75

environmental humanities 21–23, 121, 125, 130, 170–71
    deep time and 34, 163, 164, 165–66, 168, 169, 175
    postcolonialism and 16, 19, 37

environmentalism 43, 72, 74–80, 155, 225, 255
    Indigenous peoples and 18–19, 68–69, 325
    postcolonialism and 17–21
    salvage 228–30

environmental justice 14, 20, 22, 36, 72, 277

Environmental Justice (Westra) 74

epidemics 24, 42, 42n189, 79

epiphytes 175, 177, 180–81

Erceg, Diane 337

Eriksen, Anne 199n31

Ernman, Beata 27

Ernman, Malena 27

erosion 11, 129, 167, 222, 252, 290, 300

Espiritu, Peter Rockford 13

essentialism 18, 179, 273

Ethiopia 281, 304

ethnicity 28, 31, 289. *See also* race

ethnocide 252

ethnography 172, 315

Ettmer, Bernd 37

Eucken, Rudolf 57–58

Eurocentrism 6, 85, 254

Europe 58n16, 72, 97, 99, 133n88, 141, 150, 319, 345
    beech narratives and 171, 172, 175, 179
    climate change and 2, 13, 39, 40
    dams and 303–4
    India and 62, 84
    islands and 122, 124, 125
    sargassum and 195n15, 205

European Consortium for Pacific Studies (ECOPAS) 13

European Environmental Bureau 12

European Union 12, 43

evolutionary time 163, 165, 170, 175, 180. *See also* deep time

exceptionalism, Antarctic 341, 342, 344, 354

exceptionalism, human 23, 26, 95, 99, 100, 102, 131

execution 71, 77

exoticism 220, 266, 314, 344, 361, 364

exploitation 77, 97, 126, 138, 153–54, 180, 273, 287, 306, 351
    of adivasis 64, 71
    of Caribbean 204, 207, 209, 210, 211
    climate change and 43, 127
    life vs. death and 101–2

exploration 78, 125, 158, 166, 336, 338, 348–49, 363, 368, 377

Explorer (tour ship) 343

Exposure (Fleming) 7

extinction 41, 74, 154, 172, 220, 223, 231, 353

extraction/extractivism 10–11, 110, 130, 204, 231, 313
    climate change and 43, 44, 99
    in Malaysia 253, 257
    in Nigeria 78, 80
    Pacific Islands and 18, 220
    plantation ecologies and 122–23, 127

extremification 34

extremity 341, 342. *See also* Antarctica

Exxon 85, 365

Eyrie (Winton) 152, 153

Faber, Daniel 120

Fabian, Johannes 186

"A Fable for Tomorrow" (Carson) 268

INDEX 391

Al-Faisal, Mohommad   372
Falconer, Delia   142
family
  land and   10, 141, 142, 152, 156–57, 158–59,
    224–25, 230
  Winton and   34, 135, 136, 137n9, 139
Fanon, Frantz   302
In a Far Country (Maniam)   272
Farghaly, Dalia   37
farming.   *See* agriculture
Far Off Metal River (Cameron)   329–30
Farrney, Ramon   342
Fee, Margery   313
Feldner, Maximilian   80
feminism   6, 22, 168, 327, 328–29, 347
Fernea, Robert   281, 289n40
Fiji   14, 122, 123, 125, 219
Finlayson, Chris   96–97, 98
Fire Down Below (Golding)   370
fires   1–2, 28, 38–39, 123, 170, 206, 253, 298
The First Claimants of the Forest (Devi)   62
First Nations   37, 326. *See also* Indigenous
    peoples
fishing   74, 80, 126, 130, 201
  Hawai'i   222, 227, 241, 242
  Malaysia and   252, 260–61, 262, 263,
    266, 269
Flannery, Tim   123
Fleming, Rex   7
Fletcher's Island (iceberg)   363n8
Flight Behaviour (Kingsolver)   7, 30
Flock of Pelicans (Murād)   284
"Before the Flood" (Roy)   289
"flooded" (Muhammad)   269
flooding   14, 83n154
  climate change and   xviii, 38, 71, 80, 81,
    85, 93, 123
  in Hawai'i   222–23, 226, 229n30, 239,
    241, 243
  in Malaysia   252, 268–69, 270, 271, 276
  Nubia and   281, 282, 283, 289–90, 292,
    294–96, 301–2
flower garlands   232–33
Foley, Katherine Ellen   368n23
food   11, 129, 172, 179, 195, 223–24, 321, 353
food security   6, 24, 39–40, 66, 252, 271,
    276, 374
footprints   323, 340, 342, 345–46, 361
Forest Lore of the Māori (Best)   172

A Forest of Flowers (Saro-Wiwa)   78n123
forests   8, 39, 60, 62, 63, 65, 81, 170, 252.
    See also deforestation; rainforests;
    southern beech trees
Forsyth, Timothy   58n16
fossil fuel industry   7, 32, 41, 80–81, 87, 123,
    128, 275, 299
"Fosters" (Va'ai)   126
Fox, Kealoha   245
Fox, Marama   95–96, 102
fragility.   *See* vulnerability
France   124, 283, 303, 304
Freire, Paulo   7
Fricker, Helen   367
"The Frontier" (Neruda)   176
Fuegians (Yaghan)   179
fungus   179, 180, 181
future-making   195–97, 197, 199, 207–13, 300,
    306, 326, 356

Gabriel, Sharmani P.   272
Gabrys, Jennifer   336
Gandhi   60
garbage   115, 127–28, 131, 197, 201, 229, 243,
    273, 276–77, 352
Garcia Marquez, Gabriel   45
"Gardening in the Colonies" (SPAN)   19
Gardiner, Stephen   23
Garner, Helen   347, 354, 368–69, 379
Garrard, Greg   17, 18, 19
Garrido, Pao Fernández   303n114
gaze, tourist   344, 353–55
gender   28, 99, 262, 348–49
genealogies   100n31, 258–59
  beech trees and   176, 183
  Hawai'i and   36, 221, 225, 230–32, 233–36
  Māori   95, 96
  rivers and   98, 106
generalized domestication   26
Genocide in Nigeria (Saro-Wiwa)   74–75
genre fiction   30–31, 311, 312–13
genres   254
geoengineering   372
geography   44, 145n54, 234, 265, 346, 362, 366
  Aswan High Dam and   37, 283, 300
  beech trees and   164, 182
  climate change and   94, 336
  Winton and   34, 135–36, 137n9, 139, 140,
    143, 145, 148, 156–57

geohumanities   362
geological time   34, 163, 165, 167–68, 169, 170, 171, 180. *See also* deep time
geopolitics   23, 109, 166, 194, 281, 352, 361, 363
Germany   72–73, 122, 219, 337
Ghosh, Amitav   8, 9, 32, 59, 324, 329
   activism of   81–86, 87
   The Great Derangement   25, 30, 66, 81, 82–84, 86, 87, 311, 312, 330
   The Hungry Tide   81–82, 314
   petrofiction and   78
Gibson, Ross   94, 103, 115
gigantism   302–3. *See also* mega-dams
Gilligan, Carol   328
Ginn, Franklin   355
Ginsburg, Faye   315
glacial islands   363. *See also* icebergs
glaciers   297, 364
   climate change and   20, 65, 172, 315, 335, 338, 345, 361, 367
   human relationship with   346–47, 366, 371
glaciology, feminist   347
Glasberg, Elena   365
Glissant, Édouard   35, 192n1, 195, 196, 203, 204, 210, 212
globalisation   57, 231
   Antarctica and   335, 338, 341
   climate change and   22, 25, 337
   colonialism and   305, 325
   deep time and   169, 170
   India and   68, 70
   postcolonialism and   6, 17, 19, 21, 31
Global North   36, 86, 122, 255
Global South   4, 24–25, 32, 36, 86, 122, 254–55
global vs. local   182–83
The God of Small Things (Roy)   67
Golding, William   370
Gondwana continent   162, 164, 166–67, 170, 185
Gondwana Rainforests   1, 162–64. *See also* southern beech trees
Gore, Al   4
Göttsche, Dirk   338
gradualism   32. *See also* slow violence
Grand Renaissance Dam   304. *See also* dams
Grapes of Wrath (Steinbeck)   83

The Great Derangement (Ghosh)   25, 30, 66, 81, 82–84, 86, 87, 311, 312, 330
"The Greater Common Good" (Roy)   66, 303
Greek (Berkoff)   45
Green, Allyson   58
Green Deal   43
"Greenhouse Effect in New York" (Lim)   263–65
greenhouse gas emissions   39, 76, 230, 251, 271, 286, 294, 301n99, 334
Greenland   2, 3, 364
Green Party (Germany)   72
green postcolonialism   20–21
grief   42, 106n54, 347, 355, 356
Griffiths, Gareth   6
Griffiths, Matthew   256
Griffiths, Tom   355
Grovogu, Siba   24
Grunes, Marissa   368
Guadeloupe (Caribbean)   192, 194
Guha, Ramachandra   67, 255
guindo (*N. betuloides*)   176, 178, 179. *See also* southern beech trees

Habila, Helon   32, 56, 59, 76–81
Habitual Offenders Act (India)   63
Hage, Ghassan   26
Haiti   197, 199, 208
haku lei   232–33
Hale, Dorothy   58–59
The Halluci Nation (A Tribe Called Red)   322
Handley, George B.   12, 16, 21, 138, 154, 231
Hapy (Egyptian god)   294–95, 298
Haraway, Donna   100, 326–28
"Harnessing the Nile" (Penfield)   287–88, 291, 295
Harris, Stephen   34
Harris, Wilson   9, 11–12, 31
Hau'ofa, Epeli   130
Hawai'i   121, 219
   climate change and   221–24, 226–27, 245–46
   cli-po of   35–36, 235–45
   imperialism and   228–30
   and land, meaning of   224–26
   literature of   232–35
   resource management and   227–28
Hawaii2050 Sustainability Plan (2008)   221

INDEX

393

Hawaiian language 221n5, 233, 239, 244–45
Hawai'i Climate Adaptation Initiative 221–22
Hawai'i Conservation Conference 245–46
Hawai'i Sea Level Rise Vulnerability and Adaptation Report (2017) 35, 36, 221, 222–23, 226–27, 228–30
Hawai'i State Planning Act 221
Hayhoe, Katharine 297
"He ali'i ka 'āina" (Hawaiian proverb) 223–24
"Healing, Belonging, Resistance, and Mutual Care" (Magrane) 232
Healy, J.J. 5
Heat and Light (Van Neerven) 131
Heidegger, Martin 109
Heise, Ursula 165
Hellio, Claire 200
Hembemba (Winduo) 185
Hemingway, Ernest 369
Hemmings, Alan 341
Hereniko, Vilsoni 13
heroism 336, 348–49
hetero-temporalities 170, 172, 173, 174, 186. *See also* deep time
Higgins, David 15, 44
High Aswan Dam Reservoir (HADR) 37. *See also* Aswan High Dam
Highfield, Roger 65
Highlands (PNG) 166, 181, 182, 184
Hiltner, Ken 15
Himachal Pradesh (Indian state) 65, 302
Hindu nationalism 69, 70, 71
history 5, 11, 28, 86, 125, 141, 149, 166, 306, 311
    Antarctica and 336, 341, 348, 351–53, 361, 363
    Anthropocene and 93–94, 268
    Canada and 313, 329
    Caribbean and 194, 197–98, 201–3
    climate change and 25, 42, 58, 62, 84, 94, 99, 254–56, 270, 338
    cryo-, 38, 366, 374
    deep time and 15, 163, 164, 167, 168–70, 174, 176, 186
    Egypt and 281, 287, 291, 306
    Hawaiian and 221–22, 225, 228–29, 230, 232, 233–34, 235, 245
    icebergs and 371, 375, 377

Malaysia and 251, 257–59, 260, 262, 263, 265, 266, 271, 272–73
    New Zealand and 95
    Nigeria and 74, 76, 77
    Pacific Islands and 220
    of plantation ecologies 120, 122–23, 127, 129, 131
    postcolonialism and 17, 21–22, 44, 83, 94, 231
    sargassum and 35, 195, 204–5, 209–10, 212
History of the Voice (Brathwaite) 196–97
Hobbes, Thomas 345
Holland, Tom 42
home, concept of 127, 128, 131, 135–36, 138–41, 144, 157–58
homecoming 157, 263
homeland xvii, 10, 18, 81, 224, 329
    in beech narratives 172, 176–77, 178, 181
    Malaysia and 36, 258, 260, 263–65, 267, 271, 278
    Nubia and 281, 293, 306
homelessness 139
Homer 44, 139
homesickness 139n21, 264, 267
Hooker, Joseph 164, 166–67, 178–79
ho'omanawanui, ku'ualoha 224–25, 227, 232–33, 234–35, 239, 246
hope, poetics of 32, 196, 200, 204, 210–13
Houthi rebels 305
Hu, Chuanmin 200
Huang, Hsinya 232
Huggan, Graham 19–20, 32, 56, 66, 71, 103, 105, 108, 186, 329
Hulan, Renée 37–38
Hulme, Mike 45, 254
human-ice relationship 38, 336, 344–45, 346–48, 351, 355, 363, 366–67. *See also* interconnection
humanism 5, 95, 97, 99
humanities 22, 33, 56, 77–78n122, 175, 186, 200–201, 362–63, 366–67
human rights 43, 72–73, 97, 102, 120, 304, 312
humour 239–40
From Hunger to Prayer (Mackenzie) 235
The Hungry Tide (Ghosh) 81–82, 314
Hunt, Alex 20, 171
hunting 9, 11, 313, 314–15, 318, 319–21, 325n52, 326

hurricanes xviii, 38–39, 85, 194, 196–97, 199, 205n66, 206, 223
Hutton, James 167
hybridity 17, 143, 178, 183, 185
hyperobjects 168, 369, 379

ice 323, 325, 362–63
    Antarctica and 334–35, 336, 341, 361–62, 363
    climate change and 2, 20, 40–41, 157, 239, 312, 315–16
Ice (Nowra) 375–76
Iceberg Alley 378
icebergs 315
    A68 38, 364–70
    A76 378n62
    Antarctica and 363–64, 363n8
    cryobiography and 377–78
    literary narratives of 338, 345, 369–70, 373–76
    narratives of 378–79
    as resource 370–73
Iceberg Transport International 372
identity or being 28, 35–36, 67, 76, 136, 144, 201, 211
    beech trees and 178
    climate and 278
    climate change and 95, 185, 251, 349
    cli-po and 221, 232
    deep time and 169
    ecopoetics and 230–31
    interconnection and 212
    Inuit and 314–15, 317
    islands and 124, 140
    land and 10, 137, 143, 146, 147–48, 149–53, 157, 272
    language and 100–102, 239
    legal discourses of 99–100, 102–3, 116–17
    Malaysian 260, 265
    Māori 172
    in Nubian literature 293
    rivers and 95–99, 100
    Tagaq and 321–22
    water and 94, 104–7, 112–13, 115, 262, 270
    weather and 263, 264–65
Iep Jāltok (Jetñil-Kijiner) 12–13, 27
Ihimaera, Witi 376, 378
'ike 'āina (environmental knowledge) 35, 221, 234, 235, 246

Iliad (Homer) 44
imagination 31, 64, 141, 169, 197, 200, 212, 335
    activism and 56, 68, 154
    climate change and 25, 32, 37, 83–84, 255, 356
    coiled temporality and 195–96, 207–8, 209, 211
    ecopoetic 231, 232
    literature and 45, 138, 145–46, 149, 152, 159
imperial formations 121
imperialism 22, 31, 37, 59, 130, 166, 182, 336
    Caribbean and 197, 201–2
    climate change and 9, 26, 29, 44
    deep time and 170, 183
    islands and 18, 125, 220
    maps and 103, 109
    Neruda and 175–76
imperialist nostalgia 228–30
incantations 182–83
Ince, Onur Ulas 8
indentured labour 122, 129. *See also* plantation ecologies
India 56–57, 83n154, 122, 124, 273, 289n40, 302, 306, 337, 372
    climate change and 39, 40, 85
    Devy and 33, 60–65
    Roy and 67–71, 305
Indian Act (Canada) 328
Indian Ocean 3, 58
indigeneity 37, 156, 260, 272, 276–77, 326, 363
Indigenous Australians 9–10, 114, 124, 131, 142, 142n35, 145n49, 150, 156, 163
Indigenous Canadians 37–38, 326. *See also* Inuit
Indigenous Chileans 176, 178, 179
Indigenous Hawaiians 35, 36, 221, 223–25, 229, 234–38, 241–43, 245
Indigenous Indians 33, 60–64, 65–69, 70, 71, 289n40
Indigenous law 111, 113n88
Indigenous literature 104, 329
Indigenous Malaysians 252. *See also* Malays
Indigenous New Zealanders 33, 94–98, 98nn26–27, 102, 113, 172–73, 364, 376
Indigenous Pacific Islanders 219, 220, 229, 238

INDEX

Indigenous Papuans   181–83
Indigenous peoples   22, 32–33, 57, 296, 313,
   325, 328–29
   climate change and   4, 8, 11–12, 18–19, 28,
      65, 82, 94, 178, 179, 311–12
   ecopoetics and   230–31, 232, 237
   interconnection and   93n1, 99–100, 130
   living land and   9–12
   temporalities and   142, 170, 172, 180
Indigenous studies   18, 62, 241, 313, 325
Indigenous theatre   13–15, 18, 59n22
individualism   58, 83, 157
Indonesia   40
industrialism   57, 61, 351
   in Australia   129, 131
   climate change and   12, 94, 121, 168, 199,
      237, 251–52, 271, 298
   colonialism and   23, 45, 122, 231
   in Egypt   282, 285, 286–87, 290–91,
      296, 302
   in Malaysia   273, 275
Industrial Revolution   122, 298, 342
Innes, Hammond   370
interconnection   14, 81, 95, 130, 154, 312
   Antarctica and   341, 343, 355
   beech trees and   34, 172–73, 174–75, 176–
      78, 179, 182–84, 185
   Canadian literature and   37
   Caribbean and   35, 201–2, 207,
      209, 212–13
   climate change and   1, 4, 23, 25, 40–42,
      85, 93, 94, 99, 297, 337, 338, 349–50
   coiled temporality and   195, 203
   country and   10, 34, 157
   deep time and   163, 165–66, 167–69, 170,
      173, 180
   Hawai'i and   35, 224–28, 230–32, 234–36,
      241–42, 243, 246
   ice and   38, 336, 344–45, 346–48, 351, 355,
      363, 366–67
   icebergs and   373, 375–79
   Inuit and   315–16, 317–19, 321, 322–23,
      325–26, 328–29
   legal discourses and   99–100, 117
   Malaysia and   258, 259, 261, 262, 268–70
   postcolonialism and   19, 21, 27
   rivers and   33, 96–98, 104–7, 108, 112–13,
      114–15, 278, 294–96, 306
   sargassum and   196, 204–5, 210, 211–12

Winton and   34, 135–38, 142–43, 147–
   52, 158
interdisciplinarity   21, 23, 41, 165
*Interdisciplinary Studies in Literature
   and Environment* (Cilano and
   DeLoughrey)   21
Intergovernmental Panel on Climate Change
   (IPCC)   8–9, 22, 39, 87, 301n99
International Association of Antarctica Tour
   Operators (IAATO)   339–40, 354
International Majuro Declaration for Climate
   Leadership   221
Intervention (Australia 2007)   9
Inuit   37, 364
   climate change and   312, 314, 315–16, 327
   interconnection and   317–18, 319, 329
   seal hunt and   319–21
   in *Split Tooth*   322–24
   stories of   318–19
   tradition and   314–15
   See also Indigenous peoples
Ipellie, Alootook   315
ipukarea (ancestral homeland)   172
Ireland   122
Isaacs, Mark   127
Islam   281
Island Home (Winton)   34, 87, 135–36,
   138, 145
   climate change and   158–59
   human-land relationship in   136–37, 142–
      43, 146–51, 152–53
   islandness and   139, 140–41
   vision and seeing in   143–44
islandness   34, 35, 136, 139, 140–41
islands   123–24, 128–29, 157, 186, 200, 202–3,
   236, 363
   icebergs and   363–64, 369
   theory and conceptions of   124–25, 126
island studies   200
Israel   25n121, 283
Isuma Productions   314, 315

Jacquemond, Richard   285
James, Trevor   171
James I   122
Jane Eyre (Brontë)   59
Japp, Phyllis   351
Jawaharlal Nehru University   70
Jean, Michaëlle   317

Jetñil-Kijiner, Kathy xvi–xix, 12–13, 14, 14n61, 27, 32, 219
Jindyworobak Movement 150
Johns-Putra, Adeline 12, 25–26, 336, 350
Joyce, Mary C. 57
Jungle Ke Davedar (Devi) 62
justice, politics of 94, 96, 98–99, 116, 259, 328
juxtaposition 239, 297, 344

Kaani people 62. *See also* Indigenous peoples
Kagawa-Viviani, Aurora 245
Kajbar Dam 304, 305. *See also* mega-dams
Kalburgi, M.M. 69
Källén, Anna 18
kalo plant (taro) 224, 225, 226–27, 235, 241, 242
Kānaka Maoli people 35, 36, 219, 221, 221n5, 223–25, 229, 234–38, 241–42, 245. *See also* Indigenous peoples
Kanaloa (Hawaiian god) 235–38, 239, 240–41, 245
"Kanaloa 'Ai Moku" (Mackenzie) 235–38, 241
Kāne (Hawaiian god) 236, 245
Kane, Haunani 245
Kanngieser, Anja 121
Kantu people 11. *See also* Indigenous peoples
kaona 232, 244–45
Kaplan, E. Ann 254
Karpik, Joanasie 316
Keneally, Thomas 124–25
Kerpi, Peter Kama 34, 165, 181, 182–83, 184, 185
Kerr, Tamsin 145
King George Island (Antarctica) 352
Kingsnorth, Paul 155–56
Kingsolver, Barbara 7, 30
kin-making 100n31, 326
Kinsella, John 131
kinship 10, 102, 137, 156–57, 158–59, 272, 311, 317–18, 327, 330
kiore tawai (rats) 172–73
Klein, Naomi 67, 84, 219
Knickerbocker, Scott 26
knowledge 21, 100, 104, 137, 178, 257

Antarctica and 38, 337, 346, 361
cartography and 105, 109
postcolonialism and 17, 21
knowledge, Indigenous 10, 116, 178, 183, 184, 210
of adivasis 62–63
climate change and 8, 313–14
environmental 35, 65, 82, 185, 270
Hawaiian 221, 229, 234, 236, 244, 245
Inuit 37, 314–15, 316, 317–18, 323, 325–27
Māori 98n27
postcolonialism and 325–27
resource management and 227
"ko au te awa" (proverbial saying) 96–97, 99, 100–101, 102, 113, 116–17
Kronos Quartet 322
Kua Kia Soong 252
Kukum Kitchen 320
kuleana (responsibilities) 227–28, 230, 234–35
Kunuk, Zacharias 37, 313, 315, 317, 329–30
Kverndokk, Kyrre 199n31
Kwaymullina, Ambelin 10

labour 58, 63, 122, 123, 129, 335
Lake Chad 80
The Lamentations of Zeno (Trojanow) 334, 336, 338–39, 340, 342, 344–50, 351–54, 355, 356
land 11, 348–49, 363, 368
deep time and 176–77, 183
Hawai'i and 35, 223–26, 230–32, 234–35, 244
Inuit and 317, 323, 329
Malaysia and 265–66, 272, 273
as resource curse 274–77
rights 9, 10, 63, 68–69, 97, 110, 114, 116
in Winton 135–37, 138, 140–43, 145–47, 149–53, 154, 156–59
"Land" (Neidjie) 144–45
"Land and Man Unite" (Neruda) 176–77
landscape memoirs 34, 135, 137, 142–43, 145–46, 148–49, 151
The Land's Edge (Winton) 149–50
Langin, Katie 199–200
language 103–4, 108–9, 138, 146, 154, 185, 239, 244–45
being and 100–102, 108

INDEX

climate change and 33, 64–65, 67, 95
deep time and 169, 172
future-making and 207–9
interconnection and 151–52, 224–25
La Roche Qui Boit Dam 303. *See also* dams
Larsen A ice shelf 365
Larsen B ice Shelf 38, 365, 367
Larsen C ice shelf 365, 367, 370
Latin America 175–76, 180, 374
Latouche, Serge 115n106
Latour, Bruno 23, 305–6
Laudato Si' (2015) 86
Laughin, Nicholas 202–3
Laughter, Jim 7
law/legal discourses 10, 33, 95, 96–100, 102–4, 110–11, 113n87, 116–17, 372
"leaf fall" (Muhammad) 266
Leane, Elizabeth 38, 334, 344, 348, 378n62
Legba, Papa 208, 210
Lessing, Doris 8
life vs. death 101–2, 197
life writing 27, 34, 135, 145. *See also* memoirs
Lim, Shirley Geok-lin 36, 251, 258, 260–65, 278
Lindfors, Bernth 72
literacy 41, 61, 68, 234n48
Literary Activism (Chaudhuri) 57
literary fiction 8–9, 30, 37–38, 58, 77, 311–12, 314, 323, 324, 370
Literary Land Claims (Fee) 313
littoralists 135
lived experience 16, 197, 267, 314, 315, 323, 329
living land 9–12. *See also* land
"Living with the Weather" (Bate) 262
local vs. global 182–83
location, politics of 94, 315, 327
logging 15, 170, 253
Lomo'ha I Am (Winduo) 184–85
lótbòdlo (other side of the water) 197, 198
Luckman, Adrian 367
Lyell, Charles 167

Mabo, Eddie 129
Macdonald, Graeme 77–78
Macfarlane, Robert 7, 151
Mackenzie, David Keali'i 35, 221, 235–38, 239, 243

MaddAddam Trilogy (Atwood) 30, 313
Maddison, Ben 378n62
magic 295–96
magic realism 284, 285, 296, 299, 300, 374
Magrane, Eric 232
Mahood, Kim 151
Malacca (Malaysia) 258n27, 259, 260, 266
Malacca Straits 260, 263, 264, 265
malama 'āina (respect for land) 35, 225, 235, 246
Malay Annals 258–60, 266, 271
Malays 258n27, 265–67, 269–71, 273n77, 276–77
Malaysia 36, 257–62, 260–61n33, 275
climate change and 251–53, 263–65, 266–69, 271, 274, 278
Malaysian Indians 272
Mallacoota (Australia) 1
Malouf, David 147
mana 97
Maniam, K. S. 251, 260, 271–78
Manual of New Zealand Flora (Cheeseman) 173–74
Manus Islands 125
Māori 33, 95–97, 98nn26–27, 172–73, 364, 376. *See also* Indigenous peoples
Māori language 100–101, 108
maps 14, 94, 95n10, 102–5, 106, 107, 109, 334
Mapuche people 176, 177, 178, 180. *See also* Indigenous peoples
Marder, Michael 170n53, 196
Maréchal, Jean-Philippe 200
marginalisation 28–29, 75, 124, 265, 273, 284
of adivasis 63, 65
climate change and 4, 23, 43–44, 67, 198, 220, 312
of Indigenous knowledge 8, 326–27, 329
of Nubians 283, 285, 289, 300
postcolonialism and 16, 18, 22
The Marrow Thieves (Dimaline) 9, 313
Marshall, George 155
Marshall Islands xvii, 27, 121
Martin, Keavy 317, 318
Martinez, Doreen 44
Martinique 205. *See also* Caribbean
Maruia Declaration (New Zealand) 174
Maslen, Geoffrey 154–55n91
Massy, Charles 123

Mateer, John   140n24
materialism   31
materiality   94, 138, 140, 146, 148, 151, 205, 212, 362, 378
"Materializing Climate Change" (Shukin)   316
Mathews, Freya   137, 142
Matukituki Valley (New Zealand)   171–72
Mauro, Ian   315, 316
McCannon, John   37
McCarthy, Cormac   8, 30
McCaughrean, Geraldine   343
McCormack, Michael   28
McCredden, Lyn   152
McDougall, Brandy Nālani   35, 221, 235, 241–45
McEwan, Ian   7, 83
McGrath, Robin   319
McMahon, Elizabeth   128
McPhee, John   167
Mead, Philip   12
Mediterranean   205, 291, 297
mega-dams   252, 285–88, 290, 299–300, 302–4, 306. See also Aswan High Dam
Mehnert, Antonia   253
Mehrotra (poet)   57
Meister, Mark   351
mele (songs/poems)   232–33, 234
meltdowns   338, 345, 346–47. See also ice
Melville, Herman   376n54, 378–79
memoirs   27, 34, 87, 135–37, 137, 142–46, 148–49, 151–52, 312
memories   18, 100, 126, 145, 211, 278, 323
   beech trees and   173, 175, 180, 183
   Hawaiian literature and   230–31, 234, 235
   in Malaysian literature   36, 260, 263–64, 265
   Nubian   285, 289
Menely, Tobias   268
Mercator maps   334
metaphors   368–70, 376n54, 379
methane   239, 300, 301n99
Middle East   4, 120, 305, 372
Middle Passage   202, 208
migration   22, 63, 198, 220, 263
   climate change and   14, 41, 81, 85, 120–21, 245
   Malaysia and   271, 272, 273, 276

of Nubians   289, 292–93
   plantations and   122, 123–24, 238
Mika, Kasia   35
militarism   16, 84, 121, 211, 363n8, 371
   climate change and   9, 67, 120
   in Egypt   282, 305
   Hawai'i and   229–30, 245–46
   in Nigeria   72, 75, 76–77
   Pacific Islands and   219, 220
Milky Way   294
Miller, D.A.   59
Mills, Jennifer   29
mining   15, 75, 181–82
   in India   61, 63, 70–71
   Nauru and   121, 122, 123, 125, 126, 127, 129, 130
   Wright on   110, 112, 114, 131
The Ministry of Utmost Happiness (Roy)   66, 70–71
Mishra, Sudesh   99
Missing and Murdered Indigenous Women and Girls (MMIWG)   328
Mistral, Gabriela   34, 165, 180–81
Moana: The Rising of the Sea (Hereniko)   13–14
"Moa Space Foa Ramble" (Balaz)   238–41
Moby Dick (Melville)   376, 376n54, 378–79
modernisation   61, 305, 321n33
modernity   58, 76, 99–100, 130, 202, 316, 327, 374
Modi, Narendra   69
Molloy, Georgiana   155
"Moments of Initiation" (Kerpi)   183
Monbiot, George   140
"Monsoon History" (Lim)   260–62, 263
monsoons   36, 112, 253, 257, 260–63, 265, 267, 269
Montserrat (Caribbean)   205
mo'olelo (stories)   233, 234
more-than-human world.   See interconnection
Moretti, Franco   30
Morrison, Scott   28
mortality   3, 252, 270, 328
Morton, Timothy   145, 369
"Moss" (Mistral)   180–81
Mount, Dana   325, 329
Mount Pelée (Martinique)   205

INDEX   399

Movement for the Survival of the Ognoni
    People (MOSOP)   74
Mowaljarlai, David Banggal   150
mud-brick building   282, 293
Muhammad Haji Salleh   36, 251, 258–60,
    265–71, 278
Mukherjee, Pablo   19
Mumbai   85
Munif, Abdelrahman   78
Munro, Martin   209
Murād, Zakī   284
Murdoch, Rupert   85
Murphy, Patrick D.   176, 180
Murray, Neil   139, 157
music   11, 115, 150, 317, 319, 321–22, 327, 328
Myanmar (Burma)   84
"My Island Home" (Anu)   128–29, 131
"My Island Home" (Murray)   139
My Last Continent (Raymond)   340, 343, 353
"My Seditious Heart" (Roy)   69
mysticism   145, 149
mythical realism   284, 285. *See also* magic
    realism
mythology   235–38, 237, 284, 294–95, 298,
    319, 323–24. *See also* cosmology

naming   106, 114, 166, 172, 323, 366
The Nanny and the Iceberg   373–75
Napoleon's Last Island (Keneally)   124–25
NASA   2
Nasser, Gamal Abdel   282–83, 285, 286–87,
    288, 291, 302, 303
National Emergency Response Act
    (Australia)   9
National Inventory of Tribal Art   64
nationalisation   62, 283, 286, 288, 312
nationalism   17, 67, 150, 265, 278, 299, 305,
    325, 375
    Egyptian   37, 283, 284, 285, 286–89, 291,
      300–301, 302
    Hindu   69, 70, 71
National Oceanic Atmospheric
    Administration (NOAA)   2
National Self-Help Group (RSS)   69
nationhood   124, 257
Native Planters of Old Hawaii   224
Nature/Culture divide   81, 93, 179, 291, 305
    literature and   25–26, 312

postcolonialism and   17, 23, 34
rivers and   96–97, 102
See also interconnection
Nauru   33–34, 120–31
Nazism   45
Ndebele, Njabulo   57
necropastorals   242–43
"Negus" (Brathwaite)   206–8, 209, 211, 212
Nehru, Jawaharlal   287, 302–3
Neidjie, Bill   144–45, 145n49, 149, 150
Neimanis, Astrida   94, 97
neoliberalism   6, 16, 32, 41–42, 120–21
Neruda, Pablo   34, 162, 165, 170, 175–78, 179–
    80, 183
New England National Park   162–63
New South Wales (NSW)   1
New Zealand.   *See* Aotearoa/New Zealand
Nicobar Islands   84–85
Nielsen, Hanne E. F.   38, 350
Niger Delta   72, 74, 76, 78–79
Nigeria   59, 71, 73–74, 75–80
"Nigger's Leap" (Wright)   164
Nights of Musk (Oddoul)   36, 37, 284–86,
    291–93, 294, 296–302, 306
Nile Delta   282, 290–91, 293, 301
Nile River   37, 281–88, 291–98, 301–2
Nile Valley   36, 281, 282, 288, 293, 301
Ningaloo Reef   87, 156
ñirre (*N. antarctica*)   176, 178
nitrous oxide   300, 301n99
Nixon, Rob   275, 283
    on dams   287, 288–89
    on postcolonialism   17, 18, 19
    on slow violence   24, 121, 284, 294,
      297
Nkrumah, Kwame   287
Noble, Anne   335
A Nomad Called Thief (Devy)   62
nomadic narratives   271–72
nomadic tribes   33, 80, 81
nonviolence   328. *See also* care, ethics/
    rhetoric of
Noonuccal, Oodgeroo   7
"No Ordinary Sun" (Tuwhare)   105
North America   40, 58n16, 59n22, 264
Northern Hemisphere   2, 20, 166, 371
Northern Tablelands (Australia)   162–63
Norther Territory (Australia)   9, 144

nostalgia   21, 293
  imperialist   228–30
  in Malaysian literature   260, 262, 264–65,
    267, 272–73, 277
Nothofagus.   See southern beech trees
novels   83, 233, 324, 344, 373
  Antarctica and   338, 353, 355, 364
  climate change and   4, 26, 29–31, 62,
    105, 335
  postcolonialism and   31, 59, 67
Nowra, Louis   375–76
Nubia   281–83, 285, 287, 292, 294, 295, 296,
    301, 304–5
Nubians   281–82, 283, 284–85, 289, 289n40,
    291–93, 300–301, 304–5
nuclear industry   7, 18, 68, 69, 70, 121, 220,
    231, 274, 341–42
Nuliajuk (Sedna)   319, 325, 325n52
nunataks   363. *See also* Antarctica
Nüsser, Marcus   346, 366
Nuʻuhiwa, Kalei   245

O'Brian, Patrick   370
O'Brien, Susie   325, 329
ocean assemblage   201
"Oceania as Peril and Promise" (Wilson)   231
oceanic turn   200–201
Ocean Island   123. *See also* Nauru
oceans, xvii   173
  Antarctica and   341, 362–63, 364, 365,
    366, 367, 373
  Caribbean and   35, 194, 197, 210
  climate change and   11, 14, 40, 65, 127–28,
    211, 223, 238, 245, 313, 316, 325, 334
  cli-po and   235–38, 239–44
  coiled temporality and   195, 200–
    203, 211–13
  colonialism and   121, 130
  human connection with   114–15, 131, 150,
    227, 236, 239
  islands and   139–40, 231, 235
  plantation ecologies and   120, 122
  rivers and   105, 107
  sargassum and   204–5, 212
  *See also*specific oceans
Oddoul, Haggag   36, 37, 284–86, 291–93, 294,
    295–302, 305, 306
The Odyssey (Homer)   139
Oedipus Rex (Sophocles)   44–45

Ogoni people   73, 74–75. *See also* Indigenous
    peoples
Oil Encounter   78, 83
oil industry   78n123, 83, 84, 155, 365–66, 371
  Antarctica and   352, 365
  in Malaysia   274–75
  in Nigeria   72–73, 74–76, 77–80
Oil on Water (Habila)   76, 77–80
ʻōlelo noʻeau (Hawaiian proverb)   223, 226–
    27, 228, 233
1 Gigaton Coalition   305
One Hundred Years of Solitude (Garcia
    Marquez)   45
ontology   19, 33, 76, 103–4, 232, 337
  beech trees and   172, 184
  place and   34, 137, 149, 201
  rivers and   97, 100–101, 113
opacity   196, 210, 213
oppression   31, 77, 176, 265, 302
  climate change and   23, 58, 121
  postcolonialism and   6, 18, 45
oral traditions   64, 65, 233, 234, 318–19,
    325
organising   58. *See also* activism
organismic time   163, 165, 170, 171, 175, 180
orientalism   125
otherness   100, 111, 147, 176, 181, 196n18,
    289, 292–93
The Other Side of the Sea (Dalembert)   197
Otto, Melanie   11
Our House Is on Fire (Ernman et al.)   27
ownership   97
Oxfam   71
The Oxford Handbook of Ecocriticism
    (Garrard)   19

Pachauri, Rachendra   7
Pacific Islands   120–21, 125, 128, 130, 131, 219–
    20, 221n4, 364
Pacific Ocean   33, 120, 162, 237
Pacific Phosphate Company   122
Painted Words (Devy)   64
Pākehā   171, 172, 175. *See also* settlers
palm oil   122, 253, 257, 271
Pan Arab movement   283
pandemics   40–42, 44
Pangnirtung (Nunavut)   315, 316
Papa Legba   208, 210
Papillon (Charrière)   124

INDEX

401

Papua New Guinea (PNG) xvii, 35, 164, 166n26, 181–86
"Parablames" (Maniam) 274–75
paradise 124–25. *See also* islands
paradoxes 344–46
Paravisini-Gebert, Lizabeth 19
Paris Agreement (2015) 4, 86, 251
Paris Match (magazine) 319
Parrington, Mark 39
pastoralism 15, 114, 130, 131, 242–43, 267
Paton, Alan 59
patriotism 158–59
Pécresse, Jérome 304
Peel, Sidney 290, 291, 295
Pehuenche people 176. *See also* Indigenous peoples
pellín 176. *See also* southern beech trees
Pelly, David 321n33
Penfield, Frederic Courtland 287–88, 291, 295
penguins 335, 352, 353, 354, 378
peranakan (local born) 260–61n33. *See also* Malays
peripheral perception 143, 144
permission 197, 236, 237
personhood 94, 96–99, 100, 102–3, 105
PETA 327
petrofiction 78, 83
PETRONAS (petroleum company) 275
phosphate 122–23, 125, 126, 127, 129
photography 212, 318, 319, 320, 335, 345, 354–55, 368
Pidgin (Hawai'i Creole English) 233, 238, 239
pilimmaksaq 329. *See also* Inuit
Pine Island (glacier) 367
Pinnacles (Va'ai) 125–27
Pinnix, Aaron 204–5, 210
place 94, 102–3, 109, 141, 201, 230, 251, 362
   country and 10, 34
   ecocriticism and 17–18
   Malaysia and 260, 264–65, 268
   memoirs and 145–46
   postcolonialism and 19, 21, 99
   seeing and 144, 147–48, 149
   storied 35, 233, 234, 235, 246
   temporalities and 175, 180, 183
   Winton and 135, 136, 137, 138, 143–44, 152
The Plague (Camus) 45

plagues 44–45, 115
plantation ecologies 33, 120, 121–24, 127–31, 229
plants. *See* sargassum; southern beech trees
"Poem in the Matukituki Valley" (Baxter) 171–72
Poem of Chile (Mistral) 180–81
poetics 34, 103–4, 114, 203, 262
   of hope 196, 200
   rivers and 33, 95, 105, 116
   See also cli-po; ecopoetry/poetics
poetry 4, 14, 15, 59, 104–5, 108, 169, 186.
   See also cli-po; ecopoetry/poetics; southern beech trees
Point Lookout (Australia) 162–64
polar bears 312, 316, 325, 335
Polar City Red (Laughter) 7
The Politics of the Earth (Dryzek) 287
pollen 162, 173
pollution 15, 77, 97, 110, 170, 199, 242–43, 285, 349
   climate change and 3, 43
   in India 33, 60
   in Malaysia 253, 257, 259, 271
   in Nigeria 74, 76, 78, 79
   Pacific Islands and 126, 128
Poor (Ali) 285
populism 28
Position Doubtful (Mahood) 151
Postcolonial Ecocriticism (Huggan and Tiffin) 20, 56, 329
Postcolonial Ecologies (DeLoughrey and Handley) 21, 231
Postcolonial Green (Roos and Hunt) 20
postcolonial humanities 22
postcolonialism, definitions 16–17, 22, 231.
   See also ecocriticism
posthumanism 100, 327
poverty 61, 68, 70, 82, 122, 123, 220, 266, 267
Powell, Robert 340
power relations 16–17, 58, 122, 125, 157, 284, 285, 287, 300, 305–6
   Antarctica and 335, 352, 353
   climate change and 23–24, 43–44, 82, 86, 254–55, 337
   denialism and 28–29
   in India 68–70, 71
   Malaysia and 260, 266, 268, 277
practical mysticism 145, 149

Pratt, Mary Louise   103n42
"prayer" (Muhammad)   268–69
"Prayer at the Graveyard" (Kerpi)   182–83
Prentice, Chris   33
pressure of geography   136, 140, 156–57
pretrauma   254
Price, Patricia   349
prisons   124–25
production
    cultural   15, 123, 314, 355
    industrial   63, 113, 122, 129, 204, 299, 375
    knowledge   21, 337
    See also development
progress   31, 66, 149, 211, 212, 277, 306, 320,
    351. See also development
"prologue" (Muhammad)   258
Promethean discourse   291, 295, 306
property   9, 97, 98n27, 99, 100, 102, 116, 117,
    158, 274
protests   14n61, 69–70, 72, 86, 138, 156, 206,
    319, 321, 327. See also activism
proverbs   96–97, 99–102, 113, 116–17, 117, 223,
    226–27, 228, 232, 233
public health   40–42, 45, 66
Pugh, Jonathan   201
Puniwai, Noelani   245
purity   344, 376
"The Purity of Ice" (Ihimaera)   376
"Putting Feathers on Our Words"
    (McDougall)   244

Qapirangajuq: Inuit Knowledge and Climate
    Change (Kunuk)   315–17
Qassem, Muhammad Khalil   284, 285
Quajimajatuqangit (Inuit knowledge)   37,
    314–15, 316, 317–18, 323, 325–27
Quayson, Ato   75
Queensland (Australia)   1, 123, 129
"quiet village" (Muhammad)   268–69, 271
Q'um Q'um Xiiem (Jo-ann Archibald)   313

Ra (Egyptian god)   294, 298
"Rabbit" (Tagaq)   321
race   5, 19, 26, 202n48, 231, 232, 273, 281,
    344, 349n73
    Australia and   125, 131
    climate change and   28, 43
    Malaysia and   260, 265–66, 277
    postcolonialism and   31, 44

racism   26, 43, 277, 289
"Rain" (Tuwhare)   105–6, 116
rainforests   1, 38, 39, 162, 164, 165, 192n5,
    199, 253
Rajan, Rajeswari Sunder   60, 62
Ramnath, Madhu   64–65
Rancière, Jacques   108
RAND Corporation   372–73
Rashtriya Swayamsevak Sangh (RSS)   69
rats   172–73, 295, 301
Ravenscroft, Alison   113n88, 116
Rawson, Jane   30
Raymond, Leigh   27–28
Raymond, Midge   340, 342, 343, 353
realism   7, 30–31, 76, 284, 285, 291, 292n55,
    324. See also magic realism
reception studies   31
reciprocity   93n1, 150, 158, 230, 231, 262. See
    also interconnection
reefs   87, 129, 156, 223
refugees   6
    climate change and   xvii, 11, 22, 81, 120–
    21, 181
    developmental   285, 288–89, 291
    Nauru and   124, 125, 127, 128, 129–30
relation, poetics of   195, 203, 204, 210,
    211, 212–13
reliable water   36, 258, 259–60, 267, 271, 278
"Removal in Pasir Panjang"
    (Maniam)   272–78
renewable energy   252, 275, 304, 305
renewable resources   373
repetition   206–7, 211
Reports from a Wild Country (Bird
    Rose)   23–24
reproduction, sexual   224–25, 295–96
residential schools   313, 328
resilience   40, 220, 319
    of beech trees   35, 164, 170, 178
    Caribbean   194, 212
    in Hawai'i   227, 228, 245, 246
resistance   36, 69, 70, 83, 131, 155, 206, 239,
    301, 374
    Aswan High Dam and   36, 286–87
    beech trees and   177–78, 181
    of Indigenous peoples   12, 315
    postcolonialism and   16, 17, 27–32,
    45, 58, 87
    See also activism

INDEX   **403**

resource curse   275
resources   16, 102, 110, 129, 130–31, 137, 210,
    275, 287
   Antarctica and   38, 351
   climate change and   24, 43, 67, 127, 220
   Hawai'i and   222, 223, 227
   icebergs as   370–76, 379
   Indigenous peoples and   61, 62, 227,
    231, 327
   Malaysia and   252, 253, 271, 272, 274
   rivers and   98, 306
responsibility   18, 157, 259, 329–30
   climate change and   23, 84, 352
   communal   227–28, 230, 234–35
   Hawai'i   222, 223
   Inuit and   317, 318, 319
   Ogoni people and   73, 74, 75
restoration   97, 183, 209
reterritorialisation   185
Retribution (Tagaq)   321, 322
The Return (Maniam)   271–72
"return" (Muhammad)   267–68
Return to Almora (Pachauri)   7
rewilding   140
rhizomatic thought   203, 204–5
Rhys, Jean   59
The Right to Be Cold (Watt-
   Cloutier)   27, 311–12
Ritter, Harry   57
The River Gauge (Qassem)   284
"The River is an Island" (Tuwhare)   104–5,
   106–8, 116
rivers   11, 104–5, 172n65, 192n5, 199
   climate change and   81, 110, 315
   dams and   37, 68, 281, 282, 287, 288, 290,
    300, 301–2, 303, 306
   in Malaysian literature   251, 258, 259–60,
    265, 267–68, 271, 272, 273, 276–78
   Nubia and   294–96, 298
   personhood and   33, 94–99, 100–102,
    106–9, 112–14
"River Writing" (Prentice)   33
The Road (McCarthy)   30
Robinson, William   147
Rodgers, Kathleen   319–20
Rodney, Walter   7
Romantic Ecology (Bate)   262
Romanticism   15–16
Ronne Ice Shelf   378n61

Roos, Bonnie   20, 171
Ropiha, Hori   173
Rosaldo, Renato   228, 229
Ross Ice Shelf   362, 367
Ross Island (Antarctica)   361, 363
Roy, Arundhati   32, 56, 59, 66–71, 289,
   303, 305
rubber plantations   11, 266, 272
rubbish   115, 127–28, 131, 197, 201, 229, 243,
   273, 276–77, 352
Russell, Charles   5
Russian Republic of Sakha   39
Ryan, John C.   34–35

Sahitya Akademi   69
Said, Edward   125
Sainte-Marie, Buffy   322
Salleh, Ariel   168
salvage environmentalism   228–30
salvage paradigm   316
Santos Perez, Craig   26, 35–36
saprophytes   180–81. *See also* southern
   beech trees
Sardar Sarovar dam   68–69, 71. *See also* dams
Sargasso Sea   192
sargassum   193, 209
   climate change and   192, 194–95
   coiled temporality and   35, 195–96, 200,
    203–4, 211–12
   and hope, poetics of   210–13
   multi-scalar vulnerability and   197–98,
    199–200
   and relation, poetics of   204–5
Saro-Wiwa, Ken   32, 56, 59, 71–76, 77,
   78n123, 305
Saro-Wiwa, Ken, Jr.   75–76
Saro-Wiwa, Zina   75–76
Saudi Arabia   304, 305, 372, 373
Savi, Melina   356
Saxifrage, Carrie   27
scarcity   110, 178, 206, 274
Scarles, Caroline   354–55
Schlanger, Zoë   368n23
Schlegel, Christine   120
Schneider-Mayerson, Matthew   4
science fiction (sci-fi)   7–8, 26, 30, 83
Scobie, Willow   319–20
Scott Base (Antarctica)   361
Scudder, Thayer   285

sea levels 253, 278, 290
  climate change and 2–3, 11, 20, 40, 82, 85, 219
  Hawai'i and 221, 222–23, 229n30, 237, 238, 239–40, 243
  ice and 334, 365, 373
  islands and xvi, 14, 18, 27, 127, 129, 157, 220
seals 122, 315, 317–21, 325, 326–27, 351, 377, 378
seasons 270–71
seawalls xvi, 14, 238, 240, 242
seaweed. *See* sargassum
The Second Sex (de Beauvoir) 6
Sedna (Nuliajuk) 319, 325, 325n52
"Seeds and Roots" (Winduo) 185
Sejarah Melayu (Malay Annals) 258–60, 266, 271
"Selfies, Seals and Celebs" (Rogers and Scobie) 319–20
Selk'nam people 374. *See also* Indigenous peoples
Semple, Maria 343
sensuous poiesis 26. *See also* cli-po
settlement 33, 81, 85, 94–95, 97, 99, 114, 116, 121, 289
settlers 10, 18–19, 98–99, 109, 155, 175
  in Australia and New Zealand 94, 124, 158, 163, 171–72
  laws of 97, 102, 103–4, 110–11
sewage 199, 243. *See also* waste
al-*Shamandoura* (Qassem) 284
shamans 323, 325
Sharpe, Christina 202
Sharrad, Paul 33–34, 116, 182
Shawana, Joseph 320
Shearer, Christine 7
Shell (oil company) 72, 73, 74–75
Shelley, Percy 15
Shereik Dam 305. *See also* dams
Shockwave (Cussler) 343
Shukin, Nicole 316
Siberia 2, 39
sickle cell anaemia 66
Silent Spring (Carson) 6, 17, 268
Sinaa (Tagaq) 321, 322
"The Singing Bones" (Stow) 140–41
Sinohydro (Chinese company) 304, 305

Siperstein, Stephen 27
Sirb Al Balshun (Murād) 284
Sixth Assessment Report (IPCC, 2021) 39
slavery 122, 198, 202
Slemon, Stephen 300
slow violence
  Aswan High Dam and 36–37, 283–84, 301
  climate change and 24, 121, 129–30, 155, 276, 285, 297–98
  exponential threat of 294
Small Island Developing States (SIDS) 120, 220n4
Smith, Bren 27
Smith, Dick 373, 375
Smith, Jillian 312
Smith, Lawrence 306
socialisation 98–99
socialism 287, 291
social movements. *See* activism
socio-climatic literature 36, 260, 268. *See also* cli-po
Solar (McEwan) 7
solastalgia 139, 267, 356
solidarity 183, 209, 219, 231
Somare, Michael 181
Somervell, Tess 44
"Song of Lament" (Kerpi 183
songs 14, 128, 139, 182–83, 232–33, 234, 321–22, 323
Sophocles 44–45
Sörlin, Sverker 366–67
La Soufrière (volcano) 205
South Africa 5, 59, 344, 371n30, 373
South America 4, 11, 40, 162, 164, 175, 178, 192, 303, 372
Southeast Asia 3, 40, 263–64
southern beech trees
  Chilean narratives of 175–81
  climate change and 164–65, 170, 178, 186
  deep time and 34–35, 163, 164, 165, 167, 170, 173, 186
  history of 162–63, 164, 166–67
  interconnection and 172–73
  New Zealand narratives of 171–75
  Papua New Guinean narratives of 181–86
Southern Hemisphere 2, 178, 185, 364, 368, 373

INDEX

Southern Ocean 167, 344, 354
South Georgia (Antarctica) 351, 378
South Shetland Islands (Antarctica) 350, 351
sovereignty 6, 97, 102, 182, 220, 287, 374
  Caribbean and 205, 206, 211
  Hawaiian 36, 219, 230, 246
  Indigenous 15, 36, 329
  rivers and 99, 100, 103, 105, 107–8
Soviet Union 286, 287
Soyinka, Wole 6
SPAN 19
speculative fiction 7, 131, 327. *See also* climate fiction
speed 297–98. *See also* slow violence
spirituality 105n50, 110, 113n88, 152, 302
  Hawaiian 225, 234, 235, 238
  Indigenous 62, 65
  Inuit 321, 324
  Malaysian 257, 263, 271, 272, 276
  rivers and 95, 97n19
Spivak, Gayatri 104
Split Tooth (Tagaq) 322–25, 328
Stainier, Sally 35
State of Fear (Crichton) 7
Staying with the Trouble (Haraway) 326, 327–28
Steinbeck, John 83
Steinberg, Philipe 201
Stephens, Marcus 128
stewardship 18, 225, 227, 230, 246
Stiglitz, Joseph 41
Stoddart, Mark 312
Stoler, Ann Laura 121, 198–99
"story" (Muhammad) 265
storytelling 111–12, 265, 272, 284, 296, 315, 316, 318–19
Stow, Randolph 140–41
Stowe, Harriet Beecher 6
Straits Chinese 260, 260–61n33
"Strange Passion" (Winton) 143–44
St. Vincent (Caribbean) 205
"Subversion and Legitimation" (Russell) 5
Sudan 281, 282, 283, 293, 299, 304–5
Suez Canal 283, 285, 286, 288
sugar 122, 129, 203, 227, 238–39
suicide 70, 322, 374
"Sunset in Nauru" (Va'ai) 126

supercontinental thinking 165. *See also* Gondwana continent
Superfund sites 229
superphosphates 122, 123
sustainability 41, 192, 220, 303, 353
  Australia and 116, 120
  Hawai'i and 221, 222, 223, 225, 227, 242, 244, 246
  India and 65, 70
  Indigenous peoples and 8, 185, 230–31
  Malaysia and 36, 278
  Nauru and 126, 130
  seal hunting and 321n33, 327
Sutherland, Efua 7
Suzack, Cheryl 328
The Swan Book (Wright) 9, 11, 12, 110
Swart, Sandra 344
system justification 28–29
Szeman, Imre 77
Szerszynski, Bronislaw 254, 256, 270–71

Tagaq, Tanya 37, 313, 317–18, 319–28, 329–30
tanahair 36, 258, 278. *See also* homeland
Tangaroa (Māori god) 237
Tanjung Bunga (Malaysia) 262
taro 224, 225, 226–27, 235, 241, 242
Taru (Māori guide) 173
Tasmania 124, 125
Taumatamaheo Track (New Zealand) 173
tawai. See southern beech trees
Taylor, Astra 57–58
Taylor, Basil 173
Taylor, Jesse Oak 268
Te Awa Tupua Act (2017) 94, 95, 96–99, 100, 102–3, 105, 116–17
Tejgadh (Indian village) 65
te reo Māori 100–101, 108
For the Term of his Natural Life (Clarke) 125
theatre 13–15, 18, 59n22
Things Fall Apart (Achebe) 59
Thiong'o, Ngũgĩ wa 6
"This Land Is Your Land" (ho'omanawanui) 224
threat, icebergs as 370, 375, 377, 379
350.org 365
throat singing 321, 322, 326
Thumboo, Edwin 268
Thunberg, Greta 27

Thunberg, Svante 27
Thwaites (glacier) 367
tidalectics 202, 204, 213
tides 81, 82, 112, 115, 129, 152, 200, 243
Tierra del Fuego 166, 178, 179
Tiffin, Helen 6, 20, 32, 56, 66, 71, 186, 329
timber industries 184, 253, 271
Time and its People (collection) 270–71
time/temporality. *See* coiled temporality;
    deep time; monsoons; slow violence;
    wild time
Titanic 369, 370, 377
Tong, Anote 219
topophilia 180
tornadoes 84
Torres Strait 128, 145n49
tourism 6, 129, 231, 314, 316
    Antarctic 38, 334, 336–37, 339–48, 350,
        352, 352–56, 355–56, 366
    Hawaiian 222, 229, 240, 242–44
    sargassum and 195, 199, 200
"Towards the Human" (Wynter) 207
"Toward Transpacific Ecopoetics"
    (Huang) 232
tradition 314–15, 316, 322, 325, 327
transdisciplinarity 19, 33
transformation narratives 317–19, 343
translation 64, 98, 99, 100–101, 102, 103,
    108–9, 117
translation zones 103, 105, 108, 113n87
transnationalism 13, 17–18, 21, 23, 120, 124,
    131, 166, 179, 231
Treaty of Waitangi Amendment Act
    (1985) 98n26
Tredinnick, Mark 145–46
trees. *See* southern beech trees
tribal people (India) 33, 60–64, 65–69, 70,
    71. *See also* Indigenous peoples
A Tribe Called Red (The Halluci Nation) 322
Trojanow, Ilija 38, 334–35, 336, 337–39, 340,
    342, 344–50, 351–54, 355
Trouillot, Michel-Rolph 202
Trudell, John 7
"The Truly Privileged" (Maniam) 273
Trump, Donald 28
Tungijuq (short film) 317–18, 319
Tuwhare, Hone 33, 95, 104–8, 116
Twain, Mark 139–40

"Two Degrees" (Jetñil-Kijiner) 27, 32
Two-Way Thinking 150

"uncivilised art" (Kingsnorth) 155
Uncle Tom's Cabin (Stowe) 6
UNESCO 282
United Arab Emirates (UAE) 370–71,
    371n30, 373
United Nations 8, 13, 74, 87, 192n5, 219, 220,
    220n4, 251, 305
United Nations Framework
    Convention on Climate Change
    (UNFCCC) 20, 301n99
United States (US) 4, 5, 39, 124, 320
    Aswan High Dam and 286, 287
    dams in 63, 303n114
    Hawai'i and 221, 228–30, 233, 245–46
Universal Ecological Fund 4
universalism 59, 254, 255, 326
unsettlement 33, 94, 95, 103, 105, 108–9, 116
Updike, John 83
Urban, Brigitte 37
Urry, John 254
US National Ice Center 365, 366
US National Science Foundation 372
utopias 26, 45, 146, 220

Va'ai, Makerita 125–27
van der Watt, Lize-Marié 344
Van Neerven, Ellen 131
Vansleb, F. 290
van Steenis, Cornelis 184, 185–86
Vemula, Rohith 70
verbs 101, 102, 108, 224
vernacular/vernacularisms 182–83, 185
Vezins Dam 303. *See also* dams
Victorian literature 16
"villagers" (Muhammad) 269–71
Vodou cosmology 208–9
Voices from the Ridge (Kerpi) 182
volcanoes 197, 205, 211, 237
Voyage of the Iceberg (Brown) 377
vulnerability 34–35, 37, 61, 138–39n18, 147,
    164, 178, 181, 220
    Antarctica and 335, 343, 346, 348,
        349, 367
    Caribbean and 58, 194, 196–200, 205–
        6, 211

INDEX

climate change and 24, 94, 117, 148, 186, 195
Malaysia and 251, 263, 268, 271

Waanyi language 109
Wachowich, Nancy 314, 315
wahi pana (storied places) 35, 233, 234, 235, 246
Waikīkī 240, 241–43, 245
Waiting for an Angel (Habila) 77, 80
Walcott, Derek 209
"walking the border between two worlds" (Ipellie) 315
Walton, David 335
Wark, McKenzie 30
Warumpi Band 128
waste 115, 127–28, 131, 197, 201, 229, 243, 273, 276–77, 352
wastewater 199
water 6, 10, 18, 79, 94, 100, 110, 115, 202, 325
    Antarctica and 2, 363, 365, 366, 371
    beech trees and 173
    climate change and 14, 24, 40, 93, 178, 201, 211
    Egypt and 290–91
    Hawai'i and 222–23, 226, 229, 230, 235–36, 239–45
    icebergs and 370–71, 371n30
    in India 66, 68, 71, 85
    Malaysia and 36, 253, 257–60, 261–63, 265, 267–71, 277–78
    Māori and 97, 173
    Nauru and 126, 129
    Nubia and 282, 287, 292, 294, 295–97, 306
    poetics of 104, 106, 142n35
"Water Remembers" (McDougall) 241–45
Watt-Cloutier, Sheila 27, 311–12
wealth 32, 71, 123, 241, 242, 243–44, 275
weather events 38–39, 84–85, 148, 262, 290
    in Caribbean 194, 197–99, 205–6
    climate change and 3, 24, 93–94, 127, 181, 223, 268, 315, 353
    climate vs. 35, 256, 270–71
    in Malaysia 251, 252–53, 257, 264–65, 268–69, 277–78
    in Wright 111, 112, 114–15
The Weather Makers (Flannery) 123
weatherwising 270–71

Weddell Sea 378
Der Weltsammler (Trojanow) 338
Wenzel, Jennifer 83n152, 84
Westra, Laura 74, 75n110
whakapapa (Māori genealogy) 95, 96, 98, 106
whakapepeha (proverbial saying) 96–97, 99–102, 113, 116–17
whales/whaling 122, 128, 350, 351, 354, 376, 377, 378
Whanganui iwi (people/tribe) 33, 94–98, 102, 113. *See also* Indigenous New Zealanders
Whanganui River 94, 95–99, 100, 102–3, 107, 113
Whanganui River Claims Settlement Act (2017) 33
Where'd You Go, Bernadette (Semple) 343
White Darkness (McCaughrean) 343
The White South (Innes) 370
Wicomb, Zoë 57
Wide Open (Weave) 322
Wide Sargasso Sea (Rhys) 59
wilderness 17, 255, 334, 341, 351, 354
wildfires. *See* fires
wildness 136, 140, 145, 147, 149, 151, 156
wild time 34, 141–42. *See also* deep time
Wilke, Sabine 338, 349
Willcocks, William 281
Williamson, Judith 335
Wilson, Bernard 271
Wilson, Rob 231
Windless Bight (Antarctica) 361–62
Winduo, Steven Edmund 34, 165, 170, 181, 184–85
Winton, Tim
    climate change and 148–49, 153–54, 155–56
    human-land relationship and 142–43, 146–48, 149–53, 156–57, 158–59
    on vision and seeing 34, 87, 135–45, 154
Wola people 183–84. *See also* Indigenous peoples
Woldendorp, Richard 144
Woolcott, Michael 23
World Bank 286
World Expo (1992) 374–75
World Health Organization (WHO) 3, 20, 40

world-making   104, 105, 108, 109, 113, 300
World War I   122–23
World Wide Fund for Nature   12
Wright, Alexis   9, 11, 12, 33, 95, 105, 108–16, 131
Wright, Judith   163–64
Wright, Laura   255
Wright, Phillip   162–63, 163
Wynter, Sylvia   195, 207

Yaghan people   176, 179. *See also* Indigenous peoples
Yakutia (Russian Republic of Sakha)   39
yearning   151, 228, 293

Yeow, Agnes S.K.   35, 36
"You Gotta Run" (song)   322
Young, Robert J.C.   6, 17
Yusoff, Kathryn   336

Zadists   306
Zalasiewicz, Jan   167, 169
"Zeinab Uburty" (Oddoul)   284, 285, 295–99
Zeno of Elea   345, 368
Zizek, Slavoj   41
zoocriticism   21–22
zoonotic diseases   40–41, 42
Zubot, Jesse   317